Very Young Children with Special Needs

A Formative Approach for the Twenty-First Century

Second Edition

Vikki F. Howard
Stanford University

Betty Fry Williams
Whitworth College

Patricia D. Port
Deceased—Formerly with Sacred Heart Medical Center

Cheryl Lepper
Gonzaga University

Merrill
Prentice Hall

Upper Saddle River, New Jersey
Columbus, Ohio

Library of Congress Cataloging in Publication Data

Howard, Vikki F.
 Very young children with special needs : a formative approach for the twenty-first
century / Vikki F. Howard, Betty Fry Williams, Patricia D. Port ; Cheryl Lepper, illustrator.
  p. cm.
 Includes bibliographical references and index.
 ISBN 0-13-028099-2 (pbk.)
  1. Handicapped children—Education (Early childhood) 2. Child development. 3.
 Special education. I. Williams, Betty Fry. II. Port, Patricia D. III. Title.
LC4019.3 . V47 2001
371.9'0472—dc21

00-033242

Vice President and Publisher: Jeffery W. Johnston
Executive Editor: Ann Castel Davis
Editorial Assistant: Amy Shough
Production Editor: Linda Hillis Bayma
Production Coordination and Text Design: Carlisle Publishers Services
Photo Coordinator: Sandy Lenahan
Design Coordinator: Diane C. Lorenzo
Illustrations: Cheryl Lepper
Cover Designer: Jeff Vanik
Cover photo: © The Stock Market
Production Manager: Laura Messerly
Director of Marketing: Kevin Flanagan
Marketing Manager: Amy June
Marketing Services Manager: Krista Groshong

This book was set in Garamond by Carlisle Communications, Ltd. It was printed and bound by R.R. Donnelley &
Sons Company. The cover was printed by Phoenix Color Corp.

Photo Credits: p. 60, Anne Vega/Merrill; pp. 103, 147, 173, 243, 292, courtesy of the Berke family; p. 54, courtesy
of the DeWolf family; pp. 1, 47, 69, 76, 95, 123, 125, 133, 135, 150, 151, 154, 157, 163, 249, 307, 328, 355, 395, 435,
465, 466, Betsy Downey; pp. 9, 87, 284, 390, 423, 443, courtesy of the Finkel family; pp. 73, 117, 193, 456, courtesy
of the Holden family; pp. 16, 140, 326, courtesy of the Moore family; p. 199, Scott Cunningham/Merrill; pp. 312,
349, 369, courtesy of the Shafer family; p. 274, courtesy of the Simpson family; pp. 24, 207, 265, 429, courtesy of
the Waritz family; pp. 121, 178, 237, 240, courtesy of Kathy Werfelmann; pp. 119, 445, Randy Williams.

1 0 9 8 7 6 5 4 3
ISBN: 0-13-028099-2

Dedication

IN MEMORY OF PAT PORT, A BELOVED FRIEND TO US AND TO CHILDREN EVERYWHERE.

This book is dedicated to the many children, students, colleagues, parents, and family members who have taught us well throughout our personal and professional lives. They set high standards for themselves and others, respected individual differences and needs, and committed themselves unselfishly to advocate for the care and education of children. It is their lessons we have tried to share in this text and from which we continue to learn.

PREFACE

This text is a collaborative effort, not only on the part of the authors, but also because of the contributions of the many parents, professionals, researchers, and students who have added to the growing body of knowledge about how to best serve very young children with disabilities and their families. It is our intention to synthesize perspectives and information from the fields of medicine, education, intervention, psychology, law, sociology, and family life for use by those who will work with infants, toddlers, and preschoolers with special needs. It is also our goal to challenge our readers to consider the future of early intervention and their role in shaping the field of early childhood special education. We hope this text is a relevant and long-lasting resource.

The purpose of this text is to provide an introduction to early childhood professionals who plan to engage in providing services and intervention to very young children with disabilities. It is not intended as a methods text, but rather as a foundation regarding the philosophy, history, family impact, legal issues, and medical concerns that are most relevant to early services to children with exceptional needs. Though early childhood special education teachers may make up the majority of readers who use this text, the term *early childhood professional* is used to address individuals in many disciplines, including healthcare, social work, physical and occupational therapy, child care, and those who are involved in interagency services to young children and their families.

Chapters 1 and 2 provide an overview of the guiding philosophies of the text, which will be applied and reiterated throughout the book, and a review of the history of the care of young children and the growth of special services for those with disabilities. Chapters 3 through 7 provide detail on normal child development and the etiology of disabling conditions that affect the very young child with exceptional needs. Chapters 8 through 10 address how intervention and support are provided to young children and how families might best be served.

Very young children with special needs are the focus of this text, but to thoroughly understand and serve a child with disabilities, one must be knowledgeable of normal development, must understand how health and genetics affect potential, and must recognize the impact of the child's family and environment on realizing that potential. Throughout the book, the stories of families will be provided through case studies, and special issues will be identified through close-ups, in order to provide real life examples. The text attempts to be interdisciplinary, inclusive, and family-focused.

ACKNOWLEDGMENTS

The authors wish to extend their deepest gratitude to the following people for their insight, inspiration, and encouragement. Though every person listed was extremely busy, they gave generously of their time and talents. There are no words adequate to express our thanks.

Editor: Ann Davis

The parents who shared their family histories and advice: David and Priscilla DeWolf, James and Judy Holden, Marsha and James Moore, Ann and Tom Simpson, Tammy and Mitch Waritz, Kim and Mark Schafer, Amy and Michael Finkel, and Sarah and Terry Berke.

Photographers: Betsy Downey, Kathy Werfelmann, and Randy Williams

Organizations that permitted our photographers to do their work: Gonzaga University's School of Education Preschool, Martin Luther King Center, Shriners Hospital, and the Spokane Guilds' School.

Reviewers who kindly read our manuscript and provided constructive comments: Elizabeth Brennan, San Francisco State University; Barbara Lowenthal, Northeastern Illinois University; Maureen R. Norris, Bellarmine College; Gwen Russell, The University of Tennessee at Martin; and Lorraine S. Taylor, State University of New York at New Paltz.

DISCOVER THE COMPANION WEBSITE ACCOMPANYING THIS BOOK

THE PRENTICE HALL COMPANION WEBSITE: A VIRTUAL LEARNING ENVIRONMENT

Technology is a constantly growing and changing aspect of our field that is creating a need for content and resources. To address this emerging need, Prentice Hall has developed an online learning environment for students and professors alike—Companion Websites—to support our textbooks.

In creating a Companion Website, our goal is to build on and enhance what the textbook already offers. For this reason, the content for each user-friendly website is organized by topic and provides the professor and student with a variety of meaningful resources. Common features of a Companion Website include:

FOR THE PROFESSOR—

Every Companion Website integrates **Syllabus Manager**™, an online syllabus creation and management utility.

- **Syllabus Manager**™ provides you, the instructor, with an easy, step-by-step process to create and revise syllabi, with direct links into Companion Website and other online content without having to learn HTML.
- Students may log on to your syllabus during any study session. All they need to know is the web address for the Companion Website and the password you've assigned to your syllabus.
- After you have created a syllabus using **Syllabus Manager**™, students may enter the syllabus for their course section from any point in the Companion Website.
- Clicking on a date, the student is shown the list of activities for the assignment. The activities for each assignment are linked directly to actual content, saving time for students.
- Adding assignments consists of clicking on the desired due date, then filling in the details of the assignment—name of the assignment, instructions, and whether or not it is a one-time or repeating assignment.

◆ In addition, links to other activities can be created easily. If the activity is on-line, a URL can be entered in the space provided, and it will be linked automatically in the final syllabus.

◆ Your completed syllabus is hosted on our servers, allowing convenient updates from any computer on the Internet. Changes you make to your syllabus are immediately available to your students at the next log on.

FOR THE STUDENT—

◆ **Topic Overviews**—outline key concepts in topic areas
◆ **Electronic Bluebook**—send homework or essays directly to your instructor's email with this paperless form
◆ **Message Board**— serves as a virtual bulletin board to post—or respond to—questions or comments to/from a national audience
◆ **Chat**—real-time chat with anyone who is using the text anywhere in the country—ideal for discussion and study groups, class projects, etc.
◆ **Web Destinations**—links to www sites that relate to each topic area
◆ **Professional Organizations**—links to organizations that relate to topic areas
◆ **Additional Resources**—access to topic-specific content that enhances material found in the text

To take advantage of these and other resources, please visit the *Very Young Children with Special Needs,* Second Edition, Companion Website at

www.prenhall.com/howard

Brief Contents

CONTENTS

CASE STUDIES AND CLOSE-UPS

PHILOSOPHY OF EARLY EDUCATION

The potential possibilities of any child are the most intriguing and stimulating in all creation.

(Ray L. Wilbur)

The first cry in the delivery room, the sudden pause in what has been a growing frenzy of action and emotion, like a long exhalation of relief and joy; a baby is born. Parents beam, laugh, and cry; attendants share smiles and swing into action; and baby, bewildered and naked, draws in the first breath of life. Whatever this little one's life will be, it is begun; totally dependent on family, caregivers, educators, and the community. One new life, whose potential is determined not only by genetics, environment, and accidents of fate, but by the larger value and support society provides, begins its journey.

As we turn the century, early education for infants and children with special needs offers both promise and challenge. While the field is still young and discovering its knowledge-base, it is also established enough to be considered a necessary and important part of the educational system. Today, to a much greater degree than in the past, society acknowledges the need for early childhood services and values the quality of care and education provided for young children. Professional educators recognize the legitimacy and importance of study in the area of early development. Consequently, Congress has mandated the provision of services to preschool-aged children with disabilities and encouraged states to meet the needs of infants and toddlers with and at risk for developmental delays. Families can expect to become advocates for their children by providing continuous input into the manner of care received in child care, early intervention, and preschool services.

Exciting opportunities open in the field of early childhood **special education** bring serious responsibilities as well. Much is expected of early educators today. Professionals must be knowledgeable in issues important to families, must demonstrate skill in providing direct services to children, and can contribute to the growing body of knowledge about early development and care. The recent, impressive growth of early childhood special education is a legacy that professionals can advance only by understanding the philosophy and knowledge-base of disciplinary best practices. A **best practice** is a dynamic concept, changing in content as the technologies of service and education are extended through research and application. Early childhood educators should expect to be lifelong learners, keeping abreast of evolutionary changes and, at the same time, actively taking part in these changes. The current assumptions of best practice most important in the field of early childhood special education include the following:

1. A growing professional treats the field with an **attitude of science.** That is, individuals respect data-based information and evaluate the effects of new procedures, materials, or interventions by their impact on children and families being served.
2. An early childhood professional values the **inclusion** of children in natural settings where they engage in age-appropriate activities with peers of diverse backgrounds and abilities.
3. An effective professional is **culturally sensitive,** prepared to work with various populations and cultures in respectful and supportive ways.
4. A professional in early childhood education recognizes that very young children are a part of their larger family support systems and the environments that surround them. Such a professional may pro-

Building blocks of our philosophy for Early Childhood Education.

vide direct services to children, but only within the context of family needs and environmental demands, and in ways that will **empower** families.

5. An early childhood professional works **collaboratively** with experts from other disciplines to develop and provide the comprehensive services very young children need.

6. Finally, early childhood special educators must practice their profession with the highest **ethical standards** for the children and families served. Professionals must serve as **advocates** for parents and children, politically and professionally, as well as through service to their communities.

Professionals now entering early childhood special education are in the position of launching their careers equipped with skills and attitudes others have taken centuries to identify and develop. This chapter will explore these key concepts in terms of their value to professionals. These concepts also will be woven throughout the content of the text.

THE IMPORTANCE OF AN ATTITUDE OF SCIENCE

Many professionals consider education to be an art; that is, a natural aptitude or ability granted a person at birth, which flowers with opportunity and experience. Some of this may be true; certainly most professionals in early childhood education were drawn into the field by the pleasure they found in working with young children and their families. Some gifted individuals possess talents that seem especially suited to working with infants, toddlers, and preschoolers. They display tolerance, playfulness, and a keen intuition for teaching. Others may be adept at communicating with children and parents, they may be more sensitive to others' needs, or they may be more skilled at working with diverse personalities and backgrounds. However, in all fields the factor separating hobby artists from professional artists is the quality of study and effort they put into developing their natural gifts, whether they be painting, dance, drama, or teaching. Inspiration comes not from spontaneity, but from a combination of knowledge, talent, and experience.

Professional artists enhance their talents by a reflective study of the work of other artists. They strive to identify principles that will improve their craft and advance the field for others. An artful teacher who relies on raw ability alone may take years to become skillful and helpful for a variety of students. Another artful teacher who reads the professional literature, experiments with and evaluates recommended materials and procedures, and holds an attitude of science builds on natural talent to efficiently become a versatile and effective teacher.

WHAT IS AN ATTITUDE OF SCIENCE?

An attitude of science deals with what is parsimonious and empirical. **Parsimony** is the adoption of the simplest assumption in the formulation of a theory or in the interpretation of data. That is, one would look for a simple explanation before investigating more complicated possibilities. For example, if a small infant wakes crying in the middle of the night, one would first see if the child was hungry or wet. One would not immediately jump to the conclusion that the child is suffering separation anxiety or is ill with an intestinal infection. "Parsimony does not guarantee correctness—because the simplest explanation may not always be the correct one—but it prevents our being so imaginative as to lose touch with the reality of observed data" (Alberto & Troutman, 1990, p. 4). Often, what is simplest is not the most interesting. For years, psychologists told mothers of children with autism that the latter were uncommunicative and developmentally delayed because the mother's relationship with her child during infancy had been cold and rejecting. This was an intriguing theory that grew from a complicated Freudian explanation based on psychotherapy with verbal adults, but it was not the most parsimonious. A great deal of mental suffering on the part of mothers, as well as misspent therapy, might have been saved if a parsimonious explanation had been investigated earlier. While there is still no explanation for the etiology of autism, parsimony might have led professionals to investigate biochemical or physical causes earlier if complex theories of attribution had not been so appealing to earlier psychologists.

In special education, many methods of intervention have evolved from complicated theories. Some theories, because they make assumptions about activities in the brain that can neither be seen nor measured easily, are untestable. One example of such a method is patterning or neural training. Thousands of parents were trained to use patterning techniques to "train the brains" of children whose disabilities ranged from mild to very severe. Experts claimed that if parents completed rigorous schedules (several hours per day) of precise movement exercises, their children's brains would begin to function normally. Later, this method was declared to be ineffective, and a distraction from more practical and effective methods (American Academy of Pediatrics, 1982; Novella, 1996). In fact, recent research suggests that much of early education, including physical movement exercises, should be conducted within the context of natural daily routines (Mallory & New, 1994). The latter offers a more parsimonious solution to families and children.

An attitude of science is also a "disposition to deal with the facts rather than with what someone has said about them. . . . Science is a willingness to accept facts even when they are opposed to wishes" (Skinner, 1953, p. 6). An attitude of science requires one to be **empirical** (that is, to rely on observation or experimentation) and to be guided by practical experience rather than theory alone. A teacher who is empirical tries out new materials and procedures with careful observation to determine their effect on children or families using them. Based on the outcomes of such experiments, teachers decide to continue or discontinue the use of individual procedures. For example, theory (or trend) may indicate that pastel colors have a warm and calming effect on infants, encouraging their attention. To evaluate this recommendation, an empirical teacher might place an infant in a plain crib with a pastel yellow, pink, and blue mobile and observe carefully to see how much the infant vocalizes, kicks, looks at the mobile, and so on. This teacher would then compare the same infant's behavior when the baby is placed in the same crib and room with a mobile of contrasting white and black. Scientific teachers experiment to find out if a theory really applies in a particular situation, rather than accepting a theory without a verifiable demonstration.

Of course, a teacher cannot function efficiently if every piece of advice must be directly tested or experienced before it is adopted. Fortunately, "science is more than the mere description of events as they occur. Rather, empiricism is an attempt to discover order, to show that certain events stand in lawful relations to other events" (Skinner, 1953, p. 6). Other teachers and researchers work to **replicate** results, that is, to demonstrate the same results with other children and in other settings. A scientific teacher can then review research to identify data-based procedures that have been verified repeatedly through experimentation and that should work, with and without adaptation, in the teacher's own situation.

When the same results can be replicated reliably, and when there is a well-documented literature-base, the theory or principle has **predictive utility.** Such a theory provides accurate forecasts regarding how a child might respond in certain circumstances, thereby giving teachers a useful tool for supporting or modifying a child's behavior. This is not to say the data-based method selected will work with all children. However, the likelihood is increased that this method will work more often or effectively than an untested or unverified method. For example, the principle of **reinforcement** states that if a stimulus is a reinforcer, the behavior it follows is likely to increase in frequency. A teacher might find that giving requested items (a music box, for example) to Amy when she says "please" increases the rate of Amy's saying "please." The teacher might then use those items as consequences for Amy when she takes a step independently, predicting with some confidence that the music box (for example) will act as a reinforcer to increase Amy's independent walking.

"As the principle is tried over and over again and continues to produce the same results, we gain faith in it and the probability that it is indeed true for all behavior" (Whaley & Malott, 1971, p. 444). When a body of knowledge is advanced enough to provide a set of principles based on extensive research and experimentation, it becomes a **conceptual system.** A conceptual system shows researchers and teachers how similar procedures may be derived from basic principles. "This can have the effect of making a body of technology into a discipline rather than a collection of tricks. Collections of tricks historically have been difficult to expand systematically, and when they were extensive, difficult to learn and teach" (Baer, Wolf, & Risley, 1968, p. 97).

Look again at the example of Amy's saying "please." Using the music box as a consequence seems like a pretty good trick to Ms. Johnson, who is visiting that day. When she returns to her classroom, she tries the music box as a consequence for Joey to see if it will increase his babbling. Nothing happens. Ms. Johnson would have been more successful if she understood the principle behind the use of the music box. If she had the *concept* of reinforcement in her repertoire, she would have looked for some consequence that was already effective in increasing the rate of Joey's behavior. A brief observation might show that Joey reaches for a toy more frequently when the toy is squeezed to make a noise each time Joey reaches for it. Squeezing the toy as a consequence to increase Joey's babbling has a higher probability of success than playing the music box. Or, if Ms. Johnson recognized the concept that a child's frequently chosen activities or materials often act as reinforcers, she might have found that marshmallows, bouncing, or clapping would also be predictable reinforcers. Ms. Johnson's skills would have been much improved if she had a data-based conceptual system from which to work, and not just a "trick." Applied behavior analysis offers one data-based conceptual system that is of great value to educators. Behavioral approaches are parsimonious in that they deal with

Table 1–1   Basic principles of applied behavior analysis.

Basic Principle	Contingent Consequence	Effect on Future Rate of Behavior	Example
Reinforcement	When a stimulus is presented (positive) or removed (negative) contingent upon a response,	the future probability of that response *increases.*	A child who chews his carrot carefully before swallowing is given ice cream immediately after and in the future he chews carefully more often. (positive reinforcement)
Punishment	When a stimulus is presented or removed contingent upon a response,	the future probability of that response *decreases.*	A child who hits his play partner is removed from the play activity and told to watch for five minutes before he is returned to the play activity, and in the future he hits less often.
Extinction	When the contingent stimulus for a previously reinforced response is no longer presented,	the future probability of the behavior *decreases.*	A child who takes toys away from others has in the past been allowed to keep playing with the stolen toys and her rate of stealing toys increased. Now the teacher makes sure she must return any toy taken from another child and her rate of stealing decreases.

observable relationships between environmental stimuli, behavioral responses, and contingent consequences.

"For a behaviorist, all learning principles are defined on the basis of what actually happens, not what we think is happening" (Alberto & Troutman, 1990, p. 23). The basic principles of behavior analysis were developed through extensive empirical testing and were replicated in thousands of classroom, clinic, and home applications. Therefore, the principles and procedures have a high degree of predictive utility and many successful interventions have been developed based on this conceptual system. Though it is not within the scope of this text to teach the principles of behavior analysis, a few examples drawn from this discipline will help to illustrate elements of a conceptual system. The basic principles of behavior analysis include reinforcement, punishment, and extinction, though these simple principles have been extended to dozens of procedures that help children learn (see Table 1–1). Yet this conceptual system, like all others, must be challenged by scientific educators to build on and improve their ability to match intervention to the needs of children and families served. The scientific teacher builds on natural talent for working with children, families, and professionals by drawing from a knowledge-base of concepts that work because they are parsimonious, empirically derived, and replicable.

Educational research is the way in which one acquires dependable and useful information about the educative process. Its goal is to discover general principles or interpretations of behavior that can be used to explain, predict, and control events in education situations. . . . (Ary, Jacobs, & Razavich, 1996, p. 22)

Gallagher (1998) questioned whether the field of special education is at a point where its knowledge-base can be considered scientific. Certainly, to reach this goal, we must aspire to achieve two things: (1) to identify generalizations that allow us to explain, predict, and control the outcomes of our interventions, and (2) to advance progressively, that is, to lay some questions to rest as we work to solve others. Gallagher (1998) cautioned that science must never replace values as a part of the professional conversation. We hasten to add, however, that values must also not replace empiricism; it is essential that professionals balance both. We must embrace a philosophy of advocacy that also determines, explains, and makes effective our course of action.

Case Study

LIVING WITH AUTISM: INTERVIEW WITH AMY FINKEL

Autism is the third most common developmental disability, more common than Down syndrome, but the research dollars are 1% of almost any other disability. Someday, I'd like to get on the lecture tour and educate people about what autism is, because there are many misperceptions. First you get the scornful looks, like "What's wrong with you? Boy, you have a real brat!" A lot of autistic children are beautiful children and you would never guess in a million years that there was anything wrong with them because they look fine physically. When your autistic child acts out in public, you learn to develop a thick skin.

When people hear the word autism, this look of horror comes across their faces. Usually two things come to mind. Often all people know about autism is from having seen the movie *Rainman*. They think your child is like the man in *Rainman*. "Wow, I bet he knows all those dates!" Or, the other thing they envision is a child sitting in a corner banging his head against the wall; a child who refuses to be touched. Both of these visions scare people, so they treat you and your family like you have the plague.

You lose friends. Some people are fearful their child will "catch it." Certain peers don't want to come over and play with the child's sibling. You just know that the parents have thought that maybe it's not a good idea that their child develop a friendship with yours. You have to deal with that.

I would like to educate people and be more politically active. I'm currently trying to get a seat on the state advisory committee for disabilities. There are some openings coming up and I'm going to put my application in. I think school districts need to do better for these children in terms of intensity, in terms of appropriateness, and it needs to start at the federal level. I'm going to try to be more politically active. I'm going to try to speak at conventions and conferences and help families get started with their own home programs.

There needs to be an autism protocol for physicians. Speech therapists need to be able to diagnose autism because typically they are the first professionals to see these kids. Early intervention is so important, that if speech/language consultants could suggest a diagnosis and refer children, that would be a help. So many physicians are scared to diagnose with the "A-word" because they don't know how to treat it. They may cop out and diagnose pervasive developmental delay (PDD) instead, but in the long run that really does parents a disservice. There needs to be a protocol where parents can be told, this treatment works 50% of the time, this treatment is effective 47% of the time. This may work or may not work, these are the risks, these are the potential benefits, these are your options. Parents need a guide.

There is so much bad information out there. A lot of parents early on tried infusions of gamma globulin that is usually used for severe immunodeficiency disorders. The down side to that treatment is that some autistic kids who received those infusions died of anaphylactic shock. The recent hysteria over Secretin is another example of why a protocol guide is needed. So many parents tried Secretin without knowing any of the potential negative side effects and there are quite a few. We tried it for Josh, but we tried it knowing all the potential risks.

Applied behavior analysis (ABA) needs to be right at the top of the list of any recommended treatments because right now it is the only thing that makes a real impact of any significance at all. ABA and visual communication systems both work. But, a lot of parents don't know that and they'll start out with the quick, easy fixes that are cheap, but have little impact, and they'll waste valuable years with auditory integration training (AIT), they'll fly to Hawaii to swim with the dolphins, they'll go to Disneyland hoping that their child will respond like one autistic boy did who suddenly started talking when he saw the Wolfman there. That was just a fluke, but parents are so desperate for something.

Parents need solid information about ABA and need to get started with it while they try other peripheral interventions on the side as money, time, and energy permit. That's what we did. We used ABA as the cornerstone of Josh's therapy but we've also tried megavitamins, dimethyl glycine, Secretin infusion, vitamin B-6 and magnesium coupled with folic acid, and AIT. We have a friend who is from Hawaii and if we ever have an opportunity to have a vacation, I'll swim with the dolphins, you betcha! But we'll do the ABA at home first, because that, by far, has made the difference.

It helps me helping other families because it gets me off my own pity pot. One of the ways I've dealt with my despair and my anger and sadness over this is to just get busy and stay active and try to channel those negative feelings into trying to do positive things for other people. My biggest fear, though, is what the future holds for my son when I'm gone. I'm hoping that his siblings will step in and make sure that he's living in a good place, that his finger nails are clipped, that he's not dirty and his clothes are clean. But I can't count on that. You never know what life holds. You do the best you can for your kids but you never know what they're going to grow up and end up being.

That's why I decided to get started in the specialty adult family home business. I want to make an impact in this community. I want to establish really high-quality adult family homes of which Joshua will end up being a trustee. So that he'll always have one of his own homes to live in. If I make a successful business out of it, there is no reason why maybe his brother or his sister wouldn't want to step in at some point and take over the directorship of that.

Before autism, I had a normal life. I had a career in international marketing. The ironic thing is that my bachelor's degree was in liberal arts with an emphasis in marketing. I had so many interests that I was never able to focus on any one thing. I knew a little bit about everything. What Josh has done for me personally is to give me that focus and that passion. I got started a little late in life, but better late than never. I try to look at the positive . Maybe this is God's way of giving me something so I can help more people. I try not to get too philosophical about it. I'd rather not have focus if it meant I didn't have a disabled child. But I am very focused now on my career and education.

It's been tough too, in the marriage department. It's been a real struggle and I think that finally, this past six months to a year, we've finally gotten past it. Frankly, I think we had one foot into divorce court there for a couple of years. I think the only reason we didn't get divorced was that we were so busy and so devastated that neither one of us had the time to go file the papers! I guess that was good because we worked through it and we are past the worst of it now. It's forced both of us to really reach inside and be honest. It forced us to deal with a lot of stuff that most married couples don't ever have to deal with.

Josh's autism has had a huge impact on everybody. One thing I don't like is when people say, "God gave you this disabled child, because He knew your son would have a good home." I find that patronizing. One of the comments I hear a lot is, "Oh Amy, you're so terrific with Josh's autism!" I think, oh sure, drug addicts have normal children. Me, I don't do any drugs, I don't drink, I don't smoke, I exercise, but I'm the one with the disabled child. Why? "Because you have such a good home for him. God knew!" Please!

Josh Finkel on a swing

INCLUSION

Inclusion is a term generally applied to educating students with and without disabilities together within regular classes in neighborhood schools (Crockett & Kauffman, 1998). However, in practice, inclusion differs markedly from setting to setting; in some schools children are in regular classrooms on a full-time or part-time basis, in others they attend special classes within the neighborhood school, and in some cases they are even sent to segregated schools. In order to understand inclusion, we must return to its roots (Crockett & Kauffman, 1998).

Thirty years ago, parents united in advocating for children with disabilities at a time when many were totally excluded from any educational services. From 1972 though 1974, court cases regarding the right-to-education were heard in 28 states (Crockett & Kauffman, 1998). When Congress was finally persuaded to act with the original 1975 legislation of the Individuals with Disabilities Education Act (IDEA), they called for the free, appropriate education of children in the **least restrictive environment** (LRE). Prior to IDEA's passage, one million children were excluded from public school because of their disabilities (Yell, 1998). Those who attended public school often received inadequate services in isolated settings.

Least restrictive environment is the legal term used to define the rights of children with disabilities to be educated in settings where they are not segregated from children without disabilities. The law states:

> 1. That to the maximum extent appropriate, children with disabilities are educated with children who are nondisabled; and 2. That special classes, separate schooling, or other removal of children with disabilities from the regular educational environment occurs only when the nature or severity of the disability is such that education in regular classes with the use of supplementary aids and services cannot be achieved satisfactorily. (Section 34 C.F.R. 300.55o(b))

The legal provisions for the LRE have never supported an immutable rule of placement, but rather a preference for including children in regular classrooms and allowing specialized (separated) services as needed by individuals (Yell, 1995). When asked if placement of a child with a disability in the regular classroom clearly constitutes the LRE, the courts have responded with the ambiguous answer, "It depends" (Crockett & Kauffman, 1998; Zirkel, 1996). One is advised to consider how well the child is progressing in the regular setting, the preference of the parents, the availability and need for special **related services,** and other highly individualized factors. To date, the Supreme Court has declined to hear any LRE cases, though a great many lower court rulings have been made.

Fuchs and Fuchs (1998) defined inclusion as a **continuum of services** that depend on the regular classroom and a variety of options in terms of special education placements and related services. "In principle, each special education placement on the continuum (from residential facility to special day school to self-contained classes and resource rooms) offers specialized, differentiated, individualized and intensive instruction, all of which are continuously evaluated for effectiveness" (Fuchs &

Fuchs, 1998, p. 3). Within this system, teachers and students work on the general education curricula and all have the understanding that the goal of special education instruction outside the regular classroom is to move students closer to being successful in the regular classroom.

An examination of the most recent data provided by the *Reports to Congress* (1997) demonstrated trends toward placing more children in regular education settings or settings that were closer to the regular classroom (McLeskey, Henry, & Hodges, 1999). Children with mild disabilities have made the greatest progress in terms of being served most of the time in regular classrooms; these include those with speech or language disabilities, learning disabilities, health impairments, and orthopedic impairments. Children with serious emotional disturbance, visual impairments, and hearing impairments are also more likely to be enrolled in regular education settings than in the past, though a large percentage are still served in separate schools. Children with mental retardation and deaf-blindness have made progress toward moving out of separate schools but continue to have only a small percentage educated in the regular classroom. Finally, children who are multiply disabled have made the least progress toward moving into less restrictive settings.

With the most recent revision of the Individuals with Disabilities Act of 1997, early intervention also stresses "natural" settings for providing services to very young children. This means that as much as is appropriate, given individual child and family needs, infants and toddlers should be served in homes, day cares, and preschools where children without disabilities would be naturally present. But, in defense of center-based services as continued options, one parent pointed out, "Having a child with a disability is never 'natural' and the most important thing is to meet that child's needs," (J. Gately, personal communication, 1999). Perhaps what is most important about the inclusion effort, is to think of special education with its related therapies, as a service, not a place.

THE CONTROVERSY OVER FULL INCLUSION

Full inclusion occurs when a student with a disability becomes a full-time member of a program the child might attend if he or she did not have a disability, and the child is not removed for the delivery of educational, social, or related services (Fuchs & Fuchs, 1998). Full inclusion means that every student, not just students with significant disabilities, or students with mild disabilities, or students with perceptual disabilities, has an opportunity to become a contributing member of a heterogeneous group of children. Students participate in all the regular daily routines of the classroom. These routines are modified through specialized instructional or curricular strategies to meet each child's individually determined functional, social, or educational objectives. Each student has multiple opportunities during the day for naturally occurring positive interactions with students without disabilities.

Preschool programs, due to their ecology, may provide an ideal context for inclusion. According to Mallory and New (1994), preschool classrooms are predicated on social activity. Most early childhood programs are language and social skills based and have multiple daily activities in which children are encouraged to learn from contextually relevant and problem-based curricula.

With full inclusion, the general classroom teacher is the primary interventionist, and has frequent and regular consultation from educational specialists, from administrators, and from the children's parents—all of whom comprise a decision-making team supporting the classroom teacher. A child is fully included when there is access to routine curricular and extracurricular activities and the child is a part of not just the classroom, but the school and the community. In sum, full inclusion is supported education—support for the classroom teacher and support for the student.

The debate over whether inclusion or full inclusion is best for all children draws impassioned supporters from parents and professionals on both sides of the issue. Supporters of full inclusion believe that at some point its challenge to this generation of educators may be viewed as a measure of their moral resolve to build a world that is more dignified, more just, more ethical, and more practical. Since schools and classrooms are microcosms of the society, the extent to which children are isolated from each other in schools reflects society's willingness and intent to isolate this same group of individuals outside the walls of the school (Gerrard, 1994).

Full inclusion is not considered as simply a child's placement, but has to do with the integrity of the placement. When a child with a disability is placed in a regular setting without the delivery of the specialized services that define special education, everyone in the system loses—the teacher, the other students, the parents, and the children with disabilities themselves (Fuchs & Fuchs, 1998).

JUSTIFICATION FOR FULL INCLUSION

The practice of full inclusion has been variously justified by identifying social, philosophical, ethical, legal, and empirical arguments. First, if children with and without disabilities are educated together, they learn important lifelong lessons and skills necessary for sustained positive relationships with each other. That is, if individuals are expected to get along in integrated environments as adults, then they must have opportunities to learn to get along as children (Salisbury, Palombaro, & Long, 1993). In fact, some studies support the notion that facilitated inclusion models lead to a higher frequency of interactions and enhance the development of social and adaptive skills of children with disabilities (Coles & Meyer, 1991; Fox & Hanline, 1993; Hanline, 1993). For example, McGee, Paradis, and Feldman (1993) found that when children with autism were surrounded by children without disabilities, they displayed autistic behavior at a lower rate than when they were either with other children with autism or alone. When preschool children with disabilities attend inclusive programs, their peers are more accepting of them than of those in self-contained programs (Esposito & Koorland, 1989; Guralnick & Groom, 1988).

Second, since the late 1960s, the field of special education has promoted a philosophy of normalization, which is based on the practice of treating persons with disabilities as valuable members of society (Wolfensberger, 1972). When persons are segregated, labeled, or treated in any way that sets them further apart for their differences, then their worth is devalued (Lipsky & Gartner, 1989; Wolfensberger, 1983). When such a practice is commonplace, individuals with differences begin to see themselves as less valuable and to behave in ways that match their devalued status. In this scenario, young children with disabilities can achieve their highest potential only when they are provided with normal opportunities. This rationale may be the most vulnerable, and the one that leaves full inclusion open to criticism as a passing trend or frivolous sentimentality. Yet, Rainforth (1994) contended that, "philosophy is a powerful influence, perhaps *the* influence, on how individual needs of children can be met most appropriately" (p. 252).

Third, the U.S. legal system protects the equitable treatment of all citizens. The Equal Protection Clause of the Fourteenth Amendment to the Constitution provided the legal basis for the Civil Rights Act of 1965, which in turn set the stage to argue for equal treatment of persons with disabilities. In 1973, Congress wrote Section 504 of the Vocational Rehabilitation Act, indicating that no person can be discriminated against solely on the basis of the presence of a disability. The Least Restrictive Environment mandate of IDEA further added to the legal foundation for full inclusion. This collective legislation, however, has led to thousands of hearings in which parents and school districts have disagreed about the proper interpretation for specific children.

While it is important to justify full inclusion with an empirical basis, it is perhaps more important to identify strategies for improving the success of students within natural settings (Gerrard, 1994). As one father questioned, "Why must children 'prove' they are ready to be in regular classrooms? We do not ask that of any other members of our society" (J. Terhaar, personal communication, January 16, 1995). Though research on this topic is complex, preliminary findings indicate that children with and without disabilities perform at least as well in integrated settings as children who are separated based on the presence of a disability (Fox & Hanline, 1993; Hanline, 1993). Furthermore, a promising knowledge-base is evolving that provides a means of bringing services to children, rather than bringing children to services (Kamps, Leonard, Vernon, Dugan, & Delquadri, 1992).

The final rationale for advocating fully inclusive preschool programs is related to personnel issues. Arguably, segregated early childhood special education programs pose the greatest challenge for teachers. Teachers must plan for and execute educational programs that provide individual instruction for students with a wide range of ages and disabilities. The growing number of children identified with significant behavioral problems increases the chaos in a classroom where children have limited language skills and only modest development of rule-governed behavior. The impossibility of managing such a classroom is likely to lead to teacher resignations, or perhaps more damaging, teacher burnout. By contrast, inclusive classrooms can absorb children with disabilities while those typical students who follow rules, play independently, and stay on task for reasonable lengths of time, help adults by providing modeling and by requiring less management.

OPPOSITION TO FULL INCLUSION

Ample justification for full inclusion has not been matched with concomitant implementation. Reasons for this delay include practical as well as sociological barriers. Gerrard (1994) summarized six major objections to inclusion:

> **Lack of input by regular educators:** Since inclusive efforts began in earnest in the late 1980s, there has been very little input or initiative from regular educators themselves. Yet, it is the expectation of parents of children with disabilities and special educators, the forces behind

the movement, that changes take place in the regular education domain. Many regular educators resent the fact that major changes must take place in their classrooms when the practice of inclusion is really based on someone else's ideology.

Lack of empirical evidence: At this point there is a small or only suggestive research base to support full inclusion, though some argue that we cannot wait on the research (Fuchs & Fuchs, 1998). Research on full inclusion, reported to date, fails to support its effectiveness for all students (MacMillan & Gresham, 1996). Many oppose full-scale implementation of full inclusion before it is understood and demonstrated through careful controls and evaluations (McKinney & Hocutt, 1998).

Practitioner resistance: Opposition to inclusion by regular and special education teachers, who tend to prefer the pull-out model, is fierce. This resistance is likely due to educators being comfortable with what they know—and what teachers know—as separate schooling. It may also reflect the difficulty of adapting curriculum or adjusting procedures for individual needs.

Educational reform: Teachers are pulled by seemingly opposing forces. While educational reform efforts are pressing teachers to improve educational achievement, there is also a demand on schools to be leaders in promoting equity.

Protection: Many educators and parents feel that separate schooling is necessary to protect children with disabilities from rejection by their nondisabled peers.

Impracticality: Historically, children were removed from the regular classroom because it was believed that specialized education could not be conducted effectively in a general education setting. This argument is still compelling, as regular classrooms are seen as inflexible in regard to inclusion. Hence, the needs of students with disabilities cannot be fully met there.

The summarized results of 27 studies surveying almost 10,000 teachers found that though regular education teachers generally favored inclusion, fewer than a third felt full inclusion was the best placement and about 30% felt including children with disabilities would be too disruptive. Fewer than 25% felt they had sufficient time for inclusion, that they were properly prepared for inclusion, or that they would be given sufficient training (MacMillan & Gresham, 1996).

Some educators believe full inclusionists are too uncompromising and presumptive in their thinking that special education is equivalent to confinement when many parents want the options of alternative placements for their children (Fuchs & Fuchs, 1998). Full inclusionists may also be too unrealistic in their belief that regular education can accommodate for all children, despite the severity and complexity of their disabilities. Furthermore, some citizens with disabilities resent the notion that placement in special education settings is somehow immoral; members of the deaf community, for example, treasure their deaf culture.

Perhaps because these arguments have not been sufficiently addressed by proponents of full inclusion, the debate over full inclusion as a philosophy and a policy continues (Rainforth, 1994). While some schools have seized the opportunity to explore new delivery systems that permit inclusive education, a majority of educational programs either maintain or purposively reestablish more traditional segregated models. Programs that have been successful are those where individual communities have adapted methods and models of inclusion to fit their own educational structure. Hence, Thousand and Villa (1991) advocated that schools moving toward full inclusion should allow "professional educators and community members . . . the flexibility and discretion to invent unique approaches and solutions to achieving . . . quality heterogeneous schooling" (p. 559). Forest (1988) further observed that schools committed to full inclusion were characterized as "incredibly child centered systems with leadership which believes in team building, cooperation, collaboration, and learning. They are also systems that dare to talk about love and social justice" (p. 2).

Representing a far different point of view are those who believe that persons should not only be recognized by their labels and segregated accordingly, but that they should develop cultures identified exclusively by a disability (Hallahan & Kauffman, 1994). For example a large percentage of deaf persons belong to the "deaf culture," a community in the broad sense that is socially, economically, and politically entwined (Singleton, 1992). Advocates of cultures of disability cite internal pride in their "differentness" and reject the intrusive imperialism of full inclusionist proponents who would dissemble this form of segregation. Likewise, Hallahan and Kauffman argued that other disability groups (e.g., learning disabilities, behavior disorders) would be better served through creation of subcultures based on the presence of a disability.

Case Study

FULL INCLUSION FOR THE FIRST TIME: INTERVIEW WITH MARSHA MOORE

The thing that I remember most about Mike's first days of being fully included in a regular classroom was the day before school started. This sounds so silly, but it brings tears to my eyes. It was routine for the teachers to post the names of the children who were in their classes to the outside of their classroom doors several days before school started, so that the students would be able to anticipate their new teachers and see which friends would be in their classes for the upcoming school year. We had driven to school so our daughter, who was in fifth grade, could get the scoop on her teacher and classmates. Mike had already been assigned to a specific first-grade classroom, and we had been given the opportunity to meet with his teacher and visit his empty classroom several days before.

As we made our way around the school, we came to Michael's classroom. There on the door was posted the classroom list and there in the list of alphabetical names in the boys' column was Michael's name! It sounds like such a simple thing, but he was finally a part of a "real" classroom. His sisters were thrilled and brought him close in hopes that he might recognize his name. They read him the names of the other children in the class. "Mike, look, this is *your* class!" they told him proudly. This symbol, just a simple class list, communicated to us that Michael finally belonged and was not just on the periphery of life. For some reason, that little list of names signified to us the beginning of community. Michael's name was neither at the top nor the bottom, but right where it should have always been.

*Mike in
school with
classmates*

Anyway, we started school. I thought to myself, "This poor teacher, she really doesn't know what she's in for." But to my surprise, those little first graders just took Mike into their hearts and included him in all they did. They cared for him and would help him. Instead of an aide being at his side to keep him from self-stimming on his shoelaces and throwing his glasses to the ground, the kids surrounded him and helped him to learn how the real world behaves.

Michael's gains have always been painfully slow for us, but he has made gains. He makes eye contact more consistently, initiates interaction with others, and attends to books. We can take him to church and even to a full-length movie. He loves to eat out, and although he's not Mr. Manners, he no longer yells, or flaps his hands or bangs his head on the back of the chair. People are not offended by him. His behavior has changed.

Some people in the school district have told me this behavior change is probably just the result of maturation. They are not certain that full inclusion for Michael in the regular classroom has really made the difference in his behavior and think he would have probably changed as much if he had spent the last several years in a self-contained classroom. Well I can guarantee he wouldn't be the same little boy without his friends by his side to model for him and remind him when he's out of line. He had been in a self-contained special education classroom from the time he was three until he was almost seven. His behavior had escalated from baby cries and back arching, when he started preschool, to hand flapping, face smacking, and loud inappropriate vocalizations as he progressed through the system. The older he got, the harder it became for us because he was bigger and stronger and much more noticeable! It was in the regular classroom that he came to know, through the assistance of his classmates, that these behaviors weren't acceptable. That's not to say that everything is perfect and we never regress a little, but things are much better.

I can't really know what inclusion has meant to Mike. He can't tell us. I only know what it has meant to us. It's great to belong to the neighborhood school and attend PTA and bake sales with the neighbors next door and down the street. It makes us happy to know that Mike has friends, not just assigned helpers. This summer three of his classmates came to visit, unannounced. They had to come on their bikes because it was quite a way, but they knew where Michael lived and wanted to come and see how he was doing. In the morning when he walks down the driveway to catch the bus, several of his buddies leave the bus line and run up the driveway to greet him. It takes a while for Mike to get to the end of the driveway, but he grins and prances when he sees them. He is excited to get on the bus in the morning and pushes himself to get up the bus stairs, just because school is something he truly looks forward to. It's just important. It means a lot to us and a lot to Mike.

SUMMARY ON INCLUSION

IDEA supports the preference for children with mild, moderate, or severe disabilities to be placed in age-appropriate regular classrooms in their neighborhood schools; it also supports a continuum of services depending on the child's needs (MacMillan & Gresham, 1996). For now, it is appropriate that these choices of options be maintained for children and families who need and prefer them. This continuum of options from full inclusion to specialized settings and services recognizes the individual needs of children and the importance of parent preferences without condoning exclusion.

Research has demonstrated that both regular and special education preschool teachers who have been provided sufficient preservice training for inclusion felt more confident about their abilities and had more positive attitudes toward teaching children with special needs (Gemmell-Crosby & Hanzlik, 1994). Some of the more effective strategies that have been used and should be taught in preservice or inservice training include team teaching (e.g., with regular and special educators), direct service by special personnel within the regular classroom, cooperative learning, peer tutoring or confederacy training, use of parallel curricula, use of technology, and accompaniment by **paraprofessionals** (Gerrard, 1994).

Recent research also compared the progress of preschoolers with disabilities in three settings: special education only with students who were disabled; integrated special education that enrolled mostly children with disabilities and a few nondisabled peers; and mainstreamed classrooms where most of the children were nondisabled peers and a few were children with disabilities. All the children were provided with similar treatments across the different placements. The integrated special education arrangement (mostly children with disabilities) produced gains that were highest for relatively higher functioning preschoolers, while the special education and mainstream classrooms (mostly nondisabled peers) produced more gains for relatively lower functioning children (Mills, Cole, Jenkins, & Dale, 1998). These results replicated previous findings. As Bricker (1995) reminded us, the needs of the child should not be lost in a movement to advocate for one type of placement over all other considerations.

THE IMPORTANCE OF BEING CULTURALLY SENSITIVE

The United States is the most ethnically diverse country in the world, including at least a hundred different racial, ethnic, and cultural groups (Taylor, 1998). In recent years, however, trends in birthrates, immigration, family structures, and economics have greatly altered national **demographics** and will continue to do so in the future. The 1990 census revealed considerable increases in minority groups compared to 10 years before: a 53% increase in Hispanics, a 107% increase in Asians, a 13.2% in African Americans, and a 37.9% increase in Native Americans.

Such diversity has often led to conflict because of a lack of receptiveness to differences (Taylor, 1998). Interpersonal reactions to others may be negative due to a number of factors:

1. *Assumed similarity.* We assume our beliefs and values are the same as others.
2. *Ethnocentrism/denigration of differences.* We hold the attitude that our own culture/origin is superior.
3. *Anxiety/tension.* We are uncomfortable when our basic values are opposed.
4. *Prejudice.* We hold a hostile attitude toward people who belong to a different group.
5. *Stereotyping.* We make assumptions about people based on their ethnic or cultural group.
6. *Comfort with the familiar.* We are drawn to people who share similar interests and values and exclude others.

Early childhood educators must overcome such tendencies not to acknowledge and respond to the importance of a child's home language and culture. We must respect and preserve this diversity (NAEYC, 1996), celebrate our shared beliefs and traditions, and honor that which is distinctive in the many groups that make up our nation (NCTE/IRA, 1996).

Professionals serving diverse children and families must become *culturally competent,* able to transform knowledge and cultural awareness into interventions that support healthy relationships within the appropriate cultural context (McPhatter, 1997). Table 1–2 identifies knowledge that is critical in becoming culturally competent.

The challenge of becoming culturally competent begins with an honest assessment of how one deals with those who are different (McPhatter, 1997). Questions to be asked include: How much time do I spend with people who are culturally different from me? How comfortable am I in immersion experiences? What is my commitment to being culturally competent? Negative answers to these questions help identify new experiences that should be sought out to improve **cultural competence.**

POPULATION TRENDS

Early in the twenty-first century, Hispanic Americans will become the country's largest ethnic minority, accounting for 100 million or 25% of the U.S. population by 2050 (Hispanic population . . . , 1997). Hispanics include immigrants from many countries and cultures connected to Spain, Mexico, Central and South America, and

Table 1–2 Essential knowledge for cultural competence.

1. Knowledge of diverse cultures, histories, traditions, values, religions, languages, and so forth.
2. Knowledge of social problems and issues related to minority communities, such as poverty, unemployment, health concerns, and community violence.
3. Familiarity with the formal and informal resources available in diverse neighborhoods and communities, such as churches and community centers.
4. Understanding of the dynamics of oppression, racism, sexism, classism, and other forms of discrimination.
5. Knowledge of the contributions of people of color, current service issues, and obstacles to providing service.
6. Knowledge of the diversity of family structure, how these families survive and excel over time.
7. Knowledge about family functioning such as childrearing practices, methods of discipline and nurturing, how heath needs are met. Knowing "what works" within family cultures.
8. Knowledge of alternative interventions that are culturally relevant. What might be viewed as manipulative behavior might be reframed as problem-solving within the demands for survival faced by minority groups.
9. Value for the longstanding informal foster/adoption/kinship care practiced in families of color.
10. Respect for the strengths and resilience of minority families.

Source: McPhatter, A. R. (1997). Cultural competence in child welfare: What is it? How do we achieve it? What happens without it? *Child Welfare,* 76(1).

the Caribbean. Asian Americans encompass an astounding variety of people, languages, religions, and cultures with many differences among them (Lee, 1998). Though relatively small, the Asian American population is growing at a rapid pace, nearly doubling between 1980 and 1990 and expecting to double again by 2010 (Lee, 1998). By the year 2050, it is predicted Caucasians will comprise only 50% of the total U.S. population (Martin & Midgley, 1994). In many of the largest urban counties and some nonmetropolitan counties, the shift has already occurred, with no single ethnic or racial group maintaining a majority (Allen & Turner, 1990). Thirty-three states have K–12 minority enrollments of 20% or more, with minority enrollment increases in 44 states in recent years. All 25 of the nation's largest city school systems have "majority minorities" (Wehrly, 1988).

A major factor influencing ethnic **demographics** is immigration with Hispanics comprising the fastest growing minority (Martin & Midgley, 1994). Today's immigrants are less well educated, poorer, and more likely to be unemployed than past immigrants. Every year nearly two thirds of legal immigrants live and work in the United States illegally before being granted legal status. Other factors contributing to demographic shifts are the birthrate, which is slightly higher in foreign-born families than for native-born citizens, and the fact that the average age of immigrant females is younger than the average age of native-born women (Martin & Midgley, 1994).

Hispanics, like most recent immigrant groups throughout history, suffer from the highest rates of poverty, have the highest school dropout rates, and are educated in the most highly segregated schools (Garcia, 1997). In 1992, 26% of Hispanic families lived below the poverty line; in 1993, 23% of Hispanic families were headed by a female, and 72% of Hispanics held unskilled or semiskilled jobs. About 50% of Hispanics will not finish high school, 38% are held back at least one grade, and 50% are overage at grade 12. Hispanics were placed in special education six times more often than the general population. Ninety percent of Hispanic students are in urban districts and 82% attend segregated schools.

African American enrollment in public schools increased 3% between 1972 and 1992, while Caucasian enrollment dropped 14% (Orfield, Schley, Glass, & Reardon, 1994). In the 1990 census, 32% of African American families reported living below the poverty level; more than 57% of those lived in urban areas (Russo & Talbert-Johnson, 1997). Though African Americans make up 16% of the public school population, they comprise 28% of all students in special education. It is predicted that by the year 2020, children of color will make up 46% of the school population, yet fewer than 5% of teachers will be African American (Russo & Talbert-Johnson, 1997).

Unfortunately, special education services are not proportionately representative of minority populations (Rounds, Weil, & Bishop, 1994). Hispanics, African Americans, and American Indians tend to be overrepresented in special education. This is due to many confounding factors that tend to correlate with minority status: low educational attainment, language differences, lack of economic resources, and lack of health insurance, all of which may contribute to an endless cycle of educational disadvantage (Smart & Smart, 1997). Though difficult to estimate precisely, the discriminating impact of institutional biases in testing, curriculum, social expectations, and teaching strategies on the appropriate education of minority children is also apparent.

ECONOMICS

From 1950 until 1969, the average family's economic situation was improving; the poverty rate for children dropped to about 14% (Mitchell, 1995). The 1980s saw a dramatic increase in the number of children living in poverty in the United States; by the early 1990s, about 20% of all children lived below the poverty line; and by 1993, the figure for children under age 6 who lived in poverty reached 26% (Guo, 1998). An estimated seven million children under the age of 6 live in poverty in the United States, and two thirds of these children live in working families who are not on welfare (Lewis, 1997). The consequences of childhood poverty are multiple. Poor children are more likely to have a low birth weight, more likely to die in the first year, more likely to suffer hunger or abuse, and less likely to have adequate medical care. Children from poor homes start off at a disadvantage, with less access to prenatal and early health care, quality day care as infants, and quality early childhood programs (Slavin, 1998).

In this century, the number of single-parent and working poor families increased, and more and more mothers of young children were compelled to enter the labor force (Olmsted, 1992). In 1940, 87% of young children had a nonemployed parent who could provide full-time care (Hernandez, 1995). By 1989, only 48% of children under six had a parent who didn't work outside the home. The number of children who spend a significant amount of each day in professional care places greater responsibility on early educators to provide appropriate experiences for these children and their families.

The likelihood that a child will live in poverty tends to parallel the data on children from minority families. While 18% of Caucasian children are poor, 46% of African American children live in poverty; this proportion has not been lower than 40% since 1959, when the Census Bureau first started measuring childhood poverty (Mitchell, 1995). More than two out of three African American children in single-mother households are poor (Montgomery, Kiely, & Pappas, 1996). As with other trends, a disproportionate percentage of African Americans and Hispanics are among the homeless (Williams & DeSander, 1999).

Children make up the fastest growing segment of the homeless population (Williams & DeSander, 1999). Families with children represented 36% of those in homeless shelters (Children's Defense Fund, 1998). By 1997, more than a million American children were homeless, 250,000 of those were below school age (Nunez & Collignon, 1997). These children displayed a wide range of social, emotional, and academic difficulties typically seen in children who qualify for special education (Walther-Thomas, Korinek, McLaughlin, & Williams, 1996). These deficiencies include poor personal/emotional development, reduced gross motor and fine motor skills, and fewer interaction skills. Poor children also have significantly higher rates of lead poisoning which contributes to neurological damage and long-term behavior problems.

Early educators must be especially sensitive to the needs of poor and homeless children when designing programs (McCormick & Holden, 1992). That is, programs for young homeless children must be maximally flexible about scheduling, opening at earlier times and closing later, and providing respite care for parents. Programs should provide transportation or funds to cover transportation expenses. They should provide social and case-management services and emphasize special attention for specific developmental delays and emotional problems that poor and homeless children may exhibit. Staff of such programs must be sensitive to the support and encouragement needed by parents.

FAMILY COMPOSITION

Most people recognize that the traditional nuclear family of "Ozzie and Harriet" is neither predominate today, nor did it every truly exist, but perhaps many do not fully comprehend how much diversity exists. In 1992, for every 100 children born, 58 entered a broken family (Fagan & Coontz, 1997). By 1993, the proportion of young children living with one parent in the home was 21% for Caucasians, 66% for African Americans, and 34% for Hispanics (Hernandez, 1995). These statistics are significant since research indicates that children in families headed by both parents, biological or adoptive, tend to do better in terms of social adjustment and academic performance than children in either **blended families** or those headed by a single parent (Thomson, Hanson, & McLanahan, 1994). The single-parent family is a much riskier place for a child (Fagan & Coontz, 1997). Being born out of wedlock increases the risk of infant mortality and of ill health in early infancy; the rates of abuse are 13 times higher in single-mother families and 20 times higher in single-father families (Fagan & Coontz, 1997).

Most of the differences in children's outcomes are, however, explained by economic disadvantage. In other words, adoptive families and those headed by two biological parents tend to be more economically stable; though it is the resources, not the family configuration, that places children at social and academic risk. Interestingly, Thomson et al. (1994) found that in most cases parental childrearing behaviors had much less to do with children's outcomes than family income and parents' educational levels. Unfortunately, among very poor families making less than $15,000 a year, marriage has all but disappeared and among working class families with incomes between $15,000 and $30,000 a year, married parents don't exist for 45% of children.

The sharp rise in childhood poverty since the mid-1970s is accounted for in large part by the increased proportion of children living in families headed by single mothers (Montgomery, Kiely, & Pappas, 1996). Between 1970 and 1994, the percentage of children living in single-mother households rose from about 13% to about 31% (Florsheim, Tolan, & Gorman-Smith, 1998). There is substantial evidence that children growing up in single-mother families are at greater risk for developing achievement-related problems which may be due to the consequences of being financially disadvantaged (Florsheim et al., 1998). The poverty rate for children in single-mother families is five times higher than that for children in two-parent families. Over 55% of children in single female-headed families live in poverty. The majority of these single mothers are divorced or separated, but the number of never married mothers is increasing.

Adolescents in single-parent families are more likely to become adolescent parents (Moore, Manlove, Glei, & Morrison, 1998). Birthrates among teenagers in the United States are substantially higher than in other Western industrialized countries. There were 89,900 teen pregnancies in 1995; fortunately, the rate has declined in recent years (Shelton, 1998; Wetzstein, 1998). Low **socioeconomic** status for the family has also been correlated with higher risk of adolescent childbearing.

Divorce, remarriage, and never-married parenting has greatly affected the composition of American families. The term *stepfamily* is now used to include households in which there is an adult couple, at least one of whom has a child from a previous relationship (Kelley, 1996). By 1990, 20% (about 5.3 million) of married-couple households cared for at least one stepchild (Kelley, 1996). Children in stepfamilies tended to have higher rates of behavioral, health, and education problems (Kelley, 1996).

Divorce, however, does not account for all family diversity. Children may be living with grandparents, in foster care, or in residential facilities. Since the late 1980s, foster care systems in the United States have been overwhelmed by the numbers of children who need assistance (Hegar & Scannapieco, 1995). This is partly because the total number of foster families dropped from 147,000 to 100,000 between 1984 and 1990 (National Commission on Foster Family Care, 1991). Many infants and young children spend the early part of their lives in "boarder" nurseries, temporary shelters where shift changes and high ratios of children to caretakers decrease the possibility of healthy attachments (Griffith, 1992). Children lucky enough to be placed in foster care may find untrained foster parents overwhelmed by the demands of caring for children with special needs and may consequently be returned to institutional placement (Griffith, 1992).

Case Study

FAMILY HARDSHIP: INTERVIEW WITH TAMMY WARITZ

In my job as a parent advocate, I see families with many difficulties to overcome. One of the biggest problems for families of children with disabilities is finding financial resources. There are a lot of families who don't have insurance and their incomes are not low enough to meet the federal guidelines to get medical assistance, so they're really struggling to figure out how they're going to pay for the services their children need.

For a number of years, our family has made sacrifices that no family should ever have to make. Some of the things that Jennifer requires are common needs for a child with disabilities and we had to be flexible enough to ensure she received what she needed. The cost of her equipment is incredible. For example, the braces that she has on her feet have to be replaced at least once a year, sometimes twice a year, and it costs seven hundred dollars each time. We just got a brand new seat and back for her wheelchair, and it was a thousand dollars. Jennifer's chair alone cost $3500.

Our family got to a point of desperation, and my husband and I separated so that our income could be low enough to receive state funding for Jennifer's needs. At the time Jennifer had been denied state funding, we were only $147 over the monthly eligibility limit on our income. We were stuck; we were struggling just to make enough money for food, shelter, and clothing; even with two blue-collar people working. It wasn't like we had a lot of money and we were trying to cheat the system out of something. We felt like we were being punished, because we had this child with special needs, and we didn't have jobs that paid twenty dollars an hour.

Finally, our situation reached a point where I had to break down publicly. I knew there were income waiver programs available and that Jennifer met the federal criteria for such a waiver, but the state agency would not approve one. I was crying uncontrollably one day, and I told them on the phone, "My family cannot continue to live like this. We can't afford to have a single-parent household. Furthermore, it's not right that I have to continue turning down raises at work to keep the financial assistance we have. If my family cannot access a waiver, you're going to have to place Jennifer because we cannot continue to live the way that we're living."

The need for medical funding literally put us in the position to choose between Jennifer and our family, though she is part of our family. I begged, "Please don't make us make that choice." I don't know how many lawyers we saw, on a consultation kind of basis, and they never charged us anything, but they all said, "There's nothing your family can do, you just don't have an option."

Finally, the state granted an exception to policy to give us a waiver for Jennifer. Jennifer is now deemed as an individual household of one, so that our income no longer counts against her eligibility for Social Security Supplementary Income (SSI) and Medicaid. For us, the SSI, which is the check that she gets, wasn't important. It didn't matter to us whether she got one penny of financial assistance as long as she got the medical help she needed.

I think that it was fortunate I was well informed, assertive and articulate, and I also think that's why I do the work that I do. Outside my job as a parent advocate, I'm very active legislatively, and I'm thankful that I've had a supportive husband who recognized that's a need I have. We are better off because I've learned to be politically active. It's my crusade. I don't want other families to have to experience what we've gone through. I can help to lessen that hardship because I've impacted the system in changes that go beyond Jennifer to reach other families in need.

This year my husband and I filed for divorce. The stress on the family for the last nine years has taken its toll. Certainly not all of our marital difficulties were caused by challenges in state agencies, but a family can only endure so much hardship before its foundation is eroded. I believe my family has now paid the ultimate sacrifice to a system that was set up to help and support but fell short in doing so.

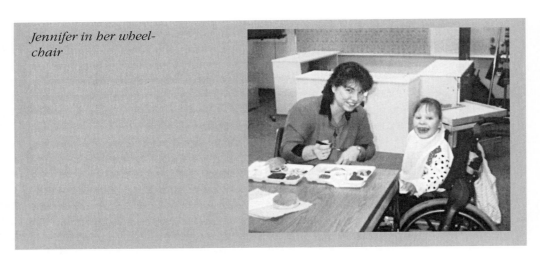

Jennifer in her wheel-chair

An emerging family option, developed out of necessity, is **kinship care** (Hegar & Scannapieco, 1995). Defined broadly, **kin** may include extended family, such as grandmothers and aunts, as well as other members of a community who are close to a family. Primary reasons for kinship care are parental drug abuse and neglect. Yet, full-time living arrangements with kin tend to have significant advantages over traditional foster care options. Children who stay with kin tend to be more stable and are associated with fewer behavioral problems than those in foster care, even though most kinship caregivers live in poverty themselves (Iglehart, 1994). Multigenerational family relationships, the sharing of childrearing and economic relationships across household boundaries, and the use of unrelated household members and parent surrogates have added greatly to the complexity of children's lives, particularly within the inner city (Hunter, Pearson, Isalongo, & Kellam, 1998).

What can professionals do to assist children whose lives are complicated by divorce or separation, who are surviving with a single parent, or whose lives in some other way no longer fit the "traditional" image? Several actions may be appropriate (Carlile, 1991), though empirical research is meager. Teachers should use instructional activities that teach children about the many different types of family structures in today's society. Numerous books deal with divorce, single parenting, grandmothers as guardians, and so on, and can be used to show different kinds of families. Teachers should modify their language and actions to match existing family patterns—inviting a grandparent to Open House, making a Mother's Day card for an aunt, speaking with foster parents at child conferences. Professionals need to make special efforts to keep communication open with both parents or other appropriate guardians. This may mean adjusting conference times, making evening telephone calls when working parents are home, or sending out multiple copies of announcements. Finally, professionals need to recognize they can provide a kind of safety net of consistency and support as children go through transitions in family situations. Yet, none of these expectations are as simple as they might appear. In order to be comfortable in this role, professionals must be secure in their own lives and careers.

SUMMARY ON DIVERSITY

This nation is rapidly becoming a people of color, with significant growth in minority populations, who are disproportionately poor and more likely to be single-parent families, in virtually every region of the country. Though the United States has moved forward in defining equity, justice, and multiculturalism, the country has done a poor job in translating these attitudes into improved educational achievement (Wells, 1988). In fact, due to significant political shifting during the 1980s, culturally diverse families have drifted further behind the mainstream economically, educationally, and perhaps most importantly, in terms of hope for improvement. Historical disadvantages for minority populations has contributed to the growth of a high-risk group who tend to suffer considerable social inequity in the education system (Slavin, 1998).

To conclude that educational underachievement and other social problems are caused by racial characteristics would be inaccurate and dangerous. The correlation between race and educational disadvantage is far more complicated, as multiple factors influence members of racial minorities in this country (Williams, 1992). Educators need greater preparation in working with families who are at risk. Family service planning and case management must become a natural part of all educational planning. Early childhood professionals need to be familiar with local resources and be able to empower families to identify and access community services. Special service delivery must reach beyond the traditional services of the school building to locations on the streets, in shelters, and within community centers. Traditionally delivered services are unlikely to reach those in greatest need if they are offered only within the agency setting. Likewise, such services will provide only part of what is needed unless they are given in conjunction with social services support. Team management and social support should include family counseling, financial assistance, job training, family planning, and housing.

As educators address the needs of the increasing numbers of children who are at risk, more comparisons will be made between minority children and children of the dominant culture. Because race is certain to be emphasized, these comparisons may unfairly foster a view that minority students are inferior and incompetent, particularly when cultural differences are viewed as deficits (McLoyd, 1990). Early childhood professionals must be careful to document the ways in which minority children achieve educationally and find methods to promote the ecological, situational, and cultural factors that encourage success. Professionals must also collaborate with other service providers to work constantly for the elimination of bigotry and discrimination, which may limit opportunities available to all children and families within this diverse population.

Slavin (1998) suggested we reduce the social inequity of education through several means. First, we need to constantly remind ourselves to think of all children as being a promise. We must identify and build on cultural and personal strengths and accept nothing less than outstanding performance; design high-quality education that is sensitive to students' needs from the beginning. Second, start early by providing early childhood programs that enhance children's preparation for elementary school while children are highly motivated and confident in their abilities to learn. Finally, overdetermine success by working on many fronts at once—addressing the multitude of needs children in poverty face.

THE IMPORTANCE OF SERVING CHILDREN IN THE CONTEXT OF A FAMILY

Empowerment is a term widely used in social science fields. According to Koren, DeChillo, and Friesen (1992), various definitions have been offered for empowerment over the past 20 years: "the reduction of powerlessness . . . gaining, developing, seizing, enabling or giving power . . . the ability to influence people, organizations, and the environment affecting one's life . . . attaining control over one's life and democratic participation in the life of one's community" (p. 306). Empowerment means increasing one's control over one's life and taking action to get what one wants (Turnbull & Turnbull, 1997). Within organizations, such as early childhood programs, one should attempt to provide families with three levels of empowerment:

1. The personal level, where individuals feel a sense of self-efficacy;
2. The interpersonal level, which is the ability to influence others; and
3. Political empowerment, the ability to effect social change and engage in social action. (Gutierrez & Ortega, 1991)

Like inclusion, the term empowerment has become a cliché, empty and scorned by those who are wary of passing fads and those who might agree with the definition, but have observed empty promise (Brinker, 1992). Early childhood professionals are challenged by law to be more inclusive of families in intervention for young children with disabilities (Sass-Lehrer & Bodner-Johnson, 1989). Bailey, Huntington, Simmeonson, and Yoder (1992) found, however, that professionals across disciplines are ill-prepared for this responsibility. Moreover, Brinker (1992) claimed the field's current knowledge-base regarding family dynamics is so weak that early childhood professionals are likely to fail in most situations when exploratory empowerment practices are attempted. In fact, Brinker (1992) was so cynical that, like opponents of full inclusion, he believed family empowerment philosophy to be motivated more by "political correctness" than by sound pedagogical practice. Even parents sometimes have rejected the term empowerment, which to them infers that professionals are condescendingly "granting" them power that belonged to them in the first place (Healy, Keesee, & Smith, 1989).

The fact that federal law requires families in early intervention to be assessed for the purpose of establishing goals for intervention implies an intent to "fix" families so they can become capable, caregiving units. While recent literature cautions against such clinical intrusiveness in families, current practices for older school-age children might be used to predict the challenge (Bailey, 1989). Twenty years after IDEA first mandated schools to include parents as equal partners in the educational process, parents largely remain either passive or adversarial in planning their children's education (Benson & Turnbull, 1986; Goodman & Bond, 1993; Turnbull & Turnbull, 1990). In fact, a study by Yanok and Derubertis (1989) found little difference between the level of participation by parents of children in regular and special education.

These findings indicate those parents who are involved in special education would be so with or without the law. A similar pattern has already been acknowledged in early intervention programs. For example, Minke and Scott (1993) found that parents rarely suggested goals in Individualized Family Service Plan (IFSP) meetings, and when they did, those goals sometimes did not appear in the final document. Even when intensive efforts were made to involve parents, there tended to be a disturbing lack of participation (Fallon & Harris, 1992).

Harry (1992) concluded that the very fact that professional behavior is prescribed by legal mandate precludes spontaneous, honest, and effective interactions. Ironically, early childhood special education law may achieve the opposite effect intended by Congress. The precise structure of special education, including clinical eligibility, written documentation of standardized tests and instructional plans with their related jargon, and "written notification" to parents, places educators and parents in two different worlds: an objective-clinical one for educators and a personal-subjective one for parents. Hence, early interventionists are at great risk of concentrating on the "letter of the law" rather than on the "spirit of the law."

WHAT IS A FAMILY?

One of the most significant shifts in special education, particularly in early childhood, is the move from focusing on the child to focusing more broadly on the child within the family system (Turnbull & Turnbull, 1997). This model recognizes that each family member is affected by other family members and events that might influence those persons. For example, if a child with a disability requires extraordinary medical attention, other siblings may be affected by loss of parental attention, perhaps by loss of financial support once available for activities or things, and by more responsibilities around the home. Similarly, the amount of involvement in programs associated with a child with a disability will be affected when caregivers are required to work extra hours to make rent payments, when they lose a job because of the need to take time off, or if they experience marital conflict. Professionals, ignorant or neglectful of the family system, will likely become frustrated when concentrating solely on the needs of a child who has been identified for services. This child-centered model (see Figure 1–1), while convenient and compatible with most professionals' training, has not been terribly effective for families who do not already possess considerable self-efficacy.

Definitions of family are influenced by culture, politics, economics, and religion. Consequently, in early childhood professions there is no consensus on criteria for membership in families (Brinker, 1992). Yet, the issue is not moot, since the scope of early childhood work relies on such a definition. For example, a broad definition of family (e.g., parents, siblings, grandparents, child-care providers, involved relatives and close friends of the family, all of whom influence the development of the child in question) would require that all these persons be considered in the development of a family service plan. A more narrow definition (e.g., blood relatives who live in the child's dwelling) reduces the scope of intervention required but may also limit possible benefits for children with special needs.

Clearly, a traditional definition of family as a nuclear construct will not suffice. According to Healy et al. (1989), a family is comprised of parents and any family or nonfamily members who have an important caregiving responsibility. This simply stated definition is consistent with the **family systems model,** which acknowledges all important influences on individuals within families. Still, society is struggling with "moral" issues related to the "goodness" or "rightness" of diverse family structures (Ingrassia & Rossi, 1994). However, early childhood educators can little afford to be

Figure 1–1
Ecological
Mapping of the
Child and
Family
Source: Adapted
from Dunst, C.,
Trivette, C., &
Deal, A. (1988).
*Enabling and
empowering
families:
Principles and
guidelines for
practice.*
Cambridge, MA:
Brookline.

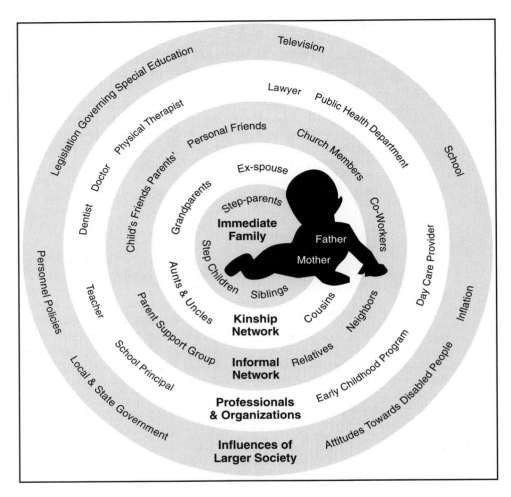

exclusive or negative when defining families. Family configurations include foster families, adoptive families, nuclear biological families, single-parent families, extended families, and same gender parents families.

While it is difficult to define families, the next step—involvement of all family members—is even more difficult. For example, the parent in parent–professional interactions has almost exclusively referred to mothers (Davis & May, 1991). In recent history, society has engaged in practices that fail to prepare men for the role of involved father, focusing on paternal attributes incompatible with the best childrearing practices (Lillie, 1993). Morgan (1993) claimed that mothers are, in part, responsible for exclusion of fathers, as women attempt to protect this one domain over which they tend to possess more power than men. Again, early educators can be most effective when they move beyond popular opinion in interactions with families. A true "family-centered" approach to early childhood compels professionals to find ways to permit fathers to be involved in decision making and child care (Davis & May, 1991; Lillie, 1993; McBride & McBride, 1993).

EMPOWERMENT

Families are empowered when their needs are met and most of the credit goes to the families themselves. When a professional can boast, "Look, they don't need me to make decisions for them, locate information, or access services," then a family is empowered. Fostering empowerment will require that educators practice in a way that they never have before. As Buysse and Wesley (1993) acknowledged, these changes cause substantial *disequilibrium* for early childhood educators whose roles are being reformed. Social service professionals, in particular, feel useful, wanted, even necessary when they can do things "for" families. It is not unusual for professionals to "need to feel needed." Yet, this very practice of apparent benevolence builds in paternalism and dependency (Dunst, Trivette, & Deal, 1988).

The desire to feel needed eventually leads to behavior that supports service providers, and agencies begin to feel that it is families' responsibility to serve the agencies' goals rather than the needs of the families. Agencies can become didactic and judgmental, labeling families as "good" or "dysfunctional" based on the agencies' definitions of what is best for children with disabilities and their families. It is not uncommon for educators and even other parents to prescribe how each family should feel, how long they should "grieve," what steps they should take to become "involved," and how they should serve professionals' needs (McGill-Smith, 1992).

Changes in the verbal behavior of service providers should reflect a new philosophy based on the preservation of families' dignity. For example, one might do away with the psychology of "death" as it relates to families with members with disabilities (Bragg, Brown, & Berninger, 1992). Professionals often label a parent who refuses to accept the opinions of professionals as "in denial," or families who seek another opinion as "bargainers," and perhaps most often to label parents who express their rights as "angry." Learning the "stages of grief" and thinking that all family behavior can fit into this model of inferred maladjustment brings one no closer to understanding individual family members. In fact, Hodapp and Zigler (1993) found that families of children with severe disabilities face problems that are "the same, only more so" than other families.

Furthermore, there is increasing evidence that families with children with disabilities exude considerable resilience, and that family resources quickly "kick in" to compensate for their new stress (Krausse, 1991). Treating families as if they are disabled because their child is disabled "undermines the intent and the effect" of family centered services (Bailey, 1989). Krausse (1991) proposed an alternative view of families, which he refers to as the "family adaptation hypothesis." This hypothesis rejects the concept of pathological maladaptation associated with the presence of a child with a disability (grief model) and acknowledges the hardiness of families to cope both initially and over time. The fundamental assumption of empowerment is that families are the center. All decisions move from the center outward; all action by the periphery is to serve the center (see Figure 1–1).

The goal of empowerment is to enable families to make decisions and take action serving their self-selected needs. According to Dunst et al. (1988):

> To the extent that professionals do not recognize and explicitly consider empowerment of families as the goal of intervention, they are more likely to fool themselves into believing they have done a good job when

in fact they have lost an opportunity to enable and empower the family and perhaps even created dependencies by engaging in noncontingent helping. (p. 7)

Noncontingent helping is defined as providing services or support for families while expecting no proactive behavior on the part of families. While seemingly "helping" families, professionals actually usurp opportunities for empowerment when family members are given no responsibility. Dunst et al. (1988) further contended that empowerment requires the fulfillment of three criteria:

1. Taking a **proactive stance;** enabling experiences and attribution of change to help the seeker. A proactive stance is one in which professionals assume that families are either competent or capable of becoming competent. Assuming that some families are incompetent and unable to change renders a professional useless for those children and their families.
2. Creating opportunities for families to display their strengths in order to gain new competencies is the responsibility of helping systems. "A failure to display competencies is not due to deficits within the person but rather failure of the social system to create opportunities." (Dunst et al., 1988, p. 4)
3. The third empowerment criterion is met when professionals enable families to acquire a sense of personal control over family affairs. "It is not simply a matter of whether or not family needs are met, but rather the manner in which needs are met that is likely to be both enabling and empowering." (Dunst et al., 1988, p. 4)

Building a climate for parent-professional partnerships is perhaps the field's greatest challenge. There is still much unknown. Most discouraging is the fact that those families who may benefit the most from family empowerment (i.e., minorities and low-income families) are the least likely to receive empowering services (Rueda & Martinez, 1992). Research efforts in the twenty-first century should be devoted to identifying methods of supporting the philosophy of empowerment and the spirit, finally, of IDEA (Nelson, Howard, & McLaughlin, 1993).

THE IMPORTANCE OF WORKING COLLABORATIVELY

An infant or toddler whose medical condition, developmental delay, or physical disability is so severe that it comes to the attention of caregivers and service providers at an early age is likely to present more complex needs than a child who does not demonstrate a disability until he or she is of school age. Very young children with medical, cognitive, or physical complications are typically at risk for developing disabilities in related developmental areas. For example, a child with abnormal muscle tone may have trouble learning to walk, may have motor problems related to eating difficulties, may not develop necessary motor movements to produce intelligible speech, and, with poor tools for communication, may be unable to demonstrate her cognitive abilities. This child has one primary disabling condition, poor muscle tone, yet the intervention services of a physical therapist, occupational therapist, speech therapist, special educator, and parents are all necessary.

While it was common practice in the past, it is unlikely that any one professional could serve this child well. Consequently, very young children with special needs are likely to have a team of specialists attending to different aspects of their care and development. An **interdisciplinary** approach combines expertise from many disciplines to scrutinize a child's various aspects of development, combining interpretation, synthesis, planning, and practices to design a plan that will promote a child's overall development (Healy et al., 1989).

When a number of professionals collaborate with a family, careful teamwork becomes absolutely necessary. Without careful coordination, there might be unnecessary duplication of services and paperwork, lack of communication with important parties, an increase in confusion and contradiction, and resultant poorer services to children and their families. A successful team approach must be organized to produce timely and accurate assessment, comprehensive and effective intervention, clear and inclusive communication, and regular evaluation and review. An effective team approach is reached only through mutual trust and respect, practice, and hard work.

Several approaches to teaming have worked well, as long as fundamental guidelines are respected. First, **consensus building** is more effective than an authoritative structure. When various professionals gather with parents, each comes with differing levels of professional status and biases. It is hard to set priorities unless each participant is willing to listen carefully to all parties and to "give and take" in regard to their particular areas of expertise. In situations with a breakdown of give and take, team coordination is at an impasse.

CLOSE-UP

TIME AS A RESOURCE AND CONSTRAINT FOR PARENTS OF YOUNG CHILDREN WITH DISABILITIES: IMPLICATIONS FOR EARLY INTERVENTION SERVICES

Society has high expectations for families who are supposed to provide shelter, food, clothing, safety, and education for their members. Time is an important element in allowing a family to fulfill all its responsibilities and for families of young children with disabilities, time can become a precious commodity. As early childhood intervention increasingly involves the family in the planning and provision of services to young children, it is critical that professionals look closely at how families view the time required for intervention and the constraints they face.

Families of 21 children of varying disabilities and severity and 19 professionals representing different disciplines participated in focus groups to discuss questions regarding family-centered intervention. A moderator in each group asked a variety of questions:

1. What defines successful partnerships and program implementation in early intervention?

2. What contributes to or impedes developing successful partnerships and program implementation?
3. How, if at all, has the early intervention program supported your child and family?
4. Think of a professional who has worked well with you and your family. What made that relationship successful?
5. Think of a professional who has not worked well with you and your family. How would you describe that relationship?
6. What would you like professionals to know about building successful partnerships with families?

Though no direct questions were asked about time, this factor was identified as critical by both parents and professionals and was discussed in several dimensions.

Parents identified four issues that support their efficient and effective use of time.

1. To parents, it was important that therapy and education activities fit into a family's routine and environment.
2. Parents believed that they knew their children best and that professionals should listen to parents and use their information as data for intervention decisions.
3. Several parents discussed how communication devices for their children (e.g., tape recorder, computer, or other technology for therapy and education activities) aided the effective use of parents' time.
4. Finally, parents asked that professionals provide sufficient time for the long process of developing and maintaining a relationship with a professional.

Parents also identified four issues that placed constraints on their time and effectiveness.

1. They cited the lack of coordination among professionals as a time waster, and recommended that parents be used more as efficient conduits of information across professionals.
2. Parents also felt overwhelmed with what they were being asked to do in their busy lives in terms of therapeutic and educational activities that left them with little time for their other children.
3. A third concern was the lack of services in local communities which caused parents to drive long distances and spend several hours a day to obtain services in different locations.
4. Finally, parents found problems related to a lack of flexible and family-centered scheduling. In scheduling appointments or services, professionals acted as if families had enough income for one parent to be a full-time caregiver to be available during the day, when often both parents worked daytime jobs and lost wages to keep appointments.

The implications of this study are several. Families want to be respected as competent, contributing members of the team with knowledge to share. Professionals need to be realistic in terms of the time and energy families can expend in providing intervention and services need to be accessible in home communities with flexible scheduling to accommodate families' responsibilities. Certainly time and consistency is required for developing productive long-term relationships between parents and professionals.

Source: Brotherson, M. J., & Goldstein, B. L. (1992). *Topics in Early Childhood Special Education, 12,* 508–527.

One father described his experience as a member of his son's individualized education planning (IEP) team (McCauley, personal communication, January 25, 1994). He requested that the team include toilet training on Sean's IEP, even though the teacher reported that his son had not had any "accidents" at school. Mr. McCauley acknowledged this observation but contended that Sean continued to have difficulty at home, and wanted to have his toileting routine continued at school. The educators refused to listen to Mr. McCauley's priorities (including the toileting training) and the IEP process eventually reached an impasse. This conflict might have been avoided had members of the team valued the input of all members and tried to accommodate as many priorities as possible from each member.

Each professional must be flexible and willing to share roles as well as information. Consider a child who presents a language delay; the teacher, the physical therapist, and the parents must all work to develop the child's language whether that is within that person's area of expertise or not. This team approach requires that each member has some working understanding of other disciplines or at least a willingness to implement suggestions made by other professionals. For example, both the speech therapist and the teacher should learn how to position a motor-involved child in the most appropriate way during all aspects of the child's home or school day. This will require some instruction and modeling by the physical therapist.

Finally, effective **group process** is essential for insuring a positive team experience. Group process includes making all participants comfortable in sharing their concerns and desires, listening carefully to all members of the team, valuing the input of all members of the team, and making decisions based on consensus. For example, parents are often intimidated when meeting with a large group of professionals and may hesitate to speak honestly and clearly regarding their priorities. If coerced into silence by intimidation or lack of opportunity, parents may leave a meeting unhappy with the planning and uncommitted to the work a plan involves. To decrease anxiety, parents should be greeted when they arrive, perhaps offered refreshments and comfortable seating, and introduced to all members of the team. These practices may seem overly zealous to some. As one educator put it, "This is not a social gathering! Do you get refreshments when you go to a law office or a dental office?" While this objection is reasonable, the goals of early childhood special education may be incompatible with the client-expert practices of many other professions. Certainly one would want to avoid the intimidation and sterility of legal and dental visits.

Professionals should refrain from using technical jargon or should take care to explain terminology carefully to other members of the team. Written plans should never be formally completed ahead of time, nor should parents be expected to sign-off at the time of the meeting. Soliciting parent suggestions and input before decisions are made is a necessary (and legally required) component of the group process. One person should act as a facilitator to make sure a meeting begins promptly, to keep the discussion on task, to see that all members have a chance to give input or to object when appropriate, and to restate or summarize when agreement has been reached. Before a meeting ends, everyone present should know what will happen next, who is responsible for each part of a plan, and when the team will meet again to review progress.

TEAMING MODELS

There are three basic team models or arrangements, and they vary in the degree to which team members are able to work together. **Multidisciplinary** teams are made up of members who work independently in providing assessment and direct services to a child and meet to share their goals and progress reports, though there is little direct coordination of efforts. For example, the psychologist may meet with a child to test intelligence and achievement levels, then meet with the team to report his results and recommendations for treatment. Members in an **interdisciplinary model** may conduct their assessments and plan goals together, but continue to provide direct services on an independent basis. For example, the speech therapist may observe while the psychologist is testing a child and check-off speech sounds, or phonemes, that the child can say, rather than duplicating the testing in a separate speech session. In a **transdisciplinary model,** professionals share roles and may combine their assessment and treatment tasks so that any one individual may be carrying out the responsibilities of a different professional. For example, the classroom teacher may be using a phoneme check-off instrument to obtain information for the speech therapist or may carry out a language program the speech therapist has recommended.

Of particular benefit to a child served by a team approach is that each team member sees the child's problem from his or her own perspective. "Early childhood education has always been an interdisciplinary field with a commitment to the education of the whole child; an understanding of the child as a complete human being is basic to the development of a program concerned with each area of development and learning" (Spodek, Saracho, & Lee, 1986). Sometimes a teacher may be intimidated by the knowledge of other specialized team members; however, the generalist perspective that a teacher brings is a necessary part of team dynamics. Specialists have in-depth knowledge of their discipline, but teachers are better able to see the whole child as he or she functions in a variety of settings, both socially and physically.

The team configuration used in a particular situation will depend on the administrative policy of the school and service agencies involved and on the comfort and cohesiveness of the professionals serving a particular child. There is no question, however, that teaming across disciplines is a necessary part of services to young children. The greater the ability of the team to interact, to share roles, and to inform each other across disciplines, the more unified and complete a child's services are likely to be. Table 1–3 summarizes the strengths and weaknesses of each of these models.

COLLABORATION IN EARLY INTERVENTION

Collaboration with other professionals is apparently not as easy as it seems. In fact, many teachers report that their jobs are made most difficult by lack of cooperation among their peers and themselves. A study of teachers' and prospective teachers' preferences for collaboration may aid understanding of issues involved in planning (Morrison, Walker, Wakefield, & Solberg, 1994). Teachers with the highest level of self-efficacy were the most amenable to collaborative problem solving. Ironically, those teachers who most believed they were capable of teaching a broad range of skills in the classroom were the most willing to work collaboratively. For example, the student teachers in this study were less willing than the practicing teachers to work with and gain assistance from other professionals. One might conclude from this study that an important barrier to collaboration is a lack of self-confidence. Yet, collaboration by all professionals, with other professionals as well as with parents, is a necessary prerequisite to an effective program.

Table 1–3 Team models.

Team Model	Strengths	Weaknesses
Multidisciplinary Team	◆ Involves more than one discipline in planning and services ◆ Pools expertise for decision making ◆ Reduces mistakes and biases	◆ May not promote a unified approach to intervention ◆ May lack team cohesion and commitment
Interdisciplinary Team	◆ Activities and goals complement and support other disciplines ◆ Allows commitment to unified service plan ◆ Information flow is coordinated through a case manager	◆ Professional "turf" may be threatened ◆ Inflexibility by professionals may reduce efficiency ◆ Role of case manager may be ambiguous, case manager may become autocratic
Transdisciplinary Team	◆ Encourages interaction within many disciplines ◆ Encourages role sharing ◆ Provides a unified, holistic plan for intervention ◆ Allows a more complete understanding of the child ◆ Leads to professional enhancement and increased knowledge and skill	◆ Requires participation by many experts ◆ Places largest responsibility on the teacher as case manager ◆ Requires a high degree of coordination and interaction ◆ Requires more time for communication and planning

In early intervention, the challenge of integrating services for families demands the most of collaborative efforts. As family needs increase, the need for increased services increases—as does the need for greater coordination of disciplines (see Figure 1–1). For example, families with multiple needs cannot be well served by autonomous narrowly defined programs. Take the following example:

Paulette is a young 28-year-old mother and about-to-be grandmother living on Aid to Families with Dependent Children (AFDC), with four children by three fathers, none of whom is part of the household physically or financially. Paulette never finished high school. Her son, Mark, 14 years old, was a chronic truant in school, and in and out of trouble in the neighborhood, which finally earned him a sentence to the Maryland Training School for Boys. Since his release, his case worker has been trying to place him in a suitable school but without success. Her oldest daughter, Tessie, is pregnant at age 13, repeating her maternal family pattern. She wants to drop out of school, but a neighbor told her about a special school for pregnant girls and Paulette is trying to get admission. The eight-year-old daughter, Marie, is doing satisfactory school work, but Paulette has noticed her late returns from school with unexplained spending money. There is a real concern that Marie is earning her money as a "spotter" for neighborhood drug dealers. The two-year-old baby of the family has started exhibiting symptoms of lead paint poisoning, caused by nibbling on flaking paint chips in their apartment. Unchecked and untreated, this could result in permanent brain damage. This is a family beset with behavioral, health, educational, housing, and financial problems. At least five different public agencies in five separate locations have some knowledge of and contact with this family. Fourteen different workers in those agencies have attempted to offer assistance during the past two years, each concerned with the specialized service agency but with little or no knowledge of efforts by the other professionals. (Levitan, Mangum, & Pines, 1989, p. 21)

This family's needs can be viewed from an ecological systems model described by Bronfenbrenner (1986). The most immediate needs, schooling for Tessie and Mark, supervision for Marie, and prevention of paint eating for the baby, are at the **microsystem** level. At the **mesosystem** level, there is a linkage between microsystems, such as a linkage between Paulette and the schools, or between the schools and the juvenile justice system. The **exosystems** are those affecting families, but with no direct relationship with agencies, such as church and neighbors. Finally, families are influenced by **macrosystems,** broad social values and belief systems of cultures and subcultures. Interdependency of agencies serving families from these multiple perspectives is a crucial philosophy. A formal link between professionals/agencies and early childhood programs serving Paulette and her family should be the service coordinator. This person is responsible for assessment of family and child needs, coordination of planning for intervention and delivery of services, as well as monitoring of services delivered.

Programs that are successful at integrating these services are correlated with such broad-based family needs as decreased birthrates in adolescents, lower incidences of low birth weight babies, increased school participation by parents, decreased drug abuse and behavior problems, increased financial self-sufficiency, and higher IQ and test scores (Voydanoff, 1994). Clearly, one professional or agency cannot possibly address all these areas. In a *metaanalysis,* Schorr and Both (1991) concluded that successfully integrated systems had the following attributes:

1. Comprehensive, flexible, and responsive
2. Child is part of family and family is part of community
3. Well-trained staff, who are accepting enough to build trusting relationships
4. Persistent and responsive to the needs of those families at greatest risk
5. Well-managed, with energetic and committed professionals whose attitudes and skills are well-defined. Professionals are willing to take risks, tolerate ambiguity, work with diverse populations, and operate with a collaborative management style
6. Client centered

In summary, collaboration as a philosophy is possible only when professionals are able to separate their own needs from those of clients, and are nonjudgmental, open-minded, and committed to providing families with the very best services possible.

THE IMPORTANCE OF ETHICAL CONDUCT AND ADVOCACY

What do **ethical conduct** and **advocacy** have to do with philosophy? Many decisions educators make, including their daily activities in a classroom, are based on a set of personal ethics or personal philosophy. Professionals, charged with working with families of very young children with disabilities, should be held to the highest ethical standards. First, educators should know and follow the ethical standards of their profession. Second, educators should actively advocate for issues that will encourage society to respond to the needs of families and children with disabilities in an ethical fashion.

Ethical professional behavior means that one will be the best early childhood professional that one can be and will support others in providing quality services with the highest ethical standards. Professional organizations serving children have already articulated high ethical and accreditation standards for those who provide services to young children. A prime example is the Code of Ethical Conduct developed by the National Association for the Education of Young Children (1997). These standards for ethical behavior in early childhood education describe professional responsibilities in regard to children, families, colleagues, the community, and society. The first principle presented in the Code expresses its ideals well:

> Above all, we shall not harm children. We shall not participate in practices that are disrespectful, degrading, dangerous, exploitative, intimidating, emotionally damaging, or physically harmful to children. This principle has precedence over all others in this Code. (National Association for the Education of Young Children, 1997)

ADVOCACY ISSUES

An advocate is someone who takes up another person's cause (Alper, Schloss, & Schloss, 1995). For what should one advocate? The president of the Association of Child Advocates, Eve Brooks, suggested getting involved with what is closest to one's heart (Himelfarb, 1992). For an early childhood professional, that may mean working and playing with one's own children or helping others in need. It may mean voting regularly and intelligently, writing one's congressman, or participating on state councils or research projects. *Putting People First* (Clinton & Gore, 1992) identified national priorities for children that few could argue against. These goals included the following:

1. Guarantee affordable quality health care through maternal and child networks and programs.
2. Revolutionize lifetime learning by fully funding Head Start, improving the K–12 education systems, and providing opportunities for college and vocational experience.
3. Make homes, schools, and streets safer for children by reducing violence and providing drug education.
4. Support pro-family and pro-children policies through tax credits for families, family and medical leaves, child-care network, and tough child-support legislation.

CLOSE-UP

HOMELESS POLICY: THE NEED TO SPEAK TO FAMILIES

Most major cities turn away approximately 30% of families who apply for shelter because they have insufficient facilities. Temporary shelters have been characterized as overcrowded with little privacy, high noise level, and short stays. Homeless children admitted to new schools face stigmatization and rejection from classmates and teachers.

In working with homeless families, practice the following:

1. Incorporate the principles of family centeredness and interdependence in service delivery;
2. Recognize diversity among families rather than treating them as a homogenous group;
3. Foster family stability, making sure families maintain current support systems, and help to establish new support networks;
4. Empower families to become self-sufficient, respecting individual dignity and including them in the development and implementation of service plans; and
5. Strengthen neighborhoods and communities through actively helping families to maintain ties with their old neighbors or relatives.

Source: Anderson, E. A., & Koblinsky, S. A. (1995). Homeless policy: The need to speak to families. *Family Relations, 44,* 13–18.

Obtaining good child care is a nationwide problem due to short supply, lack of affordability, poor regulation, frequent staff turnover, and little staff training (Ryan, 1992). An estimated 23 million children in the United States require child care. Of this number, only 8.3 million attend licensed day-care settings required to meet minimum standards for health, safety, and curriculum; the remaining 14.7 million are placed in unlicensed settings that may or may not provide adequate care. Many other children are left with friends and relatives, or even left unsupervised (Ryan, 1992). The consequences of poor child care are often troubling, leaving very young children at risk for molestation, physical injury, and even death (Hoyt & Schoonmaker, 1991). Since an enormous population of children require child care while their parents work, society must take responsibility for insuring the well-being of children in child care (Hoyt & Schoonmaker, 1991).

Although the federal government sets standards for many aspects of daily life, the regulation of child care is left to state governments. Consequently there is tremendous variability among state laws and enforcement levels (Hoyt & Schoonmaker, 1991). In fact, the Children's Defense Fund (1993, December) reported that nearly half the children in child care outside their own home are not protected by any state regulations at all. Even when states have regulations on the books, many are not able to properly inspect centers and enforce these regulations (Hoyt & Schoonmaker, 1991). In any case, as many as 80% to 90% of day-care settings are unlicensed. Yet, even a license on the wall does not guarantee appropriate care is being provided, and eight states reported that they could not even respond to all the parent complaints they received.

Who should monitor the quality of child care provided? Who should insist on high standards for programs for young children and who should police the enforcement of these standards? Parents are often ill-equipped to do so because they are victims of a provider's market; the short supply of openings available and the high cost of quality day care tend to make parents settle for availability and affordability (Hoyt & Schoonmaker, 1991). It is absolutely essential that early childhood professionals advocate for appropriate, high-quality services to very young children. Professionals have the education, the commitment, and the voice to insist that standards for child care be adequate and that society contribute to the health, safety, and education of all children regardless of race, disabling condition, or economic status. This is not a new role or futile use of energy since educators have (hand in hand with parents) accomplished extraordinary changes in terms of legal, pedagogical, financial, practical, and ethical practices in the past few decades.

Another issue that will have an impact on early childhood special education is the reform of public assistance policies at state and federal levels that require single mothers (and families) on public assistance to work and limit the length of time for which families are eligible. Such policies will most assuredly increase the need for low-cost child care, and place a further burden on a system already in crises.

To date, policy makers have not addressed this need. Therefore, it is possible that the lack of child care will result in higher rates of child neglect, homelessness, and need of special services. A professional should be an informed citizen and participate in advocacy for families through voting, writing or using electronic mail to contact congressional representatives, sending letters to the editor of the local newspaper, and using other effective ways to inform the public of issues important to families of young children with disabilities.

HOW TO GET INVOLVED IN ADVOCACY

Advocacy is a dynamic and continuous process that begins with the recognition of an unmet need and does not end until that need is met (Alper et al., 1995). An advocate's work progresses in two directions at once; as the advocate supports and obtains services for an individual, his or her work promotes changes across the system, eventually applying to large numbers of children. Effective advocacy can begin within a family, within a classroom, or within a community.

Within the local context, children with disabilities have many immediate needs, including the need for friendships, need for support in extracurricular activities, need for community access, and need for appropriate curriculum (Alper et al., 1995). Parents of children with disabilities need healthy communication between the many professionals with whom they deal, they also need emotional support, economic supports, respite care, legal protection, and information about the future. Your advocacy may begin with connecting parents with each other, arranging "buddy" systems within your class, or providing informational brochures.

On a broader level, there are numerous ways one can become involved in child advocacy (Himelfarb, 1992). Many community organizations have an interest in child issues—from Parent Teacher Associations to Kiwanis Clubs, Junior Leagues, and religious charities. Every state now has at least one organization devoted to child advocacy. These organizations may track state legislation, monitor voting records of elected officials, lobby for child issues, and fund research and education aimed at improving children's circumstances. A phone call or letter will put one in contact with a number of national organizations working on behalf of children.

A profession is more than a job. It is a long-term commitment to a field. In early childhood education, that commitment is to the well-being of children, and that well-being cannot be insured if efforts are confined to one's classroom, playground, or home. The health, safety, and education of children are dependent on society and its efforts to protect children from discrimination, poverty, disease, abuse, violence, and ignorance. Marian Wright Edelman, President of the Children's Defense Fund, gave this advice on life: "Hang in with your advocacy for children and the poor. The tide is going to turn. . . . Don't think you have to be a big dog to make a difference. You just need to be a persistent flea. . . . Enough committed fleas biting strategically can make even the biggest dog uncomfortable and transform even the biggest nation, as we will transform America. . . ." (Edelman, 1991).

In Conclusion

This chapter has summarized six of the major assumptions of early childhood special education. Over the past three decades, since early childhood education seriously began its business of serving children with special needs and their families, an increasingly liberal philosophy has evolved, in sharp contrast with the social changes in an increasingly conservative society. Already, this clash in direction has meant the closure of many early intervention programs and the reduction of funds for preschool special education programs. An assumption not discussed in this chapter is that of efficacy. There is little doubt as to the efficacy of early childhood services for very young children with special needs (Baer, 1987). Years of research have demonstrated that money and time spent in the first year of life save money and reduce the effects of developmental delays later in life (White & Casto, 1985). This is especially true of children with mild delays or those who are at risk for delays. An analogy to automobile maintenance can be made. If a problem is detected early and repaired quickly, the cost and effort are small. However, if the problem is allowed to persist, the automobile will suffer extensive damage that will subsequently be more costly and difficult to repair.

When funding for special education was generous, as in the 1970s and 1980s, schools could afford the "wait and treat later" approach because funding was available for remedial and special education. In the 1990s, money for special education has shrunk, and will continue to diminish in the twenty-first century. Therefore, more than ever, professionals must remind budget makers that when determining where to spend their bucks, they will get the biggest bang in early childhood education!

STUDY GUIDE QUESTIONS

1. What are the two important elements of an attitude of science?
2. What is the value of a conceptual system?
3. How does applied behavior analysis meet the criteria for a good conceptual system?
4. Identify the differences between inclusion and full inclusion. Where do you fall in terms of which is the more appropriate goal?
5. What are the benefits of full inclusion?
6. What barriers impede the movement toward full inclusion?
7. How has the population of the United States changed in regard to racial distribution?
8. What impact do changing demographics have on education?
9. State two reasons sensitivity to cultural differences is important in early childhood education.
10. What are the detrimental effects of childhood poverty?
11. How have families changed in recent years?
12. What can teachers do to support children from nontraditional families?
13. Why is it inappropriate to conclude that minority children are abnormal or incompetent?
14. What problems accompany a philosophy of empowerment?
15. How is family defined within a family systems model?
16. Why is noncontingent helping not helpful?
17. Describe how a professional effectively relates to empower a family.
18. What can professionals do to ensure that a team works well together?
19. Describe the differences among the three primary team models.
20. Give examples of how you could relate to a single mother of a child with Down syndrome that would contribute to a successful collaborative team.

REFERENCES

Alberto, P. A., & Troutman, A. C. (1990). *Applied behavior analysis for teachers* (3rd ed.). Upper Saddle River, NJ: Merrill/Prentice Hall.

Allen, J. P., & Turner, E. (1990). Where diversity is. *American Demographics, 12*(8), 34–38.

Alper, S., Schloss, P. J., & Schloss, C. N. (1995). Families of children with disabilities in elementary and middle school: Advocacy models and strategies. *Exceptional Children, 62*(3), 261.

American Academy of Pediatrics. (1982). The Doman-Delacato treatment of neurologically handicapped children (RE2709). *Pediatrics, 70*(5), 810–812.

Anderson, E. A., & Koblinsky, S. A. (1995). Homeless policy: The need to speak to families. *Family Relations, 44,* 13–18.

Ary, D., Jacobs, L., & Razavich, A. (1996). *Introduction to research in education.* Fort Worth, TX: Harcourt Brace College.

Baer, D. M. (1987, March). A behavior-analytic query into early intervention. Paper presented at the 19th Banff International Conference on Behavioral Science: Early Intervention in the Coming Decade. Banff, Alberta.

Baer, D. M., Wolf, M. M., & Risley, T. R. (1968). Some current dimensions of applied behavior analysis. *Journal of Applied Behavior Analysis, 1,* 91–97.

Bailey, D. B. (1989). Case management in early intervention. *Journal of Early Intervention, 13,* 120–134.

Bailey, D., Huntington, G., Simmeonson, R., & Yoder, D. (1992). Preparing professionals to serve infants and toddlers with handicaps and their families: An integrative analysis across eight disciplines. *Exceptional Children, 10,* 26–34.

Benson, H. A., & Turnbull, A. P. (1986). Approaching families from an individualized perspective. In R. H. Horner, L. H. Meyers, & H. D. Fredericks (Eds.), *Educating learners with severe handicaps: Exemplary service strategies* (pp. 127–157). Baltimore: Paul H. Brookes.

Bragg, R. M., Brown, R. L., & Berninger, V. W. (1992). The impact of congenital and acquired disabilities on the family system: Implications for school counseling. *The School Counselor, 39,* 292–299.

Bricker, D. D. (1995). The challenge of inclusion. *Journal of Early Intervention, 19*(3), 179–194.

Brinker, R. P. (1992). Family involvement in early intervention: Accepting the unchangeable, changing the changeable, and knowing the difference. *Topics in Early Childhood Special Education, 12*(3), 307–332.

Bronfenbrenner, U. (1986). Ecology of the family as a context for human development. *Developmental Psychology, 22,* 732–752.

Buysse, B., & Wesley, P. W. (1993). The identity crisis in early childhood education: A call for professional role clarification. *Topics in Early Childhood Special Education, 13,* 418–429.

Carlile, C. (1991, Summer). Children of divorce: How teachers can ease the pain. *Childhood Education,* 232–234.

Children's Defense Fund. (1993, December). Family support. *CDF Reports,* pp. 5–9.

Children's Defense Fund. (1998). *The state of America's children. Yearbook 1998.* Washington, DC: Author.

Clinton, B., & Gore, A. (1992). *Putting people first.* New York: Times Books. 47–51.

Coles, D. A., & Meyer, L. H. (1991). Social integration and severe disabilities: A longitudinal analysis of child outcomes. *The Journal of Special Education, 25,* 340–351.

Crockett, J. B., & Kauffman, J. M. (1998). Taking inclusion back to its roots. *Educational Leadership, 56*(2), 74–77.

Davis, P. B., & May, J. E. (1991, Spring). Involving fathers in early intervention and family support programs: Issues and strategies. *CHC,* 87–91.

Dunst, C., Trivette, C., & Deal, A. (1988). *Enabling and empowering families: Principles and guidelines for practice.* Cambridge, MA: Brookline.

Edelman, M. W. (1991). Ten lessons to help us through the 1990s: The state of America's children. *The Measure of Our Success.* Beacon Press, 13–15, 19, 20.

Esposito, B. G., & Koorland, M. A. (1989). Play behavior of hearing impaired children: Integrated and segregated settings. *Exceptional Children, 55,* 412–419.

Fagan, P., & Coontz, S. (1997). Q: Are single-parent families a major cause of social dysfunction? *Insight on the News, 13*(45): 24–27.

Fallon, M. A., & Harris, M. B. (1992). Encouraging parent participation in intervention programs. *The Transdisciplinary Journal, 2*(2), 141–146.

Florsheim, P., Tolan, P., & Gorman-Smith, D. (1998). Family relationships, parenting practices, the availability of male family members, and the behavior of inner-city boys in single-mother and two-parent families. *Child Development, 69*(5), 1437–1447.

Forest, M. (1988, Winter). Full inclusion is possible. *Minnesota UAP Impact, Minnesota Affiliated Program on Developmental Disabilities,* 1.

Fox, L., & Hanline, M. F. (1993). Learning within the context of play: Providing typical early childhood experiences for children with severe disabilities. *Journal of the Association for the Severely Handicapped, 18,* 121–129.

Fuchs, D., & Fuchs, L. S. (1998). Competing visions for educating students with disabilities: Inclusion versus full inclusion. *Childhood Education, 74*(5), 309–316.

Gallagher, D. J. (1998). The scientific knowledge base of special education: Do we know what we think we know? *Exceptional Children, 64*(4), 493–502.

Garcia, E. E. (1997). The education of Hispanics in early childhood: Of roots and wings. *Young Children, 53*(3): 5–14.

Gemmell-Crosby, S., & Hanzlik, J. R. (1994). Preschool teachers' perceptions of including children with disabilities. *Education and Training in Mental Retardation and Developmental Disabilities, 29*(4), 279–290.

Gerrard, L. C. (1994). Inclusive education: An issue of social justice. *Equity and Excellence in Education, 27*(1), 58–67.

Goodman, J. F., & Bond, L. (1993). The Individualized Education Program: A retrospective critique. *The Journal of Special Education, 26,* 408–422.

Griffith, D. R. (1992, September). Prenatal exposure to cocaine and other drugs: Developmental and educational prognosis. *Phi Delta Kappan,* 30–34.

Guo, G. (1998). The timing of the influences of cumulative poverty on children's cognitive ability and achievement. *Social Forces, 77*(1): 257–287.

Guralnick, M. J., & Groom, J. M. (1988). Peer interactions in mainstreamed and specialized classrooms: A comparative analysis. *Exceptional Children, 54,* 415–425.

Gutierrez, L., & Ortega, R. (1991). Developing methods to empower Latinos: The importance of groups. *Social Work with Groups, 14*(2), 23–43.

Hallahan, D. P., & Kauffman, J. M. (1994). Toward a culture of disability in the aftermath of Deno and Dunn. *The Journal of Special Education, 27*(4), 496–508.

Hanline, M. F. (1993). Inclusion of preschoolers with profound disabilities: An analysis of children's interactions. *Journal of the Association for the Severely Handicapped, 18,* 28–34.

Haring, N. G., & McCormick, L. (1990). *Exceptional children and youth.* Upper Saddle River, NJ: Merrill/Prentice Hall.

Harry, B. (1992). *Cultural diversity, families, and the special educational system: Communication and empowerment.* New York: Teachers College Press.

Healy, A., Keesee, P. D., & Smith, B. S. (1989). *Early services for children with special needs: Transactions for family support.* Baltimore: Paul H. Brookes Publishing.

Hegar, R., & Scannapieco, M. (1995). From family duty to family policy: The evolution of kinship care. *Child Welfare, 75*(1), 200–217.

Hernandez, D. J. (1995). Changing demographics: Past and future demands for early childhood programs. *The Future of Children, 145*–160.

Himelfarb, S. (1992, November). You can make a difference for America's children. *Parents,* pp. 221–224.

Hispanic population to become largest U.S. minority. (1997). *Population Today, 25*(11), 1–2.

Hodapp, R. M., & Zigler, E. (1993). Comparison of families of children with mental retardation and families of children without mental retardation. *Mental Retardation, 31*(2), 75–87.

Hoyt, M. & Schoonmaker, M. E. (1991, October, 15). The day care delusion: When parents accept the unacceptable. *Family Circle,* pp. 81–87.

Hunter, A. G., Pearson, J. L., Isalongo, N. S., & Kellam, S. G. (1998). Parenting alone to multiple caregivers: Child care and parenting arrangements in black and white urban families. *Family Relations, 47*(4), 343–353.

Iglehart, A. P. (1994). Kinship foster care: Placement, service, and outcome issues. *Children and Youth Services Review, 16*(1–2), 107–121.

Ingrassia, M., & Rossi, M. (1994, February). The limits of tolerance? *Newsweek,* p. 47.

Kamps, D. M., Leonard, B. R., Vernon, S., Dugan, E. P., & Delquadri, J. C. (1992). Teaching social skills to students with autism to increase peer interactions in an integrated first-grade classroom. *Journal of Applied Behavior Analysis, 25,* 281–288.

Kelley, P. (1996). Family-centered practice with stepfamilies. *Families in Society, 77*(9), 535–544.

Koren, P. E., DeChillo, N., & Friesen, B. J. (1992). Measuring empowerment in families whose children have emotional disabilities: A brief questionnaire. *Rehabilitation Psychology, 37*(4), 304–321.

Krausse, M. W. (1991). Theoretical issues in family research. Paper presented at the Annual meeting of the American Association on Mental Retardation, Washington, D.C. (ERIC Document Reproduction Service No. ED 337 923).

Lee, S. M. (1998). Asian Americans: Diverse and growing. *Population Bulletin, 53*(2), 2–40.

Levitan, S. A., Mangum, G. L., & Pines, M. W. (1989). *A proper inheritance: Investing in the self-sufficiency of poor families.* Washington, DC: The George Washington University.

Lewis, A. C. (1997). The price of poverty. *Phi Delta Kappan, 78*(6), 423–424.

Lillie, T. (1993). A harder thing than triumph: Roles of fathers of children with disabilities. *Mental Retardation, 31,* 438–442.

Lipsky, D., & Gartner, A. (1989). *Beyond separate education: Quality education for all.* Baltimore: Paul H. Brookes.

MacMillan, D. L., & Gresham, F. M. (1996). Full inclusion: An empirical perspective. *Behavioral Disorders, 21*(2), 145–159.

Mallory, B. L., & New, R. S. (1994). Social constructivist theory and principles of inclusion: Challenges for early childhood special education. *Journal of Special Education, 28*(3), 322–337.

Martin, P., & Midgley, E. (1994). Immigration to the United States: Journey to an uncertain destination. *Population Bulletin, 49*(2), 2–47.

McBride, B. A., & McBride, R. J. (1993). Parent education and support programs for fathers. *Childhood Education, 70,* 4–8.

McCormick, L., & Holden, R. (1992). Homeless children: A special challenge. *Young Children, 47*(6), 61–67.

McGee, G., Paradis, T., & Feldman, R. S. (1993). Free effects of integration on levels of autistic behavior. *Topics in Early Childhood Special Education, 13*(1), 57–65.

McGill-Smith, P. (1992). Can't get on the train without a ticket. *Teaching Exceptional Children, 25,* 49.

McKinney, J. D., & Hocutt, A. M. (1998). Policy issues in the evaluation of the Regular Education Initiative. *Learning Disabilities Focus, 4,* 15–23.

McLeskey, J., Henry, D., & Hodges, D. (1999). Inclusion: What progress is being made across disability categories? *Teaching Exceptional Children, 31*(3), 60–64.

McLoyd, V. C. (1990). Minority children: Introduction to the special issue. *Child Development, 61,* 263–266.

McPhatter, A. R. (1997). Cultural competence in child welfare: What is it? How do we achieve it? What happens without it? *Child Welfare, 76*(1), 255–278.

Mills, P. E., Cole, K. N., Jenkins, J. R., & Dale, P. S. (1998). Effects of differing levels of inclusion on preschoolers with disabilities. *Exceptional Children, 65*(1), 79–90.

Minke, K. M., & Scott, M. M. (1993). The development of Individualized Family Service Plans: Roles for parents and staff. *The Journal of Special Education, 27,* 82–106.

Mitchell, S. (1995). The next baby boom. *American Demographics,* 22–27, 30–31.

Moore, K. A., Manlove, J., Glei, D. A., & Morrison, D. R. (1998). Nonmarital school-age motherhood: Family, individual, and school characteristics. *Journal of Adolescent Research, 13*(4), 433–457.

Montgomery, L. E., Kiely, J. L. & Pappas, G. (1996). The effects of poverty, race, and family structure on U.S. children's health: Data from the NHIS, 1978 through 1980 and 1989 through 1991. *American Journal of Public Health, 86*(10), 1401.

Morgan, R. (1993). *The word of a woman.* New York: W. W. Norton.

Morrison, G. M., Walker, D., Wakefield, P., & Solberg, S. (1994). Teacher preferences for collaborative relationships: Relationship to efficacy for teaching in prevention-related domains. *Psychology in the Schools, 31,* 221–231.

National Association for the Education of Young Children. (1997). *Code of Ethics.* Author.

National Association for the Education of Young Children. (1996). NAEYC position statement: Responding to linguistic and cultural diversity—recommendations for effective early childhood education. *Young Children, 51*(2): 4–12.

National Commission on Family Foster Care. (1991). *The significance of kinship care: Blueprint for fostering infants, children, and youths in the 1990s.* Washington, DC: Child Welfare League of America.

National Council of Teachers of English and International Reading Association. (1996). *Standards for the English language arts.* Urbana, IL: NCTE.

Nelson, D., Howard, V. F., & McLaughlin, T. F. (1993). Empowering parents to become advocates for their own children with disabilities. *B. C. Journal of Special Education, 17*(1), 62–72.

Novella, S. (1996). Psychomotor patterning. *The Connecticut Skeptic, 1*(4), 6.

Nunez, R. C., & Collignon, K. (1997). Creating a community of learning for homeless children. *Educational Leadership,* 56–60.

Olmsted, P. P. (1992). Where did our diversity come from? *High/Scope ReSource, 11*(3), 4–9.

Orfield, G., Schley, S., Glass, D., & Reardon, S. (1994). The growth of segregation in American schools: Changing patterns of separation and poverty since 1968. *Equity and Excellence, 27*(1), 5–8.

Rainforth, B. (1994). Philosophy versus student need? A reply to Smith and Hilton. *Education and Training in Mental Retardation and Developmental Disabilities, 29,* 251–252.

Rounds, K. A., Weil, M., & Bishop, K. K. (1994). Practice with culturally diverse families of young children with disabilities. *Families in Society, 75,* 3–15.

Rueda, R., & Martinez, I. (1992). Fiesta Educativa: One community's approach to parent training in developmental disabilities for Latino families. *Journal of the Association for the Severely Handicapped, 17*(2), 95–103.

Russo, C. J., & Talbert-Johnson, C. (1997). The overrepresentation of African American children in special education: The resegregation of educational programming? *Education and Urban Society, 29*(2), 136–148.

Ryan, M. (August 30, 1992). Who's Taking Care of the Children?" *Parade Magazine,* pp. 3–5.

Salisbury, C. L., Palombaro, M. M., & Long, C. A. (1993). On the nature and change of an inclusive elementary school. *Journal of the Association for the Severely Handicapped, 18,* 75–84.

Sass-Lehrer, M., & Bodner-Johnson, B. (1989). P. L. 99–457: A new challenge to early intervention. *American Annals of the Deaf, 134*(2), 71–77.

Schorr, L. B., & Both, D. (1991). Attributes of effective services for young children: A brief survey of current knowledge and its implications for program and policy development. In L. B. Schorr, D. Both, & C. Copple (Eds.), *Effective services for young children: Report of a workshop* (pp. 23–47), Washington, DC: National Academy.

Shelton, D. L. (1998). Downward public health statistics show upbeat trends. *American Medical News, 41*(42), 35.

Singleton, P. (1992). We Can! Empowerment of people who are deaf. *OSERS News in Print, 5*(2), 12–15.

Skinner, B. F. (1953). *Science and human behavior.* New York: Macmillan.

Slavin, R. E. (1998). Can education reduce social inequity? *Educational Leadership, 55*(4), 6–10.

Smart, J. F., & Smart, D. W. (1997). The racial/ethnic demography of disability. *Journal of Rehabilitation, 63*(4): 9–15.

Spodek, B., Saracho, O. N., & Lee, R. C. (1986). *Mainstreaming young children.* Newton, MA: Allyn and Bacon.

Taylor, R. (1998). Check your cultural competence. *Nursing Management, 29*(8), 30–32.

Thomson, E., Hanson, T. L., & McLanahan, S. S. (1994). Family structure and child well-being: Economic resources vs. parental behaviors. *Social Forces, 73*(1), 221–242.

Thousand, J. S., & Villa, R. A. (1991). A Futuristic view of the REI: A response to Jenkins, Tious, and Jewel. *Exceptional Children, 57*(6), 559.

Turnbull, A., & Turnbull, R. (1990). *Parents, professionals, and exceptionality.* Upper Saddle River, NJ: Merrill/ Prentice Hall.

Turnbull, A., & Turnbull, R. (1997). *Parents, professionals, and exceptionality, A special partnership.* Upper Saddle River, NJ: Merrill/Prentice Hall.

United States Conference of Mayors. (1993). *A status report on hunger and homelessness in America's cities: A 26-city survey.* Washington, DC: Author.

Voydanoff, P. (1994). A family perspective on services integration. *Family Relations, 44,* 63–68.

Walther-Thomas, C., Korinek, L., McLaughlin, V., & Williams, B. (1996). Improving educational opportunities for students with disabilities who are homeless. *Journal of Children and Poverty, 2*(2), 57–75.

Wehrly, B. (1988). *Toward a multicultural partnership in higher education.* Macomb, IL: Western Illinois University, (ERIC Document Reproduction Service No. ED 308 731).

Wells, A. S. (1988). *Urban teacher recruitment programs.* New York, NY: Columbia University, Institute for Urban and Minority Education, (ERIC Document Reproduction Service No. ED 312 318).

Wetzstein, C. (1998). Teen births decline. *Insight on the News, 14*(44), 40.

Whaley, D. L., & Malott, M. E. (1971). *Elementary principles of behavior* (2nd ed.). Englewood Cliffs, NJ: Prentice-Hall.

White, K., & Castro, G. (1985). An Integrative review of early intervention efficacy studies with at-risk children: Implications for the handicapped. *Analysis and Intervention in Developmental Disabilities, 5,* 7-31.

Williams, B. F. (1992). Changing demographics; Challenges for educators. *Intervention in Schools and Community, 27*(3), 157–163.

Williams, B. T., & DeSander, M. K. (1999). Dueling legislation: The impact of incongruent federal statutes on homeless and other special-needs students. *Journal for a Just and Caring Education, 5*(1), 34–50.

Wolfensberger, W. (1972). *The principle of normalization in human services.* Paper presented at the National Institute on Mental Retardation, Toronto.

Wolfensberger, W. (1983). Social role valorization: A proposed new term for the principle of Normalization. *Mental Retardation, 21*(6), 234–239.

Yanok, J., & Derubertis, D. (1989). Comparative study of parental participation in regular and special education programs. *Exceptional Children, 56,* 195–199.

Yell, M. L. (1995). Least restrictive environment, inclusion, and students with disabilities: A legal analysis. *Journal of Special Education, 28*(4), 389–415.

Zirkel, P. (1996). Inclusion: Return of the pendulum? *The Special Educator, 12*(9), 1, 5.

EARLY CHILDHOOD SERVICES, YESTERDAY, TODAY, AND AROUND THE WORLD

During the 30 or so years that I have been involved in child care research and administration, the field has been plagued with claims and counter-claims, praise and denunciation, acceptance and rejection. Even so, child care has come a long way. From an obscure service that most people had never heard of or thought about, it has risen to a position of national prominence and makes every list of key issues for the present and future of our nation and the world.

(Caldwell, 1997, p. 35)

We sometimes think that the care of young children has always been in the home with mother. But, in fact, the first organization of child-care providers was established in the United States in New York City only 30 years after this country declared its independence (Neugebauer, 1990). The history of organized services to very young children began much earlier and has evolved through a variety of forms to become what we know of today as day care, preschool, kindergarten, early intervention, and other names. This chapter examines our roots and those of other cultures, in order that we might have a better perspective on where services to very young children have been and where they might be going in the next millennium.

AN HISTORICAL PERSPECTIVE

This chapter explores the history of Western culture in terms of its beliefs about the rights of young children and their families and subsequent practices that have changed as those beliefs changed. Though it would be preferable to be global in this analysis, it is undeniable that Western civilization, because of worldwide colonization from the sixteenth century, has directly influenced the evolution and predominant practice of educational services provided in almost all parts of the world today (Woodill, 1992). The chapter examines how various cultures' perspectives on raising and educating children have changed over time, and how cultures have attempted to solve both the economic and civil rights problems these issues present. In addition to looking at the history of early childhood services, relevant research in the United States and internationally is considered. Finally, the current challenges and future goals for the field of early childhood are discussed.

THE HISTORY OF CHILDHOOD IN WESTERN CIVILIZATION

This text is sensitive to the ethnocentricity of describing the history of early childhood education from the viewpoint of Western culture. However, study of this discipline reveals that to know the history of European education (and in particular that of very young children) is to understand educational practices worldwide (Woodill, Bernhard, & Prochner, 1992). Western-style cultural infusion in early education has become the dominant global model.

Lloyd deMause (1974) described the history of childhood as a series of stages in which the concept of childhood in Western civilization evolved over the last two thousand years (see Table 2–1). Each stage was marked by great changes in society—changes in the way people were governed, changes in religious beliefs and customs, and changes in the way wealth was distributed (Day, 1983). In general, children in ancient times were treated with indifference, and there was no apparent conception of childhood as a distinct human experience. Not until the period from the fourteenth to the seventeenth century did there emerge some notion that childhood was a special time. Even then, economic struggle and survival were so prominent that children tended to be treated with ambivalence and emotional distance.

In the eighteenth century, when Christian belief systems developed strongly, parents were expected to be responsible for the souls of their children, and thus formal

Table 2–1   A history of childhood.

Stages	Date	Problem	Solution
From Bad to Worse **Stage 1:** No apparent conception of childhood	To the fourth century A.D.: infanticide mode The fourth to thirteenth century: abandonment mode	Survival depends on pleasing the gods, controlling population, and maintaining a physically strong community	Eliminate extra mouths to feed, ensure that only the strongest are raised from childhood
Children Will Be Children **Stage 2:** The emergence of the idea of childhood as a special period	The fourteenth to seventeenth century: ambivalent mode	Rampant disease and hardship kill many young children	Remain detached from young children, have many but don't form bonds until they survive early childhood
Church and State Mix **Stage 3:** Parents begin to feel a responsibility for the soul of the child	The eighteenth century: intrusive mode	Everlasting salvation of the soul is highest priority, heavenly life beyond this earthly toil is the final reward	Provide an early education so that children can learn of god's redemption
Parents Know Best **Stage 4:** Parents become responsible for training the child; a recognition of independence	The nineteenth to the mid-twentieth century: socialization mode	Industrialization requires an increasing labor base; immigrant parents work long hours and neglect their children	Provide early childhood care and education to promote productive citizenship among children
Children Know Best **Stage 5:** Children know better than the parents what they need and involve parents in fulfilling those needs	The mid-twentieth century, current: helping mode	Resources are abundant enough that all people should have equal opportunity, including children	Provide early educational services to children who are poor or disabled

education for children grew more important. During the nineteenth century and through the early part of the twentieth century, the concept of childhood evolved to a point that parents were seen as responsible for training their children to be independent and to follow the rules and values of society.

STAGE 1: FROM BAD TO WORSE

From ancient civilization until the fourth century A.D., many cultures of Western civilization were characterized by their struggles to survive. The solution to crises was often ritualistic sacrifice of children to supplicate the gods or abandonment of children to ensure the survival of the strongest or perhaps to control population density (Day, 1983).

Children were also murdered in great numbers for nonreligious reasons until well into the fourth century. Cultures in Greece and Rome, among others,

??BC – 1200 AD
ABANDONMENT MODE

abandoned babies on hillsides to die, threw them into the sea or rivers to drown, and even entombed them in large pots. It is clear that children were not treated protectively or held in special regard.

Children who were born infirm, sickly, or premature were almost always destroyed. Political states like Sparta killed all but the most fit children in order to maintain strength in their society. Though infanticide became a punishable crime by the fourth century, the practice lingered in some places until the eighteenth and nineteenth centuries (deMause, 1974). In these traditional patriarchal societies, the role of women was very different from that in today's Western culture. Women who protested or cried at the slaughter of their children were subjected to fines (Greenleaf, 1978). Perhaps if mothers had possessed more control over their own destinies they could have influenced the treatment of their children as well.

In ancient times, a child was considered to be an adult by age 7 (Gordon & Browne, 1993). Formal education of children began at about this same age, though Plato and Aristotle both spoke of the need to educate younger children. Greek education, and virtually all classical European schooling that followed this model, was provided for boys of wealthy families, while girls and children of working class families were trained for domestic work or trades (Gordon & Browne, 1993). A few insightful ancient Romans provided education at home beginning as soon as a child could talk; some even used systems of rewards for their children's educational gains (Hewes & Hartman, 1974).

The fall of the Roman Empire was followed by centuries of lawlessness and anarchy; people left their villages for the protection of a local baron or king, and formal schooling ceased to exist (Gordon & Browne, 1993). With no educational system to speak of, even members of the ruling class were seldom taught to write their names or to read. Only monastery schools were available, and these were open only to those entering the priesthood. In medieval times (fifth through thirteenth centuries), childhood was viewed as a period beginning with birth and lasting just beyond infancy. Adults assumed that, in their natural state, children were basically evil and needed to be directed, punished, and corrected in order to learn to follow social rules. Youth were expected to take up the responsibilities of adulthood as quickly as possible, learning the necessary skills of a trade mostly through their parents or through apprenticeship. Survival was the primary goal.

STAGE 2: CHILDREN WILL BE CHILDREN

Well into the seventeenth century, children were commonly beaten, sexually abused, sold into slavery, and abandoned. Even children who were valued by their families were commonly sent away from home to be raised by wet nurses or other families. It was clear that parents were generally ambivalent toward their children.

1200 - 1600AD

AMBIVALENT MODE

It could be that the lack of attachment was a psychological survival technique. The rate of infant mortality was so high that more young children were lost to illness or injury than survived childhood. Consequently, it was common practice to have many children in order to ensure that a few children would live. For many years, there were no pictures made of young children nor were formal names given until children had passed the toddler stage.

The shift to a more compassionate approach to childhood began in French cities among more affluent families. The gentry of France seemed to find enjoyment in children, who were accepted for the amusement they brought their parents. Philosophers began to theorize about the effect that adult care and nurturance could have on the well-being of children. At the same time, Christian beliefs were spreading, and people began to think about the immortality of a child's soul.

In 1658, Comenius, a Czech educator, wrote *Orbis Pictus* (The World of Pictures), the first picture book for children (Gordon & Browne, 1993). The book was a guide for teachers and emphasized sensory awareness and the study of nature. Comenius believed that education should follow the natural order of things and referred to the "school of the mother's lap." His ideas were later reflected in Montessori's and Piaget's theories of the stages of development.

As an English philosopher of the 1600s, John Locke theorized that children are born neutral, rather than evil, and possess a moral and behavioral "clean slate," or tabula rasa, to be written upon by parents, society, education, and the world (Gordon & Browne, 1993). He was one of the first Europeans to promote the idea of taking the individual learner into account when planning instruction and evaluating progress. Locke recommended that instruction be conducted pleasantly in the areas of business and the Bible. Though Locke's influence was minimal during his life, his ideas were later popularized by Rousseau (Gordon & Browne, 1993).

In 1647, the Massachusetts Bay Colony enacted a law by which all communities of 50 households had to hire a teacher and open a school. If a community had more than 100 families, a Latin grammar school was required. There was no political or moral separation of Christian churches and Christian schools at this time. Indeed, the principle purpose of education was to teach children to read in order to understand the Bible and to study Christian doctrine.

Early life in New England was difficult and, though conditions had improved over the medieval period, as many as 60% to 70% of children under age 4 died in colonial towns during the "starving season" (Gordon & Browne, 1993). Puritan families showed little overt affection and children were seen as important economic tools, working the land and apprenticed into trades early (Gordon & Browne, 1993). Discipline was harsh and children were expected to obey without question.

By the beginning of the 1700s, most towns provided schooling. However, formal education was still considered unnecessary for children under the age of 6 or 7 years. It was the general belief that young children should stay in the care of their mothers until middle childhood.

STAGE 3: CHURCH AND STATE MIX

1600 – 1700AD

INTRUSIVE MODE

By the mid-1700s there was a realization that childhood was developmentally connected to adulthood (Day, 1983). This encouraged consideration of child-rearing practices, and society began to place value on disciplined activity and tasks that would foster an appropriate spirit, a fear of God, and a respect for elders. Puritan beliefs supported the idea that children possessed souls that could be saved through devotion to God. Hence, it was expected that parents ensure the education of their children so the latter could begin their studies of Christian doctrine early in life. Moral and spiritual goodness were often inspired with the birch whip; children were thrashed to drive out evil spirits and to ensure their well-being (Day, 1983; deMause, 1974).

Providing an altogether different view of education, the French scholar Rousseau became an outspoken champion for children. Rousseau departed from the view that children were simply miniature adults (Williams, 1992). In his book, *Emile,* in which he raised a hypothetical child to adulthood, Rousseau argued that children should be treated with gentle care early in life and that play and childhood experiences contributed to learning (Day, 1983; Gordon & Browne, 1993; Rousseau, 1969). Rousseau dismissed the idea that children were inherently evil, concluding, on the contrary, that they were naturally good (Gordon & Browne, 1993). The importance of beginning a child's education at birth and treating children with sympathy and compassion was stressed, providing the philosophical basis for early childhood education (Cook, Tessier, & Klein, 1992). He stood against harsh, physical punishment of children and also against education that stressed memorization and recitation. Like others, however, Rousseau was considered a radical by his contemporaries, and his ideas had little impact on educational practices during his life.

Case
Study

LIVING NATURALLY: INTERVIEW WITH DAVID DEWOLF

It's an important thing for our teachers to recognize the need for disabled children to have natural lives and not to be pushed too hard too early. From my perspective, one of the mistakes that you can make is to try so hard to overcome the disability that you push too hard. A parent or a professional can become a little bit like the doctor whose job it is to fight sickness. The doctor views the disease as an enemy and as sort of a matter of pride, decides he is not going to let this thing take his patient. The doctor uses all his ingenuity and energy to figure out ways to beat the disease.

In dealing with children with disabilities, it is healthy and appropriate to try to ameliorate the effects. Perhaps if the child has a hearing impairment one thinks, "How can I provide a hearing aid?" or, "What new technology or breakthroughs in terms of electronics or whatever can I offer that will compensate and allow the child as normal an experience as possible?"

I think, particularly for kids with a learning disability or a cognitive disability like Down syndrome, there is an impulse to accelerate the educational process, as though you saw a hill coming up ahead of you and you jammed on the accelerator to get up enough momentum so when you get to the hill your momentum will kind of carry you over the top before you've lost your steam. I think some of that is a good idea, but if you're not careful, you can make the child's academic accomplishments overshadow their right to be a child.

Children with disabilities ought to be able to kind of go at their own speed, at their own rate in what feels good to them in the same way that children without disabilities are allowed to develop whatever talents and abilities they have. That's a difficult balance to strike. I think it's the same balance you have to strike with a normal child. Do I teach my kid to play the violin at the age of four? Suppose I have a tradition in my family of violin players, can I pass that along to my child at the age of four by encouraging them and keeping at them to do this because of the great benefit that I see at the end of the process? They may resent it now, but they'll thank me for it later when they can see the fruits of all this effort. On the other hand, I can sit back and say, if he wants to, that's great, but I'm not going to push it on him. I think many of the same dynamics are present with a kid who has a disability.

The most important thing is to be sure that what you're doing is really for the child's benefit rather than for your own psychological benefit. I think that parents who have kids with disabilities are subject to the same kind of competitive streak as everybody else. Some parents want their kid to make the varsity team because it will help them get ahead. We're similarly tempted to think well, maybe most kids with this condition can only sit there and babble, but by golly, my kid is going to be able to recite the alphabet. That's not all bad, the ambitions that you have for your children to help them achieve, that's part of the reasons that kids do achieve.

But, I think you have to take stock of it periodically to say, is this really for my ego gratification or is this really because I think my child will genuinely be better for this? Also, it is very important to avoid a denial process. Just like the doctor who appropriately enough is engaged in the fight against disease and death, you can kid yourself into thinking that if you just work hard enough and do enough research in the lab you can beat it.

There is a risk that you get so infatuated with all of the compensatory mechanisms that you think if you just work hard enough and are a devoted enough parent, you can compensate for the disability so that your kid will be just like everybody else. I think that people who work with parents have to be prepared for the parent who won't allow any discussion of the child's limitations, as though it were a kind of sabotage or disloyalty if you ever suggested that something less than normal milestones was acceptable.

In the same way, the doctor occasionally has to tell the patient, "I'm sorry, but there's nothing more we can do for your father [child or husband]." There are times, I think, when you have to say, "Your child is only going to be able to do this and that's just because of the condition that he has." There was a time in which people had unrealistically low expectations of children with Down syndrome. They just wanted to warehouse these kids, or get rid of them. Children with Down syndrome were denied basic opportunities to prove what they could do. So it has become unfashionable to speak discouraging words, to say, "Hey, because your kid has this condition, this is all you should expect."

I think now there is more risk of denial. Both parents and the people who work with children who have disabilities need to accept the fact that their efforts—as worthy as they may be—may be unsuccessful, or may prove to be disappointing. They need to understand that you don't have to win this. I think it is particularly important to communicate to the child that whatever they do is acceptable. Just as the parent who wants his kid to play the violin can subconsciously—or not even subconsciously, but overtly—communicate to the kid, "Hey, if you don't do this, if you can't make the varsity team, or accomplish this particular thing which I think is so important, well, you're not really a member of this family, or you're not really worth much, or you must not be trying hard enough." A child with wonderful gifts can be destroyed by the fact that the gifts they have don't measure up to some parent's arbitrary idea of what it is to be a great kid.

Parents who want their kids to be normal have to watch that they don't place such high expectations on their child, that the child is taught in essence I'm only good to the extent that I outperform my disability expectations. If I'm just a normal handicapped kid, then it's not good enough. I suppose that's a form of equal treatment for parents who push their other kids to be extraordinary. Some parents want their kid with a disability to be extraordinary too. Just as a matter of parenting style, I think that parents have to be gently helped to accept their kids for who they are.

Teachers and other people who work with these kids can help parents see their children through fresh eyes. Parents of both normal kids and kids with disabilities get stuck with their own perceptions. They don't see their kids the way other people see them and sometimes it's very important for the teacher to say, "Gee, here's the way this kid looks to me, here's the way I perceive him or her. Maybe you're stuck on something here that doesn't really fit." No parent likes to hear that. Those are tough words to speak to any parent, but I think you can do it if you really care about the child, and if you establish some credibility with the parent. You can do it in a subtle and nonjudgmental way, and if you can help the parent get a fresh perspective, that's one of the most important things that I think that a teacher can do.

There's nothing wrong with the impulse to "save" a child; it's just that it has to take place within a context of acceptance. Life is limited and we can't have all we want all the time. A disability is a forced example of learning to accept what you're given rather than always thinking that life's going to be a series of pleasant experiences.

Robin DeWolf

Still, by the late 1700s, several authors extolled humane ways to educate children. For example, Johann Pestalozzi, an Italian-Swiss school teacher, indicated his belief in children's ability to learn through self-discovery (Cook et al., 1992). He felt that education should be based on the natural development of children, that mothers were the best teachers for very young children, and that the home should be the basic model for teaching and learning. Pestalozzi's ideas were much like Rousseau's, though he was more pragmatic and included principles on how to teach basic skills and the concept of caring for, as well as educating, children (Gordon & Browne, 1993).

Pestalozzi founded the first European school to acknowledge the developmental characteristics of children (Williams, 1992). "Papa" Pestalozzi prescribed parental guidance, strong morality and work ethic, and high intensity work training (Pestalozzi, 1915; Williams, 1992). It was Pestalozzi who coined the phrase, "education should be of the hand, the head, and the heart of the child" (Gordon & Browne, 1993). His humane attitude was a source of present day philosophy in special education where caregivers focus on unique characteristics of children in planning and conducting educational programs.

In 1799, Jean-Marc Itard undertook the first documented efforts to work with a child with special needs (Day, 1983; Itard, 1962). A child, approximately 12 years old, was found living in isolation in the forest near Aveyron, France. Victor, the "Wild Boy of Aveyron," was thought to have been raised by animals, and was described as an "incurable idiot." Itard undertook the task of humanizing the boy, and though he felt he failed, Itard's methods showed that specialized instruction could improve the abilities of children with significant developmental delays.

The first early childhood teachers in America ran "dame schools." These seventeenth- and eighteenth-century "schools" have only recently been researched, as feminist historians have studied the journals and diaries of women who ran the schools (Wyman, 1995). To make ends meet, widowed or young unmarried women held school for very young children in their homes. According to Wyman (1995), dame schools provided a transitional education to students whose mothers had too many children to care for, too many tasks, or too little time. Though no curriculum was available for children of any age, preschoolers at the dame schools were often taught fine motor skills, sewing, knitting, bread making, and rhyming songs. Because the Bible was typically the only reading material available, children learned to read from this text, mostly through rote recitation. It is interesting to note that dame teachers, because they were female, were rarely permitted to go to school themselves after completing their education in a dame school. Therefore, the academic skills taught in dame schools were, by default, rudimentary.

STAGE 4: PARENTS KNOW BEST

1800 - 1950AD
SOCIALIZATION MODE

By the nineteenth century, the American and French revolutions had changed the way Western society thought about human rights. It was believed the common person should expect freedom, and concerns were gradually raised about paternalistic treatment of women, children, peasants, and the infirm, who were often treated as property (Day, 1983). Slavery, child labor, and harsh punishment were now considered inhumane. There was movement toward social reform and new voices encouraged parents to raise their children to live self-determined and productive lives.

At the same time, American cities were becoming more industrial and great numbers of immigrants flocked to this country to seek a better life. Rapidly growing cities were heavily populated with foreigners who could barely scratch out an existence. The cities teemed with children whose parents had little time for child-rearing activities. Still, parents were assigned the responsibility for guiding their children to good citizenship; children were viewed as the product of parents' competence and attention. Yet, a growing conviction that the government should intervene in raising the neglected children of immigrants was fueled by an inspired movement to maintain cultural integrity by saving these children (Day, 1983).

Child-care centers and public schools developed in response to the needs of working families. By 1828, the Boston Infant School was established as a service to working mothers. The school cared for children from 18 months to 4 years of age. It was open for 13 hours daily in the summer and for 9 hours daily in the winter to accommodate work schedules (Day, 1983).

In 1837, the German educator Froebel created kindergartens (literally translated as "children's garden") and the model quickly spread throughout the world (Day, 1983; Froebel, 1895). Froebel had studied with Pestalozzi, and though he agreed that play should be the medium for children's learning, he altered Pestalozzi's theory to encompass the "self-actualization" of children as a legitimate goal of early childhood (Williams, 1992). Consistent with his desire to build a moral society, Froebel idealistically assumed the potential for perfection in each child. Froebel felt the role of the teacher was to bring a child's inborn capabilities to fruition. He emphasized the use of manipulatives and introduced handiwork projects for children (Williams, 1992).

Froebel started his German kindergarten with children aged 2 to 6 years, focusing on self-directed activities, self-esteem, and self-confidence. Kindergartners were encouraged to play in school, had toys as learning tools, and were educated by trained teachers who joined in the games with playful attitudes (Gordon & Browne, 1993). Furthermore, Froebel pushed the radical idea that both men and women should teach young children by being friendly facilitators rather than stern disciplinarians. "Play is the highest phase of child development—the representation of the inner necessity and impulse." [In Froebel's 1826 *Education of Man* (Gordon & Browne, 1993).]

Unfortunately, at the time of his death in 1852, Froebel's methods were still being developed, leaving no written guide to explain his ideas (Gordon & Browne, 1993).

Kindergarten in the United States

In 1856, Margaretha Schurz, a German emigrant who had studied under Froebel, opened the first kindergarten in the United States for German-speaking children in Watertown, Wisconsin (Gordon & Browne, 1993). Later, she frequently traveled to visit other kindergartens or to give inspiring talks about Froebel's system. It was Schurz's inspiration that led Elizabeth Palmer Peabody to open Boston's first kindergarten for English-speaking children in 1860.

Early kindergartens for children aged 3 and older were intended to supplement nurturance in the home environment. The goals of these early programs were moral and social growth for children. Women were hired to assist as both teachers and mother-surrogates, even though teaching had traditionally been a male-dominated profession before this time. By now, society had embraced the need for kindergartens, and as with other forms of education, it was affluent families who were the first to take advantage of these services (Cook et al., 1992). However, because Froebel's underlying philosophy was poorly translated from German to English, most American kindergartens were quite different from what Froebel had intended, and few maintained a spirit of joyous play (Gordon & Browne, 1993).

Social Reform

Following the Civil War, the view that parents were obligated to provide good child rearing was strong enough that parent manuals had been developed to outline a family's responsibilities to its children. There was an increasing emphasis on safe custodial care that could meet children's nutritional, physical, and health needs. Day-care services expanded rapidly with the support of philanthropic women and were clearly seen as a mechanism for the social reform of poor or neglected children (Day, 1983). The growth of kindergartens from 1880 to 1900 was phenomenal. Free kindergartens were established in Boston in 1877, and St. Louis Superintendent William Harris (influenced by Elizabeth Peabody) established public-school kindergartens district wide before going on to serve as United States Commissioner of Education from 1889 to 1906. As Commissioner, Harris continued to advocate for public funding of kindergartens.

> Every dollar spent at the Nursery means from one to three dollars earned by the mother while her little one is in our care. But that is not all. Every mother receives her child at night happy, clean and in excellent physical condition. The influence toward cleanliness and thrift is strong, and every mother has felt it. [From the 1888 *Second Annual Report of the South Side Day Nursery*, St. Louis, Missouri (Neugebauer, 1990, p. 6)]

In the United States, the 1890s were known as the "progressive era," and in some ways served as a turning point for early childhood education. There was a growing national concern for the means by which the poor and immigrants living in cities were forced to exist. Considerable efforts were made to enact child labor laws, establish clean milk distribution centers, and provide for the nurturance of children whose parents needed to work. Kindergartens became an instrument of social reform. These early childhood programs became known as charity kindergartens and included a day-care function (Gordon & Browne, 1993). At the same time, it was generally recognized that some people had greater knowledge and expertise in child development than others.

G. Stanley Hall began the American Child Study Movement, and though he was criticized by his peers, other child advocates and psychologists soon added to the momentum (Day, 1983; Williams, 1992). In 1892, *Children's Rights* was published by Kate Douglas Wiggen; in it she pressed for children's freedom. About the same time, William James, a noted psychologist, argued (like those before him) that children must be active participants in their education process. John Dewey echoed James as an advocate for school reform, insisting that children needed to be actively engaged in order to learn. Dewey emphasized children's direct experience with the natural world and the goal of socializing children as builders of social order and democracy. He believed children should be trained as social beings and participate in role playing and problem solving that might prepare them to handle societal problems as adults (Gordon & Browne, 1993; Williams, 1992).

By the early 1900s, there was universal acknowledgment that some form of education for 3- to 5-year-olds was beneficial. Many nursery schools and day-care programs were created, and kindergartens underwent a second evolution. Kindergarten proponents diverged into two groups. Patty Smith Hill, a student and later a colleague of Dewey at Teachers College, Columbia University, was a prominent leader of the Progressive Movement, which emphasized child-oriented rather than regimented kindergarten curricula (Gordon & Browne, 1993). (Patty Smith Hill wrote the song "Happy Birthday" and founded the National Association for Nursery Education, now known as the National Association for the Education of Young Children.) She instituted new ideas to the kindergarten model, such as free play, provided larger blocks, introduced dolls and doll houses, and gave more freedom for creative play. She also introduced the use of workbenches and tools, as well as music and dance.

By 1925, kindergarten had been transformed. Practical curricula were now more concerned with conformity than morality—a class-related value system was substituted for universal values, and an emphasis was placed on punctuality, cleanliness, responsibility, and sharing.

> Cooking classes—When these girls marry they will do the cooking. Good cooking and economical management will mean a happy and prosperous home. We teach them for 3 cents a lesson, 5 days a week. [From a 1920 brochure of Colony House in Brooklyn, New York (Neugebauer, 1990)]

Patty Smith Hill also promoted nursery schools for children too young for kindergarten and maintained Froebel's belief that young children should learn by doing in a nurturing environment (Gordon & Browne, 1993). Every day, teachers in centers and homes across the country practice the belief that early education should be a garden where adults plant ideas and materials for children to use as they grow at their own pace (Gordon & Browne, 1993). Over 90% of the eligible population in the United States now attends kindergarten. For all practical purposes kindergarten is a universal educational practice in the United States (Warger, 1988).

The Advent of Child Psychology

In the early 1900s there was a growth of child psychology, as many scholars emerged with advice regarding child-rearing and educational practices. In 1907, Maria Montessori, the first female physician in Italy and a noted educator, opened the Casa De Bambini for children of lower income, working class, Roman citizens (Gordon & Browne, 1993). She had been commissioned by the Italian government to serve the educational needs of children living in the tenements. Children from age 3 attended for 6 to 8 hours each day. The purpose of the preschool was to prepare children for common school and to train them in self-care. Many of the children were labeled mentally retarded, though Montessori sensed that they really lacked proper motivation and environment (Gordon & Browne, 1993).

Montessori believed that education begins at birth and that the early years are the most important for fostering intellectual and social development. She identified what she called "sensitive periods," in which children's natural curiosity makes them especially ready to acquire certain skills and knowledge (Gordon & Browne, 1993). Montessori also believed that any task could be reduced to a series of small steps suitable for a child's learning. Therefore, she developed materials graded in difficulty and emphasizing self-help skills. She emphasized a "prepared environment," meaning that classroom environments set the occasion for children to explore certain materials to engage in activities specifically intended to foster problem solving and concept formation. She also designed materials, classrooms, and a teaching procedure to prove her points (Gordon & Browne, 1993).

Montessori's curriculum had three major components:

1. *Exercises in practical life.* hygiene, care of clothing and living space, and skills for self-management
2. *Sensorial experiences.* didactic materials that would instruct children, such as stacking blocks, series of rods, and wooden cylinders
3. *Language development.* training on articulation, dialect, and precision in usage (Montessori, 1964)

From 1910 to 1915, Montessori gathered attention in the United States but was criticized by progressive educators as too rigid and constraining. Her work was seemingly forgotten, until interest in Montessori's methods reemerged in the early 1960s. Now, this scholar and teacher can be viewed as one of the most influential child psychologists of the century.

In 1914, behavioral psychologists Watson and Thorndike introduced the idea that child development resulted almost entirely from environmental influence (Thorndike, 1913; Watson, 1914). They were convinced that heredity was an inadequate and misleading explanation of human behavior. Thorndike explained that habits were formed by conditioning in which appropriate behavior was rewarded and unwanted behavior stopped because it was either no longer reinforced or was punished (Day, 1983). John Watson emphasized the contribution of specific environmental influences, proposing that parents could make of their children what they wished (Cook et al., 1992). B. F. Skinner was the intellectual force behind behavior analysis who proposed a natural science approach to human behavior, moving it away from its early mechanistic focus (Pierce & Epling, 1995). Skinner outlined his theory of operant behavior, discussing basic operant principles and their application to human behavior. He addressed self-control, thinking, the self, and social behaviors. Applied behavior analysis extended the application of behavioral principles to socially important problems. Today, behavioral psychology offers a vast array of effective procedures for the education and training of young children.

Gesell, a developmental psychologist, wrote *The Preschool Child* in 1923. In it, he too, emphasized the importance of the early years. Gesell stated that the preschool period "is biologically the most important period in the development of an individual for the simple but sufficient reason that it comes first in a dynamic sequence; it inevitably influences all subsequent development." He created a normative developmental approach based on keen observation of children at various ages. However, Gesell warned that his "ages and stages" concept could not be interpreted too literally. His norms were not rigid prescriptions, but rather indices of behavior likely to occur (Cook et al., 1992).

Day Care

Throughout the early 1900s, day cares were considered a component of social welfare and were designed to serve "pathological" families who were incapable of providing proper care for their children. Day care was offered selectively and restrictively to families in hardship and was seen as temporary assistance until families could care for their own children.

During the Great Depression, the need for day care was considerable, and the federal government provided Works Progress Administration (WPA) nursery schools, which hired unemployed teachers in the United States (Gordon & Browne, 1993). In 1937, there were 1900 WPA day cares serving 40,000 children in the United States.

Works Progress Administration day cares were more educational than protective or custodial, and such services were publicly supported during World War II as women were recruited to work in the war industry. The 1941 Lanham Act (Community Facilities Act) gave communities funds to provide support for the war effort; by 1942, the Lanham Act was interpreted to include funding for day care. By 1945, government funded day care was being provided for 1.5 million children across the United States. Unlike previous programs, child enrollment was based solely on whether the mothers were employed, not on the presence of family pathology. Sadly, Lanham funds were withdrawn in 1946 when the war ended, and the schools were either turned over to the states or closed (Gordon & Browne, 1993).

Following World War II, Europe emerged from the rubble to rebuild its communities. In Italy, the mothers of the village of Reggio Emilia teamed with a young teacher named Loris Malaguzzi to build a school for young children. They believed that all children had a natural ability to learn about their world and that the teacher's job was to help them explore their ideas in a myriad of ways including art, drama, and music. The approach features community commitment, supportive, amiable relationships, preparation of the environment for learning, an emphasis on art, project-based curriculum, collaboration, multiple languages of intelligence, and documentation of conceptual development (Abramson, Robinson, & Ankenman, 1995). Babies nap in floor-level "nests" so they can crawl out and explore when they awaken. Preschoolers spend weeks on projects, producing artwork and analytical thinking to solve problems they've chosen for themselves.

The Reggio philosophy produced preschools that were later taken over by the government in the 1960s and expanded to include infant-toddler centers in the 1970s. By the 1980s, the rest of the world was taking notice and incorporating these ideas (Edwards, Gandini, & Foreman, 1993).

Early Childhood Special Education

Services to young children with special needs seems to be the last piece of an elaborate early childhood puzzle. All the other pieces—education, universal education, and education of children with disabilities in public schools—had to come first. The early 1900s also witnessed a seeding of services for children with special needs through the initiation of a variety of programs both in the United States and in Europe. Just before the turn of the century, Alexander Graham Bell, inventor of the telephone and a strong advocate of oral education for the deaf, petitioned the National Education Association to establish a division for the needs of persons with disabilities. The approved division was called the Department of Education of the Deaf, Blind, and the Feebleminded, later shortened to Department of Special Education (Cook et al., 1992).

In 1904, Alfred Binet was commissioned by France's minister of public instruction to design a test to determine which children could succeed in the public schools and which children needed special attention. The philosophy of the time was to keep children with disabilities in the regular classroom, while creating a method of identification so that teachers would avoid the problem of prejudice that might occur if these children were mistaken for "slackers" or "lazy students" (Cook et al., 1992).

In 1922, the International Council for Exceptional Children was formed. Its members were an influential advocacy group who worked on behalf of children with special needs (Cook et al., 1992). The 1930 White House Conference on Child Health and Protection marked the first time special education had received national recognition in the United States. However, prior to World War II, parents were still inclined to isolate children who had severe disabilities, to institutionalize them, or to be unwilling to admit their children needed special services. At the same time, children with mild disabilities received no special services though many were placed in regular classrooms in neighborhood schools (Cook et al., 1992).

One of the earliest and most dramatic demonstrations of the importance of early intervention was reported in 1939. Skeels and Dye (1939) removed two "hopeless" babies from an orphanage and placed them under the care of adult women with mental retardation who also resided in an institution. After living on the women's ward for 6 months, the babies' IQs rose by 40 points; a few more months in this setting and their IQs rose to the mid-90s. Skeels and Dye then convinced state authorities to move 13 more children (all but two of whom were classified as mentally retarded and unsuitable for adoption) to the one-on-one care of teenage girls with mental retardation who lived at the institution.

The teenage girls were trained in simple mothering skills, and the children also attended a half-morning kindergarten program at the institution. Twelve other children under age 3 who remained in the orphanage were used as a comparison group. After 2 years, the experimental group in the care of the teenage "mothers" averaged a gain of 28 IQ points, while the comparison group that stayed with the orphanage lost an average of 26 IQ points. A follow-up 25 years later by Skeels (1966) showed the experimental group had almost all completed high school, married, and had normal children. By contrast, four of the control children were still institutionalized, and the average education of the group was only third grade. These studies provided substantial support for theories that early environmental experiences influence child development.

After World War II, the public experienced guilt over the numbers of formerly healthy young men who returned from the war in a maimed condition. Consequently, parent organizations developed and directed political pressure toward the improvement of services for people with disabilities, including children. The success of programs for individuals with sensory impairments was a boost to the efforts of advocates for special education.

By the late 1940s a number of prominent individuals such as Pearl Buck, Roy Rogers and Dale Evans, and the Kennedy family were visibly calling for better education of individuals with special needs. Parents in the 1950s were beginning to question the practice of keeping children with disabilities hidden at home, and advocacy groups such as the United Cerebral Palsy Association, the National Association for Retarded Citizens, and the American Foundation for the Blind demanded alternatives to institutionalization (Cook et al., 1992). Between 1953 and 1958, there was an increase in enrollment in special education classes by 260% (Cook et al., 1992). Thus, the age of public support of children with special needs had begun.

CLOSE-UP

THE BEST DAY CARE THERE EVER WAS

The "best day care that ever was" arose in response to the urgent need to meet production requirements during World War II. In 1943, in Portland, Oregon, 25,000 women were employed to carry out a massive undertaking: the production of tankers and cargo ships desperately needed for the war in Asia. These massive ships were completed, from start to finish, in an unbelievable four days in shipyards that operated day and night, 7 days a week. Five thousand women, working as welders, secretaries, chippers and burners, were mothers who required day care for their children.

Hence, Edgar Kaiser, general manager of the yards set about building the finest facilities for a child care program. Mr. Kaiser began by hiring the best architects to design two children's centers which would each serve 1,125 children a day, and would be open 24 hours a day, 364 days a year. The buildings were huge, with round wheel-like plans containing 15 large rooms in the spokes and a protected playground at the central hub. Classrooms were placed at the plant entrances so that every worker passed by and mothers could drop their children off in the most convenient way.

Kaiser hired only the best professionals—teachers with degrees in child development and 3 or more years experience. The educators were recruited from every major teacher-training institution in the country. When Kaiser learned what the going pay rate was for nursery-school work, he exploded, "You can't pay college graduates that!" The pay was raised to match that of other shipyard workers. One hundred teachers, 6 group supervisors, 10 nurses, 5 nutritionists, and 2 family consultants formed an astonishing concentration of experts in child care.

The classrooms were large and each had storage space and a bathroom with child-sized sinks and toilets. Windows on two sides gave the children views of the shipyards. Two bathtubs were added, high enough that adults did not have to bend over and big enough for children to splash and play in the water. The rooms were filled with carloads of nonbreakable juice glasses, self-feed bibs, cots, sheets, blocks, puzzles, easels, and play equipment.

Kaiser's day-care centers were designed for the needs of working mothers. Each child went through a health test every morning before being admitted. Children who were mildly sick attended an infirmary where nurses and a consulting pediatrician took care of the children in isolated class cubicles and infirmary teachers provided quiet bed play. The nurses also immunized the children. Three meals and two snacks were provided each day and the chief nutritionist sent parents a weekly list of meals served and suggestions for additional food to complete an adequate day's diet. Also helpful was the Home Service Food; precooked and packaged meals mothers could purchase and pick up at the center's kitchen.

The centers cared for children from 18 months to 6 years of age and expanded services for school-age children to after school, on Saturdays and during summer vacations. A commissary provided necessary items like toothbrushes and shoelaces. For a short while, a Mending Service was also in operation and parents could borrow children's books from the center's library. As James Hymes, Jr., the on-site manager put it, "We thought that anything that saved the working [mother] her time and energy meant she would have more to give to her child."

The Kaiser Centers were in operation for only 2 years, closing in 1945 when the war in the Pacific was winding down. When the staff separated, they hoped their work would provide a model for excellent day-care programs, but the Kaiser Centers were never to be replicated. Though the Kaiser Centers demonstrated that day care could be good for children and mothers, it took a special set of circumstances to bring about full support for working mothers.

Source: Zinsser, C.(1984, October).*Working Mother,* pp. 76–78.

STAGE 5: CHILDREN KNOW BEST

1950 - 2000AD
HELPING MODE

In the mid-twentieth century, new psychological theories regarding childhood became popular in the United States. Freud's psychotherapy concentrated on the affective development of individuals and its connection to early childhood experiences. This view revived a pessimistic attitude toward childhood that had been dormant since the 1700s. According to Freud, childhood was ambiguous, incoherent, and filled with conflict (Freud, 1953). Freud advocated parental permissiveness in order to free children of possible causes of conflict and subsequent neuroses (Cook et al., 1992). Early childhood education was seen as critical to the social and emotional development of children (Day, 1983).

It was also during the 1950s that Jean Piaget's work became popular in America. Providing an antidote to Freud's pessimism, Piaget proposed that children have an inborn tendency toward adaptation and that through their encounters with the environment they develop categories of knowledge that are remarkably similar among all humans. Piaget, a cognitive psychologist, suggested the purpose of education should be to provide opportunities that allow children to combine experiences into coherent cognitive systems constituting knowledge. He insisted children are active learners and initiators and should direct their own play and learning. The Perry Preschool Project, developed in the late 1950s in Ypsilanti, Michigan, is the most notable Piagetian (cognitive) program (Cook et al., 1992). However, there is no doubt that Piaget's observations of young children, their translation to theory, and subsequent recommendations for practitioners are the most significant influence of this century on early childhood education policy and practices.

Poverty and Child Development

Similar to efforts at the turn of the century to address issues of parental neglect, an interest in poverty and its effect on child development reemerged in the 1950s. During the 1950s, the term "cultural deprivation" was coined. This theory assumed that poor children suffered from a dearth of experiences necessary to meet the demands of a complex and changing world (Day, 1983). A subsequent revolution in early education occurred in America, as curricula were specifically designed for the enrichment of poor children. In 1962, the Baltimore Early Admissions project established preschool programs in public schools explicitly for poor children (Day, 1983). In the same year, the New York City schools arranged an experimental enrichment program for preschool-aged children in three Harlem schools (Day, 1983).

Such remedial efforts were bolstered by scholars like J. M. Hunt, who published *Intelligence and Experience* (1961), arguing against the concept of fixed intelligence and predetermined development. Similarly, William Fowler (1962) suggested that concept formation began during infancy, based on evidence that early verbal stimulation helped the development of memory and knowledge acquisition. This research contradicted Freud's warning that challenging young children's intellect might damage their psychological development (Day, 1983). In 1964, Benjamin Bloom published *Stability and Change in Human Characteristics* in which he claimed that 70% of a person's intellectual aptitude and 50% of the reading skill of young adults was established before the age of 9. Combined, these educators provided ample justification for early intervention (Day, 1983).

Head Start

In 1964, the United States government passed the Economic Opportunity Act (EOA), which launched President Lyndon Johnson's ambitious War on Poverty campaign. Eventually, the showcase project for the War on Poverty, the Head Start program, was initiated in 1965 (Bailey & Wolery, 1992). Head Start was the first national enrichment program of preschool education in the United States. It began as a summer program for 560,000 children whose admission was based on their poverty status. As a community action program, Head Start was designed to address the health, nutrition, and education needs of poor families, with the goal of preventing later school failure. Two key features of Head Start are parental participation and health care services.

The Head Start effort was supplemented by the 1965 Elementary and Secondary Education Act, which provided funding to support the creation of preschools for poor children to be directed by public school districts (Day, 1983). It is interesting to note that, until 1965, the federal Children's Bureau still held the position that day care would be disruptive for healthy family relations and that it should be provided only to those families who were not capable of providing adequate care for their children.

Both a strength and a weakness of Head Start were flexible guidelines that allowed individual programs to develop along a wide range of educational approaches (Zigler & Muenchow, 1992). By 1968, there were 14 different variations of Head Start in implementation across the nation. The Westinghouse Learning Corporation and Ohio University conducted an evaluation of the effectiveness of summer and full-year Head Start programs (Cicirelli, Evans, & Schiller, 1969). When the independent evaluators released the Westinghouse Report, it was very damaging to the Head Start effort (Day, 1983).

Researchers found that, despite early gains, summer programs did not produce cognitive or affective gains that persisted into the early elementary grades and that full-year programs had only marginal effects on cognitive development that could still be detected in grades 1, 2, and 3 (Smith & Bissell, 1970). Head Start was judged a failure. At the same time, Arthur Jensen (1969), a noted psychological researcher, claimed compensatory education had been tried and had failed. This fueled tremendous debate and controversy.

However, this political and philosophical controversy stimulated early educators to do more to solve the problem of equalizing educational opportunities. It became more socially acceptable to recognize that various cultures are different, not deficient (Cole & Bruner, 1972; Labov, 1972) and by the 1970s, the concept of cultural deprivation was discredited (Day, 1983).

Researchers focused on identifying which early education approaches might have the most success and extending those interventions to follow through with poor children into elementary school. By 1969, there were 21 alternative preschool and primary grade curricula being researched under the Head Start Planned Variation program and 20 educational models under Follow Through programs, which served poor children from kindergarten through third grade. In 1970, the Head Start summer programs were discontinued and replaced with full-time, year-round programs serving about 400,000 children. The long-term data on well-run model preschool programs and Follow Through programs revealed positive effects on school performance, special education placement, grade retention, teen pregnancy, delinquency, welfare participation, and employment (Haskins, 1989).

Since 1965, Head Start has provided services to 13.1 million children (Head Start: A Child Development Program, 1998). By 1993, its Congressional appropriation reached $2.8 billion a year. Head Start currently enrolls 721,000 children across all 50 states, the District of Columbia, and the U.S. territories. It also serves migrant and American Indian children. Approximately 1,400 community agencies support Head Start through their non-Federal share of 20% of cost or services. Head Start provides parent involvement, educational, medical, dental, nutritional, mental health, and social services to children and their families. Ten percent of Head Start's enrollment slots are reserved for children with disabilities. Studies have indicated that Head Start children score higher than non-Head Start children on preschool achievement tests, that they perform equal to or better than their peers when they enter school, and that there are fewer grade retentions and special class placements later in their school careers (Head Start: A Child Development Program, 1998).

Recent Day Care Efforts

In 1971, advocates for national day-care services for all families suffered a serious blow. The National Organization for Women (NOW) had argued for publicly supported, 24-hour on-demand day care as a necessary service for women if they were ever to achieve equitable freedom of opportunity. Though initially supportive, President Richard Nixon, in his first term, vetoed the Comprehensive Child Development Bill, asserting that day care would ruin the American family (Day, 1983). Since that time, the United States has failed even to establish national standards for child care, despite the increasing numbers of children who are cared for outside of the home.

Since the 1960s, child development specialists have considered day care as a means by which developmental delays associated with socioeconomic disadvantage could be remedied or prevented. Yet, day care needs continue to increase as more mothers are working and as many husbands and wives separate through divorce. By 1985, the Department of Education estimated that 2.5 million 5-year-olds were enrolled in public preprimary programs and 5 million in private schools (Warger, 1988).

Today, there is scarce and contradictory evidence on the effects of long-term day-care attendance by young children. Currently, the United States' provision of day care is shamefully inadequate in meeting the great demand that exists, and with the rising costs of day care, quality of care is out of reach for parents who must satisfy themselves with any affordable options.

1990S AND CHILD CARE

Child care came of age in the 1990s in the United States. Legislative activity escalated at both the federal and state levels, with expansion of Head Start, tax credits for families, and extension of Medicaid health insurance to all poor children. In 1991 alone, the federal government spent $8 billion on programs related to children's services (Hofferth & Phillips, 1991a). Since 1986, the Individuals with Disabilities Education Act (IDEA) has made it possible for all states to fulfill the mandate for preschoolers with disabilities ("DEC holds IDEA reauthorization hearing," January 1994). It is clear we have come far from the days when children were frequently abandoned, sold into bondage, or abused (deMause, 1974).

On the other hand, as a society, we have also greatly failed our children. Though we think of ourselves as a nation that dearly loves and cares for its children, we lag behind almost all other industrialized nations in the world in terms of the quantity and the quality of child-care services we provide and the degree of financial support our government prioritizes for children. Hofferth and Phillips (1991b) quoted Marian Wright Edelman, head of the Children's Defense Fund, who warned, "The inattention to children by our society poses a greater threat to our safety, harmony and productivity than any external enemy."

Demographic shifts occurring since 1970 have greatly increased the need for child care for normally developing children as well as for children with developmental disabilities (Landis, 1992). Increasing numbers of women in the labor force and the increasing numbers of single-parent families have contributed to a child-care crisis. According to the U.S. Bureau of Labor Statistics (U.S. Department of Labor Women's Bureau, 1997), only 13% of families fit the traditional model of working father and stay-at-home mother. Currently, 61% of married couples both work. Six of every ten mothers of children under age 6 are working (half of all mothers return to work within a year of their babies' births). The rate has been similar for women with children under age 3 (Landis, 1992).

Half of all children of working women, almost 9 million children, were cared for by a parent, relative, or in-home sitter; about 28% (5.3 million) were cared for in commercial day-care centers; and another 20% attended family day-care homes (Hofferth & Phillips, 1991a). The National Center for Education Statistics (West, 1995) found that 31% of all children under age 6 were cared for in center-based programs and 18% were in home-based, nonrelative care.

Child-care fields currently employ about 2.3 million workers and are expected to grow at a faster than average rate through the year 2005 (U.S. Department of Labor Women's Bureau, 1997). Despite the importance of their work, child-care workers averaged about $200 a week in earnings. Certified preschool teachers in public schools fared much better with wages and benefits, averaging salaries of about $750 per week. Thirty-nine states and the District of Columbia required no prior training for providers looking after children in their homes, and 32 states required no prior training for teachers in child-care centers (Children's Defense Fund, 1998). Only 6% of all child-care centers held accreditation from the National Association for the Education of Young Children (Children's Defense Fund, 1998).

THE "TRILEMMA" OF CHILD CARE

A "trilemma" has been created by the large numbers of children for whom care is neither available, affordable, nor of sufficient quality (Culkin, Morris, & Helburn, 1991). Perhaps the most pressing of these problems is affordability (Culkin et al., 1991). For example, the average family spends almost 11% on child care, the same proportion as they spend on food (Culkin et al., 1991). Low-income families spend as much as 20% to 25% of their budget on child care (Hofferth & Phillips, 1991a). Further, affordability is directly related to quality of service because a primary means of reducing costs is to increase child-to-staff ratios and to offer low pay (Culkin et al., 1991).

> "When you look at the whole concept of putting your children in someone else's hands, you think money is not an object," said Monaghan, who manages the hair salon at the Hudson's Southland store. "But then it adds up. It's amazing what you end up paying. . . . It's kind of a contradiction, and I don't know what the answer is." (Kresnak, 1999)

With labor representing the highest costs for care in centers, many facilities are able to exist only through dependence on subsidies provided by community or government sources. This dependency adds to the financial instability of the child-care delivery system (Phillips, Howes, & Whitebook, 1991). For example, since federal funding began to decline in 1981, both the quality and the number of children who could be served affordably also declined. By 1987, Head Start, the largest federally funded child-care program, was serving only 16% of the 2.5 million children eligible (Warger, 1988). Recognizing Head Start's inability to serve children adequately, Congress significantly increased its funding in 1990 (Bailey & Wolery, 1992), seeking to serve 40% of eligible children by 1991 and 100% by 1994 (Hofferth & Phillips, 1991b). However, by December of 1993, only 21% of eligible 3-year-olds and 53% of eligible 4-year-olds were being served ("Head Start quality, expansion guidelines released," February 1994).

The quality of early childhood services is clearly related to funding issues but licensing standards also influence the quality of services. The current licensing systems used by states set minimum standards, but in many cases, these are lower than standards that research would suggest for positive child outcomes (Olmsted, 1992).

EARLY CHILDHOOD SPECIAL EDUCATION TODAY

The first federal law written exclusively for services to preschoolers with special needs was the Handicapped Children's Early Childhood Assistance Act (P.L. 90-538), which was passed in 1968. This act constituted landmark legislation as it represented the first major federal recognition of the importance of early childhood special education. The purpose of the bill was to develop model early educational programs for children with disabilities from birth through age 8. These model programs were funded as 3-year demonstration grants, called First Chance projects. First Chance directors were required to include parents, to provide inservice training, to evaluate the progress of children served in the program, to coordinate with public schools, and to disseminate information (Cook et al., 1992).

The First Chance Network began in 1969 with 24 programs funded for a total of one million dollars. Of those 24 projects, 84% continued past their original three-year funding (Fallen & Umansky, 1985). By 1985, there were 173 different First Chance programs throughout the country, and by 1987, over 500 programs had been funded. These projects have developed screening and assessment devices, curriculum materials, parent training programs, and thousands of other print, audiovisual, and support materials for early childhood intervention (Heward & Orlansky, 1992).

The Economic Opportunity and Community Partnership Act of 1974 required that Head Start programs in each state reserve 10% of their enrollment slots for children with disabilities (Fallen & Umansky, 1985). By 1977, 13% of all children enrolled in Head Start programs were classified as disabled, a total of over 36,000 children ("HEW reports," 1978; Heward & Orlansky, 1992). Later, Head Start developed 14 regional Resource Access Projects which provided training and technical assistance to personnel serving children with disabilities in Head Start programs (Fallen & Umansky, 1985).

IDEA of 1975

Head Start's inclusion of children with disabilities was only the first step in extensive federal legislation to provide services to all children with disabilities. The Individuals with Disabilities Education Act (IDEA) was first passed under Public Law 94-142 in 1975 and has since evolved through several revisions. At the time, its passage provided landmark legislation that insured the free and appropriate education of all chil-

Integrated population of children at school

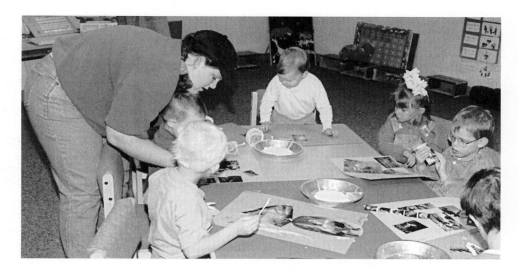

dren with disabilities. Its impact was primarily on school-aged children. However, even in its first stages IDEA recognized the importance of early intervention. IDEA was intended to apply to children ages 3 to 21, unless an individual state's law did not allow services to children starting at this young age. Financial incentives were built into IDEA to encourage the provision of services to preschoolers, and by 1985, 31 states had passed some form of preschool legislation (Bailey & Wolery, 1992).

In 1986, Congress amended IDEA, reauthorizing it under Public Law 99-457. The revised law extended all the act's rights and protections to preschoolers. When the newly revised IDEA was put in place in 1986, fewer than half the states had mandates for the education of preschoolers with disabilities; now all states have established such a mandate ("DEC holds IDEA reauthorization hearing," January 1994). Since the passage of extended services through IDEA, more than 170,000 preschool children have been added to the daily rolls of those receiving special services. Almost 400,000 preschool children were served through IDEA programs and Chapter 1 funding in the 1990–1991 school year (Office of Special Education and Rehabilitative Services [OSERS], 1992).

In addition, Part H of the 1986 IDEA amendments established new incentives for services to children with disabilities who were less than 3 years old. By December 1990, almost 200,000 infants and toddlers under age 3 were receiving early intervention through the assistance of federal funds (OSERS, 1992).

Provisions of IDEA do much to encourage the collaboration of parents and community agencies, including schools, in serving infants and toddlers with disabilities. The law makes clear that services are the responsibility of an interagency system and that resources should be shared ("DEC holds IDEA reauthorization hearing," 1994). Its emphasis is on delivery of services within the context of the family and in natural settings, which should encourage community-based, culturally sensitive, and family-driven services ("DEC holds IDEA reauthorization hearing," 1994). In addition, the revised law provides an incentive to states to address the early intervention needs of children who are

Table 2–2   Recent landmarks in early intervention services.

Date	Landmark Description
1965	Project Head Start was established to serve 3 and 4 year olds living in poverty
1968	Handicapped Children's Early Education Program established to fund model preschool programs for children with disabilities
1972	Economic Opportunity Act required Head Start to reserve 10% of its enrollment for children with disabilities
1975	P.L. 94-142, The Education for All Handicapped Children Act provided incentive funding for programs serving preschoolers with disabilities ages 3 to 5 years
1986	P.L. 99-457 amends P.L. 94-142 to require services to children age 3 to 5 with disabilities and to provide incentives for programs serving infants and toddlers who are developmentally delayed or at risk of developmental delay
1990	Head Start Expansion and Quality Improvement Act reauthorized and expanded Head Start programs through 1994
1997	P.L. 105-17, the 1997 amendments to IDEA renew early intervention efforts

Source: Adapted from Bailey, D. B., & Wolery, M. (1992). *Teaching infants and preschoolers with disabilities* (2nd ed.). New York: Macmillan.

born at-risk for developing later disabilities and delays. Table 2–2 summarizes recent legislation, including IDEA 1997, the most recent revision of this law.

Well into the 1990s, early childhood services continued to expand. In 1990, the Head Start Expansion and Quality Improvement Act reauthorized Head Start through 1994 and increased funding so that Head Start could serve more children (Bailey & Wolery, 1992). In the same year, the HCEEP was renamed The Early Education for Handicapped Children Program, which increased the emphasis on identifying and serving infants and toddlers in need, encouraging transition from medical to early intervention services, promoting the use of assisting technology, and serving children prenatally exposed to maternal substance abuse (Bailey & Wolery, 1992).

CURRENT PHILOSOPHY OF EARLY INTERVENTION

Three broad historical themes led to the current status of early intervention (Bailey & Wolery, 1992). First, society became concerned about the care and welfare of young children, as evidenced in the passage of legislation to protect and provide services to young children. Second, society demonstrated concern about the rights and needs of individual citizens and minority groups. Changes in advocacy for civil rights, individual rights, women's rights, and disability rights have set the stage for establishing legal rights and improved services for children with disabilities. Finally, a third trend was the increased focus on support for individuals and families as a primary goal of human service programs.

These themes have supported diversity in the population and the ways in which services are delivered. Heterogeneity in the kinds of children served has expanded with the inclusion of newborns and infants, the improving survival rate of medically fragile infants, the advent of children with AIDS, and the increasing numbers of children who have been affected in utero by exposure to alcohol, cocaine, or other drugs (Bailey & Wolery, 1992). Likewise, the families of these children show greater diversity than in years past.

Despite this increasing diversity, professionals in the field of early childhood share assumptions based on the accumulated knowledge of the profession, knowledge derived from research, theory, cultural values, and clinical experiences. Bailey (1989) summarized the principles of early intervention that have become generally accepted across the profession. Among these shared principles are the following:

1. The quality of a child's physical and social environment has a significant influence on the child's behavior and long-term development.
2. Early intervention is effective in reducing the impact of disabling conditions.
3. Parent involvement is essential for appropriate early intervention.
4. Early intervention is most effective when professionals work together as an interdisciplinary team.
5. Clinicians should teach to a child's strengths rather than focusing on the child's deficits.
6. Intervention must be developmentally based.
7. Individualized assessment is a necessary prerequisite to effective intervention.
8. Skills taught to children with disabilities do not generalize to other contexts unless specific planning and training is designed for such carryover.

If the current best practices in early childhood special education could be summed up in one descriptive word, that word would be *natural*. The major goals of early intervention today revolve around a philosophy of normalization. Teachers, parents, and clinicians work toward the child's acquisition of developmentally appropriate skills, they provide services in the natural setting of the home or in integrated classrooms with typical peers, and they emphasize teaching that utilizes normal routines, play activities, and natural contingencies.

Many early childhood professionals embrace the philosophy of developmentally appropriate practice (DAP). Guidelines for DAP encourage teachers to identify children's interests, to arrange the environment to facilitate exploration, and to provide motivating activities (all from the child's perspective). Learning activities and materials used are to be real, concrete, and relevant to young children (Bredekamp, 1987). While DAP guidelines provide a context that makes integration of children with disabilities feasible, some educators warn that DAP may not be a sufficient approach for children with disabilities (Wolery, Strain, & Bailey, 1992). Children with disabilities may require assistance from others, may not learn well on their own, and often their special needs interfere with their exploration and interactions.

Despite a long history of increasingly didactic services, today's wisdom of practice dictates a return to more natural settings, empowerment of the family unit, and understanding of the importance of the child's instinctive inclinations. Children are no longer viewed as isolated entities that can be separated from their environments, treated with standardized educational packages, and returned to the world as conventional, though small, adults. Instead, children and their families are now viewed as active participants in learning and in teaching.

A NATIVE AMERICAN PERSPECTIVE: INTERVIEW WITH JAMES HOLDEN

We know by many of the various demographics available today, what's happening to Native American students. They are overrepresented in remedial programs and badly underrepresented in gifted and talented programs. Unfortunately, the reality is, a lot of that, in my opinion, is because of stereotypic beliefs on the part of the educational community. That's part of it, but another part of it is how we as Native Americans look at ourselves. We tend to think, sometimes, we've lost the ability to know who we are.

Our Indian children today, and our Indian parents, are struggling with who they are. We're dealing with second, third, fourth, and fifth generation children off the reservation, and parents off the reservation. The circle of life on the reservation is pretty real, but it's also pretty short. The circle of life is you're born, you go to school if you can, you play some sports, often you drink, and you get a job. It seems to repeat itself over and over again across generations.

Unemployment's high; alcoholism is extremely high; emotional, sexual, and physical abuse is extremely high. A lot of Indians believe if they get off the reservation, that will fix them. We get off the reservation, and we run smack into this whole wall of misinformation. If you want to see a third world country, go to a reservation, but don't make a judgment about what it is you see, unless you understand what it is.

Somehow, we as a group, need to get the idea that we must and can walk in two worlds. I want to be able to work and compete in the white man's world. That's fine, there's nothing wrong with that. But I also must have the other foot firmly planted in my roots, my beliefs, and my customs. You know, if you look at the whole warrior society idea, many male Indians are still stuck in that. What's a warrior? All those stereotypes that whites have about savage warriors have some truth, because that's how we were. Do we treat females differently than our white counterparts? What do you think? Some of us are still stuck back with the warrior mentality.

So, what do we do for children? That's really what it's all about, what do we do for children, because if the water of life is our children, and I believe it is, then what are we doing for our children? We must somehow teach them it is right and just to be proud of being Indian. But we also must tell them, what being an Indian is. We can't just say it's living on the reservation. It is who and what we are as a people; our old ways, our oral traditions, our celebrations and the history of how we have been treated by the dominant culture. A lot of it is just traditional views of Mother Earth getting us back to the basics.

I think, you should start with the smallest of the small. As soon as they're in preschool, what do we teach them? Do we teach them that the girls play with the dolls, and the boys play with the blocks and all the dolls are white? Or, do we teach them it is all right, for the teacher, who is male, to put on an apron to cook, and it's okay for the girls to put on the construction outfit in play time. That's the way it should be.

Deeper than that, we have to somehow reach them with the idea that diversity is a way of life, and where your place is in that structure of diversity. Our children don't have that sense, when they go back to visit grandfather on a reservation and he's still stuck. Grandfather is still stuck with the idea that it's a white man's school system. Grandmother is stuck with showing her girls the old way because the old way's getting lost. The children today are saying, "What are you talking about, old way? If it's not video and microwave, I'm not sure I want to know it. But many of us believe there is tremendous value to honoring and understanding the old customs and ideas as a bridge to our past.

Unfortunately, one major problem of Native Americans today is that our agenda is not put on the front burner by many districts because that spot is often already taken by African Americans or other minority groups. We do not seem to have those powerful speakers and activists who can engage the system in a meaningful way to bring about change.

Reuben Holden

CROSS-CULTURAL HISTORY OF CHILDHOOD EDUCATION

Rising preschool enrollments and use of child care are cross-cultural trends (Boocock, 1995). Economic pressures have caused employment of more mothers worldwide, but there is also an international recognition of the value of early developmental experiences. Other factors such as dwindling family size and disappearing extended family support are worldwide phenomena that influence the need for early childhood services (Olmsted, 1989). We include these brief descriptions of international models, not simply to illustrate diversity and understanding, but to cultivate ideas for the evolution of preschool programs in the next millennium.

Because Western civilizations inhabited and colonized all corners of the globe during the same interval that childhood education in Western culture was evolving, and because Western industrialization has influenced almost every culture, there are distinct commonalities among early childhood services in most countries. Unfortunately, Western practices have supplanted traditional educational activities in so many cultures that knowledge and understanding of heritage and customs of various cultures has often been lost, and with their absence, the possibility of learning new and potentially powerful principles of teaching and learning are gone forever. Nevertheless, Woodill et al. (1992) compiled brief analyses of early educational practices across the world. In these summaries, the history of childhood education in non-Western cultures is almost always begun with the introduction of services by colonizers. Many of the following synopses are taken from Woodill et al. (1992) and provide a sample of cultural histories that reflect a heritage different from that of Western culture.

ALBANIA

Albania has been occupied by foreign governments since the Roman period (Dedja, 1992). The first schools were built by the Greeks, Slavs, and Ottoman Turks. However, a "collective" means has been used to educate young children since the Illyrian tribe. Children were given over to the state for their education at the age of 5, where they learned a love of work and were given military training. A national renaissance movement occurred at the beginning of the twentieth century when ideologists such as Sami Frasheri, Naim Frasheri, and Gjerasim Qiriazi envisioned a system of preschool education in the "mother's schools." Still, access to schools was limited, and in 1939, only 10% of Albanian children were considered literate.

In 1913, Parasheevi Qiriazi criticized the predominant Turkish influences, asserting that schools were too traditional and heavily affected by Moslem principles. Qiriazi believed preschools should be a transition from family to formal schooling and should emphasize moral development, good behaviors, simple handiwork, mental development, observations of nature, language and proper speech, and physical training. Qiriazi's model provided special schools for children with mental or physical handicaps. These programs would provide a curriculum of practical work skills. However, Qiriazi's curricula were never really implemented, as his work was oppressed by the reign of Ahmet Zog. At the end of Zog's reign, there were only 22 kindergartens in Albania.

Because of widespread destruction during World War II, schools in Albania closed until 1945. In 1946, following the proclamation of the People's Republic of Albania, schools became the property of the people. Nursery school, preschool, and kindergarten services were widely expanded to permit Albanian women to take an equal part in social production. However, traditional education of children, transmitted by families to young children, coexists with state-run preschools.

Until the 1990s, preschool education focused on the socialist pedagogy, whereby teachers constantly worked to link the educational activities with revolutionary practice, life, and production. For example, "preschool children participate in beautifying the kindergarten grounds, watering the plants and flowers, making excursions to work and production centers and the fields (where they learn about the work of cooperative farmers and workers), giving modest aid at building sites and during the country's political campaigns, and cleaning up around memorials, historic monuments, and their own playgrounds" (Dedja, 1992, p. 25). As the century ends, Albania is again immersed in violent civil and regional warfare. The direction this war will take preschool education is unknown.

Botswana

Traditionally, in Botswana, the families, including extended family members, have been responsible for the education of their own children (Monau, 1992). Grandparents and older siblings were responsible for basic survival needs including health, education, and socialization, while children's parents engaged in agricultural or other economic activities. Families tended to be self-sufficient, "They live, eat, work and play together, consult and help one another in all personal difficulties and share in one another's fortune or even bad luck. . . . Few couples ever live away from the immediate environment of their relatives" (Schapera, 1971, p. 926).

Monau (1992) quoted the former president of Botswana on the importance of self-reliance: "It has always been part of our custom that members of a family should help each other face and overcome the problems of life" (p. 114). This tradition was altered substantially in 1966 when Botswana became independent. Along with economic changes, Botswana experienced long and severe droughts. A subsequent migration of families, first the father and then mother and children, to the urban areas, adversely affected family structure. As women without extended families went to work to supplement their husband's meager wages, children were increasingly left in the care of older children who were too young to manage their siblings. Though many day-care programs were initiated to address this family crisis, only a small percentage of children have access to such services.

Child-care facilities that do exist are little improvement over home care by siblings. The minimum licensing standard is that teachers are able to read and write. Many are operated in garages or small houses, with perhaps a single toilet for 40 or so children. Though the state is authorized to monitor licensed programs, there is little chance that resources would be available to improve day-care programs that are found in noncompliance. While the concentration of day-care programs is largely preacademic, some are able to provide custodial care only.

One unique preschool program in Botswana is the Child-to-Child Program, in which older children in rural areas look after the welfare of younger brothers and sisters. Preschoolers attend the public schools twice a week and are "taught" by older children who select their students (usually siblings). The older students are taught to train the younger children school routines and concepts as well as rudimentary preacademics.

Certified teachers of preschool education in Botswana are trained in Lobatse. Montessori methods and curriculum form the basis of this teacher training. For several reasons, however, experts believe this method is inappropriate for the culture. Most importantly, teachers do not adapt the methods and activities to cultural conditions of the people of Botswana. Consequently, many preschool teachers, frustrated with a curriculum that doesn't "fit," resort to formal methods, whereby children are seated in rows, lectured to, and expected to engage in structured academic activities.

Early education in non-Western cultures reflects the unique heritage of each culture

PEOPLE'S REPUBLIC OF CHINA

Laing and Pang (1992) described the history of preschool education in China as a series of stages, beginning in 1949. Prior to this time, early childhood education was based on semifeudal and semicolonial styles of education. After the founding of the People's Republic of China, preschool education was reformed based on Soviet theories of education. During this first stage, preschool education grew in availability, teacher training, and research. In the second stage, "unplanned growing and consolidation," there was unchecked growth of preschool education, pushed by the extreme left. Education during this period became adult-centered, and ideas such as a children's focus, nutrition, appreciation of art and nature, and use of toys were considered capitalistic and were discouraged. The third period, "seriously damaged," began with the cultural revolution. Preschool children were given military training and taught to engage in "revolutionary criticism." Memorization and recitation from quotations of Mao and giant gymnasiums with organized sports replaced more developmental approaches to early childhood. At the same time, teacher training programs were closed as were many kindergartens themselves. Teachers were prohibited from instructing children and were reassigned to other jobs. The fourth stage began in 1976, and was termed "restoring and vigorously developing stage." Education of young children has become an important part of the overall emphasis on public education. Though not universally available, hundreds of thousands of preschools and kindergartens serve children throughout China.

The two primary foci of preschool education in China are morality (love of motherland, its people, and family) and language. Morality includes teaching children a love of work, more specifically, collective work. This also involves cultural values of altruism, modesty, ability to accept criticism, honesty, respect of adults, use of social manners, hospitality, and a sense of optimism and confidence. There are six components of China's language instruction: (1) articulate and accurate speech in the primary language; (2) enrichment of vocabulary; (3) ability to clearly express wishes and thoughts without inhibition; (4) ability to use descriptive language; (5) enjoyment of songs, stories, storytelling, and recitation of 25 to 30 simple poems; and (6) love of books and radio stories.

Teaching methods in China also vary from traditional Western methods. For example, most activities take place in large groups, with an emphasis on collective play, work, and problem solving. Children also engage in semistructured dramatic role-playing in which they practice real-life activities and language skills. Observation skills are emphasized and specifically taught, so children can use these abilities later across subject areas. Work and daily routines are used to teach good moral habits, so children can learn to be proud of their products and their ability to serve others in the collective. For example, children are assigned to "on-duty" groups, and each week the on-duty group designated is responsible for a variety of tasks (e.g., cleaning off the table, feeding the birds, washing the toys).

Many aspects of Chinese preschool education are unique. However, like most countries worldwide, there is increasing pressure for educators to reform to more Western-style methods.

INDIA

Organized education of children in India began in the nineteenth century when European missionaries introduced the notion of kindergartens (Kaul, 1992). Montessori methods were introduced in India in the 1930s by Marie Montessori herself. At the same time, Mahatma Gandhi was advocating for early childhood education, calling this preschool notion prebasic education.

In the 1940s, Tarabai Modak adapted Montessori education for tribal children. Her anganwadi (courtyard centers) literally meant to take education to the doorsteps of tribal children. A major emphasis on early childhood education began in the 1950s and 1960s when the newly independent government established a national agency under social welfare to promote preschool education. Today, however, only 12% of eligible preschoolers are served by any kind of program.

Though the preferred teaching method in India is "playway," in which activities are largely child-directed, there is considerable pressure by parents to provide preschoolers with the prerequisites for formal schooling. National objectives for pre-school are physical development, self-help habits, social skills, emotional maturity, aesthetic appreciation, intellectual curiosity, independence and creativity, and expressive communication.

In India, only half of the children enrolled in school complete the first year (Boocock, 1995). Many go to work, and often girls stay home to care for younger children in the family. The Indian government has provided a massive project through the Integrated Child Development Service, which literally gathers children in anganwadi (courtyard) centers, for several hours each weekday. The children are provided supplementary feeding, health checkups, and educational activities. This is the largest program in the world, and served 4.6 million children in 1987–1988. There has been some success in reducing infant mortality, malnutrition, and school repetition and dropout, but only about 12% of India's children are served.

JAPAN

According to Noguchi, Ogawa, Yoshidawa, and Hashimoto (1992), primitive Japan regarded children as precious, and they were reared within the protection of their tribe. In the dynasty periods (794–1185 A.D.) children of noble families were reared to be cultured women and men. Samuri warriors took charge of the state in the Middle Ages. Consequently, boys were trained to become warriors, and girls were trained to become "womanly" for the sake of the family. The Confucianists gradually changed this philosophy, beginning in the sixteenth century, when they began to advocate for early education.

Self-determination of educational practices altered in the nineteenth century when missionaries earmarked children of poor women for the first "modern" preschools in Japan. Afterwards, the first Froebelian kindergarten was introduced in 1876. The focus, child-centered education, is still considered a central feature of Japanese kindergartens. Industrialization forced an increase in the number of state-sponsored and independent early childhood programs. World War II further increased the need for early childhood care.

In the 1980s, changes in Japanese society, including smaller family size, urbanization, and improved work opportunities for women, led to reform of early childhood services. As a consequence, nursing and education in child care were unified with a new emphasis on "community-based family day care." Currently over 90% of children receive some type of preschool education. For children 3 and older, the emphasis is on life, play, and health; for children younger than 3, the emphasis is on human relations, health, and language development.

The falling birthrate in Japan has led some parents to place greater importance on the educational achievement and competitiveness of their children. However, access to special preschools (e.g., Juku, or private schools that prepare children for prestigious private elementary schools) is limited to the children of wealthy parents.

Japanese preschool is broken into two parts: the yochien, which are private, part-day programs for 3- to 6-year-olds, and the hoiku-en which are government-subsidized, full-day programs for children of all ages from families who are in need (Boocock, 1995). More than 90% of Japanese children attend one or the other before going to school. A retrospective study found that children with either preschool experience scored higher than those who had not attended preschool, but, that low-income children did best if they had attended the full-day hoiku-en rather than the private yochien (Nita & Nogano, 1975). It was concluded that the more comprehensive government-funded program might be more appropriate for these children.

Japan does have early intervention and preschool programs for young children with disabilities. These services are usually provided in special schools of three types: schools for the blind, schools for the deaf, and schools for children with physical and mental disabilities. Children with severe disabilities may be served in the home or in a hospital. Each type of school has its own course of study, relative to the disability of children enrolled.

LIBERIA

Unlike most other countries in the world, Liberia maintains a traditional educational system and, at the same time, mandates participation in modern schooling (Gormuyor, 1992). Not all, but many, ethnic groups inhabiting Liberia developed a parallel system of educating their youth. Even today, boys are educated in poros and girls are educated in sandes. In early childhood, boys are secluded from females and noninitiates in groves where they remain for their cultural education and where they will learn the responsibilities placed on them by society. Boys learn survival skills, character, appreciation of art, and to become strong and brave in order to defend their families. Similarly, girls are isolated in a sande, away from males and noninitiates. Girls are taught to perform the roles of females in society, to be loyal and faithful wives. Methods of instruction include discovery, role-playing, games, problem solving, storytelling, and learning by doing.

Historically, boys were isolated for four years and girls for three years in their respective institutions. Now, however, families are discouraged from sending their children for more than one year, and traditional education must not interfere with the children's modern Western-style education. United States philanthropic groups, American settlers, and missionaries from the United States introduced Western education to Liberia. The first Western educational attempts by colonists, often by barely literate missionaries, were provided to enable children of Liberia to read the Bible. Missions continued to provide the bulk of Western education to children in Liberia into the twentieth century.

Though public schooling increased after World War II, the country still lacks sufficient resources to ensure even elementary education for all children. Thousands of children, especially in the hinterland, go without public schooling. Preschool education in Liberia is very rare, though children four or younger may attend the kindergarten programs that do exist if they show developmental readiness. Educators in this country believe that early education is important and are working toward broadening its availability.

NIGERIA

Education in Nigeria has been traced to preliterate times when children's teachers were the mothers or grandmothers who cared for them while others worked on the farm or elsewhere (Aghenta & Omatseye, 1992). Children learned practical skills, such as interpersonal relations and adjusting to the rules and mores of society. Oral tradition constituted instruction, in which children learned through songs, folk tales, and legends. Youth were told about warriors, animals, gods, and the ancestral spirits. An emphasis was also placed on community belonging and achievement through hard work.

Traditional methods of early education were replaced by Western education in the sixteenth century when Portuguese Christian missionaries landed on the West Coast of Africa in 1515. The first school, called the Nursery and Infant Church, was started in 1842 by Methodist missionaries, who were also freed slaves from Sierra Leone. Establishment of public schools by Great Britain, which held colonial rule over Nigeria until 1960, began in the late nineteenth century. By the 1950s, universal free primary school was available in Nigeria.

Preschool programs are available only through private providers. Of these, there are two types of schools. Akara are generally run by unemployed semiliterate adults, who care for the children of working parents. School is usually held under a tree or in an unfinished building. These informal schools derive their name from the Yoruba name for fried black-eyed beans, which are given to children to try to appease them and to keep them quiet. More-affluent children attend traditional Western-style nursery schools. Activities include singing, dancing, drawing, listening to African folk tales, playing with toys, and preacademic learning. Nigerian teachers have recently modified Western curricula and activities to reflect traditional African toys and games, as well as supplanting foreign literature with meaningful African stories.

Each state in Nigeria is responsible for running schools for children with disabilities. These are usually segregated programs for children with hearing, visual, and cognitive impairments, as well as programs for the gifted. Children enrolled in state-sponsored schools or institutions usually come from a background of poverty.

SULTANATE OF OMAN

Prior to 1897, when the first Western schooling was introduced by missionaries, children of both genders were served throughout the Sultanate of Oman in kuttab (Al-Barwani, 1992). It is believed these schools began shortly after Oman embraced Islam in the seventh century. Basic education was provided to children under the age of 10, in the form of Islamic teachings, arithmetic, and reading and writing of the Arabic language. Teaching in the privately owned kuttabs took place under the shade of a tree, in a mosque, in a teacher's home, or in the courtyard. The teachers themselves were appointed, based on their age, their knowledge of Quaran, and their reputations as good citizens of the community. Until the 1970s, most children in rural Oman were still educated in kuttabs. Even now, these private schools are held during summer sessions and after school in many communities.

Between 1970 and 1990, Oman moved from having 3 to having 370 Western-style primary schools. Preschool services and day-care programs are scarce since, outside the capital city of Muscat, most women are both uneducated and unemployed. Like kuttabs, kindergartens are privately owned. In 1988, Oman adopted and adapted the kindergarten curriculum of Kuwait, which emphasized important concepts and preacademics. Methods of instruction are generally child-centered and based on relevant life experiences.

The first program in Oman for children with disabilities was established in 1989. A center was opened in Bidbid, where children from birth to age 14 are collected and taught skills to help them cope with life. Mothers of children with disabilities also receive training in methods to assist their children.

CLOSE-UP

WHO CARES FOR THE CHILDREN?

DENMARK'S UNIQUE PUBLIC CHILD-CARE MODEL

Valerie Polakow reminds us that today's anti-tax sentiment may be costing us dearly. "We might do well to pause and think about what we have lost by failing to create a publicly subsidized day-care system and a generous set of family support policies." Her article presents her first-hand account of Denmark's high-quality child-care system.

Denmark has a long tradition of public support for families and universal equity which are reflected in its social policies. The country provides a multi-tiered system of universal support policies for families, such that chronic family and child poverty has been eliminated. There is a statutory paid maternity leave of 4 weeks prior to birth and 14 weeks after birth followed by a paid paternal leave that may be taken by one or both parents for up to 52 weeks. In addition, a monthly stipend is provided, as well as housing subsidies, generous unemployment benefits, and universal health care.

A comprehensive, subsidized public day-care system serves children from 6 months of age, guarantees a slot for all 1-year-olds, and gives single parents priority placement. A variety of care options are available for children through age 6 at which time they normally begin public school. Neighborhood family day care serves three to five children in a licensed home and substitute caregivers are provided if the day-care mother falls ill. Several types of day-care centers are available, each run by teachers and paraprofessionals who are paid as unionized municipal employees. The vuggestuer are infant/toddler centers serving children from 6 months to 3 years of age. There are usually 30 to 40 children in a center, organized into smaller groups of about 10 each. The bornehaver are preschool centers for children from 3 to 6 years old. They enroll 20 to 80 students, again organized into smaller teams. The aldersintegrerede institutioner are age-integrated centers for children from 6 months to 14 years of age, which developed in the 1970s. There are also after-school centers provided for older children.

Danish centers provide high-quality care which is flexible, play-based, and developmental with a strong focus on child-centered, child-initiated learning. The Reggio Emilia approach is key to intellectual learning and music and movement are a part of daily activity. Cooperative play and socially inclusive group activities are emphasized. There is a strong bias against any form of exclusion, even for dealing with difficult children. There are also strong feelings against teaching reading or math readiness. All intervention for children who were at risk or have disabilities is carried out within the child's center where social workers and a psychologist are regularly available.

There is a national crisis in the United States in terms of available, quality, child care for both low-income and middle-class families. Yet, our public consciousness resists providing support for families. Polakow suggests we consider "Who cares for the children?" and use Denmark as a model for popular, accessible, affordable, quality care and family policy.

Source: Polakow, V. (April 1997). *Phi Delta Kappan.*

International Research on Early Childhood Programs

Boocock (1995) examined 15 major international studies of early childhood programs and came to the following conclusions. The overall availability and quality of early childhood programs is much higher in industrialized countries but there are large differences even between similar nations. For example, almost 100% of French and Belgian children are in preschools at age 3, but only 28% of Spanish and Portuguese children and only 6% of Swiss children are active in preschool at the same age. Generally, urban areas are more widely served than rural areas and children from upper and middle income levels are more likely to participate in preschool programs than are poor children. The following summarizes findings for Western cultures and developing nations.

North America

Canada's social welfare policies and programs were more inclusive than those in the United States, though less generous than those in Europe. Family care regulated by even minimal standards was of better quality than that offered in unlicensed homes. Children in child-care centers tended to have higher levels of language development and more highly developed play and activity patterns than children in family care. Across Canadian settings, the quality of care influenced the development of lower income children more than those of middle or higher income. However, as in the United States, many children receive the "worst of both worlds"—they come from low-income families and attend low-quality family care (Goclman & Pence, 1987).

WESTERN EUROPE

Nations comprising the European Community and those in Nordic areas offered the most highly developed early childhood programs in the world. The French e'cole maternelle, or nursery school is attended by nearly 100% of all 3- to 5-year-olds. French preschool teachers were paid as well as primary teachers and their programs emphasized academic activities though adult-child ratios were higher than those in the United States. The e'cole maternelle system was expanded during the 1970s and 1980s when research revealed that every year of preschool attended reduced the likelihood of school failure, particularly for those from disadvantaged homes (McMahan, 1992).

The United Kingdom had a more diverse early childhood system than France (Boocock, 1995). About 44% of 3- and 4-year-olds attended public or private nursery school and many children entered the public school system at age 4. Most families used individual caregivers called childminders and many of those with parents at home attended organized play groups several times a week. Longitudinal research on 9,000 children found that those who had any preschool or organized play group experience displayed higher cognitive development and school achievement than those who had none (Curtis, 1992). Again, disadvantaged children gained the most from such experiences. However, preschool experience did not improve social development.

In the former West Germany, about 65 to 70% of children between 3 and 6 years of age attended half-day kindergartens. Research results corroborated that of studies done in France and the United Kingdom; attending preschool improved children's readiness for school and promoted their educational success (Tietze, 1987).

Swedish child care is considered the most advanced system in the world and has been carried out since the mid-1960s (Boocock, 1995). Swedish mothers of preschool-aged children are mostly employed (86%) and full-time child care is the centerpiece of the Swedish system. Local governments provide supervised, subsidized child care through centers and family homes to almost half of children between birth and age 7, although many parents care for their infants during paid parental leaves. Swedish research found distinct advantages to children participating in early nonparental child care. Children in such care before age 1 had greater verbal facility and were rated as more persistent and independent, less anxious, and more confident than children placed at a later age (Andersson, 1992). However, research also found that the quality of care in children's own homes was a better predictor of later development than socioeconomic status or preschool experience.

Boocock (1995) cited research in Ireland that focused on impoverished children in Dublin who were provided a 2-year, half-day preschool program much like Head Start. Later measures of cognitive development, school achievement and parent involvement showed significant improvements on early standardized tests, but most of the initial gains were not maintained. By secondary school, however, the participants were more likely to stay in school and to take examinations required for further education. Data on later employment and trouble with the law showed no differences between those who had the early childhood program and those who did not (Kellaghan & Greaney, 1993).

THE PACIFIC RIM

Australia and New Zealand, though very similar to the United States, are considered Pacific Rim countries in Boocock's analysis (1995). Both countries have experienced sharply increased demands for early childhood programs. In New Zealand, 81% of young children attend some kind of organized child-care or play program. About 52% of Australian children ages 3 to 5 are similarly engaged. In addition to finding benefits for children in preschool programs, research in both countries documented parents' improved satisfaction with their lives when children spent time in nonmaternal care (Ochiltree & Edgar, 1990; Wylie, 1994).

DEVELOPING NATIONS

Preschool programs have been promoted in the developing nations of Latin America, Asia, and Africa by outside sources such as private foundations, the World Bank, UNESCO, and UNICEF (Boocock, 1995). These early childhood programs often include nutrition and health education as well as educational intervention, but overall, preschool education is limited. Research has been conducted only on specific intervention programs. The following are two examples.

The Cali project in Cali, Colombia focused on malnourished, low-income children and provided nutrition supplementation, health surveillance, child care, and education. Researchers found that the size of a child's cognitive gains was related to the length of the child's experience in the program (McKay & McKay, 1983). All children receiving nutritional supplementation made gains in height and weight, but did not gain intellectually until they also participated in preschool education. Gains in IQ persisted to age 8 and children who had had preschool were more successful in school.

In Turkey, only about 2% of children under 6 years old attended preschool programs (Boocock, 1995). During the late 1980s, a program for home enrichment was offered that trained mothers to work with their preschool children on educational activities. Children whose mothers received this training surpassed others in cognitive measures. The mothers also enjoyed higher status in the family and participated more in decision making and determining child discipline (Kagitcibasi, 1991).

SUMMARY OF WORLD CULTURES

These brief descriptions of educational history around the world illustrate the pervasive adoption of Western culture, even in some of the most remote places on Earth. Obviously, Christian religious groups, who dispatched missionaries and priests to colonies in Africa, Asia, and South America, were instrumental in converting indigenous educational methods to Western-style schooling. In most cases, traditional teaching methods were so effectively supplanted that knowledge of the methods themselves is lost or obscure. The industrial age that created a global economy and infiltration of Western culture to all parts of the world helped to institutionalize efforts begun by religiously motivated educators. Now, the information age will surely contribute to an ever-increasing uniformity of educational practices worldwide, in spite of the multicultural emphasis on valuing cultural integrity.

Boocock (1995) made the following generalizations from international research on early childhood programs:

1. There is widespread evidence that participating in a preschool program promotes cognitive development in the short term and prepares children to succeed in school.
2. There is no strong or consistent evidence that the form of preschool experience (pedagogic approach, daily schedule, or setting) influences long-term outcomes for children.
3. Preschool experience appears to be a stronger force in the lives of low-income than more advantaged children.
4. Preschool attendance can narrow the achievement gaps faced by disadvantaged children though most of these effects diminish over time.
5. Maternal employment and participation in out-of-home child care, even during infancy, appear not to harm children and may yield benefits if the child care is regulated and of adequate quality.

As in the United States, public preschool education in most countries is valued but not universally available. The education of preschool children with disabilities, if available, is usually conducted in separate school facilities that emphasize functional skill development and offer little in integration with other children. Finally, services to young children are constantly challenged to do more with fewer resources. Though the field has a substantial history and cross-cultural basis, many issues remain to be addressed.

Case Study

ADVOCATING FOR JOSH: INTERVIEW WITH AMY FINKEL

Josh started out in a self-contained preschool, and that was the impetus that got me to go back for further training. The public school system is actually responsible for me being in graduate school today. When Josh began in the self-contained preschool, I used to go a lot to observe and one of the teachers started to get upset because, even though I showed up all the time, I wasn't volunteering with the other kids or helping Josh with things. I sat and did nothing, but that was my intention. I didn't want to facilitate; I just wanted to see how things were managed with the level of staffing that was available. I felt uncomfortable helping with the other children because I didn't have access to their IEPs. I didn't know what their issues were. I knew that I didn't want someone else working with my son without my permission, so I told the teacher, "I'm sorry, I'm not here to volunteer. I'm just here to observe."

I think that made her mad, because pretty soon I got a letter in the mail from the principal stating that from now on if I wanted to come observe in the classroom, I would need to call in advance and schedule a time. The school principal continued on to say that she and the teacher would hold a meeting to decide if I could come and visit my son. I came home and became physically ill. I was throwing up, I had diarrhea, and it just hit me like a brick. "My God! Is this what I'm up against? How can this be? How can they prevent me from coming and popping in to see how my nonverbal, disabled son is doing?" I was devastated!

In the past, I've always had nothing but positive experiences with public schools. I'm a product of public schools, my other children went through public schools. My daughter was in the Able Learners Program for gifted learners, my other son barely missed Ables. I just couldn't believe my treatment. I was in shock, and physically ill.

Once I was done throwing up, I got mad. I thought, "No, this isn't right!" That's when I got a copy of IDEA. Most people would go to bed at night and read their favorite novel. I would go to bed at night and read federal legislation. I was living on two hours of sleep a night during that period of time. I was drinking a lot of coffee and I was reading legislation night, after night, after night.

It took me about two weeks to recover from that letter. I made a call to the Office of Civil Rights (OCR). I got hooked up with our local parent advocacy group, Parents Are Vital in Education (PAVE). I was mad! I put on my best suit and I marched over to the school and barged right into the principal's office. I was very professional, and I was pinching myself the whole time so I wouldn't lose my temper. I told her, "If you are going to require that I have to call in advance, and that you will have a meeting with the teacher to determine if the time I want to visit my son is appropriate, you had better damn well do that with every parent in the district, special education and regular education. Because if you don't, that's discrimination, and I'll file an OCR complaint."

I said, "Furthermore, my son is nonverbal. He can't tell me if he is being physically abused, emotionally abused, or sexually abused. He can't come home from school and tell me what he had for lunch or how his day was. Therefore, I feel I have even more reason to pop in unannounced to see how things are going. My son is incapable of communicating his school day to me."

From that point on, every time I showed up at school, it was, "Oh, Mrs. Finkel, how pretty you look in pink. Oh my! Doesn't your hair look nice today!" It wasn't a problem after that.

That was when it hit me. That was when I first discovered that knowledge is power. If I wanted to be able to advocate for my son, I needed to know what the laws were and I needed to understand the world of special education. I didn't even know what an IEP was at that time. So I got busy and I started going to every one of the PAVE meetings. After going to many of their clinics and workshops, they asked me if I wanted to be a community liaison and of course, I said I would love to. I flew all over the country attending conferences on the topic of autism and advocacy. It was really hectic trying to keep the home program running, coordinating with the school and being gone.

I'd have to schedule the red-eye flight home, because at that time I didn't feel comfortable being gone from the house over night because Josh was so dependent on me for his routine and stability. So I'd catch the early flight, attend the conference, go like crazy getting all the information I could that day and then take the last flight out to go back home that night.

The school district is actually responsible for the success I have achieved now. It was a defining moment for me when I realized what I was up against and that I had better learn how to protect my son. The only way to do that is with knowledge.

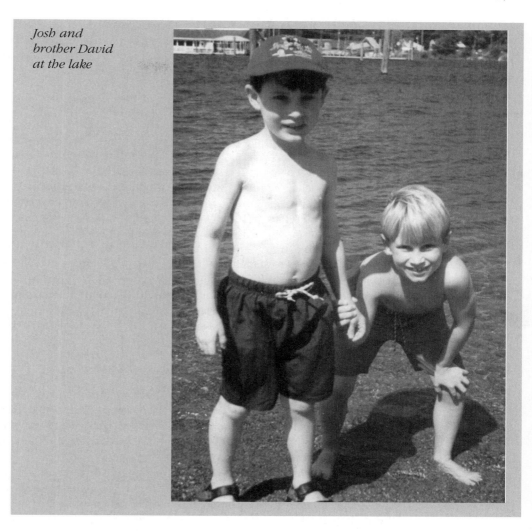

Josh and brother David at the lake

ISSUES AND CHALLENGES IN EARLY INTERVENTION

Early intervention has reached its adolescence, but there are issues and challenges that must be confronted before it can emerge into adulthood. (Thurman, 1993, p. 303)

Children and their parents are pioneers in a world where there are no precedents for such simultaneous trends as high mobility, dual-earner parents, minimal extended-family support, single-headed households, and early academic expectations, all converging on the American family, regardless of its particular form or makeup (Stegelin, 1993, p. 6).

As governments at local, state, and national levels determine policies for the coming century, they must consider a vast array of possibilities and plan for the necessary flexibility to best serve children and families. They will make decisions regarding a number of salient early childhood issues identified by Stegelin, all of which have numerous permutations:

1. Child care for children at all age levels from infancy through school age, both its quality and accessibility
2. Delivery systems for a variety of quality programs such as home-based, center-based, nonprofit, for-profit, school-based, and community-based sites, all requiring extensive collaboration among agencies
3. Funding mechanisms and wage equity—determining ways to pay for services through parent fees, family support and social welfare, employer sponsored benefits, tax credits, public vouchers, purchase of services, federal funds or subsidies, state funds or subsidies, or open enrollment in programs with sliding scales for payment dependent on family incomes
4. Accountability and standards—deciding how outcomes should be measured in terms of child gains and cost effectiveness
5. Programs for impoverished and special needs children that must address family needs as well and determine long-term gains
6. Public school early childhood programs and universal access to early education
7. Developmentally appropriate curriculum and related research in early childhood education
8. Family support systems

None of these issues is easy to resolve, particularly in a time of limited economic and human resources. Such scarcity may lead to the conclusion that only certain children and their families will be able to receive services. Programs find themselves competing for a piece of a dwindling finite pie (Thurman, 1993). Therefore, decisions must be made wisely, and eligibility criteria must be seen as aspects of a continuum that has as its basis the degree of risk to which an infant or family is exposed. An intervention model that is flexible enough to provide the degree of intervention that is necessary for different situations must be developed and supported. All of these challenges may also be seen as future goals. Advocates for early childhood care, education, and intervention have a full agenda ahead of them that might include the following.

1. **Prevention programs.** Whatever can be done, must be done to expand efforts to prevent risk to young children and their families prior to birth (Thurman, 1993). Efforts might include the provision of child-rearing and birthing classes, greater access to prenatal care, increased economic security for families, genetic counseling, and family planning.
2. **Family assessment.** Professionals need to develop more extensive ways to assess and intervene with families in greater depth (Paget, 1992). For example, it is necessary to involve family members beyond the mother, who has been a traditional focus of services; early childhood professionals may be working more directly with fathers, siblings, and grandparents. It may be wise to assess the informal support provided by friends, neighbors, and relatives.

3. **Family context.** An increasing awareness of how children with disabilities may disrupt normal family functioning and impede parental effectiveness is needed (Paget, 1992). Early childhood professionals must do a better job of working within the context of particular environmental stressors, such as poverty, unemployment, the death of a parent, family discord, divorce, single-parenting, child maltreatment and abuse, and parental deviance (Pianta & Nimetz, 1992).

4. **Transition.** Professionals need to pay more attention to transitions all along the continuum of childhood and develop deliberate and effective procedures for easing stress at times of transition (Thurman, 1993).

5. **Integration into natural settings.** The definition of mainstreaming must be relaxed to be inclusive of natural and normal experiences for young children. Too often, no real integration occurs because special programs are devised primarily for children with disabilities and only a few typical children are also enrolled. Ultimately, children are truly included only when they develop friendships—mutual child preferences characterized by reciprocity and positive affect (Howes, Droege, & Phillipsen, 1992).

6. **Microcomputer technology.** Professionals must be prepared to use computers in the best way possible to benefit young children. Computers can be used to enhance social interactions, improve attitudes toward learning, provide intrinsic motivation, facilitate cognitive development, and increase children's sense of competence. However, there is much to be learned about what support and guidance is necessary, how to select appropriate software, how to structure computer activities, and how to encourage independent work (Clements & Nastasi, 1992).

Some of these goals are already being sought in an initiative that addresses the need to improve the quality of early childhood services.

QUALITY 2000 INITIATIVE

Quality 2000: Advancing Early Care and Education is an initiative resulting from the input of hundreds of experts in early childhood education and allied fields (Kagan & Neuman, 1997). Its primary goal is that by the year 2010, high-quality early care and education programs will be available and accessible to all children from birth to age 5. The initiative outlines broad recommendations and strategies in eight essential areas where there is a need for improvement. Kagan and Neuman's (1997) summary of these areas for improvement and their associated strategies is briefly presented here.

◆ **Program quality:** address changing demographic and technological reality
   1. promote cultural sensitivity and cultural pluralism
   2. encourage pedagogical inventiveness in family child care and centers
   3. focus on improving the overall organizational climate
   4. increase the number of accredited programs
   5. link programs to networks, supportive services or other community resources
◆ **Results for children:** foster individual children's development, evaluate effectiveness and identify areas for improvement; hold practitioners accountable

  1. identify appropriate results
  2. develop appropriate strategies and instruments
  3. share results effectively, ensuring safeguards for children
- **Parent and family engagement:** involve parents and families in early care and education programs
  1. support parents as partners in early care and education programs
  2. support parents as effective consumers
  3. increase the family-friendliness of workplaces
- **Staff credentialing:** provide training and licensing for individuals who work in early care settings
  1. create early childhood administrator licenses
  2. create early childhood educator licenses
  3. create early childhood associate educator licenses
  4. maintain access to entry-level positions
- **Staff training and preparation:** address minimum competency areas and expand training for intermediate and advanced levels
  1. revise and develop staff training/preparation curricula and sequences
  2. promote the development of leaders and managers
- **Program licensing:** reduce the large number (40% of centers and 80% of family care) of unlicensed facilities
  1. eliminate exemptions
  2. streamline facility licensing
  3. enforce requirements
  4. develop national licensing guidelines
- **Funding and financing:** increase public share of costs of adequately funding childcare and increase additional research and planning
  1. estimate the actual cost of a quality early care and education system
  2. identify several revenue-generation mechanisms
  3. develop model approaches for distributing funds to parents
  4. create a targeted, coordinated funding initiative
- **Governance structures:** establish a rational governing system including boards or coordinating councils at state and local levels
  1. establish state boards
  2. establish local boards
  3. support effective federal governance

Kagan and Neuman (1997) point out that the quality of life for millions of American children depends on how we solve or fail to solve what has become a crisis of quality in early care and education. Quality 2000 recommendations would make planned, significant, and immediate advances in early care and create a true system for services.

IN CONCLUSION

The direction of early childhood special education is already shaped by its past, but what each of us does today, as a professional, also influences that future. We must commit ourselves to the humane and dignified treatment of all children, whether they are disabled or not, and to the empowerment of their parents. We must work wisely to develop policies and programs that contribute to improved education and well-being of the next generation and to their acceptance and assistance of each other. To make wise choices, we must be informed on diagnoses and treatment, knowledgeable of best educational practices, sensitive to individual needs and contexts, and open to examining evidence of effective new developments and those of other cultures.

STUDY GUIDE QUESTIONS

1. Why is an understanding of Western civilization essential for understanding other world cultures in regard to how very young children are treated?
2. Ancient Western culture was not benevolent toward children. Why? How were children treated?
3. What rationale justified the lack of attachment to children by their parents in medieval culture?
4. What motivated the educational efforts of early American colonists? Why was this purpose so important?
5. Summarize the philosophy of Rousseau and explain how his approach differed from Puritan philosophy.
6. How did social changes in industrial America change child care? What was the larger purpose of child care at this time?
7. Compare Froebel's notion of kindergarten with the practices of today in America.
8. What influence did social reformers have on early education in the late 1800s?
9. Identify the fundamental elements of Montessori's model.
10. Explain why the Skeels and Dye study was so important to early education advocates.
11. In your opinion, why is it impossible to re-create "the best day care that ever was"?
12. In what way was Freud's theory a step backwards in children's psychology?
13. How do the major conclusions of Piaget's theory reflect that of some earlier educators?
14. What were the documented long-term benefits of Head Start and Follow Through?
15. In what ways have First Chance projects influenced early education?
16. What is the relationship between provisions of IDEA legislation of 1975 and IDEA legislation of 1986 in terms of encouraging early childhood services to children who are disabled?
17. What assumptions regarding early intervention are accepted today?
18. What factors do you believe drive the current demand for qualified personnel in the field of early intervention?
19. Explain how Western notions of child care and early childhood became an influence globally.
20. What cross-cultural practices in child care might be used to enhance early childhood educational practices in the United States?
21. Why might Western educational practices be inappropriate for some cultures?
22. What are the important issues that face early intervention today?

REFERENCES

Abramson, S., Robinson, R., & Ankenman, K. (1995, Summer). Project work with diverse students; Adapting curriculum based on the Reggio Emilia approach. *Childhood Education,* 197–202.

Aghenta, J. A., & Omatseye, J. N. (1992). Preschool and primary education in Nigeria. In G. A. Woodill, J. Bernhard, & L. Prochner (Eds.). *International handbook of early childhood education* (pp. 399–406). New York: Garland.

Al-Barwani, T. (1992). Early childhood education in the Sultanate of Oman. In G. A. Woodill, J. Bernhard, & L. Prochner (Eds.), *International handbook of early childhood education* (pp. 407–416). New York: Garland.

Andersson, B. E. (1992). Effects of day-care on cognitive and socioemotional competence of thirteen-year-old Swedish schoolchildren. *Child Development, 63,* 20–36.

Bailey, D. B. (1989). Issues and directions in preparing professionals to work with young handicapped children and their families. In J. J. Gallagher, P. L. Trohanis, & R. M. Clifford (Eds.), *Policy implementation and P. L. 99–457: Planning for young children with special needs* (pp. 97–132). Baltimore: Paul Brookes.

Bailey, D. B., & Wolery, M. (1992). *Teaching infants and preschoolers with disabilities* (2nd ed.). New York: Macmillan.

Bloom, B. (1964). *Stability and change in human characteristics.* New York: Wiley.

Boocock, S. S. (1995). Early childhood programs in other nations: Goals and outcomes. *The Future of Children, 5*(3).

Bredekamp, S. (Ed.) (1987). *Developmentally appropriate practice in early childhood programs serving children from birth through age 8.* Washington, DC: National Association for the Education of Young Children.

Caldwell, B. (1997). Child care research comes of age. *Child Care Information Exchange,* 35–39.

Children's Defense Fund. (1998). *Child Care. The State of America's Children Yearbook,* 37–47.

Cicirelli, V. G., Evans, J. W., & Schiller, J. S. (1969). The impact of Head Start: An evaluation of the effects of Head Start on children's cognitive and affective development. *Report to the U.S. Office of Economic Opportunity by Westinghouse Learning Corporation and Ohio University.* Washington, DC: Government Printing Office.

Clements, D. H., & Nastasi, B. K. (1992). Computers and early childhood education. In M. Gettinger, S. N. Elliott, & T. R. Kratochwill, (Eds.), *Preschool and early childhood treatment directions* (pp. 113–150). Hillsdale, NJ: Lawrence Erlbaum Associates.

Cole, M., & Bruner, J. S. (1972). Preliminaries to a theory of cultural differences. In I. J. Gordon (Ed.), Early childhood education. *The seventy-first yearbook of the National Society for the Study of Education, Part II.* Chicago: University of Chicago Press.

Cook, R. E., Tessier, A., & Klein, M. D. (1992). *Adapting early childhood curricula for children with special needs* (3rd ed.) Upper Saddle River, NJ: Merrill/Prentice Hall.

Culkin, M., Morris, J. R., & Helburn, S. W. (1991). Quality and the true cost of child-care. *Journal of Social Issues, 47*(2), 71–86.

Curtis, A. (1992). Early childhood education in Great Britain. In G. A. Woodill, J. Bernhard, and L. Prochner (Eds.), *International handbook of early childhood education,* (pp. 231–249). New York: Garland.

Day, D. E. (1983). *Early childhood education.* Palo Alto, CA: Scott, Foresman.

DEC holds IDEA reauthorization hearing. (1994, January). *Early Childhood Report, 1*(1), 8–11.

Dedja, B. (1992). The development of preschool and primary education in People's Socialist republic of Albania. In G. A. Woodill, J. Bernhard, & L. Prochner (Eds.), *International handbook of early childhood education* (pp. 21–30). New York: Garland.

deMause, L. (Ed.) (1974). *The history of childhood.* New York: The Psychohistory Press.

Edwards, C., Gandini, L., & Foreman, G. (Eds.). (1993). *The hundred languages of children: The Reggio Emilia approach to early childhood.* Norwood, NJ: Ablex.

Fallen, N. H., & Umansky, W. (1985). *Young children with special needs* (2nd ed.). Upper Saddle River, NJ: Merrill/Prentice Hall.

Fowler, W. (1962). Cognitive learning in infancy and early childhood. *Psychological Bulletin, 59,* 116–152.

Freud, S. (1953). Three essays on sexuality. In *Standard edition, 7.* London: Hogarth.

Froebel, F. (1895). *Pedagogics of the kindergarten.* Translated by Josephine Jarvis. New York: Appleton.

Gesell, A. L. (1923). *The preschool child.* New York: Macmillan.

Goclman, H., & Pence, A. (1987). Effects of child care, family, and individual characteristics on children's language development: The Victoria Day Care Research Project. In D. Phillips, (Ed.), *Quality in child care: What does research tell us?* (pp. 89–104). Washington, DC: National Association for the Education of Young Children.

Gordon, A., & Browne, K. W. (1993). *Beginnings and beyond.* Albany, NY: Delmar.

Gormuyor, J. N. (1992). Early childhood education in Liberia. In G. A. Woodill, J. Bernhard, & L. Prochner (Eds.), *International handbook of early childhood education* (pp. 337–342). New York: Garland.

Greenleaf, B. K. (1978). *Children through the ages: A history of childhood.* New York: McGraw-Hill.

Haskins, R. (1989). Beyond metaphor: The efficacy of early childhood education. *American Psychologist, 44,* 274–282.

Head Start: A Child Development Program. (1998, November). http://www.head-start.lane.or.us/public/information/federal/HHS-brochure.html.

Head Start quality, expansion guidelines released. (1994, February). *Early Childhood Report, 5*(2), 1–3.

HEW reports 13 percent of Head Start children are handicapped. (1978). *Report of Preschool Education, 10.*

Heward, W. L., & Orlansky, M. D. (1992). *Exceptional children* (4th ed.). New York: Macmillan.

Hewes, D., & Hartman, B. (1974). *Early childhood education: A workbook for administrators* (2nd ed.). San Francisco: R & E Associates.

Hofferth, S. L., & Phillips, D. A. (1991a). Child care policy research. *Journal of Social Issues, 47*(2), 1–13.

Hofferth, S. L., & Phillips, D. A. (1991b). The editor's page. *Journal of Social Issues, 47*(2).

Howes, C., Droege, K., & Phillipsen, L. (1992). Contribution of peers to socialization in early childhood. In M. Gettinger, S. N. Elliott, & T. R. Kratochwill, (Eds.), *Preschool and early childhood treatment directions* (pp. 113–150). Hillsdale, NJ: Lawrence Erlbaum.

Hunt, J. M. (1961). *Intelligence and experience.* New York: Ronald Press.

Itard, J. M. G. (1962). *The wild boy of Aveyron.* New York: Appleton-Century-Crofts.

Jensen, A. R. (1969). How much can we boost I. Q. and scholastic achievement? *Harvard Educational Review, 39,* 1–123.

Kagan, S. L., & Neuman, M. J. (1997, September). Highlights of the Quality 2000 Initiative: Not by Chance. *Young Children, 54*–62.

Kagitcibasi, C. (1991, February). *The early enrichment project in Turkey.* Paris: UNESCO-UNICEF-WFP.

Kaul, V. (1992). Early childhood education in India. In G. A. Woodill, J. Bernhard, & L. Prochner (Eds.), *International handbook of early childhood education* (pp. 275–292). New York: Garland.

Kellaghan, T., & Greaney, B. J. (1993). *The educational development of students following participation in a preschool programme in a disadvantaged area.* Dublin: St. Patrick's College, Educational Research Center.

Kresnak, J. (1999, January 12). Clinton's child-care plan wins praise. Detroit: *Detroit Free Press.*

Labov, W. (1972). *Language in the inner city.* Philadelphia: University of Pennsylvania Press.

Laing, Z., & Pang, L. (1992). Early childhood education in the People's Republic of China. In G. A. Woodill, J. Bernhard, & L. Prochner (Eds.), *International handbook of early childhood education* (pp. 169–174). New York: Garland.

Landis, L. J. (1992). Marital, employment, and child-care status of mothers with infants and toddlers with disabilities. *Topics in Early Childhood Special Education, 12,* 496–507.

McKay, A., & McKay, H. (1983). Primary school progress after preschool experience: Troublesome issues in the conduct of follow-up research and findings from the Cali, Colombia Study. In K. King & R. Myers, (Eds.), *Preventing School Failure* (pp. 36–41). Ottawa, CN: International Development Research Center.

McMahan, I. D. (1992). Public preschool from the age of two: The e'cole maternelle in France. *Young Children, 47*(5), 22–28.

Monau, R. (1992). Early childhood education in Botswana. In G. A. Woodill, J. Bernhard, & L. Prochner (Eds.), *International handbook of early childhood education* (pp. 111–118). New York: Garland.

Montessori, M. (1964). *The Montessori method.* Cambridge, MA: Robert Bentley.

Neugebauer, R. (1990, December) Child care's long and colorful past. *Child Care Information Exchange,* 5–9.

Nita, N., & Nogano, S. (1975). The effects of preschool education. *Research Bulletin of the National Institute for Educational Research, 13,* 17–19.

Noguchi, I., Ogawa, S., Yoshidawa, T., & Hashimoto, S. (1992). Early education in Japan: From ancient times to the present. In G. A. Woodill, J. Bernhard, & L. Prochner (Eds.), *International handbook of early childhood education* (pp. 317–326). New York: Garland.

Office of Special Education and Rehabilitative Services (ED). (1992). Implementation of the Individuals with Disabilities Education Act. *Fourteenth annual report to congress.* Washington, DC: Division of Innovation and Development.

Ochiltree, G., & Edgar, D. (1990). The effects of nonmaternal care in the first twelve months of life on children in the first year of school. *Preliminary findings from a two stage study (The Australian Early Childhood Study).* Melbourne: Australian Institute of Family Studies.

Olmsted, P. P. (1989). *A look at early childhood education in the United States from a global perspective.* Paper commissioned by the National Center for Educational Statistics.

Olmsted, P. P. (1992). Where did our diversity come from? *High/Scope ReSource, 11*(3), 4–9.

Paget, K. D. (1992). Parent involvement in early childhood services. In M. Gettinger, S. N. Elliott, & T. R. Kratochwill, (Eds.), *Preschool and early childhood treatment directions* (pp. 89–111). Hillsdale, NJ: Lawrence Erlbaum.

Pestalozzi, J. H. (1915). *How Gertrude teaches her children.* (L. E. Holand, & F. C. Turner, Trans.) Syracuse, NY: C. W. Bordeen. (Originally published 1801).

Phillips, D., Howes, C., & Whitebook, M. (1991). Child care as an adult work environment. *Journal of Social Issues, 47*(2) 49–70.

Pianta, R. C., & Nimetz, S. L. (1992). Development of young children in stressful contexts: Theory, assessment, and prevention. In M. Gettinger, S. N. Elliott, & T. R. Kratochwill,

(Eds.), *Preschool and early childhood treatment directions* (pp. 151–185). Hillsdale, NJ: Lawrence Erlbaum.

Pierce, W. D., & Epling, W. F. (1995). *Behavior analysis and learning.* Englewood Cliffs, NJ: Prentice Hall.

Polakow, V. (1997, April). Who cares for the children? Denmark's unique public child-care model. *Phi Delta Kappan,* 604–610.

Rousseau, J. J. (1969). *Emile.* (A. Bloom, Trans.). New York: Basic Books. (Originally published 1762).

Schapera, I. (1971). *Married life in an African tribe.* London: Pelican Books.

Skeels, H. M. (1966). Adult status of children with contrasting early life experiences. *Monographs of the Society for Research in Child Development, 31,* (Serial No. 105).

Skeels, H. M., & Dye, H. B. (1939). A study of the effects of differential stimulation on mentally retarded children. *Convention Proceedings, American Association of Mental Deficiency, 44,* 114–136.

Smith, M. S., & Bissell, J. S. (1970). Report analysis: The impact of Head Start. *Harvard Educational Review, 40,* 51–104.

Stegelin, D. A. (1993). Early childhood policy: An introduction. In D. A. Stegelin (Ed.), *Early Childhood education: Policy issues for the 1990s* (pp. 1–18). Norwood, NJ: Ablex Publishing.

Thorndike, E. L. (1913). *The psychology of learning.* New York: Teachers College Press, Columbia University.

Thurman, K. S. (1993). Some perspectives on the continuing challenges in early intervention. In W. Brown, S. K. Thurman, & L. F. Pearl (Eds.), *Family-centered early intervention with infants and toddlers: Innovative cross-disciplinary approaches* (pp. 303–316). Baltimore: Paul H. Brookes.

Tietze, W. (1987) A structural model for the evaluation of preschool effects. *Early Childhood Research Quarterly, 2*(2), 133–153.

U.S. Department of Labor Women's Bureau. (1997, November). *Facts on Working Women.* No. 98–1.

Warger, C. (Ed.) (1988). *A Resource Guide to Public School Early Childhood Programs.* Alexandria, VA: Association for Supervision and Curriculum Development.

Watson, J. B. (1914). *Behavior.* New York: Henry Holt.

West, J. (1995). Child care and early education program participation of infants, toddlers, and preschoolers. *Statistics in Brief.* Washington, DC: National Center for Education Statistics.

Williams, L. R. (1992). Determining the curriculum. In C. Seefeldt (Ed.), *The early childhood curriculum; A review of current research* (2nd ed. pp. 1–15). New York: Teachers College Press.

Wolery, M., Strain, P. S., & Bailey, D. B. (1992). Reaching potentials of children with special needs. In S. Bredekamp & T. Rosegrant (Eds.), *Reaching potentials: Appropriate curriculum and assessment for young children, 1* (pp. 92–111). Washington, DC: National Association for the Education of Young Children.

Woodill, G. A. (1992). International early childhood care and education: Historical perspectives. In G. A. Woodill, J. Bernhard, & L. Prochner (Eds.), *International handbook of early childhood education* (pp. 3–10). New York: Garland.

Woodill, G. A., J. Bernhard, & L. Prochner (Eds.). (1992). *International handbook of early childhood education* (pp. 3–10). New York: Garland.

Wylie, C. (1994). *What research on early childhood education/care outcomes can, and can't, tell policymakers.* Wellington: New Zealand Council for Educational Research.

Wyman, A. (January, 1995). The earliest early childhood teachers: Women teachers of America's dame schools. *Young Children,* 29–32.

Zigler, E., & Muenchow, S. (1992). *Head Start: The inside story of America's most successful educational experiment.* New York: Basic Books.

Zinsser, C. (October, 1984). The best day care there ever was. *Working Mother,* 76–78.

3

HUMAN DEVELOPMENT

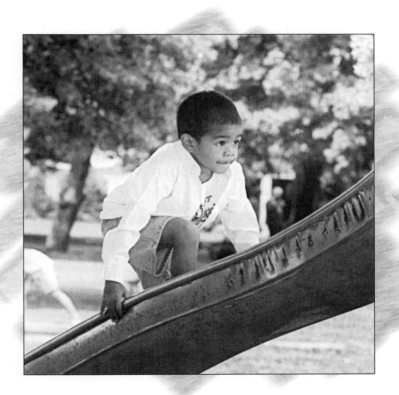

The wonder of nature, responsible for the changes that take place between human conception and the first years of school, largely awaits scientific explanation. Our understanding of human development is chiefly confined to describing the surprisingly predictable processes and stages through which the human species matures. Psychologists, linguists, biologists, geneticists, sociologists, educators, and other researchers continue to study this fascinating phenomenon. Even without complete answers, however, our present knowledge of human growth is vital to fields serving families with very young children.

THE IMPORTANCE AND USE OF KNOWLEDGE OF HUMAN DEVELOPMENT

THE IMPORTANCE OF KNOWLEDGE TO PROFESSIONALS

A thorough understanding of human development is fundamental to the competency of early childhood professionals. Without basic knowledge of the principles and stages through which infants and preschoolers pass, educators would be unable to communicate with parents, identify and assess children, design instruction, set expectations, select intervention strategies, or evaluate child and program progress. Parents turn to early childhood professionals for information and assistance, thus expecting them to be experts in normal development. To satisfy this need, educators must have at least a knowledge of developmental patterns for physical growth, as well as of cognitive, language, and social/emotional growth.

Perhaps the greatest use of our knowledge of human development is in the identification of appropriate intervention objectives and the selection of related intervention strategies. Because human development is largely predictable, it is possible to note a child's present behavior and identify the probable emerging behavior. Selecting a target behavior that is too simple or too difficult for a child would constrain that child's success and, consequently, lessen the professional's effectiveness.

Intervention strategies must also be appropriate for a child's developmental abilities. Professionals should be capable of matching materials to children's cognitive levels, giving instructions to match a child's understanding of language, determining how long a child can be expected to pay attention, and knowing the degree of social interaction that can be expected.

Knowledge of normal human development, paired with a knowledge of conditions that may lead to developmental disabilities, enables professionals to estimate the potential effects of a particular disability on a child. For example, an educator might anticipate that a child with a moderate degree of athetoid cerebral palsy will experience difficulties in expressive language and motor development. The probability of such problems should prompt this child's team to focus on intensive communication intervention and physical and occupational therapy, as well as to consider assistive devices as the child matures.

The need to cultivate a thorough understanding of how humans develop is underscored by the difficulty of such an undertaking. It often takes professionals years to master this knowledge. Fortunately, many resources regarding development are available to assist in making day-to-day and long-term decisions. While these resources are no substitute for mastery, they provide a useful supplement to a soundly established basic understanding of human development. Some basic principles of development are well established in the literature, and knowledge of these guidelines assists professionals in making daily decisions.

PRENATAL GROWTH AND DEVELOPMENT

By the time children are born, they have already undergone an average of 38 weeks of development. This period is divided into three stages: ovum, embryo, and fetus. For two weeks following the time of conception, the **ovum,** or fertilized

Figure 3–1 Developing Fetus in Prenatal Environment

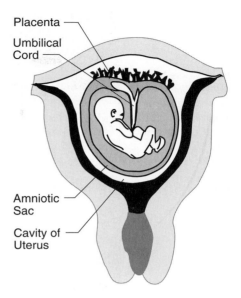

Placenta

Umbilical Cord

Amniotic Sac

Cavity of Uterus

egg, travels down one of the fallopian tubes and eventually attaches to the wall of the uterus, where it remains throughout the prenatal period.

The **embryonic stage** begins in the third week, when cell differentiation permits the emergence of a central nervous system and a circulatory system. The stage is completed by the end of the eighth week, when ossification of the bones begins. During the embryonic phase, the heart, lungs, digestive system, and brain develop from unspecified cells to well-defined structures. Muscular and nervous system development accompanies these structural changes. At the extremeties, hands, feet, fingers, and toes are formed, as well as facial features such as eyelids and ears.

The embryonic period is the most vulnerable stage of pregnancy. For one thing, many women are unaware of their pregnancies at this point, and may inadvertently cause harm to the fragile embryo. Many embryos spontaneously abort when they detach from the uterine wall and are expelled. During this early period, harmful substances (e.g., cigarette smoke, radiation) or trauma can also disrupt the structural development taking place in an embryo. Hence, embryonic damage may result in spontaneous abortion, miscarriage, or development of a birth defect.

Supporting the developing embryo, and later the fetus, are the **placenta,** umbilical cord, and amniotic sac (see Figure 3–1). The placenta is a fleshy mass made up of villi or projectiles that insert themselves into the lining of the uterus. The largest and most important of these is the **umbilical cord,** which joins the bloodstream of the embryo at the site of the child's abdomen to the bloodstream of the mother via the uterine lining. This connection permits the exchange of life-sustaining substances between the maternal bloodstream and the fetus. Though the fetal and maternal blood do not mix, it is the passage of nutrients, oxygen, and other gases through the umbilical cord to the fetus that allows the unborn baby to survive. At the same time, fetal waste products such as carbon dioxide and other metabolites pass back through the umbilical cord to be excreted by the mother. Though the placenta also serves as

Figure 3–2
Phases of Fetal
Development
Source: Adapted
from Moore, K. L.
(1983). *Before We
Were Born: Basic
Embryology and
Birth Defects* (2nd
ed.). W. B.
Saunders.
Reprinted with
permission.

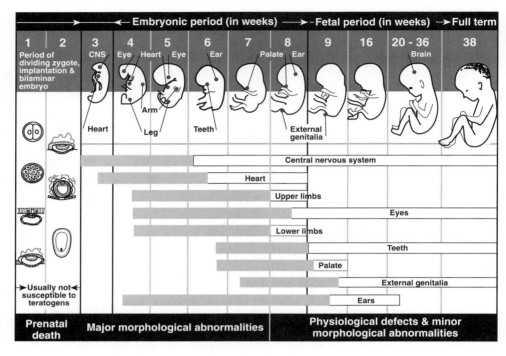

a barrier to large molecules and potentially harmful substances, it is not infallible. The placenta, unable to differentiate healthy from damaging chemicals, permits some dangerous drugs (including alcohol), hormones, and bacterial and viral organisms to cross into the bloodstream of the developing human.

Another important structure is the **amniotic sac,** which contains liquid amniotic fluid and surrounds the embryo. This sac, made pliable by the encapsulated fluid, protects the vulnerable embryo from physical shocks a mother might experience and maintains a constant temperature for the fetus.

The final and longest stage of development is the **fetal stage,** which begins in the ninth week and lasts through the ninth month. While each system was primitively developed during the embryonic stage, these systems undergo rapid growth and increase in complexity through differentiation during the final period (see Figure 3–2). At 12 weeks, a fetus resembles a human figure, and spontaneous movement of the limbs may be observed. By 16 weeks a mother can usually feel movement by the infant referred to as "the quickening." At 16 weeks, a fetus can also open and close its mouth and eyes, and grows fingernails and hair.

The age at which a fetus is considered viable, or would have the potential to live outside the womb, is about 26 to 28 weeks (24 weeks is considered the cutoff for viability). To permit independent survival, a fetus must have developed reflexes such as sucking and swallowing, and the lungs must be sufficiently developed to produce surfactant, which allows breathing without collapse of the lungs. During the final two months of pregnancy, the central nervous system, including the brain, continues to develop greater differentiation, and the fetus grows rapidly in height and weight.

Table 3–1 Patterns of perceptual development.

Sense	Ability at Birth	Patterns of Development
Vision	Research indicates range from 20/800 to 20/150 discriminates colors shows preference for patterns & three-dimensional images 20/20 at 5 years	20/100 at 1 year 20/60 at 2 years 180 visual arc at 3 mo adult-like focus at 4 mo discriminates age & gender at 5-1/2 mo recog. face from different angles at 7 mo
Hearing	40 dB threshold startle response habituation to sound soothe to rhythmic music	discriminate speech sounds (ba/pa) at 4-14 weeks 20 db threshold at 3-8 mo localize to sound and show preference for female voices at 4-6 mo
Gustatory	little research; prefers sugar solution to water	
Olfactory	little research; appears to respond differentially to odors	
Tactile	reflexive responses to touch; differential sensitivity by body parts discriminates warm and cold	decrease response threshold across first 5 days; by three days learn to habituate and is conditioned to tactile stimulation thermal regulation at 1-1/2 wks; discriminates objects tactually by 10-12 mo

CHILD GROWTH AND DEVELOPMENT

Development occurs after birth, as the complexity of each system unfolds publicly into the biological and behavioral traits that define individual children. Others may observe signs of a child's genetic inheritance through changes in physical and behavioral characteristics. Though some of these characteristics are solely determined by genetic code (e.g., eye color), others are influenced to some, as yet unknown, degree by other factors. Characteristics that are determined by both genetic and environmental factors tend to progress, though variant in rate, in a continuous and predictable pattern.

Maturation is the universally observed sequence of biological changes that take place as one ages. Maturation permits the development of psychological functions. For example, as the brain develops in the early months of life and becomes capable of understanding and producing language, infants who are exposed to language gradually develop this ability. If either language stimulation or neurological growth is missing, language cannot develop. Along with physical development is a maturation of perceptual abilities including sight, hearing, and balance (see Table 3–1). Each of these senses interacts with the other and with other developmental areas to foster normal patterns and rates of development.

Normal development refers to a sequence of physical and psychological changes that are very similar for all children. Within individual children, the extent to which environment is likely to influence this sequence, or the extent to which children will realize their potential, has been referred to as **range of reaction**

(Zigler & Stevenson, 1993). Favorable conditions enable children to reach the high end of their potential, while unfavorable conditions can depress development toward the lower end of the range.

Major indexes of developmental accomplishments, such as "Casey just took his first step yesterday" or "Adam just learned to say 'mama'!", are used to measure developmental progress. These indexes, which are identified across developmental areas (e.g., language or social skills) and across years, are referred to as **developmental milestones.** Established milestones are based on the average age at which children acquire skills or pass through stages. For example, an average child begins to take the first step at 12 months, and begins to say "mama" at 9 months. The milestones at which children are expected to achieve skills are determined by taking a representative sample of children and determining the average age that they acquire those skills.

Norms are statistically determined standard (normal) age levels for developmental milestones. For example, the norm for independent sitting is six months. Some children sit earlier, and others take longer than six months to acquire this skill, but on the average, infants learn to sit by themselves about midway through their first year. It is important to stress, however, that norms are simply averages, around which there is a **range of normalcy.** For example, slight deviations in development are known to be related to infants' sleeping posture. Since the early 1990s parents have been advised to place sleeping infants on their side or back to reduce the possibility of Sudden Infant Death. Recent research indicates that six-month-old infants who sleep face down are more developed in motor and other skills than infants who sleep on their backs or side (Davis, Moon, Sachs, & Ottolini, 1998). However, by the time these infants reach 18 months, there are no developmental differences. This research shows how prevailing is nature on child development.

Typically developing children who acquire developmental skills earlier or later than the norm will still be considered normal. It is when acquisition of developmental milestones occurs sometime beyond the range of normalcy that parents and educators should be concerned about a child's progress. For example, if a child is not sitting independently (norm is 6 months; range is 4–8 months) by 10 months of age, parents should seek professional advice. Children who exceed the norms in several areas or the expected ranges in a few areas may be **at risk** for **developmental delays.** Significant delays in acquisition of developmental milestones in one or more developmental areas would indicate developmental delay and eligibility for early childhood special education.

PATTERNS OF GROWTH

From conception throughout early adulthood, humans experience physical growth. The most obvious index of growth is in size, as measured by changes in height and weight. Height and weight measures increase rapidly during fetal development and early childhood. An increase in birth weight of 300% is expected by the time a child is 12 months of age, while height is expected to increase 200% by 24 months of age. This rate of growth slows after the first year to an almost linear rate until adolescence. While some children grow in spurts, others appear to grow steadily throughout childhood. In addition to individual genetic differences in rate and pattern of development, factors such as nutrition and health influence growth outcomes. Children from economically advantaged families tend to grow faster than children from poorer families who tend to have poor nutrition and more frequent illnesses.

SIZE

Body proportion also changes as a child ages. At birth, a child's head accounts for approximately one fourth of the total body height and weight. Gradually, the proportion of the head to the body decreases, while the proportion of the legs gradually increases. Ossification or hardening of the bones is another function of growth, beginning during the prenatal period. This skeletal development is necessary for posture and strength. During early infancy, the bones of the legs and arms are fragile, and unable to support an infant's weight. As hardening of the bones takes place, the extremities straighten and 1-year-olds are able to bear weight in standing and walking.

DEVELOPMENTAL PATTERNS

Three universal patterns of physical growth govern motor development. **Cephalocaudal** is the sequence in which growth and development of motor skills occurs progressively downward from head and neck, to the trunk, hips, legs, and finally to the feet and toes. Children first gain head and neck control, which enables them to hold their heads steady and look around; then they gain trunk control, which allows infants to turn from back to tummy, to sit, and so on. A second principle, **proximodistal** sequencing, refers to development that progresses from the center of the body, outward toward the extremities. Legs and arms, being closer to the midline of the body, can be controlled earlier than toes and fingers, as seen by gross movements of extremities in the play of young infants. A child will reach (arm movement) before grasping because the hands are farther from the center of the body, and finger control comes later.

Refinement is a third principle that is also referred to as simple-to-complex or gross-to-fine development. A child's motor development is initially concentrated on large muscle groups for sitting and walking, and then on small muscle group control for such things as scribbling and writing with a crayon. Understanding these three principles helps adults predict a child's development so that intervention is appropriately concentrated on present and emerging stages of development.

PHYSICAL GROWTH

At birth, an infant should be capable of independent functioning that is separate from its mother. Even though organ systems are not all fully developed, they should function well enough to permit growth and development. Deviations from the normal progression of growth may indicate a health problem, but more often are normal variations that relate to genetic predisposition. Again, though the normal sequence of growth and development is known, the individual timing of certain milestones is not always predictable.

Physical growth implies a biological change in the structure and mass of a person through increases in weight and size. In each of us, growth is a reaction to a predetermined, but idiosyncratic, plan. Events and relationships influence growth, though they rarely completely stop advancement. Finally, because of the nature of human growth, behavior observed and accepted during one stage of development may be considered abnormal during another stage of development.

Major organ systems develop at different rates and at different times. All of the major systems are established during fetal life and, by birth, have developed to the point where adaptation of the systems to extrauterine life can occur. Major organ systems include the respiratory, cardiovascular, gastrointestinal, renal, neurological, skeletal, and integumentary systems. Each of these systems controls different activities of normal physiological functions that are critical to a normal life.

Case
Study

THE DIARY OF ESTHER ANNA BERKE: MONTH 1

November 15–22, 1998: Esther Anna was born on November 15 at the Huang Baby Clinic in Tainan after a 12-hour labor. The Taiwanese doctors and nurses were amazed at her size, 4.5 kg (10 lbs) and 52 cm (21 inches) long. She was a "blue baby" and had to be rushed to the ICU at Shinlao Christian Hospital in Tainan. After clearing her lungs she breathed normally, and was released after two days. Mother and daughter went home on Day 3.

November 23–30: Esther Anna sleeps most of the time and appears normal, although she "quivers" occasionally. Our pediatric guide says this happens occasionally in newborn babies, so we ignored it. We weighed her at her two-week checkup, she lost 400 g (~ 1 lb).

December 1–7: Esther Anna had more episodes of "quivering," so we started to record time, date, circumstance, etc., and we started weighing her at home to monitor her condition more closely.

December 8–15: Esther Anna started having more pronounced seizures, including one where she just "froze" for 30 seconds. We started checking for her pulse when she suddenly came out of it and appeared normal. We had several neurological tests done, including an EEG and a brain ultrasound. The neurologist said she has agenesis of the corpus callosum. At her four-week checkup, she only weighed 3.8 kg.

Esther Anna was diagnosed with Aicardi Syndrome on December 15, "Black Tuesday." The neurologist examined her eyes and said he was 97% sure she has Aicardi Syndrome, a rare genetic disorder characterized by seizures, retardation, eye problems, and death by age 20. To be sure, he referred us to an eye specialist, who confirmed his diagnosis (the disease is characterized by certain peculiar lesions on the retina) and said that Esther Anna may be partially or completely blind. We start her on Depakine, an antiseizure medication.

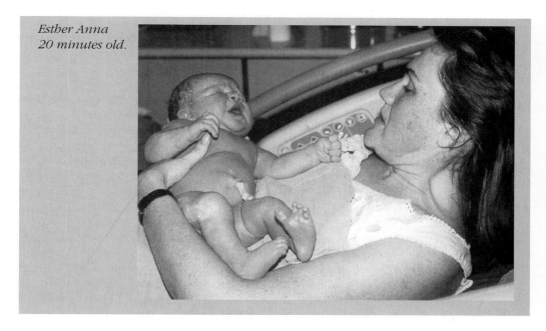

*Esther Anna
20 minutes old.*

The **respiratory system** is made of many complex structures that enable human beings to both take in oxygen, essential for cellular life, and give off carbon dioxide (a by-product of cellular function). The lungs are the main organs of the respiratory system, though healthy cardiovascular functioning is critical to normal functioning of the lungs. Adequate nutrition is necessary for normal lung growth. This factor can be very important when dealing with certain infants and children, such as those with cerebral palsy, who suffer from diseases that affect either the lungs themselves or a child's ability to sustain adequate caloric intake.

The **cardiovascular system** is comprised of the heart and the blood vessels that extend throughout the body connecting all cells to their source of nutrition. A fetal heart begins to beat at approximately four weeks of gestation. This development provides the link necessary for the placenta to adequately provide oxygen and nutrition to a fetus. These nutritional elements (oxygen, glucose, etc.) are then carried to the fetus and circulated throughout the body by the fetal circulatory system.

After birth, the act of independent respiration changes the normal blood flow. This transition occurs when the lungs expand, changing the pathway of blood to the lungs for oxygenation. Newborns consequently become self-reliant in the physiology of oxygen and carbon dioxide exchange. Deviations in development of heart structure or of the pathways for blood flow can have very significant effects on the growth of a child.

The **renal system** consists of the kidneys and bladder, as well as the tubes that connect these organs. The cardiovascular system directs blood flow through the renal organs, where the products of cell reproduction and death are absorbed from the bloodstream and excreted from the body through urine. Adequate kidney function is essential for survival, for without these organs waste cannot be eliminated. As a consequence, other vital organs would be destroyed by the toxic build-up of waste products. Kidneys, generally not completely developed by birth, mature throughout the first year of life.

The **gastrointestinal system** (GI system) both processes and absorbs nutrients taken in with food to maintain metabolism and to support growth. The system includes the mouth, esophagus, stomach, and small and large intestines. The GI system also is involved with excretion of both digestive residue and waste products absorbed from the blood as it passes through the intestinal tract. A functioning GI system is essential for life. Failure to develop, or malformations of this system, can produce significant problems related to malnutrition and failure to thrive.

Prior to birth, the **neurological system** is the fastest growing system. Rapid brain growth occurs between 18 and 20 weeks of gestation and again at about 30 weeks through the first 12 months of postnatal life. In fact, it is estimated that the brain achieves at least two thirds of its adult size by the time an infant has reached one year of age (Beck, Moffatt, & Lloyd, 1973; Langman, 1975). Head circumference is an index of brain growth. Typically, measurements of the head change rapidly during the first year of life then slow down during subsequent years.

During the first six months of life, the brain cortex increases in size and function, as **neurons** (cells responsible for receiving and sending messages) of the brain increase in number and connectedness to other neurons. Immediately after birth, the brain's cortex has little control over neonates' activities. Primitive reflexes, controlled by peripheral nerves and the brain stem, generally guide the activity of very young infants. As growth and development occur, the brain, through its developing pathways, exerts increasing control over the reflex activity of infants, facilitating the acquisition of more complex abilities. Cortical control requires the development of a **myelin sheath** on the nerves. This sheath permits electrical impulses to move quickly along the nerve fiber or axon (see Figure 3–3). That is, the more myelinization there is, the more efficient or rapid the nervous system becomes at sending/receiving messages. Hence, myelinization of the nervous system is required before complex motor skills can be developed. Lack of myelinization or damage to the myelin sheath leads to motor disorders such as cerebral palsy. Myelinization is also required before visual discrimination can be accomplished.

Increases in body size require both new bone growth and the maturation of existing bone structures. The development of new skeletal cells and connective tissue

Figure 3–3 Neural Transmission of Myelinated Axon

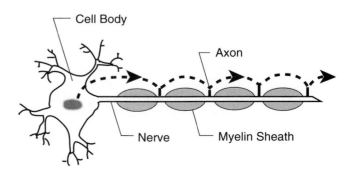

leads to this linear growth. Through maturation, tissues consolidate into a permanent shape that provides structure for the body. Bone growth follows a genetic plan that continues for up to 20 years after birth (Beck et al., 1973). Many diseases that affect children may affect bone growth. For example, chronic lung disease in premature infants increases the possibility for decreased food intake leading to poor nutrition that can adversely affect bone growth.

Muscle growth also has a role in childhood development. Muscle fibers, which have been laid down in fetal life, remain constant in number throughout the lifespan, but increase in size at varying times. Growth periods are probably most apparent during adolescence, when hormonal changes in puberty stimulate the muscle fibers to increase in size. By contrast, muscles that are unused in childhood will shrink in size, ultimately leading to atrophy with eventual loss of muscle function.

The **integumentary system** has many component structures. These include nails, hair, sebaceous glands, sweat glands, ligaments, tendons, and fat tissue. The skin is the largest organ in the body. It provides protection and structure to an individual, prevents the loss of body contents, and impedes the entrance of hazardous agents. The skin also conserves heat when the external temperature is low and allows for heat loss when the external temperature is high. In addition, the skin's ability to prevent water loss is essential for maintaining the body's steady state. This efficiency in protecting and preventing heat loss is underdeveloped in very young or immature infants. Maturity improves the ability of this system to control or prevent heat loss and maintain a normal fluid balance.

Dentition (tooth formation) is another process of growth. Primary and secondary tooth formation can be categorized into stages that consist of growth, calcification, eruption, and tooth loss. Ages at which teeth erupt are inconsistent among children, but the order in which they erupt is fairly constant (see Figure 3–4). With the exception of the first molar the teeth erupt from the incisors, or front teeth, backward in order to the molars. Significant delays in eruption may be indicative of nutritional factors or other health problems.

Weight is a growth variable that is influenced by many factors. Heredity, gestational age, maternal conditions, and environmental influences all affect weight. Weight and height, in combination, make it possible to determine normal ranges of growth for different populations. Periodic measurements of weight and height are monitored using standard charts to determine an individual child's rate of growth according to the norm (see Figure 3–5). This information is useful in determining where a particular child stands in relation to other children of the same age. Children who deviate from the norm are categorized as "large for age" or "small for age." These deviations give information related to the overall health of a particular child and indicate potential or real problems.

Growth parameters follow age-related guidelines. However, age stages are arbitrarily determined and do not generally take into account individual differences. Therefore, it is more important to follow the weight gain in a particular child than to make assumptions about health based solely on where a child lies on the standard growth curve.

Typical stages of growth include the **prenatal period** (from conception to birth), the **neonatal period** (from birth to 30 days of age), the **infancy period** (from 30 days to 12 months), the **toddler stage** (from 1 year to 3 years), the **early childhood**

Figure 3–4
Sequence of
Eruption and
Loss of Primary
Teeth and
Permanent
Teeth

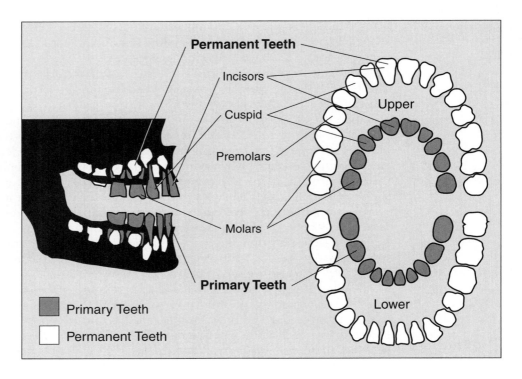

stage (from 3 years to 6 years), the **middle childhood stage** (from 6 years to 12 years), and the **adolescent stage** (from 13 years to 18 years). As mentioned, the prenatal growth period consists of the embryonic and the fetal stages of development. During prenatal care, obstetricians can determine if growth complications that may lead to problems during the neonatal period are present. During the neonatal period, babies attain stability from intrauterine to extrauterine life. Infants must transition completely from fetal circulation patterns, during which they relied on their mothers for all their metabolic needs, to assuming much of the responsibility for meeting their own needs.

An average newborn weighs between 7 and 7 1/2 pounds (3175 to 3400 g), is usually 18–21 inches long, and has a head circumference of 12–15 inches (Allen & Marotz, 1989). These newborns generally lose about 7 to 10% of their body weight during the first two to three days of life, but gradually regain that weight and stabilize their ongoing weight gain to approximately an ounce per day. **Neonates** have poor temperature control, requiring external heat management, such as extra blankets, to maintain a normal temperature of 98.6°F (37°C). Poor heat control is related to the insufficient fat stores under the skin, which produce fuel for maintaining body temperature (Dahn & James, 1972). Neonates also have a rapid heart rate and a fast but somewhat inconsistent breathing pattern. Because of their small stomach size, neonates eat small amounts frequently. Breast-fed infants may eat as often as every hour.

The infancy period (from 30 days to 12 months) is also a time of very rapid physical growth. By one year, normally progressing infants have tripled their birth weights

Figure 3–5
Typical Growth
Charts for Male
and Female
Infants

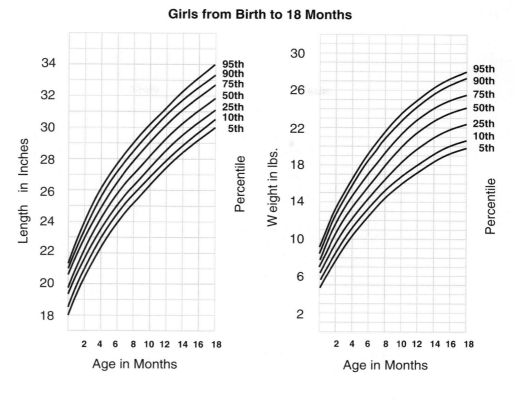

Girls from Birth to 18 Months

Boys from Birth to 18 Months

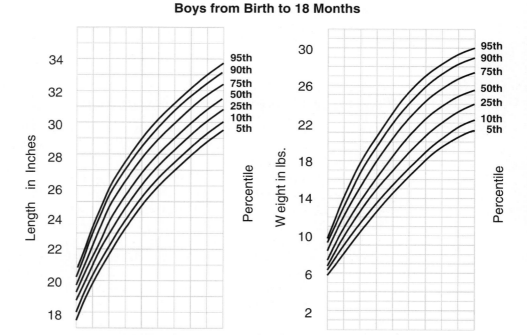

and are approximately one-and-a-half times their birth heights. The head and chest circumferences have equalized. Heart rates continue to be elevated but are less rapid, and the respiratory pattern is well established. By this time (two to three months), infants can maintain temperature stability and fat stores are sufficient to preserve heat. Skeletal and muscle growth has also occurred, enabling infants to progress through the developmental tasks that are appropriate for this age, especially those related to gross motor skills. Primary tooth eruption usually occurs, and by 12 months infants have an established pattern of three meals daily with an additional feeding before going to bed for the night. Most infants sleep approximately 12 hours each day.

Toddlers (from 12 to 36 months) generally weigh four times their birth weight (26–32 lbs) and are about 32 to 33 inches tall at the end of this stage. Head circumference is increasing, though more slowly now, and primary dentition is usually complete (Allen & Marotz, 1989). Toddlers have food preferences and may not exhibit much of an appetite. In spite of this, many toddlers' abdomens protrude and their extremities appear to have an excess of fat. Toddlers' heart rates may continue to be slightly elevated, though heart rate is decreasing to an average of about 100 beats per minute. The respiratory rate continues at about 25 breaths per minute with use of the abdominal muscles. Many toddlers have inconsistent sleep patterns and are reluctant to go to bed.

Early childhood is the period between 3 and 6 years of age. It is during this time that children begin a steady linear growth rate that will continue until adolescence. Three-year-olds will have attained about 50% of their adult height. Weight gain also continues on a steady curve, though growth may be slowed due to an enormous amount of physical activity. This increased physical activity and the increase in linear growth both require calories that are diverted away from weight gain. Brain growth has achieved approximately 90% of its total, with the head circumference reaching approximately 90% of the adult size. Organ growth continues along the same steady curve as external physical growth. The average heart rate continues at about 100 beats per minute, with the average respiratory rate between 21 and 23 breaths per minute. Young children may begin to lose their primary teeth in early childhood.

Case Study	

THE DIARY OF ESTHER ANNA BERKE: MONTH 2

December 16–23: Esther Anna's seizures decreased, but so did her appetite (one of the side-effects). She refused to eat at times, clenching her lips together and turning away when we tried to feed her. We weighed her at six weeks and she is down to 3.6 kg (she went from 10 lbs at birth to 8 lbs at six weeks old).

December 24–31: She had an MRI on December 31 to assess her brain condition. The MRI revealed at least three different brain abnormalities, including agenesis of the corpus callosum (an absence of the connection tissue that joins left and right sides of the brain is missing). These abnormalities are due to the dominant mutation on the X chromosome which causes Aicardi Syndrome. We weighed her at seven weeks and she was down to 3.5 kg.

January 1–7, 1999: The doctor inserted a feeding tube down her right nostril on January 4 at the doctor's office (fortunately we didn't have to go to the hospital for it, and we can feed her at home). She did NOT

| | like having a tube shoved down her nose, and had a Grand Mal seizure (her second one in two days!) after they inserted the feeding tube. We injected formula and/or breast milk down her nose directly into her stomach six times a day. The feeding tube was somewhat successful, she stopped losing weight but didn't gain any weight either. It extended about 12 inches out of her nose, and she sometimes batted it with her hand. The kids called her "baby elephant." |
| January 8–15: | I traveled to California on January 9 to consult with a pediatric neurologist, Dr. Berg, at UCSF Medical Center, and check out job opportunities with some private vegetable seed companies. The feeding tube falls out on Monday so the doctor re-inserts it, a very painful process. Esther Anna starts to spit up two to three times a day, and then chokes and turns blue. She has to be watched almost constantly, and Sarah brushes up on her CPR techniques. She becomes physically exhausted preparing formula (what a pain), feeding Esther Anna every 2 hours (takes 20–30 min.), and then holding her upright for a half hour afterwards to try to prevent the reflux. The most exhausting part, however, is the emotional toll. I talked to Dr. Berg but Esther's medical records (which we mailed and faxed to him 3 days in advance) never reached him so he couldn't tell us much. He is interested in her case and promises to pursue it. I return to Taiwan on January 15. |

PRINCIPLES AND PATTERNS OF DEVELOPMENT

Several principles of normal development have been derived from decades of observation of infants and young children. These principles represent our current knowledge and beliefs about human patterns of physical and behavioral development. These principles probably will be revised or replaced in the future as our understanding of very young children grows. Still, what we now know allows early childhood professionals to plan intervention and to advise parents. Assessment tools, instructional strategies, and curricular materials are based on the principles of development that follow.

INFANTS ARE HIGHLY COMPETENT ORGANISMS

As research emerges on child development, it becomes increasingly clear that even newborns possess complex skills. Young infants are capable of learning new behaviors, solving problems, and adapting to changes in their environment. Abilities that enable neonates to use perceptual and cognitive abilities to acquire vast knowledge were unrecognized by early researchers. For example, a wind-up mobile was once thought to be appropriate stimulation for a "passive" infant. Now mobiles that jingle or turn only when the infant touches the mobile are considered more appropriate since they help infants establish cause-and-effect and encourage them to take control of their environments.

INFANTS ARE SOCIALLY INTERACTIVE

Recently, educators have recognized that not only is social interaction a critical area of development but it also influences development in intellectual growth. In fact, it is possible that social competencies may be a more accurate predictor of later abilities than cognitive abilities. Evidence suggests that the need for social attachment is a biological drive. According to MacDonald (1992), human affection provides motivation for children to be compliant and accepting and correspondingly encourages adults to invest in their children. For example, in the past, parents were sometimes advised to feed a child on a fixed schedule at three-hour intervals. Considering the interactive nature of development, parents are now trained to respond to a child's cues to feed or stop feeding based on the child's facial expressions, vocalizations, or activity levels. Parents try to read a child's intent and respect the child's social communication. A child who has not experienced such interactions on a regular basis may learn to be a passive participant.

INFANTS ARE ACTIVE LEARNERS

Developmentalists believe infants are not merely passively modified by the goings-on around them, but play an active, if not always intentional, role in their own development. Early give-and-take interactions, such as pat-a-cake and peek-a-boo, between infants and caregivers provide the context for a child to learn control over the environment.

INFANT DEVELOPMENT IS MULTIDIMENSIONAL

The process by which infants' skills become more complex and integrated is a nonarbitrary sequence. Rather, this highly organized process unfolds predictably as children simultaneously grow physically and develop cognitively and socially. Behaviors in each area have an impact on behaviors in other domains, as skills develop across domains at the same time. The following example illustrates the interdependency of developmental domains. Children with Down syndrome often have cognitive delays. Their ability to problem-solve is complicated by poor language development, which is also typically delayed. Articulation difficulties may further compound the communication problems. Consequently, when this child needs help in solving a problem, she may not be able to request it in an understandable way affecting social interactions.

DEVELOPMENTAL SEQUENCING IS UNIVERSAL

Developmental milestones describe a universal sequence of steps through which children progress (see Figure 3–6). Though not all children progress through the steps at precisely the same age, the pattern of development is very reliable. When there are significant deviations in this pattern of development, a child may be at risk of developmental disability.

SKILLS BECOME MORE SPECIALIZED

As children develop, they are able to integrate more refined skills in one area with newly acquired skills in another to perform coordinated behaviors. For example, in-

Figure 3–6

Typical Motor Development Sequence

Source: Adapted from Mussen, P. H., Conger, J. J., Kager, J., & Huston, A. C. (1990). *Child development and personality* (7th ed.). New York: Harper & Row. Used with permission.

fants learn to recognize an adult's voice as their auditory discrimination improves. At the same time, facial muscle control increases to the point where a child can smile voluntarily. The result is a specialized ability to smile at "mom" when she is speaking. This acts as a way to enhance social relationships. In early childhood, children scribble nondiscriminately. Gradually, they refine this skill so that they can copy lines and circles. As children near school age, they integrate their emerging cognitive knowledge of alphabet letters with their newly refined fine motor skills. Thus, the specialization of these two domains results in handwriting.

PLASTICITY

One of the remarkable aspects of development is the **plasticity** of the human brain, by which alternate neural pathways can be formed to compensate for deficits in other portions of the brain. Damage to a specific area of the brain (e.g., language) often results in another portion of the brain developing the function of the damaged section. Another example of this flexibility is seen in infants who are blind or deaf but acquire necessary developmental skills by focusing on alternate channels of understanding.

CRITICAL LEARNING PERIODS

Interactional and developmental theorists contend that critical sensitive periods during which a child is biologically most ready to learn certain new behaviors occur throughout human development. When environmental events provide the right conditions for a particularly sensitive period, developmental progress can be maximized. However, when experiences fail to match a child's predisposition for learning, the window of opportunity is missed. Though a child will not necessarily fail to acquire the new skills, learning will take much longer than otherwise possible.

Paired with the theory of "peak" periods of learning is the need to provide diverse learning experiences involving all sensory systems. Many factors can upset the formula of optimal development. For example, Guo (1998) found poverty experienced in early childhood had a significant and lasting effect on cognitive aptitude. Another example of missed opportunity is in children who have chronic ear infections during a critical period when children learn to discriminate sounds used by others in conversations; those children may have difficulty acquiring the sounds necessary for speech.

CHILDREN UNDERGO SEVERAL TRANSITIONS

It is typical for children to undergo stages of **transition** when there are spurts of growth and development that may be followed by unpredictable behavior or regression. For example, changes in a daily pattern, such as beginning at a new day-care center, may result in behavior problems that are generally short lived. As children cognitively become more inquisitive, more mobile, and more verbal in the latter half of their second year, their behavior also becomes more unpredictable. The resolution of these problems, referred to as **consolidation,** occurs when the disorganized behavior is replaced by more advanced developmental skills. For example, a child may become better behaved when babbling is replaced by the more sophisticated means of communication, conventional words.

INDIVIDUAL DIFFERENCES AMONG CHILDREN

Children differ in such characteristics as **temperament** and gender, making each child unique. Temperament, or one's adaptation to everyday events, is partially innate and partially learned. Thomas and Chess (1981) concluded that temperament is a relatively constant trait throughout life. Differences in temperament affect the manner in which adults interact with infants and children and often result in such labels as "difficult" or "easy" baby. These responses, in turn, influence the development of a child's temperament. For example, if a cuddly, active, and smiling infant is reinforced by similar adult behaviors, the child is likely to continue being a socially rewarding companion.

Expectations of infants according to gender are obvious, even in newborns, as adults handle and talk to infants differently based on a child's sex (Rheingold & Cook, 1975). This social training appears to be so powerful that children learn to label their own and other's gender before they are able to label objects or tasks that are non-gender related (Bussey & Bandura, 1992). Evidence of the influence of childhood experiences is found in studies of hand coordination, where research consistently finds that men have greater fine motor control than women. Yet, in childhood, no such differences are found, suggesting that it is the types of activities in which males and females engage that result in significant differences as adults (Gabbard & Hart, 1995). Influences such as toy selection, play activities, playmates, adult-modeled behavior, and exposure to television all affect the degree of children's compliance to sex-role expectations.

FACTORS INFLUENCING DEVELOPMENT

There is little argument that children born into this world are at the mercy of their genetic endowment as well as the capriciousness of the world around them in terms of the rate of their development across domains. Though the search to determine the relative degree of these two factors continues, it can be assumed that to some large extent, children's development can be altered by the manipulation (intentional or not) of environmental factors. Several of these factors were discussed extensively in Chapter 1 (see Figure 3–7). For example, poverty, maternal income and education, family size, culture and race are all factors that influence both opportunity and motivation and consequently child development (Guo, 1998). The following is a discussion of important factors that affect every child's growth and development.

FAMILY STRUCTURE

As discussed in Chapter 1, American families are diverse in family structure, with a large number of families either in transition or headed by a single parent. The absence of either a dominant female or male adult figure in a child's life influences patterns of development, particularly in social and personal areas. The reconstitution of divorced families in blended or extended families results in socialization patterns that may affect children's loyalty to others, values, adaptability, and self-esteem. Research indicates that divorce has a variable influence on children, depending on such factors as age and gender of children, the presence of siblings, the psychological status of custodial parents, the intensity and outcome of custody battles, and the reconstitution of families in subsequent marriages (Monahan, Buchanan, Maccoby, & Dornbusch, 1993).

CHILD CARE

Raising children while working full time places stress on both parents, especially when the working mothers are expected to fulfill all the traditional responsibilities (Hoffman, 1989). Yet, the fact that mothers work outside the home in greater proportion than in the past does not automatically mean that children are less well nurtured. Vandell and Ramanan (1992) made a longitudinal analysis of work patterns of low-income women and related factors. These authors found that the earlier women went to work after childbirth and the more recently (relative to the time of the study) they worked, the better off the family was. These women were more educated and more intelligent, the family was less likely to exist in poverty, and the quality of home life was higher; finally, their children were more likely to do well in school academics. Thus it appears that it is the quality of child care paired with the overall richness of a child's experience that affect their development rather than their enrollment or nonenrollment in child care itself.

Figure 3–7
Pathways
Leading from
Poverty to
Childhood
Disabilities
Source: Adapted
from Sherman, A.
(1994). *Wasting
America's future:
The Children's
Defense fund
report in the costs
of child poverty*
(p. 12). Boston:
Beacon.

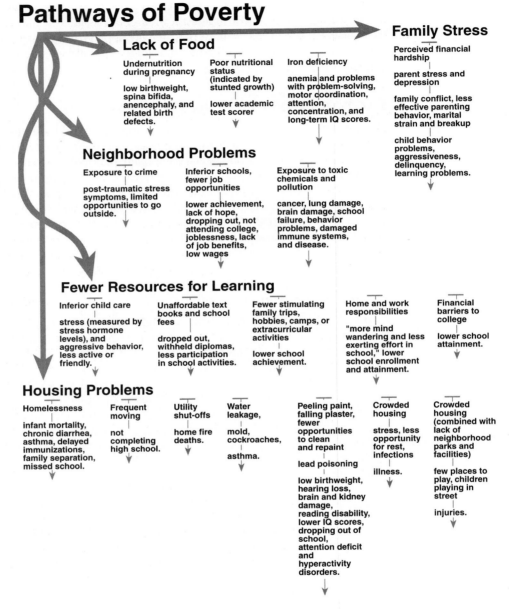

Pathways of Poverty

Lack of Food

Undernutrition during pregnancy

low birthweight, spina bifida, anencephaly, and related birth defects.

Poor nutritional status (indicated by stunted growth)

lower academic test scorer

Iron deficiency

anemia and problems with problem-solving, motor coordination, attention, concentration, and long-term IQ scores.

Family Stress

Perceived financial hardship

parent stress and depression

family conflict, less effective parenting behavior, marital strain and breakup

child behavior problems, aggressiveness, delinquency, learning problems.

Neighborhood Problems

Exposure to crime

post-traumatic stress symptoms, limited opportunities to go outside.

Inferior schools, fewer job opportunities

lower achievement, lack of hope, dropping out, not attending college, joblessness, lack of job benefits, low wages

Exposure to toxic chemicals and pollution

cancer, lung damage, brain damage, school failure, behavior problems, damaged immune systems, and disease.

Fewer Resources for Learning

Inferior child care

stress (measured by stress hormone levels), and aggressive behavior, less active or friendly.

Unaffordable text books and school fees

dropped out, withheld diplomas, less participation in school activities.

Fewer stimulating family trips, hobbies, camps, or extracurricular activities

lower school achievement.

Home and work responsibilities

"more mind wandering and less exerting effort in school," lower school enrollment and attainment.

Financial barriers to college

lower school attainment.

Housing Problems

Homelessness

infant mortality, chronic diarrhea, asthma, delayed immunizations, family separation, missed school.

Frequent moving

not completing high school.

Utility shut-offs

home fire deaths.

Water leakage,

mold, cockroaches,

asthma.

Peeling paint, falling plaster, fewer opportunities to clean and repaint

lead poisoning

low birthweight, hearing loss, brain and kidney damage, reading disability, lower IQ scores, dropping out of school, attention deficit and hyperactivity disorders.

Crowded housing

stress, less opportunity for rest, infections

illness.

Crowded housing (combined with lack of neighborhood parks and facilities)

few places to play, children playing in street

injuries.

PSYCHOLOGICAL FACTORS

The maintenance of a nurturing environment is as important to child development as health care and nutrition. From the first days of life, adults begin to nurture children through breast feeding, eye contact, smiling, kissing, and vocalizations, which in turn establish an attachment between infant and caregiver referred to as **bonding** (Siegel, 1982). Unlike other species, however, human babies resiliently retain the capability of bonding, even if parents miss opportunities in the first days and weeks of life. As infants grow, other psychological factors begin to influence development. Erikson (1963) wrote that one of the primary tasks of infants in their first year of life was to develop a sense of trust, which comes out of predictable and positive responses of caregivers and siblings.

It seems that children not only require secure social attachments, but may also need intermittent solitude as a condition of normal growth (Buchholz, 1997). Buchholz contended that greater emphasis on social interactions may actually deplete opportunities that infants have to self-regulate, organize information, and take a "psychological rest." Research citing the physiological benefits of solitude included improvements in the immune system and general functioning.

Parental style is important to nurturance of children. Adults who use warm and gentle tones to give directions and provide frequent positive feedback supporting appropriate behaviors develop the strongest levels of attachment. Kennedy (1992) analyzed the child-rearing strategies of parents whose children were rejected by their peers and found that mothers had spent less time teaching social skills to their children, were more likely to use punishment, and used less reasoning to explain discipline. At the same time, the fathers and mothers of these children did not value or spend time in child-centered activities.

Environmental deprivation and/or environmental chaos can affect social and cognitive development (Coll, Buckner, Brooks & Wei, 1998). When homeless and low-income infants and toddlers were assessed at 9 months and 18 months of age, there was a significant drop in motor and cognitive developmental scores. These findings suggest that poverty has a cummulative negative effect on development, increasing the longer children are exposed to conditions of poverty, including single parenting, violence, maternal depression, and substance abuse.

Infants and young children must also be given the freedom to explore their environments and to experiment and play with appropriate toys or materials (Allen & Marotz, 1989). For decades it has been recognized that the absence of stimulation or deprivation of experiences negatively affects development (Skeels, 1942; 1966). In Skeels's original research, 25 infants were selected from an overcrowded orphanage; 13 of them were sent to an institution to be cared for by adult women with mental retardation who provided the children with a stimulating and responsive environment. Though initially testing an average of 22 IQ points lower than the 12 infants remaining in the orphanage, a year and a half after placement in the institution, the children raised by women with mental retardation gained an average of 28 IQ points. Meanwhile, the children who remained in the overcrowded orphanage lost an average of 26 IQ points in the same interval of time.

Case Study

WORKING WITH THE FOSTER CARE SYSTEM: INTERVIEW WITH JAMES HOLDEN

I have been an early childhood special education teacher, and now I teach a regular sixth grade, but my wife and I started taking foster children before I was ever trained in education. We've probably had a couple of hundred foster children over the course of our marriage. We did foster care for years, when our family was smaller but as our own family increased to seven children, we retired from foster care for a while. At the time, we didn't feel we had a voice in what was happening to the foster children. When foster children were placed, the decisions on what was going to happen with them were pretty much controlled and dictated by the state.

For example, when we first started, in the mid-1960s, there was not a lot of emphasis on disabilities. All the children were just foster children and there wasn't really a thought given to the special needs a lot of those children had. The only special service I can remember being considered was the notion that counseling would fix whatever was wrong with foster children. Many of the children we dealt with, even then, were of mixed ethnic backgrounds, or coming out of divorce situations, so there were some emotional needs which got in the way of education. When you would have children like that you'd have a hard time.

We had not had foster children for some time when I went back to school and became a certified special education teacher. I took a teaching position on an Indian reservation and that was when we got back into the foster system. These children would show up at our house anyway. Sometimes parents would get to the point where they didn't feel like they could take care of their children, so they would bring them to our house and we'd watch over them a few days. Usually this was in a crisis situation. The school district superintendent's wife worked for the Department of Social and Health Services on the reservation, so in an emergency situation she would always place a few children with us. Finally, someone at the tribe said, "Well you're doing it anyway, you might as well get a license;" so that's what we did.

All the foster children from the reservation were high needs children. Many had parents who had used drugs or alcohol during pregnancy; the children were chemical effect, fetal alcohol syndrome, or alcohol impacted children. All kinds of differing abilities go with these problems. We no longer live on the reservation and now the children we receive tend to have health impairment or emotional problems.

Medical care is paid for through the foster care system, which is a big bonus. The difficulty is making sure you get children with special needs to the right people. The treatment can be more traumatic than just leaving them alone. For example, taking Rueben and April to an office for physical therapy is more traumatic than trying to do it yourself at home because you're taking them off of their schedules and they're being exposed to a lot of people. You also expose them to more illness and they're already medically fragile, so they can become undone by then. Doing something in an unfamiliar setting can be very stressful for these children.

Many times you get children with problems that have not been diagnosed, so you're starting from ground zero. Each child is so individual, the evaluation process can be overpowering. I know a lot of foster parents just say, "Hey, it's not worth the effort," or "I just don't have the time to do it." As the children get older you're often looking at some kind of counseling or therapy as well. Getting services is very time intensive and distracting from a normal life, whatever that is.

We often have had five foster children at one time. With the kinds of high needs children we have, that's about all a family can handle. Right now we have two children who have cystic fibrosis and fetal alcohol effect, and the other three who we're adopting are all chemically impacted from crack cocaine. My wife and I are a team. I try to deal with the bureaucracy, arrange the medical treatment, and the diagnostic testing, but she does the every day nitty gritty care of the children.

Right now, the foster care system is overloaded with these kinds of children, and many of them are not in appropriate homes. Many of the foster parents are simply not trained adequately to deal with high needs children. When they hit school, many foster parents are going to feel, "Hey, we've done our job, now do yours." If the evaluation process doesn't start until then, the child has already lost three years before we do anything with them.

Foster parents in this area have organized to try to make changes in the system. They would like to see ongoing training about ways to identify suspected abuse or neglect, and continuing training with substance abuse impacted children. AIDS is another huge part of what we're going through right now. The system will put a child with AIDS or suspected AIDS in your home and will not give you that information. I've also had a couple children who had hepatitis and they did not tell us. Those can be scary things because you're really in jeopardy. Family contact is very intimate at that level, there's no way to avoid it—so something needs to be done. Again we're balancing confidentiality rights with the rights of the caregiver and, we as a society haven't come to grips with that.

All in all, I feel the foster parent association and the state foster care workers work very well together to try and provide the best care available. But this will be an ongoing and important battle to win for the children. If we don't fight for these children, who will?

Holden children dressed in costume for Halloween.

EDUCATION

A child's educational opportunities, when good, can compensate for the types of disadvantages discussed elsewhere in this section, and, when poor, serve to exacerbate the environmental disadvantage of children and their development. The following list represents some educationally related factors that have been found to differentially influence a child's development (McLaughlin & Vacha, 1992):

1. The opportunity for preschool educational services, especially for children who are raised in poverty
2. Educational level of parents
3. Structure and curriculum focus of educational program
4. Safety of child in school
5. Opportunity for success and positive experiences in school
6. Consistency of school attendance and mobility
7. Value of a child's education to parents
8. A parent's knowledge of the educational system

CULTURE

Although cross-cultural research is in its infancy, it has revealed that universality exists in many aspects of development, just as differences have been observed in the rates of that development. For example, infants within the same culture seem to behave similarly, while behaving as a group differently than children from other cultures (Lester & Brazelton, 1982). In the past, educators tended to evaluate the development of all children according to the norms established with white middle-income children. Similarly, educational priorities favor the values of the dominant culture. For example, cooperative group behavior is highly valued in most minority groups, while Caucasians tend to value independence and competition. More recently, it has been realized that this practice gives undue priority to a single culture, while simultaneously and arbitrarily devaluing the practices of other cultures that may differentially affect child development.

TECHNOLOGY

Two major influences of the technological expansion in the last half of the twentieth century are television and the computer. While computers have become household tools for both adults and children, the long-term influence of this technology on child development is yet undetermined. Television, on the other hand, has been the center of controversy for decades. The potential influence of television cannot be underestimated, as it has been found that no other activity consumes as much time for American children as watching television (Nielson, 1988).

Of particular concern to parents and child advocates have been the correlational findings linking programming and commercials on television to aggression in children (Pearl, Bouthilet, & Lazar, 1982), unhealthy eating habits (Finn, 1977), and unwise buying tendencies (Baecher, 1983). A reduction in children's academic capacity when greater than three hours per day were spent watching television was identified by Beentjes and VanderVoort (1988). However, Henggeler, Cohen, Edwards, Summerville, and Ray (1991) concluded that family contexts (maternal life events stress and paternal marital satisfaction), when correlated with television viewing time, might be interrelated with academic performance of children (support for and active participation in studying). Though computers and television are sources of concern when overused to entertain, as in computer and video games and in many television forums, both obviously have the potential to be valuable learning tools.

MILESTONES OF DEVELOPMENT

Understanding the principles of human development is a prerequisite to interpreting the milestones that mark the developmental progression of infants and young children, including those with and at risk for developmental disabilities. Maturation across developmental domains is characterized by behavioral markers or key milestones. For practitioners working with young children with disabilities, this knowledge should be constantly at the ready—available for ongoing assessments of the headway children are making. In the absence of this knowledge, an educator's barometer of normalcy tends to drift. For example, early childhood special educators often admit that when they have an opportunity to observe typically developing children, they are reminded of the severity of their own students' delays. While the point is not to highlight individual differences, misinterpretation of development can lead to lowered expectations, oversight of potential problems, inaccuracy in educational programming, and miscommunication with families and other professionals. Since drift is possible, even for well-trained professionals, early childhood professionals should continuously recalibrate by revisiting developmental milestones.

In this section, our descriptions in each of five areas of development—motor, cognitive, language, social, and self-help—are accompanied by little theory. The absence of theory is intentional but is not meant to diminish its importance to the field of early childhood special education. Entire courses, indeed entire disciplines, have been devoted to these theories. This text's purpose, however, is to provide the elementary basis for making judgments about a child's performance in relation to typical developmental patterns and rates.

MOTOR DEVELOPMENT

Motor development provides the physical basis for movement, posture, and balance, which are critical prerequisites for acquiring concrete knowledge, producing speech, exploring the environment, carrying out daily self-help activities, and socializing with others. Normal development allows children to accomplish organized, purposeful, and efficient movement. This movement is dependent on the integration of the central nervous system and the muscular system acting together on skeletal structures (Bigge, 1991). Delayed or dysfunctional motor development can greatly influence when and how well children reach expected milestones. For example, chronic middle ear infections can disrupt functioning of the vestibular system that controls posture and balance against gravity. Delays in gross motor skills are observed in excessive falling, clumsiness, collisions with objects and may also be related to language development (Orlin & Effgen, 1997). In fact, motor delays can signal later developmental problems such as learning disabilities, mental retardation, and attention deficit disorder (Festschrift, 1994). Consequently, it is important that early childhood professionals understand motor development, recognize deviations from norms, and know appropriate intervention services that may support a child's individual motor needs.

Gross Motor Development

A review of the principles of physical development will provide a means for understanding the progress of gross motor development. It has been noted that children's muscle control progresses from head to toe (cephalo-caudal), from gross to fine, and from the center of the body toward the extremities (proximo-distal). The first of these, head to toe, is most useful in determining which skills one would expect to emerge next, based on the present level of maturity.

Head Control.   A newborn has very little intentional body control, yet does move its arms, legs, head, fingers, and toes reflexively. Because newborns are unable to independently support the weight of their heads, caregivers provide these babies with substantial head support. Soon, neck muscles develop sufficient strength and tone for turning the head from side to side in a **supine** (lying on the back) position and for greater ability to hold the head up in an upright or horizontal position. This head control becomes stronger until, eventually, infants raise their heads off a surface from a supine position and turn their heads from side to side in a **prone** (on

*Typical prone
propping position.*

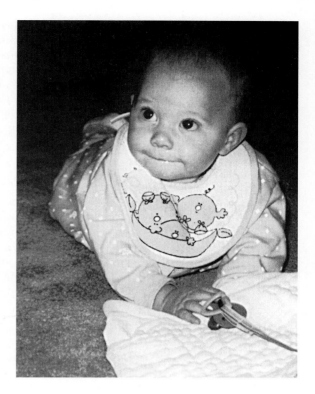

the tummy) position. An infant is said to have gained good head control when, as the infant is tilted side to side and front to back, there is no head lag and the posture of the head remains upright. A test for head control is the facilitated sit-up. A caregiver places a child supine and, taking the arms, pulls the child to a sitting position. If an infant is able to raise its head independently so the head stays parallel to the trunk, there is no head lag.

Shoulder Control. Though overlap exists in the development of neck and shoulder control, the latter cannot fully develop without an infant first achieving complete head control. At approximately two to three months of age, infants begin to assist themselves in turning their heads from side to side by propping their chests on their forearms. As muscle control is gained, infants are able to prop themselves higher and for a longer time, eventually pushing up on fully extended arms and hands (proximodistal principle in effect). Prone propping is paralleled by supine use of the arms, in which children begin to reach, first a few inches and then with fully extended arms. At this age, infants will begin to play with mobiles hung over their beds and to reach for near objects while lying on their tummies. When infants have well-developed shoulder control, they are able to turn themselves from prone to supine and back the other way. Usually, it is the front-to-back roll that emerges first since infants get an assist from their extended arms. However, by the fourth or fifth month, most infants are able to do both well since trunk control is also emerging.

Trunk Control. A neonate placed in a sitting position will droop from the waist to the head, exhibiting little resistance to gravity. At two months, an infant can hold its head upright in a sitting position and, at four months, can hold its upper body upright, but will fall over when a caregiver releases support of the waist. By six months, most infants will be able to sit independently, though they may not be able to catch themselves in a fall because protective reflexes are still immature. A strong sitter at eight months will independently get in and out of a sitting position, will reach for objects on the floor without falling over, and can stay upright when pushed gently in all directions. The last protective reaction to develop is extension to the rear, and even at eight months, an infant is vulnerable to head injuries from falls backward.

Hip Control. When an infant is independently able to get in and out of a sitting position, it is because some hip control has developed. At this time, an infant in a prone position will begin to crawl by coordinating its arms and legs to move across the floor or other surface. Later, weight bearing at the hips permits infants to resist gravity by raising their heads and lifting their trunks off the floor on their hands and knees (some infants go straight to hands and feet in a "bear crawl"). By coordinating movement of the extremities, infants of nine to ten months creep from this elevated position.

Lower Body Control. The final major gross motor development is upright mobility. Once hip control is fully developed, infants are capable of balance and stability on extended legs. Initially, standing may be possible only when knee joints are hyperextended. By 10 to 12 months though, most children can stand upright while holding on to a support. This evolves into cruising, or stepping sideways while holding on to furniture or some structure for support. Before long, a competent cruiser can be expected to transfer short distances between furniture by taking short steps without holding on. Finally, a child begins to take, first a few, and then several, independent steps.

Refinement. Once a child has learned to walk independently, the remainder of gross motor movement can be considered a refinement of the most critical skills of this domain. In fact, early childhood professionals tend to place relatively less emphasis on this domain (see Table 3–2) and more on cognitive and language skills after a child has begun to walk well. Refinement includes walking up and down stairs, running, standing on one leg, skipping, jumping, and development of recreation skills. While a child could be quite functional in life without most of these skills, a delay in development of gross motor coordination could be an early signal of generalized developmental problems later in life.

Fine Motor Skills

Like gross motor skills, fine motor development follows a predictable pattern. The most relevant principle is gross-to-fine motor skill maturation. For example, you would not expect a child to be capable of grasping objects intentionally until the child had gained shoulder control and was reaching with some accuracy. It can also be predicted that control of grasping progresses from the palm of the hand to the finger tips (proximo-distal).

Refinement of gross motor skills includes development of recreation skills.

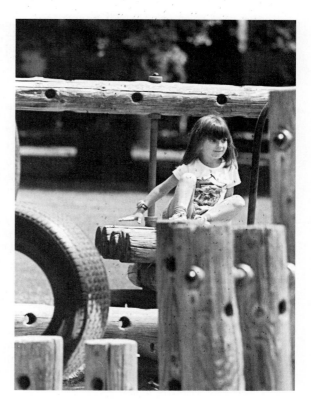

Eye Contact and Facial Expression.   In conformity with head-to-toe development, fine muscle control of the eyes is one of the first observable fine motor skills to begin developing. Within the first few days of life, neonates may be observed matching maternal eye movement. Yet, neonates have difficulty tracking, following moving objects with their eyes, and they lose contact once an object has been moved away from their midline. In just a few weeks, however, infants begin to track objects that are moved gradually from side to side and, eventually, will track 180 degrees by moving their heads to prevent loss of eye contact. Both range and duration of eye contact are important to mobility, fine motor coordination, and language development.

Reaching.   At birth, an infant's reach and grasp are entirely reflexive. Intentional reaching from a supine position begins at about two months, after an infant has gained some control at the shoulders. Infants will initially reach toward objects with minimal coordination and may bat or swing at an object but do not grasp it. Instead, infants hold their hands in a predominately fisted position. By four months, an infant's reach has become more coordinated, and the infant will unhesitatingly move its arm and hand in the direction of a desired object.

Grasping.   At the point where reaching has become a refined movement, grasping becomes intentional, now permitting infants to acquire and hold objects. Still, the

Table 3–2 Refinement of gross motor development.

12–18 months	Creeps up and down stairs
	Runs
	Throws ball overhand
	Pulls toy behind when walking
	Walks backwards
18–24 months	Kicks a ball
	Squats
	Bends at waist to pick something up without falling
	Walks up stairs alone with both feet on each step
3 years	Rides a tricycle by pedaling with alternating feet
	Catches a large bounced ball
	Broad jumps two feet
	Runs smoothly with changes in speed
4 years	Catches a thrown playground ball against body w/arms
	Walks up and down stairs alternating feet holding rail
	Jumps over a string held slightly off the floor
	Walks to the rhythm of music
5 years	Catches bounced ball
	Skips alternating feet
	Jumps rope 2–3 consecutive times
	Rides a bike with training wheels
	Skates forward a few feet
	Hits a ball with a bat or stick

unintegrated grasp reflex does not permit infants to intentionally release objects. The most primitive grasp is referred to as the palmar grasp (see Figure 3–8), in which a child acquires an object by scooping it into the palm with all fingers extended. Obviously, this grasp prevents an infant from manipulating an object in any precise fashion and play with the object is unsophisticated. Later, infants will be able to pick up and hold an object by opposing the palm with the tips of all fingers. Still there is no differentiation of finger use. A major milestone is reached when infants are able to grasp by opposing their thumbs with other fingers. This development, the prehensile grasp, is a feature unique to humans and other primates. First, the thumb opposes all the fingers, then the second and third fingers, and finally a fine pincer grasp (see Figure 3–8) is achieved.

Handedness. Handedness, or the tendency to be more skillful at using one hand/foot over the other, is a reflection of the dominance of one hemisphere of the brain over the other. In infancy, most children do not show a preference, but use both hands with equal coordination. Later, as children begin to perform more specialized hand movements, the majority show a preference for right handedness. In spite of beliefs to the contrary, right handers are not better coordinated than left handers or children who are "inconsistent" left handers (Gabbard & Hart, 1995).

Refinement of fine motor abilities is observed throughout the preschool years (see Table 3–3). The gradual refinement is facilitated by increased speed, strength, and coordination of small muscle groups. This ability is closely integrated with cognitive

A predominant flexor pattern: the infant holds its hands in a fisted position and swipes at objects.

Figure 3–8
A. Palmar Grasp
B. Pincer Grasp

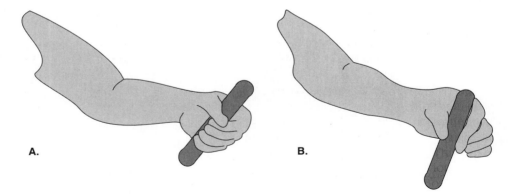

A.   B.

and perceptual development. Infants learn to pick up small objects and use their index finger to point to and probe objects. Toddlers begin to put simple puzzles together and to scribble with a crayon. Later on preschoolers learn to draw, to cut with scissors, and to form objects with clay.

Table 3–3   Refinement of fine motor development.

12 to 18 months	Holds crayon, with crayon held from radial side of hand
	Turns pages of a cardboard book
	Places a peg in a pegboard
	Builds a tower with two blocks
	Places a round form in a formboard
18 to 24 months	Imitates a crayon stroke
	Imitates vertical and circular stroke
	Completes puzzle with circle, square, triangle
2 years	Builds tower with four to six blocks
	Turns door knobs or TV handles by twisting wrist
	Unscrews nesting toys
	Turns pages one at a time
	Holds a crayon with thumb and forefinger
3 years	Cuts with scissors on a line
	Holds pencil with adult-like tripod grasp (resting on third finger)
	Folds paper
	Winds up toys
4 years	Completes puzzle of three to five pieces
	Moves paper and cuts out simple shapes (e.g., triangle)
	Draws a person with two body parts
	Makes crude objects with two to three parts with clay
	Screws together threaded objects
5 years	Prints first name
	Completes 11–15 piece puzzle
	Copies small case letters
	Colors within lines
	Opens lock with a key
	Hits a nail with hammer

Case Study

THE DIARY OF ESTHER ANNA BERKE: MONTH 3

The doctor orders Esther Anna admitted to NCKU Hospital in Tainan on Wednesday, January 27. She is dehydrated and anemic and the doctor puts her on an IV and re-inserts the nasal feeding tube. A nurse asks us why we didn't abort her! GRRR!!! Esther's right lung collapsed and she was put into the ICU. After 16 days in the hospital, Esther celebrated her 3-month birthday at home, she weighs 4.1 kg and measures 55 cm long.

February 16–21:   This is New Year's Day on the Chinese lunar calendar, Happy Chinese New Year, the Year of the Rabbit! Esther is eating well and staying healthy. Our colds are slowly improving, and Esther weighs 4.4 kg. On February 21 she weighed 4.5 kg, finally back to her birth weight after fourteen weeks! She is at the 25th percentile for weight and height for girls her age. We hope we can put some fat on her.

February 22–March 1:   Sunday February 28: She weighs 4.75 kg today, and is eating well. Esther's seizures are still a problem; she has two new types we have not seen before, and their frequency is much higher than before. Other than her seizures, she is doing well—she rolled over from her stomach to her back for the first time. We took her to a physical therapist to begin strengthening her neck muscles which are weak. We appreciate a relatively calm week!

March 2–8: Sunday March 7: She weighs 5.0 kg, and started a new drug this week—Rivotril—in addition to the Sabril. We are investigating a diet called the ketogenic diet, it is a high fat, low protein, ultra-low carbohydrate diet that has helped many people with seizures, including at least one Aicardi girl. One baby was started on it at 4 1/2 months old, using a special formula. The Johns Hopkins Medical Center in Baltimore is the world's expert on this diet. We are also investigating a holistic therapy program prescribed by the National Academy of Child Development in Ogden, Utah. They try to treat the entire child (5 senses plus mental and emotional aspects) in order to stimulate the brain to grow new connections between the brain cells. People have written us dramatic stories of how they helped their children.

March 9–15: Esther celebrated her 4-month birthday March 15 by hiking in Yu Shan (Jade Mountain) National Park. Actually she didn't hike, she and Mom stayed in the car because it was pretty cold up there for us "tropicalized" people. She weighed 5.2 kg and measured 63.5 cm, her weight is only in the 15th percentile for her age but her length is in the 70th percentile. We need to put some more fat on that baby!

LANGUAGE DEVELOPMENT

One of the most amazing phenomena of human life is the development of language. In just three-years time, infants progress from almost total reflexive responding to the development of adult-like speech. Yet, even in the first few days, infants communicate; they send messages that are understood by caregivers. For most children, this **communication** will later conform to a set of rules that guide how ideas are formed into words and put together in sentences. These symbolic systems, known as languages, differ across cultures. Furthermore, language can be communicated in writing, orally through speech, and manually (e.g., American Sign Language). All these systems have something in common. Individuals who share the language conform to the standard rules, enabling them to communicate very efficiently. However, humans do not send and receive messages through language alone. Unconventional language—body language, facial expressions, grunts, laughter, wincing, and so on—all communicate powerful messages that are "read" by the listener.

Just as musculoskeletal movement is reflexive at birth, so is the majority of neonatal communication. A newborn communicates basically in two ways—crying and not crying. Within two years, however, this child will have developed all the basic constructs of human adult language. Several theories attempt to explain the nature of linguistic development. The various theories can be viewed as complementary, contradictory, or supplemental. In fact, our current understanding of language seems to borrow from each of the most prominent theories (McCormick & Schiefelbusch, 1990). The following principles of language development are generally agreed upon by linguists.

◆ Humans are born with a certain capacity to acquire language (McCormick & Schiefelbusch, 1990).
◆ Children acquire language according to a universal pattern, which is observed across children of different languages, cultures, families, and disabilities (Chaudhary & Suparna, 1991).
◆ Children generally develop an understanding of the meaning of concepts before they learn to use the corresponding words. Moreover, a child's receptive language (words they understand) is almost always more highly developed than a child's expressive language (words they use).
◆ Social exchanges are a necessary context for language development (McDonald, 1989).
◆ Children's language development is facilitated through modeling by adults, repeated practice of sounds and words, and differential reinforcement (i.e., attending to understandable language and not attending to incomprehensible language).

The remainder of this section will be a description, rather than an explanation, of language development in children from birth to six years of age. Interactional theorists describe language as three interrelated components: form, content, and use. The form of language refers to its structure: phonology, syntax, and morphemes. Language content refers to a child's knowledge of the words and the interrelationship between words. Both receptive and expressive language are considered in language content. Finally, language use, or pragmatics, is the way in which children communicate in social contexts.

Language Form

Three aspects of language are generally considered when discussing language form. **Phonology** is the study of speech sounds. When considering the linguistic development of infants, the evolution of phonemes (speech sounds) follows a predictable pattern. The rules that govern structural patterns of language utterances and sentence grammar are referred to as **syntax.** Finally, **morphological development** refers to the evolution of word structure and word parts such as prefixes and suffixes.

Phonological Development.   The sounds made by neonates are nonspecific crying, grunting, and gurgling. Without training or direction, caregivers are typically able to differentiate types of crying sounds to determine if an infant is wet, tired, hungry, or otherwise uncomfortable. Infants begin to make vowel sounds within the first few months. Vowel sound production is referred to as **cooing.** Vowels are physically the easiest sounds to make since they require little motor control or use of the articulators (tongue, lips, palate, and teeth).

Infants begin to **babble** by about four months of age as they gain greater oral motor control. Babbling is a combination of consonant and vowel sounds (C-V and V-C) and progresses from simple to complex sound production. In the early babbling stages, infants produce a variety of sounds, some of which are not a part of their native language. Later, sounds not used in children's native language(s) drop from their repertoire and may be very difficult to acquire at an older age. By the end of the first year, infants' first words begin to appear; many of these are monosyllabic C-V or V-C combinations, for example "up" or "ma-ma." Thereafter, consonant sound production progresses along a continuum of easy to hard, relative to oral-motor complexity (see Table 3–4).

Children produce words that increase in understandability as initial sounds, ending sounds, and middle sounds of words are put together with precision. The transition to real words is remarkably fleet. At 18 months, infants' speech is only about 25% intelligible, but it should be approximately 65% intelligible by two years of age, when toddlers begin to produce two-word utterances. At four years of age, children have acquired most phonetic sounds and are producing almost totally intelligible sentences.

Syntax.   Without direct instruction, children acquire the rules of spoken syntax with surprising accuracy. It is not until after children already speak with correct syntax that the rules of grammar are specifically taught. Initially, infants rely primarily on one-word utterances, and toward the end of their second year, they rely on successive single-word utterances. Infants do not begin to put words together in phrases until late in their second year. However, this linguistic development represents a major accomplishment in a child's communicative power. The significance of two-word utterances is that these telegraphic phrases possess more meaning than either word uttered in isolation. That is, two-word phrases convey the meanings of word A and word B, plus the meaning of each word's relationship to the other. Examples of simple two-word phrases used include noun-verb: "baby eat"; verb-noun: "give ball"; noun-noun: "Daddy ball".

Sentence structure becomes complex in several ways in children's third year. At about 27 months, children begin to ask questions, though initially only by intonation. Children may ask some "wh-questions" at this time, but initially not with the verb transposed (e.g., "Where car is going?"). Wh-questions emerge in correspondence with conceptual knowledge and receptive understanding of the same types

Table 3–4   Sequence of phonological acquisition.*

Age	Sounds Produced
By age 3	p, m, h, n, w
By age 4	b, k, g, d, f, y
By age 6	t, ng, r, l, s
By age 7	ch, sh, j, o with wavy line as in *th*ick
By age 8	s, z, v, o with carrot as in *th*is
Later	Zh

*The age of acquisition may vary by as much as 3 years.
Source: Adapted from McCormick, L., & Schiefelbusch, R. L. (1984). *Early language intervention*. Columbus: Merrill.

of questions. "Who," "what," and "where," which have more concrete referents, precede "when," "how," and "why." Queries that require transposition of verbs occur when children have begun to use auxiliary verbs and copulas or linking words (e.g., "Is the bike outside?"). Tag questions are also complex interrogative forms added on after other question forms have appeared (e.g., "We are having ice cream, aren't we?").

Negative sentences also follow a pattern of increasing complexity as they gradually approximate accurate syntactic rules. To the frustration of adults, negative statements are among the highest frequency utterances made by toddlers. Children first make negative comments by placing a negative marker at the beginning of a sentence. This is followed by placing the negative marker inside the sentence next to the relevant verb, but without the use of copulas and auxiliary verbs. Finally, though not until about age four, children begin to accurately use inflections and negative markers together.

Stage I.   No want milk.
Stage II.   Kitty no eat candy.
Stage III. I can't fix the bike.

Complex sentences contain at least one independent clause and at least one subordinate or dependent clause. Sentences with more than one independent clause are referred to as **compound sentences.** Both advanced types of sentences combine two or more ideas in a single sentence through the use of conjunctions, relative pronouns, or other linguistic linkages. "And" is the first conjunction to appear and is observed in children as young as 25 months of age, though initially the "and" joins nouns (e.g., "me and Mommy") rather than clauses. **Relative clauses** that modify subjects (e.g., "I like the doll that has the green hair") appear later. By three or four, many children are using compound and complex sentences by adding elements to the beginning or end of kernel sentences. Still later (4 to 13 years of age), children add clauses internally to sentences in a process referred to as **embedding** (e.g., "I saw the girl who is in my class at the park").

CLOSE-UP

MEANINGFUL DIFFERENCES IN EVERYDAY EXPERIENCES IN YOUNG AMERICAN CHILDREN

Research is increasingly clear that a child's intellectual and social destiny is largely determined prior to entering school. In fact, for children who live in poverty, it may be impossible for educators to undo the effects of early childhood experiences with their parents. Hart and Risley (1995) found that children of university faculty parents far out-paced their same age peers from poor families when compared on language development. The implication of these findings is that, while all parents have the opportunity to provide rich intellectual experiences required for healthy cognitive development, the failure to do so may lead to deficiencies that are all but impossible to rehabilitate once children reach school age.

There were pronounced differences in the amount and quality of interactions between parents and their children as observed monthly across three years by Hart and Risley. Across three income groups, it was found that the more educated the mother, the more she spoke to her children. Welfare, working-class, and professional parents addressed their children an average of 600, 1200, and 2000 words per hour respectively. As a consequence, Hart and Risley estimated that by the time these children reached age three, the welfare children would have heard 10,000,000 words, working class children would have heard 20,000,000 words, and professional children would have heard 30,000,000 words.

In addition to the differences in number of words heard, parents of the different groups studied differed in what they talked about to their children. For example, welfare parents made positive comments to their children an average of 6 times per hour, as compared to 15 times per hour for working-class parents, and 30 times per hour for professional parents.

These linguistic differences led to significant differences in intellectual accomplishments when children were followed up in the third grade. While performance differences based on SES tended to diminish across time, differences in parental behavior remained a strong predictor of their children's cognitive success.

Hart and Risley predicted that it would take 40 hours of supplemental care every week from birth on to compensate for the observed differences in parental behavior. While this option is unrealistic, there is clearly a need for better/more parent training, mentorship programs, parental aides, and access to quality child care.

Source: Hart, B., & Risley, T. R. (1995). *Meaningful differences in everyday experiences in young American children.* Toronto: Paul H. Brookes.

Morphological Development

A **morpheme** is defined as the smallest part of a word that possesses meaning. Morphemes that can stand alone with meaning are referred to as free morphemes, while those that cannot stand alone are referred to as **bound morphemes.** While a language frequently adds new free morphemes, it rarely adds new bound morphemes. Of the two, free morphemes appear first in infants' language as their first words (e.g., bottle, Mommy, ball, cup). Not until much later (beginning at about 24 months) do bound morphemes (inflections) begin to appear (e.g., -ed, -ing, pre-). The latter, along with auxiliary verbs, are referred to as morphological inflections and emerge along a predictable pattern (see Table 3–5).

An index of the sophistication of children's language is based upon the frequency of morphemes in their utterances. **Mean Length Utterance (MLU)** is calculated by dividing the number of morphemes in an utterance by the number of utterances (at least 50). An MLU of 1.0 is observed when infants are at the one-word-phrase stage. By the time children have MLUs of 3.0 or higher, they are usually incorporating at least some morphological inflections into their phrases. When a child's MLU is greater than 4.0, the score is no longer a valid index of language development.

Morphological development appears to be particularly difficult for children with language impairments and an index that distinguishes language problems from cognitive deficits. Even children with language delays however, acquire morphemes in a normal pattern. Although many children "catch-up" in later childhood, they often retain minor deficits in morpheme development, particularly morphemes associated with verb use (Bedore & Leonard, 1998). Hence, these children, may benefit from early intervention in speech and language (Paul & Alforde, 1993).

Language Content

As mentioned earlier, content develops along two parameters: receptive and expressive language. The former typically progresses at a more rapid rate but is not necessarily a prerequisite for expressive development. In other words, children sometimes use words in their speech before they understand their meaning.

Receptive Language.   Neonates are capable of learning speech in their first days of life. Bertoncini, Bijelac-Babic, Jusczyk, Kennedy, and Mahler (1988) discovered that infants would alter their pattern of sucking when a tape emitting phonetic sounds ("ba") suddenly changed to a new sound ("da"). This ability to discriminate sounds is a necessary prerequisite to speech production. Within the first few months, a mother might notice that her child will become quiet or pause at the sound of mom's voice but not at that of a stranger's voice. Later, when infants develop some head control, they will turn their heads toward sounds by sound localization. Although infants begin to recognize familiar words in speech by about 7.5 months, it is not until the end of children's first year that they begin to acknowledge specific words. This is evident when children respond differentially to their names. Not surprisingly, one of the first words recognized by infants is the word "no."

By the end of their first year, infants recognize a few high-frequency words and can demonstrate this skill by looking directly at the named objects. One-year-olds are also learning to follow simple commands like "wave bye-bye," or "give me a kiss." However, these commands are often accompanied by gestures or signals.

Until the beginning of their second year, the difference between infants' expressive and receptive language does not appear to be great. However, after this point, receptive language far outpaces expression until about the third year of development when the gap narrows again. Therefore, the next six months represent a turning point in children's receptive language, as infants learn to follow simple novel commands that do not have gestures, such as "put the toy on the table" or "give mommy a drink." By a child's thirteenth month they begin to understand grammatical morphemes. At 16 months, infants point to body parts upon request. At the end of their second year, infants understanding of speech is nearly perfect, as they can discriminate accurate and inaccurate phonemes, morphemes and syntax (Morgan, 1996).

Until their second year, infants' word understanding is referent specific. During their second year, these same infants begin to categorize concepts by making gradually more sophisticated generalizations (Oviatt, 1982). For example, they learn that cats and dogs belong to a category of animals. Later, they learn that even though horses have some of the same characteristics as dogs, they do not belong to the same class. Still, 2-year-olds are bound by literal interpretation of adult language and are unable to solve the figurative meaning behind clichés, metaphors, or analogies. By three, young children can both interpret and use figurative speech. A child might be overheard saying, "Rover is a pig." Anaphoric terms, such as "this," "that," "it," and "there," are difficult terms to master, though 3-year-olds are typically able to solve such directions as "put the spoon there." Four-year-olds can understand passive sentences (e.g., "I had wanted to take you to the park") but use them infrequently in conversation. A 6-year-old is quite good at solving subtle messages in language, such as sarcasm and humor that rely on irony (Winner, 1988). Since children's language is still literal, transparent metaphors, such as "hold your tongue," might be understood by these youth, though it is not until much later that children are able to decode opaque metaphors, such as "smell the roses" (MacArthur, 1990).

Expressive Language. Documenting the development of expressive language is easier since one does not have to make inferences about the invisible cognitive processes that underlie this form of communication. Though children represent meanings much earlier, their first real words do not generally appear much before a child's first birthday. However, intentional pointing emerges near the end of the first year. This is a significant milestone; as it has been found that the timing of the emergence of pointing may be related to speech expression and comprehension in later childhood (Butterworth & Morissette, 1996).

Universally, the first words that infants use represent salient features of children's immediate environments. Actions and objects dominate early words, though nouns appear to be more easily learned and more frequently used than verbs. This makes sense, since objects have a concrete referent, while actions are not permanent and their dimensions change with each event. For example, "jumping" can only be la-

Tommy and his mother signing to each other.

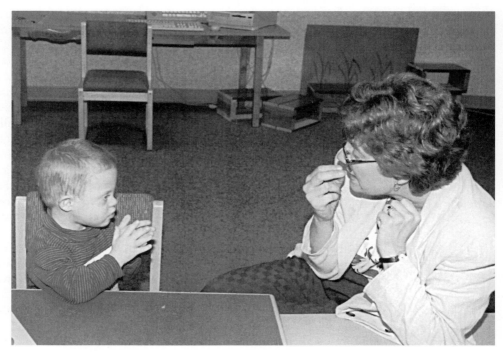

beled when someone jumps, and then the visual referent disappears. Additionally, jumping can be on one foot or two feet, executed by mom or dad, a few inches or over a high jump, and so on. Words that represent objects that move or are acted upon in a variety of different ways (e.g., baby doll) are more frequently used than objects that do not move (e.g., wall).

At 18 months, when infants typically possess a 50-word vocabulary of mostly nominals, their language content begins to change significantly. It is at this juncture in development that children begin naming many different objects that are less salient and less important. Some have referred to this transition as a "naming spurt," and it corresponds with a sudden sharp increase in children labeling everything they see (Gopnik & Meltzoff, 1992). This milestone also seems to be the threshold for combining words into successive single-word utterances and two-word utterances. Finally, at about this stage, a sharp rise in the use of both verbs and adjectives has been observed (Klink & Klink, 1990).

At two years, toddlers have acquired a vocabulary of about 300 words. With words paired together in telegraph-like sentences, children use only key words (e.g., "baby up" stands in for "the baby is standing up"). A rapid growth in novel **semantic relations** takes place in children's second year. For example, Braine (1963) documented novel use of two-word utterances of a toddler. In successive months the child used 24, 54, 89, 250, 1400, and 2500 new phrases.

Perhaps because of their limited repertoire of words, toddlers commonly **overextend** the use of words. For example, these children might mistakenly refer to all men as "Daddy" since men have physical characteristics similar to their fathers. At the same time, these toddlers might alternately look at Dad and his friend Bob when they hear their names, reflecting a lag in production as compared to cognitive understanding. **Underextensions** occur when categories are defined too narrowly. For example, very young children might use the word "chair" to refer to their highchairs and the dining room chairs but do not include the rocking chair or kitchen stool in this category. It is also common for children to use known words idiosyncratically to fill in for concepts for which they have no words.

Preschool programs commonly spend much time teaching young children color terms, a behavior that maintains very little functional value when compared to the many other conceptual categories available. Little ones can typically supply a color of an object to the request "What color is this?" by age two, though not necessarily accurately. Colors closest to primary (e.g., red-reds) are learned most easily (Andrick & Tager-Flusberg, 1986). More complex content reflecting concepts that are not concrete typically do not appear much before a child's third birthday. For example, time and space are relative terms, and words used to reflect these concepts begin to appear at about age four when concepts such as "before," "after," "next to," "in front of," "first," and "last" are observed.

Though a child's vocabulary development is influenced, to some unknown but significant degree, by experiences, the normal rate of word acquisition has been described (Reed, 1994). By two years a child typically uses 300 words, 1000 by three years, 1500 by four years, over 2000 by five years, and nearly 3000 words by age six. By contrast, a child's receptive vocabulary is approximately 20,000 to 24,000 words by age six.

Four-year-olds exhibit a variety of conversational skills.

Language Use

The final category of language function, language use, is more difficult to define, assess, and plan for instruction. This aspect of language refers to the effectiveness of the speaker in establishing and maintaining mutually rewarding interactions with others. Some children have very well-developed language form and content but are simply unable to engage others in conversations. Even as adults there are people who, for example, can talk and talk but are not desirable conversation partners because they are insensitive to the subtle rules of communication that make interactions mutually rewarding.

Three types of behavior comprise language use. **Speech acts** are the speakers' intentions or purposes for communicating. People communicate to give information, ask questions, make requests, tell a story or entertain, make protests, and show surprise, among other things. When communicating with others, people also make judgments about the listener that allow modifications to the content and style of the communication. These **presuppositions** include, but are not limited to, assessments of social status, educational or developmental level, and the intimacy of relationships. For example, one estimates the level of interest that the listener might have in a particular topic as well as the degree of background knowledge that the listener holds. If these judgments are inaccurate, one could talk over someone's head or, conversely, offend someone by appearing condescending. Finally, conversations have subtle rules, that may vary from culture to culture, that allow humans to converse in a reciprocal manner. **Conversational postulates,** as these rules are called, include skills in initiating conversations, balanced turn-taking, questioning, repairing a breakdown in conversations, maintaining interactions, and closing a conversation.

The earliest appearance of language use is in the form of conversational postulates. For example, neonates have been observed engaging in reciprocal turn-taking with caregivers in the first days of life. Eye blinking and mouth and tongue movements can become routinized back-and-forth actions between a child and caregiver. However, it will be several more years before these skills become refined. A child of nine months will play many reciprocal games, demonstrating conversation-like turn-taking (e.g., peek-a-boo). This turn-taking skill is used primitively in dialogues when a child is 18 to 24 months of age.

During the period when children first begin to use intentional communication many of their language intentions are nonverbal. For example, a child may point to a favorite doll. Yet, the purposes of this intent could be several. The child might be making a request to acquire the toy, telling mom that the doll is nice, protesting the removal of the doll, or asking if the doll is hungry. In context, a parent can interpret these limited regulatory requests. Even at this age, these same 1-year-old speakers have been observed altering their communication for their listeners.

By the latter half of their second year, children begin to use language for a variety of new functions that integrate regulatory purposes with interactional skills. At two years of age, children have learned that a single utterance can serve more than one function. Because conversation has now taken on a social purpose, toddlers need to maintain conversational topics. However, many conversations break down as children appear to flit in and out of a conversation more often than they stay on topic. Limited skills, such as repeating or imitating words or parts of words used in the previous sentence, are used to maintain conversations. These children might fix a topic breakdown by attempting to articulate with greater clarity. By contrast, 4-year-olds are capable of carrying on a conversation for several minutes, discussing the same or related topics. Skills used to fix topic breakdowns include rephrasing sentences, shortening utterances, and expanding their sentences.

Three- and four-year-old children will adapt their communication based on their perceived assessment of the listener's prior knowledge. They may give more or less information based on the extent of previous experiences their listeners are judged to possess. Furthermore, these preschoolers can be observed altering the length of sentences, affect (e.g., facial expression, voice intonation, body language), and language content when interacting with younger children or infants (Shatz & Gelman, 1973).

Factors Affecting Language Development

Multiple factors can affect the rate and pathology of linguistic acquisition. For example, many developmental disabilities can directly affect language form. Clefts of the lip and/or palate and oral-structural anomalies associated with Down syndrome influence phonological production. Cerebral palsy may result in reduced respiratory capacity that hampers speech production as well. Other developmental disabilities affect children's rate of learning and slow the acquisition of content and use. Autism, for example, is linked with aberrations in all areas of language development.

New evidence has been found that many children inherit their language deficits. In a small controlled study, Spitz and Tallal (1997) found that 50% of those infants with a positive family history of language impairments had a significant language delay themselves at two years, though development was normal in all other domains. Moreover, the children with no family history also had no delays in language development at two years. Bedore and Leonard (1998) reported that immediate family members of children with speech and language delays are two to seven times more likely than family members of children with normal language development to have language disorders themselves.

Though patterns of language development are universal (see Table 3–6), there are some cultural and sociocultural factors that influence the rate of acquisition of language (Wood, 1992). For example, Chaudhary and Suparna (1991) found that children differed across nuclear and extended families, with children from single units having more rapid language development. Lewis (1997) worried over the loss of oral traditions in African American families and recent immigrant groups, whose storytelling practices are devalued by the Anglo-American school system and obstructed by urban life. The loss of nuturance and social exchange through family lore is believed to signal the loss of critical language stimulation.

Idiosyncrasies in parenting also influence language development. Schacter and Straye (1982) described a specialized manner of interaction between mothers and infants called "motherese." Tactics of motherese were found to be correlated with the rate of language development and include use of extensions, shortened sentence length and simplified vocabulary, repetitions or rewording, and talking about events within a child's world. Though gender differences do exist in communication with infants, Klink and Klink (1990) concluded that fathers also engage in "motherese."

Children with disabilities who have language delays may require specially structured opportunities to facilitate language development. For example, children with language delays benefit from opportunities to engage in structured play with children whose language is developing normally. These peer models provide their friends more things to talk about, correct models of language structure, and appropriate ways for using language in a social situation (Roberston & Weismer, 1997).

COGNITION

The process by which human beings learn has been under inquiry and discovery for hundreds of years. The acquisition of knowledge, also known as cognition, is a complex phenomenon in which infants, children, and adults are constantly learning about their world. This development allows human beings to learn to reason (both concretely and abstractly), to think logically, and to organize information about their environment in a way that will bring order to their world. Cognitive development is closely tied to the other developmental domains. Failure to follow the normal developmental pathway can result in difficulties in social and emotional development and produce blocks to the development of communication skills.

The study of cognitive development has resulted in the evolution of many theories about learning and the conceptual frameworks that correlate with those theories. Ensuing controversy over incompatible theories, as well as questions left unanswered, both frustrate and fascinate students. Most theories are based on observations of behaviors that can be related to age, maturity, and environment. Explanations typically hypothesize a link between observed behaviors and unobservable processes. For example, if an infant loses interest in a toy that has dropped off the highchair (the observed behavior—looks away or plays with something new), one can hypothesize that the child has not yet learned that objects still exist when out of sight of the observer (the process—object permanence). All models of cognitive development deal

Table 3–6   Milestones of language development.

Birth	Responds to noises (activity stops)
	Frequent crying
	Makes vowel-like sounds "e" and "a"
1 month	Vocalizes
	Responds to voices
	Special cry for hunger
	Vocalizes pleasure
4 months	Imitates simple gestures
	Repeats syllables (da-da-da)
	Localizes sounds
	Uses vowel sounds "o" and "u"
	Expresses displeasure without crying
8–11 months	Produces consonant sounds in babbling
	Stops activity momentarily when told "no"
	Combines two syllables in vocal babbling "ba-da"
	Babbles using adult-like intonation
	Shows understanding of some words
	Waves "bye-bye"
	Plays "peek-a-boo" and "pat-a-cake"
12 months	Says 5–10 words
	Points to familiar objects when named
	Expresses wants
	Says "no" with authority
18 months	Points to two to three pictures named
	Names familiar objects upon request
	Intelligible speech 25% of time
	Imitates last word spoken
	Uses own name in conversation
24 months	"Sings" along with music
	Uses plurals
	Uses two-word phrases
	Responds to choices
	Utterances have communicative intents
	Intelligible speech 65% of time
	Overextensions (goed, feets)
3 years	Knows a few songs—approximates correct pitch
	Can carry on a conversation
	Uses four-word sentences
	Uses past tense, and present tense (-ed)
	Asks wh-questions
	Uses pronouns I, her/him, her/his, she/he
	Intelligible speech 80% of time
4 years	Says "excuse me" to interrupt conversation
	Will retell story read by someone else
	Carries out instructions with prepositions
	Participates in group songs
	Defines words
	Can tell what simple things are made of

Table 3–6 Continued

5 years	Knows birthday, phone number, and parents' names
	Uses five-word sentences
	Describes events in past/future with logical sequence
	Answers questions related to a spoken content or story
	Begins to understand abstract concepts
	Uses compound sentences with two main clauses

with how humans gather information, process it in both short-term and long-term memory, and relate it back in a relevant fashion to be used in determining and executing action.

Children appear to be born with the innate ability for learning, but this potential is developed only through interaction with the environment. Using their senses to gather and process information leads to the ability to understand relationships between themselves, objective reality, and the world at large. Furthermore, development of the intellect occurs jointly with physical growth, development of motor skills, language development, and learning social skills. Children progress serially through stages of cognitive development—learning skills and having insights in which ideas fit into their pictures of the world.

Case Study

ACCEPTANCE: INTERVIEW WITH MARSHA MOORE

When we were finally given a diagnosis for Michael, it was not good. The prognosis we were given was infantile autism with moderate to severe mental retardation. We were told that because we had a large family and much responsibility to our other children, we should consider applying for institutional placement for Michael in the state institution for the mentally handicapped. It would be several years before space would come available. Four or five years was a long time and by then we may be ready.

You know, to be honest, it was almost a relief to hear someone say that there was a place where "trained personnel" could take care of your child on an ongoing daily basis. After all, it was obvious, that after a year of sleepless nights and frazzled emotions, we were not prepared to care for him! We thought about this possibility for less than a half hour. This was truly not an option for us. We never did put our name on the waiting list. I can't help sometimes wondering what our lives would be like if we had.

The time that we received Michael's diagnosis was the saddest time in our lives. Somehow, it seemed almost too painful to feel such deep sorrow for very long. It didn't hurt as much to be angry. Part of our anger focused on the medical establishment. What stupid, uncaring human beings they were! How could anyone even suggest institutionalizing this beautiful little boy of ours? How can they predict Michael's future. We'll show them. We will prove them wrong!

I also feel resentment and anger towards others who seemed to be enjoying their lives in ways I thought would never again be possible. Did they know how precious their "perfect" children were?

*Michael Moore and
his dad.*

I put on a happy face for everyone outside the home, but often even a casual re-
mark would hurt me deeply. Friends, who were trying to be upbeat, would tell me
how lucky I was to "at least" have five "other" beautiful healthy children, as if Michael
was a puppy and the deformed runt of the litter or something, as if that should make
me happy. To me, there was no consolation.

We worried about how our extended family would react, but they were all very
supportive. I think my mom and dad knew how devastated we were, but I don't
think my brother and sisters had a clue as to what our family was going through.
We tried to keep a stiff upper lip when they'd call. We'd talk about other things
and not really cry or complain or go into detail over the phone. I think everything
was very gradual for them, seeing Michael over a period of time and realizing he
wasn't changing.

After the diagnosis, I remember working for hours out in the yard and just crying
and crying and crying. I felt sorry for myself, I felt sorry for Jim, I felt sorry that the
kids would always have a retarded brother. I couldn't imagine how Mike would be
when he was ten, just like I really can't imagine what he'll be like when he's twenty.
When you have a typical child, you imagine an adult and you assume he's going to
be bright and handsome and charming. But with Michael, I was so fearful. What
would he be like when he was 5 years old or 10 years old? The thought of having
to bathe a 10-year-old child, having to change his diaper, and wipe his runny nose
was almost scary. I thought, "I don't want this. This wasn't included in my grand
scheme of life."

Michael is ten now and I'm not horrified by his needs and he's not repulsive to
me. It's just part of my routine in life. It doesn't mean that I don't ever feel discouraged and that I don't ever feel sad when I look at him and compare him to other little boys his age, but the sadness isn't as intense now as it was in the beginning. I
find so much more pleasure in just Mike and how he is right now. I just enjoy him

for the dumb little things he does; like the smile that he gives me out of the corner of his eyes sometimes.

There is still the burden of taking care of a child with severe disabilities. Michael was up this morning at 4:30 a.m. and would not go back to sleep, so Jim brought him into bed with us. I can't sleep when the both of them are in bed with me. So I got up and I went to the grocery store this morning at 5:00 a.m. It's not what a typical family would be experiencing at this time in their life, but it's our life and I think you learn to just grow to enjoy and appreciate even the little things he does. I really can't imagine Mike any other way.

Theories of Cognition

Jean Piaget is the most well-known theorist associated with the **cognitive-developmental approach.** Piaget was originally trained as a biologist and applied many biological principles and methods to the study of human development. Many of the terms he introduced to psychology were drawn directly from biology (Slavin, 1994). He based his earliest theories on careful observation of his own three children. His theory is appreciated because of the ease in adapting constructs of the model to the descriptive observations of infants and their learning processes.

Piaget's model identified four distinct stages of cognitive development he referred to as sensorimotor, preoperational, concrete operational, and formal operational (see Table 3–7). Each stage is characterized by the emergence of new abilities and the reorganization of a child's thinking about the world. Piaget held that development precedes learning and that the developmental sequence for cognitive skills is largely fixed (Slavin, 1994).

The **sensorimotor stage** of development integrates gross and fine motor development with the senses of sight and hearing. This stage (birth to age two) consists of simple learning governed by sensations. Primitive reflex activity progresses to repetitive activity and, later, to imitation. In the reflexive stage, repetitive action of the reflexes allows infants to eventually draw associations between their activity and a response. As an example, sucking (initially reflexive) on a nipple produces a milk flow and consequently leads to a feeling of fullness. Later, infants understand (have gained knowledge about) the relationship between the act of sucking and the outcome. Such experiences are used by the developing intellect as a foundation for advancing along a progressive course to the next stage.

This stage is the beginning of voluntary behavior. Deliberate activity begins when infants learn that certain behaviors can elicit specific responses. Accommodation begins with an infant incorporating and adapting actions with the recognition that certain activities produce a specific response. An infant may begin to cry upon hearing the voice of its mother, having learned from previous experience that the general response to crying is mother picking up and cuddling the infant. This is the beginning of the recognition of sequence and is an early experience with cause and effect.

It is later that both the quality and quantity of activity can be identified. Activities such as grasping progress to shaking (as with a rattle) that produces both movement and noise. An infant learns during this progression that degrees of shaking produce different qualities of sound. It is also during this time period that infants

Table 3–7 Piaget's stages of cognitive development.

Stage	Approximate Ages	Characteristics
Sensorimotor	Birth to 2 years	***Reflex activity*** (0–1 mo.): Reflexive movement in sucking/ swallowing etc. ***Primary circular reactions*** (1–4 mo.): repetition of movements becomes more coordinated toward end of period. ***Secondary circular reactions*** (4–8 mo.): Can focus on outside world; repetition of movements that produced interesting stimulation. ***Coordination of secondary schemes*** (8–12 mo.): generalize use of acquired actions to solve new problems. ***Tertiary circular reactions*** (12–18 mo.): Exploration and experimentation of environment with previously learned schemes. ***Invention of new means through mental combinations*** (18–24 mo.): Ability to comprehend that one thing can represent another thing.

*Sensorimotor stage adapted from Hanson, M. J. (1984). *Atypical infant development*. Austin, TX: PRO-ED.

Stage	Approximate Ages	Characteristics
Preoperational	18–24 months to 7 years	***Stored imagery or representational thought*** characterized by deferred imitation. ***Symbolic ability*** characterized by pretend play and language development. ***Egocentrism***—unable to view the world from another's perspective.
Concrete Operations	6 to 8 years to 12 years	***Decentration:*** focus on several attributes of object simultaneously; ***Reversability*** of mental operations; Use of *logic* to solve problems; ***Conservation:*** amount does not change with change in shape; ***Relational thinking:*** larger, shorter, etc.; Understands *hierarchical relationships* and that objects can belong to more than one class.
Formal Operations	12 years and up	Versatile flexible thinking process. Reasoning about hypothetical problems. Systematic searching for solutions to problems. **Abstract thinking.**

Source: Preoperational, concrete operations, and formal operations adapted from Mussen, D. H., Conger, J. J., Kagan, J., & Huston, A. C. (1990). *Child development and personality*. New York: Harper.

learn separateness from other objects in their environment and realize that their environment can be controlled by their own behavior. During this stage infants demonstrate imitation, object permanence, and attachment, which are memory-related behaviors (Cohen & Gelber, 1975).

Imitation, the repetition of a sound or activity or both actions and sounds of another individual, implies there has been storage of information within an infant's brain. In fact, studies by Butterworth and Hopkins (1988) determined that infants probably have the capacity at birth for imitation; observations of even very young infants showed they can imitate the facial expressions of caregivers. This initially may be a reflexive activity but through the progression of learning is broadened and becomes more sustained to include not only expressions but verbalization and motor activity.

Object permanence can be described as the demonstration of knowledge that an object exists even though it can no longer be seen. Infants between four months and eight months will search for an object if it is at least partially exposed. Infants between eight months and one year of age will seek out an object even if it cannot be visualized at all (Ault, 1977). For example, when a rattle is placed under a blanket, an eight- to twelve-month-old infant recognizes that the rattle still exists and will actively attempt to remove the blanket and expose it. This implies that short-term memory functions and is being demonstrated on the basis that knowledge exists even without the reality of observation.

Attachment is also a strong indicator of memory in infants. Fear of strangers appears to develop between six and eight months of age and involves recognition memory. This implies that infants draw from an experience-base that recognizes the comfort in familiarity and a lack of trust in the unfamiliar. Whether this is based on sight, smell, or sound remains unclear, though it is obvious that long-term memory is being demonstrated (Seamon, 1980).

The last stage of Piaget's sensorimotor development precedes transition to the next level of learning. This stage occurs between 18 months and 2 years of age. Increased gross motor skills and past experience with achievements in behaviors increase an infant's ability to interact with the environment. An increased understanding of object permanence accompanies the initiation of intellectual reasoning. Infants can recognize that an object has singular properties that are separate from the individual possessing the object. An example of this ability is the recognition that a ball will roll even if not necessarily pushed by a person having possession of the ball. Infants at this stage begin to actively engage in manipulating their environment by attempting to remove barriers that detain them from reaching a desired goal. Toward the end of this period expressive language skills are emerging that increase the ability of young children to successfully interact with their environment.

Piaget's **preoperational stage** in cognitive development (2–7 years) is characterized by rapid intellectual development. During this period of development children view the world only in direct relationship to themselves. They seem to be unable to view a situation from a perspective other than their own, and their thinking processes are generally concrete. They are increasingly able to use language to express ideas and use toys symbolically to replace objects in play (e.g., using a broom as a "horse"). Finally, children in the preoperational stage begin to understand the relationships between size, time, and weight, and their thought processes are intuitive, based on just knowing without reasoning.

Though the final stages of Piaget's theory extend beyond early childhood, they are introduced here to show the longitudinal nature of his observations. **Concrete operations** (7–11 years) is the stage of logic. It is during this period that children can classify, sort, and organize facts about their world to use in problem solving. They continue to solve problems concretely based on perception since most have not yet developed abstract thinking. In looking at the development of memory in children at this stage, the processes of selective attention, strategies used for retention, and the duration of memory must be explored. There is no doubt that age makes a difference in the abilities of children to both attend to learning and remember what has been learned before. During this process, children also develop the ability to build on past memories and use their current environment for new learning.

Formal operations (11 years to adulthood) is the stage of adaptability, flexibility, and abstraction. During this stage, adolescents can make hypotheses and use them to think in theoretical and philosophical terms. These individuals are aware of the contradictions in life, can analyze them practically, and can act upon the conclusions.

Long-term memory ability in children is variable. Use of selective attention processes and strategies improves with age. For example, increasing evidence suggests that an infant's visual habituation, or the ability to focus without distraction, is a useful predictor of cognitive abilities in children (Hood & Murray, 1996). There is no comparison between the ability of children and adults to process information and recall the same information over time. Flavell (1971) and Flavell, Friedricks, and Hoyt (1970) determined that maturation is necessary for the development of individual awareness about memory and the relationship of meaning to performance. However, Flavell et al. (1970) also determined that young children recognize their limitations. Through this determination children learn how to use available resources to succeed in the learning process, which in turn allows them to become more adaptive to their environment (see Table 3–8).

SOCIAL DEVELOPMENT

Social development governs the emergence of individual emotions and personality. Human beings are constantly involved in a dynamic relationship with other human beings and their environment. This involvement is essential for survival. People need social relationships in order to learn the rules for adapting to community norms that govern living within a society. Social rules, however, are not always constant across settings, culture, or time. Part of social development is learning how to seek the information necessary to learn current rules and recognizing the steps that may be necessary when old rules change and new rules are adopted.

Such rules are learned through interactions with adults and other children. Among other factors, heredity, culture, economics, and the community differentially influence social development. Developmental delays can occur when infants and young children are seriously deprived of early social nurturance by caregivers. Through nurturance, caregivers provide reliable stimulation to the senses, establishing a mechanism for the development of a trust relationship. This reciprocal confidence in primary caregivers is the first step toward being able to expand and develop other attachment relationships. In more dramatic cases, infants who do not experience "mothering" with some sort of consistency fail to gain weight regardless of appropriate caloric intake, are lethargic, and do not show a normal developmental progression. Some of these infants may even die if the emotional isolation occurs over a long enough period of time.

Infants initially require an individual caregiver to provide a relationship in which learning the social rules occurs. Providing the cues for what will be the personality development of an infant, this nurturing person (or persons) represents a major

Table 3–8 Milestones of cognitive development.

Age	Behavior
1 month	Responds to voices
	Inspects surroundings
4 months	Shows anticipatory excitement
	Plays with rattle
	Repeats new behaviors
	Plays with hands, feet
4–8 months	Repeats new behaviors
	Plays with hands, feet
	Finds partially hidden object
	Indicates continuation of play by repeating movement
	Touches adult to restart activity
	Reaches for second object
	Anticipates trajectory of object
	Imitates familiar action
	Finds hidden object
	Plays 2–3 minutes with single object
	Recognizes names of family
8–12 months	Imitates new action
	Responds to simple request with gestures (e.g., "point to _____")
	Uses "tool" to retrieve object
	Knows "no"
	Responds to simple verbal request
12–18 months	Enjoys looking at a book
	Shows understanding of category
	Places round, and later square, piece in puzzle
	Stacks toys
	Imitates "invisible" gesture
	Matches objects
	Points to named objects
	Brings objects from another room on request
	Identifies at least one body part
18–24 months	Points to pictures named
	Activates mechanical toys
	Plays with playdough and paints
	Matches object to pictures
	Sorts objects
	Understands personal pronouns and adjectives
	Matches sounds to photo of animals
24–36 months	Understands the concept of one
	Identifies clothing items for different occasions
	Engages in simple make believe play
	Matches shapes and colors
	Knows gender
	Identifies body parts with function
	Sorts shapes
	Completes three to four piece puzzle
	Begins to understand long and short

Table 3–8   Milestones of cognitive development (Continued).

Age	Behavior
3 years	Completes 10% of a task with little supervision
	Counts to three orally
	Draws a circle in imitation
	Knows most prepositions
	Locates big and little
	Sorts by size
4 years	Remains on task for 10 minutes with distractions present
	Knows more and less, many and few
	Matches coins
	Draws a line between two parallel lines
	Places three simple pictures in a sequence
	Locates objects that don't belong
	Determines three ways that objects are similar or different
5 years	Completes 50–75% of task
	Determines when a task is done
	Names letters and alphabet sounds
	Counts orally to 10
	Names penny, nickel, and dime
	Reads and writes numerals to three
	Relates today, tomorrow, and yesterday to days of the week
	Copies letters and numbers
	Prints own name
	Colors within lines
	Makes judgments in time and speed
	Draws a picture to illustrate three pieces of information
	Reads simple three letter words paired with pictures
	Reads numerals on a clock face
	Names days of the week
	Counts orally to 100
	Draws a person with three to six body parts

influence in early infancy. This influence frequently remains as one of the most significant relationships throughout the life span of a person.

Social skills appear at an early age with the ability of an infant to recognize family members. These skills continue to mature throughout one's life span as different social skills are necessary at different ages. For example, it is acceptable for toddlers to hug family members and acquaintances lavishly, but in adolescence, such displays of affection are usually viewed as immature. Normal social development is achieved when an individual exercises the rules of social conduct acceptable for a given age, gender, economic status, and culture.

Human beings are accustomed to receiving "rewards" for appropriate social behaviors. This is a learned response from early infancy when interactions between infants and significant caregivers include feedback of a physical nature that becomes associated with an activity generally perceived as pleasurable. As an example, an infant initially responds physically by body movement and then with vocalization upon hearing the caregiver approach, and this activity results in the infant being picked up and cuddled. Infants soon learn which of their behaviors initiate desired responses in caregivers and incorporate these activities into their interactions with other human beings.

Young children with disabilities are at risk for the development of distorted social skills. Because all developmental areas are interlinked, an impairment in one area can significantly alter the ability of an infant or child to initiate or respond to interactions in ways that build or maintain social relationships. Physical impairments, such as cerebral palsy, may prohibit postures or gestures that progress to social interactions. Caregivers need to learn to read the signals of infants or children with disabilities and use these signals in their interactions with the child. Teaching families relevant mechanisms to establish relationships with their disabled children is one of the initial responsibilities of an early childhood educator.

As in other areas of human development, research and understanding of social development are influenced by theory. For example, Erik Erikson (1968, 1980), a psychoanalytic theorist, posited that humans progress through eight discrete stages of psychosocial development. Each stage represents contrasting constructs that form a continuum. That is, at the beginning of each stage, a person's psychosocial behavior is negative or immature; by the end of each stage, desirable resolution has occurred. At each stage, individuals can be characterized as "working to resolve" the contrasting elements. For example, infants are working to resolve mistrust into trust of other humans.

Social Play

Play is the medium through which infants and toddlers acquire and execute social relationships. It is within play activities that people behave just to enjoy or amuse themselves. Yet play is a significant precursor for both physical and mental growth and for the acquisition of normal social maturation. Playing is a form of self-expression and is required in the normal dynamic of growth as a significant part of social development (see Table 3–9). McKimmey (1993) claimed that, in addition to

Esther Anna's typical supine position.

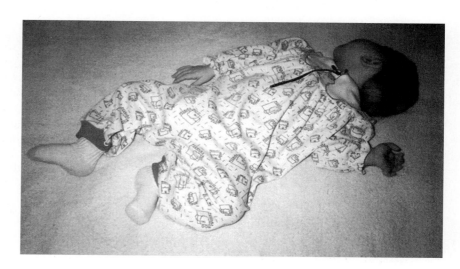

Table 3–9 Milestones of social-play development.

Age	Behavior
1–6 months	Smiles
	Regards face
	Establishes eye contact
	Laughs
	Discriminates strangers
6–12 months	Enjoys frolic play
	Lifts arms to mother
	Shows separation anxiety
	Cooperates in social games
	Tests parental reactions during bedtime
	Likes to be in constant sight and hearing of an adult
12–18 months	Difficult to discipline independent behavior
	Displays frequent tantrums
	Need and expects routines
	Shows a sense of humor
	Tends to be messy
	Enjoys being the center of attention
	Hugs and kisses parents
18–24 months	Shows jealousy at attention to others
	Desires control of others
	Enjoys solitary play
	Attempts to comfort others in distress
2 years	Distinguishes self as separate person
	Strongly possessive, dependent, clings, and whines
	Frustration tantrums peak
	Parallel play
	Values own property and uses the word mine
	Begins to obey and respect simple rules
	Takes pride in own achievements and resists help
3 years	Plays games with another person
	Takes turns in games 25–50% of the time
	Responds and makes verbal greetings
	Plays with one or two others
	Cooperates with others in group activities
4 years	Behaves according to the desires of others
	Volunteers
	Conforms to group decisions
	Takes turns in games 75% of the time
	Verbalizes feelings before physical aggression
5 years	Tries again after change or disappointment
	Leaves provoking situations
	Sacrifices immediate reward for delayed reward
	Accepts friendly teasing
	Comforts a playmate in distress
	Cooperates in group games with loose rules
	Protects other children and animals
	Offers help to others voluntarily

facilitating language, social play helps children learn sympathy, empathy, the difference between feelings and actions, ability to focus, and other social skills.

Play is universal and crosses all the physical and social boundaries of the world (Piers, 1972). Activities that are both fantasy and real constitute play. Play can be individual or collective, can involve a small or large group, and can occur anywhere and at any time. Play activities can be divided into three general groups: motor (physical exercise, action toys, etc.), intellectual (mental activities such as card and board games), and sensory (spectator activities, such as track meets, ball games, etc.). Very young children, between two and four years, generally prefer to engage in motor play activities.

Though some claim that neonates have little personality, observations of newborns reveal that they begin to engage in simple play within hours of birth. As mentioned earlier, reciprocal interactions involving facial expressions, eye movements, and sounds begin very early and serve as reinforcers to caregivers, who are drawn to this "playful" little being. Infant interactions with their environment generally remain within the context of relationships with their primary caregivers. Social-affective play may involve stretching or turning an infant's arms or legs, patting or stroking, and presenting bright objects or introducing sounds to elicit responses, such as cooing (Hughes, 1975; Johnson & Medinnus, 1974; Neisworth & Bagnato, 1987). An infant's typical response to social play is pleasure that is derived from nurturing relationships with familiar people. Thus, play provides a context for learning that emotional responses from caregivers can be provoked by smiling, cooing, and other such behaviors. In fact, some refer to play as "the work" of young children (MacDonald, 1989).

Once infants have begun to develop voluntary motor skills, play progresses to acquiring new skills. Manipulating objects repetitively brings repeated pleasure that commonly accompanies success. On the other hand, play can produce frustration when attempts to learn new skills are not immediately successful (Brooks-Gunn & Lewis, 1982). By the time infants reach one year of age, they are able to participate in imitative games. These may include repetitive games, such as pat-a-cake, itsy-bitsy spider, and peek-a-boo. Such games generally involve an infant and an adult, but they are setting the stage for the later initiation of play with other children.

Though these initial social relationships are necessary to the development of social skills, children generally learn many of the rules of social conduct from other children. Peers are less tolerant of deviations from an established standard than are adults who can reason beyond what is obvious. Social play in the preschool years can be categorized into five sequential stages: solitary play, spectator play, parallel play, associative play, and cooperative play (Cass, 1971). The rate of progress at which an individual child transcends these stages is dependent upon both the opportunities a child has for interactions and the integrity of the social contacts that are available.

In some cases, children with greater economic stability may have the advantage because more social contacts are arranged to provide the opportunities for engaging play experiences and may allow for a more rapid progression. For example, in established supervised play groups, parents have the means to take the initiative in providing toys and games that promote peer interactions.

*Mother and child engage
in social-affective play.*

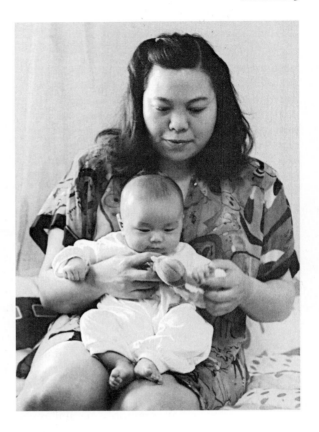

Solitary play involves both isolation and independence. This play experience can involve an individual child within the same physical area as a group of children. Children involved in solitary play are involved with their own activities and their own group of toys. They enjoy the physical presence of other children but do not speak to other children, nor do they attempt to decrease the physical distance between play areas. They also show no interest in the activities of other children that differ from their own activities. Young children will also engage in solitary play in their own homes while with a caregiver. Though engaging in independent play, a child may frequently move the activity to the vicinity of the caregiver.

Spectator play is also frequently referred to as onlooker play. This occurs when a young child observes the play activities of other children but makes no attempt to enter in the activity. This play may involve conversation about the nature of the activity between the observer and child involved.

Parallel play also involves independent play between children in a group. Children play with toys that are like those of the children around them but of their own choosing and in their own fashion. This play involves children playing beside each other but not with each other. Toddlers frequently engage in parallel play, which is consistent with their world view that objects have properties independent of involvement. Additionally, toddlers' language development is just beginning to allow for verbal expression in social context.

Toddlers frequently engage in parallel play.

Associative play occurs between the ages of 3 to 4 years. Individual children will play with other children, engaging in similar or even identical activities. Without adult facilitation, associative play generally lacks organization. Though toys may be shared, each member acts without regard for the group wishes since no group goal has been established. When an individual child initiates an activity, the entire group will typically follow this lead. During this stage, there may be occasional attempts by individual children to control both group behavior and group membership. Four-year-olds begin to establish strong preferences for associates and may begin to have a "best friend." This "friend" may change frequently during the course of a play experience, depending upon the direction of the play. Hence, children have learned initial strategies to gain power over other children; yet these young children are incapable of wielding power wisely. For example, it is typical of children of this age to be bossy and selfish, to begin to taunt and name-call, and to boast and bend the truth a little.

Cooperative play occurs when activities are organized. Children involved in cooperative play are engaged in a goal-directed activity that has been planned by the group to accomplish some defined end. Formal games become important during this stage, and the end goal frequently involves some competition. Group members have designated roles that are generally both assigned and directed by one or two accepted "leaders" of the group. Even at this age, children develop a great sense of either belonging or not belonging to cooperative play groups. During this final stage of play development, there may be gender splits with children seeking membership in same-sex groups.

Play enhances skill development in both motor activities and emotional development. Active play develops muscle control, cognitive development, and socialization. Through play, children learn about their physical world and its relationship to themselves. Intellectual stimulation is provided through manipulation of shapes and work with texture, color, and size.

Perhaps most importantly, play is the most effective medium through which children develop language (McKimmey, 1993). As early as 18 months, toddlers begin to pretend, demonstrating an awareness of symbolic thought—a prerequisite of language. Children can experiment with abstract thought through fantasy and fabrication within the acceptable context of creativity without being diverted by conformity to a norm of the society. Play becomes less spontaneous and more structured with age.

Because children are not as tolerant of violations of codes within their own play group, externally initiated codes of behavior for the group facilitate learning of acceptable social behaviors. Hence, children who are culturally different adjust more easily to new social situations when dramatic play is a part of the curriculum (McKimmey, 1993). Truth, honesty, fair play, self-control, and leadership skills are learned within the group and provide an important mechanism for teaching the standards of the society and personal accountability for individual actions.

Case Study

THE DIARY OF ESTHER ANNA BERKE: MONTH 5

March 16–30: No major changes occurred during this time. Esther continued to eat well and gain weight but had multiple seizures each day. Most seizures appeared to be painless, but one kind must hurt because it makes her cry. The doctor altered her medication again, now her daily dosage is 0.8 ml Depakine, 1 g Sabril, and 0.33 mg Rivotril. We have also started her on 250 mg of Vit. B6 (pyridoxine) each day. Some people have obtained dramatic relief from seizures with this vitamin. We haven't seen any effect yet, so we will increase the dose and see if that helps.

April 1–15: Esther weighed 6.5 kg on her 5-month birthday, for a total gain of 2 kg since she was born and 1.3 kg in the last month alone. She is now 66 cm long. This is at the 50th percentile for weight and the 80th percentile for length for her age, so she is getting bigger! We took her off Depakine, it made her very sleepy and didn't seem to help control the seizures. We also boosted her Vit. B6 to 275 mg each day.

Self-Help Development

SELF-HELP SKILLS

Self-help skills include independent feeding, dressing, toileting, and personal responsibility (see Table 3–10). The term **adaptive skills** also refers to the same set of behaviors and either term may be used by various assessment tools and curriculum packages. The acquisition of skills that enable children

Table 3–10 Milestone of self-help.

Age	Behavior
1–4 months	Coordinates sucking, swallowing, and breathing
	Recognizes bottle
4–8 months	Swallows strained or pureed foods
	Feeds self a cracker
	Holds own bottle
8–12 months	Drinks from held cup
	Finger feeds
	Sleeps 10–12 hours
	Cooperates in dressing
12–18 months	Cooperates in washing and drying
	Undoes bows and snaps
	Has regular bowel movements
	Indicates when wet or soiled
	Cooperates in dressing
18–24 months	Sits on "potty chair"
	Unzips, zips, removes unlaced shoes
	Washes and dries hands partially
	Helps with simple household tasks
	Food preferences apparent
24–36 months	Delays sleeping by demanding things
	Understands and stays away from common dangers
	Undresses with assistance
	Washes hands and brushes teeth
	Uses toilet w/assistance, daytime control
4 years old	Takes responsibility for toileting
	Serves self and helps set table
	Dresses with supervision
	Uses spoon and fork well
	Uses toilet regularly without asking
	Puts comb and brush in hair
	Puts shoes on correct feet
	Knows front from back
5 years old	Drinks from water fountain, serves self and carries tray
	Carries liquid in open container without spilling
	Wipes self after toileting
	Uses comb/brush, washes face and ears in bath, and dries with towel
	Zips up front opening of clothing
	Dresses and undresses functionally without being told
6 years old	Cuts and spreads with knife, cuts with knife and fork
	Independently washes and dries hands after toileting
	Bathes, showers, and "cleans up" independently
	Washes own hair
	Selects and uses clean and protective clothing
	Ties shoes
	Turns clothing right side out
	Uses proper brushing strokes (toothbrush)

Source: Adapted from Hanson, M.J., & Hanliner, M.F. (1984). Behavioral competencies and outcomes: The effects of disorders. In M.J. Hanson (Ed.), *A typical infant development* (pp. 109–142). Austin, TX: PRO-ED.

*Child self-
feeding.*

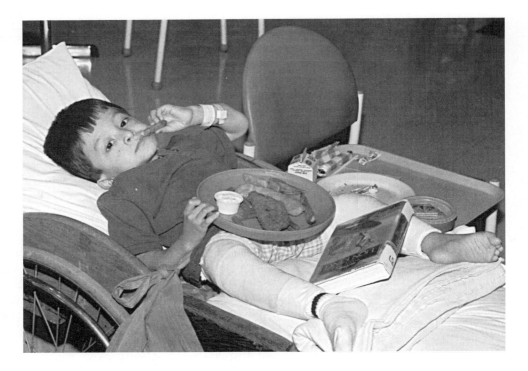

*Child self-
feeding.*

to interact independently with their environment is linked closely to both motor development and cognitive skill development. For example, children will not independently use the toilet until they:

1. Have gained sufficient muscle control to stay dry for an hour or two at a time
2. Can move themselves to the toilet
3. Are cognitively aware of the "signs" of urgency to void
4. Know what action to take to avoid an "accident"

Historically, planning for instruction of self-help skills has followed a strict developmental model, but more recent research illustrates that skills once thought to be prerequisites could be skipped for children with significant developmental disabilities. While recognizing this, the following description of self-help skills is based upon knowledge of typical developmental patterns.

Independent Eating and Drinking Skills

As in all other areas of development, a neonate eats and drinks reflexively only, though parents might swear there is some intent involved when a hungry infant wakes parents throughout the night and keeps them further vigilant during the day with demands to be fed. This aspect of child care can be exhausting for parents, as infants demand food five to eight times a day, requiring approximately 30 minutes time for each feeding.

Though the sucking reflex is present at birth, it is not until infants are four months old that they suck voluntarily with enthusiasm and vigor. Young infants consume exclusively liquid diets of either breast milk or formula for the first four to six months. At about this time, infants begin to take some responsibility for eating by holding their bottle. Simultaneously, solid pureed foods will be tolerated, though infants may remain very passive, not offering to close their lips around the spoon or to push food from the front of the tongue toward the back of their mouths.

A dramatic transition of independence takes place at about eight months of age. Infants, who now have well-developed fine motor skills, will drink from cups with help, will feed themselves finger foods (crackers, etc.), and may refuse to drink from their bottles. Very grown up now, these infants should be on the same eating schedule as adults though, like adults, enjoying between meal snacks.

By age two, toddlers are often independent eaters and drinkers. This does not mean that they can do so with grace. Using a spoon, toddlers can feed themselves. However, this level of independence is often paired with independent decision making. It is not uncommon for toddlers to maintain a narrow range of food preferences or to go through stages where they eat very little.

Three-year-olds eat well with a spoon and may be able to use a fork to stab foods. These youngsters now display some very sophisticated skills at the table, serving themselves drinks or portions of food. Additionally, vegetables become a food to avoid. Independence in the use of utensils is achieved by four years of age. Four-year-olds also enjoy helping prepare meals and are able to make simple meals, such as cereal and toast, independently by age five.

Dressing Skills

The first indication that infants are thinking about dressing skills is when they begin to tug at their feet and incidentally pull off socks or shoes. At about the same time, approximately nine months, significant progress in dressing is made when infants assist with dressing by lifting their arms to remove or put on a shirt, stepping into a pair of suspended pants or shoes, and holding still during diapering. Since undressing is easier, toddlers take off jackets, shoes, socks, and unbuttoned pants at about 18 months. Though they will try earlier, children have little success in dressing even in articles of clothing that are easy to put on (pants, loose shoes) until they are about two years of age. A two-year-old may learn to fasten large buttons and small front buttons by three years of age. Zippers and buckles are more difficult fine motor tasks that may be mastered at age four or five. Usually by the time children are four, they will be able to dress by themselves, though it is not until age five that most dressing errors (putting clothes on backwards or inside out) are recognized and self-corrected. Complex dressing tasks such as tying shoes and fixing stuck zippers emerge at five years of age but may not be mastered until age six or seven.

Toileting Skills

Toilet training begins at birth, as muscle control is gradually gained. A very young infant is seldom dry, dribbling small quantities of urine almost constantly. Gradually, muscle control permits infants to sustain first brief, and then longer, periods of dryness. By eight months, infants begin to stay dry for reasonable lengths of time and may communicate their recognition of "wetness" by pulling at their diapers. Parents should not, however, consider toilet training until at least 18 months or later if a child does not stay dry for an hour or more.

One index of sufficient bladder control is whether toddlers remain dry during their naps. Bowel control is more easily achieved than bladder control, as infants begin to have routine bowel movements one or two times a day by eight months of age. Training for bowel control can begin at 12 months and may be accomplished as early as 18 months. This process is often not completed until age three, though it is typically more easily accomplished by girls than boys. By 5 years of age, children can be expected to independently care for all toileting needs, including wiping and washing hands afterwards.

Personal Responsibility

Children can be expected from an early age to begin to take on responsibility for themselves. Toddlers, for example, can follow directions to pick up their toys, though this behavior might not become habitual until some years later. Two-year-olds will put their coats away regularly when the routine is expected. By three years of age, children can take on a variety of responsibilities, such as wiping up spills, helping to clear the table, and placing dirty clothes in a hamper.

Parents should begin brushing an infant's teeth as soon as the primary teeth begin erupting. As infants gain sufficient fine motor control, parents can ask infants to attempt to imitate tooth brushing. Though cleanliness is not the goal, as caregivers follow after children and brush with precision, children learn valuable patterns of routine daily care. Bathing and washing are similar responsibilities that can be transferred to young children. By age four, children should be able to bathe themselves and brush their teeth with acceptable proficiency. While 4-year-olds are unpredictable, 5-year-olds are generally happy to assist in the completion of jobs around the home. Given chores, children tend to be cooperative and reliable.

CONCLUSION

In the past, cognitive, linguistic, and social behaviors have been largely explained by guesses about what goes on underneath one's skin, rather than by knowledge of actual neurological or endrocrinological processes. Now, we know that the brain, in particular, is at peak capacity for learning during the very period of interest in this text. In addition to nutrition, nurturance and secure relationships with an adult(s) stimulate brain growth, which is in turn related to children's social and cognitive development. With increased understanding of the importance of these early years, policy makers must be compelled to invest in bringing educational services to all families of very young children (Lewis, 1997). Comprehensive early childhood education should help to level the field for families across economic lines.

Based on this new knowledge, early childhood educators can help families to select and design programs that more reliably influence children's acquisition of desirable behaviors. Concomitantly, professionals will need to learn more about family systems, so that we are able to respond sensitively and effectively to diverse characteristics. This issue is infinitely more complex and intractable than the mind-boggling changes in technology that we are likely to encounter in the coming decades.

Technology may influence children's development in a more direct way. Increasingly, human activities are interwoven with computers. Computers have and will continue to take over traditional routines of daily life. It is possible that such basic activities as reading, teaching, and shopping will be replaced by computers. These changes will not only influence what children need to learn, but can also influence if and how they will learn. That is, if children's early learning experiences vary significantly because of interactions with technology, their neural pathways will become hardwired differently than today's youth, who have had different kinds of experiences.

There is little question that the coming decades will bring changes in our culture, both friendly and unfriendly, that will influence the capacity of children to progress from one milestone to the next. In fact, changes may be so great that the dimensions of behavior that are now considered indexes of healthy growth will be obsolete. New expectations could evolve from changes in technology and medicine or from environmental catastrophe. Changes might also occur in how we view children, the study of children and the subsequent education of infants and preschoolers. For example, Cannella (1997) claims that the entire knowledge base of the 20th century is fraught with myopic research and practice. She proposes "deconstructing" early childhood educational thought and practice in order to create a more just and presumably more effective model of education.

Perhaps in the future, more will be expected, perhaps less, but surely different priorities will be selected for adaptation and survival in a world that is changing too

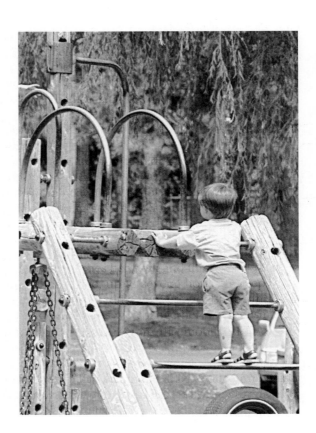

fast to describe. Will some parents continue along the current trend of expecting infants to accomplish more and more at earlier ages? Will they want children to walk at 6 months or to play the violin at 11 months? Or, will more and more parents adopt the current philosophy of "developmental appropriateness" and expect less and less of children—favoring an emphasis on "natural" evolution of learning? Perhaps the coming generation of children will struggle so hard to adapt to or survive increases in poverty, threats to safety, and diminished educational resources that such questions will seem esoteric.

STUDY GUIDE QUESTIONS

1. In what areas of development must educators have knowledge?
2. Briefly explain development during the embryonic stage.
3. Describe development of the fetus throughout the fetal stage.
4. What are the requirements for a viable fetus?
5. Why do different children grow at different rates?
6. Would you expect the same pattern of growth across all children? Explain.
7. List and explain the three universal developmental patterns of growth governing motor development.
8. Why is continual monitoring of physical growth important in the early years of life?
9. What is the function of the cardiovascular system and its relationship to the respiratory system?
10. Explain the function of the renal system.
11. Why is the gastrointestinal system important to physical growth?
12. Describe the relationship between myelinization and neurological development.
13. How is bone maturation related to growth?
14. Why is the integumentary system important—especially in early infancy?
15. How is physical growth measured?
16. Describe a "normal" newborn in the first days of life.
17. What would be a "normal" infancy growth pattern?
18. According to MacDonald (1992), what does emotional warmth or affection provide for humans? What may result if a child does not experience such affection?
19. In what way is child development sequential and universal?
20. Explain the remarkable plasticity of the human brain.
21. What is the theory of peak periods of learning?
22. Briefly explain how the following influence a child's development: family configuration and lifestyle, and child care.
23. Several factors influence bonding. Name three of these.
24. There are several educational factors believed to influence a child's growth. List five of these factors.
25. Why is it important to evaluate a child's development according to relevant culture, rather than according to dominant culture?
26. What are the correlational findings between television exposure and children's behavior?

27. Describe the sequence and age milestones of hip control.
28. Explain the progression of development from reflex to reaching to grasping.
29. What are the five principles of language development?
30. Explain the three aspects of language considered when discussing form.
31. Briefly outline the general development of phonological skills and sentence structure.
32. What is a morpheme? How do we measure the sophistication of language?
33. Describe the receptive language abilities of a child around the following ages: 1 year, 18 months, 2 years, 3 years, 6 years.
34. As children begin to develop expressive language, actions and objects dominate their early vocabulary. Explain why this may be so.
35. Describe a child's language use at the following ages: neonate; 12 months; 2 years; 3 years; and 6 years.
36. Define cognition.
37. Describe the four phases of Piaget's model of cognitive development.
38. Define accommodation.
39. What is the importance of imitation in cognitive development?
40. Define attachment.
41. Name three factors that may influence social development.
42. Identify and discuss the five stages of play.
43. How do children learn social behavior through play?
44. List the traditional skills that fall into the domain of self-help.
45. Describe a child's eating and drinking repertoire at the following ages: 4–6 months, 8 months, 2 years, 3 years, 4 years, 5 years.
46. Describe a child's dressing skills at the following ages: 9 months, 18 months, 2 years, 4 years, 5+ years.
47. When should training of bowel and bladder begin? Complete?

REFERENCES

Allen, E. A., & Marotz, L. (1989). *Developmental profiles: Birth to six*. Albany: Delmar.

Andrick, G. R., & Tager-Flusberg, H. (1986). The acquisition of colour terms. *Journal of Child Language, 13,* 119–

Ault, R. (1977). *Children's cognitive development*. New York: Oxford University Press.

Baecher, C. M. (1983). *Children's consumerism: Implications for education*. Paper presented at the Bush Center in Child Development and Social Policy, Yale University, New Haven, CT.

Beck, F., Moffatt, D., & Lloyd, J. (1973). *Human embryology and genetics*. Oxford: Blackwell Scientific Publications.

Bedore, L. M., & Leonard, L. B. (1998). Specific language impairment and grammatical morphology: A discriminant function analysis. *Journal of Speech, Language, and Hearing Research, 41,* 1185–1193.

Beentjes, J. W., & VanderVoort, T. H. (1988). Television's impact on children's reading skills. *Reading Research Quarterly, 23,* 389–413.

Bertoncini, J., Bijelac-Babic, B., Jusczyk., P. W., Kennedy, L. J., & Mahler, J. (1988). An investigation of young infants' perceptual representations of speech sounds. *Journal of Experimental Psychology, 117,* 21–33.

Bigge, J. (1991). *Teaching individuals with physical and multiple disabilities* (3rd ed.). Upper Saddle River, NJ: Merrill/Prentice Hall.

Braine, M. C. (1963). The ontogeny of Enghlish phrase structures: The first phrase. *Language, 39,* 1–13.

Brooks-Gunn, J., & Lewis, M. (1982). Affective exchanges between normal and handicapped infants and their mothers. In T. M. Field & A. Fogel (Eds.), *Emotion and early interaction* (pp. 161–188). Hillsdale, NJ: Earlbaum.

Buchholz, E. S. (Sept., 1997). Even infants need their solitude. *Brown University Child & Adolescent Behavior Letter, 13*(9), 1–3.

Bussey, K., & Bandura, A. (1992). Self-regulatory mechanisms governing gender development. *Child Development, 63,* 1236–1250.

Butterworth, G., & Hopkins, B. (1988). Hand-mouth coordination in the newborn baby. *British Journal of Developmental Psychology, 6,* 303–314.

Butterworth, G., & Morissette, P. (1996). Onset of pointing and the acquisition of language in infancy. *Journal of Reproductive and Infant Psychology, 14,* 219–232.

Cannella, G. S. (1997). *Deconstructing early childhood education: Social justice & revolution.* New York, NY: Lang.

Cass, J. (1971). *Helping children grow through play.* New York: Schocken Books.

Chaudhary, N., & Suparna, N. (1991). Early language learning in a multilingual environment. *Early Child Development and Care, 76,* 135–143.

Cohen, L., & Gelber, R. (1975). Infant visual memory. In L. Cohen & P. Salapatek (Eds.), *Infant perception: From sensation to cognition, Vol I.* New York: Academic.

Coll, C., G., Buckner, J. C., Brooks, M. G., & Wei, L. F. (1998). The developmental status and adaptive behavior of homeless and low-income housed infants and toddlers. *American Journal of Public Health, 88,* 1371–1373.

Dahn, L., & James, L. (1972). Newborn temperature and calculated heat loss in the delivery room. *Pediatrics, 49,* 504–506.

Davis, B. E., Moon, R. Y., Sachs, H. C., & Ottolini, M. C. (1998). Effects of sleep position on infant motor development. *Pediatrics, 102,* 1135–1141.

Erikson, E. H. (1963). *Childhood and society* (2nd ed.). New York: W. W. Norton.

Erikson, E. H. (1968). *Identity, youth and crisis.* New York: Norton.

Erikson, E. H. (1980). *Identity and the life cycle* (2nd ed.). New York: Norton.

Festschrift, C. (July, 1994). Primitive reflexes: Their contribution to the early detection of cerebral palsy. *Clinical Pediatrics, 33*(7), pp. 388–398.

Finn, M. (1977). *The politics of nutrition education.* Unpublished dissertation, Ohio State University, Columbus.

Flavell, J. (1971). First discussant's comments: What is memory development the development of? *Human Development, 14,* 272–278.

Flavell, J., Friedricks, A., & Hoyt, J. (1970). Developmental changes in memorization processes. *Cognitive Psychology, 1,* 324–340.

Gabbard, C., & Hart, S. (1995). A note on trichotomous classification of handedness and fine-motor performance in children. *Journal of Genetic Psychology, 156,* 97–105.

Gopnik, A., & Meltzoff, A. N. (1992). Categorization and naming: Basic-level sorting in eighteen-month-olds and its relation to language. *Child Development, 63,* 1091–1103.

Guo, G. (1998). The time of the influences of cumulative poverty on children's cognitive abilty and achievement. *Social Forces, 77,* 257–282.

Hart, B., & Risley, T. R. (1995). *Meaningful differences in everyday experiences in young American children.* Toronto: Paul H. Brookes.

Henggeler, S. W., Cohen, R., Edwards, J. J., Summerville, M. B., & Ray, G. E. (1991). Family stress as a link in the association between television viewing and achievement. *Child Study Journal, 21,* 1–10.

Hoffman, L. W. (1989). Effects of maternal employment in the two-parent family. *American Psychologist, 44,* 283–292.

Hood, B. M., & Murray, L. (1996). Habituation changes in early infancy: Longitudinal measures from birth to 6 months. *Journal of Reproductive & Infant Psychology, 14,* 177–186.

Hughes, J. (1975). *Synopsis of pediatrics* (4th ed.). St. Louis: C.V. Mosby Co.

Johnson, R., & Medinnus, G. (1974). *Child psychology: Behavior and development* (3rd ed.). New York: Wiley & Sons.

Kennedy, J. H. (1992). Relationship of maternal beliefs and childrearing strategies to social competence in preschool children. *Child Study Journal, 22,* 39–60.

Klink, M., & Klink, W. (1990). The influence of father caretaker speech on early language development: A case study. *Early Child Development and Care, 62,* 7–22.

Langman, J. (1975). *Medical embryology. Human development—normal and abnormal* (3rd ed.). Baltimore: Williams & Wilkins.

Lester, B. M., & Brazelton, T. B. (1982). Cross-cultural assessment of neonatal behavior. In D. A. Wagner & H. W. Stevenson (Eds.), *Cultural perspectives on child development.* San Francisco: Freeman.

Lewis, A. C. (1997). Learning our lessons about early learning. *Phi Delta Kappan, 78,* 591–593.

MacArthur, F. (1990). Miscommunication, language development and enculturation in L. P. Hartley's *"The Go Between." Style, 24* (1), 103–112.

MacDonald, K. (1992). Warmth as a developmental construct: An evolutionary analysis. *Child Development, 63,* 753–773.

McDonald, J. D. (1989). *Becoming partners with children: From play to conversation.* San Antonio, TX: Special Press.

McCormick, S., & Schiefelbusch, R. L. (1990). *Early language development.* Upper Saddle River, NJ: Merrill/Prentice Hall.

McKimmey, M. A. (1993). Child's play is serious business. *Children Today, 22*(2), 14–15.

McLaughlin, T. F., & Vacha, E. F. (1992). The social, structural, family, school, and personal characteristics of at-risk students: Policy recommendations for school personnel. *The Journal of Education, 174*(3), 9–25.

Monahan, S. C., Buchanan, C. M., Maccoby, E. E., & Dornbusch, S. M. (1993). Sibling differences in divorced families. *Child Development, 64,* 152–168.

Moore, K. L. (1983). Before we are born: Basic embryology and birth defects (2nd ed.). Philadelphia: W. B. Saunders.

Morgan, J. L. (November, 1996). Knowing isn't saying: Early receptive language abilities. *Brown University Child & Adolescent Letter, 12*(11), pp. 1–4.

Neisworth, T., & Bagnato, S. (1987). *The young exceptional child: Early development and education*. New York: Macmillan.

Nielson, A. C. (1988). *Nielson report on television*. Northbrook, IL: Author.

Orlin, M. N., & Effgen, S. K. (1997). Effect of otitis media with effusion on gross motor ability in preschool-aged children: Preliminary findings. *Pediatrics, 99,* 334–338.

Oviatt, S. L. (1982). Inferring what words mean: Early development in infant's comprehension of common object names. *Child Development, 53,* 274–277.

Paul, R., & Alforde, S. (1993). Grammatical morpheme acquisition in 4-year-olds with normal, impaired, and late-developing language. *Journal of Speech and Hearing Research, 36,* 1271–1276.

Pearl, D., Bouthilet, L., & Lazar, S. J. (Eds.). (1982). Report by the Surgeon General on Television Violence. *Television and behavior: Ten years of scientific progress and implications for the eighties*. Washington, DC: Government Printing Office.

Piers, M. W. (Ed.) (1972). *Play and development: A symposium*. New York: W.W. Norton.

Reed, V. A. (1994). *An introduction to children with language disorders*. New York: Macmillan.

Rheingold, H. L., & Cook, K. V. (1975). The content of boys' and girls' rooms as an index of parents' behavior. *Child Development, 46,* 459–463.

Robertson, S. B., & Weismer, S. E. (1997). The influence of peer models on the play scripts of children with specific langauge impairments. J*ournal of Speech, Language & Hearing Research, 40,* 49–62.

Schacter, F., & Straye, A. (1982). Adults talk and children's language development. In S. Moore & C. Cooper (Eds.), *The young child: Reviews of research*. Washington, DC: National Association for Young Children.

Seamon, J. G. (1980). Memory and cognition: An introduction. New York: Oxford University Press.

Shatz, M., & Gelman, R. (1973). The development of communication skills: Modifications in the speech of young children as a function of the listener. *Monographs of the Society for Research in Child Development, 38* (Serial No. 152).

Siegel, E. (1982). A critical examination of studies of parent-infant bonding. In M. H. Klaus & M. O. Robertson (Eds.), *Birth, interaction, and attachment: A round table*. Skillman, NJ: Johnson & Johnson.

Skeels, H. M. (1942). A study of the differential stimulation on mentally retarded children: A follow-up report. American *Journal of Mental Deficiency, 46,* 340–350.

Skeels, H. M. (1966). Adult status of children with contrasting life experience: A follow-up study. *Monographs of the Society for Research in Child Development, 31* (3).

Slavin, R. E. (1994). *Educational psychology theory and practice*. (4th ed.). Boston: Allyn & Bacon.

Spitz, R. V., & Tallal, P. (1997). Look who's talking: A prospective study of familial transmission of language impairments. *Journal of Speech, Language & Hearing Research, 40,* 990–1002.

Thomas, A., & Chess, S. (1981). The role of temperament in the contributions of individuals to their own development. In R. M. Lerner & N. A. Busch-Rossnagel (Eds.), *Individuals as producers of their development: A life-span perspective*. New York: Academic.

Vandell, D. L., & Ramanan, J. (1992). Effects of early and recent maternal employment on children from low income families. *Child Development, 63,* 938–949.

Winner, E. (1988). *The point of words*. Cambridge, MA: Harvard University Press.

Wood, D. (1992). Culture, language, and child development. *Language and Education, 6*(2), 123–140.

Zigler, E. F., & Stevenson, M. F. (1993). *Children in a changing world: Developmental and social issues* (2nd ed.). Pacific Grove, CA: Brooks/Cole.

DEVELOPMENT AND RISKING CONDITIONS: PRENATAL, NATAL, AND POSTNATAL

The physical connections between mothers and their infants that exist before pregnancy, during pregnancy, during the labor and delivery process, and during the immediate period after birth can affect the later physical and developmental health of children. **Prenatal** refers to the period before conception through gestation. **Natal** conditions affect the mother or the infant during the labor and delivery process, and **postnatal** conditions affect the mother or the infant after delivery and during the first 30 days after birth. A fourth term, **perinatal,** is commonly used to designate a period that actually overlaps all of the preceding periods. Technically, the perinatal period begins at the 29th week of gestation and ends between the first and fourth weeks after birth. At any time during any of these periods, problems may arise that can compromise the physical or cognitive growth of the infant. While knowing the cause or timing of injury seldom guides early childhood professionals as they design intervention plans, this knowledge can be useful to families in understanding their children.

PRENATAL GROWTH AND DEVELOPMENT

Prematurity is when a developing fetus is born prior to the 37th week of gestation. It is important to distinguish between premature infants and those who are of low birth weight, small for gestational age, or have intrauterine growth retardation. Though babies from all these categories are at-risk due to their size and other factors, premature infants have a unique set of risk factors associated with immature physical development corresponding to the gestational age of the baby.

Viability is the gestational age when a fetus can survive outside of the womb with or without medical or technological intervention. With current medical practice, a fetus is considered **viable** at a gestational age greater than 23 weeks beyond conception. In fact, the survival of premature infants is directly related to advances in neonatal medical technology. With the improved survival rates of premature infants, it has become possible to identify a normal progression of preterm growth and development. Consequently, researchers have also investigated interventions aimed at improving the quality of survival and assisting families in meeting the needs of their medically fragile infants.

While infants born between the 33rd and 36th week of gestation have increased risk compared to full-term infants, those born at less than 32 weeks are at extreme risk for significant developmental delays. The corresponding fragility of underdeveloped organ systems, particularly the brain, affects both physical growth and neurological development. Indexes used to project fetal physical growth are gestational age, birth weight, and medical conditions. Maternal and fetal conditions (e.g., maternal high blood pressure or physical anomalies such as a heart defect) can either independently or collectively influence fetal growth. In spite of preexisting conditions, appropriate interventions can alleviate or control high-risk medical conditions, while permitting infants to progress along a corrected growth curve established specifically for infants born prematurely. Furthermore, potential delays can be mediated by strong maternal language interactions, a positive home environment, and early intervention programs (Apgar, 1997).

EFFECTS OF PREMATURITY ON BODY SYSTEMS

Fetuses who will eventually be born prematurely proceed along the same predetermined pattern as that of full-term fetuses until birth itself interrupts this normal course of development. Though this interruption does not change the normal developmental sequence, it does have an impact on the schedule over which development occurs. That is, premature infants are born with underdeveloped organs, which are not sufficiently capable of meeting the demands of independent life without the support of the mother's womb. The following is an analysis of the particular organ systems that are compromised when infants are born prematurely. Note that all systems, while described in a discrete manner, are essentially linked, with insult to one or more systems affecting the development of other systems.

RESPIRATORY SYSTEM

Surfactant is a chemical agent needed for independent breathing that is not produced in sufficient quantity until the 32nd to 33rd week of pregnancy. This chemical prevents the lungs from sticking together during expiration. Without surfactant the lung surfaces stick together, causing the small airsacs to collapse. The tiny airsacs, called **alveoli,** permit normal exchange of oxygen and carbon dioxide. Collapsed alveoli cause oxygen deficiency, leading to lung disease and, if serious enough, death. Respiratory function can be further compromised by an immature nervous system. Since breathing is governed by nerve impulses, weak or absent stimulation (as is the case in prematurity) results in inconsistent patterns of breathing. Consequently, it is common for preterm infants to experience **apnea,** in which an infant stops breathing for periods of seconds or minutes.

CARDIOVASCULAR SYSTEM

Blood vessels in premature infants are unusually fragile and break easily. This fragility increases the risk of bleeding into the brain (**intracranial bleeding** or stroke) or other vital organs. A second condition associated with an immature cardiovascular system is **anemia,** since underdeveloped bone marrow is unprepared for the body's demand to produce red blood cells. These conditions place additional stress on the young heart, which is poorly equipped to meet the body's demands for oxygen and nutrients.

NEUROLOGICAL SYSTEM

The younger the fetus, the greater will be the probable impact of delivery on a developing neurological system. In particular, the relationship between cardiovascular proficiency and neurological functioning is critical. That is, the more premature the infant, the more likely it is that the blood/oxygen supply to the brain will be compromised. Hence, the brain, which itself is immature and consequently vulnerable to any interruption in the vital oxygen and nutrient supply, can incur permanent damage to its cells. Furthermore, the immature neurological system is incapable of sending or receiving messages efficiently. Thus, other systems in the body, all of which are dependent on the nerve network for adequate functioning, have decreased ability to respond to the body's demands.

RENAL AND GASTROINTESTINAL SYSTEMS

In addition to being affected by their own immaturity, the kidneys and gastrointestinal systems are seriously affected by compromised cardiovascular and neurological systems. The kidneys are unable to maintain normal sodium and calcium levels or to sufficiently filter waste. The gastrointestinal tract is capable of absorbing nutrients, but the large bowel is too short, so the passage of food is too rapid to permit sufficient absorption, increasing the risk of malnutrition. Interestingly, when the cardiovascular system is weakened (as in prematurity) infants' bodies tend to protect the organs that are the most important to survival. Accordingly, the gastrointestinal system is not considered critical to an infant's preservation, so blood flow is detoured away from the intestine to provide increased blood to the brain, heart, and kidneys.

MUSCULAR SYSTEM

Studies have documented the developmental evolution of tone, deep tendon reflexes, pathologic reflexes, and primitive reflexes for infants born between 24- and 32-weeks gestation. Ironically, while motor development in full-term infants follows a pattern of upper extremities to lower extremities (cephalo-caudal) and from the center of the body to the extremities (proximal to distal), the preterm developmental progression of tone and reflexes emerges in the opposite directions (Allen & Capute, 1990). **Micropremature infants** (24–26 weeks of gestation) show generalized **flexion** of the lower extremities at birth. These parameters give providers the opportunity to determine whether these infants are following a progressive course typical of gestational age or whether they are experiencing delays.

SKELETAL SYSTEM

Poor nutrition contributes to bone growth deficiency, which is necessary for linear growth. Most importantly, calcium loss in the newly forming bone structures (rickets) will delay both growth and maturation. A premature infant's inability to adequately coordinate sucking and swallowing, along with gastrointestinal inefficiency can cause nutrient deficiency. Height is one of the most critical measures in determining the progression of a normal growth curve in premature infants. In spite of adequate weight gain, infants who fail to grow in height (one should expect 0.5 cm to 1 cm of linear growth per week) deviate from the normal expectation.

INTEGUMENTARY SYSTEM

The skin in premature infants is extremely fragile. For a very premature infant, the skin surface provides no protection from heat or water loss and no barrier against infection. These infants are also at risk for the development of yeast infections on the skin surface. The infection can then progress into the blood stream through breaks in the fragile surface. External heat sources (i.e., isolettes), filtered air, and good hygiene practices are necessary to provide both warmth and protection for these infants.

INDEXES OF GROWTH IN PREMATURE INFANTS

As with term infants, weight is an unpredictable measure of both gestational age and maturity. Premature infants who have been under physiological stress during pregnancy will exhibit signs of lower birth weight, along with less-advanced organ function. Head circumference, as a measure of brain growth, is used to make growth predictions. **Corrected gestational age** (gestational age versus chronological age) is used to determine if appropriate growth and development is occurring. This measure is considered to be accurate at least through the first year of life. Prematurity affects growth and development, sometimes only during early life, and sometimes will alter the course of an individual's entire life. Recognition of the normal progression provides the opportunity for planning interventions and aligning resources that will promote development to the maximum potential of the affected infant.

MATERNAL CONDITIONS AFFECTING PREGNANCY OUTCOMES

PRECONCEPTUAL MATERNAL CONDITIONS

Conditions exist in some women that will affect their own health as well as the development and overall health of a fetus if pregnancy occurs. Actively educating women about these conditions and encouraging them to seek health care and counseling before becoming pregnant is a practice that early educators can adopt. Some of these conditions are diabetes, hypertension, heart disease, drug and alcohol addiction, obesity, age, and some genetic conditions (e.g., cystic fibrosis and PKU). Attention to risk factors and provision of necessary interventions significantly reduce the risks to both the mother and infant.

Socioeconomic standing is an important factor in the incidence of premature delivery. This includes race, culture, shelter, food, money, and social support structures. Poverty influences both living conditions and physical conditions that increase the incidence of prematurity. Studies show that young, single mothers with few support networks have both an increased incidence of unplanned pregnancy and a higher incidence of premature delivery and low birth weight infants (Report of Consensus Conferences, 1987). Women who are physically or sexually abused are at greater risk for low birth weight and preterm delivery (Curry, 1998). Limited economic opportunities frequently lead to poor prenatal care, poor diet, and increased complications of pregnancy (e.g., pregnancy-induced hypertension), all of which may lead to premature delivery. Consideration of socioeconomic issues prior to becoming pregnant, with an exploration of available resources, decreases the incidence of complications of pregnancy.

PRENATAL MATERNAL CONDITIONS

A **term pregnancy** averages approximately 280 days (10 lunar months or 40 weeks) and terminates in the delivery of a viable fetus that is capable of independent life. Delivery prior to the 37th week of pregnancy is considered to be premature. The number of times a woman has been pregnant **(gravida)** and the number of live infants that she has delivered at greater than 20-weeks gestation **(parity)** is important information in giving prenatal care. That is, the more times a woman has been pregnant, the greater risk for problems associated with the pregnancy than for those who have been pregnant fewer times. These problems may include faster labors with quick and uncontrolled deliveries, failure of muscle contraction of the uterus with significant bleeding, and malpositioned placentas. Previous premature delivery is related to the increased probability of a subsequent pregnancy ending in premature delivery and earlier in the gestation than the previous delivery.

Age is an important factor that can be related to the increased incidence of both premature delivery and appearance of physical and genetic abnormalities in the infant. Women younger than 20 and women over 40 have an increased risk of spontaneous abortion, toxemia of pregnancy, premature delivery, and congenital abnormalities in the fetus. These mothers frequently have other risk factors present that increase the possibility of pregnancy complications, for example, socioeconomic factors in young women and health problems (preexisting hypertension, diabetes) in older women.

Nutrition is one of the most significant factors associated with maternal/infant well-being. Poor nutritional habits along with variations in such preexisting conditions as obesity or malnutrition will severely affect a fetus both during gestation and following birth (Tiedje, Kingry, &, Stommel, 1992). Prematurity and low birth weight are determined in the first trimester, suggesting that fetal growth may be dependent on maternal nutrition before conception (Preconception, 1999). Maternal behaviors that promote malnutrition (e.g., anorexia) result in decreased stores of nutrients for the developing fetus. These infants may be born with **growth retardation** (weight is lower than the 10th percentile and chest circumference is lower than the 3rd percentile for gestational age) and may have brain injury due to diminished oxygen and nutrition supply caused by a poorly functioning placenta (Peleg, Kennedy, & Hunter, 1998).

Maternal obesity (20% over the standard weight) can also produce both maternal and fetal problems. Infants born to obese mothers may be large, thereby increasing problems with delivery. Maternal obesity may also produce **hypoglycemia** (low blood sugar) in infants, leading to serious neonatal problems. Conversely, a large percentage of women fail to have adequate weight gain; those who gain less than 21 pounds during pregnancy increase the likelihood of fetal death by 1.5 times (Tiedje et al., 1992). It appears that women who engage in regular heavy exercise throughout pregnancy actually reduce the risk of preterm delivery (Soares & Beard, 1998).

Maternal infections can play a significant role in fetal outcomes. Both bacterial and viral infections cause a multitude of disabilities for the fetus and neonate. Meningitis, cytomegalovirus, rubella, toxoplasmosis, and many other maternal infections may have a devastating affect on a newborn. Many of these can be avoided by prenatal education and attention to behaviors that place a mother at risk for contacting an infection.

Chronic diseases in mothers may have an effect on a fetus. These conditions include kidney disease, cancer, thyroid disease, Rh sensitization, hypertension, cardiovascular disease, diabetes, genetic disorders (e.g., PKU), respiratory disease (e.g., cystic fibrosis), neurologic disorders (e.g., multiple sclerosis), infectious disease (e.g., hepatitis), psychiatric disorders, and mental retardation. Some of these conditions have a known effect on developing fetuses, and through appropriate prevention measures, risk to the fetus can be decreased.

Utilization of prenatal care in which a woman's pregnancy is monitored by a health care professional is statistically the most important factor in decreasing problems associated with any of the maternal conditions. For example, early and consistent prenatal care decreases the incidence of prematurity associated with risk factors (Tiedje et al., 1992). At the same time, lack of prenatal care is one of the most reliable predictors that problems will occur. Many of the conditions discussed on the following pages could be identified through good prenatal care, thereby reducing risks to mother and infant.

COMMON CONDITIONS OF GESTATION

The following conditions are frequently seen during gestation. They lead both to the need for advanced intervention for the pregnant woman and also account for the greatest majority of premature deliveries. Education of pregnant women, through prenatal care, to look for signs of complications can decrease the incidence of problems to the fetus. Table 4–1 summarizes these conditions.

PLACENTA PREVIA

Placenta previa is a condition in which the placenta implants in the bottom segment of the uterus instead of the top segment. A normal site of implantation of a fertilized egg is in the upper half of the uterus. When a previa occurs, the placenta implants over the opening of the cervix. Many pregnant women who have a placenta previa will have several episodes of bleeding through the second and third trimesters of the pregnancy. Several factors may initiate the onset of sudden and excessive bleeding. These include contractions of the uterus, intercourse, and

Table 4–1 Conditions of gestation.

Condition	Characteristics
Placenta previa	The placenta implants in the bottom segment of the uterus instead of the top segment. Requires bedrest until the fetal gestation is sufficient for independent breathing after birth.
Abruptio placenta	The placenta separates from the wall of the uterus prematurely causing decreased availability of oxygen and nutrition, decreased blood flow to the fetal brain with decreased tissue perfusion, and even fetal death.
Toxemia of pregnancy	Causes an elevation in maternal blood pressure, decrease in urine output, and decreased ability of the kidney to conserve protein and salts, which contributes to swelling of the extremities that may advance to the liver and brain. Reduces blood flow to the uterus and the placenta then begins to shrink in size causing fetal growth retardation.
Gestational diabetes	Increased blood sugar that is initiated by the pregnancy. Infants may have complex heart defects, be very large size for age, require increased gestation for lung maturation to occur and experience an increased rate of respiratory distress syndrome.
Rh sensitization	Occurs when a pregnant female who has a negative blood Rh is exposed to positive blood Rh from her fetus. Thereafter, the mother carries an activated antibody against Rh positive, which will attack any fetus with positive blood Rh. The result of fetal exposure to the maternal antibody is profound anemia requiring blood transfusions.
Premature rupture of the membranes	The water sack that surrounds the fetus breaks prior to the 37th week of pregnancy often initiating premature delivery. Risk of infection is high.
Premature labor	Onset of regular uterine contractions that produce cervical dilatation prior to the 37th week of gestation. Attempts are made to control the progression of labor until transfer to a facility with a critical care nursery can be made.

excessive fetal activity. This bleeding is generally not painful but can result in a large blood loss over a very short period of time and places an unborn infant at high risk for death.

Ultrasound is often conducted after the woman has had an episode of bleeding and then seeks care to determine the cause. This will diagnose the condition. Women with known previa are placed in the hospital and on bed rest until the length of gestation is sufficient for the fetus to be capable of independent breathing after birth. This is to assure that immediate care is available for both the woman and the unborn infant should sudden, excessive bleeding occur from the placenta. The babies are then delivered by cesarean section, and those women who have received consistent care generally are able to carry their infants close to term before delivery is necessary.

ABRUPTIO PLACENTA

Abruptio placenta is a condition in which the placenta separates from the uterine wall before delivery of the fetus. This can occur at anytime during gestation and to varying degrees of separation. The impact on both the mother and the fetus can be significant. Partial separation of the placenta will result in vaginal bleeding, which may be small or large, and is generally associated with abdominal pain in the mother. The fetus may be affected by a decreased blood flow and may respond by either a drop or an increase of the heart rate. This change in blood flow can have a significant impact on the long-term outcome for the infant. Effects include decreased availability of oxygen and nutrition, decreased blood flow to the brain, and even death. Repeated abruptions will result in growth retardation along with any of the fetal factors of an acute abruption.

Acute and total abruptio placenta will result in fetal death. When the placenta fully separates from the uterine wall, the fetus loses the supply of oxygen and nutrients that are essential to sustain life. This condition also has significant maternal effects. Many women who have a total abruption have an increased risk of bleeding from many systems, and may even result in the death of the mother.

TOXEMIA OF PREGNANCY (PREGNANCY-INDUCED HYPERTENSION)

A major problem associated with premature delivery is referred to as **toxemia of pregnancy.** This condition presents a variety of symptoms that produce variable effects in individual pregnancies. The exact cause of the cluster of symptoms and why they occur during pregnancy remains unknown, though factors that increase an individual's vulnerability to toxemia have been identified.

As many as 10% of all pregnancies have some evidence of toxemia of pregnancy. This ratio may increase to as high as 25% in mothers who are diabetic. Maternal death from this condition may be as high as 2%, with fetal death rates being approximately 20% (Besinger, Repke, & Ferguson, 1989). Toxemia of pregnancy is present more frequently in very young women and during a woman's first pregnancy. Most of the fetal effects are a result of significant prematurity that stems from the urgency to deliver the baby to prevent maternal death and to save the infant.

Symptoms of toxemia generally include high maternal blood pressure and kidney malfunction. The kidney disorder contributes to swelling in the extremities that may advance to the liver and brain. Blood vessels constrict causing increased blood pressure and constriction of the blood vessels that provide blood flow to the uterus. The placenta then begins to shrink in size causing fetal growth retardation. However, this process does not happen quickly; rather, it occurs over an extended period of time.

MATERNAL DIABETES

Diabetes in a pregnant woman can be present prior to the pregnancy or come about during gestation. Infants of diabetic mothers, regardless of the onset, are at significantly higher risk for natal and postnatal complications.

Gestational diabetes is a condition of increased blood sugar that is initiated by the pregnancy. It is usually diagnosed during the second trimester through laboratory analysis, Generally controlled through diet, diabetes may occasionally require the use of insulin. Though the condition disappears after delivery, it does appear to be a predictive factor for the development of age-onset diabetes later in the mother's life and increases the risk of maternal diabetes during later pregnancies. Risk factors for congenital diabetes are the same as those that are predictive of later onset diabetes. These factors include advanced age, family history of diabetes, non-white ethnicity, obesity, and cigarette smoking (Hughes, Agarwal, & Thomas, 1997; Solomon, 1997).

Preexisting diabetes in a woman, who then becomes pregnant, raises many issues for maternal care during gestation. The physiological changes that occur in the human body during gestation have a significant effect on the ability of a woman to maintain normal control of her diabetic condition. Nutritional factors and insulin needs are inconsistent during the course of the gestation and will, in turn, affect fetal well-being. Precise control of diabetes decreases the risk to a fetus, but this requires a multidisciplinary approach to the pregnancy and a mother who is committed to providing every opportunity to her fetus for normal growth and development.

Infants of diabetic mothers have an increased risk for congenital abnormalities. The most frequently occurring anomalies are complex heart defects. Babies may also be born very large for their gestational age, which increases the possibility for birth trauma. Many of these infants also require a longer gestation for lung maturation to occur and, without this advantage, have an increased rate of respiratory distress syndrome. These infants will also have significant problems with blood sugar control and tend to have a decreased ability in the first few days of life to coordinate their sucking, breathing, and swallowing mechanisms which make feeding consistent.

RH SENSITIZATION

Each human being has a blood grouping that has been inherited from her or his parents. They, in turn, pass the genetic framework to their children. There are situations that arise in which the antigen of the mother and that of the unborn fetus are not compatible. When this occurs, the mother produces antibodies against the fetal blood.

Rh is a blood group or collection of molecules on the red blood cells. Blood groups used to identify a person's blood compatibility include A, B, and O, each of which can either be Rh factor positive or negative. Either the Rh factor is present (Rh+) or absent (Rh−) in an individual's blood system.

Rh sensitization occurs when a female who has a negative blood Rh is exposed to positive blood Rh. This may occur during a blood transfusion or as a result of a pregnancy when the partner has a positive Rh blood type. Sensitization may occur with any pregnancy, even those that end in miscarriage at a very early gestation. The *positive Rh antigen* crosses the placenta from the fetus, and the maternal response to this foreign protein is to produce antibodies against the perceived invasion. This is a normal response of a healthy immune system.

The initial pregnancy in which Rh-positive and Rh-negative blood are involved is not affected, but subsequent pregnancies, in which the mother now has an activated antibody against Rh-positive, will be affected if the fetus has a positive blood Rh. The result of fetal exposure to the maternal antibody is profound fetal anemia. If not diagnosed and treated in utero, the fetus may die or have problems caused by the anemia.

Progress in medical technology and public awareness has significantly decreased both the occurrence of Rh sensitization and the effects of the process on the development of an affected infant. Treatment consists of giving blood transfusions in utero or exchanging the fetal blood to prevent the breakdown of the normal blood cells. Either of these interventions support the affected fetus until the gestation has progressed to viability or the ability of the fetus to breathe outside the uterus has been determined. Severely affected infants may also require exchange transfusions because of the high levels of *bilirubin* that build up in the bloodstream as a result of the breaking apart of the affected red blood cells. Transfusion is done to prevent the effects of high bilirubin concentrations on normal brain development. Severe mental retardation and/or cerebral palsy may occur with very high levels of bilirubin. Prevention of sensitization is now possible with RhoGAM. This vaccine destroys any positive cells that enter the maternal circulation, preventing the mother from producing antibodies that will eventually destroy the blood cells of the fetus.

PREMATURE RUPTURE OF THE MEMBRANES

Premature rupture of the membranes is a common initiating factor in premature delivery. Normally, the water sack that surrounds the fetus breaks prior to the 37th week of pregnancy. This may either initiate the onset of uterine contractions and subsequent delivery or place the woman and fetus at risk for infection with the loss of the protective barrier around the infant.

The reasons for premature rupture may vary. Though most instances are not explained, an infant who has acquired an infection is thought to initiate the process in many cases. Even with a ruptured sack, the placenta and infant continue to produce fluid, and the woman continues to leak fluid throughout gestation, until delivery occurs. Any bacteria (or virus) that may be present in the vaginal tract of the mother can find their way into the uterus and come into contact with the fetus. Careful observation of the mother and infant for signs of distress or infection can delay an otherwise high risk/premature delivery. Infants who experience a premature loss of the sack are at risk of interruption of normal physical growth related to the alterations in the environment. Ironically however, rupture of the membranes tends to speed up the process of maturation of the lungs in a fetus. An infant's self-protective mechanisms sense impending delivery and actually accelerate the maturation process.

PREMATURE LABOR

Regular uterine contractions that produce dilatation of the cervix signal the onset of labor. When contractions and dilatation occur prior to the 37th week of gestation, it is defined as premature labor. While considerable variation exists across sources, it is estimated that as many as 10% of all births have episodes of **premature labor.** This rate increases when women are at risk due to aforementioned socioeconomic factors and inadequate prenatal care. That is, women receiving care tend to be educated regarding warning symptoms of labor and are more likely to seek help before labor has progressed to the point of making premature delivery unavoidable. Many women will have regular uterine contractions prior to delivery. This may result from uterine weight, fetal movement, stress, diet, exercise, and many other factors. However, unless there is cervical change and movement of the cervix from a backward to a forward position, premature labor may not be occurring.

In many cases, premature labor can be controlled with medication and bed rest. Careful monitoring of maternal conditions and the status of the fetus are critical in any situation in which an attempt is being made to stop labor. If the labor is progressing and delivery is unavoidable, current technology allows for acceleration of fetal lung maturity with medication (within 36–48 hours), which allows a woman undergoing premature labor to deliver her infant with decreased risk.

Case Study	**THE DIARY OF ESTHER ANNA BERKE: MONTH 6**

April 16–30:   The neurologist continues to tinker with Esther's medications, she is currently taking Rivotril, Vitamin B6, Sabril, and Lamictal every day. Her seizures have decreased somewhat in frequency but increased somewhat in intensity.

May 1–15:   No major changes during this time, we are busy planning Sarah's trip to the United States in June to have Esther examined by several specialists.

Esther Anna seven months old.

Table 4–2 Maternal/infant natal conditions.

Condition	Characteristics
Dysfunction of labor and/or delivery	Ineffective labor pattern, too few uterine contractions, or maternal conditions that place the mother at risk for a normal labor process. These may be malposition of the fetus, large size for gestation, and congenital defects that prevent proper positioning.
Prolapsed or entangled cord	The length of time the flow is obstructed can be a critical factor in determining whether the fetus will asphyxiate in utero and die, or whether blood flow will be resumed at a point where neurological damage may occur but the fetus will survive the insult.
Hypoxic–ischemic brain injury	Hypoxia, decreased oxygen levels, and ischemia, death of the cells and tissue due to decreased blood flow, can occur together or separately. Such neurological damage generally includes severe mental retardation, intractable seizures, and spasticity.
Meconium aspiration syndrome	The fetus either gasps before delivery (usually from asphyxia) or meconium is aspirated into the trachea and airways with the first breath of the infant whose mouth and nose have not been cleared of the amniotic fluid that contains meconium particles. This initiates a state of pneumonia.

MATERNAL/INFANT NATAL COMPLICATIONS

Labor is precarious for infants who are expected to pass from the dependent world of dark, warm liquid to a world that is bright, cold, and dry and requires an independent ability to both breathe and excrete waste products. The physiological adaptations are easier when the labor and delivery process do not place additional stress on infants.

Labor is the process in which a mother and fetus work together toward the goal of delivery of the infant. The uterus provides the contractions that produce pressure on the emerging part of the fetus to dilate the cervix. Dilatation is necessary to provide a passage for the infant from the protective environment of the uterus into the world. Labor requires that both the mother and infant participate to successfully complete the process.

Factors may occur that influence the ability of either the mother or the fetus to be effective during the labor and delivery process (see Table 4–2). Maternal factors may include an ineffective labor pattern that:

1. does not produce the uterine pressure necessary for dilatation to occur
2. has too few uterine contractions
3. is accompanied by high-risk maternal conditions, such as toxemia of pregnancy

All place the mother at risk during the labor process. Fetal conditions may also influence the course of the labor and delivery. The normal position for delivery is head down. It is possible for a fetus to present in an abnormal position. The fetus may be **breech** (bottom first), transverse (sideways), large for gestation, or have congenital defects that prevent proper positioning to occur. The health status of the fetus also influences its ability to withstand labor.

Dysfunctional labor may be improved with the use of medication to increase both the number and strength of uterine contractions. However, if medication is not effective, then delivery by cesarean section may be necessary. Medication must be closely monitored to make sure that the fetus can withstand the increased uterine pressure. In large-for-age infants, their shoulders may fail to pass below the mother's pubic bone, which can cause cord compression that, in turn, may lead to asphyxia. Assessment of the maternal pelvis (by examination) and the estimated fetal size (by ultrasound), prior to the onset of labor, may prevent a shoulder dislocation. Anticipation of this occurrence may lead health care providers to surgically deliver the infant.

PROLAPSED CORD/ENTANGLED CORD

The *umbilical cord* is the lifeline by which a fetus is connected to the placenta, which is connected to the mother. This structure contains one large blood vessel and two smaller vessels that carry oxygenated blood and nutrients from the fetal side of the placenta to the fetus. The two small vessels return blood with fetal waste products to the fetal side of the placenta, where an exchange takes place across a membrane to the maternal side of the placenta. The cord vessels are protected by a thick membranous cover and a thick jelly-like substance on the inside.

The length of any umbilical cord varies. Length of the cord may be a factor in the likelihood of becoming entangled. In many normal vaginal deliveries the umbilical cord is wrapped around the neck of an infant or, occasionally, around other areas of the body, such as the chest or abdomen. Monitoring equipment used during labor can give care providers information that an umbilical cord may be entangled with an infant's body parts.

If an infant is wrapped up in its own cord, there may be slight decreases in the fetal heart rate during a contraction. Occasionally a fetus may become entangled in the cord during gestation, decreasing blood flow through the cord. The length of time the flow is obstructed can be a critical factor in determining whether the fetus will asphyxiate in utero and die or whether blood flow will be resumed to permit the fetus to survive the insult. Even though neurologic damage is likely, infants are born without any indications of an in utero insult but display obvious and profound symptoms of neurological deficits after delivery. Symptoms of damage may include seizures, abnormalities in muscle tone, and the absence of primitive reflexes.

Abnormal positioning of a fetus may cause the umbilical cord to fall from the uterine cavity (*prolapsed cord*) after the mother's water has broken. Since, the normal position of a fetus for a vaginal delivery should be head down, when the fetus is breech or transverse, space is available for a cord prolapse.

Prolapse of the umbilical cord places a fetus at risk for loss of blood flow due to cord obstruction. The presenting part of the fetus can come to rest on the cord and blood flow either significantly decreases or stops completely. The fetus then experiences asphyxia, and death occurs rapidly. If prolapse occurs, the emerging part of the fetus must be manually held off the cord, allowing for blood flow, and delivery by cesarean section is done immediately. Infants who are delivered rapidly can expect normal recovery, but if a prolapsed cord occurs outside of the health care setting, even if the infant survives, significant neurological damage is likely.

NEONATAL CONDITIONS

HYPOXIC–ISCHEMIC PERINATAL BRAIN INJURY

Hypoxia (decreased oxygen levels) and **ischemia** (death of the cells and tissue due to decreased blood flow) can occur together or separately. This condition accounts for the largest group of infants with severe nonprogressive neurological deficits that happen prior to and during delivery. Permanent changes in the neurological structure of the brain matter follow such injuries. Such neurological damage generally includes severe mental retardation, intractable seizures, and spasticity.

Hypoxic–ischemic brain injury can occur during gestation or during the labor and delivery process. Any situation that causes a decrease in blood flow or oxygen supply or an increased level of carbon dioxide can result in the condition. The cycle is repetitive, unless intervention (change of position or supplemental oxygen) increases the blood flow again. Infants do not have the reserves of larger children and adults, and smaller decreases in central blood pressure may severely impact blood flow to the brain.

Infants who have experienced either prenatal or natal asphyxia syndrome may have problems with independent respiration and hyperactive responses to the environment. Seizures are often observed between 12 and 72 hours after birth. The earlier the onset of the seizures, the greater the insult on the neurological status of the infant. As many as 80% of these infants experience severe mental retardation, and 50% exhibit spastic quadriplegia (McCormick, 1989).

Brain damage from asphyxia can be determined by diagnostic imaging methods such as the CT Scan or MRI (described in Chapter 5). Death of the brain neurons results in the transformation of brain matter into fibrous tissue. This injured brain matter is ultimately replaced in many areas by cysts that can also be located by scanning methods. Other affected areas of the brain can be identified through the seizure patterns that emerge. Certain seizure patterns are known to evolve from specific brain areas.

MECONIUM ASPIRATION SYNDROME

Meconium is the accumulation of fetal waste products that collect in the bowel during gestation. The rectum should not relax until after the infant is delivered, but when a fetus experiences asphyxia or when an infant is overdue, the muscles of the rectum relax and meconium is passed by the infant into the amniotic fluid. This results in a green staining of the fluid, which is generally obvious with rupture of the bag of waters. Even mild asphyxia can initiate the passage of meconium and set the infant up for possible aspiration syndrome. This material contains fetal waste products as well as fetal sludge (skin, hair, cells, etc.), which can be swallowed or absorbed through the intestinal wall.

Meconium aspiration syndrome occurs when a fetus either gasps before delivery (usually from **asphyxia**) or when meconium is aspirated into the trachea and airways with the first breath of the infant whose mouth and nose have not been cleared of the amniotic fluid that contains meconium particles. This aspiration can lead to pneumonia, which may be mild to severe. Multiple physical problems can result from aspiration syndrome, affecting the respiratory system, the cardiovascular system, and the neurological system. Permanent neurological dysfunction is common.

POSTNATAL CONDITIONS

Many of the postnatal complications that infants encounter are a result of prematurity. In addition, infants affected with congenital abnormalities, congenital infections, acute infections, birth trauma, and many other factors will be found within the neonatal intensive care units in this country. The following discussion addresses only a select few of the conditions that affect these infants. Those discussed frequently result in outcomes that place these infants and young children in early intervention programs. Table 4–3 summarizes these postnatal complications.

PREMATURITY

Prematurity is the largest issue affecting pregnancy outcomes in our society. It is also the single most common cause of sickness and death worldwide. An estimated 8–10% of all births are premature, accounting for 75% of all neonatal deaths and 50% of all handicaps. Infants delivered before the 37th week of gestation also account for

Table 4–3   Postnatal conditions.

Condition	Characteristics
Prematurity	Infants delivered before the 37th week of gestation. Those infants who are both premature and growth retarded (or small for gestational age) have two factors that impact their prognoses.
Intraventricular hemorrhages	Bleeding which may cause brain damage.
Apnea of prematurity	Pauses in breathing due to position or to neurological lapses.
Respiratory distress syndrome	Difficulty breathing caused by the absence of, or a deficiency in the amount of, surfactant present in the lungs of the infant.
Bronchopulmonary dysplasia	Chronic lung disease of infancy.
Patent ductus arteriosus	A cardiac defect that frequently occurs in the very low birth weight and extremely low birth weight infant. This condition can result in increased respiratory distress.
Hypothermia	Low body core temperature which places the infant at risk for other physical problems such as increased respiratory distress, low blood sugar, and possibly for intraventricular hemorrhage.
Retinopathy of prematurity	Retinas of premature infants subjected to excess oxygen show an overgrowth of connective tissue surrounding blood vessels. This overgrowth ultimately damages vision.
Anemia	Where there is a deficiency in the number of red blood cells available to the infant.
Poor nutrition	Difficulty with sucking, swallowing, and breathing coordination, and feeding apnea requires either continuous tube feeding of mild or intermittent tube feedings.
Periventricular leukomalacia	A condition of brain development and function that is related to cerebral blood flow both prior to delivery and during the neonatal period most frequently in premature infants, most often seen, and most profound symptom is spastic diplegia.
Failure to thrive	Inability of the infant to maintain or gain weight sufficient for healthy growth and development.

A. A 25-week preterm infant on day two of life weighing 800 g (1 lb 12 oz). B. Same infant at 4 weeks weighing 1200 g (2 lb 12 oz). C. Infant at 8 weeks weighing 1900 g (4 lb 3 oz) and ready to go home.

a major portion of the health care dollars being spent within the United States. For example, the average hospital stay for infants at 24-weeks gestation is four months, with an average cost of $294,849 per survivor (Walling, 1998).

Gestational age is a critical factor in determining what problems a particular premature infant may encounter. Pregnancy dating is not a perfect science and lacks the ability to determine precisely in which week of gestation a particular infant may be. Technology currently makes it possible for survival of infants as young as 23-weeks gestation, but these infants have the potential of a multitude of problems that affect them at birth, within the first weeks of life and may follow them into their future. The risk of death or permanent disability increases significantly as birth weight declines. Follow-up of survivors who weigh less than 700 g indicates that the chances of severe neurological abnormalities is 100% (Stephens, Richardson, & Lewin, 1997).

Birth weight, along with gestation, is a more useful indicator of outcome than gestational age alone. Infants who are both premature and growth retarded (or small for gestational age) have two factors that threaten their prognoses. Infants born at less than 2800 g (6 lb 3 oz) at 38-weeks gestation are considered **low birth weight** (to varying degrees). These infants may experience many of the problems commonly associated with premature infants: respiratory distress, apnea (breathing pauses), poor temperature control, and problems with nutrition. Though survival rates for this group are as high as 95%, developmental delays are a concern (Paz et al., 1995). Such delays may result in lowered cognitive ability and poor school achievement (Apgar, 1997).

Infants delivered at less than 1500 g (3 lb 5 oz) are considered **very low birth weight.** Such infants may be both premature and/or growth retarded. These infants are at-risk for respiratory distress, bleeding within the brain and surrounding structures, infections, apnea, nutritional problems, and potential visual defects. Infants

CLOSE-UP

THE DIRECT COST OF LOW BIRTH WEIGHT

Medical and technological advances have significantly increased the survival rates of low birth rate infants, including a doubling of the survival rates of extremely low birth weight infants between 1978 and 1995 (those weighing less than 2 lbs). Because of this success, the overall number of low birth weight infants has increased, causing a dramatic impact on the cost of health care. As with other technological advances, changes in the treatment of these very tiny humans have been made in the absence of ethical debate and practical considerations. Yet, Lewit, Baker, Corman, and Sinono (1995) provide compelling evidence for a social debate over current practices.

Lewit and colleagues studied the immediate and long-term direct cost of low birth weight infants as compared to infants born of normal birth weight, all born in 1988. To establish a point of reference, low birth weight infants comprised about 7% of all infants born during 1988. Yet, the medical care of these small infants consumed 35% of all health care costs for 1-year-olds. Infants who were extremely premature and experienced respiratory distress syndrome incurred almost three times the medical expenses as other low birth weight babies.

During the preschool years the medical costs, though significantly lower for all children, continued to be almost three times higher for those born low birth weight. However, even though children born low birth weight did delay entry into kindergarten later than other children, the overall use of resources was not substantially greater than that of other children.

When these children reach school age, the medical costs were more than four times higher than that of other children. In addition, these children used substantially greater resources in school. Those born less than 2500 g were 50% more likely to be enrolled in special education, with each child in special education costing approximately 50% higher than children born of normal birth weight. In addition, more children born low birth weight repeat grades and are therefore more likely to drop out of school, have lower earnings, commit more crimes, and require more social services.

To put this dilemma into context, Lewit and colleagues indicated that the overall cost of low birth weight was about one third the direct cost of smoking and two thirds the direct cost of alcohol abuse; the cost in 1988 for low birth weight was several times the direct cost of AIDS among all persons. These figures should provide a context for discussion of ways to reduce the rate of premature birth and low birth weight. Moreover, in the face of economic limits, it may be time to consider medical/ethical policy regarding the extraordinary measures taken to preserve the lives of micropremature infants. According to the authors, "the evidence suggests that residual problems experienced by adults who were born low birth weight may be large in term of increased morbidity, lost earnings, and increased demand for health and social services."

Lewit, E. M., Baker, L. S., Corman, H., & Sinono, P. H. (Spring, 1995). The direct cost of low birth weight. *The Future of Children, 5*(1), 1–23.

who are considered growth retarded, within this context, may be at risk for developmental delays due to a history of extended insufficiency of the placenta to supply adequate nutrition to the fetus during the pregnancy. As compared to infants born at the 50th percentile, those born weighing less than 1500 g are 70–100 times more likely to die in infancy (the rate is 5–30 times higher for infants who weigh less than 1500 g) (Peleg et al., 1998).

Infants delivered at less than 750 g (1 lb 10 oz) are considered **extremely low birth weight.** Survival rates for these very fragile infants have steadily increased over the last 10 years, and now, the expectation for survival is around 70%. These infants have the highest risk factors for poor or delayed outcomes. Of the survivors, greater than 45% require some special services that includes special education (Hack et al., 1994). Those infants who escape intraventricular bleeding, chronic lung disease, and environmental factors such as poverty and child abuse have a good chance of surviving with normal cognitive and motor development (Stephens et al., 1997).

Extremely low birth weight infants frequently have some degree of intraventricular bleeding, which may cause brain damage. The effects of the bleeding are variable with deficits including a wide range of developmental delays. Visual and hearing deficits are common with these very immature infants. Retinopathy of prematurity (ROP) is a common occurrence caused by the need for long-term oxygen therapy (for apnea of prematurity) and capillary fragility, which may lead to bleeding in the capillaries that supply the retina of the eye. Hearing loss is common and is related to drug therapy necessary for survival and the neurological impact from bleeding or decreased oxygen.

Infection is a frequent complication for the extremely low birth weight infant. The immune system does not become functional for several months after birth, leaving the infant at significant risk for any environmental or human bacteria or virus. Many of the common care needs of the infant, such as intravenous feedings and airway support, place the infant at risk for the development of an infection.

Nutrition is a major complicating factor with extremely low birth weight infants. The gastrointestinal tract requires the initiation of oral feedings before maturation can occur. The ability of these infants to tolerate oral feedings is extremely variable. Lung disease places the intestine at risk for perforation because of chronic decreased blood flow and lower oxygen levels supplying the system. Lung growth is necessary for healing and this will be compromised in the presence of inadequate nutrition. The interventions to provide sufficient calories for growth impact other organs, such as the liver or kidneys. Long-term, intravenous therapy leads to poor liver function. Failure of the infant to be able to feed increases the potential for total system failure that can ultimately lead to death.

Respiratory Distress Syndrome (RDS)

Respiratory distress syndrome is a common condition found in premature infants. It is caused by the absence of, or a deficiency in, the amount of *surfactant* (a naturally occurring chemical sometimes referred to as lung soap) present in the lungs of the infant. Without sufficient surfactant to lubricate the lung tissue, premature infants are then unable to generate enough pressure to reopen the collapsed segments of the lung. This creates the condition in which there is decreased lung surface tissue available for the work of exchanging oxygen for carbon dioxide between the lungs and the blood vessels. This low oxygen state can ultimately result in neurological damage along with the advent of stiff lungs that require very high pressures to re-expand the collapsed segments.

Infants suffering from respiratory distress syndrome display symptoms of respiratory failure. These symptoms include an increased respiratory rate, retraction of the space between the ribs, audible grunting noise when breathing, and a blue-tinged or pale color to the skin, in spite of supplemental oxygen. If the symptoms persist without appropriate intervention, infants will eventually tire of their effort and quit breathing. Mechanical ventilation such as a respirator or ventilator is used to treat this disease. Recently, an artificial surfactant has been developed and may decrease the likelihood of chronic lung disease (McNab & Blackman, 1998).

Mechanical ventilation has certain risks that are inherent in its use. These include lung damage from increased artificial pressure, tearing of small airways resulting in air leaks between the external lung surface and the rib cage (pneumothorax), bleeding into the lungs from increased pressure, damage to the small capillaries that are part of the circulation pathway (pulmonary hemorrhage), and the development of cysts created in the airways from excessive pressure (pulmonary interstitial emphysema), all of which can ultimately lead to chronic lung disease of infancy (bronchopulmonary dysplasia). While oxygenation increases the survival of premature infants, those with extreme prematurity frequently acquire chronic lung disease and ROP as a side effect of the treatment itself (Stephens et al., 1997).

A relatively new treatment for infants with severe respiratory distress involves diversion of blood from the infant and conducting it through a membrane oxygenator to artificially exchange oxygen and carbon dioxide, warming the blood and returning it to the infant's body. This method, referred to as extra-corporeal membrane oxygenation (ECMO), is a heart-lung bypass procedure which greatly increases the chances of survival. However, even with the use of this sophisticated technology, developmental problems occur in approximately 20% of survivors (Wildin, Landry, & Zwischenberger, 1994).

BRONCHOPULMONARY DYSPLASIA (BPD)

Chronic lung disease of infancy is called **bronchopulmonary dysplasia (BPD),** a condition in which lung injury has occurred during the treatment of premature lung disease. This can be from the effects of positive pressure from extensive oxygen use. Occasionally a full-term infant who has had meconium aspiration or acute pneumonia from infection may contract BPD. Health care providers who treat these infants are aware of the potential implication of the treatments but are committed to providing the necessary intervention for acute respiratory failure and then deal with the effects over the course of the first two to three years of life.

Most extremely low birth weight infants will develop BPD and most require home oxygen therapy through the first year of life. Aggressive treatment of the accompanying health care problems allows for the possibility of recovery, and many infants show normal lung function over the course of early childhood.

Infants with BPD show symptoms of respiratory distress. These include an increased respiratory rate, increased effort for breathing that may be displayed by retraction of the space between the ribs, the use of abdominal and neck muscles to breathe, the need for supplemental oxygen, and pale or dusky skin color. Additional symptoms may be poor tolerance for activities of daily living and symptoms of cardiac failure, which result from the strain placed on the heart and liver by chronic low oxygen levels and the need to maintain circulation through the injured lungs.

BPD can also show up as a cluster of health problems for affected infants. These include, but are not limited to, problems with both acute and chronic infections, cardiovascular problems (including high blood pressure), kidney stones, vitamin and mineral deficiencies (which may result in bone fragility), feeding problems, and poor growth. This combination of factors then places these infants at significant risk for developmental delays. Stephens et al. (1997) found that the longer infants required mechanical oxygenation, the greater the likelihood of cognitive delay. Emotional problems, such as failure to bond, are most likely related to repeated and prolonged hospitalizations and irritability that is frequently seen in infants with chronic air hunger from lung disease.

Infants experiencing the effects of BPD can recover. Aggressive attention to the nutritional needs (allows for new lung growth) and the respiratory needs (prevents further deterioration), as well as medication to control cardiovascular effects, provide the time for healing to occur. When incorporated into the efforts of professionals, there is the need for early intervention to allow the child to develop normally within the constraints of his or her physical limitations.

Another significant problem associated with this disease is the dramatic impact on family structure. Many of the care needs of the infant may require skilled nursing. This may mean the addition of strangers to the inner family. Family systems that are already stressed may not survive the additional burdens this chronic disease places on individuals.

PATENT DUCTUS ARTERIOSUS (PDA)

Patent ductus arteriosus (PDA) is a cardiac defect that frequently occurs in the very low birth weight and extremely low birth weight infant. Because fetal circulation bypasses the heart, premature birth may prevent the natural transition to independent functioning. That is, the opening in the heart permitting the blood bypass does not close spontaneously. This condition can result in increased respiratory distress for these infants and may have to be treated with medication or, in some cases, require surgery to close the opening at one of the most vulnerable periods, within the first week or two of life.

NEUTRAL THERMOREGULATION

Low birth weight infants do not have the physical or physiological mechanisms to maintain body temperature. Heat loss occurs rapidly in these infants through **convection** (heat loss with the delivery of unwarmed gases such as oxygen), **conduction** (heat loss to unwarmed surfaces such as a mattress), evaporation (heat loss through fluid loss through the skin), and **radiation** (heat loss through dissipation from the body into the air). **Hypothermia** (low body core temperature) then places the infant at risk for other physical problems, such as increased respiratory distress, low blood sugar, and possibly, intraventricular hemorrhage. Efforts are taken to preserve body temperature during any interaction with the very immature infant.

Temperature regulation may continue to be a problem for infants with chronic diseases. Poor regulatory mechanisms in infants with neurological deficiencies places them at risk for cold stress in what may appear to be a normal environment. Other conditions that may produce temperature instability are any conditions in which there is decreased blood flow to the skin. This may occur in children who have congenital heart defects or acute and chronic infections or in infants who have problems with lung disease.

INTRAVENTRICULAR HEMORRHAGE (IVH)

The neurological system is one of the most vulnerable in any infant. This is particularly true for the premature infant. Because the rich capillary beds that lie next to the ventricles of the brain are extremely fragile in premature infants, they are prone to bleeding or leakage when there is oxygen deprivation leading to rapid changes in blood pressure (McNab & Blackman, 1998). Many factors that can influence low birth weight infants may result in intraventricular bleeding. Extremes of temperature with rapid fluctuation causes dilatation and constriction of blood vessels, which may cause leakage or rupture of the vessels. Changes in blood pressure affect blood flow in the fragile vessels, also resulting in breakage or leaking. One of the most critical factors leading to **intraventricular hemorrhage (IVH)** is the acid balance of the blood. Infants who are **acidotic** (high levels of blood acid) are predisposed to fragility of the vessels, which increases the risk of bleeding (Dijxhoorn, Visser, Rouwen, & Huisjes, 1987). Acid buildup can occur with lung disease (high carbon dioxide levels and decreased oxygen), low blood sugar, infections, and temperature instability, among other factors. The area of bleeding, the amount of affected area, the age and weight of an infant, and many other physical factors determine the amount and potential damage to function that may occur as a result of IVH. Bleeding that is acute and rapid tends to have greater impact on the overall stability of an infant in the acute phase.

Intraventricular hemorrhages are categorized into four grades. The grade of the hemorrhages can be predictive of the long-term outcome for a child, though the predictive value is not always accurate. For example, a grade IV bleed frequently results in hydrocephalus, or swelling of the fluid-filled cavities in the brain, and the subsequent need for placement of a ventricular peritoneal shunt. These infants require ongoing developmental follow-up after discharge from the hospital and are at significant risk for serious developmental delays. Injuries to infants who sustain grades I and II bleeding often resolve without permanent neurological abnormalities. On the other hand, approximately half of all children with grades III or IV bleeding develop cognitive and/or motor disabilities.

Related to IVH is a second neurological disorder that occurs in premature infants called **periventricular leukomalacia (PVL).** Also believed to be caused by rupturing of the blood vessels in the brain, PVL is associated with the development of cysts or fluid-filled holes, generally on both sides of the brain. Infants with PVL are at high risk for spastic cerebral palsy and other developmental disabilities such as cognitive, speech, and visual impairments.

APNEA OF PREMATURITY

Premature infants have a very high incidence of irregular breathing patterns. Pauses in breathing are called episodes of apnea. These may be apparent at birth for those infants that do not require ventilation or may develop over the first few days of life. This apnea results from central nervous system immaturity or may be a result of posture in the small infant. Many cases may actually be attributed to a combination of both factors. When pauses occur, the infant's response is generally a decrease in the baseline heart rate. This may be a small decrease or it may be substantial. Many infants will require stimulation by caregivers or, if the apnea is particularly severe, may require mechanical ventilation.

Initial apnea in the infant may not be severe. It is the case in which the infant does not self-stimulate (autoregulatory effect from the nervous system) and proceeds to more profound states of apnea that creates conditions requiring intervention to prevent decreased oxygen to the brain, heart, and kidneys. Failure to appropriately intervene can lead to secondary apnea (respiratory failure/arrest), which is more difficult to reverse. Apnea can lead to the build-up of acid in the blood, placing affected infants at risk for bleeding into the brain.

Several interventions are possible to decrease the incidence of apnea. These may include continuous external stimulation, such as an oscillating mattress and medications that stimulate the central nervous system to regulate respiration. These methods may be necessary for the first few months of life, until the nervous system has matured sufficiently to have acquired more consistent regulatory control. Many premature infants may be discharged from the hospital with continuous cardiac/respiratory monitoring and medication, provided their caregivers have been educated to appropriately respond to apnea events.

Case Study

THE DIARY OF ESTHER ANNA BERKE: MONTH 7

May 16–30:   Esther weighs 7.15 kg and measures 67 cm long, still at the 50th percentile for weight and at the 70 percentile for length. She is currently taking 0.125 mg Rivotril, 300 mg Vit. B6, 1 mg Sabril and 2 mg Lamictal per day.

Her seizures have decreased somewhat in frequency but increased in intensity. Sarah took the kids to America on May 29. Esther traveled well, she slept most of the trip, only waking up to drink a bottle here and there. We were concerned that the trip would really disrupt her schedule, but she adjusted quite well.

June 1–15:   Esther was examined by an eye specialist on June 9. He said that her left eye never really developed inside. He couldn't even really see an optic nerve. But she does have vision in her right eye. There is a large coloboma, but it doesn't hinder her main vision. He said she probably won't have 20/20 vision, but she will be able to see. He also said that children that grow up with vision in one eye usually are able to compensate for it quite well. Sarah is in the 5th month of her pregnancy and doing well. Sarah and the kids went to a Berke family reunion on June 13, then flew to Spokane, Washington on June 14 to see her parents and another specialist.

RETINOPATHY OF PREMATURITY (ROP)

Low birth weight infants face the possibility of permanent damage to their vision because of their size and gestational age. One third of infants born at 24 weeks develop **retinopathy of prematurity (ROP),** with this rate decreasing by one half for each additional week of gestation (Walling, 1998). This factor is variable, depending on the ventilation needs of the infant and the necessity for the use of supplemental oxygen during visual maturation which takes place between 40 and 44 weeks after conception.

Prolonged exposure of fragile blood vessels in the retina to excessive levels of oxygen constrict and disrupt later vessel development. The new blood vessels are then prone to leakage or rupture and grow outward from the retina into the interior space of the eyeball. In many cases, this overgrowth spontaneously recedes, permitting the retina to develop normally. In other instances, scars may develop on the retina, resulting in myopia, strabismus, retinal detachment and, in very severe cases, blindness.

At one time, ROP in low birth weight infants was controlled with the use of less oxygen; but decreased oxygen increased infant mortality rates and created a significantly higher incidence of cerebral palsy. Today, oxygen is administered liberally in an effort to save increasingly smaller premature infants. A mature retina is not affected by increased oxygen use. This is why few full-term infants have ROP. When given supplemental oxygen, premature infants must be closely monitored in order to keep arterial blood oxygen levels within a range to prevent **hypoxia,** while minimizing risk of eye damage from the oxygen. In cases where deterioration of the retina proceeds rapidly, surgery may be implied. Cryotherapy, freezing of the blood vessels, and laser surgery are used to encourage overgrown vessels to recede (Fleck, 1999).

ROP is currently categorized into four stages. Stage One and Stage Two damage generally resolves completely without treatment. Stage Three damage may require laser treatment, while Stage Four damage will require surgery to attempt to reattach the retina. Most infants who proceed to Stage Four will have significant visual defects from this disease in spite of the surgical intervention.

ANEMIA

Anemia is the condition in which there is a deficiency in the number of red blood cells available to the infant. This can result either because of a failure in the production of cells or because cells are being used or destroyed faster than they can be replaced. Prematurity results in infants who are affected with anemia for both of these reasons.

Since premature infants have immature bone marrow, production of red blood cells, which takes place in the marrow, is inhibited until the marrow has matured. In addition to the inability to produce new cells, premature infants are nutritionally deficient, especially in iron, which also leads to decreased blood cell production. Even with supplemental iron in the diet, premature infants often are unable to take in sufficient amounts of oral feedings to meet requirements. Infants may become symptomatic with anemia as demonstrated through decreased activity, poor feeding, increased apnea, and slowed weight gain. Premature infants require multiple blood transfusions during their initial weeks of life. Parents now have the option of requesting a Directed Donor in many hospitals. This program allows parents and close family members to donate blood to be used by the individual infant, thus decreasing parent anxiety over multiple blood transfusions.

NUTRITION

The ability to eat and digest food is critical to life. Alterations in either physical or physiological processes that affect eating or digestion place a child at risk for the development of delays or for an increase in the impact of an existing disability on the course of the child's life. Adequate fluids, sufficient caloric intake of essential proteins, fats, and carbohydrates, as well as vitamins and minerals are essential for growth and development.

Term infants are born with primitive reflexes that allow them to initiate a suck and to coordinate breathing and swallowing. These reflexes disappear as maturation occurs, and the act of eating becomes voluntary. Premature infants, dependent on gestation, may not have matured to the point of a primitive reflex state. Oral feeding for these infants is not possible. As maturity occurs, these reflexes emerge and learning to eat becomes possible.

Premature infants require a minimum of 120 Cal/kg of body weight each day for growth to occur. Chronic disease will require up to 150 Cal/kg of body weight for the same growth pattern to occur. The expectation is that the infant will gain approximately 15 g (1/2 oz) to 30 g (1 oz) of weight every day. This allows for the linear growth and brain growth that is critical to a normal developmental progression.

Difficulty with sucking, swallowing, and breathing coordination requires tube feedings. Nonnutritive sucking (pacifier) initiates a learning drive in which nutritive sucking becomes possible as a learned behavior. Factors such as fatigue, illness, and congenital defects affect the rate and success of learning.

Occupational therapy may be necessary within the neonatal period to assist in planning care for the premature or sick infant who is feeding poorly and not gaining weight. Many interventions may be tried to provide opportunities for the child to successfully feed. Infants who cannot take a minimal requirement of fluids and/or calories for normal growth may require further interventions to assist in the feeding process. This may involve the placement of a **gastrostomy tube** or a gastric button through which feedings can be given directly into the stomach, bypassing the esophagus. Even infants who are receiving primary nutrition through a feeding tube are continually orally stimulated to teach them oral feeding.

FAILURE TO THRIVE

Failure to thrive can be described as the condition of growth failure in infancy and early childhood. Parameters for determining adequate growth are dependent on placement in standard growth charts that are guidelines for a normal growth curve. Infants and young children who fall at least two standard deviations below the norm over a designated time period (generally two months) are suggestive of growth failure. This condition may be the result of a multitude of problems that affect the infant. These include, but are not limited to, inadequate economic means for adequate food, chronic disease (congenital heart defects, BPD, etc.), genetic disorders, emotional distress, and abuse. The signs of failure to thrive include decreased weight, decreased height, small head size, and any combination of these. Prolonged failure will ultimately affect brain growth, leading to more complex problems.

Failure to thrive may be termed as either **organic** (specific physical causation) or as **nonorganic** (without specific physical cause). Many physical conditions that result in poor growth can be treated with a resultant improvement in growth rates. These interventions may include increasing caloric intake through dietary changes, medications, and the treatment of other physical factors that may impact growth, such as chronic ear infections.

Nonorganic failure to thrive is the more commonly occurring condition. Nonorganic factors that influence the ability of an infant to grow normally include economics, ignorance, poor parenting skills, and ongoing family stresses. Feeding problems arise in these situations, resulting in prolonged malnutrition and, if not corrected, may lead to delayed mental development and, in the most severe cases, may even lead to death of the infant. Many of these infants appear to lose the will to live during periods of profound depression. This can be significantly affected by a nurturing attitude in a consistent caregiver.

The ability to influence failure to thrive in infancy is dependent on the age at onset, the cause, and the requirements for treatment. The earlier the infant is affected, the poorer the long-term outcome. However, Wright and her colleagues (1998) compared children identified as failing to thrive and who received regular home visits by health professionals for two years to a control group that received no intervention. Though the primary intervention consisted of dietary management, families also received input from pediatricians and social workers. At 3 years of age, 76% of the treated children had recovered compared to 55% of the control group.

Comprehensive interdisciplinary planning is necessary in severe cases of failure to thrive. Specialized dietary preparations and specialized feeding techniques may be necessary to counteract the behaviors of the infant and its aversion toward feeding. Prolonged nutritional deficits will place the child at risk for learning problems that may affect gross motor skills, expressive language, and social skills.

INTERVENTION FOR INFANTS AND CHILDREN BORN PREMATURELY

The most important factor in improving outcomes for infants who are born prematurely is to keep them healthy in early childhood. Though not all children who are premature will have the same needs, the following interventions should be considered when planning hospital follow-up (McNab & Blackman, 1998):

◆ Speech therapy for children with chronic lung disease for feeding and language
◆ Physical/occupational therapy for children with chronic lung disease who have poor exercise tolerance and tire easily
◆ Home-based therapy to avoid exposure to infants with low/poor immunity to risk of infection
◆ Emotional support to the family, including group meetings
◆ Aggressive attention to the nutritional status of infants
◆ Regular opthamological examination in children with prolonged oxygen treatment
◆ Special adaptations for children with mild/severe ROP to promote sensory integration

SUBSTANCE ABUSE AND PREGNANCY OUTCOMES

Since substance abuse during pregnancy may be associated with many disabling newborn conditions and is entirely preventable, more detailed discussion is focused in this area. Alcohol, drugs, and cigarettes are all considered teratogens. A **teratogen** is an agent introduced into the mother's womb that causes either physical or neurological harm to an embryo or fetus. While a range of environmental substances are dangerous, the most common will be discussed here.

FETAL ALCOHOL SYNDROME

Though the in utero effects of alcohol have been acknowledged for centuries (Weiner & Morse, 1988), it was not until the 1970s that the term **Fetal Alcohol Syndrome (FAS)** was officially attached to the constellation of characteristics now considered criteria for this syndrome (Jones, Smith, Ulleland, & Streissguth, 1973; Jones & Smith, 1973). Though it is believed that FAS and Alcohol Related Neurodevelopmental Disorders are grossly underrecognized and underreported, it is reported that FAS occurs in 1–3 per 1000 live births (Gardner, 1997). These statistics make FAS the leading known cause of mental retardation.

Children born with FAS may not be identified at birth, and if suspected at some later point, must be medically diagnosed with the syndrome. The three primary characteristics of FAS described by Burgess and Streissguth (1992) are:

1. Growth deficiency
2. Abnormal facial features
3. Central nervous system dysfunction

Additionally, the physician must find strong evidence of maternal alcohol consumption during pregnancy (Burgess & Streissguth, 1992). If some, but not all, of the characteristics mentioned are present at birth, and if the mother is known to have been a heavy drinker during pregnancy, these infants will be labeled **Fetal Alcohol Effects (FAE).** Though the latter is not a medical diagnosis, both the cause and the effects may be as serious as in FAS. Fetal Alcohol Effect may also be referred to as Alcohol Related Neurodevelopmental Disorder (ARND).

Infants with FAS are short for their chronological age and tend to weigh less than average. As these children age, they do not tend to catch up to their peers, but they are more likely to be closer to expected weight than height (Streissguth, LaDue, & Randels, 1988). Facial characteristics commonly attributed to FAS include a short, upturned nose, thin lips, wide set eyes, flat midface, epicanthic folds, and ear anomalies (Streissguth et al., 1988).

The average IQ of individuals with FAS was found to be around 68 (borderline mental retardation), with a range of 20 to 105 (Streissguth et al., 1988). When academic content is concrete (in early elementary), children with FAS or FAE may do quite well. However, abstract content causes such children to experience increasing difficulties (Burgess & Streissguth, 1992). It is because of the transition in intermediate school years to more abstract content that children with FAS or FAE tend to plateau in terms of academic achievement (Streissguth et al., 1988).

The behavioral characteristics of FAS are the most distressing for caregivers. Typical behavior patterns may or may not be associated with neurological damage sustained by vulnerable fetuses. That is, for a majority of infants and preschoolers with FAS or FAE, postnatal environments are chaotic and sometimes transient. These conditions alone could cause the kinds of abnormal developmental behaviors seen in children with FAS or FAE. Behaviors seen within this population (not necessarily in all children with FAS or FAE) include hyperactivity and impulsivity, language and communication difficulties (especially in social conventions), noncompliance, immaturity, and difficulty in self-regulation, judgment, and decision making (Burgess & Streissguth, 1992). Children with FAS or FAE appear to be immune to subtle kinds of consequences (e.g., praise, reprimands) that help others regulate their behavior. This combination of behaviors makes children particularly challenging to parents and educators. For example, children who are hyperactive tend to get into situations in which they are frustrated and become aggressive. Yet, it is difficult to isolate consequences that are effective in changing this impulsive behavior. As these children reach adolescence, their behavior may become more serious, as lack of judgment leads them to steal and lie (Burgess & Streissguth, 1992). These behaviors cause significant concern in terms of adaptation to vocational and community settings.

Etiology

The cause of FAS and FAE is always alcohol consumption during pregnancy. Alcohol crosses the placenta and enters the fetal blood stream. A fetus's immature liver and neurological systems are less capable of metabolizing the alcohol than a mother's systems. Consequently, the alcohol becomes toxic. There is no known safe level of alcohol intake below which point it can be said that a developing fetus would be safe. However, it is probable that such factors as the timing, duration, and overall health of a mother (e.g., age, nutrition, genetics) interact with the amount of alcohol consumed to influence fetal development (Stevens & Price, 1992). Musculoskeletal/organ anomalies, intellectual/behavioral deficits, and growth retardation are thought be linked to exposure during the first, second, and third trimesters, respectively (Gardner, 1997).

It may also be that the pattern of drinking affects neurological outcome. That is, Thomas and Riley (1998) believe that the symptoms seen in newborns going through alcohol withdrawal (from maternal alcohol consumption immediately prior to birth) are also likely to occur during gestation. Seizures, delirium tremors, and violent agitation associated with subsequent withdrawal may compound the adverse affects of alcohol exposure when women "binge drink." Though the incidence of FAS and FAE is relatively high in some ethnic groups (i.e., American Indians and Native Alaskans), the toxic risk of alcohol to a fetus appears to be the same for all women (Burgess & Streissguth, 1992).

Treatment

FAS and FAE are disabilities that require the mobilization of multiple agency resources. For example, families may require drug rehabilitation before they can be expected to nurture a child with so many needs. An early interventionist may be asked to mediate services by foster care, child protection, mental health, drug rehabilitation, public schools, public assistance, corrections, and public health. None of these agencies working in isolation is likely to be effective in meeting the plethora of needs of families who have children with FAS. Three factors have been found to improve the prospect of these children: a stable and nurturing home of good quality, having few changes of households, and not being the victim of violence (Streissguth & O'Malley, 1997).

Early intervention for children should center around social language, learning weak-rule governed behavior, and sustained attention (Howard, Williams, & McLaughlin, 1994). Specific suggestions for helping parents of children with Fetal Alcohol Syndrome/Effects include (Tanner-Halverson, 1998):

◆ Foster independence in self-help and play
◆ Give choices and encourage decision making
◆ Establish a limited number of simple rules, and use consistent language to remind children of the rules; for example, "This is your bed, this is where you are supposed to be."
◆ Use established routines so children know what to expect—advise well in advance of changes in routines
◆ Teach new skills in small pieces
◆ Be concrete and teach by showing rather than just telling
◆ Set limits and be consistent in expecting children to follow them by having predetermined consequences for both following and not following rules
◆ Review rules for getting reward and change reward often
◆ Do not negotiate rules
◆ Redirect behavior rather than threatening
◆ Intervene before behavior escalates and avoid overstimulating situations
◆ When giving instructions, repeat and ask child to repeat instructions back

PRENATAL EXPOSURE TO DRUGS

At the height of the "cocaine baby" media anxiety, it was suggested that the single most challenging educational problem of the twenty-first century would be the after effects of maternal use of recreational drugs during pregnancy (Chasnoff, 1989). Yet, longitudinal research, which has been conducted with more care and across greater numbers of children, has failed to validate early dramatic claims (Covington & Templin, 1998; Gustavsson & MacEachron, 1997). Still, there is sufficient reason to be concerned about the effects of both prenatal and postnatal exposure to such drugs as tobacco, cocaine, and methamphetamine.

Cocaine/Crack and Methamphetamine

The physiology of these drugs on adults and fetuses is similar, though the drugs themselves vary considerably in price, availability, and addictiveness. Crack is the least expensive and is a crystallized form of cocaine (the powder form). Furthermore, crack provides a more powerful, though shorter lived, high, and is significantly more addictive than either powder cocaine or methamphetamine. These drugs cause blood vessels to constrict, resulting in increased blood pressure. In a pregnant woman, the placenta itself constricts, reducing oxygen flow to the fetus.

Likewise, fetuses directly exposed to cocaine that crossed the placenta experience "highs" along with associated side effects. Since a fetus is unable to metabolize or break down the drug as easily as her mother, cocaine can stay in the fetal system for up to four times as long as in an adult's system. Primary risks to a fetus include premature birth, placenta previa (Handler, Mason, Rosenberg, & Davis, 1994), abruptio placenta, spontaneous abortion or prematurity, and possible neurological damage (Chasnoff, 1998). In spite of the apparent risks, for most infants, the long-lasting neurological consequences of drug use during pregnancy are either absent or so subtle that they cannot be detected by common diagnostic procedures (Susman, 1996).

A neonate born to a drug-using mother will not always show signs of prenatal exposure, just as some infants born to alcohol abusers do not. However, those that do have a recognizable constellation of behavioral characteristics. No abnormal attributes in appearance are associated with prenatal cocaine or methamphetamine effects. Neonates who are obviously affected appear to have poorer than normal motor performance and in their response to environment; they tend to be less cuddly and consolable and lack alertness to environmental stimuli (Delaney-Black & Covington, 1996). These withdrawal features may persist for a few days, weeks, or months. Perhaps the most enduring and disturbing behavior is hypersensitivity to stimuli, which in some children will remain a serious problem for years.

The long-term effects of prenatal exposure to cocaine, once thought to be significant, are now considered to be associated more with polydrug use (Napiorkowski & Lester, 1996) and/or environmental conditions than with permanent neurological damage to the brain by crack/cocaine alone (Hulse, 1997; Susman, 1996). Such characteristics include problem behaviors such as difficulty with habituation, short attention span, and hyperactivity, with many children classified as **attention deficit hyperactivity disorder (ADHD)** (Calhoun & Alforque, 1996; Covington & Templin, 1998; Weintraub, Bental, Olivan, & Rotschild, 1998). In well-controlled studies, where children with and without prenatal cocaine exposure are matched for such factors as poverty, age, ethnicity/race, and gender, there appears to be no significant long-term effect of the drug alone (Gustavsson & MacEachron, 1997; Susman, 1996). Yet, children who are raised in poverty and generally chaotic environments do poorly in social, language, and cognitive development, whether they are or are not exposed to cocaine. Irrespective of the cause, children in both groups may require substantial resources in order to compensate for their environmental disadvantage. Susman (1996) found that children who were prenatally exposed to cocaine, and subsequently born prematurely, faired well when they returned home to a stable and positive home environment. Thus, it appears that, more important than the drug exposure itself, is the environment in which children are raised.

Cigarette Smoking
Cigarette smoking in North America increased dramatically for females in the late 1960s when the tobacco industry began to market specifically to this gender, then decreased significantly from the 1970s to the 1980s, with men representing the largest group of quitters or abstainers (Fried, 1993). Since 1991, the incidence of adolescent cigarette smoking has risen every year, with one in five teenagers being a smoker (Blumenthal, 1998). Of these teenager smokers, approximately 76% are addicted and 70% continue to smoke into their adulthood. The relative proportion of heavy smokers favored women (57% to 31% for men) and white or Hispanic (40% and 33%, respectively, as compared to 12% for African Americans) (Blumenthal, 1998; 1993). It is estimated that 18 to 20% of pregnant women continue smoking throughout their pregnancy (Blumenthal, 1998).

A PARENT'S PERSPECTIVE ON FETAL ALCOHOL SYNDROME: INTERVIEW WITH JAMES HOLDEN

Part of the difficulty with the diagnosis of fetal alcohol syndrome is there are so many variables we don't know. We don't know how much the parents were drinking, and we know these children often had absolutely no prenatal care. April's mother just showed up at the hospital, had the baby, checked herself out and left.

April was 2–3 months old when we got her. She was in a good home, but a court order had deemed the home was not a culturally appropriate home—they wanted her in a Native American home. But, here again, I think part of the trouble of the system is, that although they offer a wide variety of training for foster parents, those folks really didn't know what to look for. They really didn't know what the danger signs would be. We got this child and we knew instantly this was not the child we had been led to believe we would be receiving.

She slept all the time, and wouldn't take any nourishment. Her little arms and legs were scrawny and she couldn't do anything that was developmentally appropriate for her age. At three months, you would expect to see her head moving, and she should be responding to light or sound, but she was lethargic; she'd just lie there and not do anything.

Within three or four weeks she started waking up and we knew immediately it was going to be a battle. She was so flighty even then. As soon as she started waking up, she would start quivering even when we were holding her. She didn't like to held, to be walked, to be rocked, to be touched, or to be cuddled. We couldn't do anything to comfort her, so she did a lot of screaming.

As we get closer to an educational experience for these children, we considered Head Start and ECAP, which are great programs, but they're already heavily weighted with children of color and children of poverty that we fear our Indian children won't have appropriate models. When we get children in kindergarten who have no social skills, who can't work with large groups or small groups, who are hyperactive, and a lot are on medications, our teachers are just totally overwhelmed.

Our children receive occupational and physical therapy, and speech therapy at home. So with three of them, we have our own little group, but there's not much interaction with other children their age. And that really concerns us, because I know there's a lot of children like that out there.

As soon as the children turn three, the therapists may want us to take them in to their offices. You can't blame them, they're getting overloaded too, there are so many of these children. So we have to find treatment for them somewhere, and we would prefer that they be in smaller sessions, but with some other children on a consistent basis. I don't see anything like that. Most of the therapists want one-on-one. So, as far as working in small groups, these children aren't doing that yet.

These children won't get into the early childhood program in the schools until they're four, unless they're identified as developmentally impaired. Our district has a propensity to identify only those children who have neurological or physical handicaps as eligible for preschool services.

Every time I go to a foster care meeting, or see other foster care folks, we're all saying the same thing. We're talking about terribly, chemically impacted children.

These are children who desperately need some kind of intervention for social and behavioral issues, but until they're four we often can't get services unless they also have a pronounced physical disability.

Holden children at the ocean.

Though cigarettes contain over 2000 active ingredients, nicotine is considered the most harmful (Zuckerman, 1991). For unborn children, exposure to tobacco that crosses the placenta causes vasoconstriction of the blood vessels and subsequent hypoxia or reduction of oxygen-carrying capacity of the hemoglobin, due to an increase of carbon monoxide, which binds with the hemoglobin (Zuckerman, 1991). Beginning very early in pregnancy, this process can have a degenerative effect (i.e., necrosis and reduced thickness) on the integrity of the placenta (Jauniaux & Burton, 1992). Several outcomes that increase infant morbidity and mortality have been associated with maternal smoking before or after birth; these include placenta previa (Handler et al., 1994), stillbirth, premature abruption, and Sudden Infant Death Syndrome (SIDS) (Gustavsson & MacEachron, 1997). The immediate risks of smoking on newborns include preterm delivery, intrauterine growth retardation, and low birth weight (an average of 200 g less than infants not exposed to tobacco) (Hakim & Tielsch, 1992; Hanrahan et al., 1992; Zuckerman, 1991).

There also appears to be a direct dose response relationship between the amount of smoking and the reduction of birth weight (Floyd, Zahniser, Gunter, & Kendrick, 1991; Zuckerman, 1991). It has been estimated that for every additional five cigarettes smoked per day, a newborn's birth weight is lowered by 26% (Kleinman & Madans, 1985). However, when mothers stop smoking either before or during pregnancy, the risk of problems goes down (Floyd et al., 1991). Apparently, the third trimester of pregnancy is the period most vulnerable to the harmful effects of nicotine (Fried, 1993).

Prenatal exposure to tobacco is also correlated with a high incidence of lung disease (i.e., bronchitis, pneumonia, tracheitis, and laryngitis), respiratory illnesses, and middle-ear disease (Floyd et al., 1991; Hanrahan et al., 1992). Nicotine is a known carcinogen and when metabolized during the prenatal period, poses an increased risk of cancer to the baby (Wise, 1998). Moreover, smoking causes a reduction in breast milk volume and is perhaps the reason why heavy smokers are less likely to breast feed and tend to wean their children sooner (Fried, 1993). As with Down syndrome, the risk of smoke-related problems for neonates seems to increase as the age of mothers increases (Wen, Goldenberg, & Cutter, 1990).

Though the findings are somewhat controversial, Lazzaroni et al. (1990) found a 16 g reduction in birth weight and 0.05 cm reduction in birth length for every hour that a non-smoking mother was exposed to second-hand smoke during pregnancy. Also challenged was the finding that the risk of childhood cancer increased substantially for children of women who smoked during pregnancy, even though they were exposed to several known carcinogens (Stjernfeldt, Lindsten, Berglund, & Ludvigsson, 1986).

In analysis of infant development, there is again a relationship between the amount of smoking by mothers and the degree of developmental delay. In general, children born to heavy smokers tend to do worse on standardized tests of development than infants born to light smokers or nonsmokers (Fried, 1993). Long-term effects of smoking (again dose dependent) indicate that when exposed, children do less well in cognitive and language domains (Zuckerman, 1991). Others have documented an increased incidence of hyperactivity, attention deficit disorders, and learning disabilities (Floyd et al., 1991; Fried, 1993).

For cigarette smoking, as with other drugs, we should caution that neurologically vulnerable infants may do just as well as uncompromised infants when exposed to a nurturing environment; ". . . responsive care taking appeared to be a protective factor for those preterm children with biologic vulnerability" (Zuckerman, 1991, p. 34). In fact, numerous intervening variables interact with prenatal smoking. For example, J. L. Jacobson, S. W. Jacobson, and Sokol (1994) argued that when controlled for drinking alcohol, childhood stature was not affected by smoking at all. Nevertheless, it has been impossible to separate the isolated and conglomerate effects of teratogens. In the meantime, it is most reasonable to assume the worst and attempt to eliminate the potential harmful effects of nicotine during and after pregnancy through prevention; when that has not happened through provision of rich childhood experiences. Finally, it is always important to note the harmful effects of cigarette smoking to persons of any age. This is particularly clear to your authors who lost their dear friend and co-author Patricia Port to lung cancer.

IMPLICATIONS FOR INFANTS AND CHILDREN PRENATALLY EXPOSED TO DRUGS

It appears that the drug most harmful to a fetus, with known long-term and significant affects, is alcohol. There is also little question that cigarette smoking poses a substantial threat to the long-term development of children. Because these drugs cross the placenta—a direct link to the mother—women who have exposed their babies to drugs are blamed and often punished for their actions. Removal of children to foster care is common; a two-fold increase in the number of children in foster care between mid-1980 and mid-1990 has been linked to labeling children as neglected or abused because of maternal drug use. Some suggest that such removal of children from their biological families is a moral obligation of society, necessary to protect children from the risk of violence and neglect associated with drug using families (National Association for Families and Addiction Research and Education, 1998). On the other hand, Gustavsson and MacEachron (1997) suggested that this criminalization of maternal drug use tends to victimize poor minority women, with foster care becoming a major form of family life for too many minority children. While this alleged victimization is clearly a social-ethical concern, it is also of practical concern as early intervention specialists will often be working in very complex social systems, chaotic family lives, and possible adversarial situations between state and family. Managing the system requires knowledge of the social welfare and child protection systems, legal rights of families and children as well as careful execution of mediation and professional cooperation skills.

Interestingly, children who have been exposed to a single drug or polydrug use (and poverty) have similar developmental implications. Deficits in social skills and mild to moderate cognitive delays are common to all groups. For early interventionists, these general intervention principles apply (Calhoun & Alforque, 1996; Gardner, 1997):

◆ Multidisciplinary intervention, including educators, social workers, behavioral specialists, and health care providers
◆ Positive, structured and predictable environment
◆ Avoidance of highly stimulating environments
◆ Direct training of social skills
◆ Adaptation of tasks to meet individual learning strengths
◆ Functional analysis of serious behavioral problems
◆ Concrete, clear, and immediate consequences for both desired and undesired behaviors
◆ Careful attention to diet and health care

IN CONCLUSION

One of the greatest challenges for society over the next decade will be to identify and plan interventions for decreasing the impact of prematurity on infants, and their families, and to influence life choices that affect the health of future children. This plan should include education toward prevention, resources toward providing assistance to families involved with children with special needs, and discussion among disciplines regarding approaches that promote optimal functioning among affected children. Alcohol and substance abuse are two factors that increase the likelihood of premature birth. Most of these highly preventable early births are the consequence of social neglect of women whose lives are challenged by health problems (including depression), poverty, abuse, and poor education. Early childhood professionals who work with children born prematurely or effected by drug abuse will also be working within the context of families who have significant needs. Moreover, medical services are likely to be an ongoing part of the lives of children who are born prematurely. Therefore, a broad understanding of social and health services will be necessary in order to serve these children and their families well.

STUDY GUIDE QUESTIONS

1. Discriminate between the terms prenatal, natal, perinatal, and postnatal.
2. Explain how prematurity influences the vulnerability of different body systems.
3. Describe the impact of maternal conditions (e.g., age, weight, and socioeconomic status) on fetal growth.
4. Describe the following conditions of pregnancy in terms of mechanism and risk to fetuses: placenta previa, abruptio placenta, toxemia of pregnancy, maternal diabetes, premature rupture of membranes, and Rh sensitization.
5. During labor itself, there are several conditions that place neonates at risk. Identify and describe these.
6. Explain how hypoxia–ischemia places a newborn at risk for developmental delays.
7. What is meconium, and when does it pose a threat to infants?
8. Discriminate between low, very low, and extremely low birth weight.
9. What is the relationship between RDS and BPD?
10. Explain the heat regulation concerns of premature infants.
11. A major concern to early childhood professionals of premature infants is IVH. Explain why this is.
12. Define apnea and describe its relationship to prematurity.
13. ROP is a common outcome of the treatment of prematurity. Explain why this is and what is being done to prevent ROP.
14. What is the relationship between nutritional needs of premature infants and anemia?
15. Define failure to thrive and explain the difference between organic and nonorganic failure to thrive.
16. What are the defining characteristics of FAS?
17. Why are children with FAS such a challenge to families and professionals?
18. Explain the way in which cocaine and methamphetamine influence a mother and fetus physiologically.
19. What are the "withdrawal" symptoms of neonates affected by cocaine/methamphetamine?
20. Explain the relationship between possible long-term behaviors associated with cocaine/methamphetamine and their treatment.
21. Summarize the influence of tobacco on unborn infants.

REFERENCES

Allen, M., & Capute, A. (1990, Supplement). Tone and reflex development before term. *Pediatrics*, 393–399.

Apgar, B. (1997). Pregnancy outcome and intelligence at age five. *American Family Physician, 55,* 1928–1930.

Besinger, R. E., Repke, J. T., & Ferguson, J. E. (1989). Preterm labor and intrauterine growth retardation: Complex obstetrical problems with low birth weight infants. In D. K. Stevenson, & P. Sunshine (Eds.), *Fetal and neonatal brain injury. Mechanisms, management & risks of practice* (pp. 11–33) Toronto: BC Decker Inc.

Blumenthal, S. J. (1998). *Young women and smoking.* Fact Sheet published by the Department of Health and Human Services: U. S. Public Health Service's Office on Women's Health. www.inwat.org/young.

Burgess, D. M., & Streissguth, A. P. (1992). Fetal Alcohol Syndrome and Fetal Alcohol Effects: Principles for educators. *Phi Delta Kappan, 1,* 24–30.

Calhoun, G., & Alforque, M. (Fall, 1996). Prenatal substance afflicted children: An overview and review of the literature. *Education, 117,* 30–39.

Chasnoff, I. J. (1989, July). *National epidemiology of perinatal drug use.* Paper presented at the conference on Drugs, Alcohol, Pregnancy and Parenting, Spokane, WA.

Chasnoff, I. J. (1998). Silent Violence: Is prevention a moral obligation? *Pediatrics, 102,* 145–149.

Chasnoff, I. J., Burns, K. A., Burns, W. J., & Schnoll, S. H. (1986). Prenatal drug exposure: Effects on neonatal and infant growth and development. *Neurobehavioral Toxicology and Teratology, 8,* 357–362.

Covington, C., & Templin, T. (1998). Prenatal cocaine exposure and child behavior. *Pediatrics, 102,* 945–951.

Curry, M. A. (1998, October). Abused women at higher risk for maternal infant complications. *Women's Health Weekly,* 6–7.

Delaney-Black, V., & Covington, C. (1996). Prenatal cocaine and neonatal outcome: Evaluation of dose-response relationship. *Pediatrics, 98,* 735–741.

Dijxhoorn, M.J., Visser, G.H.A., Rouwen, B.C.L., & Huisjes, H.J. (1987). Apgar score, meconium and acidemia at birth in small for gestational age infants born at term, and their relation to neonatal neurological morbidity. *British Journal of Obstetrics and Gynecology, 94,* 873–879.

Dixon, S. D., & Bejar, R. (1989). Echoencephalographic findings in neonates associated with maternal cocaine and methanphetamine use: Incidence and clinical correlates. *The Journal of Pediatrics, 115,* 770–778.

Fleck, B. W. (1999). Therapy for retinopathy of prematurity. *Lancet, 353*(9148), 166–167.

Floyd, R. L., Zahniser, M. P.H., Gunter, E. P., & Kendrick, J. S. (1991). Smoking during pregnancy: Prevalence, effects, and intervention strategies. *Birth, 18*(1), 48–53.

Fried, P. A. (1993). Prenatal exposure to tobacco and marijuana: Effects during pregnancy, infancy and early childhood. *Clinical Obstetrics and Gynecology, 36*(2), 319–337.

Fried, P. A., & Watkinson, B. (1990). 36- and 48-month neurobehavioral follow-up of children prenatally exposed to marijuana, cigarettes, and alcohol. *Journal of Behavioral and Developmental Pediatrics, 11,* 49.

Gardner, J. (1997). Fetal alcohol syndrome—recognition and intervention. *MCN, 22,* 318–322.

Gustavsson, N. S., & MacEachron, A. E. (1997). Criminalizing women's behavior. *Journal of Drug Issues, 27*(3), 673–688.

Hack, M., Taylor, G., Klein, N., Eiben, R., Schatschneider, C., & Mercuri-Minich, N. (1994). School-age outcomes in children with birth weights under 750 grams. *The New England Journal of Medicine, 331*(3), 753–759.

Hakim, R. B., & Tielsch, J. M. (1992). Maternal cigarette smoking during pregnancy: A risk factor for childhood strabismus. *Archives of Ophthalmology, 110,* 1459–1462.

Handler, A. S., Mason, E. D., Rosenberg, D. L., & Davis, F. G. (1994). The relationship between exposure during pregnancy to cigarette smoking and cocaine use and placenta previa. *American Journal of Obstetrics and Gynecology, 170*(3), 884–889.

Hanrahan, J. P., Tager, I. B., Segal, M. R., Tosteson, T. D., Castile, R. G., Vunakis, H. V., Weiss, S. T., & Speizer, F. E. (1992). The effect of maternal smoking during pregnancy on early infant lung function. *American Review of Respiratory Disease, 145*(5), 1129–1135.

Howard, V. F., Williams, B. F., & McLaughlin, T. F. (1994). Children prenatally exposed to alcohol and cocaine: Behavioral solutions. In R. Gardner, D. M. Sainato, J. O. Cooper, T. E. Heron, W. L. Heward, J. Eshleman, & T. A. Grossi (Eds.), *Behavior analysis in education: Focus on measurably superior instruction* (pp. 131–146). Belmont, CA: Brooks/Cole.

Hughes, P. F., Agarwal, M., & Thomas, L. (1997). Gestational diabetes and fetal macrosomia in a multi-ethnic population. *Journal of Obstetrics & Gynecology, 17,* 540–545.

Hulse, G. (1997). Assessing the relationship between maternal opiate use and neonatal mortality. *Addiction, 7,* 1033–1043.

Jacobson, J. L., Jacobson, S. W., & Sokol, R. J. (1994). Effects of prenatal exposure to alcohol, smoking, and illicit drugs on postpartum somatic growth. *Alcoholism: Clinical and Experimental Research, 18*(2), 317–323.

Jauniaux, E., & Burton, G. J. (1992). The effect of smoking in pregnancy on early placental morphology. *Obstetrics & Gynecology, 79*(5), 645–648.

Jones, K. L., & Smith, D. W. (1973). Recognition of the Fetal Alcohol Syndrome in early infancy. *The Lancet, 2,* 999–1001.

Jones, K. L., Smith, D. W., Ulleland, C. N., & Streissguth, A. P. (1973). Pattern of malformation in offspring of chronic alcoholic mothers. *The Lancet, 2,* 1267–1271.

Kleinman, J. C., & Madans, J. H. (1985). The effects of maternal smoking, physical stature, and educational attainment on the incidence of low birthweight. *American Journal of Epidemiology, 121,* 843–855.

Kline, J., Stein, Z., & Susser, M. (1989). Conception to birth: Epidemiology of prenatal development. *Monographs in epidemiology and biostatistics, Vol.14.* New York: Oxford University Press.

Lazzaroni, F., Bonassi, S., Manniello, E., Morcaldi, L., Repetto, E., Ruocco, A., Calvi, A., & Cotellessa, G. (1990). Effect of passive smoking during pregnancy on selected perinatal parameters. *International Journal of Epidemiology, 19*(4), 960–966.

Lewit, E. M., Baker, L. S., Corman, H., & Sinono, P. H. (Spring, 1995). The direct cost of low birth weight. *The Future of Children, 5*(1), 1–23.

Low, J., Galbraith, R., Muir, D., Killen, H., Pater, B., & Karchmar, J. (1982). Intrauterine growth retardation: A study of long-term morbidity. *American Journal of Obstetrics and Gynecology, 142,* 670–677.

McCormick, M.C. (1989). Long-term follow-up of infants discharged from neonatal intensive care units. *Journal of the American Medical Association, 261,* 24–31.

McNab, T. C., & Blackman, J. A. (1998). Medical complication of the critically ill newborn: A review for early intervention professionals. *Topics in Early Childhood Special Education, 18,* 197–206.

Miller, M. Q., & Quinn-Hurst, M. (1994). Neurobehavioral assessment of high-risk infants in the neonatal intensive care unit. *American Journal of Occupational Therapy, 48,* 506–551.

Napiorkowski, B., & Lester, B. M. (1996). Effects of in utero substance exposure on infant neurobehavior. *Pediatrics, 98,* 71–76.

National Association for Families and Addiction Research and Education. (1998). Silent violence: Is prevention a moral obligation? *Pediatrics, 102,* 145–149.

National Institute on Drug Abuse. (1993). *Conference highlights from the 2nd National Conference on Drug Abuse.* Rockville, MD.

Paz, I., Gale, R., Laor, A., Danon, Y. L., Stevenson, D. K., & Seidman, D. S. (1995). The cognitive outcome of full-term small for gestational age infants at late adolescence. *Obstetrics & Gynecology, 85*(3), 452–456.

Peleg, D., Kennedy, C. M., & Hunter, S. K. (1998). Intrauterine growth retardation restriction: Identification and management. *American Family Physician, 58,* 453–461.

Preconception factors may contribute to early birth, poor fetal growth. (1999, January). *Women's Health Weekly,* 13–15.

Report of Consensus Conferences. (1987). *American Nurses' Association: Access to Prenatal Care: Key to Preventing Low Birthweight,* Kansas City, MO: American Nurses' Association, 24–32.

Seel, E. G. (1986). Outcome of very very low birth weight infants. *Clinics of Perinatology, 13,* 451–459.

Soares, J. A. C., & Beard, R. W. (1998). Maternal leisure-time exercise and timely delivery. *American Journal of Public Health, 315,* 737–740.

Solomon, C. G. (1997, October). Risk factors identified for diabetes during pregnancy. *Women's Health Weekly,* 9–10.

Stephens, R. P., Richardson, A. C., & Lewin, J. S. (1997). Outcome of extremely low birth weight infants (500-999 grams) over a 12 year period. *Pediatrics, 99,* 619–622.

Stevens, L. J., & Price, M. (1992). Meeting the challenge of educating children at-risk. *Phi Delta Kappan, 1,* 18–23.

Stjernfeldt, M., Lindsten, J., Berglund, K., & Ludvigsson, J. (1986). Maternal smoking during pregnancy and risk of childhood cancer. *The Lancet, 2,* 519–520.

Streissguth, A. P., LaDue, R. A., & Randels, S. P. (1988). *A manual on adolescents and adults with Fetal Alcohol Syndrome with special reference to American Indians* (2nd ed.). Seattle, WA: University of Washington.

Streissguth, A. P., & O'Malley, K. D. (1997). Fetal Alcohol Syndrome/Fetal Alcohol Effects: Secondary disabilities and mental health approaches. *Treatment Today, 9*(2), 16–17.

Susman, E. (Sept, 1996). Cocaine's role in drug-exposed babies problems questioned. *Brown University Child and Adolescent Behavior Letter, 12*(9), 1–3.

Tanner-Halverson, P. (1998). *Strategies for parents and caregivers of FAS and FAE children.* The National Organization on Fetal Alcohol Syndrome. www.nofas.org/strategy.

Tiedje, L. B., Kingry, M. J., & Stommel, M. (1992). Patient attitudes concerning health behaviors during pregnancy: Initial development of a questionnaire. *Health Education Quarterly, 19,* 481–494.

Thomas, J. D., & Riley, E. P. (1998). Fetal alcohol syndrome: Does alcohol withdrawal play a role? *Health & Research World, 22,* 47–54.

Villar, J., do Onis, M., & Kestler, E. (1990). The differential neonatal morbidity of the interauterine growth retardation syndrome. *American Journal of Obstetrics and Gynecology, 163,* 151–158.

Walling, A. D. (1998). Outcomes of infants born at 24–26 weeks of gestation. *American Family Physician, 57*(9), 2220–2222.

Weiner, L., & Morse, B. A. (1988). FAS: Clinical perspectives and prevention. In I. J. Chasnoff (Ed.), *Drugs, alcohol, pregnancy and parenting* (pp. 127–148). Lancaster, UK: Kluwer Academic.

Weintraub, Z., Bental, Y., Olivan, A., & Rotschild, A. (1998). Neonatal withdrawal syndrome and behavioral effects produced by maternal drug use. *Addiction Biology, 3,* 159–170.

Wen, S. W., Goldenberg, R. L., & Cutter, G. R. et al. (1990). Smoking, maternal age, fetal growth, and gestational age at delivery. *American Journal of Obstetric Gynecology, 162,* 53–58.

Whitman, B. Y. (1991). The roots of organicity: Genetics and genograms. In P. J. Accardo, T. A., Blondis, & B. Y. Whitman (Eds.), *Attention deficit disorders and hyperactivity in children* (pp. 37–56). New York: Marcel Dekker.

Wildin, S. R., Landry, S. H., & Zwischenberger, J. B. (1994). Prospective, controlled study in developmental outcome in survivors of extracorporeal membrane oxygenation: The first 24 months. *Pediatrics, 9,* 404–408.

Wise, J. (1998). Carcinogen in tobacco smoke may be passed to fetus. *British Medical Journal, 317,* 555.

Wright, C. M., House, D. C., Callum, J., Birks, E., Jarvis, S., Service, P., & Terrace, D. (1998). Effect of community based management in Failure to Thrive: Randomized controlled trial. *British Medical Journal, 317,* 7158–7162.

Zuckerman, B. (1991). Drug exposed infants: Understanding the medical risk. *The Future of Children, 1*(1), 26–35.

Zuckerman, B., & Bresnahan, K. (1991). Developmental and behavioral consequences of prenatal drug and alcohol exposure. *The Pediatric Clinics of North America, 38*(6), 1387–1406.

5

CONDITIONS AFFECTING THE NEUROLOGICAL FUNCTION

Early childhood special educators are often a family's first link to intervention services and, consequently, also a first bridge between medical treatment and other professional therapies. It is critical, therefore, to have both substantive knowledge and reference information regarding the most common conditions that are associated with neurological damage. Though educators cannot be as intensely trained as medical personnel, a basic understanding of medical procedures and conditions is necessary in order to be conversant with other professionals and with parents.

Early childhood special educators may also find themselves in the role of interpreter for parents and for others who need to understand the medical nature of a child's neurological condition in order to plan effective intervention. Educators can refer to this text to refresh their own understanding of a condition, as well as to help parents interpret information given by health professionals. Though health professionals are often very direct and thorough, a parent's own ability to "hear" such information can be limited by the normal, initial emotional responses to a child's trauma or poor prognosis. Later on, early childhood special educators may be called on to fill in missing information when parents are better able to "hear" and to understand.

This chapter is devoted to understanding conditions that may affect a child's neurological functioning. This understanding includes knowledge of diagnostic testing, etiological factors resulting in damage to the nervous system, and characteristics of specific medical conditions common to early childhood special education.

The neurological system is comprised of the central nervous system (brain and spinal cord) and the peripheral nervous system (12 cranial nerves and motor/sensory nerves in the extremities). Neurological impairments can be so subtle that they can be detected by neither medical nor educational diagnostic techniques. On the other hand, significant damage to the nervous system can affect functions in all developmental domains, including movement, communication, social interactions, and cognitive functioning. Specific permutations of brain damage can also vary. Four children with a similar medical history of prematurity might have any one or all of the following neurological conditions: seizures, cerebral palsy, mental retardation, or attentional deficits. Some forms of damage to the neurological system occur very early in fetal development; other children may be affected long after birth. Causes of neurological damage include prenatal exposure to toxins, birth trauma and infections, as well as other factors.

DIAGNOSTIC TOOLS

The first step in clarifying various medical or disabling conditions is medical testing. These tests can be expensive, time-consuming, and frightening for families engaged in the process. A simple understanding of the diagnostic tools involved can help alleviate a parent's concern or lack of understanding. Diagnostic tools involve both **invasive** procedures, in which a body system must be penetrated, and **noninvasive** methods, in which the body is not penetrated.

X RAYS

One of the oldest noninvasive tools used to evaluate an individual's condition is the **X ray.** X rays are a form of invisible electromagnetic energy that have a short wavelength that bombards a specific area of the body. Because of their very short wave length, X rays are able to penetrate most substances, some substances more easily than others. The density of the tissue and the voltage power used affect the degree to which various tissues are penetrated by the X rays. These rays make certain substances fluoresce so that the size, shape, and movement of organs can be observed. The X rays themselves are invisible to the human eye but can be captured as an image on a specially coated film.

X rays are useful in detecting foreign bodies and fractures or for illuminating radioactive substances that have been introduced to the body. For example, radioactive dye may be injected into a blood vessel, and X rays can trace the resultant pathway.

Excessive exposure to X rays, especially over a short period of time, can pose a serious health hazard. X rays have the potential to damage living cells, especially those that are dividing rapidly. The risks include damage to bone marrow and other blood-forming organs, damage to genes resulting in genetic/chromosomal mutations (which can be passed to future generations), onset of fetal death or malformation, and the development of cataracts. Finally, exposure to X rays over a long period of time can be carcinogenic. Such damage is avoided by using the lowest possible radiation doses, by using a lead shield to protect tissue that is not of concern, and by avoiding X rays when there is any possibility of pregnancy.

COMPUTERIZED AXIAL TOMOGRAPHY

The **Computerized Axial Tomography** (CAT scan, also commonly known as CT) was developed in 1972 and was proclaimed the most important diagnostic device to be invented since X rays were first introduced. While operating on similar physical principals as an X ray (radiology), a CAT scan is 100 times more powerful than its predecessor. To conduct this exam, individuals are placed in a circular chamber and are bombarded with focused X rays coming from several planes (e.g., cross-sectional, horizontal). A detector, positioned opposite the X-ray source (scanner), picks up the X rays, which have been absorbed at different rates, depending on the density of the tissue through which they have passed. These measurements are reconstructed using a computer to produce clear, three-dimensional images of body tissue and structure on an oscillating screen. CAT scans are used to distinguish interior body structures such as lesions, bleeding in the brain, hydrocephalus, and tumors. An advantage of CAT scans over X rays is their ability to detect structures not visible on conventional tests and their ability to evaluate the targeted body part from many different angles simultaneously. Though more expensive and more risky (increased radiation exposure) than ultrasonography, CAT scans are considerably more accurate in detecting such problems as tumors or abscesses (see Figure 5–1).

Figure 5–1
A CAT scan slice.

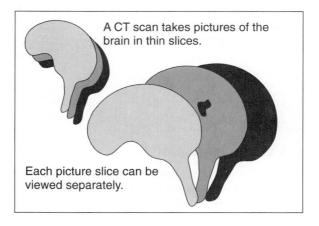

A CT scan takes pictures of the brain in thin slices.

Each picture slice can be viewed separately.

MAGNETIC RESONANCE IMAGING

Magnetic resonance imaging (MRI) is a relatively new technology that is now used widely in the diagnosis of abnormalities in cardiovascular, orthopedic, and neurological systems. Unlike CAT scans and X rays, MRI does not rely on radiation, thereby reducing the risks of radiation exposure. Instead, a powerful magnetic force is used to attract ions within cells toward the edges of an organ. An image of those ions lined up on the edges of an organ reveals whether an **anomaly** has occurred, for example, the growth of a tumor, torn cartilage, or a fracture.

During imaging, a patient lies very still inside a massive, hollow, cylindrical magnet. Children may be given a powerful sedative or even general anesthetic for the average half-hour examination. Short bursts of magnetic power are emitted. These cause the hydrogen atoms in the patient's tissues to line up parallel to each other like little magnets. The machine detects this alignment as an image and a computer processes the information in much the same way as a CAT scan but shows normal and abnormal tissues with greater contrast. The test is particularly valuable for studying the brain and spinal cord, identifying tumors, and examining the heart and major blood vessels.

FUNCTIONAL IMAGING

While X rays, CAT scans, and MRIs are useful in analyzing gross anatomical abnormalities, they are not useful in monitoring actual chemical activity. Two relatively new techniques, which have been used largely for research purposes until recently, are capable of measuring this function. **Positron emission tomography (PET)** and **single photon emission computer tomography (SPECT)** are noninvasive techniques that are particularly valuable for evaluating neurological disorders.

PET scanning detects positively charged particles that have been labeled with radioisotopes and injected into the blood. Because of their instability, these substances are taken up in greater concentration by areas of tissue that are more metabolically active, such as tumors. Detectors linked to a computer make a picture of how the radioisotopes are distributed within the body. PET scans can detect brain tumors, locate the origin of epileptic seizures, and examine brain function. Similar to the CAT scan, in producing images of the brain in several planes, the PET scan makes a biochemical analysis of metabolism rather than anatomy. PET scanning equipment is expensive to buy and operate, so it is currently available in only a few urban centers, but its contributions are so valuable that its use is likely to become more widespread in the future.

PET and SPECT are safe procedures. They require only minute doses of radiation and carry virtually no risk of toxicity or allergy. Advances in radioisotopic scanning depend on the continuing development of radioactive particles specific to certain tissues.

ULTRASONOGRAPHY

In this noninvasive procedure, high-frequency sound waves (inaudible to the human ear) are passed through a patient's skin and focused onto an organ of interest. The sound waves travel at variable speeds depending on the density of the tissue through which they are passing. For example, the waves travel through bone much faster

Table 5–1 Comparison of diagnostic tools.

Tool	Risk of Radiation	Powerful Tool	Multiple Analyses	Expensive
X ray	moderate	limited	NA	low
CAT scan	high	yes	yes	moderate
Ultrasound	none	limited	yes	low
MRI	none	yes	yes	high
PET/SPECT	low	yes	yes	high
EEG	none	yes	yes	moderate

than they travel through muscle. These sound waves bounce back to the transducer as an echo and are then amplified. A computer processes these echoes into electrical energy and displays them on a screen for interpretation. The images are displayed in real time, producing motion on a television screen. The images can then be translated into photographs for permanent examination. A distinct advantage of **ultrasound** (or **ultrasonography**) over other techniques is the absence of risk incurred by exposure to radiation as in some other diagnostic techniques (see Table 5–1).

Ultrasonography is frequently used during pregnancy to view the uterus and fetus. The technique helps in early pregnancy to establish fetal gestational age, determine if there is a multiple pregnancy, evaluate fetal viability, confirm fetal abnormalities, and guide amniocentesis. Later in pregnancy, an ultrasound may be carried out if the growth rate of the fetus seems slow, if fetal movements cease or are excessive, or if the mother experiences vaginal bleeding.

In a newborn child, ultrasound can be used to scan the brain to diagnose hydrocephalus, brain tumors, or brain hemorrhage and to determine if other organs, such as the kidneys, appear normal. A type of ultrasound is also used in echocardiography to investigate disorders of the heart valves. Doppler ultrasound is a modified version of ordinary ultrasound that can look at moving objects, such as blood flowing through blood vessels and the fetal heartbeat in pregnancy.

ELECTROENCEPHALOGRAPHY

Electroencephalography (EEG) is a conventional noninvasive procedure used to detect normal and abnormal electrical activity within the brain. EEGs detect, amplify, and measure electrical activity on the scalp produced by the brain's neurons. The analysis is typically conducted in a small room designed to eliminate electrical interference and distractions. Small electrodes are placed in a definitive pattern on the scalp but do not produce shock or otherwise aversive stimuli. While the results directly measure only surface activity, changes in electrical patterns effectively represent the activity of deeper structures. These impulses are recorded as brain waves on moving strips of paper.

This diagnostic technique is commonly used to detect the presence of abnormal brain activity that might be related to seizures. Different types of seizures emit differential brain waves. During testing, after an initial baseline is completed, various forms of stress, such as deep breathing or bright lights, may be introduced in order to elicit brain wave patterns typical of seizure disorders.

While EEGs are useful diagnostic tools, they are also more unreliable than many techniques and should be interpreted with caution. For example, approximately 20% of individuals who do not have brain damage will have abnormal readings on electroencephalography. On the other hand, a significant portion of individuals with seizures or other kinds of brain damage will have unaffected EEGs.

An EEG can also be used to evaluate hearing loss. Sounds are introduced through earphones, and the subsequently evoked electrical potentials are amplified via EEG and can then be separated from other electrical activity by computers. The resulting record reveals whether sound has been perceived by the brain.

NEUROLOGICAL DISABILITIES

The diagnositic tools described above are widely used to attempt to verify the presence or absence of unusual patterns of neurological functioning in children who have physical, cognitive, behavioral, or language development concerns. As you will see, these tools are very often too primitive to provide definitive answers, though in many cases are helpful in identifying problems. The remainder of the chapter will isolate a variety of relatively high incidence neurological disabilities that early childhood professionals are likely to encounter.

CEREBRAL PALSY

Cerebral palsy (CP) is one of the most common disabilities in our society. It encompasses a broad category of nonprogressive neuromuscular conditions affecting muscle tone, movement, reflexes, and posture. Cerebral palsy results from brain injury sustained during the early stages of development, and though the damage to the brain itself gets no worse during an individual's life, children may develop deformities across time. The original injury to the brain must occur before 16 years of age for the condition to be classified as cerebral palsy.

The incidence of cerebral palsy (approximately 1.5–2.7 per 1000 live births in developed countries and much higher in developing countries) has not changed significantly since the 1960s, even though modern medicine has improved the prognosis of premature infants below 2500 g (5.5 lbs) (Rosen & Dickinson, 1992). In fact, since 1960, there has been a 20% increase in the incidence of cerebral palsy as a result of life-saving treatment of very low birth weight infants (Bhushan, Paneth, & Kiely, 1993). The rate continues to be high because of the concomitant success in decreasing the mortality of even smaller babies, who do not respond as well as more mature infants to intensive, life-saving medical treatment. For example, from the early 1970s to the mid-1980s, the survival rate of infants with birth weights below 1500 g (3 lb 5 oz) improved in developed countries from 15–40% to 75% (Rosen & Dickinson, 1992). Infants born at very low birth weight comprise 25% of the infants diagnosed with CP in the United States each year (Adler, 1995). However, it is not just premature birth that causes cerebral palsy. Brain damage causing cerebral palsy may occur before, during, or after birth. The physical traits and etiological conditions of persons with cerebral palsy are diverse.

Cerebral palsy is categorized according to the site of cerebral damage, the extent of brain damage, and the parts of the body affected by that damage. Whatever the origin, cerebral palsy causes a functional miscommunication between a person's movement intentions and subsequent motor responses.

JENNIFER WARITZ, SEARCHING FOR A DIAGNOSIS: INTERVIEW WITH TAMMY WARITZ

Jennifer was born in Montana, in a small rural railroad town. I was very sick throughout my pregnancy, and I can remember saying, "It's just not right, something's wrong." We couldn't get a heartbeat until about six months into the pregnancy, although we had done an ultrasound so we knew she was there. Everybody thought that she was going to be a big baby and that everything was going to be okay and that I was just being paranoid.

Jennifer's delivery was a repeat Cesarean section, but when she was born she was blue, and immediately began having seizures. Of course being in a rural area, nobody really knew what was going on and they just whisked her away before we had an opportunity to hold her. She was placed in the incubator with IVs everywhere and a heart monitor, because she frequently stopped breathing and had to be resuscitated. The doctor, a long-time family friend, was almost in tears when he said, "I don't know what's wrong with Jennifer, but I don't think she's going to make it through the night." I received this message alone in my hospital room.

Jennifer remained in the hospital for another two weeks. The hardest part was to leave her there, and to go home without the baby that we had been anticipating for nine months. I returned to the hospital every day for feedings but it just got to the point that we decided we needed to take her home, regardless.

Jennifer was so fragile, she only weighed 5 lb 2 oz and had absolutely no sucking reflex at all. She dropped almost 1 lb within the first 24 hours; she was so frail, had very low muscle tone (like a limp rag doll), and was almost lifeless. At one point, we were asked to use an alarm blanket that would go off if Jennifer quit breathing. It was really a hard decision to make, but we knew that we would lie awake every night waiting for that buzzer to go off. We felt that if it was her time to go, it was her time to go, so we declined to use the alarm.

We didn't know of anybody else who had a child with these concerns so there was a period of time when we carried a lot of guilt. We used to think, "What did we do, what did we do? Why did this happen to us? Why is she like this? Why, why, why, why, why?" All these "why" questions and there were no answers. Not once did we ever get a name and a number of another family who had already experienced all this grief. It would have been most beneficial for us to have been able to talk to someone who really could say, "I understand, and know what you're feeling and going through."

It took us a good three months just to settle in with Jennifer and to feel comfortable and accepting of her. Then, the search was on. We needed to know what Jennifer's condition was; what her diagnosis was. We got connected with a genetics specialist, who told us that Jennifer had a rare condition where the surface of the brain is smooth and she would probably die before the age of two. We were told that if she lived, she would be so severely involved that it would be an extreme burden on the family and that we should consider placing her in an institution. I cried all the way home that day. My husband had an even harder time, and he began to withdraw from Jennifer, because he was afraid that he would get too attached and then lose her.

Several months later, I asked the specialist to retest. They found that she did have the ripples on the surface of the brain, but that she had microcephaly; her brain was smaller, but there was definitely a clear cranial pattern. I was told she would be severely disabled; Jennifer is moderately to severely involved, both mentally and physically.

Jennifer has very little speech; she can feed herself now, but requires assistance in order to do that. She has to have total assistance to get dressed and bathed and she's completely incontinent so she requires diapering. She's mobile in her chair and she can crawl around and pull herself up onto furniture. Her tests indicate functions somewhere between 12 and 18 months of age. Socially, she is very much aware and very connected to her environment and probably at a 24-month or above level. That's been our saving grace; she has been such a pleasant child.

Jennifer's condition was just labeled as cerebral palsy, though we were told, "We really don't think that this is what it is, but this is the best term that we can use for her right now." We went through five years of thinking that she had cerebral palsy, but every doctor we saw said, "This is the funniest looking case of cerebral palsy that I have ever seen." Finally we were told that Jennifer's features looked very similar to children who have Kabuki Makeup Syndrome, so we went to another genetics specialist.

As soon as we walked into the room, the geneticist became very excited. I mean if this man could have done backflips he probably would have. He was thrilled, "Oh my! Oh my! This is it! This is it!" He started shouting down the hall, "Bring me those papers my colleague in Germany sent me." The research was all on children with Kabuki Makeup Syndrome and this colleague of his in Germany was following one of the first Caucasian children to be diagnosed with it and had just sent him this information.

The geneticist looked for all the distinguishing features of Kabuki Makeup Syndrome; the little lines and the loops in the fingers, the S-shaped eyebrows, the way the corners of her lips turn down, the way her eyes appear to be bigger than her eye sockets, and the retardation in her bone growth. Jennifer demonstrated the syndrome, and they consider her to be one of the most involved cases of the children they know. At that time of her diagnosis, there were only 69 other children who had actually been diagnosed and most of those were in Japan.

We were pleased to have an answer, to have this diagnosis, but we didn't know anybody else with the same syndrome. There are a whole group of people who have Cerebral Palsy, and we had been really connected with them. We thought, "Oh, no, now what do we do?" But it was such a relief just to have someone say, we're almost 100% sure that this is what she has, that these are the features that match this disorder and we feel comfortable diagnosing her with this. In the meantime, the research is still continuing. The specialists think there is a large number of undiagnosed cases out there and that as the information gets out, Kabuki Makeup Syndrome will become a common diagnosis, like Down syndrome, and will also have an identified genetic link.

I have met only one other child with Kabuki Makeup Syndrome. It was such a relief to get that diagnosis and to have a clearer picture of what Jennifer's possible outcomes could be, instead of just guessing all of the time. It was probably even good that I had heard all the worst predictions possible, because I have accepted those things and I know that's as bad as it could ever be for Jennifer. So every improvement that Jennifer makes, even the smallest improvement, is like a huge milestone for us because we're just one step beyond the possibility of her needing institutionalization; we've been successful at keeping her with us at home, just as we would either of our other children.

Jennifer Waritz asleep as an infant.

REFLEXES

One way to describe cerebral palsy is as an interruption of normal reflex development. As an infant's neurological system develops, motor reflexes move from "primitive" to "voluntary." Whereas all infants differ slightly in their rate of development, a significant injury to the brain, either prenatally or postnatally, may impair the normally smooth transition to such a degree as to cause cerebral palsy.

Primitive reflexes are developed in utero and are present in the early months of life. They are responsible for involuntary motor responses to specific stimuli. For infants with intact neurological systems, the presentation of a given stimulus, such as a touch to the cheek, is predictably followed by a motor response; in this case, the head turns toward the touch and is known as the rooting reflex. Primitive reflexes may be a kind of natural "hardwiring" that equips the child with basic motor patterns and established neurological pathways. While thought to be useful prenatally (Fetters, 1984), primitive reflexes have limited utility to infants after birth. As infants mature, most primitive reflexes are neurologically integrated, giving the child control over them. Primitive reflexes gradually disappear and are replaced by postural, or adaptive, reflexes. When this does not happen, persistent primitive reflexes can interfere with a child's development of voluntary movement.

Figure 5–2
Typical moro
reflex.

It is generally agreed that reflexes are key to normal motor development. The presence (or absence) of primitive and adaptive reflexes provides a prediction of developmental potential. Predictable reflex patterns are considered "neurodevelopmental markers" and the best index of brain dysfunction, particularly cerebral palsy. For an optimistic motor outcome, primitive reflexes should appear before 3 months and disappear by 6 months; if primitive reflexes do not disappear by 12 months of age, there is a pessimistic prediction for walking (Festschrift, 1994). Therefore, early childhood educators should be aware of reflex patterns so that noticeable deviations in development can be spotted. Since the objective of subsequent neuromotor intervention is to limit the influence of atypical reflexive development, early identification provides the greatest promise of mediating motor problems.

The **moro reflex** is the most commonly used index of reflexive maturity and is present at birth (see Figure 5–2). When a child's head is suddenly dropped backwards, the child's arms fly back and out in a symmetrical **abduction** (away from body) and **extension** (straightening of the joints); then the child's arms flex and return to the body in **adduction** (toward body), as if to embrace someone. Abnormal neurological maturation is indicated when the moro response:

1. Is absent in the neonatal period
2. Is asymmetrical
3. Persists beyond three to four months of age

The **asymmetrical tonic neck reflex (ATNR),** also commonly assessed, is sometimes referred to as the "fencer's reflex." When a child's head is turned to one side, the extremities of the same side are extended, while the extremities on the opposite side of the body are flexed (bent at the joints) (see Figure 5–3). In normally developing infants, the response is usually partial or incomplete. On the other hand, when the response is well-defined and easily provoked, this is usually a sign of some negative neurological involvement. The ATNR reflex begins to disappear in the first few months. It has been speculated that the ATNR reflex can persist even into early childhood and may be the cause of mild motor problems in children who are "clumsy" or awkward in motor play (Henderson, French, & McCarty, 1993).

Other primitive reflexes seen at birth include the rooting, grasp, startle, and stepping reflexes. The **rooting reflex** occurs when an infant's cheek is lightly stroked. In response, a child will turn its head toward the touch. Stimulating the palm of an infant's hand will elicit the **grasp reflex,** or flexion of the hand. A **startle reflex** occurs when

Figure 5–3
Typical
asymmetrical
reflex.

a sudden noise or movement causes children to thrust their arms outward and then pull them back. It is apparent that if these involuntary responses were to persist, they would interfere with normal motor routines. For example, if the grasp reflex persisted, individuals would never be able to voluntarily release objects once placed in the hand's palm. The disappearance of these reflexes, mostly within the first four to six months of life, is a necessary transition referred to as **reflex integration.**

Several reflexes could interfere with walking and are typically integrated within the first six months. By holding a child in a vertical position so that the feet touch the surface, one can elicit the **stepping reflex** (see Figure 5–4). This step-like response encourages many parents to inaccurately conclude that their children are precociously ready to begin walking. The **Babinski reflex** is stimulated by stroking the sole of an infant's foot. If the Babinski reflex is present, infants will respond by spreading their toes. A third commonly assessed reflex of the lower extremities is the plantar reflex. The latter is observed when pressure applied to the ball of an infant's foot is followed by flexion of the toes around the stimulus, as if to grasp the object.

Primitive reflexes are replaced by adaptive and postural reflexes. If these reflexes do not develop appropriately, then a child's motor skills will not progress. The sucking and swallowing reflexes are *adaptive reflexes* that are present at birth, though still immature. These reflexes work in harmony when mature and are usually well-developed by six months of age. When they are fully developed, a child has good tongue control and lip closure when sucking. These reflexes are paired with the ability to move food from the front to the back of the mouth, and to control the path of food to the esophagus (rather than trachea), and to move food down the esophagus to the stomach.

Figure 5–4
Typical stepping
reflex.

While much of human movement is voluntary, a significant part of balance is reflexive. Appearance of **postural reflexes** requires the brain to integrate several modalities (sight, hearing, motor movement, etc.) simultaneously. Unlike primitive reflexes, which interfere with movement if persistent, postural reflexes actually supplement movement and help to prevent injury. A **parachute reflex** (see Figure 5–5) results when an infant is held horizontal and prone, and then lowered toward the floor. As if to break the fall, infants will extend their arms and legs toward the surface. Several reflexes evolve that permit children to maintain an upright position, as infants learn to sit and stand. Lateral head righting at two to three months is generally the first postural reflex to appear. An **equilibrium reflex** is stimulated whenever a child moves or is pushed out of a midline (vertical) position. Resisting gravity, the equilibrium reflex involuntarily causes the body to realign its trunk vertically. Similarly, when an infant's trunk is pushed out of an upright position either to the side, front, or back, the head righting reflex will attempt to hold the head in an upright position. A final and complementary reflex is referred to as **protective extension.** In this case, an infant, pushed out of midline from either a sitting or standing position, will reach out (extension) and attempt to protect itself from falling. Children will first learn to protect themselves from falls to the front, then from falls to the sides, and finally from falls to the rear.

MUSCLE TONE

Posture, consistency of muscles, and joint range of motion are all affected by dimensions of muscle tone. Three categories are generally used to define a child's muscle tone: normal, hypertonic, and hypotonic. Infants with abnormally high or tight muscle tone (**hypertonia**) show restricted ranges of motion. By contrast, **hypotonia,** or very loose tone, is seen in children who show little strength to resist gravity or joint movement. While the former have very tense muscle consistency, the

Figure 5–5
Typical
parachute
reflex.

latter tend to have flaccid muscle tone. Both hypertonicity and hypotonicity are indexes of neurological insult and are also likely to result in delayed if not abnormal motor development.

Assessment of muscle tone can be accomplished by comparative analysis of **range of motion.** One test of muscle tone is head rotation, in which the head is passively turned when flexed and when extended. The Scarf sign is a second test of muscle tone. In this test a child's arm is extended across the chest toward the opposite shoulder. In both cases, the degree to which movement is permitted or prohibited gives an index of the neurological maturity: in normally developing children, the range of motion must be neither too loose nor too tight for the chronological age of a child.

Affected Site

Cerebral palsy can be described by the extent of involvement (affected) if one imagines the body dissected vertically and horizontally (see Figure 5–6). **Hemiplegia** occurs when one side of the body is affected (double hemiplegia involves both sides, with one side more severely impaired, and the arms more affected than the legs) and is caused by traumatic brain injury in the opposite side of the brain. In **paraplegia,** the lower extremities are affected, and in **quadriplegia** (or tetraplegia), all four extremities are involved. Similarly, all four extremities are affected in **diplegia,** with greater involvement of the legs than the trunk and arms. Finally, **monoplegia** and **triplegia** have involvement of one and three extremities, respectively. It is generally believed that diplegia is associated with injury that occurs to the brain before birth, while quadraplegia and hemiplegia occur as a result of complications in the neonatal period (Cooke, 1990).

Characteristics of Cerebral Palsy

Though definitions vary, the type of cerebral palsy can generally be classified according to the type of muscle movement or muscle tone abnormality manifested. The most common descriptions of the types of CP indicate the state of muscle tone, the area of injury within the central nervous system, and the quality of muscle control.

Figure 5–6
Breakdown of
cerebral palsy
by body part.

Hemiplegia   Double hemiplegia   Paraplegia   Quadriplegia or Tetraplegia   Diplegia   Monoplegia (any one extremity)   Triplegia (any three extremities)

Hypertonia, occurs when the **pyramidal tract** (the motor cortex and spinal cord) is damaged. Eventually, hypertonia limits joint movement because of shortened muscles and ligaments. If this muscle tightness is severe, it contributes to the development of deformities of the spine, joint dislocation, and contractures (Bigge, 1991).

Infants born with cerebral palsy are initially hypotonic, but if their floppiness persists through the first year without the development of other tone problems, generalized hypotonia is diagnosed. Hypotonia is often correlated with cognitive deficit. Hypotonic infants tend to rely on external support and are delayed in the development of motor skills. They also have poor posture and hypermobile joints.

The pyramidal nerve fibers originate in the brain and pass through the spinal cord to attach to motor cells in the body. When cerebral damage occurs outside the pyramidal nerve group, it is said to be **extrapyramidal,** and the resulting condition is called **athetosis,** or **dyskinesia.** Rather than being responsible for initiation of movement, extrapyramidal nerves are responsible for controlling and coordinating posture, tone, and locomotion. Dyskinesia affects approximately 20% of all children with cerebral palsy. Athetosis, or variable muscle tone, ranges from rigid to flaccid. Injury, often due to jaundice, is responsible for athetosis, which affects all four extremities. Slow worm-like or writhing movements, more pronounced in a child's head and hands, are accentuated when children attempt to move and when they become emotional. Children with athetosis may have difficulty sitting, walking, eating, and speaking. Typically, the excessive movement associated with athetosis is not observed until the second year of life, even though abnormalities in tone, reflexes, and posture can be diagnosed earlier.

With **ataxic cerebral palsy,** which is very rare, children have difficulty balancing well while walking. The cerebellum is the site of injury in this type of cerebral palsy (Bigge, 1991). Ataxia interferes with coordination in balancing and hand use. The individual bobbles while standing and walking and tends to overshoot a target. Children with ataxia tend to exaggerate movement in an effort to balance, and the constant effort to stabilize can cause rigid movement.

Spastic cerebral palsy, in which the muscle tightens and resists efforts to move, is the most common type and results from injury to the pyramidal tract of the brain, usually due to hemorrhaging after premature birth or severe brain damage (perhaps caused by prolonged oxygen deprivation). Spastic movement has been characterized as a "jackknife" response, in which joints express hyperresistance to extension or

Table 5–2 Diagnostic criteria for severity of cerebral palsy.

Degree of Involvement	Characteristics
Severe Cerebral Palsy	1. Total dependence in meeting physical needs
	2. Poor head control
	3. Deformities, present or potential, which limit function or produce pain
	4. Perceptual and/or sensory integrative deficits which prevent the achievement of academic and age-appropriate motor skills
Moderate Cerebral Palsy	1. Some independence in meeting physical needs
	2. Functional head control
	3. Deformities, present or potential, which limit independent function or produce pain
	4. Perceptual and/or sensory integrative deficits which interfere with achievement of academic and age-appropriate motor skills
Mild Cerebral Palsy	1. Independence in meeting physical needs
	2. Potential to improve quality of motor and/or perceptual skills with therapy intervention
	3. Potential for regression in quality of motor and perceptual skills without intervention.

Source: Adapted from Grove, N., Cusick, B., & Bigge, J. (1991). Conditions resulting in physical disabilities. In J. Bigge (Ed.), *Teaching individuals with physical and multiple disabilities* (pp. 1–15). Columbus, OH: Macmillan.

flexion up to a certain threshold, and then resistance is suddenly released. The status of a child's tone may change over time; many children have hypotonia in infancy, and this progresses to spasticity.

Naturally, all movement, including that of both large and small muscle groups, can be affected by cerebral palsy. The diagnosis of just one type of cerebral palsy is rare (Bigge, 1991), and it is typical to encounter a diagnosis such as "mixed spastic/athetoid quadriplegia with underlying ataxia." Early in development, signs of neuromuscular damage include the absence of primitive reflexes or the later failure to integrate these reflexes. Hence, development of head control, crawling, sitting, and walking tends to be delayed.

SEVERITY OF INVOLVEMENT

A diagnosis of cerebral palsy is almost meaningless unless it is also paired with a description of the degree of **involvement** or the degree to which a child is affected motorically. Variations of motor involvement range from mild to severe, based on the degree to which a child's impairment interferes with independent motor and functional behaviors. Descriptions of the general characteristics of children with mild, moderate, and severe motor involvement are presented in Table 5–2.

ASSOCIATED CHARACTERISTICS OF CHILDREN WITH CEREBRAL PALSY

Because cerebral palsy results from damage to the central nervous system, interference with normal movement is almost always accompanied by collateral

Table 5–3 Signs of malnutrition.

Body Part Affected	Observable Physical Symptoms of Malnutrition	Possible Nutritional Inadequacy
Overall body	Low body weight, short stature, edema (swelling)	Calories Protein
Hair	Looseness, sparseness, dullness	Protein
Skin	Xerosis (dryness), follicular keratosis (growth, e.g., wart, lesion) Solar dermatitis (inflammation) Petechiae, pupura (easy bruising and tiny red patches)	Vitamin A Niacin Ascorbic acid
Subcutaneous tissue	Decreased subcutaneous tissue	Calories
Nails	Spoon-shaped appearance	Iron
Eyes	Dry conjunctiva, keratomalacia (cell death of the cornea)	Vitamin A
Lips	Cheilosis (fissures and dry scaling of the lips)	Iron B-complex vitamins Riboflavin
Gums	Swelling, bleeding	Vitamin C
Tongue	Glossitis	Niacin, folate, riboflavin, Vitamin B_{12}
Skeletal system	Bone tenderness	Vitamins C and D
Muscles	Decreased muscle mass	Protein, calories

Source: Adapted from Fee, M. A., Charney, E. B., & Robertson, W. W. (1988). Nutritional assessment of the young child with cerebral palsy. *Infants and Young Children, 1*(1), 33–40.

damage to other biological functions such as hearing and cognition. Furthermore, the motor involvement itself affects functioning in a number of skill areas. For example, self-help skills, such as feeding and dressing, are limited by the degree of motor dysfunction.

Difficulty in feeding children with cerebral palsy, especially those with *dystonia,* is common (Dahl & Gebre-Medhin, 1993). It has been found that approximately 50% of children with cerebral palsy experience feeding problems and 48% have growth retardation (Thommessen, Kase, Riis, & Heiberg, 1991). The most common feeding problems include poor self-feeding, poor swallowing and chewing from oral-motor dysfunction, and inordinately long feeding sessions. Frequent vomiting, dental problems that cause pain and infection, rumination, reflux, and poor appetite are also not uncommon (Dahl & Gebre-Medhin, 1993; Fee, Charney, & Robertson, 1988). Diets tend to be restricted in texture and taste, as many children are given pureed or powdered foods, which are easy to prepare and feed (Reilly & Skuse, 1992). Subsequently, children's energy intake and nutritional status are frequently compromised; two thirds of the children studied by Dahl and Gebre-Medhin (1993) were below the 10th percentile for energy intake. To assist in monitoring a child's diet, Fee et al. (1988) identified several physical characteristics that can indicate to a caretaker a child might be malnourished (see Table 5–3). Feeding difficulties apparently begin at birth when a large percentage of infants have difficulty sucking during nursing

(Reilly & Skuse, 1992). From direct observations of mealtime, Reilly and Skuse (1992) described typical mothers' behavior as mechanical and lacking in verbalization. They concluded that the stress associated with difficult feeding reduced mothers' typical nurturing. Although maternal behavior returned to normal levels as soon as mealtimes were completed, the loss of this valuable opportunity may be significant in terms of social and linguistic development.

The overall growth patterns of children with cerebral palsy are substantially depressed when compared to standardized measurements. While measurements are within the normal range by 12 months of age (when corrected for gestational age), many infants have fallen well behind their nondisabled peers in both height and weight (Reilly & Skuse, 1992).

Seizure Disorders

Approximately one third of children with cerebral palsy also have some form of epilepsy. Children with spasticity are most likely to experience seizures, while children with athetosis are least likely. The most common types of epilepsy observed are **tonic-clonic** and **partial complex seizures.**

Mental Retardation

The average incidence of severe mental retardation in accompaniment with cerebral palsy is 25%. By contrast, the majority of children with cerebral palsy have IQs above 50, in spite of the inherent bias built into intelligence tests when used for children with motor impairment. Taken as a group, however, children with cerebral palsy are more likely to have delayed development in sensorimotor behaviors (Cioni, Paolicelli, Sordi, & Vinter, 1993). This makes sense, since these infants and preschoolers are prevented from exploring and interacting with their environments to the same extent as children who have no motor involvement. Figure 5–7 illustrates the comparative results of children with cerebral palsy and nondisabled, same-age peers on measures of cognitive development.

Some types of cerebral palsy are more likely than others to be associated with intellectual deficits. For example, hemiplegia is rarely associated with cognitive deficits when it is not paired with seizures (Vargha-Khadem, Isaacs, Ver der Werf, Robb, & Wilson, 1992).

ETIOLOGY OF CEREBRAL PALSY

It has been held that premature birth and birth complications, such as asphyxia, constitute major causes of cerebral palsy. On the other hand, this assumption has been debated on the grounds that many children who experience birth-related problems do not show signs of motor involvement later in childhood (Grant, Joy, O'Brien, Hennessy, & MacDonald, 1989). Additionally, approximately half of all children with cerebral palsy are born full-term to apparently healthy mothers (Seppa, 1998). Further, it does not appear that cesarean delivery reduces the risk of cerebral palsy (Scheller & Nelson, 1994). Even Freud speculated that Central Nervous System (CNS) abnormalities preceded both birth complications and the asphyxia commonly associated with cerebral palsy. This stand was supported by a major study conducted by the National Collaborative Parental

Figure 5–7
A. Results
obtained by
infants with CP
in Scale 1,
compared with
mean step scores
(continuous line)
and standard
deviations
(broken lines) of
unaffected
subjects of Vinter
et al., 1993.
B. Results
obtained by
infants with CP
in Scale 1,
compared with
mean step scores
(continuous line)
and standard
deviations
(broken lines) of
unaffected
subjects of Vinter
et al., 1993.

Project (Eicher & Batshaw, 1993), which revealed that fewer than 10% of all cases of cerebral palsy were the result of asphyxia alone. Recent research has focused on pre-natal infections as a major potential contributor to cerebral palsy (Seppa, 1998).

Two opposing characteristics of the brain are associated with the long-term prognosis of children who have received neurological insult during the fetal or neonatal period. The developing brain is especially vulnerable to trauma or physiological disruptions. On the other hand, very young nervous systems are more plastic and may repair or compensate for damage at a rate and effectiveness that cannot be matched by older children and adults (Farmer, Harrison, Ingram, & Stephens, 1991). As a consequence, abnormal CAT scans at birth can appear normal 12 months later, with no apparent residual motor or cognitive damage (Eaton, Ahmed, & Dubowitz, 1991). Still, 36% of all cases of cerebral palsy are associated with a birth weight below 2500 g (5.5 lb), and 30% of all cases were attributed to brain damage before or during birth (Rosen & Dickinson, 1992). Among very low birth weight children, several factors have been found to correlate with positive outcomes versus those who eventually develop cerebral palsy. Neonates who spend long periods of time on a ventilator, develop widespread infection, have a severe neurological abnormality, or have residual signs of prenatal infection are at greater risk of developing cerebral palsy than infants who do not experience these risk factors (Wilson-Costello et al., 1998).

To illustrate the diversity of circumstances associated with cerebral palsy, Veelken, Schopf, Dammann, and Schulte (1993) delineated the known and probable causes of 53 children with cerebral palsy who had very low birth weight. Table 5–4 provides a sample of these causes, which range from rupture of the umbilical cord to obstruction of the tracheal tube. The resultant motor impairments range from spastic hemiplegia to severe spastic triplegia.

In addition to birth related injury, **congenital** causes are cited as a second large category responsible for cerebral palsy, though causation in many cases is based on speculation. Naeye, Peters, Bartholomew, and Landis (1989) studied over 40,000 live births, of which 150 (0.37%) were diagnosed with cerebral palsy between birth and age seven. Of those with quadriplegia, 53% had a probable congenital cause, while 35% of the nonquadriplegic cases had a verifiable congenital origin. Hence, birth asphyxia accounted for just 14% of the cases of cerebral palsy in the quadriplegic group and a negligible percentage of cases (0.01%) in the nonquadriplegia group.

Cerebral palsy can result from neurological damage after birth as well. Infections such as bacterial meningitis and encephalitis can cause severe neurological damage. Anoxia caused by submersion syndrome (water accidents) or near-suffocation is another cause of cerebral palsy. Prenatal abnormalities such as a reduced blood supply to the placenta, cysts, and abnormal brain development are also associated with cerebral palsy. To a small degree, genetic and metabolic disorders contribute to the incidence of cerebral palsy. Finally, environmental toxins such as prenatal exposure to radiation, industrial waste, and alcohol exposure have been associated with cerebral palsy (Eicher & Batshaw, 1993).

However, it is still apparent that a large percentage of cases of cerebral palsy have no known etiology. It is these cases that sometimes result in unfortunate speculation and self-blaming by families. Professionals may inadvertently add to parent's guilt by asking probing questions about prenatal and perinatal history. In most cases, while such information might be interesting, it is of no functional use and may be better left unprobed.

Table 5–4 Causes of cerebral palsy in very low birth weight infants.

Type of CP	Timing of Brain Injury	Event Related to Injury
Spastic diplegia, moderate dystonia	Prenatal	Maternal epilepsy, placental bleeding
Dystonia	Prenatal/delivery	Gross cephalic deformity, lifeless at birth
Spastic diplegia, moderate	Delivery	Cord rupture during cesarean section, hypovolemic shock
Spastic diplegia, moderate	Delivery	Marginal placenta, hypovolemic shock
Spastic tetraplegia	Delivery	Cord prolapse, lifeless at birth
Spastic diplegia, severe	Delivery	Severe and prolonged bradycardia, refusal of cesarean section
Spastic hemiplegia	Delivery/immediate postnatal	Stained amniotic fluid; no resuscitation efforts within 30 min after birth
Spastic diplegia, moderate	Neonatal	Intraventricular hemorrhaging; cerebral depression
Dystonia	Neonatal	Repeated resuscitations on day 6 following artificial airway obstruction
Spastic diplegia, moderate	Neonatal	Heart arrest on day 3, resuscitation
Spastic tetraplegia	Neonatal	Severe hypoxia; artificial airway tube obstruction on day 3
Spastic tetraplegia	Later	Encephalopathy of unknown origin in infancy, neurological deterioration
Spastic diplegia, mild	Later	Bacterial meningitis on day 42, neurological and sonographic deterioration
Spastic tetraplegia	Later	Skull fracture, subdural hematoma, neurological deterioration
Spastic diplegia, moderate	Prenatal	Severe placental bleeding, severe decelerations on cardiotocography
Spastic diplegia, moderate	Delivery/neonatal	Vaginal delivery despite breech presentation, infection with strep B
Spastic diplegia, moderate	Immediate postnatal	Severe cardiac depression after birth
Spastic diplegia, moderate	Immediate postnatal	Cardiac depression after birth, delayed airway management despite severe signs of RDS
Severe diplegia, moderate	Immediate postnatal	Defect of incubator heating and respirator during transportation resulting in hypothermia and ineffective ventilation
Spastic diplegia, moderate	Neonatal	Hyperkalemia on day 2, fall of hematocrit, IVH IV on ultrasound
Spastic diplegia, moderate	Neonatal	Severe apnea and bradycardia on day 2 after extubation
Spastic diplegia, moderate	Neonatal	Dramatic clinical deterioration with seizures day 8
Spastic diplegia, severe	Neonatal	Septicemia with thrombocytopenia on day 2 cardiac arrest, resuscitation on day 4

Source: Adapted from Veelken, N., Schopf, M., Dammann, O., & Schulte, F. J. (1993). Etiological classification of cerebral palsy in very low birthweight infants. *Neuropediatrics, 24,* 74–76.

TREATMENT OF CEREBRAL PALSY

Though many infants and preschoolers with cerebral palsy receive center-based treatment in the form of physical and occupational therapy or special education, these are also usually paired with expectations that parents complete home programs. Much research has been conducted on the efficacy of home programs; yet there continues to be a general lack of follow-through on the part of parents that is not reflective of parents' overall interest in their children's welfare (Hinjosa & Anderson, 1991). Instead, this lack of participation may be due to expectations set by therapists that were perceived by parents to be unrealistic. The following are excerpts from interviews of parents taken by Hinjosa and Anderson (1991):

> I would do it but then, as a mother, I would get frustrated . . . I was feeling like, "Wow, what is wrong with me?" It was like I was just tired, and it's like they said, "Don't try to take an hour and do it. Do it, like, when you are changing his Pampers, or when you are doing this." But, with me, when I finish his Pampers, I have to move on to something else. 'Cause I have the other child here, I can't, you know, do that. (Irene, p. 275)

> The other therapist told me, "Don't let her walk." I mean, that's like saying, "Don't let her eat." because I can't watch her all the time, and she wants to walk, you know. If it is going to make her become independent and this is what she wants to do, I'm going to let her do it! (Carol, p. 276)

In general, Hinjosa and Anderson (1991) made the following recommendations to therapists regarding expectations for family home intervention:

◆ Explore the needs of parents and assist them in developing their own interventions, which should foster their own creativity and reinforce their efficacy as the primary caregiver.
◆ Provide follow-up positive support and feedback related to family solutions and implementation of their own plans.
◆ Assist parents in developing activities that are consistent with the total family needs and that are realistic.
◆ Implement collaborative goal selection and treatment plans that are sensitive to a family's daily schedules, and recognize that parents may be unable to follow through as consistently as is recommended.

Research efforts conducted to determine the overall effectiveness of early intervention for infants and preschoolers with cerebral palsy yield mixed findings. Turnbull (1993) concluded that, while some children do no better than could be expected given natural maturation, overall those with and at risk of cerebral palsy who receive physical therapy experience substantially greater motoric development than those without physical therapy. Other researchers found that young children who received physical therapy alone, progressed at least as well in all domains as those who received short-term infant stimulation and physical therapy (Palmer et al., 1990).

For children with cerebral palsy, management of physical development is a primary focus in early intervention, as well as later education. Physical therapists may be the primary or only specialists working with families. Their role is to monitor physical development, detect changes in orthopedic status, and to plan and implement specific motor development strategies (Dormans, 1993). It may be necessary for children to wear day and/or night braces, to undergo corrective surgery, or to be fit for orthopedic equipment such as crutches, a walker, or a wheelchair. The goal of physical development however, is to facilitate the greatest amount of movement while concurrently working to diminish interfering abnormal movement or reflexes.

The primary focus of physical management is often **positioning** and handling. Positioning refers to the treatment of postural and reflex abnormalities by careful, symmetrical placement and support of the child's body. Efforts are made to adapt seating and standing equipment so that a child's skeleton can be aligned in a posture that is as normal as possible and to inhibit the interference of primitive reflexes. Parents and teachers can be trained in proper positioning techniques, but an occupational or physical therapist should be consulted for the specific needs of an individual child.

For example, a child with cerebral palsy who still has a dominant asymmetrical tonic neck reflex (ATNR) would extend the limbs on the side of the body toward which the head is turned and flex the limbs on the side of the body that is opposite. If the child is allowed to fall into this position much of the time, some muscles of the body would shorten and might cause contractures that would eventually deform the affected bones and joints. Furthermore, the child's face might be in an awkward position for speech, eating would be difficult, and the child would not be able to bring objects to the midline for functional use with both hands.

This child would best be seated in a device adapted to prevent looking to one side, thus inhibiting the ATNR. This might be done by placing blinders to the side of the child's head so that the child looks straight ahead. Any person feeding or talking with the child would approach from directly in front of the child. Now, the limbs could be used at midline in a symmetrical fashion.

A child with low muscle tone might be positioned in a standing device that provides a slight forward incline and straps to support the child's weak muscles and to encourage flexion of the head and arms. This positioning would allow stimulation of the child's weight bearing joints and limbs and keep the child upright to interact with other children and adults.

Handling involves preparation of a child for movement and positioning. A child who is hypertonic and very stiff may be difficult to dress, for example. If a parent or therapist provides gentle shaking or stroking of the child's arms before putting on a shirt, it will be much easier to bend the child's elbow and pull the shirt over as needed. Even soft lighting and music may relax the child's muscle tone in preparation for such an activity. Accurate assessment of an individual child's need for handling is best carried out by an occupational or physical therapist.

In addition to physical therapy, a nutritionist should be involved with families whose children have compromised nutritional intake. However, some general considerations for all children with oral-motor involvement were advised by Fee et al. (1988): frequent short feedings, development of a structured feeding program by a physical and occupational therapist, and increased caloric concentration of food, including nutritional formula supplements.

THE DIARY OF ESTHER ANNA BERKE: MONTH 8–9

Esther was examined by a physical therapist and a dietitian, both of whom prescribed customized programs for Esther to help her body develop. The physical therapy program will be implemented by Sarah, with help from Daniel, Abigail, and me. The diet requires Esther to eat foods high in sodium and low in potassium. She was 72 cm long (80th percentile) and weighed 8 kg (50th percentile) on her 8th birthday.

June 16–30:   Sarah left Daniel and Abigail with Grandma Appleby and flew to Utah on June 19 with Esther for an evaluation at the National Academy of Child Development (NACD). They specialize in designing holistic physical therapy programs for children like Esther. The parents become the therapists, giving the child physical therapy each day. They are cautiously optimistic about Esther's development, and design a 3 hour/day program for her that includes such things as aromatherapy (sniffing pleasant odors such as cinnamon, coffee, and myrrh), swinging in a hammock, and listening to classical music (I could handle a program like that!). On June 25 Esther was evaluated at Life Balances. They specialize in designing customized diets for children like Esther. They take a blood sample and analyze it for everything you can possibly measure in blood, then compare the results against a "normal" child of the same age and sex. They look for differences and then try to prescribe special foods or vitamins to bring the blood back into balance. Esther's blood is high in potassium (K) and low in sodium (Na), and the pH is too alkaline. Some other components are also out of balance. They prescribe an electrolyte solution that is high in Na for her, along with meat, wheat, and corn (fortunately Gerber makes a wheat- and corn-based baby cereal). High-potassium foods like bananas are off-limits to her. On June 30 Sarah and the kids return to Taiwan.

July 1–15:   The electrolyte solution helps control Esther's seizures. When a seizure starts, we dribble the solution into her mouth, and the seizure generally stops after 3–4 min. The number of seizures is quite high at first, but gradually is decreasing. After 5–6 days of electrolytes, she is almost seizure-free. We hosted the Tainan Missionary Fellowship for a 4th of July party, and she was quite the charmer, very quiet no matter who held her. However, a new type of spasm started occurring the next day in which she arches her back and thrashes around, crying. This can go on for a long time, up to several hours. It keeps her up a lot at night, and makes our schedule very erratic. I hope this is just another phase in her adjustment as we change her metabolism.

SEIZURES

As many as 1 in 10 persons has a **seizure** at least once in a lifetime. In childhood, approximately two million Americans experience recurring seizures, defining a condition known as epilepsy (Hingley, 1999). Seizures are the result of abnormal electrical discharges in cerebral neurons. Different types of seizures result from cortical involvement of different regions of the brain. The physiology of seizures, irrespective of type, is an imbalance between the usual coordinated efforts of neurons that are **excited** (activated to perform a function) and those that are **inhibited** (prevented from activating when not needed). During a seizure, the normal communication between neurons is interrupted by millions of electrical impulses occurring at the same time and are more intense than usual, resulting in abnormal brain activity which can usually be detected on an EEG.

While a person who has a seizure may have epilepsy, this is not necessarily the case. **Epilepsy** is a condition in which seizures are recurrent. Though epilepsy is not provoked by external sources (e.g., metabolic disturbances, exposure to poison, or severe insult to the central nervous system) seizures may be caused by such events. According to Brunquell (1994), all humans have a threshold for seizures, beyond which a clinical seizure will occur. Most person's thresholds are so high that normal life challenges will not push them past these limits. On the other hand, those with multiple daily seizures have very low thresholds as compared to persons who have less frequent seizures. Individual threshold levels are presumed to be both genetically determined and interactive with environmental events (Brunquell, 1994).

Though there are 30 different types of seizures, they have been grouped into three categories of epileptic seizures as recognized in the International Classification of Epileptic Seizures: *partial* (those that result from activation of one area of the brain), *generalized* (those that involve activation of the entire brain and affect the whole body), and *unclassified* seizures. In simple partial seizures, individuals may be conscious, while consciousness is impaired with complex partial seizures. Either of these two conditions may progress to a partial seizure with secondary generalization, in which an individual totally loses consciousness.

Of the seizures described above, **generalized seizures** are the most commonly discussed in educational literature, and these include the following: **absence** (petit mal), **tonic, clonic, tonic-clonic** (grand mal), **myoclonic,** and **atonic** seizures (see Table 5–5). In each of these seizures loss of consciousness is a classification criteria.

Over 150 known causes of seizures have been identified, though in 70% of individual cases it is not possible to pinpoint the cause (Hingley, 1999). Most diagnoses are related to factors also associated with other forms of neurological damage. Factors associated with the risk of seizures include perinatal trauma, fetal distress, congenital and postnatal infections (e.g., cytomegalovirus, meningitis, and influenza), teratogens, malformations or tumors, head injuries, and chromosomal abnormalities (e.g., juvenile myoclonic epilepsy resulting from an anomaly of the short arm of chromosome 6).

The relationship between seizures and mental retardation seems to be related to the presence of associated neurological disabilities or severe cognitive delay (Goulden, Shinnar, Koller, Katz, & Richardson, 1991; Shepherd & Hosking, 1989). It seems that the risk of seizures in persons with mild mental retardation who do not have cerebral palsy or other types of disabilities is low (Goulden et al., 1991). Laybourn and Hill (1994) referred to the relationship between seizures and other risk factors as "epilepsy-only" and "epilepsy-plus." Children in the latter group tend to have a poorer overall prognosis, including greater intellectual impairment, resistance to drug treatment of seizures, and other physical disabilities.

Table 5–5 Types of seizures.

Type of Seizure	Description
Absence	Sudden interruption of ongoing activity and the assumption of a blank stare for 1 to 15 seconds. Usually normal intelligence. Good response to therapy, though many have poor social adaptation and difficulty sustaining attention.
Tonic	Rigid muscular contraction, often fixing the limbs in some strained posture.
Clonic	Alternate contraction and relaxation of muscles, occurring in rapid succession.
Tonic-clonic	Rigid muscular contraction followed by the appearance of clonic activity.
Myoclonic	Sudden, brief, shock-like muscle contractions. Usually normal intelligence, but may experience delays in social development.
Temporal lobe (Psychomotor)	Repetitive movements such as chewing, lip smacking, rocking: may have bizarre sensory/emotional changes.
Atonic	Sudden reduction in muscle tone. In more severe cases, persons may slump to the ground.
Infantile seizures	Long-term prognosis is very poor, mental and neurological damage affect over 80% of cases.
Febrile seizures	Tonic-clonic seizures result from high temperatures. Usually do not require medication and terminate when fevers are gone.

On the other hand, the effects of seizures themselves on cognitive functioning are associated with the type, age of onset, and frequency of seizures. Overall, children with seizures tend to have diminished concentration and mental processing (Dam, 1990). Generally speaking, the earlier the onset of seizures, the poorer the prognosis. Furthermore, each seizure has the potential for causing further brain injury due to a depletion of neurological metabolites. Children are most at risk of further brain injury when seizures are prolonged for 15 minutes or more, in a condition referred to as **status epilepticus.**

There is some indication that children with seizures are more likely to have behavior problems than children without epilepsy. In general, Austin, Risinger, and Beckett (1992) found five factors that increased the likelihood of behavior problems:

1. Female gender
2. Families that had high levels of stress
3. Families that perceived themselves as having low levels of mastery over family events or outcomes
4. Families with little extended family support
5. High frequency of seizures

Approximately 4% of children experience **breath-holding spells** (Morelle, 1993). While these are not seizures, they are involuntary. Usually appearing before 18 months of age, breath-holding tends to disappear by age five. Typically, breath-holding proceeds from a stressful event (e.g., crying or anger) to a change in color, and then to a forceful inspiration. At other times, the breath-holding may be prolonged enough to lead to loss of consciousness, slow pulse, and incontinence. The cause of breath-holding episodes is unclear, though the incidence overlaps with some tonic-clonic seizures (Morelle, 1993), and Procopis (1992) reported a family history in about a third of cases. Medication, though sometimes prescribed, is generally neither necessary nor effective (Procopis, 1992). To assist parents, professionals should provide reassurance and information. For some children, whose temper tantrums precipitate episodes, behavioral intervention may be necessary, though the aim is to change the precipitating behavior and not the breath-holding which is involuntary.

TREATMENT

Medical treatment of epilepsy primarily includes the use of several drugs (see Table 5–6). Drugs affect children differently than they do adults. For example, Phenobarbital may cause some children to become hyperactive, whereas this drug is generally a sedative in adults (Dichter, 1994). Because of this effect, and the tendency of Phenobarbital to adversely affect cognitive functioning and memory, its use is not recommended for younger children (Dichter, 1994). Sometimes with prescribed medication, a child's seizures will be resistant to a first attempt. Adding a second drug may be successful in eliminating or reducing seizures. The goal of drug treatment is to select the medication which will have the greatest control while causing the fewest side effects. This is why, initially, many children go through a period of "experimentation" in order to find the right combination of drugs for a particular child (Hingley, 1999).

However, in 30% of cases, seizures cannot be controlled through medication (Brunquell, 1994). Recent medical advances have made surgery a more viable op-

Table 5–6 Drugs prescribed for the treatment of epilepsy.

Category A: Prescribed to compensate for depressed inhibitory neuron functioning.

Generic Drug Name	Common Product Name	Use
Barbiturates	Phenobarbital	Sedation; generalized seizures
Valproic Acid	Depakene	Multiple seizure types
Diazepam	Valium	Adjunct for generalized seizure control with other medications
Ethosuximide	Zarontin	Petit mal seizures
Vigabatrin	Sabril	Experimental drug, decreases seizures by 50% when resistant to other therapy

Category B: Drugs used to counter hyperactive excitatory processes

Carbamazepine	Tegratol	Partial and generalized tonic-clonic seizures
Phenytoin	Dilantin	Partial and generalized tonic-clonic seizures experimental for individuals who are therapy resistant
Gabapentin	Neurontin	Individuals who are therapy resistant
Lamotrigine	Lamictal	Experimental for individuals who are therapy resistant
Paraldehyde	Paral/Paraldehyde	Used rectally to stop threatening prolonged seizures

tion for persons with seizures that cannot be effectively controlled by medication (Fish, Smith, Quesney, Andermann, & Rasmussen, 1993). Procedures (i.e., video EEG, CAT scans, MRI, and PET) that have helped evaluate those who are and those who are not candidates for surgery, concomitant with improved surgical techniques, make the procedure safer than in the past. In general, surgery is more effective in improving one's quality of life if done in childhood than if delayed until adulthood (Brunquell, 1994).

New developments include a NeuroCybernetic Prosthesis (NCP) which is a surgically implanted device that stimulates the vagus nerve in the side of the neck with an electrical burst lasting about 30 seconds and occurring every 5 minutes throughout the day (Hingley, 1999). However, this treatment is currently used only for older children and adults, and has not yet been applied to very young children with difficult-to-control seizures.

Families of children with seizures can be assisted in several ways. As with other children with disabilities, there may be a tendency of parents to treat children with seizures differentially. For example, the potential hazard of having a seizure in traffic, near water, or in other dangerous situations may cause parents to become overcautious. Furthermore, when a seizure happens to occur concurrently with some action, such as enforcement of a family rule, parents may experience guilt and anxiety over future compliance requirements. The social and emotional effect of these family responses may affect sibling and peer relationships. Professionals can offer advice on the importance of consistency in child-rearing practices and normalcy of daily routines. Research indicates that children's overall developmental prognoses are best when they receive high-quality medical treatment and minimal use of drugs (Laybourn & Hill, 1994). Yet, professional educators themselves appear to lack sufficient information on seizures and often lack information regarding the needs of specific children with seizures (Laybourn & Hill, 1994). Since seizures are so common in the early childhood special education population, this knowledge deficit can prevent professionals from serving children and families well. Minimally, professionals should be well-versed on the protocol for treating children with generalized clonic-tonic seizures and aware of the symptoms of common types of seizures (see Table 5–7).

Multidisciplinary services indicated for children and families of children with seizures include medical, counseling, social skills programming, family support, education, and advocacy. According to Laybourn and Hill (1994), recent literature on family dynamics has paralleled early childhood philosophy. That is, historically, families were often viewed as needing the assistance of "experts" to help them overcome the emotional and psychological trauma and fear of public attitudes regarding their child's disability. Current efforts contrast this perspective, and focus on the positive aspect of services, which concentrate on the practical financial and medical needs of families. The latter perspective is based on actual data gathered from families who seemed to react sensibly to their children's disabilities and found friends, relatives, and professionals to be sympathetic and helpful.

In contrast, group programs designed to help parents cope with children with epilepsy are perhaps less successful. Hoare and Kerley (1992) established group counseling programs for a large number of parents whose children had recently received a diagnosis of epilepsy. Only 35% of parents expressed interest in the

Table 5–7 Treatment protocol for generalized tonic-clonic seizures.

The typical seizure is not a medical emergency, but knowledgeable handling of the situation is important. When a child experiences a generalized tonic-clonic seizure, caregivers should follow these procedures.

◆ Remain calm. Take time to reassure others that the child will be fine in a few minutes; if appropriate remind other children of the correct conduct under these circumstances.

◆ Carefully lower the child to the floor and clear the area of anything that could hurt her.

◆ Put something flat and soft (like a folded blanket) under her head so it will not bang on the floor as the body jerks.

◆ Since you cannot stop the seizure. Let it run its course. Do not try to revive the child and do not interfere with the child's movements.

◆ Turn the child gently onto their side. This keeps the airway clear and allows saliva to drain away:
 Do not try to force the mouth open
 Do not try to hold on to the tongue
 Do not put anything in the mouth

◆ When the jerking movements stop, let the child rest until she regains consciousness.

◆ Breathing may be shallow during the seizure, and may even stop briefly. In the unlikely event that breathing does not begin again, check the child's airway for an obstruction and give artificial respiration (remember—no objects in the child's mouth).

◆ Some children recover quickly after this type of seizure and others require more time. A short period of rest is usually advised. If seizures are routine, caregivers should encourage children and families to maintain daily activities with as little disruption as possible.

Source: Adapted from *Epilepsy School Alert,* Epilepsy Foundation of America, 1987, Washington, DC, Author.

therapy, and only 12% actually attended, with a high rate of attrition in the latter group. A majority of the parents indicated they were not concerned with public attitudes but desired more information about epilepsy and its management. In summary, professionals may be overly concerned with parental coping and not sufficiently concerned with becoming an information resource for parents.

ATTENTION DEFICIT HYPERACTIVITY DISORDER (ADHD)

The term *attention deficit* has been recognized for at least the last half century. In a 1902 address to the Royal College of Physicians, G. F. Still described 20 children in his clinical practice who were aggressive, defiant, and resistant to discipline; these children were excessively emotional or passionate and showed little self-control (Barkley, 1997). Furthermore, these children were described as impaired in attention and quite overactive. Because attention deficit hyperactivity disorder (ADHD) is a hidden disorder, children are often blamed for their misbehavior and adults expect that they could behave appropriately if they would "just try."

The primary symptoms of ADHD have changed very little since 1902, as was evident in the DSM-III-R Diagnostic Criteria for Attention Deficit Disorder, with and without hyperactivity, published by the American Psychiatric Association in 1987. However, in 1994, the terminology relating to ADHD changed with the APA's publication of the *Diagnostic and Statistical Manual of Mental Disorders* (1994). There is much controversy and disagreement among professionals as to the utility and meaning of this term (Bender & McLaughlin, 1995). In spite of this disagreement, descriptions of behaviors associated with the condition have remained remarkably consistent. Though the definition has remained stable, the number of children identified with this disorder has not; the overall incidence of ADHD has increased markedly in the past decade. Furthermore, increasing numbers of very young children with ADHD are being identified. Many preschoolers are now medicated daily with drugs intended to reduce activity levels and improve concentration.

CHARACTERISTICS

In interviewing parents of children with ADHD, it is revealed that even in infancy, symptoms of the disorder are manifest (Friedman & Doyal, 1992; Quinn, 1997). Early signs include squirminess, inability to adjust to change, frequent high-intensity negative moods, irregular sleep patterns (often requiring less sleep), and difficulty in feeding. These symptoms evolve into the behavioral triad defining ADHD. The primary symptoms of ADHD include inattention, impulsivity, and hyperactivity. Barkley (1993) postulated another primary symptom—poor delay of response. Inattention manifests itself when children fail to attend and concentrate on the task at hand. Preschool children often move from activity to activity, rapidly shifting their attention from one thing to another. If you ask them what they are supposed to be doing, many times they cannot tell you. These children also appear to be distracted by their own thoughts as well as the behaviors of other children and adults. What can be somewhat frustrating and promising is that these children will concentrate for longer periods of time in highly enjoyable activities such as going skiing for the first time.

Impulsivity has been viewed as another primary symptom. This can be seen when these children behave in ways that appear to others as though they do not understand the consequences of their actions. These children get into difficulty because they respond too soon and come to decisions too rapidly. They interrupt at meals, cannot take turns at preschool, and interrupt the play of others a great deal of the time. As a consequence, secondary problems evolve in self-esteem, interpersonal relationships, and learning (Fouse & Morrison, 1997).

The third primary symptom of ADHD is hyperactivity. This characteristic is the most widely known and easiest to recognize. Most parents and caregivers describe this characteristic as "always on the go," " in constant motion," "never sitting still," or "always fidgeting, talking, or making noise." Children exhibiting ADHD with hyperactivity have a much poorer prognosis than children without hyperactivity. The former are more likely to have conduct problems, to be more impulsive and to be rejected by their peers.

The newest characteristic suggested by Barkley (1993) replaces inattention with disinhibition or poor delay of response. Barkley feels that children with ADHD cannot delay their actions sufficiently and have little use for delay intervals between tasks. Barkley's contribution is based on the earlier work of Bronowski (1967, 1977), who postulated that as our language evolved, humans developed the skill to delay their response to a signal, message, or event. This ability is said to be part of the evolutionary changes of the frontal lobes. Frontal lobe differences can be seen in preschool children who cannot delay between tasks or activities or who respond too quickly to stimuli. There have been several secondary characteristics associated with

ADHD, including poor school performance, learning disabilities, delays in speech and language development, poor problem solving abilities, and slightly more difficulties in sensory and motor skills.

Etiology

Since the first edition of Barkley (1981) as well as early classic texts in the field (e.g., Ross & Ross, 1976; Safer & Allen, 1976), considerable research as to the etiology of ADHD has been carried out. This research has been somewhat inconsistent and conflicting in outcomes. Most of the senior researchers in the field view the cause of ADHD as having multiple etiologies (Barkley, 1997; Lerner, Lowenthal, & Lerner, 1995). Various data-based correlates of ADHD have included exposure to toxins in the environment (Marlowe, 1986), gender favoring males 5 to 1 (Barkley, 1997; Farley, 1997), differences in the brain's ability to use glucose fast enough to maintain normal thought (Zametkin et al., 1990), and inheritability (Anastopoulos & Barkley, 1991). In addition, several theories that have no empirical support, ranging from diet (Conners, 1980) to sugar sensitivity (Milich, Wolraich, & Lindgren, 1986), have been with us for some time and continue to appear in the popular press at this writing.

Conduct disorders, the most common childhood disorder and the most severe form of ADHD, indicates that home environment, specifically marital harmony/discord, is the best predictor of this severe chronic antisocial behavior (Murray & Myers, 1998). This finding reflects the general opinion of scientists that what is now categorized as a single ailment, will eventually prove to be several discrete but related disorders that have different causes and subsequent treatments (Friedman & Doyal, 1992). For example, it is believed that ADHD follows a genetic continuum that includes Tourette syndrome and learning disabilities (Whitman, 1991). While these disabilities can appear independently, they also overlap in symptoms and outcomes (see Table 5–8). What is certain is that this disorder starts early in childhood and will follow the person for the rest of his or her life (Barkley, 1997; Lerner et al., 1995).

Treatment

There is a wealth of data regarding the effective treatment of infants and children with ADHD. The information available today is clearly more empirically sound and is directed at both parents and professionals (see Table 5–8). The primary treatment of preference has been and continues to be stimulant medication therapy. In 1995 nearly half a million prescriptions for Ritalin or similar drugs were written for children between the ages of three and six (Gibbs, 1998). Medication has been shown to be highly effective and of assistance to young children with ADHD (Barkley, 1997). The two most common medications employed have been Cylert (Pemoline) and Ritalin (Methylphenidate). Even with such positive outcomes, the use of medication therapy is not without side effects that caregivers need to monitor (e.g., tics, weight loss, insomnia, stomach aches, headaches, dizziness, nail biting, reduced speech, irritability, nightmares, sadness, and staring). Recent research has indicated that over half of some children tested displayed the most common side-effects during medication therapy as well as with **placebo** conditions (Barkley, DuPaul, & McMurray, 1991). When two dosages of Ritalin were taken (3 mg/kg versus 5 mg/kg), the most common side-effects were decreased appetite, insomnia, anxiousness, irritability, and proneness to crying under either dosage level. However, many of these side-effects were also found during the placebo phase of the research.

Table 5–8 Infant and preschool stages of ADHD.

Age	Needs	Difficulties	Treatment Program
Atypical infants and toddlers	Self-regulation including: Arousal Deviant attentiveness Crying Irritability Sleep disorders Structure Limit setting Control issues Dependency Parental-child interactions that are clearly affected	Neurologic dysfunction Overaggressive/oppositional behavior Short attention span Hyperactivity Low threshold of frustration Temper tantrums Sleep disorders Accident proneness	Parent education and counseling Behavior modification Environmental manipulation Educational intervention—nursery school/Head Start Occupational/physical therapy Play therapy Medication Diet
Preschool	Proper nursery school placement Increasing attention span for learning Increasing social awareness and interaction	Hyperactivity Aggression Poor socialization Learning delays Developmental issues when ADHD is not the only problem	Parent and teacher education Behavior management Environmental Manipulation Proper diet Medication Other therapies as needed (OT/PT/Speech)

Source: Adapted from Quinn, P. O. (1997). *Attention Deficit Disorder: Diagnosis and Treatment from Infancy to Adulthood* (pp. 205–206). New York: Brunner/Mazel.

Another common intervention with young children with ADHD has been to employ behavioral parent training in the home (Barkley, 1997). As students become older, behavioral interventions, such as token economies and behavioral contracting, and self-management procedures, alone or in combination with stimulant medication, have been effective at school (Abramowitz, Eckstrand, O'Leary, & Dulcan, 1992; O'Leary, Pelham, Rosenbaum, & Price, 1976; Williams, Williams, & McLaughlin, 1991). As one's home environment is the best predictor of severe social maladaptation, chaotic and fractured families may require intensive support and the children need positive integrated educational experiences where they can play and work alongside appropriate peer role models (Murray & Myers, 1998).

A child with ADHD can have a devastating effect on families (Friedman & Doyal, 1992). Not only are there the predictable daily management problems that require extraordinary supervision, but parents often must deal with marital stress and guilt caused by accusatory suggestions by family, friends and professionals that the behavior problems are a consequence of misguided parenting. The following quote exemplifies the frustration felt by parents of children with ADHD (Colin, 1997):

I decide to mention Willie's behavior in school to the pediatrician. "Does every child yell like this?" I ask embarrassed.

The pediatrician tells me not to worry. "Oppositional behavior," he calls it, is common among three-year-olds and should go away on its own. He laughs when I tell him how Willie substituted "old wallpaper" for the offending "stupid idiot."

"He's obviously very creative," the pediatrician says, still smiling.

I stare at him blankly. They never call Willie creative in school. In fact, his teacher rarely says anything positive about him. Why is it so hard for her to appreciate the good things about my son—his sense of humor, his vocabulary, his wonderful singing? (pp. 24–25).

Several excellent texts are available for parents who have children with ADHD. In addition there is a wealth of information for teachers and other care providers to assist children with attention deficit hyperactivity disorder. For example, many internet sites, including parent specific websites and support networks are established. The following practical suggestions will prove useful in helping families of children with ADHD (Friedman & Doyal, 1992).

♦ Provide constant nurturance through love, support, and kindness
♦ Keep undesirable activities (e.g., car travel, shopping) brief
♦ Provide immediate (nonviolent) consequences for acting out to limit repetition of behavior
♦ Limit physical punishment and verbal violence since these are imitated by children with ADHD
♦ Limit access to violence on TV since children with ADHD are more likely than other children to be influenced by this violence
♦ Set behavioral rules and establish clear rewards for rule following
♦ Do not try to force children with ADHD to go to sleep, but set routine bedtime, where child must play quietly and independently until they are ready for sleep
♦ Daily schedules help young children predict their day and learn self-control

TRAUMATIC BRAIN INJURY

Head injuries, accounting for 40% of fatalities in children ages one to four, are caused by physical assault (abuse) 56% of the time; child abuse is the cause of 90% of cases of traumatic brain injury (TBI) (Ewing-Cobbs et al., 1998). Each year approximately 180 of 100,000 children experience a traumatic head injury (Wade, Taylor, Drotar, Stancin, & Yeates, 1998). TBI may also be the result of accidental trauma to the head such as a car accident or a fall where a child lands on their head. In children, some common causes of TBI are falls from shopping carts, walkers, and from windows (Waaland, 1990).

The outcomes and prognoses differ for the two types of head injury, with a better overall health picture for children who suffer non-inflicted (caused by other than child abuse) TBI. In 1992, Congress added Traumatic Brain Injury as a separate disability category under IDEA, defining it as:

. . . an acquired injury to the brain caused by an external physical force, resulting in total or partial functional disability or psychosocial impairment, or both, that adversely affects a child's educational performance. The term applies to open and closed head injuries resulting in impairments in one or more areas, such as cognition; language; memory; attention; reasoning; abstract thinking; judgment; problem-solving; sensory, perceptual, and motor abilities; psychosocial behavior; physical functions; information processing; and speech. The term does not apply to brain injuries that are congenital or degenerative, or brain injuries induced by birth trauma (U.S. Federal Register, 1992).

Children whose head injury is the result of a blow to the head have a specific type of brain injury that includes lacerations, contusions, external **hematomas** to the skull, scalp and brain. However, when a head injury is the result of inertia that involves rapid acceleration followed by rapid deceleration, the type of injury is more generalized as in a concussion and internal hematomas. The latter often make rapid physical recovery, and may show no evidence of cognitive processing deficits until several months later. Like seizures, brain injury that results in temporary or permanent disability may not appear on typical diagnostic tests such as MRIs or EEGs. While long-term effects include deficits in personal independence, behavioral/emotional skills, social functioning, cognitive processing skills, and motor functioning, there is no typical profile of a child who is head injured (Wade et al., 1998; Yim-Chiplis, 1998).

The symptoms of TBI generally fall into one of three categories:

◆ Physical symptoms: nausea, vomiting, dizziness, headache, blurred vision, sleep disturbance, fatigue, lethargy, and other sensory loss.
◆ Cognitive deficits: attention, concentration, perception, memory, speech/language, or executive functions.
◆ Behavioral changes or alterations in degree of emotional responsivity (irritability, anger, disinhibition, or emotional lability) (Mild Traumatic Brain Injury Committee, 1993).

The severity and manifestation of brain injury is dependent on the extent and location of damage and may range from mild to severe. With early and ongoing intervention, symptoms of brain damage may decrease, though there is considerable variability in improvement across children. This is particularly true of infants and preschoolers whose brains are still maturing at a rapid rate.

Children whose head injury is the result of physical abuse, generally have patterns of trauma that include massive retinal hemorrhages, broken bones (especially ribs), and major head trauma such as cerebral hematomas, hemorrages, **edema,** and stroke (Ewing-Cobb et al., 1998). Generally speaking, children with inflicted TBI are more likely to suffer long-term mental deficiency than children who suffer accidental TBI, possibly as a result of concomitant environmental factors which are associated with child abuse (Ewing-Cobb et al., 1998).

The term "shaken baby syndrome" is used to describe possible TBI that results from repeated severe shaking of an infant. It is hypothesized that the movement of the brain within the skull can cause serious brain injury in infants. However, some question whether the movement, without rapid deceleration or impact, such as shaking a baby's head against a pillow is sufficient to cause brain hemorrhage associated with long-term injury. Whatever the mechanism, it is clear that a child can sustain long-term brain damage even when there is no external evidence of harm.

CLOSE-UP

THE CONSEQUENCES OF CHILD ABUSE OF GIRLS

It is estimated that 1.6 million new cases of child abuse occur in the United States each year. Of these, 52% are cases of neglect, 25% are from physical abuse, and 13% are comprised of sexual abuse with girls being the most common victims. This number is even more astounding when considering that the number of serious injuries resulting from child abuse quadrupled from 1986–1993.

Putnam conducted a longitudinal study of girls who were abused and a cohort group who had not been abused. Overall, abused girls were significantly more likely to manifest physical and behavioral abnormalities. Specifically, girls who were sexually abused were more likely to have oppositional disorders, depression, suicidal tendencies, ADHD, and conduct disorders. These girls scored low on measures of frustration tolerance, appropriate social skills, attention to task, and sociability

In addition to behavioral problems, these girls exhibited an alarming rate of physical/medical problems. As compared to nonabused cohorts, there was a five-fold increase in physical problems including vomiting, headache, eating disorders, post-traumatic stress disorder (PTSD), self-injury, asthma, urinary tract infections, and skin problems.

While the emotional fallout of child abuse is great, there is also a direct fiscal cost to society. Putnam reported that $56 billion per year is spent dealing with the consequences of child abuse. These costs include long-term problems of substance abuse, violence, HIV and other sexually transmitted diseases, health care utilization, teen pregnancy, diminished academic achievement and subsequently lowered occupational status. In comparison, the total cost associated with cancer is approximately $104 billion per year. As great as these costs are, the United States is clearly not invested in solving the problems of child abuse. That is, the U.S. government spends approximately $28 per victim of child abuse on research compared to $1,735 per cancer victim. Put another way, the research investment for child abuse is approximately 5¢/$100 of cost while we spend $2/$100 of cost for cancer research.

Source: Putnam, F. (May, 1999). Childhood maltreatment and adverse outcomes: A prospective developmental approach. American Psychiatric Association Annual Meeting. Washington, DC.

There are a few general guidelines for educators who work with children with TBI, though these suggestions will not be appropriate for all variations of the disability:

◆ Provide repetition and consistency
◆ Demonstrate new tasks, state instructions, and provide examples to illustrate ideas and concepts
◆ Avoid figurative language

◆ Arrange materials and tasks to promote as much independence as possible
◆ Reinforce lengthening periods of attention to appropriate tasks; provide extra time for task completion
◆ Probe skill acquisition frequently and provided repeated practice
◆ Build in prompts and teach strategies for memory (picture cues, verbal prompts, etc.)
◆ Provide breaks to avoid fatigue
◆ Reduce unnecessary distractions

Families of children with TBI are often adversely affected by the stress of chronic behavioral and cognitive changes in their child, with parental adjustment and parent-child interactions growing worse over time (Wade et al., 1998). Unlike children whose brain injury is lifelong, those with TBI and their parents remember how they were before the trauma, and as a result have a different set of emotional and psychological needs than other children and parents. The following suggestions are made for working with families of children with TBI:

◆ Build a team of professionals including family, child, educators, and rehabilitation specialists
◆ Behavioral intervention for social/emotional problems
◆ Acquire a full assessment of the child across developmental areas
◆ Plan intervention that include a variety of learning methods and materials
◆ Conduct frequent assessments (every 30–60 days in the first year post injury)
◆ If injury is inflicted, all appropriate safety net services to child and family must be in place
◆ Provide substantial support in terms of counseling, instruction, and respite to families

CONGENITAL PHYSICAL MALFORMATIONS

NEURAL TUBE DEFECTS

The most critical time for development of the nervous system is between the third and fifth week of gestation (Avey, 1965). It is during this time that the neural groove closes and forms the vertebral column, which houses the spinal cord and is joined to the other soft tissue structures surrounding the nerves. Any disturbance in the developmental sequence will result in incomplete closure and create **neural tube defects.** The resulting abnormality can be severe (anencephaly), moderately severe (myelomeningocele), or less severe (meningocele and spina bifida occulta).

Spina bifida
Spina bifida is the term used to describe an incomplete spinal column and the relationship of the spinal cord and contents to the defect. The term is frequently used interchangeably with any of the neural tube defects. These include spina bifida occulta, meningocele, and myelomeningocele. Spina bifida affects about 1 out of every 1000 live births in the United States (Public Health Reports, 1998a). Treatment is dependent on the level along the spine at which the defect is located, as well as on the existence of other complications (e.g., **hydrocephalus** or urinary tract involvement).

Anencephaly

Anencephaly is a congenital malformation in which the brain does not develop and the skull, which would normally cover the brain, is absent. A membrane occasionally covers blood vessels that do develop within the cavity where the brain should be contained. This defect is one of the most commonly occurring neural tube defects and frequently occurs in conjunction with other midline defects of the spinal cord and the spine, which covers the cord.

Anencephalic infants will either be stillborn or die shortly after delivery. Though anencephaly and other neural tube disorders can be spotted via ultrasound, the most accurate diagnosis is made by a laboratory test for maternal or amniotic fluid alpha-fetoprotein (AFP) (Public Health Reports, 1998b). This protein increases in both the mother's bloodstream and in the amniotic fluid when a neural tube defect is present. Genetic counseling is available for families who experience this condition and can be especially valuable when planning future pregnancies. Development of anencephaly occurs between the 16th and 26th day after conception (Shapiro, 1990). No single factor seems to be responsible for the malformation, though genetic influence may be associated. There is a 5% recurrence rate within families (Shapiro, 1990). Environmental factors have also been linked correlationally to this malformation.

Spina Bifida Occulta

The normal spinal cord is fully protected by bony structures called vertebrae. **Spina bifida occulta** (see Figure 5–8) is an often unnoticed condition in which there is a defect in the vertebrae covering the spinal cord. There is neither exposure of the neural membranes nor evidence of nerve tissue involvement. Spina bifida occulta is a common occurrence and many cases of spina bifida occulta go undetected. Those that are discovered generally show skin anomalies that include abnormal hair tufts over the coccyx (tailbone) area, a dimple in this area, a "port wine" birth mark, or a cyst. Most individuals do not have any neurological symptoms that accompany the defect. Some children with spina bifida occulta have mild symptoms of neurological deficits. These symptoms may include an abnormal gait, positional deformities of the feet, and problems with **incontinence** of urine or stool.

Meningocele

The normal spinal cord is fully protected by bony structures called vertebrae. **Meningocele** is a neural tube defect that generally appears in the lumbar area of the vertebrae where the spinal cord is exposed (near the base of the spine). It is a soft tissue mass that is covered by skin and does not contain nerves or nerve roots. The cerebral spinal fluid (CSF) and meninges are affected in this defect (see Figure 5–9). Meningoceles are sometimes associated with genetic syndromes (Kousseff, 1984).

A meningocele is surgically repaired during the first few days of life. There is generally no paralysis or sensory loss and hydrocephalus rarely occurs. Occasionally there will be breakdown of the skin covering the defect, which increases the risk of infection of the spinal tract. There are sometimes nerve roots trapped within the sac, and this may cause weakness of the legs, but full recovery generally accompanies repair of the defect.

Figure 5–8
Internal schema
of spina bifida
occulta.

Myelomeningocele

Of all the defects that occur under the heading of spina bifida, myelomeningocele occurs the most frequently and has the most significant of the long-term effects. In **myelomeningocele,** both the spinal cord and its covering, the **meninges,** push through the skeletal defect to the surface (see Figure 5–10). As with the other forms of spina bifida, this can occur at any level along the spine. The higher the defect occurs in relationship to the head, the more severe the complications for an infant. Associated problems may include paraplegia, hydrocephalus, incontinence, sexual dysfunction, skeletal deformities, and mental impairment.

There is no known cause for myelomeningocele. Researchers suspect that a combination of factors that include heredity, environment, and possibly vitamin deficiency may be responsible for the occurrence of neural tube defects (Mill, 1989; Mulinare, 1988). The intake of greater than 400 µg of folic acid during pregnancy via prenatal vitamins is known to reduce the incidence of neural tube defects (Public Health Reports, 1998a). Furthermore, the incidence of neural tube disorder is higher in women of Indian or Pakistani origin, who tend to have significantly lower concentrations of red-cell folate (Michie, Chambers, Abramsky, & Skooner, 1998).

Myelomeningoceles differ in size as well as location. They may be as small as a dime or as large as an apple. The size of the defect is not always the key to the complications that may arise. Severe neurological involvement may accompany a small defect as well as one that is large.

At birth, the defect may be covered with a thin membrane. This is frequently broken during the birth process and cerebral spinal fluid leaks from the open area, placing the infant at significant risk for meningitis. A broken membrane also increases the need for surgery within the first few days of life.

Surgical repair of a myelomeningocele replaces the contents of the exposed sac into the spinal column and closes the defect. Occasionally the defect may be so large

Figure 5–9
Internal schema
of meningocele

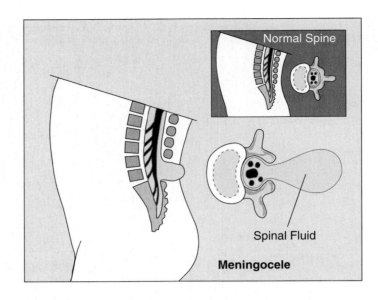

Meningocele

Figure 5–10
Internal schema of
myelomeningocele

Myelomeningocele

that it requires a skin graft to cover the open area of the back. Within the next one-
to two-week period, at least 90% of these infants will require a shunt in order to treat
hydrocephalus which appears as part of the abnormality (National Institute of Neurological and Communicative Disorders and Stroke, 1986).

Prior to 1960, most infants affected with myelomeningocele were sent home and
managed without the benefit of surgery. Fewer than 20% survived the first two years
of life, with the majority dying within the first month (Laurence, 1964). In 1959, the
University of Sheffield in Sheffield, England, developed a comprehensive plan for

*Myelomeningo-
cele before and
after surgery.*

the treatment of affected infants. This plan included repairing the spinal defect within the first few days of life, placing a shunt for hydrocephalus, and establishing a home program, using the services of a team of surgeons, physicians, physical therapists, and social workers (Sharrard, Zachary, Lorber, & Bruce, 1963). The two-year survival rate increased to over 70% but presented the community with a whole new set of issues. These included providing services for surviving children who had severe disabilities, degrees of bladder and bowel dysfunction, and lower extremity paralysis. These are the problems that continue to affect children with myelomeningocele.

Most recently, medical advances in prenatal surgery of the open lesion have improved the prognosis even further. Because the unprotected neural tissue in a fetus is progressively traumatized in utero by chronic exposure to chemicals in the amniotic fluid, prenatal repair of the opening can rescue the spinal cord from damage that would occur throughout the remainder of pregnancy. In 1998, in the first reported case of in-utero surgical repair of an open spina bifida and concomittant placement of a cerebrospinal shunt, the male infant failed to develop hydrocephalus and had met all developmental milestones (including motor) at six months, developing full use of both legs (Adzick, Sutton, Crombleholme, & Flake, 1998).

Common problems experienced by infants and children with a repaired myelomeningocele include genitourinary and orthopedic abnormalities. These problems are anticipated within the neonatal period and realized during infancy and early childhood. Defects in the upper lumbar spine area will affect hip flexion and may confine the child to a wheelchair; whereas, defects in the lower lumbar spine area may allow the child to walk with the aid of braces and crutches. Regardless of the level of the defect, many of these children also have club feet that often require casting.

Many affected children have significant problems with the genitourinary system. Because of the nerve involvement in the lumbar spine, the bladder frequently is atonic (without tone). The bladder becomes distended with urine and lacks the nerve impulses required to empty itself. This buildup of urine provides the perfect setting for bacteria to grow and chronic urinary tract infections place the child at risk for kidney disease. In addition, many of these children lack the nerve impulses for normal bowel control. Rectal muscles lack tone, allowing stool to leak, increasing the opportunity for contamination of the urinary tract with bacteria from feces. These children are also at risk for problems with skin breakdown, both from decreased circulation and decreased sensation below the level of the defect. Consequently there is a higher rate of chronic infections. Caregivers must be educated regarding the best method of promoting adequate bladder and bowel function to decrease the risks of chronic problems. Methods of prevention may include insertion of a bladder catheter, learning to place downward pressure on the lower abdomen to empty the bladder, administration of antibiotics, or in severe situations, the creation of an **ostomy.**

An ostomy is an opening made from an internal tube to an external source to allow for passage of urine or stool from the body. The formation of an ostomy is a surgical procedure. A stoma is the external opening that is on the abdomen at the site of the ostomy. The site is dependent on the reason for creation of the ostomy. Ostomies are created in the presence of many of the gastrointestinal and genitourinary defects. They may be temporary or permanent depending on the condition requiring their creation. Ostomies placed for urine diversion are generally permanent; whereas ostomies created for stool diversion may frequently be temporary until staged repairs of abnormalities can be successfully accomplished. A pouch is worn over the external stoma for the collection of urine or stool. This pouch requires careful monitoring to prevent skin irritation from urine or stool. In the absence of other disabilities, a child can be taught to monitor and maintain the external pouch. In situations in which children are neither physically nor mentally able, caregivers or even educators must be adept at both monitoring and maintaining the stoma and pouch. Careful monitoring of an ostomy can prevent foul odors, leakage, and skin irritation. This is essential to promoting self-esteem in the child and allowing a normal lifestyle.

Many children with myelomeningocele have average to above-average intelligence. This depends on the presence of malformations within the brain that correlate with the defect (e.g., Arnold-Chiari malformations). Opportunities must be provided to allow for these children to reach their full potential in the presence of extensive physical disabilities.

Infants born with myelomeningocele, as with Down syndrome and **duodenal atresia,** are those who initiated what is known as the Baby Doe legislation. These laws were enacted by the Federal Government to protect the rights of infants with birth defects to receive definitive care for correctable defects and supportive care for problems related to defects that are not correctable but are compatible with life. Health care providers and educational systems are mandated by law to serve the needs of these children. In spite of the multiple problems experienced by infants and families affected with myelomeningocele, the expectation of parents for their children can generally be a happy and independent life.

MICROCEPHALY

Microcephaly means very small head and brain. This condition can be either primary or secondary depending on the reasons for the limited brain growth. Primary microcephaly generally occurs during the first or second trimester of pregnancy and can result from genetic malformations, chromosomal abnormalities, or exposure to toxic agents (e.g., radiation, chemicals such as drugs or alcohol, and infections). Secondary microcephaly usually occurs during the last trimester of pregnancy, during the labor and delivery process, or during the period of early infancy. Some of the factors responsible for secondary microcephaly are infections, birth trauma, inborn errors of metabolism as in Hurler syndrome, and decreased oxygen supply related to many different causes (Morris & Rodger, 1998; Tam, 1997). Either primary or secondary microcephaly may result in only minor developmental delays or may range to profound disabilities and mental retardation.

Small head size in infants is usually identified with a head circumference that falls at least two standard deviations below the mean on a standard growth chart for age. Microcephalic head size also tends to be disproportionate to both the weight and the linear growth of a child. In spite of the significant difference, many of the chromosomal abnormalities that cause small head size have varying degrees of disability. Still, many of these conditions are also associated with other physical and developmental disabilities, such as cataracts and skeletal abnormalities.

The most common development of microcephaly after the second trimester of pregnancy is related to hypoxic-ischemic cerebral injury. This generally occurs during the birth process or during the neonatal period and is caused by decreased blood flow to the brain, which in turn, decreases oxygen levels (hypoxia) and causes cellular death (ischemia) from lack of oxygen and glucose. Many affected infants are full term and initially have a head circumference that is within normal parameters for height and weight. Conditions that cause hypoxic-ischemic brain dysfunction may be trauma or infection. Development of microcephaly following such events has a major impact on the long-term neurological outcome of an infant. The neurological impairment that occurs generally includes cognitive impairment, cerebral palsy, seizures, and cerebral atrophy (Hill, 1991; Volpe, 1987).

There is no medical treatment for microcephalus. Many of the children with minor impairment show some degree of autism and many are hyperactive. Both conditions increase the need for carefully planned educational opportunities that address the individual needs of a child and also assist parents with the difficult job of raising a child with special needs.

HYDROCEPHALUS

Hydrocephalus is a condition where there is an excessive accumulation of **cerebrospinal fluid** in the **ventricles** of the brain. These four ventricles are fluid-filled sacs that occupy space within and around the brain mass. The cerebrospinal fluid bathes the brain and spinal cord, providing both protection and nutrition. Though capillary circulation throughout the brain is the main source of nutrition and the elimination of waste products, there is additional diffusion of nutrients from the cerebrospinal fluid to the brain tissue.

Hippocrates was one of the first physicians to describe hydrocephalus. He felt that chronic seizures caused the condition and that treatment should be laxatives, vegetable ingestion, and sneezing (Rocco, 1985). Failure of these treatments would then require surgical intervention that consisted of opening the skull extending to the brain material itself. Additional treatment involved the frequently used approach to any disease process—"bloodletting" (Rocco, 1985).

Defined medically, hydrocephalus causes the head to increase in size beyond two standard deviations above the mean on the standard growth chart. Swelling of the ventricles can be caused by an obstruction in the drainage system, an overproduction of spinal fluid, or a failure in reabsorption of cerebrospinal fluid into the general circulation. As an example, meningitis may either cause swelling that results in blockage of the ventricles (a cause of hydrocephalus) or a blockage of the ventricles and subsequent build-up of fluid may lead to bacterial build-up and meningitis itself (an effect of hydrocephalus) (Mactier, Galea, & McWilliam, 1998). When the ventricles fill with excess fluid, they become massively dilated, placing pressure on the brain matter. If left unchecked, the brain structures may become permanently damaged, and mental retardation will occur.

Hydrocephalus may also be caused by the presence of a tumor or head trauma. Long-term outcomes for infants either born with hydrocephalus or who develop it after birth are dependent on the cause of the problem, presence of any other neurological problems, and the time frame from onset until a diagnosis is made and treatment is initiated (Jansen, 1988). Early diagnosis and treatment significantly improves the possibilities for normal development and the prevention of mental retardation. Head ultrasounds, computerized tomography, and MRI are the methods used for definitive diagnosis. The medication Diamox can sometimes aid in controlling the condition without surgical intervention by pulling excess fluid into the circulatory system, where it can be excreted by the kidneys.

Hydrocephalus before and after surgery.

Failure to control hydrocephalus medically may ultimately result in the need for surgical intervention in which a temporary or permanent shunt is placed between the ventricles and the abdominal space. **Shunting** procedures require the surgical placement of a soft pliable plastic tube between the ventricle and either the heart or the peritoneum (a closed sac lining the abdomen). Generally, the peritoneal cavity is used in children because it provides the opportunity to loop extra catheter tubing into the abdominal space, allowing a child to grow without needing replacement of the system. Most shunts have a small bubble reservoir that is seeded under the skin, usually behind the ear. This reservoir contains a one-way valve that controls the amount of cerebrospinal fluid that can be drained from the ventricle at any one time depending on the pressure within the ventricle. This reservoir also provides a method of checking on the flow of the system; this is especially useful when a shunt failure is suspected. The ease with which the valve can be pumped (gently pushed) is an aid to evaluating the shunt for free flow of fluid. Symptoms of shunt failure are similar to those of increased pressure from obstruction. This tube must be watched carefully for blockage. Symptoms of tube obstruction may include a decreased level of consciousness, vomiting, temperature instability, seizures, and if the pressure gets high enough, loss of brain mass, and even death.

Hydrocephalus may be evident on prenatal ultrasound, or it may be completely without evidence at birth. However, infants affected with significant blockage prior to birth, which has been identified by prenatal testing, may require delivery by cesarean section to attempt to preserve functional brain material and also decrease the risk of injury to a mother attempting to deliver an infant with a very large head by the vaginal route. Many cases of significant prenatal hydrocephalus will result in brain wasting from pressure during the developmental process. Surgical intervention in these cases is done not to protect the brain, but for comfort to an infant and to assist families in providing adequate physical and emotional care.

Hydrocephalus frequently occurs with other neural tube defects, such as myelomeningocele. In the latter, initial repair of the spinal defect is the first stage of surgical care, and placement of a ventricular/peritoneal shunt is the second stage. Closure of the primary defect (myelomeningocele) causes obstruction of cerebrospinal fluid that results in the need for a shunt.

Hydrocephalus is a life-long disorder, that requires consistent follow-up (Buxton & Punt, 1998). Management of the shunt, observations for function, and awareness of the symptoms of possible infections are requirements of not only the family and care providers but also of educators who may be working with these children. Awareness of symptoms that may be displayed by an individual child is part of the educational plan.

The cognitive and psychosocial development of children varies significantly, depending on the underlying cause of the hydrocephalus. Many children with hydrocephalus have normal intellectual development (Amacher & Wellington, 1984). Frequent shunt infections, plugged shunts, and other malfunctions may affect development of an otherwise normal brain. Early evaluation of possible developmental delays is necessary, and many of these children benefit from early childhood developmental stimulation programs. Shunt tubing is versatile and can withstand normal childhood activities. It is essential that children participate as fully as possible in age-appropriate activities so that the illness not be an unnecessary deterrent to full enjoyment of life.

THE DIARY OF ESTHER ANNA BERKE: MONTH 9

This month features Esther's diary from July 16–Aug. 15. These are the same notes that we show her doctor so you can see what her progress is like. In my opinion, her physical therapy program and specialized diet don't seem to help control her seizures very much. We did phase out one of her medications (Lamictal) without seeing much change in seizures, so that was good. She isn't very "stable"—her eating, sleeping, and seizure patterns change frequently. We will continue with both her customized program and her diet and see what happens. She was 75 cm long (95th percentile) and weighed 7.3 kg (20th percentile) on her 9-month birthday.

July 16–31:   Theravite and #16 are both vitamin supplements.

July 18, Sunday Seizures: 2 short hard infantile spasms (both of these were in a noisy restaurant, while she was trying to fall asleep). She's sleeping much better at night now. Hooray! She doesn't always have the cold hands and feet phenomenon with each seizure episode. She's also not as stiff as before, just likes to keep the head twisted to the right side.

July 21, Wednesday Seizures: Most seizures were intense and weird patterns. Usually flexor spasms with head turned right and tongue stuck out. These new ones extend her arms and head turns hard left and she squeals with each one. Sometimes these two alternate, sometimes there are mild flexor spasms, sometimes a longer flexor is thrown in. Things may be quiet and then all of a sudden, she does one of these extensor ones. Her arms and legs aren't always cold, but usually. (Almost) ALWAYS in the past (except for the partials she had for 2 months), the infantile spasms (flexor) would start hard and taper off gradually. She's not as stiff and arched as before, but it seems the days after a night-full of seizures, she's much more passive, not sleepy really. She's still irregular in sleeping/eating habits. Sleeps like a charm for the first few hours at night and then starts seizures.

July 28, Wednesday Diet: Finally a stool!! Very black and thick, but not hard. Not much it seems for 9 days backlog. She seemed quite relieved, however, and promptly fell asleep. Her eyes are tracking together much better but her face and lips looked really asymmetrical today. She uses her left side MUCH more than her right, except it's the left side of her face that is asymmetrical. She's not arching any more except in between the hard spasms.

August 4:   Subdued all day. Didn't try to lift her head like before. The seizures seem to be changing from the hard, short kind to the mild, long ones. Some are very mild with only her tongue sticking out and her feet lifting and thumping on the bed. Silent, otherwise. When she began the Lamictal, the end of April, suddenly the seizures became more intense and shorter. So maybe she's going back to the more "simpler" infantile spasms, but they sure last a lot longer. Hands and feet still get cold, but not every time. One series of spasms had a frequency of only every 15–20 seconds. She tried to drink a bottle in between the spasms.

Her face seems asymmetrical like before, and the flaky-type skin that was always around her eyebrows has returned. Congestion is becoming a problem. It used to happen during some seizures (we were told it was a side effect of the Rivotril). Now it's very prevalent whenever I give her drops, to the point she seems to be gasping for breath until she finally coughs . . . usually after the spasms have ended.

August 10, No seizures: Very sleepy. Arched back and fussy when awake. Hard to do NACD program, or feed. Only seems happy when drinking something. Her tongue moves a lot and she tried to get one hand in mouth. Right arm is stiff by her side, doesn't use it much at all, although kicks her right leg. (Looks like a stroke victim). Her knees stay stiff a lot of the time, feet are pointed out. Drools and spits up a lot. Head turned hard to the right. Eyes not tracking together as well as before, but better than last night. A few times this p.m., she pulled her knees up 2 or 3 times, a little like the rhythmic infantile spasms, but there were no other signs of a seizure. Deja vu. It is so similar to week of July 2–7 or 8. The long episodes of seizing and then nothing, but the arched back in exchange.

Esther Anna and her mother, Sarah.

In Conclusion

Each child affected with a neurological disability, regardless of the cause, has an individual response to his or her condition. Continuing research into causes of neurological disabilities, both physical and functional will provide educators with the knowledge-base to devise new and innovative approaches to interactions with each child and family. Prevention is the goal, but providing optimal care to affected families is a more realistic short-term objective.

One area in which early childhood professionals must become more knowledgeable is that of attentional deficits. With the present rise in incidence, which is recognized at an earlier and earlier age, children with very significant management needs cause havoc in preschool programs for children with special needs. In fact, this young population of children, who tend to be so disruptive, is more difficult to manage than older children because their language and cognitive skills are less well developed, and therefore, they are less able to understand rules and their consequences. On the other hand, because the time it takes to remediate behavioral problems is proportionate to the length of time that the behavior has been in a child's repertoire (a ratio of three months treatment for every one month that the behavior has occurred), very early treatment is crucial. One approach that holds much promise as a method of assessing and identifying effective strategies for preschool children is functional analysis. Using this method, the factors that motivate and sustain undesirable behavior are carefully observed and measured. When these factors are identified, systematic attempts are made to alter the conditions that maintain such behaviors. More research, however, is clearly needed. Therefore, future efforts in early childhood special education should be devoted to research in behavioral management of significant behavior problems, training of professionals to use such strategies, and, perhaps, widespread application in early childhood settings.

Study Guide Questions

1. Why should early childhood special educators know the etiologies and courses of disabling conditions?
2. Differentiate between invasive and noninvasive procedures. Give an example of each.
3. What are the medical uses of X rays? What precautions should be taken when X rays are used?
4. In what ways do CAT scans provide more information than X rays?
5. What are the advantages of the MRI over CAT scans and X rays?
6. Describe how PET scans are carried out. What special information do PET scans provide?
7. What are the primary medical uses of ultrasound?
8. What kind of information does an EEG provide?
9. What is cerebral palsy?
10. How has modern medicine maintained the incidence of cerebral palsy?
11. Describe the relationship between primitive reflexes and normal motor development.
12. Name and describe the primitive reflexes seen at birth.

13. What is the main difference between primitive reflexes and postural reflexes? How do primitive reflexes interfere with postural reflex development in children with cerebral palsy?
14. Name and describe three general terms used to describe muscle tone. How do the terms apply to abnormal muscle tone in children with cerebral palsy?
15. Differentiate each of the following: hemiplegia, paraplegia, quadriplegia, and diplegia.
16. Differentiate hypertonia and hypotonia.
17. Briefly describe the characteristics of athetosis, ataxia, and spasticity.
18. Compare and describe cerebral palsy that is severe, moderate, or mild.
19. What nutritional and feeding problems often accompany cerebral palsy?
20. In addition to feeding problems, what other conditions are often presented with cerebral palsy?
21. How should therapists work with parents of children with cerebral palsy?
22. What is meant by positioning and handling?
23. How are seizures activated?
24. Define epilepsy.
25. Differentiate each of the following types of seizures: absence, tonic-clonic, and myoclonic.
26. How do seizures affect cognitive functioning?
27. Summarize the chapter's advice about assisting families of children with seizure disorders.
28. What should one do if a child experiences a tonic-clonic siezure?
29. What are the characteristics of ADHD?
30. What are the recommended treatments for ADHD?
31. Why is it difficult to describe a child with traumatic brain injury? What are some common symptoms?
32. Identify five general recommendations that might be made to those who work with children with traumatic brain injury.
33. What is anencephaly?
34. What are the effects of spina bifida occulta?
35. How is meningocele treated? What are the long-term effects?
36. What is myelomeningocele?
37. How is myelomeningocele treated?
38. What physical problems are common for children with repaired myelomeningocele?
39. What is the Baby Doe legislation?
40. What is microcephaly, and what causes it?
41. What is hydrocephalus?
42. How is hydrocephalus controlled?

REFERENCES

Abramowitz, A. J., Eckstrand, D., O'Leary, S. G., & Dulcan, M. K. (1992). ADHD children's responses to stimulant medication in two intensities of a behavioral intervention program. *Behavior Modification, 16,* 193–203.

Accardo, P. J., Blondis, T A., & Whitman, B. Y. (Eds.). (1991). *Attention deficit disorders and hyperactivity in children.* New York: Marcel Dekker.

Adler, T. (1995). Infant CP protection. *Science News, 147*(8), 119.

Adzick, N. S., Sutton, L. N., Crombleholme, T. M., & Flake, A. W. (1998). Successful fetal surgery for spina bifida. *Lancet, 352*(9141), 1675–1677.

Amacher, A., & Wellington, J. (1984). Infantile hydrocephalus: Long-term results of surgical therapy. *Child's Brain, 11,* 217–229

American Psychiatric Association. (1987). *Diagnostic and statistical manual of mental disorders* (3rd ed., revised). Washington, DC: Author.

American Psychiatric Association. (1994). *Diagnostic and statistical manual of mental disorders* (4th ed., revised). Washington, DC: Author.

Anastopoulos, A. D., & Barkley, R. A. (1991). Biological factors in attention deficit disorder. *CH. A.D.D.ER, 5,* 1.

Austin, J. K., Risinger, M. W., & Beckett, L. A. (1992). Correlates of behavior problems in children with epilepsy. *Epilepsia, 33*(6), 1115–1122.

Avey, L. (1965). *Developmental anatomy: A textbook and laboratory manual of embryology,* (7th ed.). Philadelphia: W.B. Saunders.

Barkley, R. A. (1981). *Hyperactive children: A handbook for diagnosis and treatment.* New York: Guilford.

Barkley, R. A. (1993). A new theory of ADHD. *The ADHD Report, 1*(5), 1–4.

Barkley, R. A. (1997). *ADHD and the nature of self-control.* New York: Guilford.

Barkley, R. A., DuPaul, G., & McMurray, M. (1991). Attention deficit disorder with and without hyperactivity: Clinical response to three dose levels of methylphenidate. *Pediatrics, 87,* 519–531.

Bender, W. N., & McLaughlin, P. J. (1995). The ADHD conundom: Introduction to a special series on attention deficit/hyperactivity disorder. *Intervention in School and Clinic, 30,* 196–197.

Bhushan, V., Paneth, N., & Kiely, J. L. (1993). Impact of improved survival of very low birth weight infants on recent secular trends in the prevalence of cerebral palsy. *Pediatrics, 91*(6), 1094–1100.

Bigge, J. L. (1991). *Teaching individuals with physical and multiple disabilities* (3rd ed.). Columbus, OH: Macmillan.

Bronowski, J. (1967). *Human and animal languages. In honor of Roman Jakobson (Vol. 1).* The Hague, Netherlands, Mouton.

Bronowski, J. (1977). *Human and animal languages. A sense of the future* (pp. 103–131). Cambridge, MA: MIT Press.

Brunquell, P. J. (1994). Listening to epilepsy. *Infants and Young Children, 7*(1), 24–33.

Buxton, N., & Punt, J. (1998). Failure to follow patients with hydrocephalus shunts can lead to death. *British Journal of Neurosurgery, 12*(5), 399–402.

Cioni, G., Paolicelli, P. B., Sordi, C., & Vinter, A. (1993). Sensorimotor development in cerebral palsied infants assessed with the Uzgiris-Hunt scales. *Developmental Medicine and Child Neurology, 35,* 1055–1066.

Colin, A. (1997). *Willie: Raising and loving a child with Attention Deficit Disorder.* New York: Viking.

Conners, C. (1980). *Food additives and hyperactive children.* New York: Plenum.

Cooke, R. W. (1990). Cerebral palsy in very low birthweight infants. *Archives of Disabled Children, 65,* 201–206.

Dahl, M., & Gebre-Medhin, M. (1993). Feeding and nutritional problems in children with cerebral palsy and myelomeningocoele. *Acta Pediatrica, 82,* 816–820.

Dam, M. (1990). Children with epilepsy: The effect of seizures, syndromes, and etiological factors on cognitive functioning. *Epilepsia, 31*(4), 26–29.

Dichter, M. (1994). *The epilepsies and convulsive disorders.* In K. J. Isselbacher, E. Braunwald, J. D. Wilson, J. B. Martin, A. S. Fauci, & D. L. Kasper (Eds.), *Harrison's principle of internal medicine* (13th ed.) (pp. 2223–2333). New York: McGraw-Hill.

Dormans, J. P. (1993). Orthopedic management of children with cerebral palsy. *Pediatric Clinics of North America, 40* (3), 645–657.

Eaton, D. G. M., Ahmed, Y., & Dubowitz, L. M. S. (1991). Maternal trauma and cerebral lesions in preterm infants. Case reports. *British Journal of Obstetrics and Gynecology, 98,* 1292–1294.

Eicher, P. S., & Batshaw, M. L. (1993). Cerebral palsy. *Pediatric Clinics of North America, 40*(3), 537–551.

Epilepsy school alert. (1987). Epilepsy Foundation of America. Washington, DC, Author.

Ewing-Cobbs, L., Kramer, L., Prasad, M., Canales, D. N., Louis, P. T., Fletcher, J. M., Vollero, H., Landry, S. H., & Cheung, K. (1998). Neuroimaging, physical and developmental findings after inflicted and noninflicted traumatic brain injury in young children. *Pediatrics, 102,* 300–307.

Farley, D. (1997). On the teen scene: Attention disorder overcoming the deficit. *FDA Consumer, 31*(5), 32–36.

Farmer, S. F., Harrison, L. M., Ingram, D. A., & Stephens, J. A. (1991). Plasticity of central motor pathways in children with hemiplegic cerebral palsy. *Neurology, 41,* 1505–1510.

Fee, M. A., Charney, E. B., & Robertson, W. W. (1988). Nutritional assessment of the young child with cerebral palsy. *Infants and Young Children, 1*(1), 33–40.

Festschrift, C. (1994). Primitive reflexes: Their contribution to the early detection of cerebral palsy. *Clinical Pediatrics, 33,* 388–398.

Fetters, L. (1984). Motor development. In M. J. Hanson (Ed.), *Atypical infant development* (pp. 313–358). Austin, TX: PRO-ED.

Fish, D. R., Smith, S. J., Quesney, L. F., Andermann, F., & Rasmussen, T. (1993). Surgical treatment of children with medically intractable frontal and temporal lobe epilepsy: Results and highlights of 40 years' experience. *Epilepsia, 34*(2), 244–247.

Fouse, B., & Morrison, J. A. (1997). Using children's books as an intervention for attention-deficit disorder. *Reading Teacher, 50,* 442–446.

Friedman, R. J. & Doyal, G. T. (1992). *Management of children and adolescents with attention deficit-hyperactivity disorder:* Third Edition. Austin, TX: Pro-Ed.

Gibbs, N. (November, 1998). The age of *Ritalin. Time, 152* (22), 86–94.

Goulden, K. J., Shinnar, S., Koller, H., Katz, M., & Richardson, S. A. (1991). Epilepsy in children with mental retardation: A cohort study. *Epilepsia, 32*(5), 690–697.

Grant, A., Joy, M. T., O'Brien, N. O., Hennessy, E., & MacDonald, D. (November, 1989). Cerebral palsy among children born during the Dublin randomized trial of intrapartum monitoring. *The Lancet,* 1233–1235.

Henderson, H. S., French, R., & McCarty, P. (1993). ATNR: It's possible impact on motor efficiency in children. *Physical Educator, 50*(1), 20–23.

Hill, A. (1991). Current concepts of hypoxic-ischemic cerebral injury in the newborn. *Pediatric Neurology, 7,* 317–325.

Hinjosa, J., & Anderson, J. (1991). Mother's perceptions of home treatment programs for their preschool children with cerebral palsy. *The American Journal of Occupational Therapy, 45*(3), 273–279.

Hingley, A. T. (1999). Epilepsy: Taming the seizures, dispelling the myths. *FDA Consumer, 33*(1), 28–33.

Hoare, P., & Kerley, S. (1992). Helping parents and children with epilepsy cope successfully: The outcome of a group programme for parents. *Journal of Psychosomatic Research, 36*(8), 759–767.

Jansen, J. (1988). Etiology and prognosis in hydrocephalus. *Child's Nervous System, 4,* 263–267.

Jordan, D. R. (1992). *Attention deficit disorder: ADHD and ADD syndromes,* (2nd ed.). Austin, TX: PRO-ED.

Kousseff, B. (1984). Sacral meningocele with conotruncal heart defects: A possible autosomal recessive trait. *Pediatrics, 74,* 395–398.

Laurence, K. (1964). The natural history of spina bifida cystica. *Archives of Diseases of Childhood, 39,* 41–50.

Laybourn, A., & Hill, M. (1994). Children with epilepsy and their families: Needs and services. *Child Care Health and Development, 20,* 1–14.

Lerner, J. W., Lowenthal, B., & Lerner, S. R. (1995). *Attention deficit disorders: Assessment and teaching.* Pacific Grove, CA: Brooks/Cole.

Mactier, H., Galea, P., & McWilliam, R. (1998). Acute obstructive hydrocephalus complicating bacterial meningitis in childhood. *British Medical Journal, 316*(7148), 1887–1890.

Marlowe, M. (1986). Metal pollutant exposure and behavior disorders: Implications for school practices. *Journal of Special Education, 2*(2), 251–262.

Michie, C. A., Chambers, J., Abramsky, L., & Skooner, J. (1998). Folate deficiency, neural tube defects, and cardiac disease in UK Indians and Pakistanis. *Lancet, 351*(9109), 1105.

Mild Traumatic Brain Injury Committee. (1993). Definition of mild traumatic brain injury. *Journal of Head Trauma Rehabilitation, 8*(3), 86–87.

Milich, R., Wolraich, M., & Lindgren, S. (1986). Sugar and hyperactivity: A critical review of the findings. *Clinical Psychology Review, 6,* 493–513.

Mill, J. (1989). The absence of a relationship between the periconceptional use of vitamins and neural-tube defects. *New England Journal of Medicine, 321,* 430–435.

Morelle, M. J. (1993). Differential diagnosis of seizures. *Neurologic Clinics, 11*(4), 737–754.

Morris, A. A. M., & Rodger, I. W. (1998). Leukotrienes and the brain. *Lancet, 352*(9139), 1487–1488.

Mulinare, J. (1988). Periconceptional use of multivitamins and the occurrence of neural tube defects. *Journal of the American Medical Association, 260,* 3141–3145.

Murray, B. A., & Myers, M. A. (1998). Conduct disorders and the special-education trap. *Education Digest, 63*(8), 48–54.

Naeye, R. L., Peters, E. C., Bartholomew, M., & Landis, J. R. (1989). Origins of cerebral palsy. *American Journal of Diseases of Children, 143,* 1154–1161.

National Institute of Neurological and Communicative Disorders and Stroke. (1986). *Spina bifida: Hope through research.* Bethesda, MD: National Institute of Health.

O'Leary, K. D., Pelham, W. E., Rosenbaum, A., & Price, G. H. (1976). Behavioral treatment of hyperkinetic children: An experimental evaluation of its usefulness. *Clinical Pediatrics, 15,* 510–515.

Palmer, F. B., Shapiro, B. K., Allen, M. C., Mosher, B. S., Bilker, S. A., Harryman, S. E., Meinert, C. L., & Capute, A. J. (1990). Infant stimulation curriculum for infants with cerebral palsy: Effects on infant temperament, parent-infant interaction, and home environment. *Pediatrics Supplement, 85*(3), 411–415.

Procopis, P. G. (March, 1992). Breath-holding attacks in children. *Modern Medicine of Australia,* pp. 36–37.

Public Health Reports (1998a). Please, more folate. *Public Health Reports, 113*(4), 293.

Public Health Reports (1998b). FDA study finds test kits effective in spotting birth defects. *Public Health Reports, 113*(5), 382.

Putnam, F. (May, 1999). *Childhood maltreatment and adverse outcomes: A prospective developmental approach.* American Psychiatric Association Annual Meeting. Washington, DC.

Quinn, P. O. (1997). *Attention Deficit Disorder: Diagnosis and Treatment from Infancy to Adulthood.* New York: Brunner/Mazel.

Reilly, S., & Skuse, D. (1992). Characteristics and management of feeding problems of young children with cerebral palsy. *Developmental Medicine and Child Neurology, 34,* 379–388.

Rocco, C. (1985). *Historical background: The treatment of infantile hydrocephalus.* Boca Raton: CRC.

Rosen, M. G., & Dickinson, J. C. (1992). The incidence of cerebral palsy. *American Journal of Obstetrics and Gynecology, 167,* 417–423.

Ross, D. M., & Ross, S. A. (1976). *Hyperactivity: Research, theory and action.* New York: John Wiley.

Safer, D. J., & Allen, R. P. (1976). *Hyperactive children: Diagnosis and management.* Baltimore: University Park.

Scheller, J. M., & Nelson, K. B. (1994). Does Cesarean delivery prevent cerebral palsy or other neurologic problems of childhood? *Obstetrics & Gynecology, 83*(4), 624–630.

Seppa, N. (1998). Infections may underlie cerebral palsy. *Science News, 154*(16), 244–245.

Shapiro, K. (1990). Anencephaly. In M. Buyse, (Ed.). *Birth defects encyclopedia* (pp. 139–140). Dover, MA: Center for Birth Defects Information Services, Inc.

Sharrard, W., Zachary, R., Lorber, J., & Bruce, A. (1963). A controller trial of immediate and delayed closure of spina bifida cystica. *Archives of Diseases of Childhood, 38,* 18–25.

Shepherd, C., & Hosking, G. (1989). Epilepsy in school children with intellectual impairments in Sheffield: The size and nature of the problem and implications for service provision. *Journal of Mental Deficiency Research, 33,* 511–514.

Tam, D. A. (1997). Microcephaly in Hurler syndrome. *Clinical Pediatrics, 36,* 51–52.

Thommessen, M., Kase, B. F., Riis, G., & Heiberg, A.(1991). The impact of feeding problems on growth and energy intake in children with cerebral palsy. *European Journal of Clinical Health, 45,* 479–487.

Turnbull, J. D. (1993). Early intervention for children with or at risk of cerebral palsy. *American Journal of Diseases of Children, 147*(1), 54–59.

U.S. Federal Register, 57 (189), September 29, 1992, p. 44802.

Vargha-Khadem, F., Isaacs, E., Ver der Werf, S., Robb, S., & Wilson, J. (1992). Development of intelligence and memory in children with hemiplegic cerebral palsy. *Brain, 115,* 315–329.

Veelken, N., Schopf, M., Dammann, O., & Schulte, F. J. (1993). Etiological classification of cerebral palsy in very low birthweight infants. *Neuropediatrics, 24,* 74–76.

Volpe, J. (1987). *Neurology of the Newborn.* Philadelphia: W.B. Saunders.

Waaland, P. K. (1990). *Pediatric traumatic brain injury.* Rehabilitation Research and Training Center on Severe Traumatic Brain Injury, Virginia Commonwealth University, Richmond, VA.

Wade, S. L., Taylor, H. G., Drotar, D., Stancin, T., & Yeates, O. (1998). Family burden and adaptation during the initial year after traumatic brain injury in children. *Pediatrics, 102,* 110–116.

Whitman, B. (1991). The roots of organicity: Genetics and genograms. In P. J. Accardo, T. A. Blondis, & B. Y. Whitman (Eds.), *Attention deficit disorders and hyperactivity in children* (pp. 37–56). New York: Marcel Dekker.

Williams, B. F., Williams, R. L., & McLaughlin, T. F. (1991). Treatment of behavior disorders by parents and in the home. *Journal of Developmental and Physical Disabilities, 3,* 385–407.

Wilson-Costello, D. Borawski, E., Friedman, H., Redline, R., Fanaroff, A. A., & Hack, M. (1998). Perinatal correlates of cerebral palsy and other neurologic impairment among very low birth weight children. *Pediatrics, 102,* 315–323.

Yim-Chiplis, P. K. (1998). The child with traumatic brain injury returns to school. *Pediatric Nursing, 24,* 245–248.

Zametkin, A. J., Nordahl, T. E. Gross, M., King, A. C., Temple, W. E., Rumsey, J., Hamburger, S., & Cohen, R. M. (1990). Cerebral glucose metabolism in adults with hyperactivity of childhood onset. *New England Journal of Medicine, 323,* 1361–1367.

6

INBORN VARIATIONS OF DEVELOPMENT

My child will never be considered a poster child. She does not give professionals the satisfaction of making great progress, nor is she terribly social. But I need the same type of investment by professionals as any other parents of children with disabilities. The most important thing any educator can do for me is to love my Mary.

Carol Maloney, Mother of daughter with Rett Syndrome

When one considers all the ways in which human development, from embryology to birth, might vary, the fact that so many children are born without apparent disabilities is miraculous. This chapter is devoted to the description of variations in development that originate before a child's birth. These variations do not insinuate devaluation, inferiority, or undesirability of persons born with differences. Rather, the variations in development result in patterns of physical and/or behavioral characteristics that enable professionals to reliably group children according to similarities. Sometimes specific treatments are implicated when a child has membership in a certain group. For example, children with cystic fibrosis usually receive postural drainage treatments because respiratory congestion is always a symptom of the disease. Usually, however, membership in itself tells us very little about the specific treatments to be used for a child because individual differences are so great. Furthermore, most treatments are not universally effective for all children with the same characteristics. Anyone who has worked with children with autism can verify that determining what reinforcers, activities, and instructions work for one child will not necessarily provide guidance for another child with the same label. This chapter includes an introduction to basic genetics, which helps in understanding the causes of genetic deviations in development. The third section of this chapter is devoted to common disabilities that have no known etiology. It is probable that most of these disorders will eventually be linked to genetics. This chapter intentionally includes more information than will seem necessary for a foundations text. That is because this text is intended as a reference for later use by early childhood professionals. It is clear from working with parents that the more they can learn about their child's disability, the more capable they feel. Thus, it is the responsibility of professionals to become as knowledgeable as possible and to be able to help parents seek further information and resources.

Still, it should be noted that the following descriptions are generalizations based on current understanding of groups of children with categorical disabilities. It would be a mistake to assume that one could make specific educational or programmatic recommendations for individual children based on the characteristics and types of treatments described in the following chapter. This general information provides a beginning point. Beyond that, families and early childhood professionals must define programs based on the unique characteristics of children and their families.

GENETICS

Genetics is the study of heredity and variations in the characteristics of organisms, both plant and animal. In humans, genetic research provides information about development and diseases. Understanding gene physiology and function in relation to human growth and development is necessary to understand how individual variability occurs. Treatment and sometimes prevention of disabilities and diseases are made possible by recognizing the role that both genes and the environment play in human development.

Chromosomes are the basic genetic units and stay constant in number within a species and across generations. The first link between genes and chromosomes was made in 1911 by T. H. Morgan, using saliva from a fruit fly (Risley, 1986). **Genes** are regions of a chromosome made up of molecules that collectively define a particular trait.

In a process known as gene mapping, specific genes are linked to individual chromosomes and chromosomal regions (Guyer & Collins, 1993). For example, the gene for muscular dystrophy is located on the "p21" region of the X chromosome. The gene is labeled Xp21. By contrast, Prader-Willi syndrome occurs when a region of the 15th chromosome is missing or deleted. The deleted region is called 15q11-13.

Recently, the study of genetics has been facilitated by new technologies. As a result, the genes responsible for many inherited traits such as Huntington's disease, fragile X syndrome, Duchenne muscular dystrophy, and cystic fibrosis have been isolated. Isolating and identifying genes, understanding their mutations, and learning about their protein products have increased knowledge about disabilities and diseases. This molecular approach is unlike past approaches to genetics, thus the term "new genetics" has been applied (Thompson, McInnes, & Willard, 1991).

The Human Genome Project is an example of new genetics. This is an international project whose goal it is to map and sequence the entire genetic code of human chromosomes by the year 2005. Mapping the human genome will lead to prediction, understanding, and, eventually, to the prevention or curing of many human disabilities and diseases (National Institute of Health [NIH], 1990). This knowledge brings with it numerous ethical questions about how such information should be used. Public dialogue, education, and policies are needed to address the social, legal, and ethical implications of the Human Genome Project. To date, however, participation by society at large in directing this project has been very limited.

Behavioral genetics represents another emerging area of genetics. This subdiscipline is so named because researchers seek the identification of genes associated with behaviors, such as violence, mental illness, and alcoholism. A majority of studies, however, refute the notion that genes, by themselves, cause behavior. Many geneticists warn that research in behavioral genetics should be reviewed critically. It is agreed that scientific and popular media should emphasize that rarely do genes alone determine behavior; rather, genes interact with the environment to cause variations in behavior. "Genes act in environments, and as a result, changing the environment can often change the effect of the gene" (Billings, Beckwith, & Alper, 1992, p. 236).

CELLULAR ACTIVITY OF GENETICS

The human body contains more than a billion miles of **deoxyribonucleic acid (DNA),** with an average cell possessing more than a meter of this substance. DNA is a nucleic acid compound that carries the chemical coding needed to transmit genetic information from generation to generation. A chromosome is a chain of DNA. Human cells possess a total of 46 chromosomes, or 23 pairs of chromosomes (see Figure 6–1). That is, each member of a chromosome pair has matching genes at the same location and in the same sequence. Of the 23 chromosomal pairs, 22 are called **autosomes.** The 23rd pair is comprised of two sex chromosomes: X and Y. The X and the Y chromosome combination determines the gender of an individual—XX in females and XY in males.

Alleles are one of two alternative versions of a gene, with complementary alleles residing on each of the two chromosomes in a pair. A **homozygote pair** will inherit identical alleles for a certain trait, such as two genes for cystic fibrosis. A **heterozygote** has two different alleles for a particular trait, such as one normal gene and one gene for

Figure 6–1
Drawing of the
individual
chromosomes.

cystic fibrosis. **Genotype** refers to the combination of alleles inherited for a particular trait within an individual; **phenotype** refers to the observable expression, or appearance, of the genotype in an individual. When speaking of whole chromosomes, the term **karyotype** is used to describe the number and configuration of the chromosomes. Some genetic testing is done to examine the whole chromosome for variations that may indicate problems. For example, when a child is suspected of having Down syndrome, an analysis of the child's karyotype will be conducted to determine if there is an extra chromosome or extra chromosomal material causing this genetic difference.

The purpose of cell division is to ensure growth, development, and repair of an organism. The two types of cell division are mitosis and meiosis (see Figure 6–2). **Mitosis** produces two identical daughter cells each containing the full set of 46 chromosomes. This occurs in all body cell reproduction. Chromosomes replicate and the cell divides once to create two identical cells, as in the regeneration of skin cells. **Meiosis** produces sex cells, called germ cells, or **gametes,** each with only one half the full complement of chromosomes (one from each chromosome pair). These cells are involved in reproduction. A sperm is a male gamete, and an ovum is a female gamete. When these cells join during conception, the resultant cell(s) will have a full set of chromosomes—one of each chromosome pair from each parent. Abnormalities in chromosome number or structure can arise during either of these processes of cell di-

Figure 6–2
Comparison of mitosis and meiosis cells.

vision. An example is Down syndrome, in which the 21st chromosome, usually in maternal meiosis, does not divide, resulting in three 21st chromosomes, or trisomy 21.

SINGLE GENE DISORDERS

Single gene inheritance is the type of inheritance described by Mendel's principles. Such variations are mutations of genes. This may involve one or both genes of a chromosome pair. Examples of single gene disorders are cystic fibrosis, hemophilia, and sickle cell anemia. The occurrence of abnormalities varies. For example, in hemophilia, the occurrence rate is 1 in 10,000 live births. By contrast, sickle cell disease occurs once in every 400 live births among African Americans (Thompson et al., 1991).

There are about 4000 observable single gene characteristics, 3000 of which are considered genetic disorders. In several hundred of these diseases, the biochemical defect has been identified, and in many, as mentioned above, the responsible gene has been isolated (Thompson et al., 1991). Single gene disorders are transmitted from one generation to another in three ways: recessive, dominant, and sex linked. A **recessive gene** is one whose genetic information is typically overruled by genetic information of a more dominant gene. Usually, it takes two recessive genes, one from each chromosome of a pair, in order for the trait to be expressed. On the other hand, only one **dominant gene** is typically needed for that gene's trait to be expressed. The terms recessive and dominant describe only the phenotypic expression, or observable trait; they do not describe what is happening at a molecular, or biochemical, level. For example, in the case of inheritance of a single recessive gene, the characteristic trait(s) of the disorder is usually not expressed. Nevertheless, at the biochemical level both the dominant and recessive genes are being expressed. The phenotype may also be a combination of recessive and dominant genes acting together (Thompson et al., 1991). **Sex-linked disorders** are transmitted on either the X or Y chromosomes. However, most sex-linked disorders are inherited on the X chromosome. Hemophilia and color blindness are examples of sex-linked genetic differences.

Recessive Gene Inheritance

Tay Sachs, phenylketonuria (PKU), cystic fibrosis, and sickle cell anemia are a few of the many recessive single gene disorders (see Figure 6–3). As mentioned, usually a recessive gene is expressed only if it is inherited from both parents. For example, if

Figure 6–3
Pattern of inheritance of autosomal recessive genes.

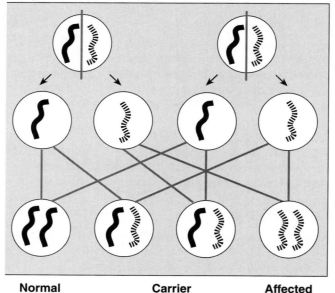

Autosomal Recessive Inheritance Pattern

Disorders are caused by a pair of altered genes on the autosomes.

Parents

Both parents are carriers of the altered gene (though they are clinically normal).

Gametes

Children

When both parents are carriers, there is a 25% risk of having an affected child (male or female) with each pregnancy.

Normal (25%) **Carrier** (50%) **Affected** (25%)

the recessive gene for sickle cell anemia is inherited from both parents, the person will show signs of the disease. In this case, the offspring have a 25% chance of receiving two recessive genes and, consequently, of having the disorder. If just one affected gene is inherited, the person will not show signs of the disease except at the biochemical level. This is because the gene is paired with a dominant gene, and the dominant gene is the one phenotypically expressed. This person is a **carrier,** and although carriers have no signs or symptoms of the disease, they may transmit the gene to their offspring. There is a 50% chance of inheriting one gene and becoming a carrier and a 25% chance of not inheriting the gene from either parent.

Dominant Gene Inheritance

Huntington's disease, familial hypercholesteremia, and some forms of muscular dystrophy are examples of dominant single gene disorders (see Figure 6–4). Dominant genes are phenotypically expressed whenever they appear. Persons having just one of the genes will show signs of the disorder. Therefore, if one parent has the dominant gene and the other parent does not, the offspring have a 50% chance of receiving the dominant gene. Early identification of the possession of dominant gene disorders can help parents decide whether or not to prevent the inheritance. At this

Figure 6–4
Pattern of inheritance for autosomal dominant genes.

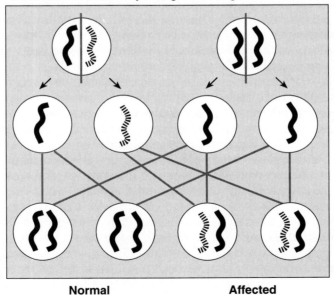

Autosomal Dominant Inheritance Pattern

Disorders are caused by a single altered gene on one of the autosomes.

Parents
Either parent may have the gene, or the disorder may be due to a new gene alteration (mutation).

Gametes

Children
When one parent is affected, there is a 50% risk of having an affected child (male or female) with each pregnancy.

Normal (50%)   **Affected** (50%)

{ **Normal Gene**   ⟩ **Affected Gene**

time, prevention of transmission can only occur when parents decide not to reproduce or, once conception has taken place, to abort a fetus with a genetic disease.

Recessive and dominant traits are not strictly determined by the presence or absence of a normal/abnormal gene. As with most things in nature, heredity is not so simple. If one normal and one mutant gene are present, then the result of their combined production of genetic material is what determines the dominant or recessive nature of the trait (Thompson et al., 1991). For example, if there is enough gene product between the two genes to provide for normal functioning, then the mutant gene and its related disorder are overruled and therefore recessive. For the sake of illustration, let's say hypothetically that syndrome Q needs 56 out of 100 units of normal gene product in order for the syndrome to be expressed. From the mother, who is a carrier of the mutant gene, the fertilized cell receives 10 units of normal gene product and 40 units of mutant Q gene product. From the father, who is not a carrier, the fertilized cell receives 50 units of normal gene product. Since there are 60 units of normal gene product, the offspring of this union will yield sufficient gene product for the gene trait to function normally. In this child, the gene for syndrome Q is recessive.

If there is not enough genetic product between the two chromosomes to function normally, then the gene and the disorder are said to be dominant. For example, in sickle cell anemia, a recessive gene produces abnormal hemoglobin. If that gene is inherited from each parent, then the blood will make abnormal hemoglobin. In this case, the person has sickle cell anemia. On the other hand, if one abnormal gene and one normal gene are inherited, the blood will contain some normal and some abnormal hemoglobin. Although both genes are functioning, the person will show no symptoms of the disorder because there is enough normal hemoglobin produced to outweigh the effects of the abnormal gene. These individuals do not have sickle cell anemia, but they are carriers of the recessive gene and can therefore transmit the gene to their children.

Sex-Linked Inheritance

Sex-linked disorders have the affected gene on either the X or Y chromosome. Most sex-linked disorders are related to the X chromosome. Hemophilia and Duchenne muscular dystrophy are examples. The incidence of these types of disorders is highest in male offspring. Males inherit X-linked diseases from their mothers, the source of their X chromosome. In males, such diseases are usually more significant since there is no complementary X chromosome. Females, with two X chromosomes, are usually not affected because the second X chromosome compensates for the recessive gene on the affected X chromosome. Only a few genetic disorders are X-linked dominant. In this case, an affected male parent passes the disorder on to all daughters but none of the sons. This is because the son receives his X chromosome from the mother and the Y from the father. The daughter, on the other hand, receives one of her two X chromosomes from the father and, because it is dominant, will have the disorder. However, such diseases are usually of a less severe nature in females because they possess two X chromosomes. The normal X chromosome helps counteract the abnormal member of the pair (see Figure 6–5). Fragile X and Duchenne

Figure 6–5
Sex-linked chromosomal disorders.

X-linked Recessive

Either parent may have the gene present on the **X** chromosome.

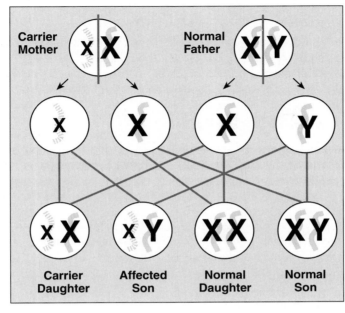

Parents

Since females have two **X** chromosomes, in order to be **affected** they must have an altered pair of genes. (Only one **X** chromosome is altered here.)

Gametes

Children

When a woman has an altered gene on only one **X** chromosome, she is a carrier (usually not affected) and with a normal father, they have a 25% risk of having an altered son.

Key: **X** Normal X chromosome.   **Y** Normal Y chromosome.

X Affected X chromosome.

muscular dystrophy are similar in that females are usually carriers, but may show mild symptoms of the disorders. In these cases, the unaffected/normal X chromosome may not completely compensate for the affected X chromosome, and some form of the disorder is manifest.

CHROMOSOME DISORDERS

In **chromosome disorders,** whole chromosomes or chromosome segments are responsible for a problem rather than a single gene or combination of genes (see Figure 6–6). These variations can include an extra chromosome, extra chromosome material, structural abnormality, or absence/deletion of a chromosome. Turner syndrome is an example in which there is a whole or partial absence of one of the two X chromosomes. Chromosome disorders of this nature are common, occurring in 7 out of every 1000 births. It is estimated that 50% of all spontaneous abortions in the first trimester are due to these chromosomal abnormalities.

Figure 6–6
Chromosomal
disorders.

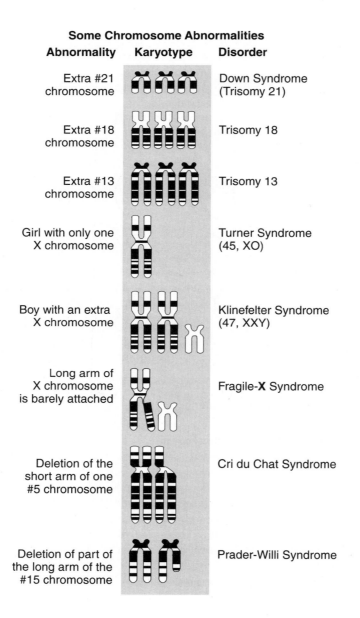

Some Chromosome Abnormalities

Abnormality	Karyotype	Disorder
Extra #21 chromosome		Down Syndrome (Trisomy 21)
Extra #18 chromosome		Trisomy 18
Extra #13 chromosome		Trisomy 13
Girl with only one X chromosome		Turner Syndrome (45, XO)
Boy with an extra X chromosome		Klinefelter Syndrome (47, XXY)
Long arm of X chromosome is barely attached		Fragile-**X** Syndrome
Deletion of the short arm of one #5 chromosome		Cri du Chat Syndrome
Deletion of part of the long arm of the #15 chromosome		Prader-Willi Syndrome

MULTIFACTORIAL DISORDERS

Multifactorial disorders account for two types of genetic problems: congenital disorders and the predisposition to a disease, usually with onset in adulthood. Congenital disorders account for malformations such as cleft palate, spina bifida, and various heart anomalies. Prenatal environmental factors may also be involved in these disorders. Many diseases do not appear until adulthood. These are exacerbated by a probable genetic predisposition to acquire the disease. A few examples that are currently believed to be affected by genetic predisposition include heart disease, obesity, arthritis, some forms of cancer, and metabolic problems, such as diabetes mellitus. It is also believed that lifestyle moderation, such as diet and exercise, can affect the course of some of these diseases.

GENETIC TESTING

One American in 100 is born with a serious genetic disorder, which may be chromosomal, sex-linked, or multifactorial (March of Dimes [MOD], 1992). Genetic testing and counseling are conducted for people who have questions and concerns about problems that may affect their offspring. There are several reasons to consider genetic testing: family history of genetic disorders, a child with a genetic disorder, two or more miscarriages or a baby that died in infancy, ethnic origin (e.g., sickle cell anemia is more prevalent among African Americans), first cousins planning to have a child together, and pregnancy of a woman over age 35.

Analysis of blood samples can detect genetic disorders. Hemophilia, Tay Sachs disease, cystic fibrosis, sickle cell anemia, and Duchenne muscular dystrophy are detected in this way. Blood samples also show if a person is the carrier of a recessive gene that could be passed on to offspring. Amniocentesis, chorionic villus sampling, and, more recently, fetal blood sampling from the umbilical cord are prenatal tests that can be used for early detection of abnormalities (Sach & Korf, 1993). **Amniocentesis** is a painful and risky procedure that removes fluid from the sac surrounding the fetus. A long, thin needle is inserted through the abdomen to withdraw approximately four teaspoons of amniotic fluid. Of every 400 amniocentesis tests performed by a qualified physician, one spontaneous abortion is likely to occur. Amniocentesis can reveal chromosomal, metabolic, and biochemical disorders. For example, DNA tests can be conducted to detect such problems as cystic fibrosis or sickle cell anemia. Down syndrome is the most common chromosomal problem detected with this procedure. **Chorionic villus sampling (CVS)** is conducted vaginally or abdominally and requires a small tissue sample from the chorion or outer sac that surrounds the fetus. Chorionic villus sampling can be conducted earlier in fetal development than amniocentesis, but the risk to a fetus is higher. **Fetal blood sampling** (also called percutaneous umbilical blood sampling) can be conducted even earlier than CVS, and detects the same problems. A needle is guided into the abdomen, through the uterus to the umbilical cord, from which a blood sample is withdrawn.

Other prenatal tests include ultrasound and alpha-fetoprotein screening (AFP). Ultrasound is used to visualize the fetus and its developing organs. Congenital malformations, such as spina bifida, can be detected using this procedure. **Alpha-fetoprotein (AFP)** screening is a blood test conducted to detect neural tube disorders, such as malformations of the spinal cord, the spinal column, and the brain. This test, however, produces many false positives since the level of AFP fluctuates during pregnancy. For this reason, AFP testing is usually used as a screening tool leading to further diagnostic tests, such as those mentioned above.

GENE THERAPY

Though gene therapy is presently experimental, discoveries of the new century may provide treatments for various genetic disorders. One type of gene therapy introduces a normal gene into a cell nucleus to replace an abnormal gene. The cell can then function normally. For example, in diabetes mellitus, in which the body is unable to produce insulin, a gene that provides the genetic information needed to initiate insulin production might be introduced. However, the inserted genes are not passed on to the next generation because normal genetic material is not placed in the germ cells. For now, because such therapy is so exploratory, education and caution are necessary to facilitate judgment regarding the relative benefits and risks of therapy compared to the prognosis for the disease (Haan, 1990).

Germ line therapy introduces genes into the germ or sex cells, as well as into the somatic cells. The consequences of this therapy may be profound. Future generations would be influenced if such therapy is successful, and stability of the entire gene pool could be compromised by eliminating certain genes while potentially creating other new abnormalities. For this reason, and because it is believed that there is a risk of serious ethical abuse, most geneticists agree that this type of therapy should not be undertaken (Haan, 1990; Sach & Korf, 1993), even if it could be successful in reversing the effects of a serious genetic defect in some children.

GENETIC VARIATIONS IN DEVELOPMENT

CYSTIC FIBROSIS

Cystic fibrosis (CF) is the most common fatal genetic disease in the United States. Approximately 1 in 23 persons in the United States is a carrier of the CF gene (Cystic Fibrosis Foundation [CFF], 1999a). Cystic fibrosis affects the exocrine glands, which secrete body fluids. In children with cystic fibrosis, the **exocrine glands** overproduce a thick, sticky mucus that eventually clogs the lungs and blocks functioning of the pancreas. Also affected are the sweat glands, which produce perspiration containing two to five times the normal amount of sodium (Anfenson, 1980).

Characteristics

Individuals with cystic fibrosis produce an excessive amount of thick, sticky mucus (CFF, 1999b). In the lungs and respiratory tract, this mucus blocks airways and interferes with breathing, eventually resulting in respiratory failure. This mucus further inhibits the pancreas from releasing enzymes to the digestive tract necessary for breaking down foods (CFF, 1999b). Consequently, children with cystic fibrosis are unable to sufficiently metabolize fats and proteins. The sweat glands' tendency to excrete abnormally high amounts of sodium provides the basis for the "sweat test," the primary diagnostic measurement for cystic fibrosis. Because of an excessive release of salt, exposure to fevers and extreme heat are two conditions that can be especially harmful. Heat can cause serious depletion of sodium and may result in confusion, seizures, and other electrolyte imbalance problems.

As a consequence of these physiological disturbances, children with cystic fibrosis have chronic symptoms of persistent coughing, recurrent wheezing, repeated respiratory infection, excessive appetite, poor weight gain or even weight loss (CFF, 1999c). The progression of cystic fibrosis symptoms varies across individuals with the disease. Some children may be affected primarily in the respiratory system; in others the pancreas and digestive systems might be more significantly affected. No diagnostic tests have yet been devised to predict the course that will be taken in specific patients with cystic fibrosis. In the past, it was very unusual for those affected by cystic fibrosis to live long enough to go to school; most died in infancy (CFF, 1999c). However, with recent treatment advances, there has been a substantial improvement in life expectancy. Although 30 years ago the life expectancy of persons with CF was 8 years, today it is 30 and continually increasing with medical advances (CFF, 1999b).

Dibble and Savedra (1988) described numerous secondary physical complications that have emerged concomitant with improved survival of patients with cystic fibrosis. For example, there is an increased incidence of respiratory dysfunctions: lung infections, bloody mucus, and pneumothorax (rupture in the lung releasing air into the chest cavity). As the life expectancy of patients with cystic fibrosis increases, so does the probability of their developing diabetes; as many as 40% to 60% of persons with cystic fibrosis may acquire hyperglycemia.

Etiology

Cystic fibrosis is an autosomal recessive gene, transmitted genetically to offspring when both parents are carriers. Carriers inherit a single cystic fibrosis gene located on one of the two number 7 chromosomes. For these individuals, the second chromosome 7 remains unaffected and blocks the expression of the harmful gene. A child afflicted with cystic fibrosis has two cystic fibrosis genes, one present on each chromosome 7.

Treatment

Diagnosis of cystic fibrosis is usually made by the second or third birthday, though for some children symptoms may go undiagnosed for months or years. Treatment of cystic fibrosis involves a multidisciplinary approach to address the numerous issues likely to arise for both child and family. Professionals likely to be included on the team are a medical director, nurse, physical therapist, clinical pharmacist, respiratory therapist, nutritionist, social service worker, geneticist, and possibly others, all of whom will work together with a patient with cystic fibrosis on long and short term treatment goals. Typical family routines in daily treatment of children with cystic fibrosis include:

1. Adequate nutrition with a high carbohydrate and protein diet, adequate salt intake, pancreatic enzyme preparations, supplemental doses of fat soluble vitamins, and adequate fluid intake. Chronic malnutrition is prevalent in children with cystic fibrosis. Most can compensate for the nutritional deficiency through the consumption of energy-dense foods and pancreatic enzyme supplements. Others require a surgically implanted gastrostomy which permit nighttime or daytime food infusions. The latter can aid in normal growth and overall health status (Rosenfeld, Casey, Pepe, & Ramsey, 1999).

2. Ninety percent of children/adults with cystic fibrosis die of lung disease or gradual decline of lung function caused by repeated bacterial infection (McCarthy, 1999). Therefore, prevention of infection through frequent bronchial drainage treatments, aerosol inhalation therapy, use of antibiotics, and a mist tent while

sleeping or resting is a key aspect of treatment. Young children may need to be taught to cough expectorant into a tissue, but in no way encouraged to suppress coughing either physically or by using cough suppressants (CFF, 1999c). Some children may take as many as 25 pills per day, requiring adult supervision during the preschool years.

3. Promoting healthy development by encouraging normal social relationships, reinforcing self-image, continued contact with supporting agencies, continuous support when children are hospitalized, and emphasis on a child's identity as a "typical child" whenever appropriate. Even though children with CF may have limited stamina, they should be encouraged to engage in regular exercise which helps loosen mucus.

Although treatment practices are limited and a cure still undiscovered, many advances were made in the 1980s and 1990s. Advances that have improved life quality and expectancy include the mucous thinning drug Pulmozyme, approved in 1993, and new antibiotics such as INS365 which stimulates cells to secrete chloride which in turn makes mucous less thick and sticky (CFF, 1999b). Since the 1989 identification of the abnormal protein causing cystic fibrosis, many new treatment methods have been researched. Such experimental methods as genetically bypassing the problems caused by the abnormal protein or therapeutically altering the defective protein in the bloodstream are being investigated ("Scientists Forecast," 1989). One other experimental approach is gene therapy, considered "the ultimate 'correction' strategy." This potential cure for CF has yet to be perfected, but important steps were taken throughout the 1990s. To accomplish the cure, scientists manufacture normal genes in a laboratory and deliver the genes through a variety of methods such as nose drops or tube entering the lungs. The normal genes would correct the damage done by the defective CF cells. However, much work remains to be done before gene therapy cures CF (CFF, 1999a).

In the preschool years, children with cystic fibrosis may or may not display symptoms that affect their daily lives. Some children may have frequent and serious lung infections that could interfere with typical social and cognitive opportunities. Monitoring developmental progress and providing enriching educational programs should be a priority for educators of young children with cystic fibrosis. Other than constraints that might be placed on children by their medical condition, intervention should be developmentally and socially relevant.

Though cost varies from one family to another, depending on the severity and stage of the disease, family economics are almost always strained by this disease (Stullenbarger, Norris, Edgil, & Prosser, 1987). The cost of hospitalization is so high that families without medical insurance usually suffer financial crisis (CFF, 1999c). The social effects of cystic fibrosis on the entire family can also be difficult. Parents, siblings, and the children themselves are emotionally affected. Though families of children with disabilities are as resilient to life's challenges as other families, and though new technology offers unprecedented hope for a cure to cystic fibrosis, adjusting to the possible loss of a child or sibling with cystic fibrosis can begin as early as preschool. Finally, genetic counseling has also proven to be an effective means to alleviating fears and guilt in parents of children with cystic fibrosis (March of Dimes [MOD], 1987).

Down Syndrome

DOWN SYNDROME

Down syndrome was one of the first causes of mental retardation to be categorized as a syndrome. Identified in 1866 by Langdon Down, the syndrome has variously been termed cretinism, unfinished or ill-finished child, and mongolism. Down referred to the syndrome as a retrogression to the Mongoloid race, since children and adults resembled persons of this ethnic group in several phenotypic ways. This name remained common in educational and medical communities until the 1960s, when it was replaced with the more dignified label Down syndrome. The prevalence of Down syndrome ranges from 1 in 600 to 1 in 1000 live births. This incidence makes Down syndrome the second largest genetic cause of mental retardation, after fragile X syndrome.

CLOSE-UP

GENETIC SCREENING

While some genetically caused disabilities are largely impervious to the demographic characteristics of their victims, others are quite selective. For example, many genetic disabilities are gender specific, choosing either male or female victims almost exclusively (e.g., muscular dystrophy and fragile X syndrome). Some genetic diseases are more prevalent in specific racial groups. Cystic Fibrosis is more common in persons of European descent. Two other diseases that are ethnically specific are Tay Sachs Disease and Sickle Cell Anemia, commonly found in persons of Jewish and African descent respectively.

O'Sullivan, in studying the history of these diseases, found evidence that preference had been given to the research and resultant screening and treatment of some of these culturally based diseases over others. She concluded that genetic study should be governed more carefully by ethical considerations than it has in the past. This is especially true given the genetic breakthroughs in the last decade (e.g., gene cloning, gene therapy, and the Human Genome Project) that have the potential for extreme ethical abuse and catastophic consequences.

As evidence of a lack of ethical guidance O'Sullivan compared Tay Sachs disease to sickle cell disease. Tay Sachs causes progressive degeneration of the nervous system, leading to blindness, deafness, hydrocephaly, and eventual death in the preschool years. Sickle cell disease affects the circulatory system of its victims, where misshapen red blood cells cause infection, ulcers, blood clotting, painful "sickle cell crises" and eventual death in adolescence or early adulthood.

While both are autosomal recessive, single gene disorders, the prevalence within their high-risk groups is very different. In Ashkenazi Jews, the rate of live births is about 1 in 4100, while sickle cell disease is found in about 1 in 500 African American infants. Although the natural incidence indicates that sickle cell disease occurs at a much higher rate, screening methods applied to the diseases have resulted in almost complete eradication of Tay Sachs disease since the 1970s when screening methods were begun, while there has been a very small drop in the incidence of sickle cell disease. The latter is due to a natural decline rather than because of screening efforts.

In the case of Tay Sachs, the voluntary screening program was conducted in a very sensitive manner and often within the context of cultural practices, such as using community matchmaker to ensure that carriers did not marry each other. By contrast, a national compulsory screening program for sickle cell disease begun in the 1970s was abandoned by 1980 because of poor implementation. While couples who were carriers received inadequate education and genetic counseling, the test results were frequently used to turn down insurance, employment, and Air Force applicants. Possibly due to such mismanagement, this screening tool was also perceived as a racist attempt to limit the African American population in the United States.

While she does not accuse anyone of racism or unethical practice, O'Sullivan implies that the differential approaches and subsequent effectiveness were related to some degree of cultural bias. O'Sullivan suggests that by presenting undergraduate students with this ethical paradigm and others, they will become more active and ethical professionals once they become the researchers, practitioners, and socially active citizens who will decide what we do with the genetic breakthroughs of the coming decades.

O'Sullivan, H. (1998). Use and design of genetic screening programmes: A study. *Journal of Biological Education, 32,* 97–103.

Characteristics

Though more than 50 traits have been associated with Down syndrome, individuals with this disability may have a few or many of the known characteristics (Fishler & Koch, 1991). Mental retardation ranging from mild to severe is present in almost all individuals with Down syndrome. However, with changing educational practices over the last century, children's educational opportunities combined with innovative teaching methods have greatly improved the cognitive expectations and achievements of children with Down syndrome. Phenotypic characteristics include short stature and clubbed short fingers, epicanthal folds (skin at inner corner of eye forms a fold, making eye appear to be slanted), sloping forehead, flat **occipital** lobe, ruddy cheeks, speckled iris, malformed ears, flat nose bridge, upward tilt to nostrils, simian line in palm (a single deep wrinkle running across the width of the palm), third toe longer than second, and a gap between big toe and next one. A high palate and small oral cavity often lead to tongue protrusion.

Medical conditions also commonly accompany this disability. Neonates often have life threatening conditions, such as duodenal atresia where the small bowel is partially or fully blocked, and patent ductus arteriosis, in which the duct connecting a fetus's blood system to the maternal blood supply does not close automatically after birth. Because of these and other medical conditions, the life expectancy of children with Down syndrome was only 9–12 years in the early part of this century. Chronic heart problems and depressed immune response resulting in frequent upper respiratory infections often led to premature death. In a more recent analysis, Eyman, Call, and White (1991) concluded that while medical problems do affect the overall life expectancy of persons with Down syndrome, restricted mobility and poor eating patterns of infants are more significant risk factors. Most individuals who do not have significant associated disabilities have an overall life expectancy of greater than 50 years.

One of the most dominant physiological characteristics is hypotonia, or low muscle tone. Consequently, infants with Down syndrome typically have delayed motor and speech development. Children also have a high incidence of hearing impairments with a tendency toward high-frequency hearing losses (Marcell & Cohen, 1992). Because the hearing losses tend to be conductive, the susceptibility of these children to middle ear disease may be a related factor. Visual impairments are also more common in children with Down syndrome than in typically developing children.

As the life expectancy of individuals with Down syndrome improves, researchers have identified specific areas of premature aging. These differences range from the innocuous, such as accelerated aging and turnover of red blood cells (Wachtel & Pueschel, 1991), to the dangerous, as with premature deterioration of the thyroid function, leading to hypothyroidism in a large percentage of adults with Down syndrome (Pueschel, Jackson, Giesswein, Dean, & Pezzullo, 1991). Of greatest concern is the tendency toward premature dementia in middle age, leading to behavioral deterioration (Evenhuis, 1990).

A child with Down syndrome.

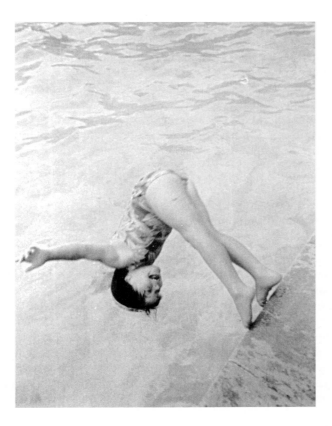

Figure 6–7
Diagram of cell division leading to Down syndrome.

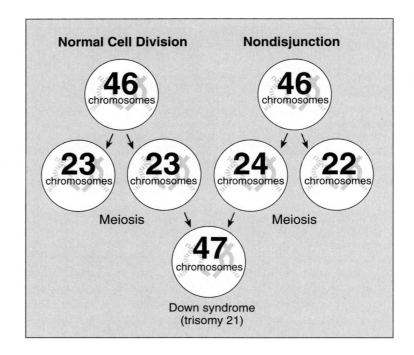

Etiology

The discovery of chromosomes quickly led to the identification of genetic anomalies causing Down syndrome. Instead of the normal complement of 23 pairs of chromosomes in each cell (46 total), most individuals with Down syndrome have an extra 21st chromosome, and 47 total chromosomes. The three 21st chromosomes, referred to as **trisomy 21,** are always associated with at least a few of the physical or behavioral characteristics described earlier. In addition, two other chromosomal defects can cause Down syndrome:

1. A **translocation** trisomy is the existence of extra chromosomal material that has become attached to another chromosome. The size of the misguided genetic material may vary from an extra piece to an entire chromosome.
2. In **mosaicism,** a portion of cells have 46 chromosomes and another percentage (usually 10% to 12%) of the cells have the extra 21st chromosome (47).

The genetic history of each of these types of Down syndrome also varies. In typical trisomies, the extra 21st chromosome is associated with **nondisjunction during meiosis** (Figure 6–7). In other words, when cell division takes place to create either an ovum or sperm, there is an incomplete detachment of the 21st pair, with one cell receiving 22 chromosomes and the other 24. In Down syndrome, the cell with 24 chromosomes (including the extra 21st) combines with a normal compliment of 23 chromosomes.

Translocation trisomies are typically genetically transmitted from a carrier parent to an affected child, and occur in approximately 5–10% of cases of Down syndrome. Research indicates that the different causes of Down syndrome described above are associated with differences in developmental and physical characteristics (Fishler & Koch, 1991; Johnson & Abelson, 1969). Specifically, Fishler and Koch (1991) observed that, on the average, children with mosaicism and translocations, had fewer physical traits associated with Down syndrome and greater intellectual potential (Fishler & Koch, 1991). This finding conflicts, however, with Johnson and Abelson (1969), who found that individuals with mosaicism had the lowest average intellectual functioning of the three types of Down syndrome.

Why some gametes have aberrant cell division, resulting in extra chromosomes, is still unknown. However, for some time, researchers recognized the contribution of maternal age to the incidence of Down syndrome. Generally speaking, as women grow older, the odds of conceiving a child with Down syndrome grow progressively more favorable (Chan, McCaul, Keane, & Haan, 1998). Women older than 35 years of age are considered high risk and may generally be advised to undergo prenatal testing such as amniocentesis when pregnant. A second factor associated with the incidence of Down syndrome is maternal exposure to low level radiation over a long period of time. Neither maternal age nor radiation exposure is an explanation for nondisjunction, but knowing their relationship to Down syndrome is useful in genetic counseling for women considering pregnancy.

Other Trisomy Disorders

While Down syndrome is the most common live birth trisomy, other trisomy conceptions are common, and some occur even more frequently than trisomy 21. However, most of these chromosomal anomalies are spontaneously aborted because their characteristics are incompatible with life. Other fetuses may survive the pregnancy but may be stillborn or will likely die within a few days or weeks of birth. Trisomies 13, 16, and 18 are the most common of these chromosomal anomalies.

Treatment

Early intervention for children and their families should focus on several dimensions. For parents, education regarding the etiology and long-term outcomes is needed. Parents may want to read literature or be put on mailing lists for magazines or newsletters, join support groups, or join the National Down Syndrome Society, a powerful advocacy group.

Intervention goals for children will likely be comprehensive, with early emphasis on motor and language development. Physical and occupational therapists and communication specialists should be involved. Speech development is often impeded by both cognitive delays and oral structural problems. However, Steffens, Oiler, Lynch, and Urbano (1992) found that the patterns of vocal development in children with Down syndrome paralleled those of normally developing children, even though the average rates of development in the former were slightly slower. **Augmentative or alternative communication** (sign language, communication boards, and other devices) can reduce frustration and enhance language development. Feeding may also be an issue, since children tend to be underweight in infancy. Later, as toddlers and preschoolers, hypotonicity and slow metabolic rates sometimes contribute to an excessive weight gain (Chad, Jobling, & Frail, 1990). According to Chad et al., regular exercise should be scheduled to both reduce body fat and correspondingly increase energy levels.

There is increasing evidence that, with certain instruction (i.e., early intervention, use of behavior analytic methods, and integration), many preschool and elementary students are able to stay at or above grade/age expectancies in some academic areas, notably in reading (Rynders & Horrobin, 1990). As children with Down syndrome grow older, their relative intellectual abilities diminish compared to the rate of progress made by typical children (Rynders & Horrobin, 1990). Even so, children with Down syndrome now being served in public schools are accomplishing feats once believed impossible. The potential of such children (indeed all children) is undoubtedly limited by our own boundaries in educational technology.

Fragile X
Syndrome

FRAGILE X SYNDROME

Until recently, the prevalence of mental retardation in males had been explained by social and behavioral gender differences (De La Cruz, 1985). The identification of fragile X syndrome challenged that assumption. This syndrome was first identified in 1969 when Lubs discovered the genetic abnormality in the X chromosomes of a mother and her son. Now, fragile X syndrome is considered the leading known cause of mental retardation (Dykens, Hodapp, Ort, & Leckman, 1993; Keenan et al., 1992; Santos, 1992). Fragile X is believed to account for 40% of the X-related forms of mental retardation and 10% of all cases of mental retardation (Rogers & Simensen, 1987). Additionally, fragile X may be even more prevalent than these statistics indicate since many carriers who have the anomalous chromosome but do not have mental retardation go undiagnosed (Santos, 1992; Sudhalter, Cohen, Silverman, & Wolf-Schein, 1990). Yet, many early childhood professionals do not have a good understanding of this disability. Wilson and Mazzocco (1993) found that only 36% of professional educators responding to a survey had knowledge of fragile X, while 64% were knowledgeable about Down syndrome, which appears to be less prevalent.

Characteristics

Prior to its identification, and even now, children with fragile X syndrome were misdiagnosed with ADHD, autism, nonspecific mental retardation, pervasive developmental disorder, learning disability, and emotional impairment (Schmidt, 1997). These "misreads" suggest the variability and severity of characteristics for this syndrome. The fragile X mutation ranges from partial to full, with the full mutation obviously corresponding to more apparent and severe syndrome related characteristics. Females who are affected by fragile X generally express either mild to moderate forms of mental retardation. Only half of those females with a full mutation are recognized as having a disability, though most have some learning problems (Turner, Robinson, Wake, Laing, & Partington, 1997). Males, on the other hand, tend to range from borderline to profoundly mentally retarded (De La Cruz, 1985; Sudhalter et al., 1990; Wolff, Gardner, Paccia, & Lappen, 1989). Of males with the fragile X chromosome, 80% express mental impairment, whereas only 30% of females with the fragile X chromosome are mentally retarded (Keenan et al., 1992). Furthermore, longitudinal documentation indicates a steady deterioration in mental functioning as these children age (Keenan et al., 1992; Santos, 1992; Simensen & Rogers, 1989). Unvalidated theories regarding this alleged decline include progressive neurological deterioration (Santos, 1992), increased emphasis on cognitive/reasoning skills as children age (Santos, 1992), and failure of the rate of intellectual growth to keep pace with expectations of standardized IQ tests (McClennen, 1992). Fragile X has a specific pattern of learning characteristics. Strengths include relatively strong language and visual skills, while weaknesses include difficulty with grammar and math (De La Cruz, 1985; Keenan et al., 1992). Males in particular have difficulty in processing novel sequential information, short-term memory, and problem solving that requires complex generalization (Reiss & Freund, 1990).

Even though the most predominant characteristic of fragile X syndrome is mental retardation, all body systems are affected, including the hormonal, neurological, and cardiac functions. Most children with fragile X have a normal appearance at birth (Keenan et al., 1992). Prominent physical features are most apparent in postpubertal males. Characteristic features in adults include a long face, large ears, prominent forehead, underdevelopment of the midface region, prominent jaw, and enlarged testicles (De La Cruz, 1985; Meryash, 1985; Santos, 1992; Simensen & Rogers, 1989). Meryash (1985) also noted that a majority of individuals with fragile X tend to be short in stature. The variability in facial features of females with fragile X makes it difficult to use physical features as an index in diagnosis (Rogers & Simensen, 1987).

As with intelligence, researchers have recorded a progressive degeneration of adaptive behavior in males with fragile X syndrome (Dykens et al., 1993). After making steady gains in adaptive behavior until early adolescence, skills then begin to decline. Several behavioral phenomena are associated with the syndrome, though considerable variability exists among individuals with fragile X. Many express distinctly autistic-like characteristics, such as unusual hand mannerisms (hand flapping and hand biting), stereotypic behaviors (rocking), and speech and language disorders (perseveration, echolalia, dysrhythmia, and inappropriate speech) (Keenan et al., 1992; Meryash, 1985; Sudhalter et al., 1990). Other traits include hyperactivity, attentional deficits, bizarre responses to their surrounding environments, hypersensitivity to environmental stimuli, emotional problems, motor delays, poor eye contact, and social avoidance (Hagerman, 1992; Keenan et al., 1992; Meryash, 1985; Santos, 1992; Simensen & Rogers, 1989; Wolff et al., 1989).

Females may also have social difficulties, including problems with peer relationships, shyness, depression and mood disorder, loneliness and a tendency to withdraw and act uncomfortable around others (Mazzocco, Baumgardner, Freund, & Reiss, 1998). While social skills tend to be most affected by the fragile X chromosome, other adaptive behaviors appear to be especially well developed relative to mental impairment (Dykens et al., 1993). Whether institutionalized or not, males have strong daily living skills in areas such as toileting, personal grooming, and domestic responsibilities.

Etiology

Fragile X syndrome derives its name from the form of its mutation on the X chromosome. The "fragile" site on the X chromosome is located on the long arm at the Xq27 gene (Keenan et al., 1992; Meryash, 1985; Rogers & Simensen, 1987; Simensen & Rogers, 1989). This long arm may be separated or connected by only a thin strand (Meryash, 1985). Though most prevalent in males, fragile X, more so than any of the other X-related chromosomes, also affects females (Meryash, 1985; Simensen

& Rogers, 1989). Sudhalter et al. (1990) noted that 1 in 1350 males and 1 in 2033 females have the hereditary abnormality. However, since females possess two X chromosomes, the one intact X chromosome tends to overrule the effects of the fragile X chromosome. Santos (1992) explained the incidence of fragile X characteristics in females as a selective inactivation of the normal X chromosome, which then allows expression by the other X chromosome at the fragile site. By contrast, males have only one X chromosome and are therefore always vulnerable to the defective genetic anomaly.

Fragile X is of a familial nature, transmitted from generation to generation in a unique fashion (Santos, 1992; Wolff et al., 1989). The defective chromosome is most commonly transmitted by the mother who may be affected or unaffected; however, it has been noted that unaffected males may transmit the fragile X chromosome to their daughters (Santos, 1992). Furthermore, genetic studies of families with the fragile X chromosome revealed that as the affected chromosome is transmitted from generation to generation, the incidence of fragile X syndrome increases in frequency and severity (Turner et al., 1997). The site of the X chromosome responsible for its fragility is normally comprised of a region of repeated proteins of 20–40 in length. Across generations, this region can slowly increase in length, gradually becoming less stable. When duplicates lengthen past 50 or so repeats, each subsequent generation can suddenly expand rapidly to 200. Two hundred repeats appears to be the threshold for manifestation of the symptoms of fragile X and represents a full mutation.

The fragile X chromosome travels through families in an unusual manner. A typical family pedigree is one in which all children of female carriers of the syndrome have a 50% chance of inheriting the gene from their mothers. Males who are carriers will pass the gene to their daughters, but obviously may not pass the gene to their sons. When a male carrier passes the abnormal gene to his daughter the likelihood of mental retardation is low. On the other hand, mental retardation is common (55%) in the daughters of females who inherited the abnormal fragile X gene from their carrier fathers (Meryash, 1985; Santos, 1992). Therefore, mental retardation is more likely to occur when the female transmits the mutated X chromosome.

Treatment

Fragile X syndrome is rarely detected at birth and may not be identified until school age in affected children with mild disabilities. Among the various professionals that should be involved in treatment are health professionals, child study teams, therapists, and educators (Keenan et al., 1992). Medical treatment of the syndrome itself is limited, though stimulant medication, such as Ritalin, has been somewhat effective in controlling behaviors associated with hyperactivity and attentional deficits (Santos, 1992). The primary treatment for fragile X syndrome is educational, with early childhood special education providing the greatest promise for long-term adaptive and intellectual benefits. Because there is considerable variability within the population of individuals with fragile X syndrome, components of educational programs should be designed to fit children's behavioral needs and not the disability itself. It is likely that components would include functional skills training, physical therapy, and speech therapy (McClennen, 1992; Meryash, 1985).

Genetic counseling of families with the mutant X chromosome is very important. Because of the unique pattern of transmission and the tendency of the syndrome to be underdiagnosed and silently carried by females, it is important to educate both nuclear and extended families when the syndrome is positively diagnosed. In instances where extensive genetic counseling and follow-up family education and prenatal screening were implemented there has been a dramatic reduction in the incidence of fragile X syndrome (Turner et al., 1997).

Duchenne MD

MUSCULAR DYSTROPHY

Several hereditary muscle wasting diseases fall under the category of muscular dystrophy. The factor that unifies these disorders is the progressive loss of muscle tissue which is concurrent with increases in fat and connective tissue and subsequent muscle weakness (Emery, 1998). The most common form of progressive muscular disease is Duchenne muscular dystrophy. Approximately 1 in every 3500 males is born with Duchenne muscular dystrophy (Shapiro & Specht, 1993). A milder but similar disorder, Becker muscular dystrophy, affects 1 in 30,000 male children. Though the severity of this disease is most prominent during the school age years, its onset is generally early childhood.

Characteristics

The course of Duchenne muscular dystrophy follows a fairly predictable pattern (Lynn, Woda, & Mendell, 1994; Shapiro & Specht, 1993). Usually in early childhood (ages three to six), children begin to have weakness in gross motor activities like running and jumping, and they fall often. The disability is positively identified when children rise from the floor using the Gower's maneuver or are unable to get up without using their arms for support. Children tend to waddle when walking and gradually develop **scoliosis** (spine curvature of the lower back). This misalignment of the body is a primary cause of respiratory disease, as the bellows of the lungs are compromised by the child's posture. As the muscles weaken, **contractures** form in the lower extremities. Between the ages of 8 and 12, children physically deteriorate rapidly and usually are unable to walk by the age of 12. Many children with Duchenne muscular dystrophy develop some degree of mental retardation, ranging from mild to moderate, due to the course of the disease. By middle to late adolescence, muscle tissue is almost completely replaced by fat or fibrous tissue. Children usually die before the age of 20, due to respiratory and heart failure. However, some individuals live into their 20s and are able to go to college or seek other occupations.

Those children with muscular dystrophy who are able to walk after the age of 15 are categorized with Becker muscular dystrophy (Lynn et al., 1994). Such individuals tend to have a much slower disease progression and may live to be 40 or 50 years of age.

Etiology

Duchenne muscular dystrophy and Becker muscular dystrophy are both X-linked recessive inheritance patterns. Males who receive the affected genes (p21 region of X chromosome) are severely affected, while females who carry the gene are either normal or only mildly affected (Shapiro & Specht, 1993). Though females who carry the genetic mutation pass it on to 50% of their offspring, the gene responsible for Duchenne muscular dystrophy is randomly inactivated in half of the males who receive it. Approximately one third of all cases of Duchenne muscular dystrophy are the result of a new mutation of the Xp21 gene and not the result of family history (Emery, 1998). For these reasons, genetic counselling for Duchenne-type dystrophy is very difficult.

Treatment

There is presently no available treatment that will slow the progress of muscle wasting in children with Duchenne muscular dystrophy. However, treatments are available to assist families and children to cope with the disease. Sometimes, surgery for scoliosis is done to improve children's comfort and appearance, though this is not believed to return muscle strength nor prolong walking. Sometimes the aggressive use of tendon-transfer operations and bracing can prolong children's ability to walk for one to three years (Shapiro & Specht, 1993). While seemingly a modest goal, this accomplishment can be very meaningful to children and their families.

Treatment priorities for families are related to maintenance of function and comfort of the children and emotional support for the families:

1. Provision of a well-balanced diet with adequate fiber to avoid constipation
2. Discouragement of long periods of bedrest which can accelerate weakening of the muscles
3. Encouragement of everyday activities within child's limits (e.g., supervised swimming)
4. Passive exercises by parents or caretakers to prevent contractures demonstrated by a physical therapist
5. Immediate treatment of respiratory infection including antibiotics and postural drainage
6. Use of lightweight splits or orthoses can prolong walking
7. Implementation of an intervention program that addresses all areas of development, including language and social and cognitive domains

Several types of experimental research are investigating complex treatments for children with muscular dystrophy (Emery, 1998). Gene therapy involves implanting normal muscle cells into the muscles of boys with Duchenne muscular dystrophy. So far, there is insufficient evidence to determine if such attempts will assist in the recovery of muscle function. Drug therapy, such as the use of steroids, is experimental in nature, is often accompanied by undesirable side effects and has yet to yield long term benefits for the disease.

Severe symptoms of muscular dystrophy and related **myopathies** may begin in early childhood. For early educators, the goals of intervention are very different than for children with cognitive disabilities. Yet, Emery (1998) reported that up to one third of boys with Duchenne type dystrophy have had some degree of cognitive disability. Therefore, an intervention plan should be global. Management of muscular function and alignment requires the ongoing participation of a physical therapist. Early interventionists should seek family input in determining educational priorities. Family support and interagency coordination will assist families to make short- and long-term decisions regarding the education and care of their child.

Case
Study

THE DIAGNOSIS: INTERVIEW WITH
TOM AND ANN SIMPSON

Tommy Simpson was born with Down's Syndrome. I was only 34 when he was born and since we did not anticipate any problems, I hadn't had any extra tests or anything like that. When I was seven months pregnant, the doctor thought the baby might be breech so he suggested I have an ultrasound to determine his position. The medical technician took a long time doing the ultrasound; he checked and rechecked his figures two or three times, then told us the doctor would need to talk to us. Later, we were told the doctors suspected the baby was a dwarf.

By the time the baby was born, we knew there might be something wrong, but I had decided it really didn't matter. I was just worried about having the baby and making sure we loved him. The rest didn't seem to matter so much, and I remember my labor coach thought that was wrong. She said, "If there are any problems you should have the information, know about it. You should be investigating." I just felt that I wanted to wait until the baby was born and then deal with it.

No heart problems had been found, so we expected no problems with the birth itself. My mom came out a week and a half before the baby was born so she and I ran all over town and had a lot of fun. I taught class the evening he was born, came home, and by about eleven o'clock, I knew the baby was coming. We went to the hospital and my labor was pretty easy. I don't think the nurses expected anything unusual; I don't think there was anything on my chart.

The birth came quickly. Smack! and not even the resident was there. I was just so happy and the nurses were really proud they had delivered him. He had come easily, but he was very blue and almost inert. The nurses worked on him and even when he was picked up, he was still very inactive. I remember by the time the doctor and my labor coach rushed in, it was all over. The doctor looked at the baby, and checked me over, but he didn't say anything. Still, I think he suspected. He said he was going to call the genetics counseling expert.

The baby came, but he wouldn't nurse and he opened one eye just a little bit. The nurses had to put him under special lights because he had jaundice. The genetics counselor and his assistant wanted to talk to my husband and me together. Now, I knew there was something wrong. When I called Tom he literally ran out of the house and left the door wide open, even in the cold. I held the baby and tried to get him to nurse, as they were talking to us. I was sharing the room with another woman, my labor coach was there, and the nurses were there. It was a difficult moment and I didn't have any privacy.

The doctor said they thought the baby had Down syndrome, and we'd heard of it, but we really didn't know what it meant. I remember we all started bawling, even with my roommate on the other side of the room, and it seemed so weird. I would have done things differently, but at the time when it's happening to you, you just take what's coming no matter how uncomfortable it is.

After the nurses knew, they switched us to a private room, but I wished they'd put a no visitors order in. I still had too many visitors and calls. We'd all waited for this baby for a long time, and not that many people expected anything to be wrong, so people kept calling and coming. I didn't deal with that very well. We all cried; everybody was so sad. The worst thing was the baby wasn't doing very well.

His breathing was high and shallow and he never nursed. The nurses had to keep sticking him for blood samples, because his skin was so thick, and he had a heart murmur so they thought he might have a heart problem. He went into the Intensive Care Unit that evening. I cried, and cried, and cried, and cried. It was ten o'clock at night and I didn't want to call my husband and mother because I knew they were both tired. I went down to see Tommy in the nursery about two in the morning, but it was so hard having him taken away.

People would visit me and I would try to be sociable and that was difficult too. Most people were understanding when I told them the baby had Down syndrome but I didn't really talk too much about it. You know it's funny, because now it's not upsetting to me, but those first few months I was terribly upset. I could cope, but I was really upset about it, and had a hard time talking about it. Now it seems like he's a neat little kid and we love him for just who he is, but it was so hard at first.

After Tommy was born with Down syndrome, and we went home from the hospital, my mom acted as my gatekeeper. She was great. She hardly let anyone talk to me by phone, and I really appreciated that because I didn't feel like talking to too many people.

One of my sisters called and said, "Well it's not like it's a tragedy or anything."

But I thought, "Oh, honey, it is; this is."

She reminded me she'd volunteered for Special Olympics, and she had a friend with a child who had Down syndrome and I said, "Did you know them when the baby was born?"

No, she'd met them when the child was five years old. I said, "Ask them what it was like when their child was born."

But my sister went on, "Oh, it's no big deal, it's not a tragedy, it's great."

I told her, "You need to understand that you've invalidated all of my feelings. Ask your friend."

Later she talked to her friend who confided that she had felt much of the same thing. I learned you do work through it, but you also have to recognize that sadness and disappointment are valid. It is a tragedy. Tommy is not going to go to college, he's not going to do a lot of things. He is a neat kid. But he's not going to do those things that you don't realize you expect for your child in your life.

Tommy Simpson
and his dad.

Table 6–1 Metabolic disturbances.

Disability	Characteristics	Cause	Treatment
Hypoglycemia	Decreased glucose for cells: If untreated can cause cerebral palsy, mental retardation, failure to thrive. Symptoms of glucose depletion: sweating, poor color, decreased attention, jitteriness, sleepiness/lethargy, seizures.	Metabolic error, other disease processes, genetic defect, stress, nutritional deficiency, infection.	High protein diet, education of all caregivers including educators on symptoms and treatment of hypoglycemia.
Galactosemia	Inability to metabolize galactose found in milk produced by mammals. If ingested, galatose builds up and becomes toxic. Toxic levels cause MR, failure to thrive, liver disease, cataracts, and if untreated—death.	Genetic disorder.	Lifelong elimination of galactose completely from diet. Casein hydrolysate and soybean formulas are used as milk substitute. Must educate child and other adults on safe foods. If not treated early, child will need comprehensive early intervention (cognitive, nutritional, visual etc.).
Hypothyroidism	Inadequate production of thyroid hormone. Causes deficiencies in skeletal formations, height, lethargy, abnormal facial features (broad flat nose, wide set eyes, coarse features), developmental retardation, motor, language, visual delays.	Unknown; possibly genetic.	Thyroid replacement therapy; with treatment, children score within normal limits. Early intervention for children not treated early. PT/OT, nutritionist, visual specialist. Speech/Language.
Thalassemia	Insufficient production of amino acid compounds decreases the production of hemoglobin. Mild to severe anemia is the result. Failure to thrive, poor appetite, can lead to mild-moderate developmental delay, cardiac conditions.	Genetic; can occur in conjunction with sickle cell disease.	Diet control to reduce the amount of iron; health maintenance in nutrition and feeding; in severe cases, routine blood transfusions.

PHENYLKETONURIA

Phenylketonuria (PKU) is an inherited autosomal recessive inborn error of metabolism. Though many other metabolic disorders exist, PKU serves to illustrate issues surrounding metabolic errors (see Table 6–1). This error results in the inability of individuals to use the essential amino acid phenylalanine. Buildup of phenylalanine results in mental retardation from defective **myelinization** in the brain and degeneration of both gray and white matter (Hayes, Rarback, Berry, & Clancy, 1987).

Many infants born with phenylketonuria are blond with blue eyes and have a fair complexion. Symptoms of untreated cases are vomiting, failure to thrive, short stature, a distinct odor to urine and sweat, seizures, and a rapid progression of mental retardation (Hayes et al., 1987). This disorder may occur as frequently as 1 in every 15,000 live births in the United States (Nyhan, 1990).

Though previous family history is a marker for diagnosis, this defect cannot be detected by prenatal amniocentesis. Therefore PKU cannot be diagnosed prior to the delivery of an infant. All newborns between 48 and 72 hours of age are initially screened for phenylalanine levels through a simple blood test obtained by sticking the infant's heel. All specimens are sent to a state sponsored laboratory in order to increase the standardization of results. Results are available within two to three weeks of birth.

PKU was the first inherited disease that could be successfully treated with diet. The goal of diet therapy is to restrict the oral intake of phenylalanine, thereby preventing excess buildup in the blood that will cause mental retardation, while still providing an adequate diet for normal growth and development (Hayes et al., 1987). Any solid foods that are high in protein (cow's milk, meats, dairy products, etc.) are excluded from the diet of children with PKU (Hayes et al., 1987). Most states within the United States offer assistance to families affected with PKU by providing the dietary supplements essential for normal growth and development. The most commonly used products for infants and children are Lofenalac, a low phenylalanine formula that is used with infants, and Phenyl-Free, a food source that is used with older children.

Current screening programs and available treatment have significantly decreased the incidence of retardation caused by PKU. However, failure to detect the disorder in a newborn (an example may be when there is a home delivery) will result in retardation. Initially, the only symptom may be irritability. This may rapidly evolve to severe vomiting with the sudden onset of seizures. Once neurological symptoms appear, normal recovery without retardation is rare. Affected children also have a decreased life span (Nyhan, 1990).

Families with children affected by PKU require counseling and education as well as positive, ongoing reinforcement of dietary goals to be successful with control of the disease. Success of children and families is dependent on understanding the diet and the reasons for restrictions, making sure that the diet is age-appropriate through the developmental years and decreasing exposure to infections for an affected child (Hayes et al., 1987). As children get older, it may become increasingly difficult to adequately monitor the diet. Therefore, the entire family must have a commitment to success. Some research has suggested that for PKU (unlike galactosemia) dietary restrictions can be lifted later in life.

SICKLE CELL DISEASE

Sickle Cell

Sickle cell disease causes its victims to experience chronic and often painful episodes for which there is currently no cure and only limited treatment. Though sickle cell disease does affect individuals of other ethnicity to a much smaller degree, this genetic disorder affects 1 in every 400 African American infants (Gil, Abrams, Phillips, & Williams, 1992). Furthermore, because most

Figure 6–8
The sickle
cell process.

Sickle Cell Process

Typical round-shaped red blood cells. Blood flows easily to all levels of the circulatory system

Abnormal sickle-shaped red blood cell. Blood clogs easily and results in pain.

of the largest cities in the United States have a high ratio of African American residents, the incidence of sickle cell disease is likely to be higher in urban than in rural areas (Brown, Armstrong, & Eckman, 1993).

Characteristics

The name of the disorder is derived from its principal characteristic. Abnormal sickle-shaped red blood cells proliferate and eventually clog the blood supply system (see Figure 6–8) causing unpredictable acute and chronic tissue death in all major organs of the body (necrosis) (Thompson, Gil, Abrams, & Phillips, 1992). The most prominent feature of sickle cell disease is chronic pain. Approximately 20% of individuals with sickle cell disease have frequent and severe painful episodes referred to as **sickle cell crisis** (Shapiro, 1989). This pain is most likely to occur in one's abdomen, back, extremities, and chest. Several other complications can accompany sickle cell disease: infections, meningitis, spleen dysfunction, enuresis, delayed physical growth, and bone inflammation and decay (Hurtig & Viera, 1986). Blood vessel blockages in the brain eventually result in seizure activity and stroke even during childhood (Adams, McKie, & Hsu, 1998).

Because research is so limited, few conclusions are made regarding cognitive and behavioral associates of sickle cell disease (Brown et al., 1993). Four physiological aspects of sickle cell disease have been documented, which Brown and colleagues believe can eventually compromise an individual's cognitive functioning:

1. Numerous tiny strokes in the central nervous system, specifically the brain
2. Anemia
3. Malnutrition
4. Compromised blood supply to the brain

In spite of these potentially harmful conditions, research to date indicates that children with sickle cell disease appear to suffer no loss of intelligence and no reliably measured deficit in academic performance as compared to peers without sickle cell disease (Brown et al., 1993). Furthermore, it seems that, psychologically, children with sickle cell disease may be no more likely to experience coping problems than children who are healthy (Armstrong, Lemanek, Pegelow, Gonzalez, & Martinez, 1993). On the other hand, extensive testing of preschoolers with sickle cell disease revealed significant deficiencies in both motor and cognitive readiness skills on the *Pediatric Examination of Educational Readiness* (Chua-Lim, Moore, McCleary, Shah, & Mankad, 1993). In this same study, measurements using the *McCarthy Scales of Children's Abilities* confirmed that intellectual abilities were within normal range. Brown et al. (1993) noted that such research is complicated by variables that, in themselves, could account for academic and social problems, namely, poverty or social class, absenteeism caused by frequent hospitalizations, family structure, and absence of support networks. All these characteristics are associated with cognitive and social difficulties; they also happen to be disproportionately characteristic of minority populations.

Etiology

Sickle cell disease is genetically transferred to the child. The disease is caused by a mutation of genes on the 11th chromosome (Nagel, 1993). According to Pollack (1993), 8% of the African American population carries the sickle cell gene. Three types of sickle cell disease exist (Brown et al., 1993; Pollack, 1993). Sickle cell anemia, the most severe, is homozygous (both 11th chromosomes affected) and is caused by two abnormal genes on the 11th chromosome. Two other heterozygous (only one 11th chromosome contains sickle cell anomaly) genotypes (HbSC and HBS-thalassemia) also result in some form of sickle cell disease. Nagel (1993) explained that the latter result from a multigene interaction, with different gene combinations producing a gradient in severity of the disease across affected individuals. Therefore, the course of the disease is unpredictable, ranging from mild to severe symptoms (Chua-Lim et al., 1993).

Treatment

The highest mortality rates from sickle cell disease are in the first five years of life because of suceptibility to infections, and again near adulthood because of multiple system failure (Serjeant, 1985). Newborn screening and aggressive medical care have increased the life expectancy and quality of life of patients with sickle cell disease. However, very little is known about sickle cell disease, in spite of the fact that it is two times more prevalent than cystic fibrosis and nine times more common than phenylketonuria (PKU) (Brown et al., 1993). Brown and colleagues noted that research on sickle cell disease lags far behind that of other congenital illnesses, implying that there is a link between the oversight of researchers and the ethnicity of its victims (see Table 6–2).

Diet is a concern in children with sickle cell disease who tend to expend energy more quickly and to possess less body fat than other children (Koop-Hoolihan, Van Loan, Mentzer, & Heyman, 1999). An overexpenditure of energy compared to nutrient intake is thought to be responsible for growth retardation. Consequently, chil-

Table 6–2   Comparative table of screening paradigm for Tay Sachs disease and sickle cell disease.

	Tay Sachs Disease	Sickle Cell Disease
Ethnicity	Ashkenazi Jews	African American
Screening	Voluntary	Compulsory in several states
Effectiveness	65% reduction in births from 1970–1980	No Effect; Abandoned in 1980
Education	In all cases, thorough education emphasizing lack of blame to carriers	No accompanying education
Screening organization	Community-based plan to conduct screening	National screening funded by federal government; state controlled

dren are often encouraged to take vitamin supplements, though with limited success. Therefore, support and planning from a nutritionist should be a part of intervention plan for children with sickle cell disease.

Pain coping methods, as with other types of chronic pain, often involve positive thinking/self-statements (Thompson et al., 1992). However, for preschoolers, the degree to which such an intervention might work is limited by their cognitive development. Those who have knowledge of the course of their illness and some sense of control over treatment are more likely to fair better than those who are more fatalistic (Werthorn & McCabe, 1988). This is an example for which empowerment is both necessary and ethical.

Parents of children with sickle cell disease may cope with medical and disciplinary problems differently than parents of healthy children. Armstrong et al. (1993) found that in families in which there was significant lifestyle disruption, parents tended to cope by focusing on their child's medical rather than emotional needs. However, parents of children with sickle cell disease also tended to be more aware of effective and less punitive disciplinary practices than parents of healthy children. These parents endorse the use of praise and mild punishment, perhaps because of their reluctance to inflict any more pain than necessary on children who already suffer from random and unavoidable pain caused by the disease itself.

TURNER SYNDROME

Turner Syndrome

Henry Turner first described Turner syndrome in 1938 (Williams, Richman, & Yarbrough, 1992). Found only in women, this disorder results when one of the two X chromosomes is absent (50–55%), partially absent (12–20%), mosaic where only a portion of the cells have a missing X chromosome (30%), or in rare instances, translocated. In most cases, there is a single X chromosome, and the characteristics of Turner syndrome are more severe than in partial or mosaic cases. The incidence of Turner syndrome is relatively rare, occurring in 1 to 4 cases per 10,000 live births (Hall & Gilchrist, 1990).

Characteristics

Girls and women with Turner syndrome are short in stature and fail to develop ovaries. One of the diagnostic characteristics of Turner syndrome is immature development of reproductive organs, with most women being infertile. Additionally, webbing of fingers, toes, and/or neck is not uncommon. Some individuals with

Turner syndrome have kidney (Williams et al., 1992) or heart abnormalities (Downey et al., 1991).

The reported average IQ ranges from 90 to 95 (range 50–140), which is well within the normal intellectual range, though slightly lower than average (Rovet, 1990, 1993). Moreover, a distinctive pattern of cognitive functioning has been observed in girls with Turner syndrome (Downey et al., 1991; Rovet, 1993; Williams et al., 1992). Visual memory, visual-constructional reading and arithmetic abilities tend to be significantly lower than that of typical children. In school, children with Turner syndrome tend to have lower academic achievement than their peers (though not significantly lower than siblings), and as adults, they generally attain significantly lower occupational status.

Individuals with Turner syndrome tend to have delayed social maturity, possibly stemming from peer interactions that are disrupted by the odd appearance and unusually short stature of these girls. Furthermore, girls with Turner syndrome tend to lack subtle social awareness skills, such as being able to "read" facial affect (Mazzocco et al., 1998). In spite of these findings, Rovet (1993) noted that adolescent girls with Turner syndrome tended to view themselves as intelligent, well behaved, and having normal appearance. Nevertheless, girls with Turner syndrome do seem to have a higher incidence of significant behavior problems than their peers as well as hyperactivity, depression, and loneliness (Mazzocco et al., 1998).

Etiology

Turner syndrome is not considered to be familial. Therefore, after one child is born with Turner syndrome, subsequent pregnancies do not carry an increased risk of the disorder (Hall & Gilchrist, 1990). Unlike Down syndrome, absence of the X chromosome is not thought to be associated with maternal age. This may be because the absent X chromosome is paternally (father) initiated approximately two thirds of the time (Mathur et al., 1991) and has been associated with advanced paternal age (Hall & Gilchrist, 1990).

Interestingly, most fetuses (98–99%) with a missing sex chromosome spontaneously abort, as compared to a spontaneous abortion ratio of 15% of all conceptions (Hall & Gilchrist, 1990). Hence, Turner syndrome has been estimated to represent as many as 1% of all conceptions. This disability can often be identified prenatally by ultrasound and confirmed through either amniocentesis or chorionic villus sampling.

Temple and Carney (1993) hypothesized that the absence or reduction of sex hormones, normally stimulated by both X chromosomes, adversely affects brain development during fetal growth. The impact of hormone deficiency is thought to be quite specific, resulting in the unique cognitive profile described above. That is, Turner syndrome is thought to be the result of absence of a "Turner" gene(s) rather than the absence of the X chromosome per se (Zinn, Page, & Fisher, 1993). In cases where two normally functioning chromosomes are present, these genes "turn on" growth production hormones necessary for healthy fetal development.

Treatment

Early intervention and family support may contravene some of the expected social and cognitive problems associated with Turner syndrome. Preschool intervention might focus on readiness for mathematics and reading skills and opportunities to model and reinforce appropriate social skills. However, because of the type of intellectual deficits described above, it is very likely that cognitive problems will not surface until children begin academic tasks in school.

When girls with Turner syndrome reach puberty, hormonal replacement is usually recommended. The replacement therapy may continue into adulthood. In rare cases, spontaneous menstruation begins, and these girls are more likely to be fertile than others.

SYNDROMES WITH UNKNOWN CAUSES

Though the syndromes described above have a known etiology, there are a host of other disabling conditions whose origin continues to baffle researchers. In fact, a large majority of children have no known cause for their mental retardation. Environmental deprivations, such as nutrition, affection, and stimulation, may be the primary cause of most cases of mild to moderate mental retardation. On the other hand, it is likely that those syndromes that are distinctly articulated (e.g., autism) from others have some type of genetic or multifactorial origin. For example, genetic research has recently led to the identification of very common disabilities such as fragile X syndrome as well as more rare anomalies such as Prader-Willi syndrome (see Table 6–3).

AUTISM

Although autism is relatively rare (5–60/10,000 depending on the definition used in identification), it is a highly visible disability. In fact, the characteristics of autism are neither discrete nor unchallenged (Wing, 1997). Some children who are identified with autism in infancy or early childhood are later identified with other disabilities. Other children who have not been labeled autistic possess behaviors termed "autistic-like." According to the American Psychiatric Association (DSM IV, 1997), autism is classified as a pervasive developmental disorder (PDD). Historically, however, such terms as childhood schizophrenia, childhood psychosis, atypical personality disorder, and symbiotic psychosis were used to identify persons who are now labeled autistic.

Though autism has been categorized by others in various ways, Wing (1997) described this disability as a spectrum of disorders which have a triad of common characteristics: social interaction, communication, and behavior. In an attempt to avoid the pitfalls of labeling children across the spectrum when current criteria and identification practices appear to be arbitrary, difficult to apply, and will change as children age and in move to different environments, Wing provided a subgrouping based on the aspect of social impairment alone.

1. *Aloof group:* Children appear indifferent to others though they may tolerate physical affection from others. The more severely disabled children in this subgroup tend to have little or no speech and few functional skills apart from ambulation and often engage in repetitive body movements including self-injury. More mildly aloof children with autism tend to have mild learning disabilities, and though they typically have language, it is generally delayed in onset with abnormalities such as echolalia common. Behaviorally, these children often

Table 6–3 Low incidence inborn variations in development.

Disability	Characteristics	Cause	Treatment
Cornelia de Lange Syndrome	Facial anomalies (long eyelashes, thin lips, confluent eyebrows, upturned nose, small face) microcephaly, mental retardation, hearing loss, severe language delays (superior language in rare cases) stereotypy sometimes evolving into self-mutilation	Unknown	Family support; Speech/Language focus, behavioral intervention for stereotypy (self-mutilation usually does not occur until after early childhood), comprehensive early intervention
Prader-Willi Syndrome	Stage I: Neonatal-hypotonia, weak/absent cry, large head, feeding problems, failure to thrive Stage II: Childhood-overeating is dominant trait, pear-shaped body, short stature, almond-shaped eyes Stage III: Adolescent-significant behavior problems, mild/moderate MR, good self-help, weak social skills	Missing portion of long arm of 15th chromosome (15q11–13). Paternal in origin. Father is carrier.	Family respite care/support groups, early management of insatiable appetite (nutritionist, environmental controls, behavioral self-management), social skills training, exercise programs in early childhood (swim, dance, soccer etc.)
Rett Syndrome	Normal development (infancy) Stage I: Onset of developmental deterioration (6–18 months). Very intrusive stereotypy begins (i.e., hand wringing) Stage II: Rapid deterioration for a few weeks to months Stage III: Relative stability with some developmental growth for up to 10 years Stage IV: Regression—sometimes to primitive language and motor state	Unknown; possibly metabolic	Medication for seizures; PT/OT, nutritional monitoring for failure to thrive, music therapy to increase movement and social relatedness, family support and collaboration
Williams Syndrome	Failure to thrive, cardiac problems, elfin-like appearance (small chin, large ears, blue iris, wide mouth, wide set eyes, broad forehead); mild-moderate MR, remarkable verbal proficiency, deficit in nonverbal ability; hypersocial, friendly, talkative, affectionate; later behavior problems; impulsive, hyperactive, self-destructive	Deletion of genes on chromosome 7	Nutritionist, focus on strengthening talents in language and social affability; PT/OT, later behavioral self-control instruction to manage activity level; parent counseling to avoid guilt when behavior problems arise—reassure parents that this behavior is a predictable sequelae to the syndrome

experience sleep disturbances, limited food tolerance, and motor stereotypies such as hand-flapping and rocking. For these children, daily activities must be highly routinized or they become agitated and act out.

2. *Passive group:* Children in this subgroup do not initiate interactions but do not reject approaches by others. The diagnosis may be missed entirely in the primary years, though eventually they are identified because of learning and social interaction problems.

3. *Active but odd:* While children in this subgroup often have fluent speech with good grammar, their communication is typically repetitive and lacks reciprocity. The play and interests of these children is similarly narrow, perseverating on topics such as train timetables, mathematical calculations, or dinosaurs. These children also exhibit difficult behavior such as frequent and severe temper tantrums, aggression, and egocentricity.

4. *Loners:* This high functioning subgroup of children tend to have fluent speech, but prefer to be alone, lack empathy, and are socially egocentric. Many individuals in this group achieve successful careers as adults and can learn to apply the rules of social interaction by direct instruction.

About two thirds of children with autism are identified in infancy when caregivers note such behaviors as disinterest in toys, indifference to caregivers or physical contact, aberrant sleep patterns, excessive crying, irritability and stiffness, and an avoidance of eye contact (Mauk, 1993). Development may appear normal in the other third of children with autism until 12 to 18 months of age, at which point language and social skills may regress or fail to progress (Wing, 1997). Like many other disabilities, boys are three to four times more likely to be affected with autism than girls. Early childhood, from ages 2–5 tends to be a period of intense behavioral disturbance, with relative improvement between ages 6–10, and the sometimes reappearance of behavioral problems in adolescence and early adulthood (Wing, 1997).

Finally, most persons with autism have some degree of mental retardation. Andolsek (1998) reported that 75% of children with autism have mental retardation, while 40% of individuals with autism have IQs below 50. Though the range is very broad, the combination of mental retardation and other behavioral and language disabilities often results in profound developmental needs. According to Eaves (1992), autistic development is not consistent with developmental patterns in other forms of mental retardation, but can be "described as strange, distorted, even bizarre" (p. 70). **Savant** behavior, in which an individual shows extreme aptitude in one area (e.g., music or mathematics) along with autism, is very rare.

Case Study

JOSH'S DIAGNOSIS: INTERVIEW WITH AMY FINKEL

Getting the diagnosis of autism was really difficult. We started recognizing that there was a problem when Josh was about 18 months old, because there was no speech, no words, nothing. We'd go to the physicians and they'd tell us, "Don't worry, he has two older siblings who do the talking for him. Don't worry, he'll talk. It's really common when kids have an older brother or sister to have a speech delay." So we'd go home thinking, okay, nothing's wrong, everything's fine. Then, as Josh got to be two, we went again to the doctor's. "Are you sure nothing is wrong? He's still not talking. He's mute. What's going on here?"

"Well," they said, "He's had a lot of ear infections, maybe he has a hearing impairment or maybe there's a lot of fluid built up in his ears." So the first thing we did was to go to the ear, nose, and throat doctor. We had a special hearing test done. Because Josh was totally nonverbal, we couldn't rely on the standard hearing test with the head phones. They actually gave him some anesthetic, knocked him out, attached electrodes to his brain, and then introduced a sound into the ear canal and his brainwaves were monitored to show whether or not he was hearing properly. The results of that test came back normal. So we thought, okay, Josh has an older brother and an older sister, his hearing is fine, we won't worry about it.

But, at about two-and-a-half, there was still no speech and there were some odd behaviors that were emerging. Josh was very much a loner. He didn't like to play with the other kids, he quit responding to his name. He would over-selectively attend to toys, but he wouldn't play with them appropriately. He would line up his toys, in a certain way. He'd line them up perfectly so that one end of a toy had to be touching each wall. If you walked through the room and accidentally kicked a toy out of the way with your foot, Josh would come unglued and obsess on starting all the way from the beginning and putting everything back in that special order. That was really a big problem.

Josh was also enthralled with certain things in the environment, like dirt. Inside, he'd play in the dirt around all my house plants and I couldn't get him away from it. Outside, he'd sit in the pea gravel and swim in it, and we'd couldn't get him out of it. He wouldn't swing on the swing or go down the slide. He wouldn't interact at all with other children, including his brother.

Josh Finkel

There was no communication, not even pointing. Josh wouldn't take me by the arm and pull me over to show me something like other kids would do. For me, it was scary. If he was crying, I had no idea what was wrong. I didn't know if he had a really bad stomach ache, or had hurt himself, so I was constantly inspecting his body, looking for some sign of something being wrong. I became paranoid and I would take him into the doctor all of the time until it got to the point that the doctor would think, "Oh no! There's that Mrs. Finkel again, thinking there's something wrong with her son!"

So we went back to the doctor, begging, "Look there *is* something wrong with our son. There's something wrong!" They said, "Don't worry, he's got an older sister and an older brother. Einstein didn't start talking until he was five. He's had lots of ear infections. Don't worry, it's just a speech delay. Go home and leave us alone!"

Then finally, when Josh was almost three, I could no longer be in denial. There were just too many bizarre things going on in addition to no speech. Basically, we went to the doctor again and threw a temper tantrum right there in the doctor's office. We refused to leave until they told us what was wrong with our son or referred us on until someone could tell us what was wrong. Otherwise Josh probably would have been four years old before we knew what was wrong. We got the actual diagnosis just before his third birthday. It took us well over a year and a half to get that diagnosis, and we only got it as the result of throwing a tantrum in the office and refusing to leave.

The doctor had very little bedside manner when he told us Josh's diagnosis, and I think in retrospect, I'm glad he was as brutally honest as he was, because it got me busy. He said, "Your son is autistic and probably retarded. He'll never go to college. You'll have to take care of him the rest of your life. He'll never get married, he'll never have his own children. He'll probably never have a job."

At the time I thought the doctor was cruel and heartless and maybe he could have said things a little more gently. He stripped us of all the hopes and dreams that we had, that any parent has for his child. The next day, what was most devastating with the diagnosis of autism, was that nobody could tell us what to do about it.

We asked our physician. We asked different people in our community, "What is autism? What can we do?" No one had a definite answer for us; no protocol. So we were left devastated by the diagnosis and then very much alone in the community in terms of where do we go for resources? Where do we find out what the treatment is? What do we do for our son? It was devastating.

Etiology

There is no known cause of autism, though historically parents, mothers in particular, were blamed for their child's autistic behaviors. It was believed that women who failed to show love and nurturance psychologically impaired their child to such a degree as to cause autism. Thankfully, today, few women are accused of this misguided and harmful assumption.

Autism is often associated with chromosomal anomalies, such as Cri du chat, fragile X syndrome, Williams syndrome, Down syndrome, XXY, congenital rubella, and PKU (Wing, 1997). In fact, there is evidence that genetic factors contribute to many cases of autism. For example, the risk of reoccurrence in families with autism is 200 times higher than in the general population (Piven, Palmer, Jacobi, & Childress, 1997). Some researchers found that relatives of children with autism often exhibit characteristics that are milder and nonpathological, but qualitatively consistent with those of children with autism (i.e., lack of emotional responsiveness, oversensitivity, special interest patterns, and oddities in social communication). Other researchers have failed to replicate such findings (Piven et al., 1997). Providing further evidence to the gene theory, Holden (1997) reported the preliminary identification of a gene linked to autism; one that regulates seratonin (a chemical neurotransmitter) in the brain. Gene mapping found that children with autism are more likely to have a shortened form of the seratonin transporter gene. Evidence that this is the culprit gene has been supported by studies that show that certain antidepressant drugs such as Prozac which increase the availability of seratonin also suppress the symptoms of autism. However, even if this gene is associated with autism, it is likely to be one which acts in concert with others, since 16% of the general population also has the shortened gene version.

Nongenetic disorders also resemble autism, if only for a period of time; these include Rett syndrome, fetal alcohol syndrome, severe mental retardation, severe deafness and blindness, and deaf-blindness (Mauk, 1993). One theory is that excessive testosterone in the fetus causes brain anomalies and subsequent cognitive dysfunction consistent with autism (Tordjman, Ferrari, Sulmont, Duyme, & Roubertoux, 1997). Epilepsy has been associated with a large percentage of children with "setback" autism (Wing, 1997). Most theories, however, have either been discredited (as in maternal neglect) or remain unvalidated. Mauk (1993) concluded that current evidence leads to a hypothesis that autism is the expression of multiple etiologies. In other words, there may be no such thing as "autism," but many different brain disorders may be expressed similarly enough to fall under the autism umbrella (see Table 6–4).

Treatment

One of the first steps to treatment is the exclusion of other potential causes of autistic behavior. For example, Eaves (1992) noted that the self-abuse in autism may mimic the tongue, finger, and lip biting of those with Lesch-Nyhan syndrome or otitis media, which commonly leads to head banging. Given the present limitations in behavioral and medical technology, autism is a lifelong condition, usually requiring very substantial resources. Treatment is likely to be complex, and no single intervention strategy will work with all children. In fact, even for a single child a strategy that seems to be effective at one point may lose its potency over time or overnight.

Generally, intervention should be directed at development of present skills (e.g., converting speech fluency into reciprocal social interactions) while minimizing limiting behavior such as sterotypy and self-injury. Behavioral intervention, involving systematic training, has been most effective in teaching new sets of skills while reducing intrusive behavior. However, even those methods are rigorous, slow to show improvement, and difficult to maintain over long periods. With the intense behavioral characteristics and limitations of technology, autism is considered one of the most demanding of developmental disabilities for families (Brown, 1999). The availability of multidisciplinary personnel, including a communications specialist, early childhood

Table 6–4 Frequency of secondary disabilities associated with autism.

Deafness	20%
IQ above 100	5%
IQ between 70–100	20–30%
Severe MR	30–35%
Mild MR	30–35%
Seizure disorder	25%
Affect isolation	88%
Perceptual inconsistencies (visual/hearing/touch)	80%
Stereotypy/twiddling	82%
Self-injury	65%
Nonverbal	50%
Echolalia	75%

educator, social worker, counselor, respite care worker, and behavioral specialist, is desirable. Though one should not presume that a family will need emotional help, some may benefit from ongoing counselling and all will benefit from ongoing support. In addition, parents should be cautioned when investigating costly but questionable dietary, medical, or other unconventional methods that promise a "cure" for their children (Andolsek, 1998). Rhythmic entrainment (Orr, Myles, & Carlson, 1998) is such a method, where externally produced music is thought to re-entrain the body to its natural rhythmic patterns (50–65 beats per minute) of the heartbeat and aid in relaxation. While this method seemed to be effective in reducing self-injurious behavior in a small number of experimental subjects (e.g., Orr et al., 1998), further empirical evidence should be required of this and all intervention methods before being widely accepted by educators or recommended to parents.

Because one of the most common deficits of autism is social adaptation, many educators are aware of the research that the optimal educational environment is an integrated one with peers trained to act as social models. In such cases, educators need to provide specific instruction for peers on both social interaction skills and attitude (Clark and Smith, 1999). Parents are a necessary part of planning, since they can educate both teachers and peers on their child's social and communication repertoire and strategies. Specific target skills between model peers and children with autism are turn-taking, sharing, initiating and maintaining play, asking for help, using conversation skills and being appropriately affectionate (see Table 6–5). To facilitate these interactions, language boards and other augmentative communication systems such as sign language can be used to mediate conversations (Cafiero, 1998). When taught to use visual cues early, children with autism have the possibility of generalizing this skill to picture reading systems, self-management systems using visual reminders, and language boards in social interactions.

According to Dawson and Osterling (1997), there are six elements common to effective programs that educate children with autism.

1. Curriculum content that addresses children's ability to attend to critical environmental stimuli, imitate others, and to produce and understand language
2. Highly structured and supportive teaching environment that plans for skill generalization (i.e., uses natural daily routines)

Table 6–5 Communication deficits in autism.

Aspect of Speech	Communication Deficits
Speech phonology (speech sounds)	Impaired receptive and expression in children with the mixed receptive-expressive syndrome and, especially, with severe verbal word deafness in which phonological decoding may be so compromised as to preclude speech comprehension and verbal expression
Prosody (rhythm and melody to speech)	In children with speech: singsong or rising intonation, high-pitched voice or monotonous, "robotic"
Syntax (grammar and word order)	Impaired reception and expression in children with the mixed receptive-expressive syndrome and with less severe verbal auditory word deafness
Semantics (vocabulary and meaning of language)	Impaired expression and reception in all children with autism—e.g., impaired comprehension of questions, open-ended questions and nonliteral language such as irony, sarcasm and jokes; word-retrieval problems and unusual, pedantic word choices; echolalia; difficulty formulating coherent discourse; narrow range of topics
Pragmatics (communicative and conversational use of language)	Impaired receptive and expressive communication in all persons with autism—e.g., impaired interpretation of tone of voice, body posture and facial expression; gaze avoidance; failure to answer; speaking to no one in particular; failure to initiate, pursue or terminate conversations; difficulty with taking turns; poor maintenance of topic; perseveration and ceaseless questioning

Source: Taken from Andolsek, K. M. (1998). Characteristics and symptoms in patients with autism. *American Family Physician, 57,* 809–811. [Reprinted from Rapin, I. (1997). Autism. *New England Journal of Medicine, 337,* 97–104.]

3. Predictable and routine classroom environment
4. A functional approach to behavior problems teaching relevant skills
5. A planned transition from preschool to elementary school
6. Family involvement

In a study designed to test the validity of these elements, Schwartz and Sandall (1998) followed three children with autism from preschool through early elementary school. Each of the children displayed very different symptoms and functional levels, though all were initially noncompliant or combative. The preschool program used a blend of applied behavioral analysis and family focused developmental approach as well as instructional methods that were effective and systematic. Imbedding these procedures into natural integrated preschool classrooms, the classes focused on social, communication, and play skills. When followed several years later in elementary school, all children were thriving in inclusive classrooms with minimal to no special education support. It was concluded that the key to their sustained social and cognitive progress was in controlling noncompliant/violent behavior in the preschool years.

TOURETTE SYNDROME

Like autism, Tourette syndrome is a bewildering and sometimes devastating disability. Until 1972, the syndrome, also referred to as Gilles de la Tourette Syndrome after the French researcher who identified the disorder in 1885, was thought to be quite rare (50 known recorded cases). At that time, the Tourette Syndrome Association was initiated by a distraught father of a child with Tourette syndrome. Now, the syndrome is identified in as many as 1/200 children (Leckman et al., 1998). The most obvious characteristic of individuals with this disorder is the expression of tics. While 4% to 23% of all children experience tics (Torup, 1972), Tourette syndrome represents the most severe expression. The average age of tic onset is five, though they can appear between ages two and seven and are three times as likely to affect boys as girls. The period of most severe tic behavior is about age 10, with nearly half of children becoming tic-free by 18 years of age (Leckman et al., 1998). Manifest in the form of motor movement or vocalizations, tics have a sudden, unpredictable onset and are purposeless and irregular. Factors such as stress tend to increase the frequency, while sleep thwarts their appearance (Lerer, 1987).

Characteristics

As children age, the intensity and form of symptoms also change. Because Tourette syndrome is so misunderstood by educators, children often go undiagnosed for years or suffer the misdiagnosis of learning disability or Attention Deficit Disorder (ADD) (Rosen, 1996). The most common early symptoms involve eye movement, as in eye blinking (Murray, 1997). Eventually, children may have whole body involvement including jumping, kicking, spitting, smelling, squatting, and licking. Between the ages of 8 and 15, vocal tics may also appear and include barking, whistling, echolalia, grunting, coughing, snorting, and humming. Examples were provided by Santos and Massey (1990, p. 71) " 'shut up,' 'stop that,' 'oh, okay,' and 'I've got to.' " The frequency of tics can vary from a few times when children are tired or tense to 100 times per minute in those most severely affected (Murray, 1997).

One of the more disturbing tendencies of Tourette syndrome is a disinhibition of aggression, where children may be unable to avoid destructiveness such as crushing an egg or a lightbulb when placed in their hand (Rosen, 1996). Throughout one's lifetime, tic patterns may vary, and in the early stages of the disorder, remissions may occur in which children are symptom free (Bronheim, 1991; Lerer, 1987).

Until recently, researchers had not acknowledged an "aura" experienced by many individuals with Tourette syndrome that sends them a message to perform a tic or ritual behavior (Murray, 1997). Their inability to ignore or defy these messages causes individuals another form of anxiety. In instances where persons are able to temporarily avoid performing a tic, the self-control is exerted at great expense. That is, the urge, resisted at one point, must be eventually performed, usually in a more severe form.

In addition to tics, approximately 50% of all children with Tourette syndrome have learning disabilities (Burd, Kauffman, & Kerbeshian, 1992). Burd et al. found a mean IQ of 94 in a sample of 42 children with Tourette syndrome. These findings suggest that the intelligence profiles of individuals with Tourette syndrome spans the normal range. Difficulty in basic writing skills, including handwriting, may lead to placement of children in special education programs (Rosen, 1996).

Either as a direct or indirect consequence of the syndrome, attentional deficits and impulse control are also common in children with Tourette syndrome. Knell and Comings (1993) provided some evidence that Attention Deficit Hyperactivity Disorder and Tourette syndrome are genetically linked. Unfortunately, medical treatment for attentional difficulties may produce the onset or exacerbate the symptoms of Tourette syndrome.

Obsessive compulsive behavior is a third associated disorder in 55% to 74% of cases of Tourette syndrome (Walkup et al., 1988). The impulse to complete tasks to perfection or to complete certain rituals, such as "evening up," in which actions or materials must be symmetrical, is a unique form of obsessive behavior found in persons with Tourette syndrome (Walkup et al., 1988). Understandably, individuals may experience excessive fear of expressing their tics or compulsive behaviors in public (Walkup et al., 1988). In addition to the movement characteristics of Tourette syndrome, these children are particularly vulnerable to psychological distress, including frustration, low self-esteem, anger and hyperactivity (Rosen, 1996). Often ridiculed by their peers and misunderstood by teachers, children experience serious anxiety related to social encounters (Bronheim, 1991; Burd et al., 1992; Lerer, 1987; Levi, 1991).

Etiology

Approximately one third of all children with Tourette syndrome also have **coprolalia,** the involuntary use of vulgar or obscene gestures or language (Levi, 1991). Yet, with concentration, children may be able to suppress tics, though compromising their ability to attend to other tasks (Bronheim, 1991). Because of these characteristics, some claimed that the disorder is psychological and that the behaviors are purposeful rather than physical. However, it is now widely accepted that the actual cause is an autosomal dominant genetic disorder (Rosen, 1996). Kurlan (1992) hypothesized that the defective gene thought to cause Tourette syndrome results in developmental damage to the area of the brain responsible for primitive motor, vocal, and emotional processes (basal ganglia). He further hypothesized that male sex hormones adversely affect this abnormal brain development, while female sex hormones beneficially influence this development, explaining the differential incidence of Tourette syndrome across genders.

While the precise cause of this disorder is unknown, it is possible that a combination of factors contribute (Cohen, Detlor, Shaywitz, & Leckman, 1992). For example, Bower (1990) concluded that the basic cause of Tourette syndrome is a genetically caused deficiency of seratonin (chemical) in the brain (neurological), which controls emotions and initiates responses to external stimuli (environmental). According to this theory, individuals with Tourette syndrome inherit two defective genes (one from each parent). It was postulated that approximately 15% of the general population carries at least one of these genes, and that half of the carriers have addictive, compulsive, emotional, or learning problems.

Treatment

This disorder can cause heartache for parents as well as children with the disorder. To know that one's child will be ridiculed or mistreated is a lifelong frustration for parents. Children and parents can be comforted by knowing that tics are out of the control of an individual with Tourette syndrome. Informing teachers and parents of other children may also reduce the stigma of tics. Santos and Massey (1990) recommended consideration of the following factors in planning intervention for a child with Tourette syndrome:

1. Family's ability to cope and provide support
2. School responsiveness
3. Peer group response
4. Choice of vocation and acceptance in the work force
5. Need for intimacy and long-term relationships
6. Family planning
7. Access to legal or advocate services

Generally, stress, anxiety, tiredness, and excitement exacerbate the symptoms of Tourette syndrome. Helping families to manage their children's activities to moderate situations that might cause overexcitment, tiredness, and anxiety should be an intervention goal. On the other hand, relaxation tends to reduce the symptoms. Teaching families and children techniques for motor and emotional relaxation will provide children with a mechanism for preventing or minimizing symptoms.

In the most severe cases, medication is the treatment of choice, either for the tics or the associated attentional deficits. For example, Haloperidol, the drug of choice for over three decades, initially diminishes symptoms in 70% of individuals but concurrently introduces the risk of side effects, such as lethargy, weight gain, poor school performance, and depression, as well as a variety of neurological symptoms (Murray, 1997; Santos & Massey, 1990). The most serious side effect of Haloperidol is a neuromotor disorder called tardive dyskinesia. Recently, drug alternatives that may be both more effective and reduce side effects have been explored with some success (Sallee, Nesbitt, Jackson, Sine, & Sethuraman, 1997).

Though relief may be gained from medication, the symptoms rarely subside entirely (Bronheim, 1991). Because of the dangerous side effects, Santos and Massey (1990) recommended that medication only be used when the symptoms of Tourette syndrome are so serious that they compromise a child's development. As an alternative, behavioral self-management interventions have been effectively used to limit the onset of some of the associated disorders (obsessive-compulsive and attentional), though these treatments may be too sophisticated for preschool age children.

Case Study	**THE DIARY OF ESTHER ANNA BERKE: MONTH 11–12**
	Sept. 16—Oct. 15: Esther continues to be unstable, rarely showing the same patterns more than 2 days in a row. She only gained 100 g for the month, weighing 8.6 kg on Oct. 12 (only the 35th percentile for her age) and measuring 76 cm (the 85th percentile for her age). If she gets much longer she won't fit in the stroller (it is a twin stroller!). She started a new drug, prednisone, an anabolic steroid, on Oct. 14, it makes her cranky and arch her back/neck a lot, but it seems to reduce the frequency of her seizures (too early to tell for sure). At times her right

arm and leg become very stiff and she doesn't move them, almost like a person with a stroke, we're not sure why. Sarah's mother has agreed to come for 3 weeks to help when the new baby is born, she will arrive Oct. 28. Otherwise, Esther's diet continues, her latest blood test showed almost everything was "normal," which was good, except her white blood cell count was high (sign of an infection?). Her diet seems to be helping "normalize" her blood, especially her sodium/potassium levels. The dietitian wants to run an amino acid profile on her blood as well.

Oct. 16–Nov. 15:   Happy birthday, Esther Anna! She was one year old on Nov. 15. She measured 76 cm long and weighed 8.3 kg. Pictures of her birthday party will be available soon. We want to move to America, but have decided to wait until next year after Joel gets a little bigger. We need some stability in our lives right now. We want to gain better access to the latest information and experimental treatments for Aicardi Syndrome (there will be a big conference on Aicardi Syndrome in July 2000).

She is tapering off prednisone now, she is much happier, let me tell you! I think it helped her, she seems to have fewer seizures and to sleep longer at night. Sarah's mother came Oct. 28 for 3 1/2 weeks to help, that was a real blessing. We had some cupcakes with candles to celebrate her birthday. At one year old, she still doesn't respond to many stimuli, and she can't hold up her head or move her arms or legs in a coordinated manner.

Esther Anna (top) and her baby brother.

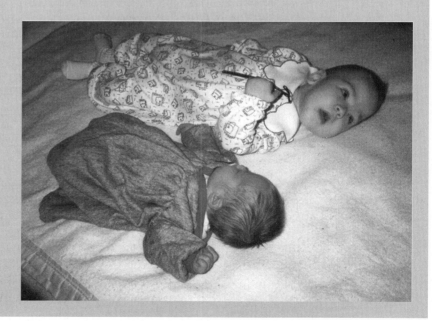

PHYSICAL ANOMALIES

CONGENITAL HEART DEFECTS

Congenital heart defects are a problem for a significant number of infants and young children. It is estimated that approximately one out of six infants are born with congenital heart disease, and approximately 3% of newborns have a major heart anomaly (Copel, 1999). Furthermore, many genetic disorders and other physical abnormalities are accompanied by heart defects (see Table 6–6). Most of these infants are ill enough within the neonatal period to require intervention. Consequently, it is estimated one third of all deaths due to congenital anomalies between five months gestation and one year after birth are the result of cardiovascular abnormalities (Copel, 1999).

Congenital defects are generally categorized into either cyanotic or noncyanotic abnormalities. Categorization is dependent on the heart's ability to direct blood flow to and from the lungs and then to the general circulation. Situations in which blood bypasses the lungs result in decreased oxygen available to cells and produce a blue-tinged color to the skin, known as **cyanosis.** Diagnosis followed by appropriate treatment is the key to decreasing the general adverse effects of congenital heart defects.

Understanding the differences between fetal circulatory patterns and those required of an infant after birth provides a means for understanding how an affected fetus can survive a significant defect through the period of gestation. Fetal circulation consists of parallel circuits. When fetal blood bypasses the lungs, either the right or left ventricle will pump blood directly to the general circulation (see Figure 6–9). The pressure in either ventricle during this period is similar. This parallel structure allows for fetal survival in spite of a variety of significant cardiac defects. Even if one of the ventricles is completely obstructed, the other ventricle can maintain sufficient blood flow with little effort.

Table 6–6 Metabolic and genetic conditions associated with congenital heart disease.

Disability	Heart Defect(s)	Cause
Down syndrome	Atrial-ventricular canal defects, ventricular septal defects, patent ductus arteriosis, atrial septal defect, tetralogy of Fallot	Extra 21st chromosome
Turner syndrome	Coarctation of aorta	45, X chromosome
Marfan's syndrome	aortic root dissection, mitral valve prolapse	mutation of gene on 15th chromosome
Williams's syndrome	supravalvular aortic/pulmonic stenosis, systemic hypertension, thickening of atrial wall and coronary arteries	deletion or translocation on chromosome 7
Cri-du-Chat syndrome	Ventricular/atrial septal defects, bicuspid aortic valve, tetralogy of Fallot, patent ductus arteriosis	mutation of 5th chromosome in 5p region

Source: Khan, A. (1999). Genetic and metabolic testing in congenital heart disease. http://www.rchc.rush.edu/genetic.htm

Figure 6–9
Fetal circulatory
patterns.

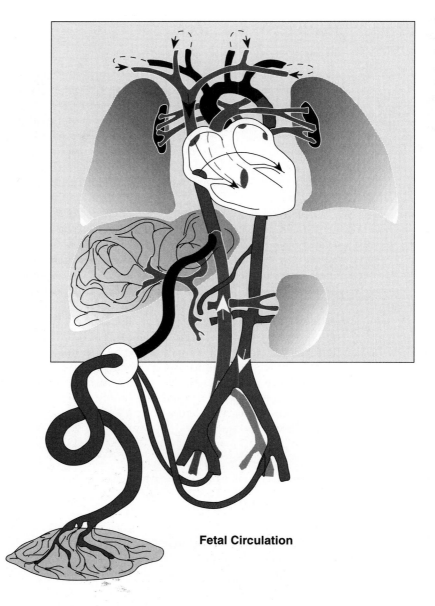

Fetal Circulation

  The birth process results in a remarkable change in the blood flow pattern of
the infant. With the infant's first breath, blood flows into the lungs and the blood
flow from the placenta ceases (see Figure 6–10). At the same time, an increase in
the independent breathing of newborns results in oxygenation of the blood from
the infant's own lungs, which, in turn, causes closure of the ductus venosus and
the narrowing of the ductus arteriosus. Finally, changes in intracardiac pressures
result in the functional closure of the foramen ovale. These changes dramatically
increase the work of the heart, especially the left ventricle. It is with this demand

Figure 6–10
Establishment of independent heart and lung function in infants changes the direction of blood flow.

Postnatal Circulation

that many congenital defects will produce symptoms that lead to recognition of an existing cardiac defect.

Most congenital cardiac defects produce symptoms that are diagnosed within the first week of life. Symptoms may include respiratory distress, a heart rate over 200 beats per minute, a heart murmur, difficulty with feeding, and failure to gain weight. Many of these may persist into childhood (depending on the defect) with the addition of exercise intolerance, poor physical growth, delayed development, recurrent infections, squatting, clubbing of the fingers and toes, and increased blood pressure. Many of these children also have chronic behavior problems, possibly related to repeated hospitalizations.

Certain cardiac defects are known to be associated with specific genetic malformations and maternal conditions. For example, there is an association between Down syndrome and *endocardial cushion defects*. Males have an increased risk for *coarctation of the aorta, aortic stenosis,* and *transposition of the great vessels;* whereas, females have an increased incidence of *atrial septal defects.* When a mother is diabetic, there is a high risk for significant multiple cardiac defects in the fetus. Congenital rubella is associated with narrowing of the pulmonary arteries and patent ductus arteriosus. Lesions associated with prematurity or low birth weight are also found with an increased incidence of both patent ductus arteriosus and ventricular septal defects.

Endocardial cushion defects occur when there is abnormal development of the septa between the atria and the ventricles, which includes a malformed, deficient, or abnormally attached **mitral valve.** This abnormality results in mixing of oxygenated and nonoxygenated blood between the right and left atria and the right and left ventricles with incompetent valves. This defect may appear as an isolated cardiac defect but more commonly is associated with other malformations and very frequently with Down syndrome.

Cleft Lip and Cleft Palate

Cleft lip and **cleft palate** (roof of mouth) are commonly occurring defects that may be present as often as 1 out of every 700 live births (Eliason, 1991). Cleft lip and/or palate may occur as an isolated defect (lip or palate), in conjunction with each other, or associated with other congenital abnormalities. It appears that approximately 20% of children with cleft lip/palate have additional congenital malformations such as skeletal malformations, mental retardation, cardiovascular problems, gastrointestinal malformations, or facial anomalies (Milerad, Larson, Hagberg, & Ideberg, 1997). A cleft is a division or split that occurs between two tissue planes. Many recognized congenital syndromes have this associated defect (e.g., trisomy 13, 15, or 21). The clefts that appear in either the lip or palate are separate defects but there may be a relationship due to the fact that the disruption in normal development occurs during a relative time period in gestational development, between the 5th and 13th week of gestation.

Formation of the lip and palate occurs in stages from about the fifth to twelfth weeks of gestation. It is during this time that the normal fusion process fails, with a cleft occurring. The specific cause for a lip/palate defect is not generally known but may be related to prenatal exposure to teratogens (i.e., maternal alcohol consumption), other anomalies, or possibly to genetic factors (since an increased incidence has been noted in families) (McInerny, 1985). Teratogens have also been connected to the incidence of clefts. For example, benzodiazepines, drugs prescribed to reduce anxiety, insomnia or epilepsy in women, are sometimes taken in the first trimester of pregnancy before realizing that they are pregnant (Dolovich et al., 1998).

The cause of isolated defects is different than those appearing with multiple congenital anomaly syndromes, of which more than 300 have been identified (Cohen & Bankier, 1991). Ethnic origins also appear to have some relationship to the occurrence of isolated defects. That is, Native Americans have the highest incidence, while African Americans have the lowest (Vanderas, 1987).

Cleft lips and palates are classified as unilateral (affecting one side) or bilateral (affecting both sides) and as either complete or incomplete. Approximately 25% of all reported cases involve an isolated cleft lip with another 25% involving an isolated cleft palate (Hardy, 1988). The occurrence of a cleft lip without a cleft palate decreases the potential difficulties that face affected infants.

Clefting of the lip involves a split that affects the lip and gum and may extend upward into the nose. In cases involving bilateral lip clefts, the defect may be extensive enough to join together at a point behind the gum. In these cases a section of the lip and gum appears to hang freely from the septum of the nose. The majority of infants with a bilateral cleft lip also have a cleft palate. The impact of such extensive abnormalities on appearance presents significant problems for families. In many cases the disfigurement is initially so overwhelming that parents experience difficulties in looking past the defect to the infant, and initiation of parent/child bonding is interrupted.

Facial disfigurement (with resulting parental rejection) and feeding difficulties are the two most significant problems that face an infant affected with an isolated cleft lip. Society places a great deal of importance on external appearance, and the face is central to this view. It is vital that health care providers, extended family members, and other individuals involved in providing service give support during the initial bonding experience of new parents of an infant with a cleft lip. This will allow for every opportunity to get past negative feelings and promote bonding.

Infants with a cleft lip may have difficulty establishing a normal feeding pattern. Interruption in the integrity of the lip produces the challenge of providing optimum nutrition to foster the necessary growth required before surgical repair can be attempted. Feeding devices are available that can use either breast milk or prepared formulas to promote a feeding pattern that is as close to normal as possible. Many infants with an isolated cleft lip can successfully breast feed. These infants feed using structures within the mouth to express milk from a nipple. Tongue movements assist with this process and, though helpful, the lip is not essential to establish a successful suck. Referral to appropriate experts within the community can provide support for a successful feeding experience for an infant with an isolated defect.

A cleft palate involves a split in the hard or soft palate or, in some cases, both. Infants who are born with a cleft palate experience a wider variety of problems than do those infants born with an isolated cleft lip. These include facial deformities, speech impairment, hearing loss, infections, feeding problems, and learning disabilities that may or may not be related to either speech or hearing problems.

The potential for failure to thrive because of a decreased ability to eat is a significant problem for infants born with a cleft palate. Feeding problems are generally a result of the physical defect but may also be related to other disabilities. Normal sucking requires the tongue and/or the palate to stabilize the nipple and then to suck milk. This is dependent on the method chosen to feed an infant—breast or bottle. Cleft palates prevent nipple stabilization and create an abnormal suck. Devices such as extended nipples placed on squeeze bottles, flexible tubing placed next to a breast and connected to a bottle of pumped milk, and standard nipples with enlarged holes are available to assist with feeding. Each defect may require adaptation of feeding devices and techniques. Evaluation by an occupational therapist should be made prior to initial discharge from the hospital after birth, and a method of feeding devised. This plan includes parental instruction and referral to appropriate resources within the community for ongoing follow-up.

Another significant problem associated with cleft palate is acute and chronic middle ear infection. Acute infection may be a single episode in a susceptible infant that can be cleared with antibiotic treatment. Chronic infection results from a defective opening between the bacteria laden oral cavity, up the eustachean tubes, to the middle ear space. Surgical repair of the cleft does not significantly decrease the incidence of infection (Yetter, 1992). Therefore, conductive hearing loss from repeated infections is a common occurrence. Though the procedure is controversial, many infants will be placed on preventive antibiotic therapy and may even have drain tubes surgically placed through the ear drum, in an effort to reduce infection and subsequent hearing loss.

Speech delay also frequently accompanies a cleft palate. Sucking is necessary to develop muscles used to make speech physically possible. Alterations in the normal sucking process delay the muscle development. Moreover, the presence of a single cavity (nose and mouth) alters the normal sound production. Both the medical condition and the possibility of social isolation decrease the opportunities these infants have for verbal interaction with the adult world, a vital link to the development of speech.

Another problem faced by children with a cleft palate is related to the normal progression of tooth eruption. Dentition is not only delayed, but in many cases, normal tooth formation may be absent. Early evaluation by a dentist with appropriate referral for orthodontics is part of the teaming approach necessary to meet the total needs of an infant and family.

Hearing loss and speech delay lead to speech-related learning disabilities. These may be influenced by the social isolation that frequently results from the facial disfigurement that is part of this defect. In addition, educators sometimes make erroneous assumptions about intelligence in children with facial defects. Richman (1978) found that teachers both underestimated ability and had lower expectations for performance from students with moderate or severe facial disfigurement.

Families of infants who have a cleft palate require a multidisciplinary approach to meet their needs. This teaming should include the primary care physician, plastic surgeon, public health nurse, speech pathologist, audiologist, dentist, social worker, occupational therapist, and educator. Team collaboration provides for long-term planning to assure that both actual and potential needs of infants and families can be met.

Children whose defects have been successfully repaired may continue to experience alterations in social interactions and with learning. Persistent problems with articulation and with hypernasality of the voice may lead to ongoing anxiety in group interaction and to low self-esteem. Stereotyping must be avoided and identification of personal biases toward the importance of physical attractiveness are important topics in discussion within the team when planning the approach to services for each infant and family affected by this defect.

In Conclusion

Scientific discoveries such as gene therapy, gene cloning, and genetic selection in fertility are likely to alter the "natural" genetic course of the human species. Many disabilities could go the way of Tay Sachs, becoming selectively eliminated from the gene pool. Others could be treated by replacing defective genes with normal genes to prevent a disease such as sickle cell anemia. Whether these imminent changes will eventually be healthy for our species or harmful is a question seldom asked. When we get to the point of asking "Do we want 'this variation' or, 'that variation'?" Will we be active participants or spectators in a dialogue regarding the ever expanding knowledge or technology of genetic manipulation?

For example, Pueschel (1991) argued against the practice of using prenatal diagnosis to detect Down syndrome, on the grounds that the overriding purpose is to determine whether or not an abortion is needed. The arguments for prenatal screening and selective abortions of affected fetuses include the following.

1. It benefits the individual woman and her family.
2. It benefits society because such procedures have a eugenic effect in eliminating defective genes from the gene pool.
3. It reduces the financial burden to society.
4. It is preventive medicine.
5. It increases the quality of life for the family.
6. The fetus has a right to be born healthy (Pueschel, 1991, p.186).

Pueschel pointed out various unforseen and ultimately questionable outcomes of prenatal diagnosis. For example, many physicians have been found liable for "negligent genetic counseling" when there was a "wrongful birth" of a child with Down syndrome. Other medical personnel have lost court battles because a specific diagnostic test that might have detected Down syndrome was not conducted. In the latter, parents claimed that they were deprived of the opportunity to make a decision to terminate the affected fetus.

A second issue surrounds the practice in our society of deeming genetic difference as a negative. Many of the arguments mentioned above, for example, are a part of the mythology surrounding persons with Down syndrome. The thoughts of Pearl S. Buck (1973) regarding her daughter illustrate the belief that lives can be richer, not necessarily worsened, by the membership of persons with disabilities:

> In this world, where cruelty prevails in so many aspects of our lives, I would not add the weight of choice to kill rather than to let live. A retarded child, a handicapped person, brings his own gift to life, even to the life of normal human beings. That gift is comprehended in the lessons of patience, understanding, and mercy, lessons which we all need to relive and to practice with one another, whatever we are.

A study conducted by Meryash (1992) may shed the most light on this issue. When women were asked what factors would influence their decision to abort a child with fragile X syndrome, the most salient answer was a fear that the parents' social lives might be disrupted. It is worth noting that women who were more likely to select abortion were (1) more highly educated, (2) had a greater knowledge of fragile X, and (3) had other children with disabilities. Furthermore, the women identified the advice of their physician as an important factor in making a decision to abort. The latter is of concern to Pueschel, who fears that professionals who do not know or work with children with disabilities will be unfairly negative. "Genetic research has the potential for misunderstanding and misapplication; there may be a time when we are tempted to cross the line from curing or preventing a medically burdensome disease to enhancing genetic traits. Society must be able to place wedges in this potential slippery slope."

STUDY GUIDE QUESTIONS

1. How is individual variability related to treatment and prevention?
2. What is genetics?
3. Describe the basic mechanisms of inheritance. Define the following terms in the course of your answer: (1) chromosomes, (2) genes, (3) traits, (4) genetic mapping, (5) chromosomal region, (6) deletion, (7) mutation, (8) protein product, (9) "new genetics," and (10) the human genome.
4. What is the interplay of genetic codes and environmental factors on the cause and treatment of genetic diseases?
5. Describe cellular activity. Define the following terms in the course of your answer: (1) DNA, (2) nucleic acid compound, (3) alleles, (4) homozygote, (5) heterzygotes, (6) genotypes, (7) phenotypes, (8) mitosis, (9) meiosis, (10) gametes, and (11) errors in cell division.
6. How many chromosomes are there within a cell structure? How many of these are autosomes? What is the 23rd pair?
7. Describe single gene disorders.
8. Discuss the relationship among the following: dominant and recessive traits; male and female sex-linked traits.
9. Define chromosome disorder.
10. Define multifactorial disorders and congenital disorders.
11. What are the major types of genetic testing, and which genetic diseases can be most readily diagnosed?
12. What is the purpose of gene therapy? What are the social and ethical implications of gene therapy and advanced genetic testing?
13. What roles do the exocrine glands and the pancreas play in the development of the symptoms of cystic fibrosis?
14. What is meant by "secondary physical complications" in cystic fibrosis?
15. Briefly describe the etiology and treatment of cystic fibrosis.
16. Describe the most common characteristics of Down syndrome and the possible degree of variation from child to child.
17. What are the primary medical and educational issues facing persons with Down syndrome?
18. Differentiate between translocation and mosaicism.
19. Describe the chief characteristics of fragile X syndrome.
20. Briefly describe the etiology and treatment needs of children with fragile X syndrome.
21. Describe the primary characteristics, etiology, and treatment of Duchenne muscular dystrophy.
22. How does the buildup of phenylalanine cause mental retardation?
23. What preventive and treatment procedures are used to reduce rates of mental retardation from PKU?
24. What are the characteristics of sickle cell disease?
25. The treatment of sickle cell disease has developed slower than other "lower incident disorders." Why might this be?
26. Describe Turner syndrome: (a) etiology, (b) chief characteristics, and (c) treatment.

27. What are the characteristics of autism?
28. What is it about autism that makes this disability especially challenging for parents? For educators?
29. What general recommendations can be made in the treatment of children with autism?
30. What is the most common manifestations of Tourette syndrome?
31. What percentage of children with Tourette syndrome also experience learning disabilities? What implications does this have for instruction or treatment?
32. How does fetal heart circulation differ from heart function after birth? How does this protect the unborn child?
33. What are the symptoms of congenital cardiac defects?
34. At what point in development is a cleft lip and/or palate formed? What can cause this to happen?
35. Why is counseling especially important for families of very young children with cleft lips and/or palates?
36. What significant problems are associated with cleft lips and/or palates?

REFERENCES

Adams, R. J., McKie, V. C., & Hsu, B. F. (1998). Prevention of a first stroke by transfusions in children with sickle cell anemia and abnormal results on transcranial Doppler ultrasonography. *The New England Journal of Medicine, 339*, 5–11.

American Psychiatric Association. (1987). *Diagnostic and statistical manual of mental disorders* (3rd ed.). Washington, DC.

Andolsek, K. M. (1998). Characteristics and symptoms in patients with autism. *American Family Physician, 57*, 809–811. [Reprinted from Rapin, I. (1997). Autism. *New England Journal of Medicine, 337*, 97–104.]

Anfenson, M. (January, 1980). The school-age child with cystic fibrosis. *The Journal of School Health*, 26–28.

Armstrong, F. D., Lemanek, K. L., Pegelow, C. H., Gonzalez, J. C., & Martinez, A. (1993). Impact of lifestyle disruptions on parent and child coping, knowledge, and parental discipline in children with Sickle Cell Anemia. *Children's Health Care, 22*(3), 189–203.

Billings, P. R., Beckwith, J., & Alper, J. S. (1992). The genetic analysis of human behavior: A new era? *Social Science and Medicine, 35*(3), 227–238.

Black, S. (1992). The genetics of fragile X syndrome. In B. B. Shopmeyer & F. Lowe (Eds.), *The fragile X child* (pp. 3–17). San Diego: Singular Publishing Group, Inc.

Bower, B. (July, 1990). The ticcing link. *Science News, 138*, 42–44.

Bronheim, S. (1991). An educator's guide to Tourette syndrome. *Journal of Learning Disabilities, 24*, 17–22.

Brown, G. (Jan/Feb,1999). The sometimes son. *Humanist, 59*(1), 46–47.

Brown, R. T., Armstrong, F. D., & Eckman, J. R. (1993). Neurocognitive aspects of pediatric sickle cell disease. *Journal of Learning Disabilities, 26*(1), 33–45.

Buck, P. S. (1973). *The child who never grew*. New York: Day.

Burd, L., Kauffman, D. W., & Kerbeshian, J. (1992). Tourette syndrome and learning disabilities. *Journal of Learning Disabilities, 25*, 598–604.

Burd, L., Randall, T., Martsolf, J. T., & Kerbeshian, J. (1991). Rett syndrome symptomatology of institutionalized adults with mental retardation: Comparison of males and females. *American Journal of Mental Retardation, 95*, 596–601.

Cafiero, J. (1998). Communication power for individuals with autism. *Focus on Autism & Other Developmental Disabilities, 13*, 113–122.

Cantu, E. S., Stone, J. W., Wing, A. A., Langee, H. R., & Williams, C. A. (1990). Cytogenetic survey for autistic fragile X carriers in a mental retardation center. *American Journal on Mental Retardation, 94*, 442–447.

Chad, K., Jobling, A., & Frail, H. (1990). Metabolic rate: A factor in developing obesity in children with Down syndrome. *American Journal on Mental Retardation, 95*(2), 228–235.

Chan, A., McCaul, K. A., Keane, R. J., & Haan, E. A. (1998). Effect of parity, gravidity, previous miscarriage, and age on risk of Down's syndrome: Population based study. *British Medical Journal, 317*(7163), 923–924.

Chua-Lim, C., Moore, R. B., McCleary, G., Shah, A., & Mankad, V. N. (1993). Deficiencies in school readiness skills of children with sickle cell anemia. *Southern Medical Journal, 86*(4), 397–401.

Clark, D. M., & Smith, S. W. (1999). Facilitating friendships: Including students with autism in the early elementary classroom. *Intervention in School and Clinic, 34,* 248–251.

Cohen, D. J., Detlor, J., Shaywitz, B. A., & Leckman, J. F. (1992). Interaction of biological and psychological factors in the natural history of Tourette Syndrome: A paradigm for childhood neuropsychiatric disorders. In A. J. Friedhoff & T. N. Chase (Eds.), *Gilles de la Tourette syndrome (Vol. 35,* pp. 31–40). New York: Raven.

Cohen, M. M., & Bankier, A. (1991). Syndrome delineation involving orofacial clefting. *Cleft Palate Journal, 28,* 119–120.

Cole, M. (1991). New factors associated with the incidence of hypoglycemia: A research study. *Neonatal Network, 10*(4), 47–50.

Copel, J. A. (1999, October). *Congenital heart disease: Vol. 1.,* No. 6. http://hygeia.org/poems6.htm.

Crews, W. D., Bonaventura, A., Hay, C. L., Steele W. K., & Rowe, F. B. (1993). Gilles de la Tourette disorder among individuals with severe or profound mental retardation. *Mental Retardation, 31*(1), 25–29.

Cystic Fibrosis Foundation. (September, 1999a). *Gene therapy and cystic fibrosis.* Cystic Fibrosis Foundation, Bethesda, MD.

Cystic Fibrosis Foundation. (September, 1999b). *Facts about cystic fibrosis.* Cystic Fibrosis Foundation, Bethesda, MD.

Cystic Fibrosis Foundation. (September, 1999c). *Teachers guide to cystic fibrosis.* Cystic Fibrosis Foundation, Bethesda, MD.

Dawson, G., & Osterling, J. (1997). Early intervention in autism. In M. J. Guralnick (Ed.), *The Effectiveness of Early Intervention* (pp. 307–326). Baltimore: Brooks.

De La Cruz, F. F. (1985). Fragile X syndrome. *American Journal of Mental Deficiency, 90,* 119–123.

Dibble, S. L., & Savedra, M. C. (1988). Cystic fibrosis in adolescence: A new challenge. *Pediatric Nursing, 14,* 299–303.

Dolovich, L., Addis, A., Vaillancourt, J. M. R., Power, J. D. B., Koren, G., & Einarson, T. R. (1998). Benzodiazepine use in pregnancy and major malformations or oral cleft: Meta-analysis of cohort and case-control studies. *British Medical Journal, 317,* 839–843.

Donaldson, M. D. C., Chu, C. E., Cooke, A., Wilson, A., Greene, S. A., & Stephenson, J. B. P. (1994). The Prader-Willi syndrome. *Archives of Disease in Children, 70,* 58–63.

Donnell, G., & Ng, W. (1990). Galactosemia. In M. Buyse (Ed.), *Birth defects encyclopedia* (pp. 763–764). Dover, MA: Center for Birth Defects Information Services, Inc.

Downey, J., Elkin, E. J., Ehrhardt, A. A., Meyer-Bahlburg, H. F. L., Bell, J. J., & Morishima, A. (1991). Cognitive ability and everyday functioning in women with Turner syndrome. *Journal of Learning Disabilities, 24*(1), 32–39.

Dussault, J., Coulombe, P., & Laberge, C. (1975). Preliminary report on a mass screening program for neonatal hypothyroidism. *Journal of Pediatrics, 86,* 670–674.

Dykens, E. M., Hodapp, R. M., Ort, S. I., & Leckman, J. F. (1993). Trajectory of adaptive behavior in males with fragile X syndrome. *Journal of Autism and Developmental Disorders, 23,* 135–145.

Eaves, R. C. (1992). Autism. In P. J. McLaughlin & P. Wehman (Eds.), *Developmental disabilities: A handbook for best practices* (pp. 68–81). Stoneham, MA: Butterworth-Heinemann.

Eaves, R. C., & Hopper, J. (1987–88). A factor analysis of psychotic behavior. *Journal of Special Education, 21,* 122–132.

Edell, B. H., & Motta, R. W. (1989). The emotional adjustment of children with Tourette's syndrome. *The Journal of Psychology, 123*(1), 51–57.

Eliason, M. J. (1991). Cleft lip and palate: Developmental effects. *Journal of Pediatric Nursing, 6*(2), 107–113.

Emery, A. E. H. (1998). The muscular dystrophies. *British Medical Journal, 317,* 991–996.

Evenhuis, H. M. (1990). The natural history of dementia in Down's syndrome. *Archives of Neurology, 47,* 263–277.

Eyman, R. K., Call, T. L., & White, J. F. (1991). Life expectancy of persons with Down syndrome. *American Journal on Mental Retardation, 95*(6), 603–612.

Fajans, S., & Floyd, J. (1976). Fasting hypoglycemia in adults. *New England Journal of Medicine, 291,* 766–772.

Fisher, D. (1991). Clinical review 19: Management of congenital hypothyroidism. *Journal of Clinical Endocrinology and Metabolism, 72*(3), 523–529.

Fisher, D. (1983). Second International Conference on Neonatal Thyroid Screening: Progress report. *Journal of Pediatrics, 102,* 653–654.

Fisher, D., & Foley, B. (1989). Early treatment of congenital hypothyroidism. *Pediatrics, 83*(5), 785–789.

Fishler, K., & Koch, R. (1991). Mental development in Down syndrome mosaicism. *American Journal of Mental Deficiency, 96,* 345–351.

Gene that causes cystic fibrosis identified. (1989, September). Cystic Fibrosis Foundation Commitment, p. 1.

Gil, K. M., Abrams, M. R., Phillips, G., & Williams, D. A. (1992). Sickle cell disease pain: 2. Predicting health care use and activity level at 9-month follow-up. *Journal of Consulting and Clinical Psychology, 60,* 267–273.

Gray, N. T., Bartlett, J. M., Kolasa, K. M., Marcuard, S. P., Holbrook, C. T., & Horner, R. D. (1992). Nutritional status and dietary intake of children with sickle cell anemia. *Journal of Pediatric Hematology/Oncology, 14*(1), 57–61.

Guyer, M. S., & Collins, F. S. (1993). The Human Genome Project and the future of medicine. *AJDC, 147,* 1145–1151.

Haan, E. A. (1990). Ethics and the new genetics. *Journal of Pediatric and Child Health, 26,* 177–179.

Hagberg, B., & Witt-Engerstrom, I. (1986). A suggested staging system for describing impairment profile with increasing age towards adolescence. *American Journal of Medical Genetics, 24,* 377–382.

Hagerman, R. (1992). Medical aspects of the fragile X syndrome. In B. B. Shopmeyer & F. Lowe (Eds.), *The fragile X child* (pp. 19–29). San Diego: Singular Publishing Group.

Hall, J. G., & Gilchrist, D. M. (1990). Turner syndrome and its variants. *Current Issues in Pediatric and Adolescent Endocrinology, 17*(1), 1421–1440.

Hardy, J. D. (1988). *Hardy's textbook of surgery,* 2nd ed. Philadelphia: J. B. Lippincott.

Hayes, C., Rarback, S., Berry, B., & Clancy, M. (1987). Managing PKU: An update. *Maternal/Child Nursing, 12,* 119–123.

Holden, C. (1997). A gene is linked to autism. *Science, 276,* 905.

Huk, S. G. (1989). Transient exacerbation of tics in treatment of Tourette's syndrome with Clonidine. *Journal of the American Academy of Child and Adolescent Psychiatry, 28*(4), 583–586.

Hurtig, A., & Viera, A. (1986). *Sickle cell disease: Psychological and psychosocial issues.* Urbana, IL: University of Illinois Press.

Johnson, R. C., & Abelson, R. B. (1969). Intellectual, behavioral, and physical characteristics associated with trisomy, translocation, and mosaic types of Down syndrome. *American Journal of Mental Deficiency, 73*(6), 852–855.

Keenan, J., Kastner, T., Nathanson, R., Richardson, N., Hinton, J., & Cress, D. (1992). A statewide public and professional education program on fragile X syndrome. *Mental Retardation, 30,* 355–361.

Klein, R. (1985). Infantile hypothyroidism then and now: The results of neonatal screening. *Current Problems in Pediatrics, 15*(1), 1–58.

Knell, E. R., & Comings, D. E. (1993). Tourette's syndrome and attention-deficit-hyperactivity disorder: Evidence for a genetic relationship. *Journal of Clinical Psychiatry, 54*(9), 331–337.

Koch, R., Acosta, P., Donnell, G., & Lieberman, E. (1965). Nutritional therapy of galactosemia. *Clinical Pediatrics, 4,* 571–578.

Koop-Hoolihan, L. E., Van Loan, M. D., Mentzer, W. C., Heyman, M. B. (1999). Elevated resting energy expenditure in adolescents with sickle cell anemia. *Journal of the American Dietetic Association, 99,* 195–199.

Krener, P., & Adelman, R. (1988). Parent salvage and sabotage in the care of chronically ill children. *American Journal of Diseased Children, 142,* 945–951.

Kurlan, R. (1992). The pathogenesis of Tourette's syndrome: A possible role for hormonal and excitatory neurotransmitter influences in brain development. *Archives of Neurology, 49,* 874–876.

Lambert, E., Canent, R., & Hohn, A. (1966). Congenital cardiac defects in the newborn: A review of conditions causing death or severe distress in the first month of life. *Pediatrics, 37,* 343–352.

Leckman, J. F., Zhang, H., Vitale, A., Lahnin, F., Lynch, K., Bondi, C., Kim, Y., Peterson, B. S. (1998). Course of tic severity in Tourette syndrome: The first two decades. *Pediatrics, 102,* 14–20.

Lerer, R. J. (1987). Motor tics, Tourette syndrome, and learning disabilities. *Journal of Learning Disabilities, 20,* 266–267.

Levi, S. L. (1991). The Tourette Syndrome Association, Inc. *Journal of Learning Disabilities, 24*(1), 16–22.

Liu, J. E., Gzesh, D. J., & Ballas, S. K. (1994). The spectrum of epilepsy in sickle cell anemia. *Journal of Neurological Sciences, 123,* 6–10.

Lynn, D. J., Woda, R. P., & Mendell, J. R. (1994). Respiratory dysfunction in muscular dystrophy and other myopothies. *Clinics in Chest Medicine, 15*(4), 661–674.

Marcell, M. M., & Cohen, S. (1992). Hearing abilities of Down syndrome and other mentally handicapped adolescents. *Research in Developmental Disabilities, 13,* 533–551.

March of Dimes. (1992). *Genetic testing and gene therapy* (No. 09-576-00). White Plains, NY: Author.

March of Dimes. (1987). *Genetic counseling.* Spokane, WA: March of Dimes Birth Defects Foundation.

Mathur, A., Stekol, L., Schatz, D., Maclaren, N. K., Scott, M. L., & Lippe, B. (1991). The parental origin of the single X chromosome in Turner syndrome: Lack of correlation with parental age or clinical phenotype. *American Journal of Human Genetics, 48,* 682–686.

Matson, D. (1969). Neurosurgery of infancy and childhood. Springfield, IL: Charles G. Thomas.

Mauk, J. E. (1993). Autism and pervasive developmental disorders. *Pediatric Clinics of North America, 40*(3), 567–578.

Mazzocco, M. M. M., Baumgardner, T., Freund, I. S., Reiss, A. L. (1998). Social functioning among girls with fragile X or Turner syndrome and their sisters. *Journal of Autism and Developmental Disabilities, 28,* 509–516.

McCarthy, M. (1999). Inhaled antibiotics effective for cystic fibrosis. *The Lancet, a*(9148), 215.

McCauley, E., Kay, T., Ito, J., & Treder, R. (1987). The Turner syndrome: Cognitive deficits, affective discrimination, and behavior problems. *Child Development, 58,* 464–473.

McClennen, S. (1992). Cognitive characteristics, assessment, and intervention in fragile X syndrome. In B. B. Shopmeyer & F. Lowe (Eds.), *The fragile X child* (pp. 33–58). San Diego: Singular Publishing.

McInerny, T. G. (1985). Cleft palate repair—surgical procedure and nursing care. *AORN Journal, 42,* 516–527.

Meryash, D. L. (1985). *The fragile X syndrome.* (Report No. MF01/PC05). Silver Spring, MD: American Association of University Affiliated Programs for Persons with Developmental Disabilities. (ERIC Document Reproduction Service No. ED 276 194).

Meryash, D. L. (1992). Characteristics of fragile X relatives with different attitudes toward terminating an affected pregnancy. *American Journal of Mental Retardation, 96,* 528–535.

Miculan, J., Turner, S., & Paes, B. (1993). Congenital hypothyroidism: Diagnosis and management. *Neonatal Network, 12*(6), 25–33.

Milerad, J., Larson, O., Hagberg, C., & Ideberg, M. (1997). Associated malformations in infants with cleft lip and palate: A prospective, population-based study. *Pediatrics, 100,* 180–187.

Mitchell, S., Korones, S., & Berendes, H. (1971). Congenital heart disease in 56,109 births. *Circulation, 43,* 323–330.

Murray, J. B. (1997). Psychophysiological aspects of Tourette's syndrome. *The Journal of Psychology, 131,* 615–621.

Nagel, R. L. (1993). Sickle cell anemia is a multigene disease: Sickle painful crises, a case in point. *American Journal of Hematology, 42,* 96–101.

National Institute of Health. (1990). Ethical, legal and social implications of the human genome initiative. *NIH Guide for Grants and Contracts, 19*(4), 12–14.

New treatments predicted. (September, 1989). *Cystic Fibrosis Foundation Commitment,* p. 6.

Norwood, W. (1991). Hypoplastic left heart syndrome. Annuals of Thoracic Surgery, 52, 688–695.

Nyhan, W. (1990). Phenylketonuria. In M. Buyse (Ed.), *Birth defects encyclopedia,* pp. 1382–1383. Dover, MA: Center for Birth Defects Information Services, Inc.

Orr, T. J., Myles, B. S., & Carlson, J. K. (1998). The impact of rhythmic entrainment on a person with autism. *Focus on Autism and Other Developmental Disabilities, 13,* 163–167.

O'Sullivan, H. (1998). Use and design of genetic screening programmes: A study. *Journal of Biological Education, 32,* 97–103.

Pauls, D. L., & Leckman, J. F. (1986). The inheritance of Gilles de la Tourette syndrome and associated behaviors: Evidence for autosomal dominant transmission. *The New England Journal of Medicine, 315,* 993–997.

Pediatric Pulmonary and Cystic Fibrosis Clinic. (1987). *"Our job is caring. . . ."* Spokane, WA: Deaconess Medical Clinic.

Perry, A. (1991). Rett syndrome: A comprehensive review of the literature. *American Journal of Mental Retardation, 96,* 275–290.

Piven, J., Palmer, P., Jacobi, D., & Childress, D. (1997). Broader autism phenotype: Evidence from a family history study of multiple-incidence autism families. *The American Journal of Psychiatry, 154,* 185–190.

Pollack, C. V. (1993). Emergencies in sickle cell disease. *Emergency Medicine Clinics of North America, 11*(2), 365–378.

Pueschel, S. M. (1991). Ethical considerations relating to prenatal diagnosis of fetuses with Down syndrome. *Mental Retardation, 29*(4), 185–190.

Pueschel, S. M., Jackson, M. D., Giesswein, P., Dean, M. K., & Pezzullo, J. C. (1991). Thyroid function in Down syndrome. *Research in Developmental Disabilities, 12,* 287–296.

Reiss, A. L., & Freund, L. (1990). Fragile X syndrome. *Biological Psychiatry, 27,* 223–240.

Richman, L. (1978). The effect of facial disfigurement on teachers' perception of ability in cleft palate children. *Cleft Palate Journal, 15,* 155–157.

Risley, M. S. (1986). *Chromosome structure and function.* New York: Van Nostrand Reinhold.

Rogers, R. C., & Simensen, R. J. (1987). Fragile X syndrome: A common etiology of mental retardation. *American Journal of Mental Deficiency, 91,* 445–449.

Rosen, A. R. (1996). Tourette's syndrome: The school experience. *Clinical Pediatrics, 35,* 467–470.

Rosenfeld, M., Casey, S., Pepe, M., & Ramsey, B. W. (1999). Nutritional effects of long-term gastrostomy feedings in children with cystic fibrosis. *Journal of the American Dietetic Association, 99,* 191–196.

Rovet, J. F. (1990). The cognitive and neuropsychological characteristics of females with Turner syndrome. In D. B. Berch & B. G. Berger (Eds.), *Sex chromosome abnormalities and human behavior* (pp. 38–77). Boulder, CO: Westview.

Rovet, J. F. (1993). The psychoeducational characteristics of children with Turner syndrome. *Journal of Learning Disabilities, 26*(5), 333–341.

Rynders, J. E., & Horrobin, J. M. (1990). Always trainable? Never educable? Updating educational expectations concerning children with Down syndrome. *American Journal on Mental Retardation, 95*(1), 77–83.

Sach, B. P., & Korf, B. (1993). The human genome project: Implications for the practicing obstetrician. *Obstetrics and Gynecology, 81*(3), 458–462.

Sallee, F. R., Nesbitt, L., Jackson, C., Sine, L., & Sethuraman, G. (1997). Relative efficacy of haloperidol and pimozide in children and adolescents with Tourette's disorder. *The American Journal of Psychiatry, 154,* 1057–1062.

Samuels, M. (1988). Hypoglycemia. In S. Silverstein and D. Frommer (Eds.), *Emergency management of metabolic and endocrine disorders* (pp. 61–75). Rockville, MD: Aspen Publishers, Inc.

Sancho, S., Mongini, T., Tanji, K., Tapscott, S. J., Walker, W. F., Weintraub, H., Miller, A. D., & Miranda, A. F. (1993). Analysis of dystrophin expression after activation of myogenesis in amniocytes, chorionic-villus cells, and fibroblasts. *The New England Journal of Medicine, 329*(13), 915–920.

Santos, C. C., & Massey, E. W. (1990). Tourette's syndrome: Tics, jerks and quirks. *Postgraduate Medicine, 87*(1), 71–74.

Santos, K. E. (1992). Fragile X syndrome: An educator's role in identification prevention, and intervention. *Remedial and Special Education, 13,* 32–39.

Schimke, R. (1990). Thyroid, iodide transport defect. In M. Buyse (Ed.), *Birth defects encyclopedia* (pp. 1675–1676). Dover, MA: Center for Birth Defects Information Services, Inc.

Scientists forecast new approaches for developing treatments. (September, 1989). *Cystic Fibrosis Foundation Commitment,* p. 2.

Schmidt, M. (1997). Fragile X syndrome: Diagnosis, treatment and research. *JAMA, 277,* 1169.

Schwartz, I. S., & Sandall, S. R. (1998). Outcomes for children with autism: Three case studies. *Topics in Early Childhood Special Education, 18,* 132–144.

Segal, S. (1989). Disorders of galactose metabolism. In Scriver, C., Beaudet, A., Sly, W., & Valle, D. (Eds.), *The metabolic basis of inherited disease* 6th ed. (pp. 453–480). New York: McGraw-Hill Information Services Company.

Serjeant, G. R. (1985). *Sickle cell disease.* New York: Oxford University Press.

Shakir, K., & Amin, R. (1991). Hypoglycemia. *Critical Care Clinics, 7*(1), 75–87.

Shapiro, A. K., & Shapiro, E. S. (1980). Tic, Tourette, or movement disorder? A guide to early diagnosis. *Diagnosis, 55,* 77–84.

Shapiro, B. S. (1989). The management of pain in sickle cell disease. *Pediatric Clinics of North America, 36,* 1029–1045.

Shapiro, E., & Shapiro, A. K. (1981). Tic disorders. *Journal of the American Medical Association, 245,* 1583–1585.

Shapiro, F., & Specht, L. (1993). The diagnosis and orthopaedic treatment of inherited muscular diseases of childhood. *The Journal of Bone and Joint Surgery, 75*(3), 430–454.

Simensen, R. J., & Rogers, R. C. (1989). School psychology and medical diagnosis: The fragile X syndrome. *Psychology in the Schools, 26,* 380–389.

Sobel, E., & Saenger, P. (1989). Hypothyroidism in the newborn. *Pediatrics in Review, 11*(1), 15–20.

Steffens, M. L., Oiler, D. K., Lynch, M., & Urbano, R. C. (1992). Vocal development in infants with Down syndrome and infants who are developing normally. *American Journal on Mental Retardation, 97*(2), 235–246.

Stullenbarger, B., Norris, J., Edgil, A. E., & Prosser, M. J. (1987). Family adaptation to cystic fibrosis. *Pediatric Nursing, 13,* 29–31.

Sudhalter, V., Cohen, I., Silverman, W., & Wolf-Schein, E. G. (1990). Conversational analyses of males with fragile X, Down syndrome and autism: Comparison of the emergence of deviant language. *American Journal of Mental Retardation, 94,* 431–441.

Temple, C. M., & Carney, R. A. (1993). Intellectual functioning of children with Turner syndrome: A comparison of behavioural phenotypes. *Developmental Medicine and Child Neurology, 35,* 691–698.

Thompson, M. W., McInnes, R. R., & Willard, H. F. (1991). *Genetics in medicine* (5th ed.). Philadelphia: Saunders.

Thompson, R. J., Gil, K. M., Abrams, M. R., & Phillips, G. (1992). Stress, coping, and psychological adjustment of adults with sickle cell disease. *Journal of Consulting and Clinical Psychology, 60,* 433–440.

Thorpe-Beeston, J. (1991). Maturation of the secretion of thyroid hormone and thyroid stimulating hormone in the fetus. *New England Journal of Medicine, 324*(8), 532–536.

Tordjman, S., Ferrari, P., Sulmont, V., Duyme, M., & Roubertoux, P. (1997). Androgenic activity in autism. *The American Journal of Psychiatry, 154,* 1626–1627.

Torup, E. (1972). A follow-up study of children with tics. *Acta Paediatricia Scandinavica, 51,* 261–268.

Turner, G., Robinson, H., Wake, S., Laing, S., & Partington, M. (1997). Case finding for the fragile X sndrome and its consequences. *British Medical Journal, 315*(7117), 1223–1226.

Ulstrom, R., & Sockalowsky, J. (1990). Hypoglycemia, familial neonatal. In M. Buyse (Ed.), *Birth defects encyclopedia* (pp. 921–922). Dover, MA: Center for Birth Defects Information Services, Inc.

Vanderas, A. P. (1987). Incidence to cleft lip and palate among races: A review. *Cleft Palate Journal, 24,* 216–225.

Virtanen, M. (1988). Manifestations of congenital hypothyroidism during the first week of life. *European Journal of Pediatrics, 147*(3), 270–274.

Wachtel, T. J., & Pueschel, S. M. (1991). Macrocytosis in Down syndrome. *American Journal on Mental Retardation, 95*(4), 417–420.

Waisbren, S., Normal, R., Schnell, R., & Levy, H. (1983). Speech and language deficits in early treated children with galactosemia. *Journal of Pediatrics, 102,* 75–84.

Walkup, J. T., Leckman, J. F., Price, A., Hardin, M., Ort, S. L., & Cohen, D. J. (1988). The relationship between obsessive-compulsive disorder and Tourette syndrome: A twin study. *Psychopharmacology Bulletin, 24*(3), 375–379.

Webster, C. D., Konstantareas, M. M., Oxman, J., & Mack, J. E. (1980). *Autism: New directions in research and education.* New York: Pergamon.

Werthorn, L. A., & McCabe, M. A. (1988). Emerging ethical and legal issues in pediatric psychology. In D. Routh (Ed.), *Handbook of pediatric psychology* (pp. 567–606). New York: Guilford.

Williams, J. K., Richman, L. C., & Yarbrough, D. B. (1992). Comparison of visual-spatial performance strategy training in children with Turner syndrome and learning disabilities. *Journal of Learning Disabilities, 25,* 658–664.

Wilson, P. G., & Mazzocco, M. M. (1993). Awareness and knowledge of fragile X syndrome among special educators. *Mental Retardation, 97*(4), 221–227.

Wing, L. (1997). The autistic spectrum. *The Lancet, 350,* 1761–1766.

Wolff, P., Gardner, J., Paccia, J., & Lappen, J. (1989). The greeting behavior of fragile X males. *American Journal of Mental Retardation, 93,* 406–411.

Yetter, J. F. (1992). Cleft lip and cleft palate. *American Family Physician, 46*(4), 1211–1219.

Zinn, A. R., Page, D. C., & Fisher, E. M. C. (1993). Turner syndrome: The case of the missing sex chromosome. *Trends in Genetics, 9*(3), 90–93.

SENSORY IMPAIRMENTS AND INFECTIONS

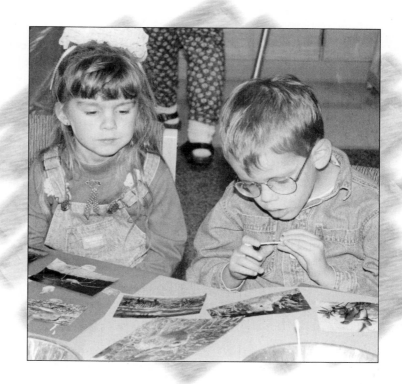

This chapter is devoted to the effects of bacterial and viral infections on developing fetuses, neonates, and infants. While some of the diseases resulting from these invasive organisms are negligible, other infections can cause severe and multiple disabilities or even death. Though there are many other causes of vision and hearing losses, sensory impairments, especially in vision and hearing, are often the result of a significant infection in a neonate or young child.

HEARING IMPAIRMENTS

Hearing is the act of receiving and processing sound vibrations. The auditory mechanisms within the ear permit humans to discriminate differential sound waves within their environment. Yet, a large number of children have degraded or impoverished hearing which affects their ability to remember, requires more time and effort to process incoming auditory information, and consequently interrupts their ability to communicate effectively (Jerger & Martin, 1995). Approximately 1 child in 22 experiences some type of hearing loss at birth or soon after (National Institute of Health Consensus Statement [NIHCS], 1999). Of those, 65% are born with a hearing loss, and another 12% develop this disability within their first three years of life.

HEARING PROCESS

The auditory mechanism is functionally separated into three components: external, middle, and inner ear (see Figure 7–1). The **external ear,** consisting of the auricle, auditory canal, and **tympanic membrane,** is responsible for collecting sound waves. Physical energy is channeled down the auditory canal, where it vibrates the tympanic membrane (eardrum).

The **middle ear** cavity lies beyond the tympanic membrane. Sound vibrations are mechanically transmitted from the tympanic membrane to stimulate, in sequence, three tiny bones: the malleus (hammer), incus (anvil), and stapes (stirrup). The latter is attached to a small opening that leads to the inner ear, referred to as the oval window. The **eustachian tube** intersects the middle ear to form a continuous passage to the throat. The purpose of the eustachian tube is to equalize internal and external air pressure on the tympanic membrane. Excessive buildup of pressure within the middle ear can cause the sensitive tympanic membrane to rupture.

Sound waves traveling to the **inner ear** from the vibration of the eardrum and bones of the middle ear are transmitted through the oval window to the **cochlea** (see Figure 7–2).

Figure 7–1
Anatomy of the ear.

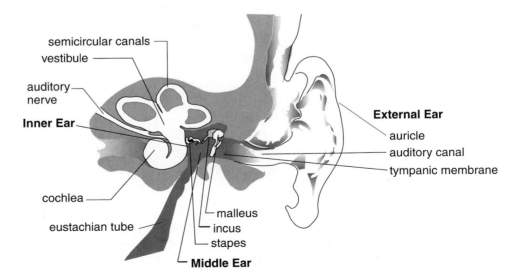

Figure 7–2
Pathway of
sound through
outer, middle,
and inner ear.

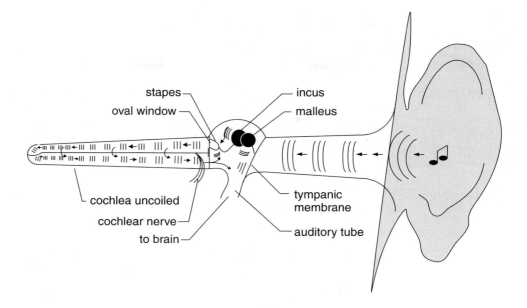

Tiny nerve endings within the cochlea, referred to as hair cells, are stimulated by the movement of cochlear fluid. The resulting energy (now electrical) is transferred to the temporal area of the brain via the eighth cranial nerve, or **auditory nerve.** Contained within the inner ear are the **vestibule** and the three **semicircular canals;** these structures also contain neural hair cells. Movement of these cells, caused by forces of gravity and motion, provides information through the eighth cranial nerve to the brain regarding the body's equilibrium status.

Hearing Loss

Sounds are heard along two dimensions: loudness and pitch. Pitch is determined by the frequency of sound waves. Normally, speech sounds range between frequencies of 500 and 2000 cycles per second. Loudness, or sound intensity, is measured in decibels (dB), and hearing is considered normal when sound is audible at 10 dB. Hearing losses, which range from slight (sound audible at 15–25 dB) to profound (sound audible at more than 90 dB), are the result of a variety of insults to the auditory system.

Approximately 50% of hearing losses have an unknown cause. The etiology, location, and severity of damage to the ear are variables used in determining immediate and long-range treatment for children with hearing loss (see Table 7–1). A **conductive hearing loss** is one that disrupts mechanical conduction of sound as it is transferred from the outer ear through the middle ear. Though several factors can contribute to a conductive hearing loss, most causes can be treated effectively and efficiently through medical intervention. Furthermore, the degree of hearing loss for most conductive etiologies ranges from mild to moderate. The most common cause of hearing loss is **otitis media,** or middle ear disease.

Table 7-1 Factors that place children at risk of hearing loss.

Prenatal/Natal Period	After Neonatal Period	Treatments
TORCH Diseases	Head Trauma†	Cochlear Implants
Cytomegalo Virus*		
Rubella*	Neurodegenerative Diseases	Assistive Devices (Hearing Aides)
Herpes*		
Toxoplasmosis*	Childhood Diseases	
Syphilis*	Mumps*	
Otitis Media*	Measles*	Vibrotactile Aids
Craniofacial Anomalies	Bacterial Meningitis*	
Cleft Palate†	Noise-Induced Hearing Loss	
Tinnitus (ringing in the ears)		
Otosclerosis		
Genetic		
Waardenburg Syndrome		
Usher Syndrome		
Treacher-Collins Syndrome		
Albinism		
Down Syndrome†		
Family History		
Low Birth Weight (<1,500)†		
Hyperbilirubinemia†		
Severe Depression at Birth		
Ototoxic Drugs		

Source: Adapted from Northern, J., & Downs, M. (1984). *Hearing in children* (3rd ed.). Baltimore: Williams & Wilkins.
*Covered in this chapter.
†Covered elsewhere in this text.

Otitis media is the most common cause of conductive hearing loss in children. Either viral or bacterial infections cause a buildup of fluid in the middle ear and eustachian tube, which reduces mobility of the membranes and bones necessary to adequately transfer sound intensity to the inner ear. Symptoms of otitis media are a red, bulging tympanic membrane, frequent ear pulling, and irritability. A single infection usually will result in only temporary and mild hearing loss. However, chronic middle ear disease (serous otitis media) can result in a more persistent and significant hearing loss that might substantially interrupt normal acquisition of language. Treatment of otitis media includes myringotomy (tubes placed through the eardrum to drain fluid), antihistimines (to reduce swelling of the eustachian tube), and antibiotics, which will generally work with bacterial infections, even though most middle ear infections are viral.

Conductive hearing losses are common in children with a variety of disabilities. For example, children with Down syndrome are at increased risk of middle ear infection for two reasons:

1. A depressed immune response system
2. An anomoly resulting in a more horizontal than normal eustachian tube, which prevents adequate drainage of the middle ear

Similarly, serous otitis media is quite common in children with cleft palates, whose eustachian tube drainage is hindered by the palate malformation.

Sensorineural hearing losses result from damage to the cochlea or auditory nerve hindering the brain from receiving sound messages. Genetic inheritance accounts for well over half of known abnormalities that result in serious sensorineural hearing loss. There are several hundred known genetic syndromes, with recent research showing that many of these are the consequence of multiple gene involvement (Current progress, 1995). Noise, such as jet engine, rifle fire, and loud music can cause sensorineural hearing loss or "noise induced deafness." Unlike conductive hearing losses, sensorineural hearing losses require amplification or surgery to improve hearing.

Intrauterine infections also account for a large percentage of serious sensorineural hearing impairments. Toxoplasmosis, maternal rubella contracted during the first trimester, herpes, mumps, syphilis, and cytomegalovirus are all associated with malformations that result in hearing loss. Meningitis, a bacterial infection, is the leading postnatal cause of hearing loss, accounting for 10% of acquired deafness in the United States (Kaplan, 1997). Bacterial meningitis affects the structure of the delicate snail-shaped cochlea.

Neonates and premature infants are at risk of acquiring hearing losses. For example, asphyxia of infants during delivery may damage the cochlea, resulting in sensorineural hearing loss. High bilirubin levels resulting in severe jaundice may also cause permanent damage to the central nervous system. Other neonatal factors include cerebral hemorrhage, apnea, and, in some cases, antibiotic drugs, which can become toxic.

Case Study

MADDY'S MENINGITIS AND ITS EFFECTS:
INTERVIEW WITH KIM SHAFER

When Maddy was only two months old, she woke one day, listless and not herself. Just to be safe, I took her into the doctor's office who didn't seem that concerned until he touched the top of her head. Within 30 seconds he was back in the room telling me that we were going to the hospital by ambulance and that she possibly had meningitis.

It was then I learned about that soft spot on the top of her head and how important it was. It's where the skull has not completely closed. And that soft spot actually tells you if there is any swelling in the brain. Usually, it should be soft and dipped, but this time it was swollen which meant the fluid and swelling from Maddy's spine had already built up around her brain.

So, we spent 12 scary days in the hospital and Maddy seemed to come back pretty fast. We knew another baby was in the hospital at the same time fighting for her life, so we thought we were pretty lucky. Lots of prayers were answered.

Two days after she was released from the hospital, we went to her doctor for a check-up. We were thinking that we'd have to take Maddy to physical therapy or occupational therapy because the meningitis caused her to lose all her muscle control so she was like a newborn again. She couldn't lift her head or roll over, so we expected that challenge, but it was something we were okay with. I remembered there had been a test done in the hospital, and I asked the doctor if he'd gotten the results back. Oh, Gosh! it was like he'd forgotten, so I figured it must not be a big deal. I had just sent my husband and my other daughter to the restroom.

But when the doctor came back into the room, he said the two sentences that I will never forget in all my life. "It looks like she's going to be deaf. The other doctor is concerned with the results of the test." I was just standing there thinking, what did he just tell me? I was thinking that my husband was not there, and my kids wouldn't understand this. I was alone and terrified and confused, and I'd have to repeat this to my husband when he came back to the room. I felt so all alone and not sure what this was all about.

I had never known a deaf person in my life. I'd never had that exposure; neither had my husband. We went out to the parking lot, cried our eyes out and said, "Okay, where do we go from here?"

Then, in the mail we got this letter that told us that the Deaf Service Center had sign language classes and they would make home visits where they came out to your house and actually sat down with you. We started sign language classes there once a week. Maddy and I would go and she'd play in the other room and I'd sit down with a couple of other parents. The other parents were a great resource for me because they had already gone through the things I was now going through. We became really close friends and learned sign language together.

Maddy started the sign language program when she was about four and a half months old and by seven months old she was starting to sign. "Wow! She's communicating! This is really cool!" Her first words were "more," because she could get more, and "candy." At that time, Maddy also got hearing aids.

We used the hearing aids, but at 18 months, the ear, nose, and throat specialist said, "You know, they have a great device called a cochlear implant that you should think about because the hearing aids don't seem to be working." I was thinking, Gosh! she's only 18 months old, have we really given this a good try? I mean she couldn't yet communicate back to us. So we asked the sign language therapist if she could really tell us whether Maddy was hearing or not? I just wasn't ready for an implant yet, so I put it off.

Mark, Kim,
Amanda, Cassie,
and Maddy Shafer.

IDENTIFICATION OF HEARING LOSS

Though the critical period of language development is during the first three years of life, the average age at which children are diagnosed with a hearing loss is close to age three (NIHCS, 1993). The National Institute of Health concluded that one factor contributing to delayed identification is the practice of screening only high-risk children—thereby eliminating up to half of those infants with hearing impairments. Early identification of hearing loss would enable families and practitioners to plan and implement a remedial program to enhance cognitive and social development. Management of hearing loss within one year of birth appears to alleviate most of the adverse affects on communication, psychological problems, and functional capabilities (Kennedy, Kim, Dees, Campbell, & Thornton, 1998).

Two tools are considered the most efficient in screening newborns for hearing loss because they measure brain activity rather than physical responses to sound (NIHCS, 1993). The first, auditory brain stem responses (ABS), can be done without sedating an infant and is highly accurate. Sounds are presented through earphones while an infant sleeps and their brain responses are measured through electrodes taped to the infant's head. Evoked otoacoustic emissions (EOAE) is a relatively new screening procedure that is less costly and less complex while still being highly sensitive. In this case, a tiny microscope is placed in the ear canal to detect sounds "sent-out" by the movement of cochlear hair cells in the inner ear.

After children are six months old, it is possible to conduct behavioral testing in which they are trained to consistently respond to the emission of a noise. However, this procedure requires well-trained professionals and is less reliable when used with infants who have developmental delays.

DEVELOPMENTAL IMPLICATIONS AND RESOLUTIONS

Children with hearing losses are identified early when they fail to startle, do not localize sounds, and have delayed acquisition of language milestones. In some cases hearing losses are misdiagnosed as cognitive delays. The developmental domain most directly affected by hearing loss in infancy is language. However, children with hearing losses generally score within the normal intelligence range when tested on nonverbal measures. Social skills may also be affected since interpersonal communication is considered an essential component of social interactions.

Two factors are related to the interaction between hearing loss and developmental progress. First, since it is estimated that the ability to learn language peaks between age 2 and 4, it is critical to identify hearing loss early and to provide adaptive intervention at the earliest possible age. Second, the age of onset and degree of hearing loss influence the degree to which children's language and cognitive skills will be affected. Because of this relationship, it is believed that a large percentage of preschoolers with hearing impairment could be dually diagnosed with learning disabilities (Mauk & Mauk, 1992).

There are several augmentative communication systems that should be considered early. Sign language systems, which use hand gestures to communicate, include American Sign Language (ASL), Signing Exact English (SEE-II), and cued speech. American Sign Language is considered a unique language with its own sentence and word structure (syntax and morphology) and is widely used by adults with deafness.

This language is the most efficient manual communication system. By contrast, SEE-II resembles spoken and written English in sentence/word structure and usage and may therefore facilitate the acquisition of written language skills and academic skills.

It is important that children with hearing losses not only learn manual sign, but also be taught to make use of residual hearing, speech (lip) reading, and oral speech to communicate. Since most individuals in our society communicate through speech and do not know manual sign, children will be most able to communicate with hearing persons if they also learn to supplement sign with conventional language modalities. Yet, even the most observant and well-trained deaf children will not catch a majority of speech messages when relying only on residual hearing and speech reading. **Total communication** combines manual sign with oral methods of communication and is the most frequently adopted approach.

Assistive devices for children with hearing losses include hearing aids, which amplify the sound. These devices should be fitted at an early age to encourage hearing perception and listening skills necessary for language development. Hearing aids assist but do not replace natural hearing abilities. However, significant progress has been made in eliminating irrelevant background noise (What's New, 1999). "Completely-in-the-ear-canal" (CIC) aids and the invention of directional microphones allow for more natural amplification. Yet, young children do not automatically link the sounds heard through amplification to the sounds' sources. They must be taught to pay attention to sounds, to orient toward sound sources, and to discriminate between relevant and irrelevant noises. Various amplification devices are available and must be matched specifically to each child's characteristics: age, degree of hearing loss, family environment, and cognitive abilities.

Preschool programs serving children with hearing impairments require some unique considerations. Harrington and Meyers (1992) made the following recommendations:

◆ Access services by personnel with certification competencies for teachers of preschool children with hearing impairments as delineated by the Council of Education for the Deaf.
◆ Use transdisciplinary teaming, including an occupational therapist, physical therapist, psychologist, social worker, counselor, audiologist, speech-language pathologist, educator of the deaf, and a parent, to collaborate in assessment and planning.
◆ Obtain oral interpreters and/or sign interpreters as needed for children with profound deafness in mainstream settings.
◆ Adapt classrooms so that ceilings and walls use acoustical tiles, floors are carpeted, and visible fire alarm systems are installed.
◆ Furnish classes with amplification systems (e.g., FM auditory training system), captioning equipment, computer software designed for children with hearing impairments, and telecommunication devices (TDD) to interact with parents who are deaf and members of the deaf community.

As noted by Harrington and Meyers (1992), accommodation of classrooms for children with hearing impairments is expensive and will challenge service providers who are already uncertain of financial resources. Moreover, controversial findings on the relative benefits of mainstreamed versus self-contained programs for children with hearing impairments fail to provide overwhelming support for such costly modifications in regular classrooms. While some argue that integrated programs will lead to greater social and emotional competency as well as improved communication skills in a mainstream setting (Ryalls & Larouche, 1992), others argue that the effect is just the reverse. Opponents of mainstreaming believe that children with hearing losses will be so isolated from their peers who lack the skills to communicate effectively, that they will suffer socially and emotionally. In one study, self-reporting children who were hearing impaired and educated in mainstream settings rated their self-confidence and social competence higher than their peers in residential programs (Cartledge & Cochran, 1996). While more study is needed, it does at least appear, that placing students in mainstream settings does not harm them socially as many educators and parents are concerned.

Educating children with multiple disabilities poses more complex educational considerations. For example, children who are hearing impaired with learning disabilities may fail to thrive in highly structured environments which do not give them the opportunity to learn to adapt to natural changes in their environments (Mauk & Mauk, 1992). These children also tend to experience a greater degree of failure, whether mainstreamed or segregated, and therefore require opportunities that enhance their level of success and self-esteem.

INFORMING AND WORKING WITH PARENTS

Unless the cause of hearing loss is known, parents of children with hearing losses should receive genetic counseling since a large percentage of these children have inherited their disability. Very early in a child's life, parents of children with deafness must make a decision regarding linguistic instruction that will influence their child's entire life. Those parents who prefer their children be given every chance to become a part of the hearing world are likely to choose an educational program that emphasizes oral communication or total communication. Other parents might feel that a mainstream education would result in social and communicative isolation, particularly since communities of deaf individuals are often very active socially and rely on sign language for communication. While a self-contained manual language does not necessarily preclude integration, this approach is usually paired with a philosophy of isolation and specialized educational programs. Still other parents, due to an absence of community resources or their economic circumstances, feel that they have little choice other than to accept the only services that are offered. Parents must be provided with objective information on the implications of educational choices—and the advocacy skills to negotiate alternative services in areas of restricted options. The National Institute on Deafness and other Communication Disorders (NIDCD, 1999) is one of the most comprehensive resources for parents and educators of children with hearing losses. Through a variety of coordinated programs, NIDCD is engaged in continuing education, research, and dissemination of research and information. Linking parents to this and other helpful resources is made easier through emerging technology such as the Internet.

VISUAL IMPAIRMENTS

Visual acuity is measured by comparing the distance at which a person is able to see an object with clarity to the distance at which a person with average visual acuity (20/20) clearly sees the same object (see Figure 7–3). For example, what a person with 20/70 vision sees clearly only to 20 feet, a person with average visual acuity would be able to see accurately as far away as 70 feet. A visual impairment is legally defined as a visual acuity of 20/200 or less in the best eye with correction. Additionally, those whose peripheral field of vision is 20 degrees or less are considered legally blind, even though visual acuity might be normal (see Figure 7–4). **Low vision** is assessed when visual acuity is 20/70 or worse in the better eye with correction.

While legal blindness is a relatively low incidence disability (1 in 1000), approximately 30% to 70% of children with severe visual loss experience one or more other disabilities (Kirchner, 1988). Unfortunately, the incidence of visual impairments has not declined, but may be rising in the United States. For example, recent advances in medical technology, which allow very premature and low birth weight infants to survive, has radically increased the incidence of children with retinopathy of prematurity (Uslan, 1983). Also, research has demonstrated a relationship between

Figure 7–3
Visual acuity:
20/20 vision
compared to
20/70 vision

Figure 7–4
Peripheral
vision

poverty and the incidence of visual impairments, and poverty rates for young children continue to increase (Chalifoux & Fagan, 1997). Thus, it can be projected that the incidence of visual impairments will also increase. On the other hand, many causes of visual impairments might be considered preventable. Goldstein (1980) estimated that two out of three of the cases of blindness worldwide might be prevented through control of infection and malnutrition.

It is believed that newborns have a visual acuity of 20/200 and that children do not develop normal visual acuity until about age five (Allen & Marotz, 1989). This "developmental visual impairment" combined with infants' cognitive immaturity make assessment of mild to moderate visual impairment unreliable before six months of age. More important to children and their families than the clinical determination of visual disability is the retention of functional visual abilities. According to Hoon (1991), professionals should emphasize to parents the importance of maximizing a child's residual vision for use in everyday activities rather than focusing on visual deficiencies.

VISUAL PROCESS

Entering light initially strikes the **cornea** of the eye, which serves both a protective and refractive function. The cornea bends the angle of light and channels that light through the fluid-filled anterior chamber. Once the light strikes the **lens,** accommodation takes place, in which the lens changes shape, becoming more or less spherical depending on the nearness of an object or the intensity of light. The elastic properties of the lens permit it to cause a constriction of the iris, which widens the pupil (opening in the eye) to regulate the amount of light entering the vitreous humor (**accommodation**). The **vitreous humor** is a second fluid-filled space lying behind the eye's lens, which maintains the internal pressure of the eye and shape of the eyeball. The rays passing through this chamber intersect at a focal point on or near the **retina.** The retina is a complex neurological network directly linked to the central nervous system; neural fibers from the retina gather to form the **optic nerve,** which transmits an electrical image to the occipital portion of the brain (see Figure 7–5). Here the visual cortex of the brain perceives and interprets the images.

Refractive Errors

Defects in the curvature of cornea and lens or abnormal eyeball shape change the focal point of light rays and are referred to as refractive errors. **Myopia,** or nearsightedness, results when the shape of the eyeball is abnormally long (or less frequently due to corneal or lens curvature), causing the image of a distant object to converge in front of the retina. Infants who are nearsighted see near objects normally, while images of distant objects are distorted. The opposite is the case of **hyperopia,** or farsightedness, in which far objects are seen with greater acuity than near objects. In this case, the eyeball shape is abnormally short, and the image converges behind the retina. To remediate hyperopia and myopia, eyeglasses or contacts with an appropriately adjusted spherical (section) lens are placed before the eye. **Astigmatism** is caused when the cornea is abnormally shaped. An oval-shaped cornea will cause the light to be refracted unevenly. The fuzzy distortion that results from astigmatism can be corrected by using eyeglasses or contacts with parabolic- or toric-shaped lenses.

Figure 7–5
Visual process
and eye
anatomy

Errors in Binocular Vision

Six sets of muscles permit the eyes to act in concert to follow a moving object and to focus images correspondingly on both retinas. A disruption in this coordination will upset the correspondence and result in a double image being perceived by the cortex. In a chronic situation, referred to as **amblyopia,** the brain will suppress one of the images and the affected eye will begin to deteriorate in performance. **Strabismus,** also resulting from muscle dysfunction, is when the two eyes do not focus on the same image. One eye may be focused directly at an object and the other eye is turned elsewhere. Strabismus can usually be corrected through lenses, surgery, or muscle exercise programs. Untreated strabismus may progress into amblyopia.

Central Nervous System Dysfunctions

In instances where the eye physiology is not impaired, yet a child experiences loss of visual ability, there may be damage to the central nervous system. Damage to the optic nerve or the cerebral tissue within the occipital portion of the brain may cause **cortical visual impairments.** These visual losses may be complete or partial, though researchers have not been able to link the amount or type of loss to specific type of central nervous system damage (Hoon, 1991). Cortical visual loss may be paired with intrauterine and postnatal infection (e.g., syphilis, meningitis), traumatic brain injury (e.g., drowning), perinatal injury (e.g., anoxia), and seizures. Often, this type of visual impairment involves damage to the brain. Mental retardation may accompany cortical visual impairments.

Rhythmic eye twitching or tremors are referred to as **nystagmus.** The etiology of nystagmus may be either neurological or muscular, with the former generally associated with more serious visual impairments.

CAUSES OF VISUAL IMPAIRMENT

Perhaps half of all cases of blindness may be genetic in origin (Bateman, 1983). Two common genetic causes of visual impairments are associated with genetic syndromes: albinism and Down syndrome. Down syndrome is a chromosomal aberration that is commonly associated with such visual disorders as severe myopia, cataracts, amblyopia, strabismus, glaucoma, and nystagmus (Shapiro & France, 1985). All children with Down syndrome should have regular ophthalmological examinations. Visual impairments accompanying **albinism** are related to a lack of melanin or pigmentosa. The eyes of a child with albinism lack color and are extremely sensitive to light, requiring tinted lenses. Nystagmus is also frequently associated with albinism.

The most common cause of congenital visual impairment is exposure to infections. Rubella may lead to retinopathy, cataracts, glaucoma, and structural malformations. Cytomegalovirus, toxoplasmosis, herpes simplex, and congenital syphilis are associated with visual impairments ranging from lesions to central nervous system malformations. Researchers are also just beginning to understand the relationship between HIV infection and visual impairments in children. Visual impairments can also be the result of exposure to dangerous chemicals prenatally (e.g., alcohol) or postnatally (e.g., lead).

A **cataract** is a clouding or opacity of the lens. The location and degree of deviation from transparency caused by the cataract(s) will determine the amount of distortion and obstruction of vision. The treatment of cataracts involves surgery to remove the portion of the lens affected. Corrective lenses are necessary to compensate for the lens removed in surgery.

Glaucoma is caused by a buildup of pressure in the anterior chamber of the eye. In most cases, the onset of glaucoma is unrecognized until much damage has already been done to peripheral vision. Untreated, glaucoma will cause continued serious visual loss or blindness. However, medical treatment (usually medication) can arrest the otherwise progressive degeneration of vision. Since children with other visual losses often have secondary visual problems, they should be observed throughout childhood for signs of glaucoma (i.e., excessive tiredness, severe headaches, dizziness, loss of field vision, and tearing).

Late visual bloomers include those children who, like children with motor, language, and social developmental delays, experience maturational delays in visual ability (Harel, Holtzman, & Feinsod, 1985). These children appear to be blind at birth and during their first months of life, but they typically develop normal visual ability by 18 months to 3 years. Research on delayed visual development is sparse, though it seems that the syndrome is associated with delays in development of specific processes of the central nervous system (e.g., myelination).

DEVELOPMENTAL IMPLICATIONS AND RESOLUTIONS

Children with visual impairments, particularly those with other disabilities, display unusual patterns of eye contact. Yet, one of the first intentional acts of infants is eye gaze. Normal language, cognition, and social skill development, are dependent on eye gaze which sets the occasion for social and language interactions and provides visual memory that enables infants to feel "safe" in exploring their world (Morse, 1991). To mediate the visual attentional differences in children with visual impairments, Morse made the following recommendations to caregivers: develop a trusting interpersonal relationship; establish routine play and social interactions; use clear, colorful (if relevant), and closely spaced cues to attend; reduce irrelevant sensory information.

Children who are visually impaired will usually experience delays in other areas as well, even when they possess normal intelligence. Muscle tone is likely to be hypotonic since normal mobility is generally impeded (Teplin, 1983). Because language development depends on imitation of mouth movements as well as nonverbal language cues, children who are visually impaired often experience delays in speech development as well as in conversational abilities. This inability to see nonverbal cues and subtle forms of language may result in self-orientation or social isolation (Hoon, 1991). Finally, children with blindness frequently present stereotypical behaviors such as rocking or postural abnormalities (Batshaw & Perret, 1988).

One factor affecting the interaction between visual impairments and later functioning is the timing of onset. **Congenital** (born with) blindness and **adventitious** blindness (developed later) differentially affect the type of intervention a child might need. Because adventitious blindness occurs after a child has had visual experiences, such children are able to "picture" images of their world conceptually, if not visually, after sight is lost.

The primary goal of early intervention is to have children make the best use of their residual vision. According to Morse (1991), special training is needed to teach infants with blindness to "pay attention." Paying attention requires that infants learn to screen out irrelevant sensory stimuli while vigilantly seeking new information. Additionally, infants must learn to use previously gained information in new situations to make decisions. Very young children can be motivated to use their residual vision if caregivers limit the amount of assistance provided to that which is necessary to ensure safety and success. Beyond that, infants and toddlers should be encouraged to explore, to move independently about their environments, and to risk an occasional bump or bruise to increase mobility.

Prevention of secondary disabilities requires an interdisciplinary approach to give attention to physical development, language acquisition, and social skills. Caregivers can assist in facilitating normal development in other areas by providing enriching experiences with activities, materials, and interactions that make use of residual vision as well as tactile, auditory, kinesthetic, and olfactory senses.

INFORMING AND WORKING WITH PARENTS

As with any disability, team members who interact with parents should be considerate enough to present any new information related to the visual impairment more than once. It is almost certain that parents who receive a large amount of technical information, especially if this information leads to emotional reactions, will be unable to focus on the details of the conversation. Using the concept of anticipatory guidance, team members can time the delivery of information to intersect with parents' ability to "hear" and a child's need for services. This practice, of course, assumes the need to tailor timing to suit individual children and their families (Hoon, 1991).

Furthermore, information givers should be knowledgeable enough to be able to answer most questions that parents might ask. However, it is worse to give misinformation than to give no information, especially regarding developmental predictions of children's future visual abilities or related developmental prognoses. Whenever possible, vision specialists should assist in informing parents. It may also be appropriate and necessary to explain the nature of the visual loss to children themselves. For example, children with congenital blindness may not recognize a deficiency until they are told and realize how they are different from their peers.

The absence of visual referents that are gained from cumulative visual experiences prevents children with visual impairments from developing conceptual, perceptual, sensory, and body awareness of space and environment. Hence, a primary objective of early intervention should be to train **orientation** skills, which will enable young children with visual impairments to achieve **mobility.** Orientation training is necessary to enable young children with visual impairments to gain a sense of position in space. Children are taught to take advantage of other senses such as touch, smell, and hearing to replace sight. Mobility training should be coupled with orientation, that is, teaching children their location in the room as well as how to move around their environment. According to Clarke (1988), orientation and mobility technology underwent an exciting evolution during the 1980s (see Table 7–2).

Curriculum specifically designed for infants and toddlers includes precane skills, sensory awareness, trailing, using a sighted guide, and environmental familiarization. Advances in mobility devices for very young children generally consist of modified adult devices, such as shortened long canes, or devices specially designed for children, such as a push toy that provides both support and protection for a toddler who is blind. Selection of appropriate orientation and mobility adaptations should be based on several factors identified by Clarke (1988): a child's motor skills, degree of visual loss, concern for safety of the child and others, adaptability of the child to change required for continuous accommodation, need for formal training, degree of independence in travel required, cost (which can range from several thousand to just a few dollars), the need for maintenance, and the availability of technology.

Table 7–2   Mobility devices for infants and preschoolers.

Types of Devices	Product	Advantages
Electronic Travel Aids (ETAs): Electronic devices that detect obstacles and provide users with auditory and/or tactual signals.	Laser Cane: Nurion; Sonicguide: Wormaid International	May be used to teach concepts and stimulate reaching prior to locomotion.
Suspended Movement Devices: Devices suspended from an overhead support that allow freedom of movement within a limited space.	Baby Swings: "Jolly Jumpers"	Provide upright movement experiences in space.
Infant Walkers: Wheeled devices with seats that allow infants to propel themselves with their feet.	Commercial Walkers	May stimulate child due to change in environment.
Scooterboards: Small wooden, foam, or plastic platforms on wheels.	Cookie Monster Crawl-Along: Educational Teaching Aids Midline Positioning Scooter: Achievement Products	Allow for independent mobility in prone, supine, and seated positions; provide trunk support for creeping; allow hands to be free to manipulate objects.
Wheelchair Devices: Manual or battery-powered devices that transport nonambulatory children.	Manual Devices: Toddler Cart: Achievement Products Powered Devices: Amigo Mini: Amigo	May allow greater independence and exploration.
Cruising Surfaces: Surfaces used to pull to standing position and maintain balance while stepping.	Playpen; Cribs	Provide comfort and stability while moving about the environment. Help child to learn about the arrangement of space. Provide a training ground for learning to trail.
Push Toys (supported/stooped): Low, weighted toys or objects used for support while walking in a stooped posture.	Large Wooden Trucks; Large Beachballs	Allow child to practice balancing in semi-upright posture. Serve as bumpers to protect child from obstacles in path.
Orthopedic Walkers: Therapeutic support devices, without seats, used to assist in walking.	Children's Full Body Suspension Walker: Achievement Products	Serve as bumpers to protect child from obstacles in path.
Walking Hoops and Guiding Sticks: Hoops and sticks used to encourage walking without direct physical contact with another person.	Hula Hoops; PVC Pipes	Offer security and support while learning to walk without physical contact with another person.
Riding Roll Toys: Wheeled children's riding toys that are propelled by pushing with the feet.	Tyke Bikes: Environments, Inc.	Are "normal" devices used by nondisabled children. Serve as bumpers to protect child from obstacles in path.

Table 7–2 Mobility devices for infants and preschoolers. *(continued)*

Types of Devices	Product	Advantages
Push Toys (supported/upright): Wheeled children's push toys that offer support while walking upright.	"Tuff Stuff" Shopping Cart: Kaplan	Serve as bumpers to protect child from obstacles in path. Are "normal" devices used by nondisabled children.
Walking Ropes: One or two ropes, running horizontally, that serve as tactual guides while walking or running.	Rope Clothesline	Provide practice in trailing. Guide child in a straight line while walking or running.
Cane Instruments: Non-rolling devices that may be used in the environment as a bumper and a probe much as a long cane is used.	Hockey Sticks Plastic Baseball Bats	Are "normal" devices used by nondisabled children.
Canes: Standard canes modified for young children.	Collapsible or Rigid Canes: White Cane Instruments for the Blind (WCIB)	May be arced side to side to clear a complete path in front of child. May encourage confidence while walking independently. May help child to avoid the development of inappropriate gait patterns. May eliminate the need to remediate skills later on.

Source: Adapted from Clarke, K. L. (1988). Barriers or enablers: Mobility devices for visually impaired and multiply handicapped infants and preschoolers. *Education of the Visually Handicapped, 20,* 115–133.

Orientation and mobility (O & M) specialists are available and should be regularly consulted for selection, adaptation, and evaluation of mobility devices for specific children (Clarke, 1988). Guide dogs are not an option for infants and toddlers since canines cannot be assigned until children reach age 16. However, preparation in orientation and mobility, even in early childhood helps prepare children for independent movement and eventual guide dog ownership if needed.

A parent's role in facilitating language in infants who are visually impaired may be particularly difficult. As mentioned, vision is important to nonverbal communication (e.g., gestures, smiling, facial expressions) and to help parent-child dyads in communication regarding a mutual focus of attention. In the absence of these important communication tools, it appears that children who are visually impaired tend to have delayed language development, particularly in the area of pragmatics (Kekelis & Prinz, 1996). Communication of young children with visual impairments tends to be egocentric. Furthermore, parents, teachers, and other adults tend to limit the opportunities for meaningful conversation by visually impaired children by taking many more conversational turns and by using more directives and labeling, and less commenting and questioning than are provided for sighted children. Because infants and children who are visually impaired do not spontaneously give the same feedback in conversation as sighted children, it is important to teach parents (and teachers) to share conversational turns equitably, to ask meaningful questions and wait for the answers, and to make relevant comments and expect relevant comments about mutual experiences.

Table 7–3 Factors leading to disadvantage in children who are visually impaired.

Risk Factors	Cause(s)	Outcome
Limited financial resources	As child: Greater likelihood of only one employed parent As adult: Unemployment, underemployment	Lack of assets and material possessions; dispossession of hopes and dreams
Substandard housing	Limited financial resources; negative attitudes of landlords	Run-down, overcrowded houses—especially detrimental to children who are visually impaired, who benefit from quiet areas to study; more likely to live in high-crime areas, further limiting mobility
Educational deficits	Disability-Specific areas of education are usually neglected; often fail to learn appropriate social mannerisms	Limited self-confidence; poor social adaptation; leads to sedentary, isolated lifestyles
Poor health, physical or mental	Isolation; disease process that leads to visual impairment	Negative feelings of emotional well-being
Family difficulties	Parental: Stress of adjusting to child with disability Child: Overprotection	Parental marital discord Limited independent living skills—causing further familial hardship

Source: Chalifoux, L. M., & Fagan, B. (1997). Labeling children who are visually impaired "disadvantaged." *Journal of Visual Impairment and Blindness, 91,* 531–539.

As compared to children who are sighted, those with visual impairments may face a lifetime of "disadvantage." Chalifoux and Fagan (1997) described a paradigm of poverty associated with children who are blind that conspires to limit the potential of these children (Table 7–3). Knowledge of such disadvantage can help educators anticipate and act to prevent such factors from adding further handicaps to children who are visually impaired.

Chalifoux and Fagan made several recommendations for actions that can be taken to mitigate the factors that lead to the developmental and economic deprivation of children who are visually impaired.

◆ Early education should be organized around hands-on experiences in all important environments, where sighted persons engage in running commentaries about the world these children are experiencing.

◆ Planning for adulthood should take place in early childhood, where parents learn to become active in planning transitions that will lead to independent, confident children.

◆ Involvement in recreational activities that involve risk taking, fitness, and social integration.

◆ Families require social support, respite, and sufficient financial security which often requires the involvement of extended family members and community agencies.

◆ Children require early and ongoing social skills training to emphasize social awareness, pragmatic interaction skills, and avoidance of stereotypic behavior.

<table>
<tr><td>Case
Study</td></tr>
</table>

EARLY DIAGNOSIS: INTERVIEW WITH MARSHA MOORE

Almost from the very beginning, before he was three weeks old, I had the sinking suspicion that there was something really wrong with Michael. He did not respond to me. He did not quiet to my voice or touch. He would not, maybe could not, make eye contact. He cried day and night, even during bath time or while nursing. He did not nurse well. He was stiff and would not cuddle, but rather would arch his back and flail his arms and hands. He was our sixth child and we were experienced parents, but Michael was not like the rest. We took him several times to our new hometown general practitioner. The doctor believed that Michael was "just colicky," and prescribed a medicine to relieve him (and I suppose the entire family) of the discomfort we all felt.

When Michael was almost four months old, we returned to Denver to visit our previous pediatrician. At first, the appointment was relaxed and friendly. We exchanged small talk about our new home in Wyoming and our other children. Once the examination began, it was apparent that our doctor had that same sinking notion that something was just not right. He examined Michael for several minutes, and then called in his physician's assistant and one of his nurses. All three continued to examine Michael, coaxing him to track their pen lights and a squeak toy; pulling him to sit and checking out his fat, pink perfect little body. I continued to jabber on nervously about all my motherly concerns. In my heart I hoped that I had been foolish to feel so anxious. They said little to each other and absolutely nothing to Jim or me. Perhaps we were expected to read minds! Finally our doctor turned to us and said, "I think Michael is blind."

We had seen Michael reach for toys. We had seen him stare into the lights over the kitchen countertop. We had seen him focus on his Mobil over his crib. And although both eyes often crossed and at times seemed disconnected, I still could not believe the diagnosis of "blind." Later we would find that his vision problems were just the "tip of the iceberg."

Before we left to return home, our pediatrician arranged for us to see a pediatric ophthalmologist, and a neurologist and to get a CT scan at a nearby hospital. We had driven almost five hundred miles for medical information and did not want to go home without some answers. It was almost 9 p.m. by the time we left the neurologist's office. Michael had been poked and prodded for almost 12 hours and was tired, over stimulated and literally "strung out." Jim and I were numb. How could all of this be happening to us?

The results of the CT scan and both examinations were inconclusive. Michael's eyes were healthy. He had strabismus, but there seemed to be no physical reason why he would not be able to see. There was a question, however, as to whether his brain could "see" and whether a label of cortical blindness would be appropriate. The neurologist was guarded in his prognosis. The CT scan showed irregularities in Michael's brain. He acknowledged that Michael's development was a little slow, but we were assured that there was little reason to worry. We were instructed to contact a therapist who worked in the outskirts of Denver. Mike's condition was not "that" delayed and would probably improve as he matured with added infant stimulation. Somehow, neither Jim or I was convinced.

We drove all night and arrived home early the next morning. We said little to each other during the trip back. I cried, and he sighed! We both recognized that this was only the beginning.

Michael was five months old when he began with his first therapy session in Denver. The therapist was a true godsend. Because we lived so far away, she scheduled the entire afternoon for Michael. We brought the whole family to his first appointment. Therapy was definitely going to be a group effort! All winter long, we worked with Michael on a daily basis, going through the routines that the therapist had taught us and improvising along the way, but we saw little change. Michael had learned to independently roll over, but still was unable to sit up by himself. He could not yet position himself on hands and knees. He was not even belly crawling. His mode of transportation was either to roll from place to place or to arch and push himself on his back. I spent many hours on the floor with him, trying in every way I knew possible to encourage him to explore his world. I would leave little trails of marshmallows and graham crackers all over the carpet in hope that he would be motivated to creep to get them. We sang to him, read to him, stacked blocks with him. We bought bags of lentils and rice for him to play in. We made pudding finger paints. We purchased vibrating pillows and hot and cold water bottles. At ten months, he was still crying through the night, and although I was still nursing him, he had never made eye contact with me.

He had earlier made somewhat of a small "breakthrough" with Jim. When he was almost eight months old, Jim was playing on the sofa with him; talking, growling, tickling him, when suddenly, Jim whispered "Look, look." I looked over to see that Michael was staring intently at Jim's face. Jim was beaming and did not move for fear

Michael Moore
plays the piano at
home.

that Mike would lose contact. It took only a few seconds before Michael began to cry big alligator tears. Why was this connection so frightening to Michael? Why did he pull away from us so? What was wrong with *us?* We both felt so helpless!

Our first Wyoming winter seemed very long and very bleak for a multitude of reasons. I stayed in telephone contact with our Denver pediatrician and with the therapist, but was not able to get back to Denver until April, when the snow finally melted and the roads cleared. At that time, Michael saw a battery of specialists at Denver Children's Hospital. He would be a year old in May and there was still no conclusive diagnosis.

We scheduled a week long hospital assessment again in July and saw several different "developmental" authorities who worked out of other clinics. These trips were so difficult for Mike. He was in strange places, with strange people, strange routine, strange food. He seemed so disoriented and fussed or cried constantly. Yet, this time we received a diagnosis. Finally, after fourteen months, we had a name to give to what was happening with Mike: infantile autism with severe mental retardation. We were relieved and very sad. How could Michael ever enjoy this type of existence? How could his life be worth anything? We felt so angry. This wasn't fair! What did Michael ever do to deserve something like this? What did any of us do to deserve this? Where do we go from here?

INFECTIONS IN EARLY CHILDHOOD

Human beings have been afflicted with both common and complex ailments since the beginning of recorded history. Sore throats, earaches, coughing, and fevers commonly interfere with the normal activities of daily living, and are those symptoms that cause the most concern for parents of young children (Kai, 1996). These are generally symptoms indicating an invasion by biological agents. The interaction between humans and the microorganisms that cause infection is complex. These **biological agents** cause damage to human cells by either living on cells or by causing inflammation of the cells. **Inflammation** is caused by the **toxin** given off by the particular **organism** causing a specific infection. This toxin acts like a poison to human cells. Biological agents may travel throughout the body via the bloodstream or by way of the lymph system. The effect of an infection on a particular individual is dependent on the agent involved, the overall health of the individual when exposed, and the age of the person affected.

For some infecting agents, premature babies, term newborns, infants, and young children are affected differently than older children and mature adults. Reactions among very young children may include lowered rather than elevated body temperatures, a decrease instead of increase in the total white blood cell count, and a more rapid progression of an infecting agent producing more significant symptoms. In addition, very young children have immature immune systems and are less capable of dealing with an infection than an individual with a mature and healthy system. Individuals with compromised immune systems, such as infants with chronic diseases, are also at a much higher risk of developing infection. As a result of these factors, neonates, infants, and young children may have more frequent episodes of significant infections that require more extensive interventions. Biological agents that

*Due to complica-
tions associated
with meningitis,
this child lost part
of both legs in
early childhood.*

may cause infections in humans include bacteria, viruses, mycoplasmas, fungi, protozoa, rickettsias, and nematodes. Two of the most common infectious agents are
bacteria and viruses.

BACTERIAL INFECTIONS

By adulthood, everyone has experienced an infection. In spite of this, few have actually seen what causes the illness. **Microbes,** or germs, are so small that they can only
be seen through a microscope, and **bacteria** are microbes that are found abundantly
in nature. Many bacteria are incapable of causing disease, and live in harmony with humans. Yet, even bacteria that generally are beneficial can cause significant infections in
humans under the right circumstances by becoming **pathogenic** (disease causing).

Pathogenic bacteria create infections that continue to be a significant cause of infant **morbidity** and **mortality** in the United States, constituting approximately 20%
of neonatal deaths each year (Magid, 1995). Such infections can occur either prior to
delivery from an infected mother or shortly after delivery from exposure to infected
persons or objects in the environment. An infant's condition can be profoundly affected, depending on the particular organism responsible for a specific infection and
the time between exposure to infection and initiation of appropriate treatment. For

example, infants infected by **group B streptococcus** may show subtle objective symptoms such as mild respiratory distress, but the infants deteriorate quickly if not treated, to the point that death may occur. Medical care providers need to use observable signs along with a maternal history and a review of risk factors when deciding whether to start early and aggressive treatment.

A history of poverty may place a child at risk for the development of infections. For example, childhood vaccination is significantly lower for children who are poor and live in inner cities, and for minorities (i.e., African American and Hispanic) (Kenyon, Matuck & Stroh, 1998; Vaccination Coverage, 1998). A direct relationship exists between socioeconomic status and low birth weight, as well as the development of both prenatal and postnatal infections (Hughes & Simpson, 1995). The greater the degree of poverty, the lower an infant's birth weight, and consequently the greater the vulnerability to infection. Poverty is also linked to many of the maternal conditions that lead to infection such as low birth weight, poor nutrition, environmental injustice (e.g., toxic waste dumps, pollution, crime), lack of prenatal care, drugs, alcohol, smoking, and inadequate attention to chronic disease states, such as hypertension. Appropriate assessment of the physical condition of an infant at delivery provides health care workers with the information necessary to determine risk factors that may indicate the presence of a bacterial agent. Keys to effective treatment of an infected infant are awareness of the possibility of infection, assessment of presenting signs and symptoms, and aggressive treatment of any suspected infection in an at-risk infant.

Infants born through infected amniotic fluid or those who acquire a bacterial infection shortly after birth are at high risk for disability or death from the infection. Initial symptoms of an infection include temperature instability, poor feeding, respiratory distress, low blood sugar, and lethargy. Symptoms may also be as subtle as a lack of appropriate response to environmental stimulation. Multiple physical system failure can occur very rapidly in an affected newborn. In those infants with multiple system involvement for whom death does not occur, there can be significant long-term developmental effects. Those disabilities occurring most frequently include visual impairment, hearing loss, and mental retardation. Such secondary disabilities may be the result of the infectious process or a result of the treatment used to save an infant's life. Infants experiencing infections at birth, or shortly afterwards, warrant early screening for developmental progress, identification of potential problems, and possible initiation of early intervention programs to provide the opportunity for full development.

Table 7–4 TORCH infections.

T	Toxoplasmosis
O	Other (Varicella-Zoster, Mumps, Rubeola, Syphilis, Hepatitis, HIV/AIDS)
R	Rubella
C	Cytomegalic Inclusion Virus (CMV)
H	Herpes simplex

CLOSE-UP

APPROPRIATE PRINCIPLES IN THE USE OF ANTIBIOTICS IN CHILDREN

HIV/AIDS emerged as the most deadly epidemic of the second half of the 20th century, even though its devastation trails far behind viral and bacterial epidemics in human history. However, the discovery of antibiotics in this same century yielded astounding progress in controlling diseases that once presented ominous health threats. Now, as we enter a new millennium, overuse of the very antibiotics that saved countless lives, threatens to place humans at even greater health risk. Antibiotics like penicillin have been effective in destroying bacterial infections such as otitis media, pneumonia, and sinusitis in their human hosts. However, bacteria are incredibly adaptive and in less than 50 years, almost all common microbes have managed to mutate into antibiotic resistant strains.

Three factors have led to the overuse of antibiotics. First, there are two types of antibiotics, wide spectrum and narrow spectrum. The former are useful in treating a wide variety of bacteria, while the latter are useful in treating very specific bacteria. While wide spectrum antibiotics are often prescribed for the sake of expedience, their overuse hastens the resistance of bacteria. Second, American families have become overdependent on antibiotics in order to keep children in school/daycare so that parents (both of whom usually work full time) can avoid taking time off work to care for sick children. Parents have increasingly put pressure on health care providers to prescribe antibiotics for children, even when the infections are minor or when antibiotic prescriptions are inappropriate (i.e., for viral infections that are unaffected by antibiotics). Third, congregation of children in daycare centers has accelerated the spread of antibiotic resistant bacteria. Similarly, the American work culture, which places a premium on work productivity has created "toxic environments," where people go to work when they are ill rather than take time off to get well or return to work before they are well, thereby spreading the disease resistant bacteria. This practice may be further compounded with the possibility that this return to work is abetted by wide spectrum antibiotics.

Some specialists warn that we may be evolving, health wise, into a "postantibiotic era," where few effective treatments are available to patients with microbial infections. In order to prevent this from happening, several steps need to be taken: (1) prescription of narrow spectrum antibiotics; (2) educate parents (and physicians) that viral infections will not respond to antibiotics; (3) encourage parents to resist repeated dependence upon antibiotic prescriptions for mild bacterial infections, even if it means the illness would last longer and possibly delay return to work/school.

Source: Green, M. (1997). Appropriate principles in the use of antibiotics in children. *Clinical Pediatrics, 36,* 207–209.

VIRAL INFECTIONS

Viruses are the smallest infectious agents and are more difficult to identify and control because of their unique properties. Like bacteria, viruses are biological agents but differ from true microorganisms. A virus consists of genetic material, either DNA or RNA, and an enclosing shell of protein. Genetic materials contained in a virus's DNA or RNA make the virus capable of reproducing and attaching itself to susceptible cells. Most viruses have specific cell preferences where they will attach and reproduce. Examples of cell preferences may be nerve, muscle, or blood cells. Once in a host individual, viruses can survive in an inactive state for extended time periods with activation and occasional reactivation periods that produce the disease itself. Other viral infections do not produce recognizable diseases in the infected individual but create a *carrier* state enabling an individual to transfer viruses to others.

Prevention of many dangerous viral diseases has been accomplished largely through the development of **vaccines.** These consist of either active viral replications that have a decreased capability of causing infection and disease or an inactive virus introduced into the human being to activate the immune system to produce **antibodies.** Through a series of childhood immunizations, many common viral diseases such as polio and smallpox have been nearly eliminated or greatly reduced in early childhood (see Figure 7–6). Once established, antibodies prevent an acute infection if the individual is exposed to an active virus of normal virulence. Potent drugs are continuously being

Figure 7–6
Recommended immunization schedule

	Diphtheria, Tetanus, & Pertussis (DTP)	Polio	Measles, Mumps, & Rubella (MMR)	Tetanus Diphtheria	Haemophilus Influenzae Type B (HIb)	Hepatitis B
Birth - 2 weeks						shot
2 months	shot	oral			shot	shot
4 months	shot	oral			shot	
6 months	shot	oral			shot	shot
12-15 months			shot		shot	
15-18 months	shot					
4-6 years	shot	oral	shot			
10-12 years						* shot
14-16 years				shot		
Based on National Standards						

* shot If not done earlier, 3-dose series between 11-12 years of age.

shot immunization delivered by shot

oral immunization taken orally

Table 7–5   Characteristics/outcomes of congenital infections.

	Toxoplasmosis	Chickenpox	Hepatitis B	Syphilis	HIV/AIDS	Rubella	CMV	Herpes
Blindness	X	X		X		X	X	X
Deafness	X	X		X		X	X	X
Retardation	X	X		X		X	X	X
Seizures	X	X		X		X	X	X
Liver affect			X	X	X		X	
Spleen affect			X	X	X		X	
Hydrocephalus	X	X		X			X	X
Microcephaly	X	X		X		X	X	X
Jaundice			X		X		X	
Brain atrophy	X	X		X		X	X	X
Transmitted at birth		X	X	X	X	X		X
Transplacental	X	X	X	X	X	X	X	?
"Shed" virus			X	X	X	X	X	X
Hydrops				X				

developed to counteract specific viral agents. The success of these drugs in preventing or controlling viral infections has been variable. When prevention is not possible, antiviral drugs specific to a given virus itself can shorten the duration of some viral diseases (Margo & Shaughnessy, 1998). Many serious viral infections such as hepatitis B and HIV with neither vaccination or cure, fall into this category.

Viral infections and many of the common congenital disabilities related to specific agents are frequently discussed under the umbrella of the *TORCH infections. (See Table 7.4)* Many professionals add syphilis to this group as a separate entity and refer to them as the STORCH infections. In this text, syphilis will be included under other infections (O). The letters TORCH represent toxoplasmosis (T), other infections (O), rubella (R), cytomegalic inclusion virus (C), and herpes (H). Because of the variability in pathology and outcome of these infections, they are usually discussed as independent entities (see Table 7–5).

Toxoplasmosis

Pregnant women must be especially careful to avoid infection by **toxoplasmosis** (*Toxoplasma gondii*), a **protozoan,** acquired by humans from contact with the feces of infected cats or birds and from the ingestion of raw or partially cooked meat. This infection is discussed as part of the TORCH viral infections since the protozoan acts upon the RNA and DNA of the cell in the same manner as viruses. Likewise, antibodies are developed following acute infections.

This infection can be acquired by a pregnant woman during any stage of pregnancy and subsequently transmitted to an unborn fetus. Maternal infections during either the first or second trimester appear to be most commonly associated with infections that cross the placenta **(transplacental)**. This occurs when the protozoa cross from the maternal side of the placenta to the fetal side, infecting the developing fetus. Congenital toxoplasmosis infections (acquired before birth) can cause significant abnormalities. Fetal conditions resulting from an acute infection are dependent on the gestation of the fetus at the time of infection.

Prevention of toxoplasmosis can be accomplished by educating women of child-bearing age to avoid the ingestion of undercooked meat and contact with excrement from cats and birds. It is also important to recognize that, in rare instances, untreated maternal infections can affect subsequent pregnancies with fetal infections and an increased incidence of in utero fetal death.

Fetal effects of congenitally acquired toxoplasmosis often include a classical triad of hydrocephaly, cerebral calcification, and **chorioretinitis** (inflammation of the retina and blood vessels that supply the retina with nutrition) with resulting visual impairment. Other features commonly associated with congenital toxoplasmosis include microcephaly, deafness, seizures, **encephalitis,** enlargement of the spleen and liver, anemia, jaundice, and mental retardation. The infection itself may not always be apparent at birth and frequently the onset of symptoms is delayed for several months. Treatment of an infected mother may include drug therapy, but most drugs are not effective at treating an infected infant. Though these agents are useful in destroying the harmful protozoa, damage already done to the infected infant cannot be reversed.

The prognosis for infants born with congenital toxoplasmosis infection is poor. As many as 15% of infected infants who are born alive will die within the neonatal period, and 85% of the survivors have severe developmental delays and vision problems (Leclair, 1980). Long-term care includes ongoing assessment for detection of developmental problems and initiation of early intervention programs.

Rubella

Rubella, also known as German measles, generally causes minor illness in children but is much more of a problem for a pregnant woman. This viral infection has been preventable by immunization since 1969. A woman may be susceptible if she has not had rubella in the past or has failed to develop sufficient antibodies due to inadequate immunization. An exposed, pregnant woman may pass the infection to her fetus through the placenta. Fetal effects are thought to be the most devastating during the first trimester when the virus attacks the developing organs and tissues of the embryo; however, evidence suggests that rubella transmitted during the fourth and fifth month of pregnancy also results in fetal infections and significant fetal effects.

Stillbirth is a common outcome of congenital rubella infection. Other common fetal effects include microcephaly, cataract formation, significant cardiac anomalies, and deafness. Many infants born with congenital infection also demonstrate intrauterine growth retardation. Infants born with congenital rubella syndrome who suffer from severe intrauterine growth retardation, microcephaly, and other symptoms of central nervous system disease have an 80% mortality rate within the first year of life (Bolognese, Aldinger, & Roberts, 1981). This risk is especially true if these infants also suffer from associated defects such as cardiac malformations. Such abnormalities may be particularly difficult to manage because of the constellation of life-threatening problems associated with rubella syndrome.

Some infants born with congenital rubella have no apparent symptoms at birth. Yet, 70% of these infants will show effects of the disease before reaching five years of age. The effects most frequently seen include hearing loss, cataracts, and autism, abnormal behavior patterns, impulsivity, hyperactivity, and learning disabilities

(Mauk & Mauk, 1992). The long-term outlook for children with congenital rubella often involves multiple disabilities and requires intensive intervention.

Of concern is the finding that infants with no obvious effects at birth can shed large amounts of active virus for up to 18 months, infecting others, without caregivers being aware of the condition. Shedding occurs through the infant's urine, stool, and saliva. Individuals coming into contact with shedding infants need to be aware of the infection in order to take appropriate personal precautions to prevent the spread of active virus. Health care professionals and caregivers who are not adequately immunized or who have not had a previous rubella infection should refrain from contact with an infant with rubella syndrome. Even though rubella has been almost entirely eradicated through early childhood vaccinations, publicity on the possible effects of the MMR (Measles, Mumps & Rubella) immunization has led to a decline in MMR immunizations since 1997 (Thomas, Salmon, & King, 1998). This decline will almost certainly lead to an increase in the number of cases of congenital rubella. Individuals placed within situations in which exposure may occur (e.g., daycare settings or classrooms) should establish whether they have adequate immunity. This can be done through laboratory testing prior to involvement.

Treatment recommendations:

◆ A neonate born with rubella needs to be isolated from contact with other infants and nonimmunized children and adults for up to a year
◆ Assessment of the physical and developmental needs of the affected infant is necessary so appropriate early intervention can be planned
◆ Special attention must be paid to any associated defects, especially cardiac, that place infected infants at a higher risk for secondary infections
◆ Attention to nutrition should be vigilant, as poor feeding can lead to failure to thrive
◆ Early eye and ear examinations to determine visual and hearing needs
◆ Referrals to community agencies that provide services for infants with significant disabilities are almost always necessary

Cytomegalic Inclusion Virus
Cytomegalic inclusion virus is the most common congenital viral infection. Approximately 80% of adults have antibodies in their blood for human **cytomegalic inclusion viral infection (CMV)** though the causative infection may have produced no noticeable symptoms. Between 10 and 15% of infants infected with CMV at birth will be affected, while the remaining 85–90% of infected infants are asymptomatic (Mauk & Mauk, 1992). Moreover, a large segment of the general population tests positively by the end of adolescence, indicating a past primary infection. This medium-sized virus is one of the four herpes viruses seen in humans; the three others are herpes simplex, varicella-zoster (chickenpox), and Epstein-Barr virus. A pregnant woman who becomes infected with CMV, or who experiences a reactivation of a past CMV infection can transmit the virus to her unborn child. Such transmission can cause serious consequences, including brain damage. Prevention of CMV infections is a prime goal of research, though, to date, no effective prevention or treatment has been established.

Live CMV virus can be transmitted throughout pregnancy, producing congenital neonatal infections at any point prior to delivery. Reported rates of transplacental transmission to a developing fetus differ significantly, from 20% to 45% (Preece et al., 1983). Studies have not indicated that primary infection during the first trimester produces more serious complications for the fetus than infection later in the pregnancy (Preece et al., 1983). This finding does not change the fact that in known infections, fetal effects may be predicted based on the gestational age of the pregnancy when the infection occurred. There is no question, however, that cytomegalovirus can cause a significant interruption in the normal developmental progress of a fetus.

Specific congenital anomalies that have been noted in neonates born with congenital CMV infections include microcephaly, deafness, chorioretinitis, optic atrophy, enlarged liver and spleen, platelet destruction, calcifications in solid organs (such as the liver) and the brain, seizures, Dandy-Walker malformations (cystic formations that replace solid structure of the brain), intrauterine growth retardation, congenital heart defects, and abdominal wall defects. Even infants who show no apparent infection at delivery have shown delays in speech and language development on follow-up.

Current medical treatment for a symptomatic infant is limited. Generally, care is supportive, aimed toward treatment of the symptoms presented by an individual infant. **Antiviral** drugs may be used, especially in infants with life-threatening infection, who display central nervous system symptoms. However, the adverse effects of these drugs must be carefully considered to determine whether the benefits outweigh the risks. Infants born with microcephaly as a result of congenital CMV infection frequently display significant developmental impairment. This finding supports the suggestion that the microcephaly is the result of intrauterine viral encephalitis. Encephalitis frequently results in brain cell death, which causes a halt in brain growth or shrinking of brain tissue.

Infants born with congenital CMV infection shed live virus through urine, stool, and other body fluids, including saliva, throughout their lifetime. Nursing mothers with current infections will also shed live virus through their breast milk, though this resolves once the active infection state is over. The definitive diagnosis of a suspected neonatal infection is made through isolation of the virus from a urine or saliva sample. No specific isolation of infected infants or children is required; however, pregnant women should not care for infected children. Caregivers who are pregnant can also acquire an infection through the handling of infected breast milk. Awareness of an infection or of those infants and children affected with congenital disease is critical in preventing the infection of a pregnant caregiver. The suggestion that a relationship exists between recurrent CMV infections and the development of acquired immune deficiency syndrome (AIDS) in at-risk individuals is also being explored.

Extensive resources may be necessary to meet the developmental needs of infants born with congenital CMV. Assessment of an infant to determine risk for developmental delay and to identify interventions is essential before initial discharge from the hospital. Reassessment of an infected infant must be done at intervals to determine if appropriate programs are in place to meet individual and family needs. Visual screening to identify impairments is a high priority. If problems are detected, neurological assessment determines if visual disturbances are a result of physical or cortical damage and can determine appropriate methods for early intervention.

Developmental impairments related to hearing loss also require monitoring. Current research attempts to identify the best method of early diagnosis of sensorineural hearing loss resulting from congenital CMV infection, especially in infants who present with **asymptomatic** congenital infection. These infants appear to be at significantly increased risk for late onset hearing loss (Hicks et al., 1993).

Initiation of physical and occupational therapy programs to improve outcomes need to be established and undertaken within the parameters of providing service to the entire family unit. Support services should be provided to parents or caregivers with realistic information based on individual evaluation regarding an infant's long-term outcome.

Herpes

Genital **herpes** infections are among the most common venereal diseases in the United States. Approximately 40 million people have herpes. In adults, the virus produces itching, burning, soreness, and small blisters in the genital area. The blisters burst to leave small, painful ulcers, which heal within 10 to 21 days. Subsequent attacks tend to occur after sexual intercourse, after sunbathing, or when the affected person is run down. There is no cure for herpes, and sexual activity should be avoided until the symptoms have disappeared.

Herpes simplex virus types 1 and 2 are closely related and share 50% of their basic genetic code (Grossman, 1980). Herpes simplex type 1 is generally associated with oral lesions but can also be present with infection at other body sites. Herpes simplex type 2 is typically associated with genital infection and, as with type 1, can also occur at other body sites. Herpes belong to a larger group of viruses that have common features; included in this category are CMV, varicella-zoster (chickenpox), and Epstein-Barr virus (mononucleosis).

Both primary infections and reactivation of the dormant virus result in shedding of live virus. This shedding is of critical importance to a pregnant woman since acquisition of the virus during pregnancy may have adverse effects on a fetus. Although transmission is rare, congenital herpes usually occurs when a woman has her first herpes episode early in pregnancy (Planned Parenthood, 1998).

Neonatal infections are usually acquired during passage through an infected birth canal in a normal vaginal delivery. This makes it vital that pregnant women with a history of genital herpes and their health care providers be certain that no lesions are visible (indicating an active infection) in the birth canal. The presence of lesions or a herpes-positive culture is an indication for delivery by cesarean section.

Women who have a primary herpes type 2 infection during pregnancy may experience more spontaneous abortions and more premature deliveries than those with reactivation of the dormant virus during pregnancy. There have been reports of this virus crossing the placenta, but such cases are rare. In most cases, affected newborns are exposed to the shed virus in the birth canal. Approximately 33–50% of infants who undergo vaginal birth when the mother is experiencing her first episode of genital herpes will acquire the disease.

Neonates exposed to herpes infection generally are without any identifiable symptoms at birth. Symptoms include infection of the central nervous system. These symptoms may include irritability, vomiting, and the onset of seizures (Gast, 1983). It is difficult to diagnose very young children, who may also show symptoms of other disorders and then progress rapidly to herpes encephalitis or meningitis though this is not the generally recognized course of the disease (Margo & Shaughnessy, 1998). Usually encephalitis does not develop until later in the pattern of herpes infection (Whitley, Yeager, & Kartus, 1983). A rapid progression of the disease decreases the likelihood of success of the treatment.

It is estimated that 50% of neonates who acquire a herpes infection will die. Of those who survive, approximately 30% will have major neurological deficits as a result of the infection (Gast, 1983). Structural damage in the brain results from viral destruction of the gray and white matter. Hence, normal brain growth will be retarded, producing conditions such as hydrocephalus with frequent seizures, reduction in cortical growth with concurrent visual and hearing impairment, and mental retardation.

Specific focal areas of brain infection may frequently be determined in the presence of seizures by EEG (Whitley, Soong, & Linneman, 1982). This finding was the result of research showing that certain types of abnormal electrical activity are associated with herpetic lesions within the brain (Kohl & James, 1985; Whitley et al., 1983). Measurement of seizure activity utilizing electroencephalography may be useful in tracking herpetic lesions and determining if there is any extension, especially during episodes of reactivation. Antiviral agents have been developed to treat herpes simplex infections in neonates, infants, children, and adults.

Infants who survive systemic herpes infections require developmental assessment and appropriate referrals for services prior to discharge from the hospital. Early intervention planning includes provisions for vision, hearing, physical, and occupational therapy. Caregivers need to be aware that these infants and children can shed active virus from lesions during reactivation phases and should take the appropriate steps to avoid infection. Protection includes covering the lesions and preventing direct contact of the affected area by other children and adults. Since many of these children also have frequent episodes of seizure activity, protective measures (e.g., head gear, removal of dangerous items) may be indicated.

OTHER VIRAL INFECTIONS

Under the "O" or "Other" category of TORCH are a variety of diseases, many of which are common childhood illnesses, such as chickenpox and mumps. Usually, though not always, these illnesses cause only temporary problems for an infant. Even when exposed in utero, there may be no long-term effects to an infant. However, HIV/AIDS, syphilis, and hepatitis are also among the "Other" diseases, and in almost all cases, these illnesses cause severe disabilities and/or death.

Chickenpox, Mumps, and Measles

Chickenpox is typically a childhood disease but when a pregnant woman becomes infected, her unborn child is at serious risk because of the infection. **Varicella-zoster** (Herpes virus varicella or V-Z virus) is a member of the DNA herpes viruses. Primary infections of varicella virus (chickenpox) produce immunity, though late reactivation of dormant virus residing in nerve cells can result in shingles (zoster) in an older child or adult. However, there is no documentation of adverse effects of reactivated virus with the presentation of shingles in a pregnant woman, fetus, or neonate. Susceptible individuals who experience prolonged contact with infected persons are at a very high risk for developing infection. Vaccinations are available for all three of these diseases.

Pregnant nonimmune women should avoid contact with people known to be infected with chickenpox. Because the virus is so capable of invading and causing infection, most individuals have acquired immunity through past infection before reaching the childbearing years. Therefore, chickenpox (V-Z virus) rarely occurs during pregnancy. Its incidence is as low as 1 to 7 cases in 10,000 pregnancies (Herrmann, 1982). Yet maternal infections can occur at any point during the pregnancy of a nonimmune mother and will have a significant effect on the neonate. Though rare, older children who develop infection can experience the same complications from the disease. Developmental disabilities in older children are generally related to the effects of encephalitis.

The more serious neonatal effects of V-Z infections result from a maternal infection early in the pregnancy and lead to congenital effects. Congenital varicella-zoster syndrome can result in a condition in which the brain stops growing and shrinks; the remaining space is taken by fluid-filled cysts. Microcephaly, chorioretinitis, cataracts, auditory nerve paralysis, and mental retardation with concurrent seizures can be the consequence. Other frequently occurring effects include limb deformities (most commonly involving one extremity), absence of fingers/toes, and eye abnormalities. In some cases, congenital infection is followed by skin scarring that frequently occurs on the limb that is deformed (Herrmann, 1982).

Another childhood disease that presents risks for pregnant women is mumps, a communicable virus causing swelling of one or both of the parotid glands that are located at the junction of the lower jaw and the neck. Currently, mumps are preventable through immunization with the live attenuated mumps virus vaccine that induces antibody production and protects an individual against acute infection. Acute mumps infections are generally self-limiting, lasting 9 to 14 days, with few complications. The most common residual effect of a mumps infection is deafness (Korones, 1988). There do not appear to be any specific congenital malformations associated with maternal mumps. However, infants exposed to mumps infections require early hearing screening with consistent follow-up. Identification of hearing impairments necessitates inclusion in early intervention programs to prevent secondary delays in other areas of development.

Measles virus, also called hard measles, is a communicable virus, like the mumps virus, that also produces a highly contagious infection. The virus is generally spread by droplets carried through the air, thus infecting susceptible individuals through the respiratory tract. Measles vaccine, introduced in 1963, has greatly reduced the incidence of epidemic outbreaks of measles in the United States. Underdeveloped countries have not enjoyed the same progress. Without the availability of vaccine or the advances in technology, these countries experience high infection rates with a significantly increased incidence of related morbidity and mortality.

The incidence of measles infections among pregnant women has decreased as in the general population. Fetal effects from maternal measles appear to be few. There is an increased incidence of preterm delivery during acute maternal infections, but there is no reported evidence of fetal malformations.

Measles infections in infants and young children are consistent with the infection rate of the general population. Those infants and children who do become infected are predisposed to otitis media as a complication of the infection. Pneumonia and encephalitis also occur and are potentially lethal in combination with the measles. A long-term effect of infection includes hearing impairment from ear infections. Viral encephalitis associated with measles can also cause visual impairment and interruption in normal brain growth.

Syphilis

Syphilis is a disease that can produce serious illness when contracted by either adults or children. It is generally considered a sexually transmitted disease but can be acquired by contact with infectious lesions that may be present on the mouth, skin, or other mucous membranes. The virus can also be transmitted to a fetus through transplacental passage. Syphilis can also be contracted by an infant through contact with a lesion during the birth process. The disease is caused by a very mobile bacterium, which was identified in 1905 by Schaudinn and Hoffmann, two German scientists. As far back as the late 1400s, the disease represented a widespread health problem throughout the world (Pusey, 1933).

After the discovery of penicillin in the late 1940s, primary and secondary syphilis infections decreased in the United States until 1977, when the incidence began a steady increase until 1990. Since that time, the incidence has declined by approximately 50%, even though the rate is still high with an overall incidence of 0.05% of live births (Division of STD/HIV, 1995). A primary infection consists of the development of a lesion, also called a **chancre,** at the site of the contact with an infected person. This chancre is generally painless but highly infectious. There may be the development of multiple chancres with a primary infection. If a primary infection is not detected and appropriately treated with penicillin, it will progress to a secondary, or disseminated, infection. The latter is a **systemic** response to the infection that can have serious effects on many organ systems, especially the kidney and brain. Individuals treated during the secondary stage may continue to have effects from damage to organ systems that occurred during the active infection. In untreated individuals syphilis will progress to **tertiary** disease, late syphilis, which is clinically evident with severe degeneration of organ systems and leads to significant disabilities.

Pregnancy has no effect on the normal course of syphilis. Pregnant women who acquire an infection require the same diagnosis and treatment course as those individuals who are not pregnant. Furthermore, untreated infection will profoundly affect the outcome of pregnancy since the syphilis bacterium is able to cross the placenta at any time. Asymptomatic infections can occur, making it more important that laboratory testing of all pregnant women takes place.

Although a high percentage of fetuses affected with syphilis do not survive pregnancy, those infants who do are frequently affected with intrauterine growth retardation and 20% are born prematurely (Issacs & Moxon, 1991). Congenital effects from maternal syphilis generally produce significant disabilities. Central nervous system development is altered, resulting in severe mental retardation, visual and hearing impairments, and frequently seizures. Normal bone growth is also altered, resulting in orthopedic malformations; and aberrant tooth formation.

It has been determined that congenital syphilis results in 40% of term deliveries to women with untreated syphilis; perinatal death occurs in 20% of these pregnancies (Issacs & Moxon, 1991). Neonatal effects of congenital infection generally consist of enlargement of the liver and spleen, jaundice, and swelling and destruction to the head of the femur, resulting in major orthopedic deformities. Another common finding is moist skin lesions, particularly located over the palms of the hands and on the soles of the feet. These lesions are highly infectious and caution is vital to prevent spread of the infection in a nursery population.

The degree of developmental disabilities of survivors of congenital syphilis infections is dependent on the gestational age of the fetus when the infection first occurred. Those infants who acquired infection during the first or second trimester of the pregnancy are at highest risk for significant neurological delays and for visual and hearing impairments. Inadequate treatment allows a congenital infection to progress toward tertiary infection as it does in the adult. The profound developmental delays caused by this progression leave these infants in need of multidisciplinary services for the infant and family.

The goal of treatment is prevention of both primary infections and further progression of the existing disease state. Comprehensive prenatal care allows for diagnostic testing to determine infection and aggressive treatment to prevent fetal involvement and the subsequent significant affects of congenital syphilis infections.

Hepatitis

Hepatitis is a viral infection that produces systemic damage to the liver. It is a complex disease involving several subtype categories that produce similar symptoms but leave different long-term effects. Many children will be without symptoms; some may proceed to severe, overwhelming, and fatal acute infections; and others suffer progressive, chronic liver failure with **cirrhosis.** There is a significant connection between hepatitis B in infancy and later development of liver cancer; in developing countries where hepatitis B is endemic, liver cancer is one of the most common forms of cancer (American Liver Foundation, 1996).

Hepatitis A virus (HAV) is generally a mild disease and has been referred to as infectious hepatitis. This virus is transmitted through personal contact with food handled by an infected individual. Poor personal hygiene, poor sanitation, and overcrowding greatly increase the potential for spreading HAV infection. HAV infection in children is rarely fatal. Chronic liver disease may result, but less than a 0.1% overall mortality rate has been reported (Klein, 1988).

Hepatitis B virus (HBV) is a major health problem throughout the entire world. In the United States, about 140,000 new cases occur each year (American Liver Foundation, 1996). Though the virus does not cross the placenta in all cases when mothers are carriers, it does cross 6% of the time. However, as many as 90% of exposed infants acquire the disease as they pass through the birth canal when the newborn is exposed to the virus from the carrier mother's blood or vaginal fluids. Although potentially fatal in infancy, newborns who are immediately administered hepatitis B immune globulin and vaccine are effectively protected. Most carriers eventually die from chronic active hepatitis, cirrhosis, or primary liver cancer. The surviving affected infants can potentially transmit hepatitis virus to family members, personal contacts, and health care providers. This includes daycare providers, teachers, and other children involved in the daycare setting.

Hepatitis B virus is a DNA virus that replicates in the liver. It can infect all body fluids including tears, gastric juices, urine, saliva, and semen. Transmission can occur through puncture wounds, blood transfusions, small cuts, and abrasions and also by absorption through mucous membranes, such as in the mouth or vagina

(Boehme, 1985). Screening of pregnant women to determine both acute infection and antibody status is critical. Many of those mothers infected with HBV will not have any symptoms. The Centers for Disease Control suggest that all pregnant women have prenatal screening and absolutely recommend that women who are in risk categories be screened and followed. Women at high risk include:

1. Those of Asian, Pacific Island, or Alaskan Eskimo descent
2. Woman who are Haitian or sub-Saharan African by birth
3. Women with acute or chronic liver disease or a history of undiagnosed jaundice
4. IV drug users
5. Those with personal contacts with HBV carriers
6. Those with multiple episodes of venereal disease or those who are prostitutes
7. Women who are sexual partners of hemophiliacs
8. Individuals who work in dialysis or renal transplant units
9. Individuals who work or live in an institution for persons with mental retardation
10. Health care professionals

Laboratory testing identifies women who are in an acute phase of infection through a positive hepatitis B surface antigen. This antigen is present on the surface of the virus and can be detected in the patient's blood serum. The presence of surface antigen indicates acute infection or a carrier state. Those individuals with a positive antigen will be tested for hepatitis B antigen. This is found only in individuals with a positive serum, and its presence is associated with active viral replication indicating the most highly infective state. It is during this time that a pregnant mother is at the highest risk to transmit infection to her fetus. Transmission may occur in as many as 90% of cases (CDC, 1988; Edwards, 1988).

Hepatitis B vaccine provides active immunity against the virus and is administered at birth, one month, and six months of age. Vaccinations can dramatically reduce the incidence of vertical transmission (mother to fetus) but can also reduce the incidence of transmission by other care providers who may contact the infection through provision of services. Teachers, daycare providers, health care workers, social service agency workers, and any other individuals who may have reason to provide service to individuals or families with HBV infections need to strongly consider seeking immunization against the virus. The potential for acquiring HBV virus is significant. Though not as widely publicized, the potential loss of productive individuals and resources is as high as the loss encountered with acquired immune deficiency syndrome.

Human Immunodeficiency Virus/Acquired Immune Deficiency Syndrome

The disease known in our society by the familiar term AIDS is the outcome or clinical manifestation of infection by a virus called the human immunodeficiency virus (HIV). Persons infected with HIV are said to be HIV positive, and in the early stages of the disease infants are usually nonsymptomatic or the symptoms are mild. As the disease progresses, the symptoms worsen. The most severe manifestation of the disease is referred to as Acquired Immune Deficiency Syndrome or AIDS. Children have a shorter incubation period (12 months) between acquisition of HIV and a transition to AIDS than do adults (8–10 years) (Simonds & Rogers, 1992). In spite of evidence of significant underreporting, there were 7,472 cases of pediatric AIDS in the United States in 1996 (CDC, 1996). There were no known cases reported before 1982. The disease is one that has disproportionately affected poor young minority women (Women and HIV, 1998). It is the third leading cause of death in women 24–44, but the number one cause of death in African American women, who accounted for 56% of female cases in 1996; Hispanic women accounted for 20% of all female cases.

Almost 93% of childhood AIDS cases occur by transfer of the virus from an HIV positive mother (1) through the placenta, (2) during childbirth, or (3) through breast-feeding (Landry & Smith, 1998). Though the role of the placenta in transmission of the AIDS virus is unknown, it is believed that the transfer of the virus occurs either late in pregnancy or during labor (Women and HIV, 1998). However, only about one fourth of HIV positive mothers transmit the virus to their unborn child. The remaining cases are accounted for by infection through blood products, such as blood transfusions in hemophiliacs or child sexual abuse. It has also been found that 14% of infants who are breastfed by HIV positive women contract the disease in this manner. Yet, in a sad acknowledgement of the desperate conditions elsewhere in the world, women in developing countries are advised that the benefits of breastfeeding outweighed the risk of infection (Women and HIV, 1998).

Currently, the HIV infection cannot be identified in the nursery population, even though they typically display behavioral characteristics such as irritability, inconsolability, poor feeding, and disrupted sleeping patterns that are similar to neonates who are drug exposed. Yet, it has been determined that all infants born to HIV-infected mothers have antibodies to HIV. Even so, there are no known cases of casual transmission of the HIV virus to caregivers in nursery, daycare settings, or schools (Wolters, Brouwers, Civitello, & Moss, 1995). While precaution in handling bodily fluids is the same as with children with hepatitis B, childcare workers need not be afraid to hug or engage in the human contact needed by children.

Because of the relationship between poverty, drug use, and HIV infection, infants and children infected with HIV represent a population already removed from mainstream health care. Furthermore, social and economic factors influencing families increases the likelihood that these children will not receive optimal treatment. Many times, maternal risk behaviors continue following childbirth, reducing the probability for either monitoring or intervening in the physical and developmental progression of childhood. Many of these children are abandoned in health care facilities or exposed to poor sanitation and overcrowding that speed up the progression of the infection. On the other hand, the life expectancy for infants and children with HIV infection continues to improve, with 50–60% surviving past age six (Meyers, 1994).

HIV infection in children is classified according to the rate at which the disease is progressing. In the best case, the disease is *static,* and infants and children gain developmental milestones, even though they tend to start behind and their rate of gain is slower than expected (Brouwers, Belman, & Epstein, 1994; Gay & Armstrong, 1995). When the disease is not static, it is either plateaued or subacute. In both cases, children tend to lose previously gained milestones, with the loss being more rapid in the subacute form. Eventually, children experience severe deficits in cognitive, motor, social, and expressive language skills. Some children also experience autistic-like behaviors such as flat affect, loss of speech, and lack of interest in others (Wolters et al., 1995). Developmental function, both cognitively and behaviorally, is affected by slowed or interrupted brain development (myelinopathy) and later abnormalities that include brain atrophy and calcification (Gay & Armstrong, 1995).

In addition to behavioral declines, children's health progressively worsens. Symptoms include failure to thrive, enlarged lymph nodes, enlarged liver and spleen, enlarged heart, chronic bacterial infections, respiratory infections, diarrhea, and fevers. For unknown reasons, survival times are shorter for children infected prenatally or during the first year of life, compared to those who contract infection during later childhood and adulthood. *Pneumocystis carinii* pneumonia is the most common complication of the syndrome that affects survival in very young children.

Failure to thrive is a major problem affecting infants and young children with AIDS. Lactose intolerance and subsequent diarrhea are common findings among the affected pediatric population. Oral lesions due to yeast infections often result from prolonged antibiotic therapy. These lesions are very painful and may cause oral aversion and reduce the child's ability to maintain adequate food intake to support continued health. Consistency in caregivers is important to develop positive relationships that allow for optimum feeding practices.

Current practice for the care of infants of mothers who are either HIV positive or have AIDS is that of support and observation. These infants are usually not treated with antiviral medications unless symptoms develop. Once conversion to HIV positive occurs, medications are initiated to attempt to slow the progression of the disease.

Many medical centers are experiencing an increasing number of infants being abandoned after delivery by positive HIV mothers who are drug abusers and who are unable to care for their children. Many of these infants experience conditions related to premature birth or other conditions, including drug addiction, that place them at increased risk for developmental disabilities along with their HIV status. Placement in foster care settings can provide the opportunity to deal with problems that arise as a result of the progression of the HIV status to AIDS.

Advocacy for infants and children affected with both HIV and AIDS is the prime role for those involved with planning care for these children. Prevention of the progression of HIV and AIDS is the goal, but providing a quality of life to those currently affected is the issue. Utilizing a multidisciplinary approach to the many problems encountered by this population is essential for establishing a systematic plan for meeting all the physical, developmental, and emotional needs of these children. An early first step is assessment of family resources and priorities. Family-centered intervention that is coordinated across many agencies should be based upon a respect for family expectations and goals. "Family" might include nonnuclear members, because of the illness or death of one or both parents.

Treatment suggestions:

◆ Physical therapy for progressive hypertonicity and eventual loss of ambulation
◆ Language intervention for loss of ability, especially expressive and attentional problems
◆ Psychological intervention to deal with stress of living with a terminal illness which possesses strong social stigmatization
◆ Social worker to help child deal with the probable loss of one or both parents
◆ Continuous communication with health care providers as to the physical condition of child

Figure 7–7
Brain with
uninfected
meninges

MENINGITIS / ENCEPHALITIS

Meningitis and **encephalitis** are both infections that involve the central nervous system with particular concentration in the brain. Though the factors causing these infections may occasionally appear to be the same, the implications for treatment differ depending on the infecting agent. The brain is protected by a fluid-filled sac that surrounds it and the spinal cord. Moreover, the brain matter is intertwined with blood vessels that provide blood flow for the transport of food and oxygen. In the absence of infection involving the central nervous system, pressure is maintained at a steady state, permitting normal blood flow (see Figure 7–7).

Meningitis

Meningitis is a condition in which infection occurs as the result of the entry of bacteria around the surface of the brain, producing inflammation of the *meninges,* the coverings that surround the brain and spinal cord (see Figure 7–8). The meninges are three membranes (i.e., dura mater, pia mater, arachnoid) that are between the skull and brain and also between the vertebral column and the spinal cord. It is in this area that the cerebrospinal fluid flows over the surface of the nervous system. *Cerebrospinal fluid* is a clear, colorless, odorless fluid that resembles water and contains glucose, proteins, salts, and white blood cells. Its function is to protect the nerv-

Figure 7–8

Brain showing
swollen and
infected
meninges

ous system from injury by acting as a shock absorber. It also carries oxygen and nu-trition to the nerve cells and takes waste products away to be reabsorbed in the cir-culatory system. Small blood vessels that are part of the skull's lining act as the mech-anism for exchange.

Meningitis does not refer to the guilty organism, rather to the condition that re-sults from a bacterial or viral infection. For example, in 10–20% of the cases of bac-terial meningitis, *streptococcal pneumoniae* is the infecting agent (Mactier, Galea, & McWilliam, 1998). With meningitis, swelling occurs and there also is degeneration of some of the surrounding nerve cells. It is this swelling and nerve destruction that cause the neurological disabilities that follow in 20–30% of acute cases of meningitis (Arditi & Mason, 1998). On occasion there may also be an invasion of the infection into the brain matter itself through tears in the meninges. This increases the poten-tial of permanent brain and nerve injury. Acute meningitis may produce significant symptoms in children; in 10% of cases, meningitis leads to death within a very short period of time (Arditi & Mason, 1998).

Acute bacterial meningitis is generally a disease of the young or the chronically ill (Sadovsky, 1998). Immaturity of the immune system in the very young and the compromised immune system in children with such disabilities as head trauma, spina bifida, and sickle cell anemia, places these individuals at greater risk for developing meningitis. Recurrent otitis media is also a condition related to a higher rate of meningitis (Arditi & Mason, 1998). Other factors that are risks for children but not adults include maternal education level, poverty, and lack of a primary care physician. However, the strongest risk factor for meningitis in children under 18 years of age is maternal smoking, with the risk increasing proportionately with the number of cigarettes smoked each day (Sadovsky, 1998). As many as 37% of cases of meningitis in children can be linked to maternal smoking.

About 45–145 cases of bacterial meningitis occur for every 100,000 people per year, and approximately 90% of these individuals survive the infection (Arditi & Mason, 1998). Of those affected, approximately one fourth will have some degree of residual effect (Arditi & Mason, 1998). Residual damage ranges from very minor dysfunctions to significant multiple disabilities.

The initial symptoms include fever, vomiting, severe headache, anorexia, and drowsiness (Mactier et al., 1998). The actual diagnosis of meningitis is made through laboratory testing along with a physical examination. A **spinal tap** may reveal cloudy cerebrospinal fluid due to the increased number of white blood cells present in the fluid. Occasionally, the fluid may appear bloody because the tiny blood vessels in the skull's lining break from the increased pressure. Blood and spinal fluid cultures will determine which bacterium is responsible for the current infection. Powerful antibiotics that would be effective against any of the possible organisms are used until a specific organism is identified.

Survivors of acute bacterial meningitis may have long-term effects generally associated with the central nervous system. Seizures are common and may be resistant to normal anticonvulsant therapy. The intractable nature of the seizures may be the result of specific focal areas of the brain that have been attacked by the disease. Bilateral deafness may occur as a result of pressure placed on the auditory nerve by inflammation of the meninges. Deafness may also be caused by antibiotic therapy needed to eradicate the bacteria. Hydrocephalus frequently occurs because of scar tissue formation in the subarachnoid space that permanently affects the normal fluid pathways for cerebral spinal fluid. Occasionally, brain abscesses may develop that produce symptoms much like those of a brain tumor.

Children with disabilities from meningitis will require extensive services. In addition to the described effects of the infection, many of these children suffer from hyperactivity (along with their seizures), motor involvement (particularly cerebral palsy), and mental retardation.

Treatment considerations:

◆ Environmental safety measures are necessary to protect these children from injury during seizures and during periods of erratic behavior
◆ Programs to deal with hearing impairments and visual problems may be part of the general plan when determining services
◆ Physical therapy for children with spasticity, ataxia
◆ Consideration of shunt in infants and children who experience hydrocephalus

Encephalitis
Encephalitis is generally an inflammation of the brain and spinal cord (see Figure 7–9), which may occur as a result of viral or bacterial infection spread by the circu-

Figure 7–9
Brain affected
by encephalitis

latory system or from movement of infection up neural **axons** to the brain. The infecting agent disperses throughout the brain and to the meninges causing inflammation. A majority of cases of encephalitis are associated with the childhood viral diseases mentioned earlier in this chapter.

Most cases of encephalitis in the United States occur during the summer since the major transmitting source is the mosquito (Whaley & Wong, 1989). Some kinds of viruses that eventually lead to encephalitis selectively attack specific types of neurons (as in polio), while others, such as the herpes virus, establish focal areas of infection dispersed throughout the brain. The manner in which dispersion occurs determines the outcome of the nervous system function following an infection.

Encephalitis can be diagnosed when an individual has symptoms of early onset meningitis, but a spinal tap cannot confirm the presence of bacteria. In other words, ruling out meningitis is one part of the diagnosis of encephalitis because symptoms of the two diseases appear to be so similar. Additional diagnostic findings may be a normal white blood cell count and an elevated protein level in the spinal fluid. In this disease, early symptoms include an unsteady gait and seizures, with the later onset of a decreased level of consciousness. Medical measures are initiated to prevent further deterioration of the physical condition. Viral cultures will identify agents responsible for acute encephalitis, or occasionally a brain biopsy itself may be necessary to identify the virus producing the illness. Most cases of viral encephalitis will recover without significant long-term effects. This is not the case with herpes encephalitis; all virally induced encephalitis can potentially lead to permanent and significant damage. Furthermore, infants born to virally infected mothers and have experienced in utero viral encephalitis with subsequent interruption in brain growth will be born with severe neurological damage.

Effects of encephalitis on central nervous system function may include severe language disorders and muscle weakness or paralysis on one side of the body. Frequently, focal seizures occur, and EEG findings are sometimes abnormal, indicating the presence of a seizure disorder. Infants and children may experience impairments in vision and hearing, especially with herpes encephalitis. Reactivation of the virus, after the initial recovery from the illness, may further damage the nervous system. Affected children also have an increased incidence of behavior problems and hyperactivity, requiring environmental precautions to assure their safety. Depending upon the severity of the infection, children may experience mental retardation with all the adverse affects of developmental delay.

Case Study

Maddy's Cochlear Implant: Interview with Kim Shafer

I just wasn't ready for the cochlear implant at first. My husband was ready though. He said, "I've read about these things, and I've seen the results." But we went on with hearing aids and sign language until just before Maddy's third birthday. Then I was ready. I had seen enough. One of my friends had a daughter just about a year older than Maddy and I'd seen her have the implant and be successful with it.

It wasn't the device that scared me, it was the surgery. I would be taking a beautiful child who is perfect in every other way and letting the doctors cut her head open and take out a piece of her skull. What if something happened on that surgical table? I was scared to death. Maddy is my baby, and I don't have a replacement for her. I think I needed that extra year to think about the cochlear implant, because when Maddy was almost three years old I was ready.

We went in for the surgery and I didn't cry when I saw her the night before. They took her into surgery and it just seemed like all of a sudden the doctor was back saying, "It went great!" They actually tested the electrodes in the surgical room so they could tell whether they were going to work or not. After the surgery, we had to wait for the incision to heal. It was about a five inch cut that went from the bottom of her ear all the way to the top of her head.

The internal unit of the cochlear implant is a magnet and on the end of that is a group of electrodes that lead down into the cochlea in the middle ear. The cochlea has the hair cells that make it possible for most of us to hear normally. The sound bounces off those hair cells and goes into the brain. But Maddy's hair cells were damaged. They think it was probably not the medication she got for the meningitis, but from the swelling the meningitis caused. So, in the cochlear implant, that group of electrodes in the cochlea takes the place of those hair cells.

On the left side of Maddy's head, she also has an external unit. After the incision healed, they actually attached the external unit it was held in place by the magnet inside her skull. We think that is so cool! The hole on the side of it is the microphone. All the environmental sounds go in through that microphone, down the wire—to a speech processor she wears in a little fanny pack. I'm trying to work with Advanced Bionics Corporation who makes Maddy's implant, to produce a pouch that is more efficient. We need something that doesn't stick out when Maddy wears a tight fitting shirt. She always looks like she's pregnant, you know? But that's a small price for what she's gained from this.

The speech processor has an on/off switch, a volume control, and a sensitivity dial, which at her age, she doesn't use because I don't know that she can really gauge that. An older person will be able to tell whether environmental sounds are too much external noise. If they want to focus on communication, they will turn the processor's sensitivity down. Then the background noise will be diffused so that they can focus on a conversation.

So all the sound goes in the microphone, down to the processor, and within seconds comes back out, goes through the skull to energize the hairs on the cochlea and then she hears. Maddy has been working on understanding all that sound. That's what a new baby does when we repeat words to them and pretty soon they start to imitate. That's what Maddy's been doing for the last two years—repeating sounds back to us. Her language has gained in leaps and bounds.

I'm very proud of Maddy, she's doing a great job. When we were getting ready for the cochlear implant, we saw a great video that had some awesome examples of a little girl who had the implant and her success. It showed a teenager in sports wearing only a headband to keep the headpiece on. The message was that anything that is your goal in life and you want to accomplish you can still do it with the cochlear implant. Well I know it's true. I really believe that the cochlear implant will help deaf kids to accomplish their goals and dreams even more so because they won't have that communication gap. Sign language is wonderful and I don't want Maddy to stop that. She has wonderful friends still using sign language, but to be able to communicate by voice and having people understand you and you understanding them is such a huge leap.

Maddy Shafer and the family pet.

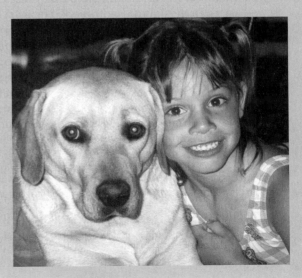

IN CONCLUSION

Technological advances continue to increase the degree of independence and integration of persons with significant hearing losses within society. For example, cochlear implants are electronic devices that can be implanted by surgery to transform sound vibrations into nerve impulses for transmission to the brain. Such transmission stimulates nerve cells for children with bilateral sensorineural hearing loss. The devices do not restore normal hearing, but when used with speech reading, allow a greater understanding of speech. To date, however, cochlear implants have not been a panacea.

Other innovations, such as computer-assisted instruction, have been targeted at increasing language and communication skills for children with deafness but have yet to fulfill their promise. For example, as recently as 1986, Allen noted that on the average, students with deafness read at the fourth grade level upon graduation. Though research is still exploratory, preliminary findings suggest that interactive videodisk (IVD) programs may be an efficient means of teaching children with and without hearing impairments such skills as signing and language patterns (Stewart, Gentry, & McLeod, 1991). Interactive videodisk programs have the advantage of permitting children to control a wide range of visual instructional stimuli, to respond to instructional cues, and to immediately receive interactive feedback. Stewart et al. (1991) noted that presently IVD technology may not be practical since, in terms of development and production, it is quite expensive. Moreover, videodisks, once pressed, cannot be edited or revised, unlike computer programs.

People with deafness differ from people with other disabilities in that they have developed their own social communities of peers and deaf culture. Segregation of this culture, largely self-selected, has led to controversy that directly affects parents of very young children with deafness. Even among those who are deaf, persons who acquire deafness adventitiously may be excluded (Darrow, 1993). In fact, Janesick (1990) argued for recognition of the Deaf community (big "D" for congenital deafness) as a distinct cultural and linguistic minority. Contending that inclusion in this community is something to be proud of, proponents of the movement shun attempts to bridge the communication gap.

Incidence trends, coupled with the finding that between 50% and 75% of children with blindness also have other disabilities (Sykanda & Levitt, 1982). Kirchner (1988) indicated that service systems are already overstretched and that if these trends continue, educational systems will be severely taxed.

As children reach preschool and school age, parents will be faced with placement decisions. In the past, most children with blindness were sent to residential schools for the blind. However, with recent inclusion practices, it seems likely that most children with blindness will be served in regular classroom settings, even if these children also have other disabilities. Parents need to be aware of placement options, the implications of these options, and strategies to advocate for the choices made for children with visual impairments. Beginning early with low vision tools (e.g., Braille, large print text, electronic systems, etc.), social skills training, and mobility and orientation training can increase the degree of independence and social competence experienced in these settings by children with visual impairments.

Rapid advancements in electronic/computerized capacities will likely continue to open new doors to academic, domestic, and vocational opportunities for persons with visual impairments. Very young children with visual impairments should be introduced to computer systems. Likewise, team members will be pressed to keep pace with developments in technology that might increase independent functioning while being practical and cost effective for families.

Procedures for treating many once untreatable causes of visual impairment will continue to evolve. Like other forms of early intervention, the cost of remediating loss of vision may be far less than the costs of long-term specialized intervention for children and families.

Each of the infections described in this chapter may have effects ranging from mild to devastating. The most effective way of decreasing the incidence of infections and their effects on children is through education. Many, though not all, infections can be prevented through a more cautious approach to living within our environment and within our society. Both a recognition of cause and an understanding of the nature of the action of bacteria and viruses can make a difference in the approach to prevention and treatment. Important advances have already nearly eradicated diseases such as rubella that place unborn children at risk of disabilities. Even AIDS, the most frightening epidemic of the late twentieth century could be wiped out with adequate education and preventative intervention.

STUDY GUIDE QUESTIONS

1. Into what three components is the auditory mechanism functionally separated? Describe the three practical functions of these components.
2. Along what two dimensions is sound heard?
3. What is the difference between a conductive hearing loss and a sensorineural hearing loss? What are common causes of a conductive hearing loss? Of a sensorineural hearing loss?
4. List the symptoms of otitis media and describe treatment for the infection.
5. What developmental domains are most affected by loss of hearing?
6. Name some sign language systems. Which is the most commonly used approach? Explain the debate in favor of and opposed to manual sign.
7. What are some disadvantages to using hearing aids?
8. List some considerations that should be made when serving preschool children with hearing impairments.
9. Discriminate between blindness and low vision.
10. Describe the visual process.
11. Describe three refractive errors in vision.
12. Name and explain two visual errors caused by a disruption in muscle coordination of the eyes.
13. What are cortical visual impairments?
14. What are common causes of visual impairments?
15. Define and give a brief description of each: glaucoma and cataracts.
16. What recommendations should be given to caregivers in working with children with visual impairments?

17. What is the difference between congenital and adventitious blindness?

18. What might be included in programs specifically designed for infants and toddlers with visual impairments? What factors should be considered in selection of appropriate orientation and mobility adaptations?

19. In what ways are children who are visually impaired disproportionately faced with a lifetime of "disadvantage?" How can educators intervene to limit this disadvantage?

20. Define biological agents. How do these agents cause damage to human cells? How do they travel throughout the human body?

21. When do pathogenic bacterial infections occur? What circumstances may affect an infant's outcome?

22. Explain the relationship between socioeconomic status, low birth weight, and infection.

23. Why is appropriate assessment of the physiological status of an infant at delivery important? What are the keys to effective treatment of an infected infant?

24. List the initial symptoms of an infection. What interventions are warranted for infants experiencing infections at, or shortly after, birth to provide opportunity for full development?

25. What are viruses and how do they differ from bacteria? How has prevention of viral diseases been accomplished?

26. What are the TORCH diseases? Briefly describe the cause, course, symptoms, and outcomes of each.

27. Explain what is meant by "shedding" of a live virus. How does shedding occur?

28. List characteristics of women who may be at high risk for contracting hepatitis B virus. What individuals should most strongly consider immunization against this virus?

29. How do social and economic factors contribute to placing children with HIV at high risk for disease progression?

30. Explain the differential causes, courses, and outcomes of meningitis and encephalitis. What is the difference between viral meningitis and bacterial meningitis?

REFERENCES

Allen, K. E., & Marotz, L. (1989). *Developmental profiles: Birth-to-six*. Albany, NY: Delmar.

Allen, T. (1986). Patterns of academic achievement among hearing impaired students: 1974 and 1983. In A. Schildroth & M. Karchmer (Eds.), *Deaf children in America* (pp. 161–206).

American Liver Foundation. (1996). *Hepatitis B: Breaking the cycle of infection from carrier mother to newborn*. http://gf.ucsf:edu/alf/info/hepbcycle.html.

Arditi, M., & Mason, E. O. (1998). Three-year multicenter surveillance of *pneumococcal* meningitis in children. *Pediatrics, 102*, 1087–1098.

Bateman, J. B. (1983). Genetics in pediatric ophthamology. *Pediatric Clinics of North America, 30*(6), 1015–1031.

Batshaw, M. L., & Perret, Y. M. (1988). *Children with handicaps: A medical primer*. Baltimore: Paul H. Brookes.

Boehme, T. (1985). Hepatitis B: The nurse-midwife's role in management and prevention. *Journal of Nurse-Midwifery, 30*(2), 79–87.

Bolognese, R., Aldinger, R., & Roberts, N. (1981). Prenatal care in the prevention of infection. *Clinics in Perinatology, 8*(3), 605–615.

Brouwers, P., Belman, A., & Epstein, L. (1994). Organ-specific complications: Central nervous system involvement: Manifestations, evaluation and pathogenesis. In P. A. Pizzo &

C. M. Wilfert (Eds.), *Pediatric AIDS: The challenge of HIV infection in infants, children, and adolescents* (pp. 433–455). Baltimore: Williams & Wilkins.

Cartledge, G., & Cochran, L. (1996). Social skill self-assessments by adolescents with hearing impairment in residential and public schools. *Remedial & Special Education, 17,* 30–37.

Centers for Disease Control. (1988). Prevention of perinatal transmission of hepatitis B virus: Prenatal screening of all pregnant women for hepatitis B surface antigen, recommendations of the Immunization Practices Advisory Committee. *Morbidity and Mortality Weekly Report, 37*(2), 341–351.

Centers for Disease Control. (1989a). *Hepatitis Surveillance Report No. 52,* Atlanta 1989. United States Department of Health and Human Services.

Centers for Disease Control and Prevention (1996). *The Florida AIDS, STD, and TB Monthly Surveillance Report,* 139. Atlanta: U.S. Department of Health and Human Services.

Chalifoux, L. M., & Fagan, B. (1997). Labeling children who are visually impaired "disadvantaged." *Journal of Visual Impairment and Blindness, 91,* 531–539.

Clarke, K. L. (1988). Barriers or enablers: Mobility devices for visually impaired and multiply handicapped infants and preschoolers. *Education of the Visually Handicapped, 20,* 115–133.

Current progress in finding genes involved in hearing impairment. (1995). www.boystown.org/deafgene.registry.

Darrow, A. (1993). The role of music in Deaf culture: Implications for music teachers. *JRME, 41*(2), 93–110.

Diienstaf, J., Wands, J., & Koff, R. (1986). Acute viral hepatitis. In Isselbacher, K. (Ed.), *Harrison's Principles of Internal Medicine,* (11th ed.). New York: McGraw-Hill.

Division of STD/HIV Prevention. (1995). *Sexually transmitted disease surveillance.* U.S. Department of Health and Human Services, Public Health Service. Atlanta: CDC.

Dubow, S. (1989). "Into the turbulent mainstream"—A legal perspective on the weight to be given to the Least Restrictive Environment placement decisions for deaf children. *Journal of Law and Education, 44,* 215–228.

Edwards M. (1988). Hepatitis B serology: Help in interpretation. *Pediatric Clinics of North America, 35*(3), 503–515.

Gast, M. (1983). Herpes update 1983. *Missouri Perinatal Progress, 5*(4), 1–4.

Gay, C. L., & Armstrong, F. D. (1995). The effects of HIV on cognitive and motor development in children born to HIV-seropositive women. *Pediatrics, 96,* 1075–1080.

Goldstein, H. (1980). The reported demography and causes of blindness throughout the world. *Advances in Ophthalmology, 40,* 1–99.

Green, M. (1997). Appropriate principles in the use of antibiotics in children. *Clinical Pediatrics, 36,* 207–209.

Grossman, J. (1980). Perinatal viral infections. *Clinics in Perinatology, 7*(1), 257–271.

Harel, S., Holtzman, M., & Feinsod, M. (1985). The late visual bloomer. In S. Harel & N. Anastasiow (Eds.), *The at-risk infant: Psychosocial medical aspects* (pp. 359–362). Baltimore: Paul H. Brookes.

Harrington, M., & Meyers, H. W. (1992). Preschool programs for the hearing impaired: Young children with hearing disabilities deserve special attention. *Principal, 34–36.*

Herrmann, K. (1982). Congenital and perinatal varicella. *Clinical Obstetrics and Gynecology, 25*(3), 605–609.

Hicks, R., Fowler, K., Richardson, M., Dahle, A., Adams, L., & Pass, R. (1993). Congenital cytomegalovirus infection and neonatal auditory screening. *The Journal of Pediatrics, 123*(5), 779–782.

Hoon, A. H. (1991). Visual impairments in children with developmental disabilities. In A. J. Capute & P. J. Accardo (Eds.), *Developmental disabilities in infancy and early childhood* (pp. 395–411). Baltimore: Paul H. Brookes.

Hughes, D., & Simpson, L. (1995). The role of social change in preventing low birth weight. *The Future of Children, 5,* 50–63.

Issacs, D., & Moxon, R. (1991). *Neonatal infections.* Oxford: Butterworth-Heinmann.

Janesick, V. J. (1990). Bilingual multicultural education and the deaf: Issues and possibilities. *Journal of Educational Issues of Language Minority Students, 7,* 99–109.

Jerger, S., & Martin. R. (1995). Childhood hearing impairment: Auditory and linguistic interactions during multidimensional speech processing. *Journal of Speech and Hearing Research, 38*(4), 930–949.

Kai, J. (1996). What worries parents when their preschool children are acutely ill, and why: A qualitative study. *British Medical Journal, 313,* 983–987.

Kaplan, S. L. (1997). Prevention of hearing loss in meningitis. *Lancet, 350*(9072), 158–160.

Kekelis, L. S., & Prinz, P. M. (1996). Blind and sighted children with their mothers: The development of discourse skills. *Journal of Visual Impairment & Blindness, 90*(5), 423–437.

Kennedy, C. R., Kim, L., Dees, D. C., Campbell, M. J., & Thornton, A. R. D. (1998). Controlled trial of universal neonatal screening for early identification of permanent childhood hearing impairment. *Lancet, 352*(9145), 1957–1965.

Kenyon, T. A., Matuck, M. A., & Stroh, G. (1998). Persistent low immunization coverage among inner-city preschool children despite access to free vaccine. *Pediatrics, 101,* 612–617.

Kirchner, C. (1988). National estimates of prevalence and demographics of children with visual impairments. In M. D. Wang, M. D. Reynolds, & H. J. Walberg (Eds.), *Handbook of special education: Research and practice* (Vol. 3, pp. 135–153). Elmsford, NY: Pergamon.

Klein, M. (1988). Hepatitis B virus: Perinatal management. *Perinatal/Neonatal Nursing, 1*(4), 12–23.

Kohl, S., & James, A. (1985). Herpes simplex virus encephalitis during childhood. Importance of brain biopsy diagnosis. *Journal of Pediatrics, 107*(2), 212–215.

Korones, S. (1988). Uncommon virus infections of the mother, fetus and newborn: Influenza, mumps and measles. *Clinics of Perinatology, 15*(2), 259–272.

Landry, K., & Smith, T. (1998). Neurocognitive effects of HIV infection on young children: Implications for assessment. *Topics in Early Childhood Special Education, 18,* 160–169.

Leclair, J. (1980). Control of nosocomial neonatal viral infections. *Critical Care Quarterly, 3*(3), 71–77.

Mactier, H., Galea, P., & McWilliam, R. (1998). Acute obstructive hydrocephalus complicating bacterial meningitis in childhood. *British Medical Journal, 316*(7146), 1887–1890.

Magid, M. S. (1995). *Pediatric pathology.* r.med.cornell.edu/CUMC_Pathnotes/Pediatrics.

Margo, K. L., & Shaughnessy, A. F. (1998). Antiviral drugs in healthy children. *American Family Physician, 57,* 1073–1078.

Mauk, G. W., & Mauk, P. P. (1992). Somewhere out there: Preschool children with hearing impairment and learning disabilities. *Topics in Early Childhood Special Education, 12,* 174–196.

Meyers, A. (1994). Natural history of congenital HIV infection. *Journal of School Health, 64,* 9–10.

Morse, M. (1991). Visual gaze behaviors: Considerations in working with visually impaired and multiply handicapped children. *Re:view, 23*(1), 5–15.

Naeye, R., & Blanec W. (1970). Relation of poverty and race to antenatal infection. *New England Journal of Medicine, 283*(11), 555–560.

National Institute on Deafness and Other Communication Disorders (March, 1999). www.nidcd.A l /articles/article4.html.

National Institute of Health Consensus Statement. (March, 1993). *Early identification of hearing impairment in infants and young children.* Volume 11(1), 1–25. Bethesda, MD: NIH.

National Institute of Health Consensus Statement. (March, 1999). *Facts about deafness.* www.nih.org.A l /articles/article5.html.

Planned Parenthood Federation of America. (1998). *Herpes: Questions and answers.* http://plannedparenthood.org/sti-safesex/herpes.htm.

Preece, P., Blount, J., Glover, J., Fletcher, G., Peckham, C., & Griffiths, P. (1983). The consequences of primary cytomegalovirus infection in pregnancy. *Archives of Disease in Childhood, 58,* 970–975.

Pusey, W. (1933). *The History of Syphilis.* Springfield, IL: Charles C. Thomas Publishers.

Ryalls, J., & Larouche, A. (1992). Accoustic integrity of speech production in children with moderate and severe hearing impairment. *Journal of Speech and Hearing Research, 35,* 88–96.

Sadovsky, R. (1998). Tobacco smoke exposure and meningococcal disease risk. *American Family Physician, 57,* 2848–2849.

Seigel, D., & Washington, A. (1987). Syphilis: Updated approach to an old disease. *Postgraduate Medicine, 8*(1), 83–90.

Shapiro, M. B., & France, T. D. (1985). The ocular features of Down's syndrome. *American Journal of Ophthalmology, 99,* 659–663.

Simonds, R. J., & Rogers, M. F. (1992). Epidemiology of HIV in children and other populations. In A. C. Crocker, H. J. Cohen, & T. A. Kastner (Eds.), *HIV infection and developmental disabilities: A resource for service providers* (pp. 3–4). Baltimore: Paul H. Brookes.

Stewart, D. A., Gentry, C. G., & McLeod, R. (1991). Using instructional design principles to produce an IVD to enhance the linguistic environment of deaf children. *Journal of Special Education Technology, 11*(3), 121–135.

Sykanda, A. M., & Levitt, S. (1982). The physiotherapist in the developmental management of the visually impaired child. *Child: Care, Health and Development, 8,* 261–270.

Teplin, S. W. (1983). Development of blind infants and children with retrolental fibroplasia: Implications for physicians. *Pediatrics, 71,* 6–12.

Thomas, D., Salmon, R. L., & King, J. (1998). Ratso f first measles-mumps-rubella immunisation in Wales. *Lancet, 351*(9120), 1927.

Uslan, M. (1983). Provision of orientation and mobility services in 1990. *Journal of Visual Impairment and Blindness, 77,* 213–215.

Vaccination coverage by race/ethnicity and poverty levels among children 19–35 months—United States, 1997. (November 1998). *Morbidity and Mortality Weekly Report, 47*(44), 956–960.

Whaley, L. F., & Wong, D. L. (1989). *Essentials of pediatric nursing* (3rd ed.). St. Louis: C. V. Mosby.

What's new in audiology and hearing screening. (March, 1999). Hearing health. file:///A l /articles/article7.html.

Whitley, R., Soong, S., & Linneman, C. (1982). Herpes simplex encephalitis-clinical assessment. *Journal of the American Medical Association, 247*(3), 317–320.

Whitley, R., Yeager, A., & Kartus, P. (1983). Neonatal herpes simplex virus infection: Follow-up evaluation of vidarabine therapy. *Pediatrics, 72*(6), 778–785.

Wolters, P. L., Brouwers, P., Civitello., L., & Moss, H. A. (1995). Receptive and expressive language function of children with symptomatic HIV infection and relationship with disease parameters: A longitudinal 24-month follow-up study, *AIDS, 11,* 1135–1144.

Women and HIV. (1998). *Online Psych.* www.onlinepsych.com.

DISCRETIONARY PROGRAMS FOR INFANTS AND TODDLERS WITH SPECIAL NEEDS

Shortly after her first birthday, Dawn was diagnosed with cerebral palsy. Her parents are confused, overwhelmed, and at a loss to know where to turn for information and help. Louis and Jeffrey are twins. At 6 months, Jeff is holding up his head, sitting unsupported, reaching for mom and dad, and chubby from many happy mealtimes. Lou has met none of these

*milestones. He is generally irritable and fussy, has problems sucking his
bottle, and difficulty raising his head, arms, or legs. His parents cannot figure out the difference in their boys. Both [Dawn and Lou] of these children
are candidates for early intervention. Dawn has a definite diagnosis: a
brain abnormality. Although Lou's pediatrician says it is too early to know
for sure, he has symptoms that show he is at risk even without a diagnosis.
That makes him eligible for early intervention, too.*

(D'Amato & Lynn, 1999, pp. 52)

Early intervention is often used to describe special services to very young children, particularly from birth, through age two. However, this simple definition does
not do enough to convey its many implications. Early intervention also means professionals working in partnership with parents of children with special needs to help
their children develop knowledge and skills (North Carolina, 1998). It is not unusual
for parents to act as teachers or therapists, carrying out intervention programs at
home that have been planned with specialists. Early intervention involves a comprehensive cluster of services that incorporates goals in education, health care, and
social service for young children and their families (Hanson & Lynch, 1995). Sometimes an early intervention program actually provides wrap-around services that
might mean family counseling, health care, therapy, and parent classes are all provided in the same building. Early intervention focuses on the life of the family (Sontag & Schact, 1994) and is designed and delivered within the framework of informing and empowering family members (Berry & Hardman, 1998). Parents learn how
to access resources and advocate for their children.

The intent of early intervention is multifaceted, but all these efforts work toward
moderating or minimizing the effects of a disabling condition on the child's growth
and development and preventing or reducing an at-risk condition (Hardman, Drew,
& Egan, 1999). Early intervention is a directed, purposeful process with the aim of
developing, improving, or changing conditions within an individual, in the environment, or with interactions with others (Umansky & Hooper, 1998). For early childhood professionals, early intervention is the heart and soul of what they do (Umansky & Hooper, 1998).

After 50 years of research in special education, early intervention is recognized as
effective for (1) ameliorating and even preventing developmental disabilities, (2) reducing later grade retention of children, (3) reducing educational costs to school programs, and (4) improving the quality of family relationships (Salisbury & Smith,
1993). The most effective programs for early intervention share these characteristics:
they occur early in the child's life; they operate from a structured and systematic instructional base; they prescriptively address each child's assessed needs, and they include normally developing children as models (Salisbury & Smith, 1993). Perhaps
most importantly, children in early intervention programs show the most progress
when their parents are involved in reinforcing new skills in the home and other natural settings.

Early intervention for infants and toddlers differs from traditional educational services in several ways that are important for understanding current practice. First, it is
sometimes difficult to diagnose a disability in a very young child. Since children don't
mature at the same rates, some developmental lags may naturally or spontaneously

disappear by the time a child is school age (Lerner, Lowenthal, & Egan, 1998). For example, many children are saying their first words by 18 months, but some may be 3 years old before this happens. Assessment of cognitive abilities and language sometimes does not accurately predict a child's later performance. Even physical problems may not show up before 6 months of age because some time must pass before the primitive reflexes are expected to disappear. Though a specific diagnosis is not possible, a very young child may be identified as "developmentally delayed," communicating a need for special services without applying what may be an incorrect label or category for the disability.

Second, the primary responsibility for the care of infants and toddlers usually falls to the parents or to a consistent caregiver selected by the parents. Often parents will take off several weeks of work to be with a newborn or they may ask grandparents to become caregivers, before they are ready to turn an infant over to a nonfamily member. The most natural environment for caring for a child younger than three years is often in a child's home. Even a child in commercial day care usually has contact with only a small number of people to interact with an infant or toddler every day and to do so in a familiar and secure environment. It is only reasonable to expect special interventions to be carried out by these same people and to be incorporated into the **natural routines** of daily life. Parents and caregivers may find themselves the mediators of treatment or instruction designed by others. It is essential that professionals work as partners with families in treating a child's special needs (Thompson et al., 1997).

In addition, since so many basic skills are established in the earliest stages of development, intervention may have to address a multitude of domains. Movement, language, self-care, and cognition may be affected in different ways by the same disability and may require assistance from a number of specialists. A child with cerebral palsy, for example, may not learn to sit up, to hold a spoon, to form words, or to put together a simple puzzle without specific accommodations, instruction, or treatment. In many cases, when children with disabilities are identified before age 3, there are extensive medical needs involved as well. Consequently, a team of professionals may be required to consult or provide treatment to one child. Often these individuals represent different disciplines, and even different agencies, and the coordination of their services becomes complex. Among the support services that may be provided are speech pathology, audiology, psychological services, physical and occupational therapy, recreation, social work, counseling, and medical services (Committee on Children with Disabilities, 1999).

Finally, very young children are vulnerable to the influence of their surrounding environment. For example, an impoverished home may mean that the child's nutrition is put at risk; a lack of transportation may mean that appointments with a therapist will be missed; exhausted parents may mean an increased likelihood of abuse or neglect; and overly protective parents may keep the child from necessary experiences or from reasonable expectations. The child's prognosis is greatly dependent on the parent's ability to provide for and cope with the child's special needs. It becomes critical to assess each family's health and resources and to provide support for their needs in order to benefit their child.

These attributes mean that early intervention must be designed to be family-centered, must attend closely to service coordination, and must encourage family empowerment in all aspects of decision making and delivery of services. It means that a child's disability may be defined noncategorically and that the family's needs may be just as important as the child's. These multiple factors play a large part in how IDEA legislation governing services to infants and toddlers differs from the laws dealing with preschoolers, from age 3 to 5. The specific mechanisms included in IDEA which foster successful early intervention include the possibility of noncategorical eligibility, the team development of an **Individualized Family Service Plan (IFSP),** and the designation of a **service coordinator.**

The goal of IDEA, Part C, early intervention for infants and toddlers with disabilities, is to:

◆ Enhance the development of infants and toddlers with disabilities and to minimize their potential for developmental delay.
◆ Reduce the educational costs to our society, including our Nation's schools, by minimizing the need for special education and related services after infants and toddlers with disabilities reach school age.
◆ Minimize the likelihood of institutionalization of individuals with disabilities and maximize the potential for their independent living in society.
◆ Enhance the capacity of families to meet the special needs of their infants and toddlers with disabilities.
◆ Enhance the capacity of state and local agencies and service providers to identify, evaluate, and meet the needs of historically underrepresented populations, particularly minority, low-income, inner-city, and rural populations.

In order to achieve these goals, effective early intervention is guided by five general principles which are reiterated in the practices related to IDEA's regulations (Salisbury & Smith, 1993):

◆ Least restrictive and most natural environment: Good services promote the potential of intervention within normal routines and environments that stimulate child initiations and choices. Programs work on establishing skills that will prepare a child for the next, less restrictive setting.
◆ Family-centered services: Delivery models recognize that the child is part of a family, are responsive to family priorities, concerns, and needs, and encourage family involvement in the intervention.
◆ Transdisciplinary service delivery: Team members share roles with each specialist helping other members of the team learn about his or her discipline and how to assist a child or family.
◆ Empirically and value-driven practices: Features such as safe, healthy, barrier-free, environments that promote engagement are delivered by professionals guided by values such as mutual respect, caring, and sensitivity.
◆ Developmentally appropriate and individually appropriate practice: Methods that promote children's self-initiated learning and age appropriate interests are combined with specially tailored curriculum and instruction to meet specific needs.

Specific regulations for implementing IDEA, Part C, formally describe the appropriate delivery of services for all infants and toddlers who are disabled or at risk for disability and assure the rights of these children and their families. Table 8–1 summarizes family rights in early intervention.

Table 8–1   Family Rights in Early Intervention (North Carolina, 1998).

1. Receive a free, multidisciplinary assessment of the child to determine eligibility for special services.
2. Participate with the team of people who determines whether the child (and family) is eligible for special services.
3. If the child is eligible, participate in the planning and delivery of services and have an IFSP developed at no cost.
4. Receive early intervention services.
5. Have family needs assessed and addressed.
6. Receive help in the form of service coordination for child and family needs.
7. Receive help for transportation if that is necessary to benefit from services prescribed.
8. Have rights protected within the process of referral, assessment, and developing the IFSP.
9. Have qualified professionals working with the child and the family.
10. Have services provided (as much as is appropriate) in places that are typical for children of the same age without disabilities.
11. Resolve disputes with other team members or agencies through mediation, due process, or legal action if necessary.
12. Have plans developed for the child to transition to preschool services at age 3.

IDEA, PART C REGULATIONS

The Program for Infants and Toddlers with Disabilities (Part C of IDEA) assists states in providing comprehensive programs of early intervention for infants and toddlers with disabilities, ages birth through 2 years, and for their families [National Early Childhood Technical Assistance System (NECTAS), 1999]. Each participating state must assure that early intervention will be available to every eligible child and his or her family. The governor of each state designates a **lead agency** to operate the program and appoints an **Interagency Coordinating Council (ICC)** to advise and assist. Currently all states participate, receiving annual funding based on the census figures of the number of children, birth through age 2 years, in their general populations (NECTAS, 1999). Lead agencies vary by state, as do specific definitions of who is eligible for services. In 1998, about 197,000 infants and toddlers were directly served.

The purpose of Part C of IDEA is to develop a "system that provides early intervention services" and to "encourage States to expand opportunities for children under 3 years of age who would be at risk of having substantial developmental delay if they did not receive early intervention services." Eligible infants and toddlers are those under 3 years of age who need early intervention for one of two reasons; they display delay in one or more areas of development or there is a diagnosis of a physical or mental condition that has a high probability of resulting in developmental delay. Services must be family-directed and to the "maximum extent appropriate, early intervention services are provided in natural environments." These special services, evaluation, assessment, and planning take place only if the family approves and only with the family's participation.

Several factors may influence the extent to which families will agree to participate in the special services available to their very young children (Baird & Peterson, 1997). These factors include the nature of the family's concerns about their child, their level of stress and degree of support, their beliefs and values, their education level, their prior experience with children, and their rapport with those who provide services. For example, a family may be too emotionally involved in dealing with their child's diagnosis to make long-term plans. Other families may be so overwhelmed by immediate day-to-day survival that they cannot attend to other issues. On the other hand, some families will be eager to become involved. It is incumbent upon the service provider to respect the central, active role the family plays in the care of their child with special needs.

Family-Centered Early Intervention

Family-centered services have evolved from the original concept of parent involvement, when parents were encouraged to participate in activities that professionals felt were important (McWilliam, Tocci, & Harbin, 1998). Traditional approaches to early intervention were "expert driven, deficit oriented, and child-centered" without considering the important impact families had on their children (Wehman, 1998). Legislation in the 1960s and 1970s first mandated an educational role for parents as teachers of their own children (Wehman, 1998). In the 1970s, the law provided parents of school-aged children with disabilities with the right to participate in the educational planning process. In the 1980s and 1990s, legal policies established the family unit, rather than the child, as the focus of services (Wehman, 1998). Consequently, early intervention specialists sought to build partnerships with and to empower families (McWilliam et al., 1998). Today, families themselves are considered the recipients of early intervention services.

There are several benchmarks of best practice in family-centered early intervention (Baird & Peterson, 1997). For example, programs recognize and respect family members as experts on their child, the family as the ultimate decision maker, and the family as the constant in a child's life. Early interventionists must also honor the family's choices regarding their level of participation and understand the need for a collaborative, trusting relationship. Professionals need to respect differences in families' cultural identity, beliefs, values, and coping styles.

Family-centered services are constantly being redefined by practice. Today, to be family-centered means to be willing to orient services to the whole family, rather than just to the child (McWilliam et al., 1998). It means being sensitive and establishing enough trust and good rapport with parents to be able to ask them about their own concerns. Being family-centered requires a lack of distance between professionals and clients, to become concerned family friends, not just therapists or teachers. Several characteristics of effective family-centered service providers have been identified (McWilliam et al., 1998):

◆ *Positiveness:* thinking the best about families. The philosophy of positiveness includes a belief in parents' abilities, a nonjudgmental mind-set, an optimistic view of children's development, and an enthusiasm for working with parents.
◆ *Sensitivity:* walking in the parents' shoes. Service providers must understand families' concerns, needs, and priorities. They must expand their own sensitivity, understand cultural differences, work through interpersonal challenges, and recognize parents' aspirations.
◆ *Responsiveness:* doing whatever needs to be done. Responsiveness requires flexibility, not pushing an agenda, attending to parents' concerns, and taking action when parents express needs.

◆ *Friendliness:* treating parents as friends. This entails developing a reciprocal relationship, building trust, taking time to talk and listen, encouraging parents, offering practical help, and conveying caring for both parents and child.

◆ *Child and community skills:* being practical. This skill requires an awareness of how the economy influences the cultural climate, a familiarity with people and agencies in the community, and a desire to collaborate with other professionals for the mutual benefit of serving families.

One service provider summarized her understanding of her role this way:

> I let them know that my role is not only to work with their child, but to help their family be a family that feels better about itself—be a family that feels like it's more knowledgeable about how to care for this child and to work on whatever goals or whatever challenges it's facing at this point, or things that they've always wanted to do and just couldn't figure out how to make it all work together. (McWilliam et al., 1998, p. 213)

Several elements of IDEA, Part C, support a family-centered approach, but perhaps the most integral of these structures are service coordination and the IFSP (Thompson et al., 1997).

Service Coordination

Imagine a family of a child with significant disabilities receiving early intervention services from three different agencies. There is likely to be confusion and frustration regarding scheduling of appointments, payment for services, and overlap of information and recommendations for home intervention. The first attempt by Congress to create an early intervention model that was comprehensive also created the need for a new method of managing the various agencies involved in service delivery for infants and toddlers with special needs. Thus a *"case manager"* role was designated in IDEA to assume the responsibility of overseeing the delivery of services to which children and their families are entitled. Specifically, "One person, together with the family, actively advocates for services in response to changing needs, and is responsible for implementation of an integrated program of services, in consultation with colleague specialists" (Division of Early Childhood, 1987). The law further stated that the professional most relevant to the needs of a child and family should serve as that family's case manager. For example, a physical therapist would be most appropriate for a child with muscular dystrophy, while a speech therapist would serve as the case manager for a child with a cleft lip and palate.

Several questions arose simultaneously with the requirement to provide case management. Educators and families asked: Who selects the case manager, the family or the agency? Can families serve as their own case manager? How many children should a case manager serve? What are the qualifications of a case manager? Partly as a result of the ensuing debate to resolve such questions, terminology in the law was changed from case manager to **service coordinator,** which reflects a less clinical and more pragmatic approach to delivery of services. Principles of service coordination generated by parents through a research survey lend understanding to family preferences regarding their relationship with a service coordinator (Early & Poertner, 1993). Parents indicated the following:

1. Parents should have a major role in determining the extent and degree of their participation as service coordinators.
2. Service coordinators should have frequent contact with children, families, and other key participants.
3. A single service coordinator should be responsible for helping families gain access to needed resources.
4. Parents and child should be involved in decision making.
5. Service coordinator roles and functions should support and strengthen family functioning.

Legally, service coordinators have responsibility for ensuring that seven major components of program delivery are completed according to federal and state laws:

1. Coordinating the performance of evaluations and assessments.
2. Facilitating and participating in the development, review, and evaluation of individual family service plans.
3. Assisting families in identifying available service providers.
4. Coordinating and monitoring the delivery of available services.
5. Informing families of the availability of advocacy services.
6. Coordinating with medical and health providers.
7. Facilitating the development of a **transition plan** to preschool services if appropriate.

It is not necessarily a service coordinator's responsibility to directly provide these services, rather that person makes sure families have access to these services. In fact, the primary goal of service coordinators is to foster family empowerment. Strengthening a family's abilities to coordinate their own services promotes human development and helps build the overall capacity of individuals, families, and communities.

Service coordinators can empower families in several important ways. They can improve families' capacity to master a broad range of skills by providing information to increase knowledge of their child's disability, giving choices and encouraging families to make their own decisions regarding types of services, and showing parents how to access information or perform certain intervention strategies independently. Service coordinators can also improve liaisons and linkages to mobilize social supports within a family's community. Both **primary social supports** (i.e., close family, friends, and neighbors) and **secondary social supports** (e.g., health care providers, educators, and therapists) can provide families with a network capable of enabling them as caregivers of a child with special needs (Dunst, Trivette, & Deal, 1988). Just as service coordinators themselves must be careful to honor the privacy of families, they can work to protect families from other sources of unwarranted intrusion. Being careful to avoid paternalism, service coordinators can serve as advocates for family rights. Finally, service coordinators may be able to minimize stress by making essential resources available in a manner that eliminates or reduces unnecessary work or anxiety.

Early on, Berzon and Lowenstein (1984) described the personal characteristics of a case manager. These seem equally appropriate for today's service coordinator:

> To be effective, the case manager. . . must possess a high threshold for frustration, a high tolerance for ambiguity, an ability to measure barely perceptible increments, a sense of humor and an ability to turn to others for support. Personal flexibility, creativity, and persistence are also important. (p. 54)

Such recommendations reflect the importance of engaging in positive, proactive behavior. However, maintaining this attitude has not always been easy for public service professionals. Maroney (1986) described four perspectives taken by many professionals toward parents; some of these views would interfere with the effectiveness of service coordinators:

1. Viewing families as problem-causing and interfering
2. Viewing families as resources to children (with no needs of their own)
3. Viewing families as team participants
4. Viewing families as needing resources (for themselves, independent of child)

Reading "case manager" as "service coordinator," Donner and colleagues (1993) made sense when they pointed out, "It is not enough for case managers to have the skills to do the tasks of their job, they also need attitudes that support families." These attitudes include: being positive; assigning no blame, no matter what; acknowledging that parents are trying; treating families as the experts on their needs; looking at the world from the parents' perspective; setting priorities based on family desires; and being sensitive to cultural, environmental, racial, religious, and sexual orientation differences.

Interagency Coordination
To manage the complex services promised for infants and toddlers, a unique governing body was created for early intervention. At the federal level, Part C is coordinated by an Interagency Coordinating Council (ICC), comprised of representatives from different governmental agencies that provide services to infants and toddlers with disabilities and led by the U.S. Department of Education (USDOE). Money allocated under Part C flows from USDOE to each state's lead agency for the administration of early intervention programs. Many states and territories selected their own Department of Education to administer Part C, while approximately the same number of states designated their Department of Health as the lead agency (Colarusso & Kana, 1991). The remaining states and territories designated other agencies such as Mental Health, Mental Retardation, or Human Resources as their lead agencies (MHLP, 1990). Appointed by the governor, the lead agency provides a single line of authority and is responsible for planning and implementing state and federal Part C regulations. The primary duty of the lead agency is to develop interagency agreements between those parties involved in delivery of services. Agreements must stipulate procedures for such actions as resolution of disputes and payment of service providers.

The governor of each state appoints members to the State Interagency Coordinating Council (ICC). State ICCs advise and assist their lead agencies in planning for implementation and oversight of Part C requirements. Membership to this committee must include parents of children with disabilities, service providers from public or private early intervention programs, a representative from the state legislature, a person involved in early intervention personnel preparation, a state insurance representative, and representatives from other state agencies. In addition to these state level ICCs, many states have created other levels of administration by appointing regional and local ICCs. The latter usually include similar proportionate representation and perform the duties of forming local interagency agreements and coordinating and delivering services to families.

Interagency Services

When agencies need to coordinate their services to meet the needs of a particular child, it is the lead agency's responsibility to initiate the formal agreement regarding who delivers and pays for early intervention services. Part C funds were not intended to supplant services and funding already provided by public agencies even though the latter might be contracted to provide services to children identified under Part C. For example, if an interagency agreement is formed with the Public Health Department, which already provides audiological assessment and treatment to the community, then Public Health and not the lead agency for early intervention is responsible for the cost of such services. Depending on the services provided and the individual situations of families served, various financial arrangements can be made to ensure that no family is denied services for which they are eligible. Sources of funding include local, state, or federal funding through agencies providing services, a family cost-sharing using a sliding scale, private insurance, and Medicaid (Colarusso & Kana, 1991). Colarusso and Kana (1991) identified a number of federal agencies that should be able to contribute to early intervention services through interagency collaboration. These included such programs as: Services for Deaf-Blind Children and Youth; Head Start Program; Medicaid; Maternal and Child Health Block Grants; Child Welfare Services Program; Alcohol, Drug Abuse and Mental Health Block Grant Program; Community Health Service Program; Indian Health Service Program; Indian Health Care Improvement Act; Migrant Health Services Program; and Health Care for the Homeless Program, Homeless Assistance Act. All these programs have the potential to provide funding for services to infants and toddlers eligible under Part C. The way in which state and local agencies choose to use these and other state and local services varies according to availability and the priorities of ICCs.

In spite of the obvious need to coordinate services across agencies in order to meet the spirit of IDEA, this is the element of the law that has been least effectively implemented (Harbin, Gallagher, Lillie, & Eckland, 1990). Aside from the task of accepting parents as equal partners, the collaboration of multiple agencies in delivery of early intervention is the next greatest challenge. Each of these relationships involves sharing power where power has not been shared in the past.

Eligible Children

Unlike IDEA regulations for older children, each state was given the responsibility of determining specific eligibility guidelines for early intervention services. In addition to serving children with developmental delays, states have been permitted by Congress to serve children who are at risk of developing a delay later in childhood, defined by IDEA as "an individual under 3 years of age who would be at risk of experiencing a substantial developmental delay if early intervention services were not provided" [Section 632(1)]. Infants and toddlers with developmental delays and those with **established risk** must be served by states that receive Part C funding. Two other risk categories are discretionary and served at the will of each state: **biological/medical risk** and **environmental risk.**

Developmental delay.   Infants and toddlers who experience delayed progress or who have fallen significantly below the age-related norms in one or more areas have a developmental delay, which may be in communication, physical development, adaptive behavior (feeding, dressing, toileting, etc.), cognition, and social/emotional development. Approximately 4% of infants and toddlers fall into this category.

Established risk.   Children who have a diagnosed condition that gives them a high probability of later delays in development have an established risk. Conditions such as Down syndrome, PKU, muscular dystrophy, and sickle cell anemia are examples. Approximately 1% of all infants and toddlers have an established risk condition.

Biological risk.   Medical conditions that threaten to compromise a child's health, particularly perinatally, are predictive of later delays. For example, children born anoxic, with low APGAR scores, prematurely, or those who experience meconium aspiration are at risk for cerebral palsy and other developmental delays but may not have an identified disability or delay (approximately 2% to 3% of infants and toddlers).

Environmental risk.   An increasing proportion of children in our society grow up in conditions that place them at risk of developmental delays. Children who live in poverty, whose parents abuse drugs or alcohol, whose primary language is not English, or who are abused are examples of children who are environmentally at risk. It was predicted that by 2000, 38% of children under age 18 in the United States would be from ethnically and linguistically diverse groups where poverty is especially prevalent (Bosch, 1998). Poverty is especially high among ethnic-minority groups, approximately 58% of impoverished infants and toddlers are in families of color, and the risk of disabilities is much higher because of poverty (Bosch, 1998).

Those who are environmentally at risk represent at least 25% of the United States' infants and toddlers. Most states are reluctant to or financially unable to serve so many at-risk children and have elected not to offer services to this population though the law encourages it (Bosch, 1998). The number of eligible infants and toddlers, with documented developmental delay and physical or mental disabilities has been about 250,000, but fewer than that number received services through IDEA, Part C (Bowe, 1995). If so few children with measurable disabilities were served, perhaps it is unfeasible to try to expand the definition for eligibility to environmentally at risk children (Bosch, 1998).

This situation is unfortunate since experts agree that children at risk are more vulnerable to the progressive effects of environmental factors and may have greater problems later on in life than children with diagnosed disabilities (Weiner & Koppelman, 1987). At the same time, it is these same at-risk children who are most amenable to intervention and such intervention should lead to long-term cost-effective results. Economic benefits accrue to society first because so many more children fall into the at-risk groups and, secondly, because relative benefits to our society are gained through prevention of delays (i.e., in children who are at risk for developmental disability) as opposed to remediation of disabilities. Still, in times of fiscal restraint, it is unlikely that the potential long-term cost savings to our society will influence voters to fund expensive preventive educational programs.

In addition to the new categories of services that might be provided under Part C, wisdom prevailed in the labeling of children served. Rather than giving children categorical labels, such as "seriously emotionally disturbed" or "mentally retarded," children and their families are simply identified as "eligible," with services determined and resources allocated according to assessed need. A simple designation of "eligible" avoids the issues of discrimination, testing error, and lowered expectations that are associated with categorical labeling.

Procedural Safeguards

States are required to establish a system that protects the fundamental rights of families and children who are eligible for services under Part C. The intent of **procedural safeguards** is to ensure both that the intended services are not denied to families with eligible children and that an impartial hearing can be requested when families believe their rights are violated. These safeguards are very much like those found under Part B of IDEA. Federal law and regulations stipulate the following due-process rights (MHLP, 1990):

1. *Access to Records:* Upon the request of parents, all documentation regarding screening, evaluation or assessment data, eligibility determination, development and implementation of Individualized Family Service Plan (IFSP), or other written, audiotaped, or videotaped communication regarding their child and family must be made available for examination.

2. *Notice:* Before initiation or refusal of services (i.e., identification, eligibility, service provision, or placement), parents must receive prior written notification.

3. *Confidentiality:* All personally identifiable information regarding a child or family member must be kept confidential. Only after parents have given written consent can information be released, and then it can be released only for the specific purpose for which the permission was given.

4. *Written Parental Consent:* Parents must give written consent before an agency can conduct an assessment or provide services to infants and toddlers. Additionally, agencies must ensure that parents are informed of their right to withdraw consent at any time. This right would be of little value to families who do not understand what "consent" means. Therefore, service providers need to explain information in a family's native language or mode of communication and then ask questions to make sure that family members have understood. As in Part B, states have the right to contest a parent's refusal of an evaluation by filing for a due-process hearing. However, most professionals feel that only in extreme cases (e.g., suspected child abuse or neglect) should a parent's decision to refuse evaluation be challenged.

5. *Surrogate Parents:* Just as with school-age children with disabilities, the state has the responsibility to appoint surrogate parents for any eligible child whose parents cannot be found or are not known or if the child is a ward of the state. This surrogate is responsible for representing absent parents in duties related to evaluation, eligibility, placement, IFSP development, and so on. The

state may not appoint a surrogate simply because the parents are considered to be irresponsible.

6. *Continuity of Services:* Analogous to the "stay put" principle, the continuity-of-services right assures that children and their families will continue to receive services throughout any legal proceedings. However, given joint agreement of parents and service provider, services may be withdrawn or changed. If a child has received services, and access to services is the issue under consideration, all services not in dispute should be provided.

7. *Prompt and Unbiased Dispute Resolution:* Mediation. The latest revision of IDEA features mediation as an initial process to resolve disputes. Mediation allows both parties to discuss issues and to attempt compromise. Mediation is free and each state can supply names of mediators.

8. *Impartial Hearing:* Both agencies and families may file for an impartial administrative hearing if the rights of either are perceived to have been violated. Each state determines if the regulations for a fair hearing under Part B are to be used or if new regulations will be devised for infants and toddlers. Parents must receive written notification of the resolution within 30 days of filing a request for hearing.

9. *Right to Appeal:* Parents or schools may file a civil action in state or federal courts to appeal a resolution made during the administrative hearing.

10. *Procedures for Resolving Systemic Problems:* Parents and others have the right to file a complaint if it is believed that the state has failed to implement any Part C regulation(s). The state must arrange an independent investigation, with results (and resolution if necessary) completed within 60 days of the complaint.

It is the obligation of each service provider to ensure that due-process rights are made clear to parents. These regulations are complicated and can be intimidating for early childhood professionals and must, therefore, be doubly obscure for many parents new to this field. The fact that professionals have the privilege of working more closely with parents in early intervention than with parents of older children provides greater opportunity to enhance families self-advocacy by clarifying the law as much as possible.

ASSESSMENT

Although IDEA previously permitted the delivery of services to infants, toddlers, and their families before an IFSP was completed, amendments since then require that an IFSP be developed and have the written consent of parents before services can be delivered. In fact, the entire process of determining eligibility, planning a child's program, implementing the plan, and reviewing progress is similar to that of older children with disabilities (see Figure 8–1).

Differing from assessment of older children, the evaluation process in early intervention has two distinct but interrelated aspects: child assessment, and family assessment. The primary purposes of assessment are to determine if infants are eligible for services and to provide sufficient information to plan intervention for a child and family (Lerner et al., 1998). Once a child is determined eligible for services and

MADDY'S PROGRESS: INTERVIEW WITH KIM SHAFER

We enrolled Maddy in a special early intervention program, the Spokane Guilds' School, at 2 years old because she had a lot of frustration. She had this huge vocabulary of sign language and she babbled. Her mouth moved like yours and mine, but she couldn't hear it, and she thought she was saying the same things I was. So when she was playing with other kids and she'd say "yababbadabbadabba" and when they didn't answer, she'd bonk them on the side of the head like, "why aren't you paying attention to me?" Whoa, this wasn't socially acceptable, so we got her into the special program. I thought that maybe by having her in a preschool program early, she'd understand that there's a routine to things and there are certain things that are okay and not okay.

Maddy did very, very well there. The Guilds' School is just an amazing school, it's just awesome. But, when your child is 3 years old they have to go into a different setting and the families are scared because they've had all their services provided in one place. It's kind of a scary thing when you go into some of the school districts and they don't have a program for 3- to 5-year-olds.

Maddy started in public school when she was 3 years old. Linwood Elementary had a deaf/hard-of-hearing preschool and her preschool teacher had been there for years and she was just a wonderful teacher. Her teacher used to be a sign language interpreter, so she incorporated the sign language with the verbal language. Maddy went there from 3 years old and she still goes there, but this last year I saw such a huge leap with her language—her verbal language, her auditory language; her skills just kept increasing.

But, I thought that making a leap from the preschool, where she's getting mainly sign language, to going into a mainstream kindergarten would be a real struggle. I wanted something kind of in the middle. My next door neighbor is one of the directors of Head Start, which includes a great program called CAPE—Cooperative Approach to Preschool Education. The program serves kids from 3 to 5 or 6 years old. So we're there now with 6 other CAPE kids, kids with disabilities, and 12 kids who are low income Head Start students, 18 kids in all. There are two lead teachers, a special education teacher, a speech/language therapist, occupational therapist, physical therapist and an aide. There are usually 6 hands-on adults to 18 kids which is a great ratio.

Maddy's language is getting clearer and clearer as she echoes the kids around her because there isn't sign language there. For the most part, she has to depend on her voice and her implant to hear. So it's been a really great resource for her.

Our other excitement is being selected winners by *Ladies' Home Journal* for an essay contest titled "My Daughter and What I Hope for Her in the Next Century." Your daughter had to be turning 1, 5, or 10 years old in the year 2000. My Mom suggested that I enter, so of course I put it aside until the night before it was due, then I whipped out this two page essay, showed it to my mom and she started bawling. I said, "Perfect!" sent it in and we won! We got this call saying that out of a thousand entries, we were one of six winners. The magazine is going to do a story on Maddy's life, each year for the next ten years.

Every year, someone from the magazine back in New York will come out and do a photo session and update as they follow Maddy's life. The one thing I was asked that I really hadn't given any thought to was "Are you nervous at all about if you have any problems that come up in your life? It's going to be in a magazine!" But I thought, you know, you can't predict the future, you just need to live your life the best you can.

Maddy, Cassie, and Amanda Shafer (left to right).

the IFSP is developed, assessment is necessary to measure progress and evaluate the effectiveness of the services provided. Federal regulations also require evaluation and assessment to be conducted in a nondiscriminatory manner.

IDEA GUIDELINES FOR ASSESSMENT

Each lead agency is to adopt nondiscriminatory evaluation and assessment procedures. The public agencies responsible for the evaluation of children and families are to ensure, at a minimum, that:

1. Tests and other evaluation procedures and materials are administered in the native language of the parents or other modes of communication, unless it is clearly not feasible to do so.
2. Any assessment and evaluation procedures and materials that are used are selected and administered so as not to be racially or culturally discriminatory.
3. No single procedure is used as the sole criterion for determining a child's eligibility.
4. Evaluation and assessments are conducted by qualified personnel.

Figure 8–1
Diagram of
identification,
eligibility,
programming,
and review for
early
intervention
services.

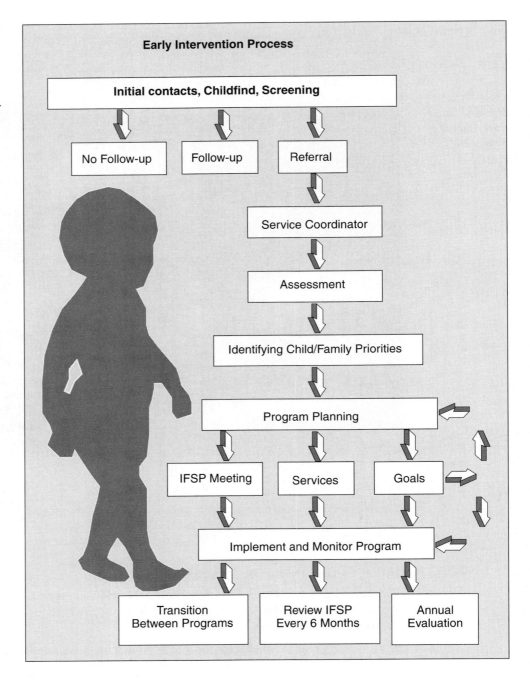

Two basic approaches may be used to conduct assessments. Formal assessments are more contrived and generally involve the use of standardized tools. Informal assessments are more consistent with current early childhood practices that place emphasis on "natural" methods. While there are advantages and disadvantages to both formal and informal evaluation, there is generally much to be gained from combining the two approaches.

Simeonsson (1986) described three methods of assessment. A **psychometric approach** is used to compare a child to normal standards of development, intelligence, or achievement in order to determine performance discrepancies. In a **behavioral assessment,** practitioners examine factors that govern children's behavior under given conditions. In this approach, the goal of assessment is to determine the controlling impact of setting conditions and consequences on behavior. An important step in behavioral assessment is to carry out a **functional assessment** which involves manipulation of those conditions in order to alter the observed behavior. For example, if a child is 18 months old, and not attempting to make sounds, it may be observed that the child is placed in a playpen for much of the day at a child care center and that when she does attempt to communicate, caregivers often overlook her verbalizations. It would be recommended, therefore, that caregivers provide multiple opportunities for interaction throughout the day and that they begin to consequate verbalizations by imitating or expanding on her communication attempts. A child's age is irrelevant in the **qualitative-developmental assessment** approach. Early interventionists examine a child's skills, as well as the child's approach to people and tasks. This global approach to assessment provides rich information for program development, which is particularly useful in family-centered intervention.

In addition to these three approaches, a fourth, the **ecological approach,** is used by many early interventionists (Carta, Sainato, & Greenwood, 1988; Sexton, Thompson, Perez, & Rheams, 1990; Thurman & Widerstrom, 1990). Ecological evaluations focus on children, their environment, and the interaction between the two. This approach provides information that is especially useful in program planning. Since a child's behavior and development are influenced by multiple factors, all these variables need to be considered in evaluation. Therefore, the key to ecological evaluations is to comprehensively analyze a child's real environment, taking into account a wide range of variables, including resources and materials, child behaviors, social relationships, and family/adult behaviors in order to develop a very specific profile.

Child Assessment

It is the purpose of child assessment that most often determines the type and scope of procedures to be used. That is, eligibility is usually determined by a somewhat formal set of procedures, while program design typically involves relatively informal measurement conditions.

Eligibility Determination

Two stages may be involved in eligibility determination. **Screening** is a relatively quick preliminary evaluation used to determine if a child should be referred for more in-depth assessment. Because full evaluations are costly in terms of time and money, screening helps to identify those children who are most likely to need services. There is, however, a drawback to this efficiency. By definition, screening tools are less accurate than follow-up assessment and, therefore, overlook many children who might actually benefit from special services.

Positive screening results lead to a **multifactored diagnostic evaluation** involving professionals from all relevant disciplines. This evaluation must be completed within 45 days of referral. In early intervention, this **multidisciplinary team** almost always includes parents, an educator, and a communication specialist. The purpose of a team approach to assessment is to have adequate expertise represented in all program areas.

State regulations guide practitioners in determining what data are needed in order to make an eligibility decision. Formal assessments use standardized tools, which compare a child's behaviors to those of a standard norm. For example, a 10-month-old child's language behaviors are compared to the average language behaviors of children at 10 months of age. With average being the "standard," a significant deviance from the standard indicates that a child may be either delayed or precocious. Standardized tools are also administered in a precise manner and scored according to a set of standard procedures. That is, any variation made in giving the test that is not provided for in the testing manual, such as timing, use of materials, or instructions, renders the results unusable for comparison purposes. Informal assessments may include the use of commercially available or curriculum-referenced tools. Also used are interviews with parents, narrative descriptions of behavior, checklists, and rating scales. These data should be combined with more formal assessment data to make an eligibility determination. If a child is found to be eligible, programs have 45 days from the initial referral to plan and hold an initial IFSP meeting. Services would begin immediately following parental approval of the IFSP.

PROGRAM PLANNING

The most efficient assessment combines eligibility determination with programming evaluation. Due to the developmental nature of both assessment and curriculum design, it is relatively easy in early intervention to use a curriculum-referenced tool to accomplish both purposes. A curriculum-referenced tool is linked to intervention objectives so that the assessment itself is sensitive to relevant behaviors. In early intervention, these tools are generally very practical and measure behaviors in all relevant developmental areas. Some tools are specifically designed to measure very small steps in learning for children with significant disabilities. Others are closely linked to broad developmental milestones and their associated learning objectives.

Day-to-day assessment provides input for dynamic decision making regarding the appropriateness of a child's objectives, intervention strategies, and programming alternatives. Research consistently indicates that continuous measurement (daily or several times a week) is the most effective schedule for assessing child progress on learning objectives. Furthermore, direct observation methods are most useful for daily data collection. Counting the frequency or rate of behaviors (e.g., number of times in a day that child wets), measuring the length of time that a behavior occurs (e.g., duration of independent sitting before falling sideways), and assessing the magnitude of behaviors (e.g., how far will a child reach across midline to grasp a toy) are examples of direct data collection.

Curriculum-based tools are also useful for measuring child progress on outcome objectives specified on IFSPs. Review of each IFSP must take place at least every six months since children can progress so rapidly through developmental stages at this early age. The comprehensive reevaluation must be completed at least annually. While it is possible for children to become ineligible for services through rapid development, the at-risk clause of Part C permits agencies to continue services should families be interested.

Family Assessment

To a large extent, family focus is based upon the provisions of IDEA. Development of IFSPs must include statements about family priorities, which necessitates the assessment of families. However, family assessment is the most sensitive and least well evolved component of early intervention programs (Hanson & Lynch, 1989). Yet, families are especially vulnerable during initial diagnostic stages because they are entering a new arena in which they must rely on the integrity and proficiency of strangers. Therefore, parents should only be evaluated voluntarily; assessment for the purpose of defining a family as it relates to care of a child with disabilities is an intrusion to which families of young children without disabilities are not subjected. For these reasons, educators are cautioned to fulfill this legal requirement with wisdom and empathy.

Any family assessment that is conducted must be voluntary on the part of the family. If an assessment of the family is carried out, the assessment must be conducted by personnel trained to utilize appropriate methods and procedures, be based on information provided by the family through a personal interview, and incorporate the family's description of its strengths and needs related to enhancing the child's development.

All aspects of a family's conduct that might influence their ability to meet the needs of their child with disabilities may be considered in the assessment. IDEA directed professionals to include a statement of family strengths and weaknesses on the IFSP (see Figure 8–2). Traditionally, a deficiency model focused attention on family needs rather than on their strengths. A more proactive way of looking at families is to concentrate on their relative strengths in formulating plans. Toward that end, the 1991 amendments to IDEA redirected educators to include a family-directed assessment of their respective resources, priorities for services, and concerns. Areas of family assessment may include domestic, child-parent interactions, educational, vocational, health, financial, and social domains. Again, while it may not be the responsibility of educational service agencies to provide for all the needs of a family, it is our responsibility to help establish linkages between families and corresponding services that will enable them to meet the needs of their child without special needs more effectively.

One approach to family assessment is a traditional format in which professionals survey parents through a standard protocol. In other words, all parents are asked a set of questions regarding specific skills, interests, and needs. Families might be interviewed or asked to fill out a written survey. Either way, professionals take the risk of offending parents who, while seeking help for their children, find the intrusion into their personal and family circumstances unwarranted. The following real account of a parent whose child was enrolled in a public program for low-income families illustrates the point.

Figure 8–2
Comparing
family strengths
and
weaknesses.

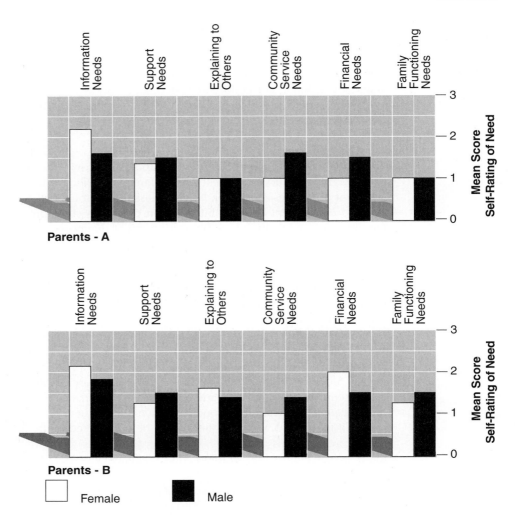

I wanted my son in an integrated preschool program but was unprepared for the ordeal. The application process included an assessment of my very personal circumstances. I was asked questions related to the adequacy of our housing and food, whether or not I am on welfare or on legal probation, how I discipline my family, and if we use drugs, alcohol, or birth control.

This parent was from a middle-class family and, therefore, was not accustomed to being treated as if her privacy was less important than the organization's right to ask such questions. It was also apparent that the questions were viewed as perfectly legitimate for families who lived in poverty. While persons who have low incomes are often subjected to intrusive questioning in order to receive other public services, the very implication that a family is deficient could place a barrier between professionals and that family.

Figure 8–3
Relationship between outcome of needs assessment and level of intrusiveness.

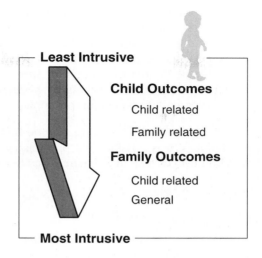

Beckman and Bristol (1991), warned that assessment of families for the purpose of identifying needs of families as opposed to their children's needs could be unwittingly intrusive (see Figure 8–3). Take for example, a child who has cerebral palsy. Traditionally, professionals would concentrate on child-centered needs as they pertain to a variety of developmental areas but, particularly, motor development. Motor assessment, conducted by a physical therapist, can be viewed as minimally intrusive. When the physical therapist attempts to determine if family members have the time, resources, or skills to conduct necessary motor development activities at home then the presumption on family privacy becomes more substantial, though perhaps not unreasonable. Using the same child with cerebral palsy as our example, if the physical therapist concludes that the child requires a wheelchair, the family might be asked about their financial capacity to purchase this child-oriented equipment. Obviously, financial questions can become quite sensitive but, under the circumstances, relevant. The most obvious intrusion and least justifiable questions surround general family needs. For example, the physical therapist, in recognizing that this child is underweight and tends to have chronic upper respiratory infections, might infer that the family lacks the resources to provide adequate nutrition or health care. Asking questions regarding employment status, health care insurance, and mealtime habits represents a very delicate assessment issue that should only be approached with the greatest sensitivity. It is recommended that professionals conduct this assessment informally and only after establishing good rapport with family members (Beckman & Bristol, 1991). Winton and Bailey (1988) suggested an informal four-stage process that should be initiated only after professionals and parents have built rapport with each other.

> **Phase I:** *Put family at ease:* Describe the purpose, structure, and confidentiality of interview.
> **Phase II:** *Interview:* Family members should do most of the talking after being asked open-ended questions and encouraged to discuss issues that are of importance to them.

Phase III: *Summary, priority, and goal setting:* Thoughts and feelings of family members are summarized and needs listed in order of priority. Though professionals may help to articulate family goals, the family itself is given the responsibility for achieving the goals.

Phase IV: *Ending interview:* After summary and articulation of goals, family contributions are acknowledged, while they are encouraged to provide continuous input to the plan.

Even this amount of structure may be both unnecessary and too overbearing for some families. It is possible that professionals who provide a continuous sounding board and use an IFSP in a dynamic manner will be as effective as those who use a more structured approach.

IFSP DEVELOPMENT

The IFSP is a form of documentation that reflects the emphasis on family-centered intervention highlighted throughout this text. IFSPs are created for infants and toddlers and their families when eligibility for early intervention is established. This legal document is the early intervention analog to an Individualized Educational Program (IEP) used with older students, but is more holistically conceived than the latter. Reflecting the rate of change in infants and toddlers, IFSPs are reviewed at least every 6 months or more often if needed.

The required components of an IFSP include the following:

1. A statement of child's developmental status in the areas of communication, physical, social/emotional, cognitive, and adaptive behavior, based upon the completion of a multidisciplinary assessment.
2. If family agrees to its inclusion, a statement of family priorities, concerns, and resources, as they relate to enhancement of their child's development.
3. A statement of the major outcomes (goals) that the child is expected to achieve, with the criteria for mastery, timelines for implementation and expected completion, and procedures for measuring progress included.
4. A statement of the specific early intervention services that must be provided to meet the aforementioned child and family goals. Included are the frequency, duration, location, and method of delivering these services; the payment arrangements, if necessary; and when deemed necessary, a specification of "other" services that may be needed by a family, but are not explicitly provided under Part C, and the steps that will be taken to secure those services. While these services may be written into the document, this does not mean that the services must be provided at public expense. Such services might include helping families to identify an agency to provide financial assistance, arranging for the child to access medical-health care services, or helping to prepare insurance papers.
5. Statement of the dates when services will be initiated and the anticipated duration of services.
6. The name of the service coordinator responsible for assuring that assessment, program planning, and program implementation are provided according to the law.

7. Statement of the steps that will be taken to ensure that a child makes a smooth transition from early intervention services to preschool education once a child reaches age three. This includes training parents for the legal and programmatic changes expected.

While IFSPs are intended to serve as a blueprint for services and as a legal agreement with families, there was a conscious effort in developing IDEA to avoid some of the pitfalls of legislation regulating the adoption of IEPs in this country. The emphasis is rightly placed on substance of intervention rather than on paperwork compliance.

Selecting IFSP Objectives

As in all areas of education, there is an increasing emphasis on planning children's programs to focus on real life (Notari-Syverson & Shuster, 1995; Stremel et al., 1992). In the past, objectives for very young children were often based on skills that were evaluated on standardized tests but had little to do with the actual daily activities of infants and their families. For example, parents might be asked to take time each day to teach their child to point to the object named in a set of pictures taken from a commercially available program. Often taught as an isolated skill, parents not only spent time on behaviors that had little meaning for their child, but there was little chance that such skills would generalize outside the teaching situation. Such activities were contrived in many ways and failed to meet the five guidelines for developing objectives outlined by Notari-Syverson and Shuster (1995):

1. *Functionality:* skills needed to operate as independently as possible in daily routines
2. *Generality:* general rather than specific skills that can be adapted to meet individual needs and used in many situations
3. *Ease of integration:* skills that will be used naturally in activities and social interactions
4. *Measurability:* skills that can be seen/heard and counted or measured
5. *Hierarchical relationship:* increasingly complex skills that are logistically sequenced—each new skill building upon a previously learned skill

To provide a sounding board for determining whether or not goals and objectives selected for very young children adhere to the above criteria, Notari-Syverson and Shuster developed a checklist (see Table 8–2). The answer to each question should be "yes" if the goals and objectives meet real life needs.

Natural Routines or the Context for Objectives

Naturally occurring routines are well suited for the integration of skill domains. For example, bathing can be the context for language, social interaction, motor (fine and gross) execution, and cognitive growth, as well as for self-help skill development. Instead of planning for integration, skills targeted on IFSPs are often designed to teach skills in isolation (Stremel et al., 1992). The point of having objectives written so that they can fit into daily caregiver routines is to increase both their relevancy for children and the likelihood that parents will have a reasonable chance of

Table 8–2   Checklist for Writing IFSP Goals and Objectives for Infants and Young Children.

Functionality

1. *Will the skill increase the child's ability to interact with people and objects within the daily environment?*
    The child needs to perform the skill in all or most of the environments in which he or she interacts.
    Skill: Places object in container.
    Opportunities: Home: Places sweater in drawer, cookie in paper bag.
                                              School: Places backpack in cubby hole; trash in trash bin
                                              Community: Places milk carton in grocery cart, soil in flower pot
2. *Will the skill have to be performed by someone else if the child cannot do it?*
    The skill is a behavior or event that is critical for completion of daily routines.
    Skill: Looks for object in usual location
    Opportunities: Finds coat on coat rack, gets food from cupboard

Generality

3. *Does the skill represent a general concept or class of responses?*
    The skill emphasizes a generic process, rather than a particular instance.
    Skill: Fits objects into defined spaces.
    Opportunities: Puts mail in mailbox, places crayon in box, puts cutlery into sorter
4. *Can the skill be adapted or modified for a variety of disabling conditions?*
    A child's sensory impairment should interfere as little as possible with the performance.
    Skill: Correctly activates simple toy
    Opportunities   Motor impairment—Activates light, easy-to-move toys (e.g., balls, rocking
                                              horse, toys on wheels, roly-poly toys.)
                                              Visual impairment—Activates large, bright, noise-making toys (e.g., bells,
                                              drums, large rattles)
5. *Can the skill be generalized across a variety of settings, materials, and/or people?*
    The child can perform the skill with interesting materials and in meaningful situations.
    Skill: Manipulates two small objects simultaneously
    Opportunities   Home: Builds with small interlocking blocks, threads lace on shoes
                                              School: Sharpens pencil with pencil sharpener
                                              Community: Takes coin out of small wallet

Instructional Context

6. *Can the skill be taught in a way that reflects the manner in which the skill will be used in daily environments?*
    The skill occurs in a naturalistic manner.
    Skill: Uses object to obtain another object
    Opportunities: Uses fork to obtain food, broom to rake toy; steps on stool to reach toy shelf.
7. *Can the skill be elicited easily by the teacher/parent within classroom/home activities?*
    The skill can be initiated easily by the child as part of daily routines.
    Skill: Stacks objects
    Opportunities: Stacks books, cups/plates, wooden logs

Measurability

8. *Can the skill be seen or heard?*
    Different observers must be able to identify the same behavior.
    Measurable skill: Gains attention and refers to object, person, and/or event
    Nonmeasurable skill: Experiences a sense of self-importance
9. *Can the skill be directly counted (e.g., by frequency, duration, distance measures)?*
    The skill represents a well-defined behavior or activity.
    Measurable skill: Grasps pea-sized object
    Nonmeasurable skill: Has mobility in all fingers

Table 8–2   Checklist for Writing IFSP Goals and Objectives for Infants and Young Children. *(continued)*

10. *Does the skill contain or lend itself to determination of performance criteria?*
    The extent and/or degree of accuracy of the skill can be evaluated.
    Measurable skill: Follows one-step directions with contextual cues
    Nonmeasurable skill: Will increase receptive language skills

Hierarchical Relation Between Long-Range Goal and Short-Term Objective

11. *Is the short-term objective a developmental subskill or step thought to be critical to the achievement of the long-range goal?*
    Appropriate: Short-term objective: Releases object with each hand
                                 Long-range goal: Places and releases object balanced on top of another object
    Innapropriate: The short-term objective is a restatement of the same skills as the long-range goal with the addition of an instructional prompt (e.g., short-term objective—activates mechanical toy with physical prompt. Long-term goal—independently activates mechanical toy) or a quantitative limitation to the extent of the skill (e.g., short-term objective—stacks 5 1-inch blocks: long-range goal—stacks 10 1-inch blocks).
                                 The short-term objective is not functionally or conceptually related to the long-range goal (e.g., short-term objective—releases object voluntarily; long-range goal—pokes with index finger).

Source: Notari-Syverson, A. R., & Shuster, S. L. (1995, Winter). Putting real life skills into IEP/IFSPs for infants and young children. *Teaching Exceptional Children*, 29–32. Used with permission.

working instruction of objectives into their already demanding lives. On the other hand, Stremel et al. (1992) cautioned that even when objectives are written according to the "family-child routine" standard, parents must be systematically taught to incorporate the objectives into daily activities.

Case Study

ISOLATION: INTERVIEW WITH MARSHA MOORE

The most difficult thing for me after Michael's diagnosis was the deep sense of guilt I felt. Somehow, I must not be doing all the things that I had done with the other kids. Somehow I had lost my touch. What was wrong with me? Why couldn't I bond with this little boy? Why didn't he know me as his mother? Even though I understood that there was a physical and neurological justification for Michael's delayed development, I felt that somehow the environment I had provided for him just wasn't adequate. I felt responsible for his slow progress, and I think some of the frustrations that I experienced came from the fact that I assumed others looked at me and thought that I must not be doing enough.

After his diagnosis, I made the decision that no one would ever be able to say, "she didn't try"! So I set up a family schedule to work with him. Intervention was a day and night process for the entire family. Mike hated it. His brothers and sisters hated it. His dad hated it. I hated it. I think back now and realize that we were really overstimulating him. The specialists had told us to bring the world to Michael and that's what we did. Lucky that Michael was a tough little guy. He survived in spite of us all! During this time, we were living in a very small mining town in north-eastern Wyoming. We felt physically isolated from medical facilities, shopping, entertainment, civilization in general. We often awakened to find antelope in the back-yard! We were socially isolated, as well. Because we had been transferred to the area shortly after Michael's birth, we had only a few acquaintances and no close friends. Our life seemed to be such a struggle, and although we lived there for almost three years, I can only remember bits and pieces about anything during that time. It sounds strange, but when the kids reminisce about neighbors, teachers, and schoolmates I have a difficult time placing names and faces. For three years, I missed a precious part of life with my husband and my five other children. I guess I didn't have the energy. I suppose my fear and sadness nearly consumed me. All I could think about was helping Michael to "get well."

Perhaps other things really weren't of any importance at that point in time. I think all parents want their circumstances to be the story of a miracle. I wanted Michael's story to have a happy ending. You know, the wonderful stories you see on TV, or read about in the newspaper. You think, "my story will be the one that they print, and it will be the miracle."

SERVICES DELIVERED

Several of the components of IFSPs mimic those of Individualized Education Plans (IEPs) which will be covered in Chapter 9. However, there are three distinct differences. First, the identification of a service coordinator described earlier in this chapter is different. Second, the services for which children and their families are eligible include some services unique to infants and toddlers. Finally, IFSPs must include a plan for a child's transition into other programs once they reach age 3. While transition plans are also used for school-age students, it is only when students reach age 14 and are preparing for transition to adulthood that such a plan is required in the IEP.

When children are found eligible for early intervention, assessment of services includes both those that will directly benefit that child and those that will support a child's family. The latter services are intended to indirectly benefit an eligible child by enhancing a family's capability of meeting the child's needs. In other words, if a family or family member has a need that is so great that it prevents nurturance of the child with special needs, that family need is as important to address as the developmental needs of the child. While this practice makes sense, provision of **tertiary services** to families is both costly and complicated, as described earlier in this chapter.

Services to infants and toddlers and their families can be provided through a myriad of models and agencies. Though, traditionally, public and private agencies have been centralized educational facilities, the law permits considerable flexibility in delivery models. Table 8–3 describes some example programs. It is clear, however, that those who crafted Part C envisioned the coordination of multiple resources; both public and private agencies are to be involved when indicated by the needs of families.

Children who are eligible for early intervention may receive the following types of services if the services themselves render a child's program "appropriate."

Table 8–3 Models for Intervention with Infants and Toddlers.

Model Program	Type of Service	Description
The SKI*HI model is operated out of Utah State University in Logan, Utah (Strong et al., 1994).	The purpose of SKI*HI is to provide home-based intervention to infants and preschoolers who have hearing impairments.	A Parent Advisor, along with parents and other members of a multidisciplinary team, assesses children, plans programs, and provides appropriate home-based services. In addition to Parent Advisors, other professionals from SKI*HI make home visits when appropriate. Team members may consist of speech therapists, occupational therapists, social workers, and so on. Finally, a large percentage of children, especially those who are older than three, receive some additional form of center-based education. Over 260 agencies in the United States, Great Britain, and Canada have been trained to replicate SKI*HI components, serving over 5000 children annually (Strong et al., 1994).
The Pueblo Infant Parent Education Project (PIPE) was initiated as a demonstration project and, after funding ran out, was adopted by the state of New Mexico for continuation (PIPE, 1984).	The needs of Pueblo families with children with disabilities could not be served in a traditional manner, so project staff work indirectly with families by training Community Health Representatives (CHRs).	Project staff provide monthly inservices to CHRs, as well as individual supervision. These CHRs have more intimate access and validity within their community by virtue of their own Pueblo membership. Thus, paraprofessionals provide the cultural linkage between a public educational agency and families of infants with disabilities. Home visits are made to conduct assessments, to train parents to implement child intervention programs, and to give ongoing emotional support to family members. In addition, parent group meetings are facilitated by a social worker from Indian Health Services.
Project Fair Start, funded by the Ford Foundation, was launched in the early 1980s to give children who were at risk due to poverty a chance to succeed once they reached school age.	Programs targeted very poor families, with very young children, and were served by members of their own community who understood the needs, values, and traditions of their peers. Widely diverse groups were served, from migrant farm workers to Haitian immigrants and inner city teen parents.	Programs held a preventive focus on pregnancy and infancy, offering education, support, and information about appropriate services. Programs targeted low-income groups who are underserved by traditional health and needed support services because of geographic, cultural, economic, or cognitive barriers. Multidisciplinary content, incorporating information about health, nutrition, child development, and social services were provided. Implementation was through personal contact with paraprofessional outreach workers who are members of the community (Larner et al., 1992, p. 7).
The Toddler-Parent Play Group Program was described by Popowicz and Haas (1991).	The caregiver is the primary communication partner. The speech/language therapist and family specialist act as participant observers. Intervention techniques involve incidental teaching modeled by therapists.	Toddler-Parent Play Groups were intended to facilitate a nonthreatening child-parent form of intervention in which caregivers were assumed to be the "experts" in their child's development. Therapists acted as facilitators to target interventions and then model for parents. Yet, therapists only "told" parents how to interact when parents asked directly. Indirectly, parents were encouraged to analyze their own skills in being responsive, empathetic, setting rules, negotiating, and selecting tools for social play.

1. Audiology
2. Service coordination (automatically provided to all families eligible for services)
3. Family training; counseling and home visits
4. Health services deemed necessary to enable infants and toddlers to benefit from the other early intervention services. (This may include clean intermittent catheterization or consultation by health care providers concerning the special medical needs of children eligible for services that will influence the delivery of those services. Specifically, services that are purely medical in nature and surgical services are excluded, as are devices that are used to control or treat a medical condition, as well as medical-health services such as immunizations.)
5. Medical services only for diagnostic and evaluation purposes
6. Nursing services
7. Nutrition services
8. Occupational therapy
9. Physical therapy
10. Social-work services
11. Psychological services
12. Special education
13. Speech-language pathology
14. Transportation (direct and related costs of travel) necessary to enable the child and family to receive early intervention services
15. Vision
16. Assistive-technology devices

This list of services to children is not exhaustive. Other services such as respite care and other family support services should be provided when they are appropriate. In contrast to the services articulated for children, the law is vague about the kind of services that must be made available to families or family members in order to enable the families. In theory, families should receive those services that will permit them to adequately meet the needs of their children with disabilities. The law is so broadly stated that professionals worry about the fiscal and logistical nightmare of serving some families who might be very needy.

Unlike service providers for school-age children under special education law, service providers may charge a fee to families of eligible infants and toddlers (Tucker & Goldstein, 1991). However, services that cannot be charged for under any circumstances are evaluation/assessment and service coordination. Moreover, guidelines that are established to determine payment may not be used to deny services to children or families because of their inability to pay for those services.

A SAMPLE IFSP

A family-centered IFSP should be positive, written with understandable language, and balanced in scope with specifics (McWilliam & Ferguson, 1998). There should be no professional jargon or doubletalk. What the family wants must be reflected on the IFSP, and what is written on the IFSP should show up in practice. Figure 8–4 is an example of an IFSP that should be examined part by part.

At the first, identifying information must be included in order to insure continued contact and monitoring of progress. This section would not only include the child's

Figure 8–4 Individualized Family Service Plan

Identifying Information

Child's Name: *Karmen Lynn Burch*　　　Nick name: *Bitsy*
Date: *10-1-99*

Gender: Male ___ Female *X*　　　Date of Birth *4-2-97*

Social Security Number: *371-16-5499*

Insurance type:　　　__ private (company and policy #) _____
X Medicaid　　　　　__ Champus　　　__ none　　　　__ other

Child's Primary Language/: *American Sign Language/English*
Mode of Communication

Initial Referral Date: *10-2-98*
Initial Referral Source: *Jackson County Health Department*

Does the child have a medical diagnosis? *X* Yes　　　__ No

If yes, what is diagnosis? *Bilateral, severe, hearing loss as a result of prenatal rubella infection*

Child's Primary Care Physician: *Glenn Stream, Jackson Clinic South*
Phone: *(517) 499-5228*

Is the child eligible for IDEA Part C services? *X* Yes　　__ No

Parent/Guardian/Surrogate/Caregiver Information

Name: *Barbara Benson, Guardian*　　　Relationship to the child: *grandmother*
　　　and
Name: *Laura Burch, Parent*　　　　　Relationship to the child: *mother*

Address: *S. 8167 5th St., Apt. #40*　　County: *Jackson*
City: *Jackson*　　　State: *MI*　　Zip: *49200*
Telephone: Day: *(517) 554-9191*　　(Night) *(517) 554-4252*
Best time to call: *7-9 a.m. and 6-9 p.m.*
Primary language/mode of communication: *English*

Service Coordinator Name: *Cheryl Tully*　Telephone: *(517) 768-2367*
Agency Name: *Michigan Deaf Services*
Address: *8237 Miller Ave.*　　City: Jackson　　State: MI　　Zip: *49200*

　　　Child's present level of performance

Child strengths:
Bitsy is a happy baby who seldom fusses. Her motor skills are good, she is running, climbing furniture, sleeping in a youth bed, putting together preschool puzzles. She feeds herself and is toilet trained during the daytime (sleeps in diapers). Her inoculations are up to date, vision is average, and though her height and weight are at about the 20th percentile, she appears healthy. Using the Brigance Inventory for Early Development, Bitsy scored at her age level in fine and gross motor and cognition. Bitsy is learning to communicate through American Sign Language and uses about one dozen signs.

Child concerns:
Bitsy was born 4 weeks prematurely, affected by maternal rubella. Her mother was 15 at the time of the birth and had received almost no prenatal care until the 7th month of gestation; father was not identified. Bitsy was treated in the NICU for almost two weeks before she was sent home. She has severe, bilateral hearing loss and does not make any speech sounds. She has very high activity levels and a very short attention span. She scored below the age 1 year level on the Brigance in the areas of receptive and expressive language. She has been fitted for hearing aids but refuses to wear them. Her grandmother and mother have decided against the use of a chochler implant.

Figure 8–4 Individualized Family Service Plan (Continued)

Family Assessment:

Family strengths:
Bitsy's mother, Laura is attending an alternative high school program that will allow her to complete her degree by next year. She also works fulltime as a waitress at the Highland Club, on the 6 p.m. to 2 a.m. shift and helps support Bitsy and Barbara, Bitsy's grandmother. Laura has relinquished Bitsy's guardianship to her mother Barbara. Barbara is on disability because of crippling arthritis. She stays home with Bitsy in the two-bedroom double-wide mobile home they share with Laura. Barbara transports Bitsy to doctor's appointments and to twice weekly speech and language therapy. Bitsy's maternal uncle, Benjamin often visits on weekends and brings his 4 year old daughter and 5 year old son along as playmates for Bitsy.

Family concerns:
Because of Bitsy's high activity levels and her lack of receptive language she is challenging for her grandmother, Barbara to control. In addition, Barbara's arthritis periodically flares up, making it physically difficult to care for Bitsy. The family would also like to have Bitsy in an environment where she would have other children to play with and could receive daily instruction in sign language and speech. A priority for the family would be at least a half-time preschool program and afternoon daycare for Bitsy while Laura is attending school. There are also concerns about continuing Medicaid services and the paperwork that accompanies it. Barbara and Laura feel they do not know enough sign language to use with Bitsy as she continues to add to what she knows.

Major Outcomes:

We would like to see Bitsy use American Sign Language fluently enough that her expressive and receptive language will be improved to a level expected for her age.

We would like to see Bitsy's attention span increased to age-appropriate levels, so that she can sit and work on an interesting, developmentally appropriate project with an adult or small group of children for up to 10 minutes at a time. This might mean listening to a story, cutting out play dough, or using finger paints.

We would like to obtain preschool and daycare services appropriate to Bitsy's needs that would provide grandmother with respite during the day while Bitsy's mother is attending high school.

We would like to increase Bitsy's use of her hearing aids so that she wears them on a daily basis.

We would like to enroll Barbara and Laura in weekend sign language instruction so they can add more signs to what they use at home with Bitsy.

Intervention Services Needed:

Continued speech therapy and sign language instruction for Bitsy.

Behavioral intervention planning and consultation to Bitsy's grandmother and mother, as well as to any new caregivers, to motivate increased attending and appropriate behavior.

Instruction in sign language for Bitsy's grandmother, mother, and new caregivers.

Special educational instruction in a group setting.

Strategies Activities, and Services:

Deborah Tully and Barbara Benson will begin the enrollment process for Bitsy to attend the Jackson Early Start Center, which provides early intervention services in an integrated preschool program. Speech and language therapy will be provided on-site and the Center's behavioral interventionist will work with the teacher and at home on Bitsy's ability to stay with a task for appropriate lengths of time, to follow simple instructions, and to wear her hearing aids.

Service Initiation and Duration:

Early Start Services will begin 10-5-99 and continue until 4-2-00 at which time Bitsy may begin transition to Head Start or Lynwood Deaf Preschool.

Barbara Benson and Laura Burch will attend parent sessions at the Southern Michigan Deaf Education Association Center in Chelsea, held every Saturday morning. Sign language instruction is provided and childcare for Bitsy is also available at the center.

The meetings also provide a parent network for families with deaf children. A deaf adult will act as a mentor and will meet with the family at their home one evening a week to provide additional sign language training and to advise the family on Bitsy's care and education.

Service Initiation and Duration:

Southern Michigan Deaf Education Association Center meetings will begin 10-3-99 and continue until 1-8-00 at which time the family and service coordinator will discuss the need to continue.

Transition Services:

The service coordinator will arrange for Barbara and Laura to visit two possible preschool programs for Bitsy to attend when she turns 3. One is an integrated Head Start program which provides speech therapy and employs staff who sign. The other is a self-contained preschool program at near-by Lynwood Elementary School which serves only deaf children. Total communication and language instruction is emphasized and all teachers are certified as teachers of the deaf.
Transportation for Bitsy will be provided by the local school district.
The service coordinator will be responsible for providing complete records to the receiving program and will identify the main contact person who will follow-through with the family.

Evaluation:

The IFSP team will meet again in March, 2000 to discuss progress made on the outcomes identified. We will determine at that time if continued behavioral intervention is needed in the home and if sign language instruction for the family should continue. We will also be prepared to make a final decision on which program Bitsy will transition to.

Service providers:

Type of Service	Person Responsible	Funding Source
Center-based early childhood education	Margaret Devon	Early Start
Family support and sign language instruction	Matthew Liese and Barbara Benson	Michigan Deaf Services
Service Coordination	Cheryl Tully	Michigan Deaf Services
Audiology and Speech and Language Assessment	Mary Manix, Jackson Clinic South	Medicare
Medical records and billing to Medicare	Nora Fishback, Jackson Clinic South and Barbara Benson	Jackson Clinic South
Transition services	Cheryl Tully and Laura Burch	Michigan Deaf Services
Medical treatment	Glenn Stream, Jackson Clic South	Medicare

This plan was developed by the following IFSP team members:

Name	Title
Barbara Benson	Grandmother/Guardian
Laura Burch	Mother
Cheryl Tully	Service Coordinator
Mary Manix	Speech and Language Specialist
Matthew Liese	Michigan Deaf Services Coordinator
Pamela Kruse	Deaf Education Teacher
Margaret Devon	Early Start Coordinator

name, but also the parent's or guardian's. It is sometimes the case that a foster parent or surrogate parent should also be identified since many at-risk children do not reside with their biological parents. Notes describing the parent or guardian's primary language, work and home phone numbers, and best time to call may improve later follow-up. It also important to note significant extended family or non-related kin who may be a significant part of the child's family. Grandparents, live-in partners, step-siblings, and so forth may play an important role in the child's life.

The name of the service coordinator must also be included. It is helpful to the family to also include the coordinator's contact information, such as agency address and phone number here on the IFSP. It may be wise to spell out the coordinator's responsibilities on the IFSP so that roles and expectations are clear to all involved.

A section is devoted to describing the child's present level of performance. This should include the results of any evaluations, assessments, and observations made on the child. The family's input regarding the child's strengths and needs would also be recorded in this section. Results from formal evaluations should be indicated as scores, percentiles, age equivalents and so on, but should also be summarized in everyday terms that are meaningful to the family and other professionals involved. Areas to describe include communication, cognition, social/emotional, motor skills, and adaptive skills. Physical development including vision, hearing, and health are also included. Relevant medical information including a birth history should be reported.

An assessment of the family is important, but as noted earlier, can be completed only with parent or guardian's consent. Items to consider for this section might be a description of who makes up the immediate family? what is the neighborhood or community like? what friends or relatives are important in supporting the family? and what things does the family like to do together? how is the child cared for during the day? and what are the child's most natural settings? Checklists might be used to indicate needs for transportation, housing, information on the disability or delay, training, help with insurance, Medicaid, or SSI, recreation, child care, and so on. Parents or caretakers should be given the opportunity to raise their own concerns about the child or their family's needs.

The IFSP must clearly state the major outcomes that express what the team wants to see happen for the child in the next six months. Also addressed are outcomes for the child's family. These outcomes must be related to the assessment information on the child's strengths and weaknesses and should reflect the family's concerns and priorities. The goals must be *functional* for the child and *age appropriate* (Umansky & Hooper, 1998). It is important to consider the context in which the child lives and what skills are needed for the child to be more successful in natural settings. For example, perhaps a family priority for a child is to become toilet trained because that will allow greater access to a regular daycare program. If a young child needs to develop fine motor skills, it makes more sense to work on dressing skills like fastening Velcro than to have her sorting nuts and bolts. Functional goals make caring for the child easier by helping the child be more independent.

Outcomes should also be realistic (Umansky & Hooper, 1998). Goals that are achievable give the family a greater sense of self-efficacy. One way to assure this is to think of six-month outcomes as steps needed to reach long-term goals. For example, a family may want a child who is currently nonverbal to speak. The first step toward that may be to teach the child to communicate through a picture exchange system in which a picture card is selected to indicate a desire for a snack or a toy.

The next time new six-month outcomes are set, the child may be ready to use a communication board or signs to indicate wants. Later, these pictures or signs may be paired with vocalizations and gradually those vocalizations are shaped to be meaningful words. But the first achievable step may be using the picture exchange. This *task analysis* (breaking an ultimate skill into its manageable subskills) should be done with the team so that all members can identify where the outcome is leading, and will recognize achievement of intermediate goals as substantive progress.

The IFSP must next indicate the intervention that is required to reach these outcomes. What type of service will be devoted to each outcome targeted? (For example, speech and language therapy, social work, medical services, transportation) Who will provide this service and when and where will these take place? A child might be served at home, in family day care, in an outpatient facility, in an early intervention class, or in a hospital, depending on the child's level of need and the intensity of services required. What type of assistive technology or specialized equipment or curriculum are needed to support the intervention? How often each week and for how long during each session will specific therapies or experiences be provided? It may be wise to also indicate how these services will be funded. Will private insurance, Medicaid, or family savings be needed? Who will make arrangements for this funding?

The IFSP team must also discuss the settings in which intervention might be provided. In the spirit of the least restrictive environment (LRE), the team should consider the most natural settings where services could be delivered. This would usually mean in the child's home or care setting. It might also mean in a community program such as Head Start or in an early intervention classroom or even in a hospital setting if the child's needs can only best be served in a more structured setting. It may be the case that a child's needs will be such that a center-based program which can provide intensive therapies is more appropriate. IDEA prescribes "the provision of early intervention services for any infant or toddler occurs in a setting other than a natural environment only when early intervention cannot be achieved satisfactorily for the infant or toddler in a natural environment" [Section 635(a)(16)]. The decision must be based on what children need. The team will indicate what options were discussed to reflect the most appropriate and natural setting and why other sites were rejected. It is also helpful to indicate any special adaptations, transportation, materials, equipment, curriculum, and so on that would be necessary to allow children to function in the setting selected.

A section must be devoted to plans for eventually transitioning to school services provided for children from age 3. Transitions might include changes in a child's teacher and other personnel, scheduling, transportation, expectations of children and their families, service delivery models, and philosophy of education. To make the movement from early intervention programs to preschool programs smooth, Part C requires that a specific transition plan be developed and included in the IFSP. Planning is to take place at least 90 days before a child's third birthday; the family, a representative from the child's early intervention program, and a representative of the school district are to meet to plan transitional activities (Rosenkoetter, Hains, & Fowler, 1994).

Transition plans need to consider a number of things. There should be procedures identified to help the child adjust to, and function in, a new setting. There will need to be a smooth transmission of information about the child to the local educational agency to ensure continuity of services, including evaluation and assessment information and copies of IFSPs that have been developed and implemented earlier.

Planning for these transitions should begin as early as possible to identify a setting that is most appropriate (Donegan, Fink, Fowler, & Wischnowski, 1995). Early childhood educators should work closely with parents to develop a plan that will facilitate adaptation to each child's new environment. The goal of transition planning is to enable children to be as successful as possible in their future environments. This means anticipating the skills needed of children and families in future preschool settings. It also requires coordination between early intervention programs and preschool programs to ensure that schools receiving young children understand a particular child's and family's needs and subsequently develop appropriate individualized programs.

The transition plan itself should answer the following questions (Destafano, Howe, Horn, & Smith , 1991, p. 69):

1. What services are available?
2. Which services are appropriate?
3. What steps must be taken before a child can enter the next program?
4. What skills does the next program require?
5. What additional skills does a child need?
6. What can the current program do to help a child succeed in the next program?
7. What is the next program not able to do to make sure a child succeeds?

An often overlooked section of the IFSP that should be included is evaluation (Umansky & Hooper, 1998). The team should discuss how the actions planned accomplished the desired outcomes and make any modification that seems necessary to make the IFSP more effective. Questions to ask include, Was intervention carried out as it was planned in the IFSP? What changes in the child's skills occurred and were they the result of the intervention? Where unexpected or undesired outcomes observed? Did we actually achieve intended outcomes? Was the family satisfied with intervention? Were family priorities addressed? The crux of evaluation is "whether families think their child received the services they felt were needed and whether they perceive those services as having a positive impact on development and behavior" (Bailey et al., 1998).

Finally, the IFSP provides a space for all those who were involved in its making to indicate their participation. Team members must include the parents or guardians and early interventionists. The planning might also involve other family members (such as grandparents), individuals invited by the family, specialists knowledgeable in the child's area of disability, medical personnel, and a parent advocate.

Case Study

TREATING JOSH'S AUTISM: INTERVIEW WITH AMY FINKEL

We probably spent six months of sixty hours a week in intensive research, after Josh's diagnosis. We talked to everybody on the phone; we made trips to Seattle to talk to a specialist, Dr. Alan Unis at the C.H.D.D.; we went to the Mayo Clinic to talk to their top people; we talked to parents across the country. We devoured books on the subject. Finally what we came across was something known as Applied Behavior Analysis (ABA), or the Lovaas Method. Applied Behavior Analysis/Lovaas Method/Discrete

Trial Teaching Methodologies was really the only thing we found that had any kind of reputable data to back it up whatsoever.

We did try some peripheral therapies, such as Secretin I.V. infusions and megavitamin therapies. Anytime something came up, a prospective cure or treatment, we did a cost-benefit analysis to figure out the potential risks or side-effects and the potential benefits. We looked at each treatment individually and decided the ones we wanted to try.

But the major treatment we selected was ABA which involved starting a home-therapy program, hiring therapists, and engaging in intensive one-on-one instruction for our son about 40–45 hours a week. The hardest part was envisioning in my head how we were going to do this. Just the physical arrangement of it: the people coming to my house; what they would be doing with my son; where they would do it. I remember distinctly the day I finally decided that we didn't have a choice, we had to do it, and I took the spare room apart.

It was a nice little guest room and I dismantled it to turn it into the therapy room. I remember it was as if we were doing everything in slow motion; carrying the bed out, taking the pictures off the wall. It was very surreal. We were told, in the beginning, to start out really bare, nothing on the walls. Anything that Josh might want to play with or that might be used as reinforcers for him were put up high on a shelf so that if he wanted them, he would be forced to communicate for them in some way.

Once the therapy room was set up, we hired a professional from outside the area to come in and hold a workshop so that my husband and I could be trained in the Lovaas methodology. We were lucky with the first therapist that we hired. She was a young intern at the University Programs in Communication Disorders where she worked three days a week with Josh in speech therapy.

Josh, back at that time, was pretty much an animal. He had no communication skills at all. If he didn't want to do something, he threw major temper tantrums. But we noticed that Robin, the speech intern, kept her cool, kept calm, kept working with him and by the end of the session, she'd get some results from him, after she wore him down. We decided, right then and there, that Robin would be the first person we'd hire.

We had no idea what Robin was going to do or what we were going to tell her to do, but we were just looking for someone we trusted with our son and that we thought had some basic skills. We were primarily tuned in to the speech therapy end of things at that time. Robin couldn't work for us while she was still working at the clinic, but we kept bugging her until she was done with her internship, and she agreed to come work for us in our home.

Robin really was a God-send because in the beginning we were just scared to death. The idea of someone being alone with my child in a room was frightening. What would they do to Josh? What would Josh do to them? We really had no clue. But Robin knew that we had to start with imitation skills. She gave us homework assignments. My husband taught block imitation and I taught gross motor imitation. We each did five or six hours a week; that's all we could handle in the beginning. Then Robin would come and help us through it—we helped each other, really, to learn the techniques. Giving us those little homework assignments in the beginning gave us something constructive to do, because we really hadn't known what to do to help our son.

That's how we got started with the home program. Then we all got training and learned more until Robin found someone she knew so we hired our second therapist. Over a period of six months, we went from about ten hours of therapy a week up to 40–45 hours and we had a team of five therapists working in our home, seven days a week.

This was really tough to finance and we covered it out of our private funds. We had a small savings we had planned to use to buy a little lake place and a boat. We used that for that first year. The Department of Developmental Disabilities helped cover about 20% of the staffing just by providing respite care worker hours. The first thing we did was to cancel our cable, cancel our newspaper, cut back on all discretionary expenditures; we didn't go out to dinner, we had no more vacations, we ate a lot of chicken and potatoes that year.

But everything we read pointed to the need for early intervention. We were scared to death. We didn't know exactly what to do, but we knew we needed to do it fast. We knew we couldn't wait. We felt really fortunate that we had a savings account that we could draw on that first year because a lot of families don't.

We started the program with an animal. Josh had no communication skills whatsoever, he ate with his hands, he was tantruming all the time, he was swimming in

Josh Finkel reading at school.

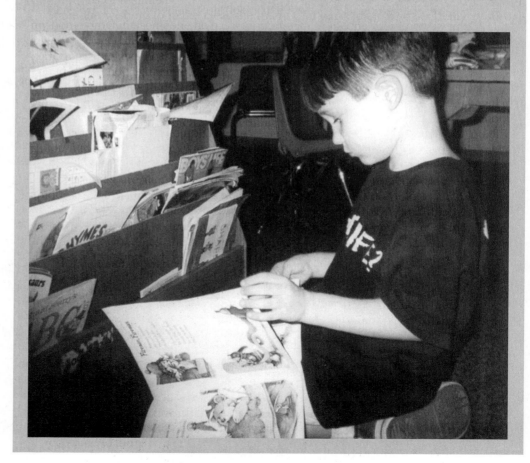

dirt, he was not potty-trained at all, and he urinated on himself and smeared feces on the wall. He was an animal. Now, after three years, he has a vocabulary of over 300 words.

Josh has a number of questions he can answer and a number of phrases and words that he can say. He can tell me what he wants, he can say "I want muffin please." You can ask him if he wants something and he can say "Yes, please," or "No thank you."

He now eats with a spoon and a fork. Josh is in a regular Kindergarten classroom with typically developing peers. He can swing on the swing sets, and he can slide down the slides. On the playground, now, you can't tell that he is disabled. He plays appropriately with his brother. He gives me hugs and kisses. He is 90% potty trained. He knows math, he knows his ABCs, and he knows prepositions and pronouns. The difference is just night and day.

EFFECTIVE FAMILY-CENTERED EARLY INTERVENTION

If early intervention has served its purpose well, then both child and family outcomes should be positive. Though child outcomes are more clearly measurable, it has been challenging to determine if families have been well served. Bailey and his colleagues (1998) recommended that several questions be answered in assessing family outcomes:

1. Does the family see early intervention as appropriate in making a difference in their child's life? Do families think their child received the services they felt were needed and did those services have a positive impact on their child's development and behavior? Dimensions that might be measured would include the type and amount of services provided, the quality of services, the extent to which these services affected the child, and whether the goals on the IFSP were attained.
2. Does the family see early intervention as appropriate in making a difference in their family life, beyond the impact on their child? To evaluate, one would have to ask if needs for information, social support, finances, child care, and so on were met. Were the services provided culturally and personally appropriate or acceptable to the family? Were family goals on the IFSP attained?
3. Does the family have a positive view of professionals and the special service system? Ideally, families should report that encounters with service providers were supportive, responsive, and respectful, and that the system was accessible and helpful.
4. Did early intervention help enhance an optimistic view of the future? Turnbull and Turnbull (1997) defined hope as the "belief that you will get what you want and need" (p. 41). In order to assess this, one must ask, what expectations do families have for their children and how strongly do they believe they will reach them?
5. Did early intervention enhance the family's perceived quality of life? What is the family's perception in regard to their independence, standard of living, productivity, relationships, health, safety, leisure, and life satisfaction?

In general, despite the trauma and disappointment associated with the early diagnosis of a child's disability, early intervention may be one of the most positive experiences that parents of children with disabilities ever encounter (Bailey et al., 1998). Unfortunately, this initially positive view seldom endures as a child ages. It is incumbent upon all early interventionists to find ways to support positive relationships between families and their children's service providers. The support provided can have enormous impact on the home environment for a child. One parent put it eloquently:

> Provide me with some ray of hope. Robbing me of hope is the worst thing you can do to me. Remember that after I leave your office, I will create an atmosphere at home of hope or despair, and surely one of hope is better for my child. You can give me hope through your attitude and what you say. Your belief that my child could defy the statistics will soften the facts that you must tell me. (Alexander & Tompkins-McGill, 1987, p. 362)

STUDY GUIDE QUESTIONS

1. What is meant by early intervention?
2. What rationale were provided as the basis for Part C in IDEA?
3. What are the five general principles which guided the IDEA regulations in regard to early intervention?
4. What are the ideals of good family-centered practices?
5. What kinds of tasks are accomplished by a skilled service coordinator?
6. Define and give an example of each of the four categories of eligibility under Part C.
7. If a child is identified with a hearing impairment, what type of professional would be most appropriate for service coordinator?
8. How would you deliver service coordination to families if you wanted to comply with family preferences identified by Early and Poertner?
9. Memorize the procedural safeguards and be able to explain the meaning of each in terms of preserving the rights of families.
10. Know the regulations regarding assessment procedures under IDEA.
11. What are the legal timelines from referral of a child to delivery of services?
12. How is ongoing assessment useful in working with infants and toddlers?
13. Why is it advised that family assessment be family-directed?
14. What are the principle steps taken by Winton and Bailey to put parents at ease in conducting assessment?
15. Identify the required components of IFSPs.
16. Develop five goals/objectives, keeping in mind the five principles developed by Notari-Syverson and Shuster.
17. Explain the rationale for using natural routines in planning IFSP objectives.
18. Explain the purpose and legal requirements of transition planning.

REFERENCES

Alexander, R., & Tompkins-McGill, P. (1987). Notes to the experts from the parent of a handicapped child. *Social Work, 32,* 352–361.

Bailey, D. B., McWilliam, R. A., Darkes, L. A., Simeonsson, R. J., Hebbeler, K., Spiker, D., & Wagner, M. (1998). Family outcomes in early intervention: A framework for program evaluation and efficacy research. *Exceptional Children, 64* (3), 313–328.

Baird, S., & Peterson, J. (1997). Seeking a comfortable fit between family-centered philosophy and infant-parent interaction in early intervention: Time for a paradigm shift? *Topics in Early Childhood Special Education, 17*(2), 139–165.

Beckman, P. J., & Bristol, M. M. (1991). Issues in developing the IFSP: A framework for establishing family outcomes. *Topics in Early Childhood Special Education, 11*(3), 19–31.

Berry, J., & Hardman, M. L. (1998). *Lifespan perspectives on family and disability.* Boston, MA: Allyn & Bacon.

Berzon, P., & Lowenstein, B. (1984). A flexible model of case management. In B. Pepper & H. Ryglewicz (Eds.), Advances in treating the young adult chronic patient. *New Directions for Mental Health Services, no. 21* (pp. 49–57). San Francisco: Jossey-Bass.

Bosch, L. A. (1998). Early intervention in the new millennium: the critical role of school social workers. *Social Work in Education, 29*(2), 139–144.

Bowe, F. (1995). *Birth to five: early childhood special education.* New York: Delmar.

Carta, J. J., Sainato, D. M., & Greenwood, C. R. (1988). Advances in the ecological assessment of childhood instruction for young children with handicaps. In S. L. Odom & M. B. Karnes (Eds.), *Early Intervention for infants and children with handicaps* (pp. 217–239). Baltimore, MD: Paul H. Brookes.

Colarusso, R. P., & Kana, T. G. (1991). Public Law 99–457, Part H, infant and toddler programs: Status and implications. *Focus on Exceptional Children, 23*(8), 1–12.

Committee on Children with Disabilities. (1999). The pediatrician's role in development and implementation of an Individual Education Plan (IEP) and/or an Individual Family Service Plan (IFSP). *Pediatrics, 104*(1), 124–127.

D'Amato, E., & Lynn, V. (1999). Early intervention: What's it all about? *The Exceptional Parent, 29*(7), 52–54.

Destafano, D. M., Howe, A. G., Horn, E. M., & Smith, B. A. (1991). *Best practices: Evaluating early childhood special education programs.* Tucson, AZ: Communication Skill Builders.

Division of Early Childhood (DEC). (1987, March). Position statement and recommendations relating to P.L. 99–457 and other federal and state early childhood policies.

Donegan, M. M., Fink, D. B., Fowler, S. A., & Wischnowski, M. W. (February 1995). Making the transition to group care. *Exceptional Parent,* 29–31.

Donner, R., Huff, B., Gentry, M., McKinney, D., Duncan, J., Thompson, S., & Silver, P. (Winter/Spring, 1993). Expectations of case management for children with emotional problems: Parent perspectives. *Focal Point,* 5–6.

Dunst, C., Trivette, C., & Deal, A. (1988). *Enabling and empowering families: Principles and guidelines for practice.* Cambridge, MA: Brookline.

Early, T. J., & Poertner, J. (Winter/Spring 1993). Case management for families and children. *Focal Point,* 1–4.

Hanson, M. J., & Lynch, E. W. (1989). *Early intervention.* Austin, TX: PRO-ED.

Hanson, M. J., & Lynch, E. W. (1995). *Early intervention: Implementing child and family services for infants and toddlers who are at risk or disabled,* 2nd ed. Austin, TX: PRO-ED.

Harbin, G. L., Gallagher, J. J., Lillie, T., & Eckland, J. (1990). *Executive summary: Status of states' progress in implementing Part H, P.L. 99–457, infants and toddlers.* Chapel Hill, NC: Carolina Institute for Child & Family Policy.

Hardman, M. L., Drew, D. J., & Egan, M. W. (1999). *Human exceptionality: society, school, and family,* 6th ed. Boston, MA: Allyn and Bacon.

Larner, M., Halpern, R., & Harkavy, O. (Eds.) (1992). *Fair Start for children: Lessons learned from seven demonstration projects.* New Haven: Yale University Press.

Lerner, J. W., Lowenthal, B., & Egan, R. (1998). *Preschool children with special needs: Children at-risk, children with disabilities.* Boston: Allyn & Bacon.

Maroney, R. M. (1986). *Shared responsibility: Families and social policy.* New York, NY: Aldine.

McWilliam, R. A., & Ferguson, A. (1998). The family-centeredness of individualized family service plans. *Topics in Early Childhood Special Education, 18*(2), 69–83.

McWilliam, R. A., Tocci, L., & Harbin, G. L. (1998). Family-centered services: Service providers' discourse and behavior. *Topics in Early Childhood Special Education, 18*(4), 206–232.

MHLP: Early Intervention Advocacy Network Notebook. (January, 1990). *Guide to Part H Law and Regulations.* 2021 L Street N. W., Washington, D.C. 20036.

National Early Childhood Technical Assistance System. (1999). Overview of the Part C program under IDEA. http://www.nectas.unc.edu/partc/ptcoverview.html.

North Carolina. (1998). *Early intervention in North Carolina.* http://www.dhhs.state.nc.us/dcd/icc_par.htm#FREI

Notari-Syverson, A. R., & Shuster, S. L. (Winter 1995). Putting real life skills into IEP/IFSPs for infants and young children. *Teaching Exceptional Children,* 29–32.

Popowicz, L., & Haas, J. (November 1991). *Toddler-Parent playgroups: Empowering parents in language intervention.* Paper presented at the Annual Convention of the American Speech-Language-Hearing Association. Atlanta, GA.

Pueblo Infant Parent Education Project (PIPE Project). (1984). *Final Report to U.S. Department of Education.* Grant No. G008100234.

Rosenkoetter, S. E., Hains, A. H., & Fowler, S. A. (1994). *Bridging early services for children with special needs and their families: A practical guide for transition planning.* Baltimore: Paul H. Brookes.

Salisbury, C. L., & Smith, B. J. (1993). *Effective practices for preparing young children with disabilities for school.* (ERIC Document Reproduction Service No. ED 358675) ED358675.

Sexton, D., Thompson, B., Perez, J., & Rheams, T. (1990). Maternal versus professional estimates of developmental status for young children with handicaps: An ecological approach. *Topics in Early Childhood Special Education, 10*(3), 80–95.

Simeonsson, R. J. (1986). *Psychological and developmental assessment of special children.* Boston: Allyn and Bacon.

Sontag, J., & Schact, R. (1994). An ethnic comparison of parent participation and information needs in early intervention. *Exceptional Children, 16*(5), 422–431.

Stremel, K., Matthews, P., Wilson, R., Molden, V., Yates, C., Busbea, B., & Holston, J. (Dec., 1992). *Facilitating infant/toddler skills in family-child routines.* Paper presented at Council for Exceptional Children/Division of Early Childhood International Conference on Children with Special Needs. ERIC Reproduction Services Document No. 353736.

Strong, C. J., Clark, T. C., Johnson, D., Watkins, S., Barringer, D. G., & Walden, B. E. (1994). SKI*HI home-based programming for children who are deaf or hard of hearing: Recent research findings. *The Transdisciplinary Journal, 4*(1), 25–36.

Thompson, L., Lobb, C., Elling, R., Herman, S., Jurkiewicz, & Hulleza, C. (1997). Pathways to family empowerment: Effects of family-centered delivery early intervention services. *Exceptional Children, 64*(1), 99–113.

Thurman, S. K., & Widerstrom, A. H. (1990). *Infants and young children with special needs.* Baltimore: Paul H. Brookes.

Tucker, B. P., & Goldstein, B. A. (1991). *The educational rights of children with disabilities: A guide to federal law.* Horsham, PA: LRP Publications.

Turnbull, A. P., & Turnbull, H. R. (1997). *Families, professionals, and exceptionality: A special partnership* (3rd ed.). Upper Saddle River, NJ: Merrill/Prentice Hall.

Umansky, W., & Hooper, S. R. (1998). *Young children with special needs* (3rd ed.). Columbus, OH: Merrill/Prentice Hall.

Wehman, T. (1998). Family-centered early intervention services: Factors contributing to increased parent involvement. *Focus on Autism & Other Developmental Disabilities, 98*(13), 80–87.

Weiner, R., & Koppelman, J. (1987). *From birth to 5: Serving the youngest handicapped children.* Alexandria, VA: Capital Publications.

Winton, P., & Bailey, D. (1988). The family-focused interview: A collaborative mechanism for family assessment and goal

MANDATED SERVICES FOR YOUNG CHILDREN

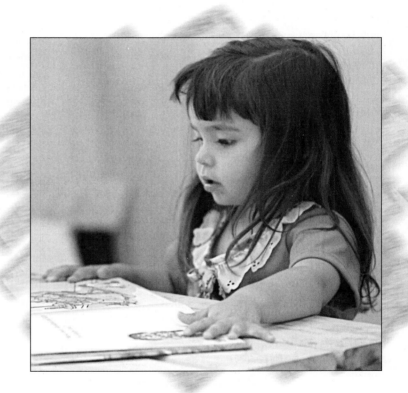

Most IEPs are useless or slightly worse, and too many teachers experience the IEP process as always time consuming, sometimes threatening, and too often, a pointless bureaucratic requirement. The result is a quasi-legal document to be filed away with the expectation it won't be seen again except, heaven forbid, by a monitor or compliance officer. The point of the IEP exercise seems to be to complete the given form in a way that commits the district to as little as possible, and which precludes, as much as possible, any meaningful discussion or evaluation of the student's real progress. (Bateman, 1995, p. 1)

Transition from those services provided through infant and toddler programs to pre-school special education for children ages 3–5 years, means transition to the public school system, which can too often be a rocky road (Turnbull & Turnbull, 1997). While early intervention has adopted a family-centered approach in which services are assured for both the family and the child, special education services to children from 3 years to age 21 are focused primarily on the student. This shift takes place as planning moves from the Individualized Family Service Plan (IFSP) to the Individualized Education Plan (IEP). It means moving away from intensive family ownership and involvement, a direction which creates a challenge for many parents. Families who have become accustomed to high-quality early intervention services may quickly become disenchanted with special education programs where the student is the central focus and family-centered planning is not the rule (Pruitt, Wandry, & Hollums, 1998).

Is the contrast an appropriate one? Certainly it is not by intention. In the larger sense, the Individuals with Disabilities Education Act (IDEA) has done more to validate the role of parents as educational decision makers for their children and to encourage collaboration between parents and professionals than any other legislative mandate, court ruling, or public policy. IDEA explicitly calls for the active involvement of parents in all aspects of educational programming for their children with disabilities. In fact, the 1997 revision of IDEA (PL 105-17) demands even greater parent involvement than in the past. As Turnbull and Turnbull (1997) contended, parents accustomed to family-centered early intervention programs are beginning to demand that such collaborative practices continue throughout their children's education.

It may be the case that millions of families of children with disabilities feel "disenfranchised and alienated from educational systems designed to help their children" (Kroth & Edge, 1997, p. 14). If professionals dominate the decision-making process and student-centered practices act to exclude family-centered input, then the potential for profitable family interactions in educational planning and implementation is lost and IDEA is not well served. Active parental involvement in the educational process benefits children both academically and socially, but too many educators fail to understand the need to encourage parental participation (Pruitt et al., 1998). This lack of understanding may foster unsatisfactory levels of communication and collaboration.

A CHANGE OF PERSPECTIVE

Schools that are making positive strides do so by responding to the qualities, needs, and characteristics of families (D'Angelo & Adler, 1991). Special educators who wish to strengthen their partnerships with parents can take specific steps to do so. Epstein (1992) suggested six types of parent involvement that should be encouraged:

1. Parenting: establishing supportive home environments;
2. Communicating: designing effective forms of interactive communications;
3. Volunteering: organizing parent help in the school environment;
4. Learning at home: assisting families with homework and other related activities;
5. Decision making: including parents in school decisions; and
6. Collaborating with the community: integrating community resources to strengthen school programs.

Professionals need to increase communication with families, use parent networks, and learn to understand family views and strengths in shared decision making (Pruitt et al., 1998).

When Pruitt and her colleagues interviewed 78 families with children in special education, they found almost 27% of respondents said they just wanted educators to listen to them. When asked what can educators do to be more sensitive to the needs of your family?, one mother responded:

> Taking input from the parents on what works. There are a lot of parents in special ed that don't keep it together. It is an overwhelming experience to have a handicapped child. Sometimes I think parents get written off as being out of line with things. Teachers must remember that there is a lot of value to what the parents say—even though they are hysterical or not rational—because they really do know that child. They may not be coping well right now, but they do know best.

Another 23% of the parents interviewed indicated that the quality and quantity of communication between parents and professionals should be improved. The respondents felt professionals should use a more humane demeanor with parents, interact in an honest manner, and treat parents with dignity and respect. A father stated:

> Please don't talk to me like I'm an idiot or assume that I know what you are talking about. Another thing is sometimes I get the feeling that the professionals are talking to each other and not me. It's discouraging. Another thing I might say is that instead of telling me what you are going to do with my daughter, ask my opinion, give me some say in her education and placement. I don't know what all my options are and it's tough.

A mother of a student with a behavior disorder gave this feedback:

> Understand that while you may have my child in your classroom for 7 hours and are tired, I have him for the other 17 hours he is out of school. I may not always be full of energy, but I am human, so treat me the same way you would treat a friend. Speak to me in the tone and language that you like to be spoken to. I am no dummy, but I think we all can do without so much professional jargon.

Other parents' recommendations to professionals included increasing knowledge about various disabilities, treating the child with respect, and improving the IEP process. A parent suggested:

> Read the IEP. I took my daughter to school before school started, so she would know who her teachers were and could identify them. They hadn't even gotten her IEP, so they really didn't know her. I'm asking, who would be responsible for adapting her curriculum and keeping track of that. And they're asking me, How much adaptation do you think she'll need? I'm thinking, I don't know; I'm not the teacher!

Parents and professionals must be equal partners in a team striving for the same goals. Though the family-centered focus of early intervention may change as the child enters special education in the school system, the advantages of family-professional partnerships do not change. Early childhood professionals must "acknowledge that parents have equitable, collaborative roles because they possess critical information about their child, without which the educational process cannot be complete" (Pruitt et al., 1998). This is also an essential requirement of IDEA.

PARENT RIGHTS AND RESPONSIBILITIES

Parent involvement is so essential to the process of planning and providing services to a child in special education that IDEA is quite explicit about those rights to participation in the decision making (ERIC Clearinghouse on Disabilities and Gifted Education, 1999). Parents have the right to:

1. A free, appropriate public education for their child, at no cost to the family and designed to meet the unique education needs of the child.
2. Request an evaluation if they suspect the child needs special education or related services.
3. Be notified whenever the school wants to evaluate the child, change the child's placement, or refuse the parents' request for an evaluation or change in placement.
4. Informed consent that is voluntary and may be withdrawn at any time.
5. Obtain an independent evaluation if in disagreement with the school.
6. Request a reevaluation if the child's present education program is no longer appropriate or if 3 years have passed and current information is not sufficient for new decision making.
7. Have the child tested in the language he or she knows best, including sign language if appropriate.
8. Review all of a child's school records, including teachers' classroom notes.
9. Be fully informed of legal rights and due process provided by law.
10. Participate in the development of the IEP and in making placement decisions.
11. Request an IEP meeting at any time they feel it is needed.
12. Be informed of the child's progress at least as often as parents of children who do not have disabilities.
13. Have the child educated in the least restrictive environment possible that provides all the supports needed to participate with children who do not have disabilities.
14. Voluntary mediation or a due process hearing if needed to resolve differences with the school.

On the other hand, parents also have responsibilities in regard to their involvement in educational decision making (ERIC Clearinghouse on Disabilities and Gifted Education, 1999). Parents should work to develop a partnership with the school, to share relevant information and observations that can be helpful in planning the child's program. They need to ask for an explanation of any aspects of the program they don't understand, especially educational or medical jargon. They need to monitor the IEP goals and objectives to be sure they are specific and agreeable. Parents should examine and think about the IEP carefully before signing it. They must make sure their children are included in regular school activities as much as is appropriate, including nonacademic areas such as lunch, art, music, and physical education. Parents should request periodic reports on their child's progress, or if the child is not progressing, they should suggest changes in the program. Parents need to work directly with school personnel to resolve conflicts over assessment, placement, or educational program. Parents have to keep good records so they don't forget important information that has not been written down. Finally, parents should join a parent organization where they can share their knowledge, experiences, and support. Their organized efforts may be the force that brings about needed changes to strengthen services to children.

When the provisions of IDEA are fully implemented, both letter of the law and the spirit of the law are protected. When this is the case, there is a supportive and mutually respectful relationship between families and professionals from the start (Beach Center on Families and Disabilities, 1999). The process of decision making will be collaborative and information about current best practices will be shared among the team members. The process is ongoing, dynamic, and individualized, with family-initiated goals and objectives given priority. Meetings and documents are jargon-free and technical information is explained when necessary. Professionals and families discuss all the options for a range of service settings, considering the advantages and disadvantages. In short, a true team implements IDEA as it applies specifically to a child.

RECENT AMENDMENTS TO THE IDEA

When President Clinton signed PL 105-17 on June 4, 1997, significant amendments to IDEA went into effect [National Association of State Directors of Special Education (NASDSE), 1997]. Most of the original procedures already outlined in the legislation were retained, but several new principles were added to Part B, the section that deals with assistance for education of children from age 3 to 21 years. Some of the modifications were significant; others simply fine tuned processes already laid out [National Information Center for Children and Youth with Disabilities (NICHCY), 1997]. The revisions showed a clear mandate to expand the active role of parents; to increase the involvement of a child with a disability in the general education setting, curriculum, and assessment procedures; and to appropriately treat behavior problems. This chapter will examine these major changes in detail, but some minor highlights of the amendments should be briefly mentioned (Pacer Center, 1999).

Developmental Delay

States and local school districts may now apply the definition of developmental delay to children from ages 3 to 9 years. This term is used when a definitive diagnosis has not been made, but a child shows pervasive delay across domains. A child's delays in physical skills, cognitive ability, communication skills, social or emotional development, and adaptive behavior can be enough for the child to qualify for special education services, even though a specific disabling condition has not been identified.

Private and Charter School Enrollment

When the local school district has been given proper notice, funds can now be distributed to private schools that provide special education services to eligible children. A child can receive services on private school premises, even in parochial schools. Likewise, Child Find services are also extended to private schools in order to identify eligible children.

The local education agency (LEA) is required to provide services to children enrolled in charter schools that are public schools in the local district. The LEA must also provide special education funds to charter schools.

Services to Prisoners

Special education must be provided to persons under the age of 21 who have been identified for special education and now reside in prisons. This includes children, who because of their crimes, have been incarcerated in adult prisons. Though this may not directly affect preschool children, it may certainly have an impact on their parents and the professionals who serve their families if a parent or sibling is incarcerated. The long-term dynamics of the family situation might be greatly improved if members are receiving an appropriate education, even while in prison.

Reevaluation

Amendments to IDEA now encourage the use of existing evaluation data on a child when those are provided by parents or through classroom-based observations. If this information is sufficient and all parties (including parents) agree, then new evaluations may not have to be made when children enter new programs or when the IEP is up for its third year review.

More significant amendments deal directly with the development of the IEP and its provisions, with due-process rights for parents and their children, and with inclusion in general education. These will be addressed in appropriate sections of this chapter.

THE INDIVIDUALIZED EDUCATION PROGRAM

Barbara Bateman and Mary Anne Linden, in their book, *Better IEPs* (1998), suggest that all professionals must obey the "IDEA Commandments":

    I. Thou shalt base all eligibility decisions on professional judgment, not on quantitative formulae.

    II. Thou shalt open wide the door unto very needed service and placement for each eligible child.

    III. Remember thou that categorical delivery of services is an abomination.

    IV. Each IEP shall be based solely upon the child's needs. He or she who looks instead to availability of services shall know the inferno.

    V. Maketh every IEP in the image of its child. An IEP like unto another is a graven image. Despised by all who know IDEA.

    VI. Place not all children in the same setting, but make available the entire continuum of alternative placements.

    VII. Thou shalt not exclude parents from decisions that affect their children.

    VIII. Thou shalt not burden parents with the cost of their children's special education and services. (Ask the Expert, 1999).

The IEP is perhaps the principal component of IDEA in terms of classroom services. This document details a specific plan used by preschool education team members on a daily basis. The IEP is specifically outlined in IDEA regulations and contains the following parts:

1. A statement of the child's present levels of performance
2. A statement of annual goals
3. A statement of short-term instructional objectives
4. A statement of educational services and related services to be provided
5. The date when services will begin and their duration
6. A description of the extent to which the child will be included in regular education settings
7. A statement of evaluation procedures

In addition to these components, the newest revision of IDEA requires the IEP team to consider the following and address needs that are apparent (Pacer Center, 1999):

1. Behavior strategies and supports for a child whose behavior impedes the learning of others
2. Language needs if the child has limited English proficiency
3. Communication needs of a child, with specific factors to consider if the child is deaf or hard of hearing
4. Provision of Braille for a child who is blind (unless the team determines it is not appropriate)
5. Needs for assistive technology devices or service

The 1997 revision of IDEA also expands the composition of an IEP team (Pacer Center, 1999). In addition to the parents who are now to be included in placement decisions for their child, teams must include at least one special education teacher and now, at least one regular education teacher if the child participates in regular education. As before, a local school district representative who can commit special education services is to be involved, but now, that person must also know about the general curriculum and local resources. One of these members must be able to interpret evaluation results; others must have knowledge or special expertise on the child's needs, including persons who provide related services and know the child. The family may invite additional persons and the child should be involved when appropriate. In all cases, a child's parent or guardian must consent to the IEP, by officially signing it, before it is implemented. Formats for IEPs vary widely and may go beyond the basic requirements of the law. (A sample IEP is shown in Figure 9–1.)

Ideally, an IEP spells out where a child is developmentally, where a child should be going, how she or he will get there, when the child will reach specific goals, and how to tell if she or he has arrived (Heward & Orlansky, 1992). To ensure that an IEP is continuously relevant, it must be reviewed at least once a year by a child's team. In addition, parents may request a review prior to the annual review date.

Several factors are key to writing a functional IEP. These include:

1. A complete description of the child's current skills and behaviors on which to base future instruction
2. The writing of clear instructional objectives

Figure 9–1 Individualized Education Program

Child's Name: Jennifer Lovinger **Birthdate:** 6-19-97 **Age:** 38 mos **School:** Pine Valley, Preschool (3-5)

Parents/Guardians: Lyle & Julia Lovinger **Address:** W. 1125 Post, Pine Valley **Telephone:** 328-3520

Reason for referral: Jennifer is an adopted child whose mother was addicted to alcohol and cocaine. Jennifer showed evidence of both in her bloodstream at birth. She was premature and seized at delivery. She continued to have tremors for several days as well as increased extension. Jennifer was slow to develop physical skills and lacks age-appropriate self-help skills. She is very active, difficult for the parents to control, and has frequent temper tantrums.

Present levels of performance:

Strengths: Jennifer's performance on the test of intelligence fell within the average range expected at this age. She was able to follow directions, imitate line drawings, and complete fine motor tasks. Jennifer is able to place shapes in a box, turn pages of a book and use a peg board competently. Her mother reports that Jennifer can turn door knobs and television and radio dials, and She can manipulate blocks. Jennifer's gross motor skills appear to be at developmentally appropriate levels; she walks, jumps on two feet and runs with ease. She likes to throw objects and follows them visually. Jennifer sings preschool songs she learned from the television. She has good receptive and expressive language skills. Jennifer has normal hearing and vision.

Areas of concern: Jennifer's self-help skills are delayed and she is not cooperative in tasks such as washing hands unless it is done very quickly. Jennifer's toilet training is delayed and she does not indicate wet or soiled pants. Jennifer still does not hold her own glass when drinking and must be fed with a spoon. She also does not assist in undressing herself. Jennifer has a low frustration tolerance and does not adapt to new situations well. She tantrums frequently, banging her head and biting herself when upset. Her activity level is high and it is difficult to maintain sustained attention to a task. Jennifer does not tolerate sensory stimulation well. She appeared to be tactilely defensive when touched and overreacted to different textures.

Statement of Major Annual Goals	Specific Education of Related Support Services Needed to Meet Annual Goals	Person(s) Responsible for Providing Services—Beginning and Ending Dates
1. Establish self-help skills, including self-feeding, toileting, and hygiene.	A detailed task analysis for each skill area will be used and Jennifer's entry level to each task identified. A system of graduated guidance will be used within self-help routines in the classroom and at home. Completion of each task and independent completion of any step in a task will be consequated with praise and access to a reinforcing activity.	Occupational therapist, special education teacher, and parent. Initiation of service: 9-6-99 Ending date: 8-15-00
2. Reduce temper tantrums in intensity and frequency (to a rate of no more than once a month).	Jennifer will be differentially reinforced for co-operative behavior and for using appropriate ways to say, "no." Each time a temper tantrum occurs, Jennifer will be placed in a chair away from other children and entertaining activities for one minute.	Any classroom staff who are present when these behaviors occur and parents at home. Initiation of service: 9-6-99 Ending date: 8-15-00

3. Increase sustained attention to tasks up to a duration of 15 minutes.

Provide structured one-on-one tutoring for short periods each day, initially with the teacher or paraprofessional, later using peer tutors. Use child-selected high-interest materials and allow Jennifer to switch to various objects or toys, gradually requiring longer contact before switching is possible.

Special education teacher and aide.

Initiation of service: 9-6-99
Ending date: 8-15-00

Related Annual Goal	Observable Behavior	Conditions	Criterion	Evaluation & Measurement Procedures—Review Dates
1. (a) Establish self-help skills	Jennifer will unbutton and remove her coat, take off her hat, and hang both in her cubby	With no teacher assistance other than verbal direction at the beginning of class each day and after outdoor play	Within three minutes of entering the classroom at least twice each day	The parent will record completion of the task and time required at entry each morning and the aide after outdoor play on a record sheet kept in Jennifer's cubby. Reassess procedure in one month.
1. (b) Establish self-help skills	Jennifer will remove her underpants and urinate in the toilet	When taken to the bathroom after snack, after lunch, after nap, and at any time she requests to use the toilet	Within five minutes of arrival at the bathroom each time she is taken	The aide will record time and success using a data sheet kept in the bathroom. Review progress in two months.
1. (c) Establish self-help skills	Jennifer will turn on water, use soap, scrub, and dry her hands	With verbal reminders and physical prompting when needed, after toileting and before eating snack and lunch	Requiring no more than one physical prompt and two verbal reminders	The aide will record number of verbal and physical prompts required. Review in two months.

Figure 9–1 Individualized Education Program *(continued)*

Related Annual Goal	Observable Behavior	Conditions	Criterion	Evaluation & Measurement Procedures—Review Dates
2. (a) Reduce temper tantrums	Jennifer will say "No"	When she does not wish to participate in an activity	Without crying, hitting, or running away	Teacher will observe circle time each day and record number of invitations to participate given to Jennifer, times "No" is used and number of times crying, hitting, or running away occurs. Reassess in one month.
2. (b) Reduce temper tantrums	Jennifer will participate	In circle activities when invited to by the teacher	With appropriate singing, talking, or hand movements requested	Teacher records number of invitations to participate given to Jennifer, and if she complied appropriately or not. Review in one month, expand to table activities when possible.
3. (a) Increase sustained attention	Jennifer will manipulate, watch, or listen to a toy	Which she has selected while working one-on-one with the teacher, aide, or peer for a 15-minute session	For three minutes before switching to another toy	The teacher or aide will use 10-second interval recording to note engagement. Review in one month.
3. (b) Increase sustained attention	Jennifer will sit quietly	During story time	Without leaving her seat for three minutes	Aide will use 10-second interval recording to note quiet sitting.

Recommendations and justification for placement:
Jennifer will be integrated into a combination Head Start/School District preschool which serves primarily typical 3- to 5-year-old children from low-income families. This will allow Jennifer to observe appropriate peer models, to have opportunities to learn social and academic skills in preparation for kindergarten, and to engage in age-appropriate activities. A special education teacher is available to work directly with Jennifer and to advise on behavioral and self-help skills. The combination program also offers parent training and support for Jennifer's family.

Date of IEP meeting: August 20, 1999
Persons present—Name/position
Cheryl Howard, Special Education Teacher
Corrine Fry, Occupational Therapist
Betty Port, School Psychologist
Pat Lepper, School District Representative
Parent Signature
Lyle Lovinger   Julia Lovinger

3. The designation of specially designed instruction and related services
4. The identification of the appropriate and least restrictive setting for educational inclusion.

PRESENT LEVELS OF PERFORMANCE

The first step in IEP development is to translate student evaluation results into practical planning information. IEP teams must use current information, state performance in concise and clear language, and identify specific skills. Teams draw from standardized test scores, medical records, observations, specialist's reports, and parent input. Crucial questions to be addressed are the following:

1. What is the student's current level of mastery in each specified skill area?
2. What is the nature of the specifically designed instruction that should be provided in each skill area? (Strickland & Turnbull, 1990)

Areas to be evaluated include speech and language, motor, sensory, cognitive, social, self-help, and play skills, as well as other skills particular to a child's disabling condition. Performance levels should be stated in the positive so that a child's strengths and resources are examined. If there are delays in any area, the kind of intervention recommended for improving that specific skill area should be noted. For example, rather than stating that fine motor skills are not age-appropriate, the present levels of performance should identify concretely what a child can do: "Amos can manipulate large puzzle shapes, use a spoon for eating, and stack blocks. He has not yet acquired the skills to fasten buttons and zippers, use a pencil to draw shapes, or lace his shoes, but these skills could be taught directly by his parents with the assistance of an occupational therapist."

INSTRUCTIONAL OBJECTIVES

Goals and objectives should be developed collaboratively by the child's IEP team and should consider the assessment information gathered to document a child's present level of performance and the parents' needs and preferences. In general, goals and objectives should address the following areas identified by Noonan and McCormick (1993):

1. Skills that are partially acquired or skills that are demonstrated in some contexts but not others (and can be improved upon or extended)
2. Skills that will permit a child to participate in routine daily activities with nondisabled peers (thus allowing inclusion in a least restrictive setting)
3. Skills that would be instrumental in accomplishing the greatest number of other skills or functional tasks (for example, basic fine motor skills like grasping can lead to self-feeding, dressing, playing with toys)
4. Skills a child is highly motivated to learn (activities that are self-reinforcing)
5. Skills that will increase opportunities for interactions with nondisabled peers (such as language and play)
6. Skills that will increase participation in future environments (such as handraising and taking turns needed in a kindergarten setting)

An IEP must include specifically developed short-term instructional objectives. These statements describe the expected outcomes of educational intervention within a short-term time frame of one to three months and assist in planning daily activities (Bailey & Wolery, 1992). Any good objective contains three main components: the observable behavior that a child is expected to perform, the conditions or situation under which the behavior is expected, and the criterion or how well the child must perform the behavior (Mager, 1962).

An observable behavior is one that can be seen or heard and, therefore, can be measured. "Being kind to others" is a description, not a behavior on which several people could agree. "Handing a toy to another child" is a behavior that could be observed and counted and that most people would accept as a demonstration of kindness. Usually objectives should contain action words that indicate a distinct movement, such as naming, reaching, or stacking. For example, the goal of "joining" in circle activities should be restated as the following behaviors: "sits in small group, answers questions, sings songs, moves fingers and hands with the music." By observing these behaviors, it would be clear that a child is joining in circle activities.

The second key component of a good objective is a description of the conditions under which the behavior is expected. Conditions are the situation in which learning is to be demonstrated and might include the materials used, the setting in which a behavior is to occur, or the people who would be present when the behavior is performed. Compare these two conditions under which a child is expected to count objects: "Charles will touch and count out loud the number of blocks up to three blocks that appear one at a time on the computer screen." "Charles will stand at the calendar in front of the circle group and count off each date of the month in order, stopping with today's date." Both are good descriptions of conditions, and in both cases, the child is expected to count, but the task of counting under the first set of conditions is probably much easier than performance under the second set of conditions. The second set of conditions implies a much more sophisticated knowledge level and would be influenced by more variables, including the changing number of days in a month, the size of the audience, and the use of numerals rather than semiconcrete images.

Conditions may describe the level of assistance or cueing that will be provided, the kind of audience that will be present, the mode in which the response will take place, and the kind of environmental contingencies present. An example of level of assistance might be: "Using his crutches, Tommy will walk with a friend from the school door to the swings," or at a later time, "Tommy will use a cane to walk alone from the school door to the swings." The kind of audience that will be present makes a difference as well. It is one thing for Darette to sing "Itsy Bitsy Spider" to her mother during bath time, and another for Darette to sing "Itsy Bitsy Spider" on stage for all the parents during the spring festival. The mode of performance can also differ; for example, it is important to indicate if the child will be drawing, using a computer keyboard, or orally telling a simple story. The kind of contingencies needed to ensure a particular performance may vary a great deal as well. For example, Arnold may eat all his soup when he is given a bite of ice cream after each bite of soup, or when he is simply praised after each bite. All these factors can have a substantial impact on the quality and strength of a child's overall performance.

The criterion of an instructional objective expresses how well a behavior is to be performed to be considered sufficient. Criteria, in some cases may be stated as percentage correct, duration of performance, level of proficiency, topography, or intensity. For example, "Katie will turn and make eye contact when her name is called by the teacher, 90% of the time." "Jacob will walk, using only his wheeled walker for assistance, a distance of 20 feet across the classroom." "Amy Jo will remove her coat, with assistance unbuttoning, and hang it in her cubby within five minutes of entering the classroom."

Criteria should be stated in such a way as to identify consistent levels that are likely to be used and reinforced (Bailey & Wolery, 1992). A child who touches a toy but does not shake it, lift it, listen to it, or in some way have fun with it is not really likely to play with the toy because of its own reinforcing properties. A better criterion for interacting with a toy might be to make it react in some way (rattle, roll, ring, etc.) because it is the toy's reaction that will eventually maintain the behavior of playing with toys.

Criteria should also reach for a high level of proficiency or automaticity that encourages **generalization** and independent functioning. For example, if the criterion for using "please" is "for 20% of the times a spoonful of food is offered during feeding," then a child is not likely to use the word "please" very often or under new circumstances. On the other hand, if a child is expected to use "please" 90% of the times any adult or child offers toys, food, activities, music, or television, then the child is likely to use "please" very often. "Please" will become automatic when choices are given and may generalize to become a word to request items or activities before they have been offered.

GUIDELINES FOR DEVELOPING GOOD OBJECTIVES

In summary, any time specific instructional objectives are developed, they should be worthwhile. It is perhaps because so many IEPs are written without thought to individual needs or attention to detail that many teachers see IEPs as a waste of time. The initial investment of thought and time in developing a truly individualized IEP pays off in long-term achievements for the teacher, parent, and child. Bailey and Wolery (1992) suggested the following guidelines for good objectives:

1. They should be developmentally appropriate; that is, they should address skills typical for a child's age and matched to a child's development.
2. Objectives should be functional. They should include skills that help a child be more independent, help a child learn a more complex skill, help a child move to a less restrictive environment, or help the family care for the child.
3. Objectives should include skills valued by the parents and significant others.
4. Objectives should be realistic and achievable.
5. Objectives should vary according to a child's stage of learning, including acquisition, mastery, and generalization.

SPECIAL EDUCATION AND RELATED SERVICES

The next step in IEP development is to decide what strategies, procedures, and materials will help a child achieve the instructional objectives that have been identified and how progress will be monitored (Noonan & McCormick, 1993). That is, an intervention team decides what to teach in order to attain the stated objectives; how to modify or adapt curriculum content, materials, and procedures; and how to arrange the environment to facilitate skill acquisition and generalization.

Special education is, by definition, specially designed instruction that includes adaptations that are significantly different from modifications normally made for typical students and are necessary to offset or reduce the adverse effect of a child's disability (Strickland & Turnbull, 1990). For example, specially designed instruction might include the use of a communication board to help a child initiate interactions and respond to peers in the classroom, the use of peers to model and reinforce offers to play or share toys, or the use of switch-activated toys as reinforcing consequences for verbalizations. Instruction can be modified according to:

1. Levels of assistance provided
2. The kinds of extrinsic motivation used
3. The arrangement of the environment and materials
4. The programming of opportunities for generalization

It is essential that specially designed instruction be both systematic and naturalistic (Noonan & McCormick, 1993). Students should be exposed to routine schedules, methods of instruction, and management strategies. Systematic instruction emphasizes consistency but does not require unnatural and mechanistic instruction. Educational plans should not be so rigid as to rule out regard for the interests and spontaneity of young children.

For example, specially designed instruction will often include providing assistance through prompting. Prompts may be verbal, gestural, auditory, movement, or picture cues that help a child respond without making errors. Prompts also include models and physical manipulation when necessary. Carefully programmed materials insert and then fade out prompts in such a way that a child can move errorlessly through each lesson.

Specially designed instruction almost always involves "reinforcement-rich" environments in which a child's appropriate responses may be positively **consequated,** making it more likely that the behavior will be repeated. Many natural reinforcers are available, including smiles, hugs, a favorite toy, or a special game. Sometimes the environment must be arranged to make it easier for children to obtain reinforcement for their efforts. For example, teaching during natural routines such as lunch, using age-appropriate and interesting materials, and presenting tasks through fun games and activities all make it more likely that a child's responses can earn reinforcement (Noonan & McCormick, 1993).

Finally, specially designed instruction must address the transfer of skills to other settings, other caregivers, and other appropriate situations. This *generalization* of newly mastered skills is ensured only through systematic and naturalistic procedures. Special education approaches should include the following generalization procedures (Stokes & Baer, 1977):

1. Common materials should be used both in training and in nontraining situations. For example, if a child is learning to use a straw at school, the family should use straws at home too.

2. Naturally occurring contingencies should be emphasized. For example, a child learning to climb steps should be encouraged to climb the steps of a slide and enjoy the quick trip down the slide as a natural reward for her work.

3. Contrived contingencies should be designed to be subtle or not too obvious, so that they can be gradually reduced. For example, a child might get a big hand-shake for speaking in front of the group but, later, receive a brief squeeze on the hand and, still later, a pat on the hand for the same behavior. Finally, just a wave or salute would be sufficient to maintain the behavior.

4. Generalization should be mediated by providing strategies that assist a child in new situations. Singing the alphabet song in order to remember alphabetical order while in the library is a good example of a strategy most people use.

5. One should use variety in the kinds of prompts, reinforcements, and corrections used from time to time. For example, when giving directions to move from circle to table work, a teacher might sometimes say, "Please sit in your chair at the table," and other times, "Walk to the table quietly."

Related services are those additional support services that allow children to benefit from their educational experience. For example, a child who uses an electric wheelchair may require special lift-van transportation in order to attend school, a child who requires catheterization may need a nurse or paraprofessional to assist in the mechanics of emptying the bladder, and a mobility specialist may train a child who is visually impaired to use a cane to find her way around the school building so she can move independently from the bus to her classroom.

The provision of services to a wide range of eligible children and their families involves the coordinated efforts of many related personnel, including but not limited to, audiologists, nutritionists, nurses, occupational therapists, physicians, psychologists, physical therapists, social workers, speech-language pathologists, and vision specialists (Brown & Rule, 1993). Table 9–1 identifies examples of the related services each professional might provide. All of these personnel concentrate on working with families, addressing child development needs, and coordinating services. In addition, paraprofessionals contribute significantly to preschool education in both home and center settings by providing support to teachers and parents or by directly aiding children in daily activities (Brown & Rule, 1993).

LEAST RESTRICTIVE ENVIRONMENT

Another key feature of the IEP is the designation of an appropriate and least restrictive educational setting. IDEA makes it clear that children with disabilities should be placed, to the greatest extent appropriate, with peers who are not disabled. The new revisions of IDEA require even stronger adherence to this principle. The IEP must include an explanation of the extent to which the child will *not* participate in a regular class. This means more detail must be provided than in the past in regard to any limits placed on regular classroom participation (this would apply, for example if a preschooler had the opportunity to be in a regular Head Start or Kindergarten program) (NASDSE, 1997). Children are also entitled to participate in extracurricular activities, so modifications should be made to allow a child to take part in a class field trip or afterschool program, for example. Children should be served in a setting as

Table 9–1 Personnel and Related Services

Professional	Examples of Services Provided
Audiologist	Auditory training, speech-reading, and listening-device orientation and training
Nutritionist	Assess food intake, eating behavior, and feeding skills; provide nutrition information and early intervention
Nurse	Advise parents and caregivers on basic health needs; develop medical plans to treat developmental problems
Occupational therapist	Enhance sensory function and motor skill; select, design, and build assistive seating and orthotic devices
Physician	Provide a "medical home," comprehensive medical care, diagnosis, and treatment; instruct parents and caregivers in health care
Psychologist	Assess psychological and behavioral needs and resources; plan and provide psychological and developmental interventions
Physical therapist	Recommend or build adaptive equipment and mobility devices; recommend and implement environmental modification; teach handling, positioning, and movement techniques to facilitate motor functioning and posture
Social worker	Make home visits to evaluate living conditions and parent-child interaction patterns; provide counseling; mobilize community resources
Speech-language pathologist	Assess and diagnose communication and oral-motor abilities; provide appropriate therapy for oral-motor and communication skills
Vision specialist	Assess visual functioning; provide communication-skills training, orientation and mobility training, and independent living skills training

Source: Adapted from Brown, W., & Rule, S. (1993). Personnel and disciplines in early intervention. In W. Brown, S. K. Thurman, & L. F. Pearl (Eds.), *Family-centered early intervention with infants and toddlers: Innovative cross-disciplinary approaches* (pp. 245–268). Baltimore, MD: Paul H. Brookes.

Case Study

Transitioning to Public School: Interview with Tom and Ann Simpson

Tommy just turned three and he learned to walk this summer. He used to really hate physical therapy and he's always had low muscle tone, even for a Down syndrome child. We've started taking gymnastics classes and he really likes all that. His fine motor skills are pretty good; he learned to eat right away, but he's real motivated to eat. He's always the best eater in his group. He was the last child in his group to learn to walk, but he was the first child to be able to eat.

Tommy's very social. He likes other children and he behaves appropriately. He goes to music class and we're in gym class and he really acts out a lot less than some of the other normal children. He follows directions to some extent. We have a lot of fun with him because we do all of the preschool things. We go to the library. We go shopping. We go to music class. He does all of that and likes all of it.

I don't think we've really had to readjust our routine for him, except that he's sick an awful lot. He's been in the hospital a couple of times. We did have to adjust to take him to therapy which he started when he was just a week or two old. There have been several really kind people along the way, who helped us and his therapist was one of those. He started in a private school intervention program when he was about five months old.

Now, Tommy will be starting with the school district preschool program and I'm nervous about it. There have already been several miscommunications between me and the school about where he's supposed to go for testing and everything. I thought, "Oh my God, what's this going on?" So I just called the teacher and said my son's coming into your program, can I see your classroom? I could tell that most parents don't do that, but I felt I needed to do it. So Tommy and I were introduced to the teachers and the children and it made me feel more comfortable.

Tommy's new school is in our neighborhood, and they will bus him from our house or from my babysitter's house. I felt good about his school; the kids in his special preschool class were verbal and at Tommy's level. I feel he needs to be with the normal kids in his neighborhood school.

I've been to a workshop on transitioning to the public school and I guess I know as much as anyone else does about what's going to happen. But I decided that I wasn't going to sit passively and wait. I've talked to other parents who live in this area. It's funny, even before Tom was born, we'd see the bus come and the neighbor's wheelchair come out and I remember thinking, "I wonder who that is." We didn't know our neighbors yet, and they are quiet people. But I talked to the father once about where his daughter went and he had been happy with the local school program.

The school system is a big bureaucracy and you've got to interface through all these people, but what you need is a manual to know who to talk to. I don't have much blind faith that it's all going to work out okay. I guess I watch each step a lot more and talk to people more, and am a lot more proactive. But yet I don't want to just beat those guys up, because I know what it's like. I work in a big bureaucracy too. I know how those things happen, but I also know I have a duty to my child and to myself, to be on top of these things too.

Getting Tommy into school reminded me of when Tommy was born. If you put yourself in the hands of the system you need to know it's designed for its own expediency rather than for your experience and comfort. One thing I have learned is be proactive about getting my needs and my child's needs met, but always try to be polite about it. I've talked to a lot of parents who just will take whatever comes, and I guess I'm not willing to do that.

close as possible to that which the student would be assigned if there was no disability (perhaps the neighborhood daycare or a school's Montessori classroom) (LD OnLine, 1999). The committee should try to arrange such placement in a neighborhood school, or at least consider and try to limit the time and distance a student must be transported. As much as possible, a child would be removed from the normal school setting (such as school-sponsored childcare) only if the nature and severity of the disability was such that education with normal peers couldn't be achieved even with supplementary aids and services (LD OnLine, 1999).

The newly revised IDEA does not consider placement just a place. It is important that the student participate in the typical preschool curriculum as much as possible (Etscheidt & Bartlett, 1999). Several sections of the amended IDEA relate to enabling a child to participate and progress in a general curriculum. The IEP must contain a statement of the supplementary aids and services that should be provided on the child's behalf to allow for integration in regular activities such as kindergarten. The law also calls for identifying strategies to deal with special factors such as behavior problems that would otherwise prevent a child from participating in the general curriculum with nondisabled peers. Likewise, IDEA now requires that all students participate in statewide assessments that are required of nondisabled students and be provided supports or adaptations that will allow this kind of assessment to be given (Etscheidt & Bartlett, 1999). Finally, the IEP team must include a regular education teacher if the child is already participating in regular education. This emphasis on inclusion should support thorough transition planning and supportive services as a child moves into less restrictive settings.

The emphasis on preschool integration into natural child settings and regular education programs has presented a considerable challenge to many public school preschool programs. Not all public schools offer programs to nondisabled preschoolers, so innovative administrators must work to develop partnerships with community programs that might serve children with disabilities in integrated settings. At the same time, a continuum of services must be available so that a child who needs more intensive therapies and special education can also be appropriately served. In many cases, public schools have partnered with Head Start; in other instances, the schools have enrolled normal peers to be a part of a special education preschool offered at the school.

There is good reason for the law to require placement in the least restrictive setting; placing a child with a disability in an environment populated only by other children with disabilities may result in a limited educational experience (Thurman & Widerstrom, 1990). Such a setting does not provide typical role models who facilitate learning language, peer interaction, and other functional skills. Segregation also does not encourage acceptance by peers and adults, nor is it compatible with society's emphasis on pluralism. Finally, no clear evidence exists to suggest that a child with disabilities is better served within a self-contained program, while the benefits of peer modeling and interaction are well documented. Thus, placement in integrated preschool settings is recognized as a goal for children with disabilities.

Still, it would be unwise to place children in settings that do not meet their most pressing needs and the preferences of their parents. A preschool setting is not least restrictive if it fails to provide appropriate services and support. Therefore, the concept of least restrictive should *not* be considered equivalent to providing one program for all children. Legislation and litigation uphold the need to provide a variety of possible placement opportunities. Hence, least restrictive environments are best facilitated through a continuum of program options which allow a child to enter at any point needed and move on to more or less segregated settings when it is appropriate.

For example, a child who is born with a serious medical problem or physical disability may require a longer than normal hospitalization with the extensive involvement of a team of medical personnel. The hospital or residential setting would be considered the most restrictive on a continuum of placement options but, at this point in the child's life, would be the only appropriate setting for providing the care needed. When this child's health status reaches a satisfactory level, the hospital is likely to discharge the child to home care, sometimes accompanied by medical equipment, such as a respirator or heart monitor. Often, visiting nurses will be assigned to work with the parents and child in the home, and if the child's health continues to be fragile, other early childhood professionals may also provide in-home services.

As the child's strength and stamina increase, placement in a center-based program where the parents and child can work with therapists and special equipment becomes a reasonable option. Perhaps, at first, the child attends only three mornings a week and a physical therapist provides therapy and parent training in a setting where several other families are also present. When the child acquires mobility and speech and language skills, placement in an intensive program five mornings a week might be preferred. As the child grows more independent and shows stable health, placement in a full-time integrated preschool might allow more normal peer interaction. Eventually, this preschooler enrolls in the neighborhood kindergarten program, with consultation from relevant specialists (Table 9–1).

As long as an integrated preschool program is properly structured and children are provided training and reinforcement for interaction, this option is clearly the ethical and developmental preference (Thurman & Widerstrom, 1990). A greater availability of child care and other preschool programs for children without special needs makes inclusive settings more accessible to young children with disabilities. However, preschool settings and their curricula should be scrutinized along several dimensions to determine their appropriateness for a particular child and family. Factors that warrant careful consideration are the following: the instructional methods used, experiences and activities provided, how generalization of skills is promoted, the physical environment, curricular adaptations, data collection and evaluation, and the use of technology (Sandall, 1993).

To insure that schools have an entire range of placements available, IDEA requires school districts to provide a continuum of alternative programs (Yell, 1998). This allows parents and professionals to choose from a number of options that come closest to meeting a child's need for services and the right to be educated with normal peers. These options might include (LD OnLine, 1999):

1. Direct instruction or consultative services within regular classrooms
2. Regular classroom instruction and specialized instruction within a resource room
3. Part-time specialized instruction in a special education classroom with some time in the regular classroom

4. Primary instruction in special education with some integration with normal peers at nonacademic times
5. Full-time special education and related services
6. Separate public or private day school in a special education facility
7. Public or private residential facilities
8. Homebound services
9. Hospital services

Often, preschool services are not available in the public school on a regular basis to nondisabled peers. In this case, the school district may develop agreements with Head Start or other preschools to provide a setting that serves both typical children and children with disabilities so that the setting can be as natural as possible.

Even with the emphasis on a least restrictive environment, a child's team needs to remember that the regular setting is not always appropriate and should not be chosen if (Yell, 1998):

1. The child with disabilities will not receive educational benefits in the regular setting.
2. Any marginal benefit would be significantly outweighed by the more significant benefits possible in a more specialized instructional setting.
3. The child would be such a disruptive force in the general education setting that services could not be adequately provided.

The least restrictive and most appropriate setting is one where critical goals for the child can be achieved. When a decision of the Sixth Circuit Court used the analogy that a child with a disability is not entitled to a "Cadillac education," but only to a "serviceable Chevrolet," it may have given some school personnel the impression that it was all right to provide less than an individual child needed as long as it was in keeping with what nondisabled children were receiving (Hurder, 1997). This is not the case, and any child whose disability is so severe that he or she can not learn in the regular curriculum must be given whatever specialized services will support that child's educational potential (Hurder, 1997).

Instructional Methods

Early interventionists need to be proficient with a variety of instructional methods in order to meet the needs of children with different disabilities, age levels, cultural beliefs, and family values (Sandall, 1993). Yet, sometimes, educational philosophy dictates which instructional approach is used (Sandall, 1993). A *developmental* perspective is associated with enrichment activities that emphasize a stimulus-rich environment with age-appropriate activities and toys. Play and self-expression are encouraged. The **behavioral** perspective is associated with direct-instruction methods that include a systematic analysis of objectives, sequencing of learning steps, and systematic reinforcement of desired behaviors. Activities and learning tasks are generally **teacher-directed.** The **interactional** and **ecological** perspectives place more emphasis on how children and their environments influence each other. These latter perspectives are more often associated with responsive and active-learning techniques, such as milieu teaching, in which the environment is arranged to stimulate a child's interest and behavior on which a teacher can elaborate. These programs

Figure 9–2
The Preschool
Continuum of
Least Restrictive
Settings

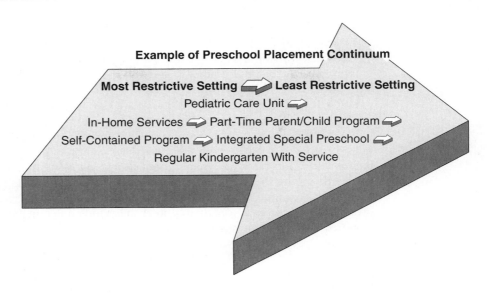

Example of Preschool Placement Continuum

Most Restrictive Setting ⇨ **Least Restrictive Setting**
Pediatric Care Unit ⇨
In-Home Services ⇨ Part-Time Parent/Child Program ⇨
Self-Contained Program ⇨ Integrated Special Preschool ⇨
Regular Kindergarten With Service

would also be described as **child-directed** and emphasize natural events and routines. Still other programs focus on parents as teachers and emphasize parent-child interactions and support systems for families.

An appropriate program for preschool children with disabilities provides a balance of both highly structured (teacher-directed) activities and less structured (child-directed or developmental) activities. Such scheduling allows direct instruction on specific skills that provide opportunities for skill acquisition, proficiency, and generalization within natural situations. For example, a specific language curriculum could be used during circle time, and a child with a language disability would be systematically prompted to respond appropriately. During free play, the same child might be encouraged to verbalize about an object or activity that is self-selected.

In addition, generalization is best facilitated if instruction is carried over between both center and home. A center-based program provides opportunities for special instruction and socialization, while well-informed parents can intervene by continuing contingencies for specific behaviors during daily routines in the home setting. For example, a child who is learning to fasten clothing may be highly motivated to button a jacket when the whole class is going outside to the playground. The child's teacher uses this opportunity to instruct by providing partial prompts of physical assistance, as needed during coat buttoning. At home, the parents may use the same system of partial prompts to help the child learn to button clothing in the morning and then, as a reinforcer, allow the child to play outside for a while before boarding the bus for school.

Experiences and Activities

Early development occurs primarily within social contexts (Sandall, 1993). It makes sense then that intervention programs promote social behaviors between infants and their parents/caregivers and between preschoolers and their peers. Activities should also promote engagement or active involvement with the environment (Sandall,

1993). A range of experiences should be provided to accommodate different capability levels and varied interests.

Consider, for example, a 4-year-old child, Jonathan, with autism who is included in a preschool program for other 4- and 5-year-old children. This child is mobile only with the use of a walker, has no expressive or receptive language skills, and engages in **self-stimulation.** Most of the children are able to sit quietly in circle time and listen to the teacher read a story. Jonathan will turn away from the teacher and flap his hands and fingers in this situation. Adjusting for this individual child's interests will help Jonathan participate with the group. For example, using concrete objects or a flannel board increases Jonathan's attentiveness, allowing him to hold something in his hands during the story decreases self-stimulation, and letting Jonathan push the appropriate computer key as the story is told allows him to respond. The other children may even prompt Jonathan to keep his hands quiet as they listen to the story. None of these adaptations makes the story less appropriate or less interesting for Jonathan's peers and may, in fact, improve their attention and participation as well.

Generalization

A consistent finding in the research literature is the poor generalization of newly acquired behaviors to functional, less-structured settings by individuals with disabilities (Sandall, 1993). Consequently, programs for young children should emphasize functional, meaningful behaviors that will have many opportunities for practice across settings, people, and materials (Sandall, 1993). Settings should use natural activities, materials, and routines to promote generalization.

A preschool setting considered as a placement for a child with disabilities should be evaluated according to these factors. For example, are all the children responsible for putting away toys, setting the table for lunch, and dressing themselves for recess (all functional behaviors)? Are the children encouraged to play with each other, to verbalize their needs, to engage in group activities (vital for socialization)? Do children take part in regularly scheduled activities such as hand washing, story time, outdoor play, and snack time (routines)?

The Physical Environment

The preschool environment should foster security and trust by being safe, warm, inviting, secure, and predictable (Bailey & Wolery, 1992). Personal identity, opportunities to develop control over their physical surroundings, and a rich and stimulating environment should also be a part of preschool designs (Bailey & Wolery, 1992). The environment should contain child-sized furniture, child-centered displays of their own work, personal storage spaces, and a shelter for escaping from overstimulation. Numerous activity areas should be available for arts and crafts, reading, sand and water play, housekeeping and dramatic play, woodworking, and outdoor exercise.

Different areas of a room may be more conducive to specific behaviors and routines or specialized instruction. For example, noisy block play should be located away from language activities where a therapist is working on the production of specific speech sounds. A one-way mirror could be located conveniently so that parents may observe instruction or evaluation without distracting a child. Finally, traffic patterns may have to be arranged to accommodate orthopedic equipment such as standing tables or wheelchairs. For some children, it may be necessary to have a ramp to access playground equipment.

Curricular Adaptations

A variety of supports and resources are needed to help adapt activities for individual children (Sandall, 1993). These include access to specialists and technical assistance and availability of specialized materials to accommodate for sensory, motor, health, or other specialized needs. In addition, all services should be delivered at locations close to the family.

For example, specialized feeding equipment, such as a nonslip plate with a lip to catch food, a built-up spoon handle, and a cutaway cup might allow a child to self-feed at lunch with other children. Therapy mats and bolsters should be a part of the classroom furnishings so that physical therapy can be provided without removing a child from the classroom. When not used for therapy, the equipment might make a nice obstacle course for all children. A computer with a touch screen could be used to help a child with severely limited movement to demonstrate cognitive skills and also for art activities or games with the other children.

Data Collection and Evaluation

A necessary component of any preschool program is a set of procedures for collecting and using data to monitor the effects of program efforts (Sandall, 1993). Data should be collected regularly and systematically and used in making educational decisions. Such data might be collected through direct observation of specific child behaviors, through the use of developmental checklists, through permanent product samples, such as videotapes or audiotapes, and through family reporting. Irrespective of the method, it is critical that data be linked to a child's goals or program and used to adjust program activities in accordance with changes in a child's development.

For example, a goal for Courtney, a child with Down syndrome, is to increase verbal interactions with peers. Her preschool teacher decides to observe Courtney on the playground and record how often she asks to play with other children during the daily 15 minutes of outdoor play. The teacher quickly discovers that across a week, Courtney initiated requests to play an average of only once a day, and in every case, the peers failed to accept her as a playmate. The teacher then devises a strategy to verbally prompt and praise such requests and to praise peers who play with Courtney. Further data collection shows that requests to play have risen to an average of five per day. Now the teacher can fade out her prompting while continuing to praise interactions with all children.

Assistive Technology

Finally, when determining the appropriateness of a placement setting, one should consider technological interventions that may benefit young children. Technology can allow young children opportunities for play, socialization, language, and manipulation of the environment (Sandall, 1993). For example, some simple electronic switches can be activated with as little as an eye blink or a puff of air to operate toys that teach cause and effect. Augmentative communication devices, such as an electronic board that speaks when a child touches a picture, allow children who have no capacity for speech or signing to interact with others in a variety of settings. Many

Table 9–2   Assistive Technology Web Sites

Web Site	Description
Applied Science and Engineering Laboratorles http://www.asel.udel.edu/atonline/assistive.html	An on-line database on assistive technology.
Equal Access to Software and Information http://www.rit.edu~easi/indes.html	Promotes access through workshops, publications and videos, e-mail lists, an electronic journal, and conferences.
Jim Lubin http://www.eskimo.com/~jlubin/disabled.html	A resource to useful information created by a person who is, himself, physically limited.
National Center to Improve Practice http://www.edc.org/FSC/NCIP/	Provides discussion forums to exchange information and build knowledge.
Trace Research and Development Center http://www.trace.wisc.edu/tcel/	Provides databases, web sites, and full text documents on assistive devices.

Source: Adapted from Lahm, E. A., & Nickels, B. L. (1999). Assistive technology competencies for special educators. *Teaching Exceptional Children, 32* (1).

preschool language programs are now available on personal computers and can be used with groups of children to stimulate language skills.

The new IDEA requires that IEP teams must consider what assistive technology is appropriate as a supplementary aid or intervention (Lahm & Nickels, 1999). Such devices include high and low technology: "any item, piece of equipment, or product system, whether acquired commercially off the shelf, modified, or customized, that is used to increase, maintain, or improve functional capabilities of a child with a disability" (Lahm & Nickels, 1999, p. 57). Assistive technology service is also encouraged. These services can help evaluate needs; purchase or lease devices; select, design, fit, customize, adapt, maintain, or replace devices as needed; train a child or the child's family, and train professional staff who work with the child. Table 9–2 provides a list of assistive technology web sites that might help a team in making decisions.

Supplementary Aids and Services

Assistive technology is only one part of a full range of aids and services that may enable a student to benefit from an educational program without significant disruption (Etscheidt & Bartlett, 1999). The IEP team should discuss aids in terms of several dimensions: the physical, instructional, social-behavioral, and collaborative. The physical dimension includes factors such as mobility, room arrangement, lighting, acoustics and seating. The instructional dimension involves factors related to lesson planning, methodology, and assessment. The social-behavioral dimension relates to services or aids that would reduce disruptive behavior. The collaborative would address how multiple personnel are coordinated and how time for collaboration is arranged.

In summary, all these factors—experiences and activities, instructional methods, generalization, physical environment, curricular adaptations, data collection and evaluation, and technology—should influence the final placement of any preschool child requiring special education. The critical piece of any IEP is the shared goal of enhancing the child's development and learning (Sandall, 1993). This outcome is reached only through the careful planning of instructional objectives, the deliberate selection of special education and related services that support those objectives, and the appropriate placement of the child in the least restrictive setting that will promote the child's involvement and progress.

CHALLENGING BEHAVIOR

Challenging behavior is behavior that interferes with children's learning and development, that is harmful to the child or to others (Bailey & Wolery, 1992). It may include self-injury, negative peer interaction, disruptive behavior, tantruming, and noncompliance (Chandler, Dahlquist, Repp, & Feltz, 1999). The most recent revisions of IDEA require that appropriate strategies, including positive behavioral interventions and supports be identified in the IEP. The amendments further require that a functional behavioral assessment be conducted when developing behavioral intervention plans for a student with challenging behavior. A functional assessment assists educators and others working with a child to understand the factors that produce and support challenging behavior. It is a process for determining the relationship between events in a person's environment and the occurrence of challenging behaviors (Rogers, 1998). The result is a clear definition or description of the behaviors, predictions as to the times and situations in which the behavior might happen, and identification of the function the behavior serves for the child; that is, one child might tantrum to escape a demanding situation while another might tantrum to get adult attention.

Take for example, Frank who was a 3 year old, developmentally delayed child, whose parents were both developmentally delayed as well. He was referred for a functional assessment for the following behavioral concerns:

> At school, Frank appeared "unmotivated" and stood apart from activities that took place; he held his hands clasped behind his back and refused to participate. Teachers reported that at times he would engage in these behaviors for as long as 1 hour, 45 minutes. The only activity he joined in was snack time. At home, the parents reported that they were frustrated by Frank's behavior; he would scream, throw objects, bite, kick, hit, bang his head against objects, the floor, and the wall, and he would refuse to follow his parents' directions. (Rogers, 1998, p. 32)

Frank's team completed a functional assessment in the home. First, they interviewed family members and caregivers about their concerns regarding Frank's behavior. They asked questions about the frequency, intensity, and duration of his inappropriate behaviors. The team also asked about strategies that had been used to control the behavior, situations in which the behaviors were seen, the child's preferences, the child's means of communication, and relevant background like his medical condition.

Next, the team undertook a motivation assessment. Parents, caregivers, teachers, and other service providers rated each specific behavior and identified the situations where it was likely to occur. This was followed by a setting-event checklist that asked about situations that occurred before and seemed to set the stage for the behaviors. For example, if Frank missed a morning nap, would he be more likely to whine to get mother's attention?

Finally, direct observations were made of Frank under several different circumstances. The team found that at school Frank's behavior was to escape activities; at home he misbehaved to get attention or tangible items he wanted and to escape demands made by his parents. Interventions could then be designed to change the environmental variables that contributed to his challenging behavior and to provide support for appropriate behavior that achieved the same function as the challenging behavior (Chandler et al., 1999). Interventions were designed so that Frank could escape tasks or request attention and tangibles through more acceptable means.

There are several advantages to functional assessments (Chandler et al., 1999):

1. It is a proactive approach, teaching children what they should do, rather than punishing children for engaging in challenging behavior.
2. It focuses on prevention as well as remediation by arranging antecedents and consequences that may be related to appropriate behavior.
3. It provides team members from a variety of disciplines with a common language and approach for addressing challenging behavior.
4. It provides teams with a method of assessment that works for any child's challenging behavior, regardless of age, disability, or setting.
5. It provides teams with consistent methods for selecting interventions for behavior.

CREATING QUALITY IEPS

Bateman (1995) outlined practices that support the development of sound IEPs. The first step is for the school to provide an appropriate time and a comfortable place for the meeting to occur, keeping in mind that this should be mutually agreeable with the parents. The focus of the meeting must be on the special needs of the student and how those will be addressed. She suggested a strategically placed photo of the youngster to keep participants from wandering off that topic. Members should be aware of their enormous power to arrange for services that are needed; they should not limit themselves to fitting the child into existing school services when those really don't suffice. All of the student's needs must be addressed, not just the academic ones.

Bateman (1995) recommended starting with a blank piece of paper rather than letting a required form drive the discussion. The team should pretend they are "describing the student to a volunteer who has never met the student and is going to take him or her camping for a week." Next, the team should complete the statement: "We are individualizing Johnny's program because _____." This will help identify the child's unique needs. At the same time, the team may be detailing each need in terms of the child's present level of performance. Enough information should be provided so that the present level is readily understandable and the information is precise enough to allow the team to measure later progress. When words don't seem to be enough, a work sample might be provided. The team should not forget to address social-emotional-behavioral areas as well.

The next question the team asks is "What will the district do about this?" for each need described. The team should be "as creative, flexible, innovative, and often inexpensive as the team's brainstorming and combined wisdom allow" (Bateman, 1995). The answer to this question will include identifying special education services and related services the child needs. It will also include how teachers who will be working with the child can be prepared and will identify any modifications that will need to be made for participation in regular education settings.

Bateman (1995) suggested approaching goals and objectives by asking "If the service we are providing is effective, what will we see in Todd's behavior that tells us so?" It is important when stating goals and objectives to remember that you will be checking to see whether the student actually reaches them.

Kroeger, Leibold, and Ryan (1999) suggest recognizing that everyone on an IEP team is a significant stakeholder in the process. The team's job is to set a vision for that student, keeping in mind the child's gifts, abilities and strengths. This starts with a listing of all the positives a student may possess, a "list in progress" of strengths that may lead the group toward interventions best suited to that child. What follows this is identification of specific concerns, brainstorming about how to intervene in areas of need, and a specific plan of action. It is essential that each participant be invited to express his or her viewpoint on all the concerns so that information is complete and decisions are made collaboratively.

What are the quality indicators of an exemplary IEP meeting? Consider the following descriptors (Beach Center on Families and Disabilities, 1999):

◆ The process is ongoing, dynamic, and individualized.
◆ Family-initiated goals and objectives are given priority.
◆ Meetings and documents are jargon-free and use clear explanations.
◆ There is a mutually respectful relationship between families and professionals.
◆ Families are a part of the collaborative process and share equal decision-making responsibilities.
◆ Current best practices are discussed and a range of service settings are considered.

Case Study

INTEGRATING JOSH: INTERVIEW WITH AMY FINKEL

Getting Josh integrated into a regular classroom was a real battle. The only way that he could be successful in a regular classroom was with one of his own aides, in other words, someone from my home-therapy program. Expressive language has always been the main focus that we have been after for Josh. Learning prepositions, learning math, and so on, was all great, but I wanted him to have functional speech. An untrained aide, or someone who didn't have a significant amount of hours with him here in the home, would have no clue what he was trying to say, because at that time, a lot of the words he said were really gross approximations of words. Unless you were pretty familiar with his speech patterns, you would have no idea what he was trying to say.

The first year, the school district refused to pay for a private aide, let alone hire someone from my home program. They said that was a conflict of interest, which we felt was ridiculous. So, we actually paid out of our own funds and got them to agree to let one of our home team members accompany Josh to school. He was only in school two afternoons a week at that time.

The next year, I decided, wait a minute! We were paying $30,000 a year for 40 hours of instruction a week; what's the school going to pay for? It just so happened that there were several landmark cases that had just been won by parents here in Washington state that year. I got the transcripts of the cases and I presented them, along with a financial argument to the school district. I pointed out that legally my son is entitled to a free appropriate education (FAPE), therefore, they should be paying for everything. All we were asking the school district to do was to pay for the Educational Aide at school. I negotiated with them that we would continue to pay for the home program; we just wanted the district to pay for the little piece of the pie that served Josh in school. I said, "If you don't, then we certainly have the option to come back and ask you to pay for everything Josh is entitled to under FAPE." It was a subtle threat.

I prepared for that IEP meeting for months. I went without sleep for weeks at a time and I walked into that meeting with stacks of case law, quotes from professionals all across the country who talked about the need for 40 hour a week programs for children with autism. The school district agreed to our request.

Here we are today where Josh does have his own classroom aide, someone from my home program, someone he has a rapport with, someone who knows what his skill levels are on a daily basis. So when he is in the school setting, he is always required to perform to the level he is capable of, so there is no regression or backsliding. Most importantly the aide is there to immediately reinforce expressive language.

Josh also attends the extended school year (ESY) summer program. That was another interesting battle. Josh starts the ESY program the Monday after the regular school year lets out and goes right up until the Friday before the next regular school year begins. Schools traditionally use regression/recoupment formulas to qualify children for ESY (which means that data must be collected which prove that the children lose skills over the summer that they don't readily recover in the fall). I feel these formulas are illegal because they don't take into consideration each child's unique needs. With autism, once regression has occurred, you've lost valuable time. With autism, you can't have one set of standards in one place and another set of standards in another setting; intervention needs to be constant, year round. There are quite a few studies and a number of professionals that have written on the necessity for 12 month schooling for children with autism.

Again, that was another killer IEP meeting and I had to threaten due process. I said, "My son will be in ESY. Regression/recoupment formulas are illegal because they don't take into account my son's unique needs. Also with autism, there is a limited developmental window of opportunity. ESY is not going to do him any good when he is 12 years old. He needs every bit of intervention he can get now." I won ESY on those three points.

I don't anticipate that it will be a problem keeping him in regular education because the language in P.L. 105-17, IDEA, is so clear on that. However, I'm sure that as he gets older Josh will need to be pulled out of the regular classroom from time to time. My biggest fear for him is when he reaches junior high and high school and the peer stuff starts. On one hand, I want him to progress as much as he can, but on the other hand, if he progresses only to a point where he is still naive about his condition that might save him from some pain.

My fears are about how he'll be treated by peers. We already had an incident last year where there was a little girl who didn't want to sit next to Josh on the bus, and she was making fun of him. "He's such a pain!" she said. It starts early and kids can be cruel. No kids want to be different, they all want to fit in.

I went to a conference where an adult man with autism talked about his experiences. He had several suicide attempts because he was recovered enough that he was painfully aware of his peers teasing him and how different he was. I think that would be the hardest part. That's why it is so important, now while he's little, that he's in an integrated classroom.

There already are three or four peers who really like Josh and that he gets along well with. Hopefully, as they grow up together in public school, there will always be a couple of "watch-dog" kids that will be his friends and companions.

Josh's older brother David and I are going to go into Josh's classroom to give presentations later this month. One thing that is really cool to a kindergartner is a second-grader, like David. So David can talk to them about his brother Josh and relieve some of their fears and tensions. We'll use a classic example where you hold up a can of vegetables that most kids don't like, such as spinach, but we'll have cleaned out the can and filled it with candy that the kids don't see. We'll ask, "Do you want any?" and of course the kids will say, "Icky, no!" Then we'll show them what is inside, and teach them that you can't tell a book by its cover.

We'll also do a felt board activity where we have a whole bunch of different shapes hodge-podge on the felt board. But we'll show them how to put the shapes together to make this neat train. Even though everybody is different, if you all come together, you can really go places.

Josh playing during school recess.

BEST PRACTICES IN PRESCHOOL INTERVENTION

Since the late 1960s, programs for young children with disabilities have proliferated (Karnes & Stayton, 1988). A model program may be defined as one in which the content and operational strategies are clearly conceptualized and defined in a manner that assures internal consistency and coherence (Peterson, 1987). A number of early intervention models have been developed that capture the best of what is known about how to serve young preschool children with disabilities. These models can be characterized by the following (Thurman & Widerstrom, 1990):

1. *Integrated:* Typical children and children with disabilities are served in the same settings; there is supported placement in generic early childhood service sites.
2. *Comprehensive:* A full array of professional services is offered through a transdisciplinary approach and using direct instruction for generalized responding.
3. *Normalized:* Instruction is stressed across a number of settings, age-appropriate materials and strategies are used, contrived reinforcement and aversive control is avoided, and parents are supported.
4. *Adaptable:* Flexible procedures are employed within noncategorical models; emphasis is on the functionality of behavior rather than its developmental form or sequence.
5. *Peer and family referenced:* The curriculum is validated in reference to the child, family, and community; parents are full partners in decision making.
6. *Outcome-based:* There is an emphasis on development of skills for future usefulness; transition is carefully planned.

Preschool models are sometimes identified by the location of their service delivery: center-based, home-based, or a combination of the two. Recently, the distinction of family-focus has emerged to identify intervention programs that concentrate on supporting the family rather than providing direct services to children. Table 9–3 describes exemplary programs for each of these types.

The most common setting for serving preschoolers with disabilities is in **center-based programs** (Bailey & Wolery, 1992). These children are served in a central location, usually a public school where they attend for 3 to 5 days each week during the school year. Center-based programs can offer a wide range of family services and supports as well as direct services to children. Children who attend group sessions also have increased opportunities for social interaction, which can facilitate their transition into kindergarten settings.

There are several advantages to training parents to be teachers for their own children in **home-based programs** (Shearer & Shearer, 1979). First, learning takes place in children's natural environments, eliminating the problem of transfer from school to the home. Secondly, there is direct and constant opportunity to intervene on behavior as it occurs naturally. Thirdly, behaviors learned in the natural environment tend to be maintained more easily. Finally, training parents gives them the skills to deal with new behaviors as they occur. The Portage project offers an outstanding model for such an approach.

Programs that use both center-based and home-based strategies are able to maximize the benefits of both models. Combination programs can offer a wide range of family services and supports, both at their central location and in the home. The

Table 9–3 Model Preschool Programs

Program	Description
Center-Based Programs	
The Direct Instruction model (Bereiter & Engelmann, 1966) was developed to serve low-income preschoolers and later expanded through the federally funded Follow Through program to serve low-income children from kindergarten through third grade.	The program emphasizes academic competence through the development of language, reading, and math skills. The curriculum is highly teacher-directed with instruction in small groups, maintaining a fast pace for unison responding, carefully sequencing the introduction of new skills, scheduling consistent review, and providing positive consequences to motivate children. Specific instruction might total an hour a day, with a teacher and paraprofessional teaching two groups concurrently, while a third group works independently at learning or activity stations.
The High/Scope Perry Preschool Project began in 1962 as an intervention program for economically disadvantaged children (Weikart, 1988).	The program uses the High/Scope Curriculum (Hohmann, Banet, & Weikart, 1979), which is organized around Piagetian principles. Primary emphasis is on problem solving, independent thinking, social development, and relationships. The guiding principle is that children's knowledge comes from direct experience with real objects, talking about real experiences and ideas, and from the application of logical thinking to these events. The daily routine is primarily a plan-do-review sequence in which children make choices and carry out their activities, then recall and represent their experience verbally, pictorially, or through a model.
The Infant, Toddler, and Preschool Research and Intervention Program (D. Bricker & W. Bricker, 1971, 1972, 1973; W. Bricker & D. Bricker, 1976) began in Nashville, Tennessee, at George Peabody College in 1970 (Thurman & Widerstrom, 1990). About 25% of the children served were typical, about 25% were at risk for developmental delays and about half of the group were children with categorical disabilities.	Activities include group and individual language training, gross and fine motor experiences, self-directed tasks, a consistent environment maintained with contingency management techniques, opportunities to develop appropriate cognitive skills, and training in adaptive skills needed for transitions into other settings. Although the program is child-oriented, there is a heavy emphasis on parent involvement. Parents are asked to participate in their child's classroom at least once a week and project staff provide parent training, counseling, and advocacy.
The Model Preschool Program for Children with Down Syndrome and Other Developmental Delays was one of the original centers funded by the 1968 Handicapped Children's Early Education Assistance Act (Fewell & Oelwein, 1991). It began at the University of Washington Experimental Education Unit and has been replicated throughout the United States and in many foreign countries.	The program uses a test-teach-test model relying on curriculum-based assessment, systematic and individualized instruction, and guidance through stages of learning, including acquisition, fluency, transfer, and generalization of basic skills. Parents attend their children's classes, master instructional strategies used in the classrooms, and are trained in developmental, academic, and behavioral management techniques used at school.

(continued)

Table 9–3 Model Preschool Programs *(continued)*

Program	Description
Home-Based Programs	
The Portage Project was initially funded in 1969 by the Bureau of Education for the Handicapped as one of its first demonstration projects (Shearer, 1979). By 1979, seventy Portage-based replication sites had been subsequently established in the United States and a number in other countries, such as Ecuador, Great Britain, Japan, and Canada.	The model provides comprehensive services to a rural area in which no educational service had been previously provided to preschool children with disabilities. A teacher trains parents in their homes to work with their own children. Teachers meet with each child's family in a one-day-per-week visit (Shearer & Shearer, 1979). Ongoing assessment, curriculum planning, and weekly objectives for parents were provided. Parents maintain a behavioral log describing the activities used and their child's accomplishments.
Combination Center- and Home-Based Programs	
The Multi-Agency project for Preschoolers (MAPPS) project was developed at Utah State University and works with agencies, including rural preschools for the developmentally delayed, Head Start programs, the Navaho Reservation, Air Force Family Support Centers, and high school programs for adolescent mothers and their families (Karnes & Stayton, 1988).	The MAPPS project serves over 500 children, of whom 20% are Navajo and another 20% Hispanic or African American. The children have a wide variety of disabling conditions or are at risk for developmental delay. Parents may choose to have their infants served in the home or in a center; most of the toddlers are served through a combination of home plus center. Children from three to five years of age are mainstreamed into existing preschool and day-care programs.
The project for Expanding Developmental Growth through Education (EDGE) is a program for children with Down syndrome. It provides home instruction to infants and center-based preschool instruction to children over 30 months of age (Thurman & Widerstrom, 1990). Project EDGE was first funded through the Handicapped Children's Early Education Program and was based out of the University of Minnesota.	Rynders and Horrobin (1975) described Project EDGE's basic principles in regard to how mothers should work with their young children. These include: affectionate sensorimotor interaction, an emphasis on speech and language, flexible structure, involvement of nondisabled siblings, and novelty of activities. Mothers are expected to engage in specified training activities for one hour each day using the EDGE curriculum and simple materials. Daily home stimulation continues even after the child begins attending the center-based preschool. Project EDGE staff provide maternal tutoring and other services, such as respite care and a mobile education unit to lessen maternal stress.
Family-Focused Programs	
The Supporting Extended Family Members (SEFAM) project is unique in that it does not provide direct services to children. Instead, services are provided to family members who are traditionally underserved: fathers, siblings, and grandfathers (Karnes & Stayton, 1988).	The SEFAM programs supplement direct service programs for children with disabilities and their families. Staff routinely provide information and referral for family members to auxiliary services such as respite care or recreational programs that would benefit the family system. The SEFAM project is based on a family systems orientation. Family members' needs are assessed through formal instruments and addressed through group meetings and newsletters.

center component allows an efficient use of staff time and ease of supervision. Team members can work closely together but, because of the added home component, can involve parents in both planning and implementation of services. The center services allow children opportunities for socialization, while home services provide for those who are too young or too fragile to take part in group activities.

Family-focused programs are designed primarily to provide assistance and support to family members rather than direct services to children. In most cases, children with disabilities may be attending center programs or receiving intervention through other outlets.

SUCCESSFUL INCLUSION

Drinkwater and Demchak (1995) described meaningful preschool inclusion of children with disabilities as involving all children in age-appropriate groups and activities that their peers are enjoying. All the children should follow the same schedule, use the same materials, and participate as fully as possible. This does not eliminate adaptation or assistance, but does so in a manner that minimizes the differences between children and maximizes the peer interaction. Teachers in these settings use the least intrusive natural prompts and contingencies they can to help children actively participate. Drinkwater and Demchak (1995) use an example of a child who cannot walk to circle time being encouraged to get there as independently as possible, even if it means using a walker, rather than being carried to circle. Another example they provide: Though other children are expected to cover the entire paper with finger paint, a child with motor disorders might be allowed to make any marks on paper he can.

Meaningful inclusion also encourages social and communicative reciprocity (Drinkwater & Demchak, 1995). Teachers can do this by training nondisabled peers to initiate play activities, share toys and respond to their disabled peer's initiations. Teachers must also make sure that a child with disabilities has some means of communicating, either by using signs, gesturing, or pointing to pictures. Nondisabled peers may need to be taught to recognize these communication attempts. When scheduling, teachers can make sure some activities require cooperation, such as bouncing objects with a parachute where everyone holds on to some part of the parachute to make it go up and down. It also helps if the child with a disability is given responsibilities, such as being a line leader or passing out snacks.

Another factor to consider is the appearance of a child with a disability (Drinkwater & Demchak, 1995). Unpleasant characteristics such as being dirty, being messy at snack, or wearing diapers may influence staff and other children negatively. Teaching grooming skills, using a napkin, and having a private changing area could do much to reduce a child's stigma and to encourage interaction.

At the same time, meaningful inclusion also addresses the goals and objectives identified in a child's IEP. Teachers need to look at the basic instructional strategies they are using to be sure they are facilitating growth (Thompson et al., 1993). Questions to ask might include:

◆ Is there a range of appropriate materials for the age group and learning tasks?
◆ Is the child positioned, handled, and moved in a way that is functional and age-appropriate?

♦ Are materials cues, contingencies, and fading of prompts used appropriately?
♦ Is a child's attention span accommodated and is enough practice provided?
♦ Are positive methods used to deal with problem behavior?
♦ Are IEP goals and objectives embedded in functional, naturally occurring activities?

Case
Study

JENNIFER WARITZ, THE EDUCATION EXPERIENCE: INTERVIEW WITH TAMMY WARITZ

Jennifer began her early education at a private school for children under the age of three who have disabilities. She attended twice a week, for a couple of hours at a time and I was deeply involved in her therapy program. It was the most nurturing place we could ever have been. Sometimes it was difficult for us to see other children who weren't as involved as Jennifer, but it was also hard to see children who were more involved. We knew the pain those families were feeling.

The private school was such a supportive and caring environment, a loving and warm place to be. Everyone was very accepting and they not only worked with Jennifer, they worked with the family. We learned so much from being there. I guess that's why I do the parent advocacy work that I do today. I want to see the system change for families so they don't have to struggle for the services they need. Jennifer had physical therapy, occupational therapy, and speech therapy twice a week. Her team of professionals taught me so much, helped me learn the system, and helped me gain the knowledge that I needed. They recognized that I was going to be Jennifer's real "case manager," her advocate for the rest of her life, because she doesn't have a voice for herself.

When Jennifer turned three, she was transitioned into a public school self-contained program. That was a scary time for us, because we were leaving the private school where we had been very much involved. (I'm not sure that it's natural for families to separate when the child is only two or three years old.) That Fall, the big yellow school bus pulled up in front of the house, and we were expected to put her on the bus and wave good-bye. The first day I followed the bus to school to make sure that she got off at the right stop; it was still a huge transition for the family.

Jennifer spent two years in a self-contained program, and then the school district initiated a cooperative venture with Head Start to provide an integrated preschool program. The integrated program was originally set up for children who were much less involved than Jennifer, but I asked for Jennifer to be included, even though I was nervous about the change and wanted to make sure that Jennifer could still go back to the self-contained program if the integrated preschool didn't work for her.

I was afraid of how the other children would treat Jennifer and I was also worried about how the other parents would react to her. I was afraid there would be so much going on in the regular classroom that she wouldn't be able to learn. For the first three years of her life, all her teaching had been one-on-one, and even in the self-contained program, there had been only six to eight students at one time. The Head Start classroom served twelve children, was a regular preschool, and was very energetic, so I was really afraid that Jennifer's needs weren't going to be met.

In fact, Jennifer made more gains in the integrated program in the first year than she had made during her two years in the self-contained program. The social interaction was so important for her. Even though she wasn't on the same level and couldn't do some of the same things, she was always right there with her peers. Jennifer developed a vocabulary of five to ten words and was introduced to a communication board to help her express her needs and wants. We asked that Jennifer stay in the program an additional year where she continued to develop and make gains that allowed her to be moved right into a regular kindergarten classroom the next year.

Moving into kindergarten was even more difficult, because now there was only one teacher and maybe an aide if the teacher was lucky. We requested a full-time aide to assist Jennifer in that environment, because we couldn't expect the teacher to meet her needs. Jennifer spent half her day in the regular kindergarten and the other half of her day in a self-contained program for children with developmental impairments. I wanted both programs because of Jennifer's involvement; there are things that she needed to learn in order to be as independent as possible. She deserved the dignity to learn these self-help skills without her peers looking on. The self-contained program provided her with the occupational, physical, and speech therapy she still needed.

Currently, Jennifer is spending about two hours a day and lunch time with her first-grade class. Her aide is still there with her, but we made it clear that we didn't want that person attached to her side, that Jennifer needed to be free to interact

Jennifer Waritz

naturally in her environment. That's what we've really focused on trying to do. When I went to the first-grade open house, I really didn't know quite how it was going for Jennifer, but there was her own little desk with her name tag and the same little books that everybody else had. When I looked on the other desks in the classroom, I saw they were all doing journals and Jennifer had one too. Sometimes an adult had helped Jennifer do her journal, but I could see there were children who'd also helped her. In almost every journal on the other students' desks was at least one page with a sentence written about Jennifer in the book. I realized, "She really does belong. She is a member of this classroom."

IN CONCLUSION

The purpose of early childhood special education is the provision of appropriate intervention services that will ultimately assist all children with disabilities. Four fundamental assumptions support this purpose:

1. Children who have disabilities or are at risk for having disabilities need and have a right to specialized services to enhance their development and the likelihood of success.
2. Families of children with disabilities often experience special needs and stresses.
3. The provision of earlier services can mean the achievement of optimal outcomes for children and families.
4. Because of the unique characteristics, needs, and resources of each child and family, no one curriculum or set of services could be expected to meet the needs of all. An individualized approach to service planning and delivery, therefore, is essential. (Bailey & Wolery, 1992, p. 34)

Given these beliefs, several basic service goals for early intervention are apparent (Bailey & Wolery, 1992). First, it is essential that families are supported in achieving their own goals; professionals must serve children in ways that are consistent with family structures, values, needs, and functions. Assisting children in their development requires the promotion of child engagement, independence, and mastery across all the key domains; the final measure of a child's development is successful interaction within a great variety of physical and social environments. Special education must always recognize the primary goal of helping children live lives that are as normal as possible, incorporating all children and their families into mainstream settings and activities. Finally, early intervention must address the prevention of new disabilities or future problems.

Beyond these primary goals for children with disabilities, each early childhood professional must also accept responsibility for pursuing goals important for the culture as a whole (Bailey & Wolery, 1992). The services mandated through IDEA are very new in the history of this society and as such must be protected and supported if they are to be maintained. It is important that special educators continue to increase the public's awareness and acceptance of people with disabilities and their need for early intervention. It is essential that special educators continually and consistently attempt to improve the quality of early intervention services through research and evaluation. Finally, professionals must be active in communicating best practices and disseminating professional knowledge to others in order to promote the availability of quality services. Early childhood professionals must advocate not only for the children and families in their direct care but also for future populations who will face the same challenges.

STUDY GUIDE QUESTIONS

1. What issues exist in respect to working with families of preschool children with disabilities?
2. What should professionals do to ease the transition to preschool special education?
3. What are the essential components of an IEP?
4. Generate an original example of a clear statement of present levels of performance.
5. Develop a good objective to describe communication targets for a 4-year-old child with moderate retardation. Be sure to include the behavior, the conditions, and the criterion.
6. Look carefully at the objective just written, what guidelines for an instructional objective does it already address? How could it be improved it to meet the remaining guidelines?
7. What are the critical characteristics of specially designed instruction?
8. Describe how one might ensure the generalization of conversational skills for a 3-year-old child.
9. Describe three specialists who might provide related services to a preschooler (and family) with a hearing impairment. What kinds of support might they provide?
10. Sometimes the same setting is least restrictive for one child but not for another. Give an example of a child for whom a self-contained preschool program for hearing impaired children might be most appropriate and one of a child for whom it is not.
11. What is the purpose of a functional behavioral assessment? How might it be carried out?
12. Briefly describe how a teacher-directed program might be different from a child-directed one. What would be the possible advantages and disadvantages of each?
13. How do center-based and home-based programs differ? Design a combined program that would maximize the advantages of each.

REFERENCES

Ask the Expert. (1999). Barbara Bateman & Mary Anne Linden answered your questions on Writing Effective IEPs. http://www.ldonline.org/ld_indepth/iep/iep.html.

Bailey, D. B., & Wolery, M. (1992). *Teaching infants and preschoolers with disabilities.* 2nd ed. New York: Macmillan.

Bateman, B. D. (1995). Writing Individualized Education Programs (IEPs) for success. *Secondary Education and Beyond.* Learning Disabilities Association, http://www.ldonline.org/ld_indepth/iep/success_ieps.html.

Beach Center on Families and Disabilities. (1999). *Quality indicators of exemplary IFSP/IEP development.* http://www.lsi.ukans.edu/Beach/html/9i.htm.

Bereiter, C., & Engelmann, S. (1966). *Teaching disadvantaged children in the preschool.* Upper Saddle River, NJ: Prentice Hall.

Bricker, D. D., & Bricker, W. A. (1971). Toddler research and intervention project report: Year I. *IMRID Behavior Science Monograph* (No. 20). Nashville, TN: Institute on Mental

Retardation and Intellectual Development, George Peabody College.

Bricker, D. D., & Bricker, W. A. (1972). Toddler research and intervention project report: Year II. *IMRID Behavior Science Monograph* (No. 21). Nashville, TN: Institute on Mental Retardation and Intellectual Development, George Peabody College.

Bricker, D. D., & Bricker, W. A. (1973). Infant, toddler and preschool research and intervention project report: Year III. *IMRID Behavior Science Monograph* (No. 23). Nashville, TN: Institute on Mental Retardation and Intellectual Development, George Peabody College.

Bricker, W. A., & Bricker, D. D. (1976). The infant, toddler and preschool research and intervention project. In T. D. Tjossem (Ed.), *Intervention strategies with high risk infants and young children*. Baltimore: University Park.

Brown, W., & Rule, S. (1993). Personnel and disciplines in early intervention. In W. Brown, S. K. Thurman, & L. F. Pearl (Eds.), *Family-centered early intervention with infants and toddlers: Innovative cross-disciplinary approaches* (pp. 245–268). Baltimore: Paul H. Brookes.

Chandler, L. K., Dahlquist, C. M., Repp, A. C., & Feltz, C. (1999). The effects of team-based functional assessment on the behavior of students in classroom settings. *Exceptional Children, 66* (1), 101–122,

D'Angelo, A., & Adler, C. R. (1991). Chapter 1: A catalyst for improving parent involvement. *Phi Delta Kappan, 72*(5), 350–354.

Drinkwater, S., & Demchak, M. (1995). The Preschool Checklist: Integration of children with severe disabilities. *Teaching Exceptional Children, 28* (1), 4–8.

Epstein, J. L. (1992). *School and family partnerships*. Baltimore, MD: Johns Hopkins University Center on Families, Communities, Schools, and Children's Learning.

ERIC Clearinghouse on Disabilities and Gifted Education. (1999). What are your rights, as a parent, in the special education process? ED419326 98 Rights and Responsibilities of Parents of Children with Disabilities. *ERIC Digest* #E567. http://www.ed.gov/databases/ERIC_Digests/ed419326.html.

Etscheidt, S. K., & Bartlett, L. (1999). The IDEA amendments: A four-step approach for determining supplementary aids. *Exceptional Children, 65*(2), 163–174.

Fewell, R. R., & Oelwein, P. L. (1991). Effective early intervention: Results from the model preschool program for children with Down syndrome and other developmental delays. *Topics in Early Childhood Special Education, 11*(1), 56–68.

Heward, W. L., & Orlansky, M. D. (1992). *Exceptional children*. 4th ed. New York: Macmillan.

Hohmann, M., Banet, B., & Weikart, D. P. (1979). *Young children in action: A manual for preschool educators*. Ypsilanti, MI: High/Scope Press.

Hurder, A. J. (1997). The Individuals with Disabilities Education Act and the right to learn. *Human Rights, 24*(1), 16–17.

Karnes, M. B., & Stayton, V. D. (1988). Model programs for infants and toddlers with handicaps. In J. B. Jordan, J. J. Gallagher, P. L. Hutinger, & M. B. Karnes (Eds.), *Early childhood special education: Birth to three* (pp. 67–108). Reston, VA: Council for Exceptional Children.

Kroeger, S. D., Leibold, C. K., & Ryan, B. (1999). Creating a sense of ownership in the IEP process. *Teaching Exceptional Children, 32*(1), 4–9.

Kroth, R. L., & Edge, D. (1997). *Strategies for communicating with parents and families of exceptional children*. 3rd. ed. Denver: Love Publishing.

LD OnLine. (1999). *Individualized Education Program: The process*. http://www.ldonline.org/ld_indepth/iep/iep_process.html.

Lahm, E. A., & Nickels, B. L. (1999). Assistive technology competencies for special educators. *Teaching Exceptional Children, 32*(1), 56–63.

Mager, R. F. (1962). *Preparing instructional objectives*. Belmont, CA: Fearon.

National Association of State Directors of Special Education. (1997). *Comparison of key issues: Current law and 1997 IDEA amendments*. Washington, D.C.: Author.

National Information Center for Children and Youth with Disabilities (NICHCY), (1997). *The IDEA amendments of 1997*. Washington, D.C.: Author.

Noonan, M. J., & McCormick, L. (1993). *Early intervention in natural environments, methods and procedures*. Pacific Grove, CA: Brooks/Cole.

Pacer Center. (1999). Pacer Center looks at IDEA '97. http://www.pacer.org/idea/pacer_idea97.htm

Peterson, N. L. (1987). Early intervention for handicapped and at-risk children: *An introduction to early childhood special education*. Denver, CO: Love.

Pruitt, P., Wandry, D., & Hollums, D. (1998). Listen to us! Parents speak out about their interactions with special educators. *Preventing School Failure, 42*(4), 161–167.

Rogers, E. L. (1998). Functional assessment in the home. *Preventing School Failure, 43* (1), 31–33.

Rynders, J. E., & Horrobin, J. M. (1975). Project EDGE: The University of Minnesota's communication stimulation program for Down's syndrome infants. In B. Z. Friedlander, G. M. Sterritt, & G. E. Kirk (Eds.), *Exceptional infant: Assessment and intervention* (Vol. 3). New York: Brunner/Mazel.

Sandall, S. R. (1993). Curricula for early intervention. In W. Brown, S. K. Thurman, & L. F. Pearl (Eds.), *Family-centered early intervention with infants and toddlers: Innovative cross-disciplinary approaches* (pp. 129–151). Baltimore: Paul H. Brookes.

Shearer, D. E. (1979). Introduction. *Portage project readings*. Portage, WI: Portage Project.

Shearer, D. E., & Shearer, M. S. (1976). The Portage Project: A model for early childhood intervention. In T. D. Tjossem (Ed.), *Intervention strategies for high risk infants and young children*. Baltimore: University Park.

Shearer, M. S., & Shearer, D. E. (1979). The Portage Project: A model for early childhood education. *Portage project readings*. Portage, WI: Portage Project.

Shearer, D., Billingsley, J., Frohman, S., Hilliard, J., Johnson, F., & Shearer, M. (1970). Developmental Sequencing Checklist. Unpublished manuscript, Portage, WI: The Portage Project, Cooperative Educational Service Agency No. 12.

Stokes, T. F., & Baer, D. M. (1977). An implicit technology of generalization. *Journal of Applied Behavior Analysis, 10,* 349–367.

Strickland, B. B., & Turnbull, A. P. (1990). *Developing and implementing individualized education programs.* 3rd ed. Upper Saddle River, NJ: Merrill/Prentice Hall.

Thompson, B., Wickham, D., Wegner, J., Ault, M., Shanks, P., & Reinertson, B. (1993). *Handbook for the inclusion of young children with severe disabilities.* Lawrence, KS: Learner Managed Designs.

Thurman, S. K., & Widerstrom, A. H. (1990). *Infants and young children with special needs, a developmental and ecological approach.* 2nd ed. Baltimore: Paul H. Brookes.

Turnbull, A. P., & Turnbull, H. R. (1997). *Families, professionals, and exceptionality: A special partnership.* Upper Saddle River, NJ: Prentice-Hall.

Weikart, D. P. (1988). Quality in early childhood education. In C. Warger (Ed.), *A resource guide to public school early childhood programs* (pp. 63–72). Alexandria, VA: Association for Supervision and Curriculum Development.

Yell, M. L. (1998). The legal basis of inclusion. *Educational Leadership, 56*(2), 70–73.

TEAMING WITH FAMILIES

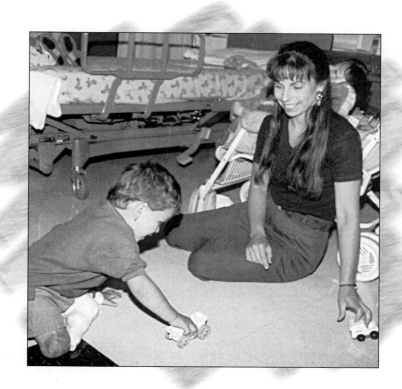

Our daughter at age three fell into our family pool. As she lay in critical condition for three days, my thoughts and my prayers were that she would live. After three days, we were told that our daughter would survive. Then the words I dreaded came. But more horrifying than I ever imagined. My daughter would never walk again. I would never hear her little voice. Severely brain damaged, they said. I was so alone. I wasn't a nurse, nor a doctor and had little experience. Yet I wanted to take this medically fragile child home and care for her. But how? Who would help me? (Beach Center on Families and Disability, Summer 1998)

The poet, Maya Angelou, captured our concern for families, "At our best level of existence, we are parts of a family, and at our highest level of achievement, we work to keep the family alive." This may be the best definition of family-centered practice (Beach Center on Families and Disability, Summer 1997). Perhaps the most extraordinary outcome of legislation supporting services for very young children with disabilities and their families has been the requirement of interdisciplinary and interagency cooperation with families. Our nation has come a long way from days when parents were shamefully considered the cause of their children's disabilities to a point where families are viewed as partners or collaborators in the decision making and treatment of their children's special needs (Turnbull & Turnbull 1996). In recent years, no education legislation has been passed by Congress that did not foster collaboration (Dettmer, Dyck, & Thurston, 1999).

Family-centered practice and philosophy embrace the following key components (Beach Center on Families and Disability, 1998):

1. Focus on the family, not just the child.
2. Emphasize mutual respect and teamwork.
3. Organize assistance according to individual family needs.
4. Consider family strengths, talents, resources, attributes, and aspirations.
5. Address family needs holistically (not focusing on one member).
6. Give families information in a supportive manner.
7. Recognize that there are typical family reactions to exceptional circumstances.
8. Structure the delivery of services to make them accessible without undue disruption of the family integrity and routine.

Family-centered principles encourage delivering services in natural, least-restrictive settings. They encourage identifying both formal and informal family supports in the home and in the community. These principles require professionals to be culturally sensitive, competent, legally accountable, and well-trained. Family-centered also means being cost-efficient and working to support in-home and community placements. Finally, it means using people-first language that refers to the person before the disability. In short, these principles increase family empowerment (Beach Center for Families and Disability, 1999).

Family empowerment is "a process through which people become more able to influence those people and organizations that affect their lives and the lives of those they care about" (Vanderslice, 1984). It generally means promoting access to resources, competence, and self-efficacy (Heflinger & Bickman, 1997). Family empowerment fosters a relationship in which professionals view families as part of an equal, reciprocal partnership (Swick, 1996). One of the most important functions of empowerment is to provide skills that promote self-sufficiency. Empowerment may grow through a family's changes in self-perception, increased self-confidence, ability to set goals, acquisition of skills to attain goals, and the opportunity for supported practice (Dunlap, 1997). One of the most dramatic changes in a family may be a transition from isolation to independence, from feeling alienated to feeling a part of the solution (Dunlap, 1997). Strategies that promote family empowerment include:

1. Involving families in developing plans to address critical needs
2. Personalizing contacts between helpers and families where there is mutual trust and support

3. Networking with other families for problem solving and enrichment
4. Enabling action through provision of child care and transportation where needed
5. Offering a variety of meaningful activities such as home visits, group meetings, individual conferences
6. Focusing on prevention of risk factors
7. Advocating for collaborative community services

When parents of children with developmental disabilities were asked to identify the most important aspects of support programs, they identified empowerment among their highest ratings (Herman, Marcenko, & O'Hazel, 1996). They said services should be guided by the principles of family-centered care and should result in families and individuals who are integrated into their community, carry out the tasks of family life independently and autonomously, and make productive contributions to society. They also emphasized the need to be connected with other parents and stressed the importance of healthy interpersonal relationships with staff.

RELATING TO FAMILIES

Special education services have a history of stereotyping parents in ways that have not been productive. The challenge for current practitioners is to overcome these assumptions. From 1960 through 1980, a large body of research was compiled that indicated families of children with disabilities, as compared to families of children without disabilities, were at increased risk for stress (Kazak, 1986) and depression (Cox, Rutter, Newman, & Bartak, 1975), had different family coping strategies or styles (McCubbin et al., 1982), had less family cohesion (Darling, 1979), had more family strain (Roth, 1982), and experienced greater social isolation (Breslau, 1983). Subsequently, both researchers and theorists assumed that these families had an increased risk of family dysfunction. Research in the 1990s, which focused less on the pathology of deficiency, has been more expansive and indicates that many of the early research assumptions can be and should be questioned. It now appears that the psychosocial functioning of families of children with disabilities is more like that of families of children without disabilities than it is different from them. Though extensive needs are expressed by all families, those with children who have disabilities face a different, though not necessarily extraordinary, set of obstacles.

Like other families with various needs, the impact of a disability may be negative, positive, or mixed (Turnbull & Turnbull, 1996). Some studies indicated that divorce or disruption of marriage was disproportionately high when there was an exceptional child in the family (Gath, 1977; Murphy, 1982; Reed & Reed, 1965), but more recent studies have indicated that the divorce rate is not higher for these families (Benson & Gross, 1989) and that these marriages are sometimes strengthened because of a shared commitment for their child (Kazak & Marvin, 1984). Singer and Nixon (1996) found that exceptionality can simultaneously strengthen and impair a couple's relationship. On the other hand, some researchers found no differences in personal relationships between families who had exceptional children and those who didn't (Abbott & Meredith, 1986; Young & Roopnarine, 1994).

One mother shared how her daughter's disability changed her life:

> In my house there is an eight-by-ten picture of me taken on my wed-
> ding day. It is just my face, looking somewhat seriously into the camera.
> When I am in a particularly melancholy frame of mind, it is sad for me to
> see it, for the woman in that picture is gone. . . . I was 23, my husband Jim
> had just turned 22 and we knew little about anything then. Eleven months
> later, . . . Maggie was born. She was not a planned child, and I do not think
> much else in my life has been since that day. As my husband peered into
> the nursery he saw Maggie turn, in his words, "navy blue." He came run-
> ning into my room yelling, "There's something wrong with the baby!" and
> my life changed forever. . . . I wish that the woman in that picture could
> have left me less suddenly, less painfully. But the person she left behind is
> smarter, wiser, more confident. . . . She has tested the love of her family
> and friends and has found it to be strong and enduring. She knows there
> is little life can put in her path that she will not be able to face and con-
> quer head on. (Klemm & Schimanski, 1999, pp. 109–110)

Mothers typically assume the responsibility for caring for their family needs, including the special needs of a child with a disability (Traustadottir, 1991). Fathers tend
to spend a comparable amount of time in child care whether their children are disabled or not (Turbiville, 1995), about two-thirds less than mothers (Young & Roopnarine, 1994). However, when fathers take on greater participation, it relates to higher
marital satisfaction for both parents (Willoughby & Glidden, 1995). It's important,
therefore, that efforts to empower a family are directed to both parents when both
are present (Turnbull & Turnbull, 1996). Yet, fathers tend to feel left out for several
reasons: (1) services are often scheduled during the day when they are at their place
of employment; (2) professionals in early intervention tend to be overwhelmingly
women, making a male uncomfortable in communicating; and (3) service providers
may discourage a father's interest unintentionally by coming to expect mothers to be
the main family spokesperson (Beach Center on Families and Disability, 1995).

Research on siblings in families with children who are disabled is similarly mixed.
Some studies showed that siblings have a higher incidence of emotional and behavioral problems (Orsillo, McCaffrey, & Fisher, 1993) such as lower self-esteem
(McHale & Gamble, 1989), but other researchers have not found greater problems
(Gath & Gumley, 1987). Carr (1988) found siblings actually had fewer behavioral
problems than the siblings of children without disabilities. Opportunities for positive
contributions by siblings are apparent; enhanced maturity, social competence, insight, tolerance, pride, advocacy, and loyalty are all attributes that might evolve from
growing up with children who have special needs (Meyer & Vadasy, 1994).

Thirteen-year-old Matthew (Fennel, 1999) wrote this about his sibling:

> My brother Alex and I used to roll around on the ground for hours
> while I tickled him. We had so much fun. As we got older, I realized that
> Alex was different from other kids. It never changed my love for him, but
> we could not share in things as much as we used to. Because of his
> autism, Alex cannot speak. Nor can he understand many words that are

said. . . . Though Alex is unable to speak, he is able to tell us things in other ways. His autism has shown me how to love. In a way, autism could help the world to be rid of hatred and anger. (p. 132)

Extended family members may also be an important part of the family unit as well as a source of support; this is especially true in some minority cultures (Turnbull & Turnbull, 1996). Grandparents often participate in a wide range of everyday tasks related to family care (Able-Boone, Sandall, Stevens, & Frederick, 1992). In African American families, for example, the grandmother may be the family matriarch who provides shelter, care, and advice on a daily basis. The whole family may be called into action; grandmother may accompany the parents to planning meetings and doctor's visits, an aunt may arrange transportation, and cousins may babysit siblings left at home. This kind of support makes economic sense and encourages the well-being of the parents and the child with a disability. It may also mean that more people care and advocate for the child with special needs.

Whether discussion focuses on families of children with disabilities or families of children without disabilities, the reality is that many family units are not composed of two parents. While statistics vary, it is now probable that professionals supporting families will be working with many families that consist of one parent with one or two children, headed by either a mother or father. Furthermore, in two-parent households, it is likely that families will consist of a blend of children from at least one previous marriage and will consequently include multiple family systems. Other family configurations include:

◆ Extended family members as primary caregivers (grandmother, grandfather, aunt, or uncle)
◆ Same sex parenting partners
◆ Families without homes
◆ Families built through adoption or foster care

Each of these family configurations adds to the complexity of interactions between families and professionals. Table 10–1 highlights some of the factors that may be involved in diverse family structures and the impact of these variations on family relationships with professionals.

While family service programs have historically been based on a traditional family model, it is only realistic to define families more broadly today. Dettmer and colleagues (1999) recommend an inclusive definition of family that was articulated at the Second Family Leadership Conference:

A family is a group of people who are important to each other and offer each other love and support, especially in times of crisis. In order to be sensitive to the wide range of life styles, living arrangements, and cultural variations that exist today, family . . . can no longer be limited to just parent/child relationships. Family involvement . . . must reach out to include mothers, fathers, grandparents, sisters, brothers, neighbors, and other persons who have important roles in the lives of people with disabilities. (Family and Integration Resources, 1991, p. 37, as cited in Dettmer et al., 1999)

Table 10–1 Variables that make family–professional interaction challenging

Situation	Impact
Family structure	Loyalties, power, complex and varying rules under similar conditions, transitions between dwellings, availability of equipment
Child care requirements	Availability of child care for infants, toddlers, and young children with disabilities; debates with child care providers about the realities of serving children with disabilities; financial burdens
Single-parent families	Time and resource management, single-parent income, transportation issues, ill child responsibilities, possible conflict with personal goals, increased need for respite care
Nontraditional partnerships	Prejudice of service providers and local community, debates over "proper parenting authority," legal authority issues
Poverty	Prejudice of service providers toward poor persons, lack of transportation to get to and from services, possible lack of phone services, possible lack of a permanent address
Substance abuse	Immediate impact on the person suffering the abuse, subsequent impact on immediate and extended family members, inability to keep priorities in desired order, secondary health issues, guilt, shame
Foster care	No long-term goals or personal authority, lack of accurate history

PARENTAL RESPONSES TO DIAGNOSIS OF A DISABILITY

For many families, life becomes more difficult from the first moments a disability is diagnosed. After a review of the literature, Moore, Howard, and McLaughlin (in press) concluded that all families have needs; it just so happens that for families of children with disabilities, the obstacles are those of a child with special needs. Other families must deal with issues of poverty, mental illness, child abuse, divorce, drugs, or death of family members, but not of a child with a disability. According to Moore et al., these factors do not make families special, unusual, dysfunctional, or in any way homogeneous. There are, however, some shared reactions to crisis that should be recognized.

Parents unexpectedly faced with the loss of hopes and expectations often proceed through several common stages, ranging from total disbelief and bewilderment to the ability to grasp and control the situation. While every parent or couple responds to a diagnosis of a disability in accord with their own external and internal resources, researchers have found some common themes experienced by many parents. These phases or stages were first identified by Dr. Elizabeth Kubler-Ross in her classic research with cancer patients over two decades ago (Kubler-Ross, 1969) and were initially referred to as the grief cycle.

Over the last decade, professionals working with parents of at-risk infants or infants in crisis have recognized that many, though not all, parents proceed through the same or similar phases (Featherstone, 1980; Turnbull & Turnbull, 1985). Today, many early childhood professionals refer to Kubler-Ross's reaction cycle as **stage theory response.**

Stage theory response is useful primarily to parents who find that naming their complex emotions helps order them and enables them to talk with others who have similar experiences. Knowledge of stage theory response also helps professionals validate parental emotions. However, when it is used to label parents or to associate a pathology with a particular stage, stage theory response is badly misused. Perhaps most important, it is necessary to realize that passage through grief, like any other life passage, is not a sign of dysfunction but of normalcy.

The stages, or phases, described are neither sequential nor of equal duration, intensity, or frequency in reoccurrence, either within or across families. Parents often report that the stages overlap and almost always reoccur, often at periods of significant transition. Studies by Allen and Affleck (1985) indicated that for some parents, a stage may last one day or one year. What is important to know and remember about the grief or adjustment process is that knowledge of the process often helps parents to understand that these common emotional behaviors are shared by many others in similar circumstances. The key components of the stage theory, or grief process, as described by Kubler-Ross and subsequent researchers (Francis & Jones, 1984; Seligman & Darling, 1989) are shock and denial, anger and frustration, volatile emotions (hope, isolation, depression), bargaining, and, finally, acceptance or reestablishment. Cook, Tessier, and Klein (1992) outlined several ways in which early childhood professionals can support parents through each of these stages (see Table 10–2).

Table 10–2   Stage theory response and how professionals should support parents

Stages and Responses	Support Needed
Shock, Disbelief, and Denial: May be accompanied by feelings of shame, guilt, and unworthiness. Parents may try to deny the existing problems. Parents may go from doctor to doctor seeking opinions. Some may refuse to accept guidance.	Convey to parents that these feelings are appropriate. Listen with acceptance. Help parents focus on ways professionals can work with them to benefit the child. Become active listeners through patience and practice.
Anger and Resentment: Parents may direct anger at the very professionals who are trying to help and be suspicious about a professional's motives. Verbal abuse is common and parents try to prove the professional to be wrong about their child.	Professionals must be understanding, compassionate, and gently caring. They should get parents busy with child activities that cannot fail. Refuse to blame or react to unreasonable demands.
Bargaining: Parents may work diligently as if to say, "If I do everything you tell me to do, then this problem will go away." If progress is not rapid, they may become severely depressed.	Be empathetic, recognize and accept the natural feelings of parents. Convey an attitude of interest and caring.
Depression and Discouragement: Hopelessness overtakes parents but may make them more likely to request assistance. Parents may be saying "good-bye" to the normal image of the child they held. Parents can begin to focus on productive solutions.	Focus on the positive but avoid over-eagerness to get on with the intervention. Give parents activities that will be successful to avoid self-doubt. Avoid all criticism as well as unwarranted praise. Provide access to parent support groups.
Acceptance: Parents have an increasing willingness to do practical, useful activities. The child's needs are recognized, not denied. There may be a conviction that much needs to be done and will make a difference.	Encourage the parents to be patient and set realistic goals. Help parents read their child's cues. Praise the parents for the child's progress. Focus on positive interaction techniques.

Source: Adapted from Cook, R. E., Tessier, A., & Klein, M. D. (1992). *Adapting Early Childhood Curricula for Children with Special Needs.* Upper Saddle River, NJ: Merrill/Prentice Hall.

Anderegg, Vergason, and Smith (1992) studied the grief process with 130 parents. Their work led to the development of a slightly different model still supportive of earlier work. This later research indicated that parents and extended family members pass through three phases:

1. Confronting (denial, blame/guilt, shock) *
2. Adjusting (depression, anger, bargaining)
3. Adapting (life-cycle changes, realistic planning, adjusting expectations)

A number of factors account for a family's ability to reach a point of adjustment and acceptance. Among the most significant factors are the characteristics of a child's exceptionality, the degree of exceptionality, and, in particular, the demands of an exceptionality (Turnbull & Turnbull, 1996). Werner and Smith (1982) found that family configuration (e.g., single-parent family, blended family), family size, and the socioeconomic status also affected a family's ability to cope and adjust.

Again, the apparent usefulness of stage theory research is that it gives parents a description of what is happening to them during a period that is otherwise overwhelming and foreign. It provides parents with descriptive language that links their experiences with the experiences of veteran parents. The passage from diagnosis to adaptation is cyclical and complex. Some parents feel they never really move out of a low-grade sadness that seems to permeate their lives. The important thing to remember is that shifts usually take place. The early panic that follows a diagnosis of an infant in crisis usually changes and develops according to healthy patterns of adaptation.

Still, it is necessary to be cautious in applying stage theory response to any particular parent or family. Parents arrive at adjustment in many ways and the sequence and time needed are different for every parent (Allen & Affleck, 1985; Bradley, Knoll, & Agosta, 1992; Schell, 1981). Stage theory response has a distinct psychiatric flavor, which may imply that parents are maladjusted and need counseling when, in fact, they are responding normally (Roos, 1985).

Case Study

JOSH'S FAMILY: INTERVIEW WITH AMY FINKEL

That first year, Josh's older brother, David was essentially neglected. I had so much to do focusing on my disabled child. I started to see by the end of the year that David was starting some attention-getting behaviors. It woke me up to the fact that I had two other children who also needed me. So we've made a real effort to do things just with David, and just with Josh's older sister Rebecca. Rebecca is a musician so we get a baby-sitter and go to her concerts and do things just for her. We enrolled David in soccer, summer camp, and different things that are just for him. I try to go out of my way to give quality one-on-one time with each of them. That's helped a lot.

I think the largest impact of Josh's disability has been on David because he is so close in age (the boys are only 18 months apart). One of our biggest fears in the future for Josh is, what's going to happen to him when we are gone? David has heard us go through the early diagnosis. He was here when all the crying and the screaming was going on because we were in such despair. One night we were lying in bed watching a movie and David said, "Mom, I don't know how to hire a therapist.

How do I hire a therapist? What do I tell them to do?" He had internalized some of our fears. He felt responsible for his brother.

Another time, David had a friend spend the night and Josh started making some strange sounds. David's little friend started mocking Josh, by making the same sounds and teasing him. David told him to stop it and his friend started to cry. David, matter of factly, said, "It's okay. You have to understand my brother is disabled. You need to be nice to him. But it's okay, everybody makes mistakes." It was so sweet. Some of his friends come over and they ask questions about Josh. After a while they warm up to him and it's okay. I think David is going to grow up to be a real champion of the disabled. He has a compassionate heart. We talk to him a lot about issues involving people who are disabled.

I know also the time will come when David is 15 or 16 that he will be at an age when it is uncool to have a disabled brother. He'll have some friends over and he is not going to want his disabled brother around. It wouldn't be normal if that didn't happen. He'll go through that stage where he is trying to impress a girl and he won't want to admit that he has a disabled brother. We'll deal with that when the time comes and hopefully we'll have a solid foundation. I think he's already learned a lot of valuable lessons in life that a lot of kids and a lot of adults unfortunately never learn.

David once said, "Mom, I promise you when I grow up, I'll make sure my wife will let Josh live with us. I'll find a wife that understands about my brother."

David (left) and Josh (right) Finkel at home playing.

FAMILY HARDINESS

In addition to the basic needs or desires of all families, researchers have identified stressors that may be prominent in families of children with disabilities. **Acute stressors** occur as periodic incidents related to a child's disability; **chronic stressors** include concerns about the future, financial limitations, and society's acceptance of human differences; and last, **transition stressors** are linked to significant milestones, such as entry into school, that occur throughout a child's lifespan. Put in the context of need, Failla and Jones (1991) concluded that, based on these unique stressors, there is a need for **family hardiness.** Hardiness was defined as a constellation of three dimensions that includes:

1. A sense of control or the ability to influence events rather than being controlled by them
2. A commitment to becoming actively involved in events and viewing them as meaningful
3. Recognition of life changes as opportunities for growth and development, not a burden to bear (Kobasa, Maddi, & Puccetti, 1982; Pollack, 1986)

Throughout the course of a child's life, services and providers will come and go. The primary functions and needs of a family may vacillate. Cultural and community norms may expand or contract, and society's acceptance of exceptional persons is uncertain. Funding and research in the area of early childhood education and intervention will undoubtedly pass through highs and lows. What will remain constant in all this will be the children and their families, however formed.

Family hardiness might best be fostered through connections with other parents who have had similar experiences. These parents can teach others about professionals they never knew existed, words and acronyms that are unfamiliar, and reactions from friends and families that can't be anticipated (Klemm & Schimanski, 1999). Other parents provide information and emotional support as a family learns about a disability and what it will mean. Several important resources help connect parents:

◆ Beach Center on Families and Disability
   3111 Haworth Hall
   University of Kansas
   Lawrence, KS 66045
   (785) 864-7600 (phone and TDD)
   (785) 864-7605 (FAX)
   E-mail: beach@dole.lsi.ukans.edu

◆ National Parent Network on Disabilities
   1130 17th Street NW, Suite 400
   Washington, DC 20036
   (202) 463-2299
   (202) 463-9403 (FAX)
   web site: www.npnd.org

◆ Parent to Parent of New York State
   500 Balltown Road
   Schenectady, NY 12304
   (518) 381-4350
   (518) 382-1959 (FAX)
   web site: http://www.parenttoparentnys.org

BARRIERS TO COLLABORATION

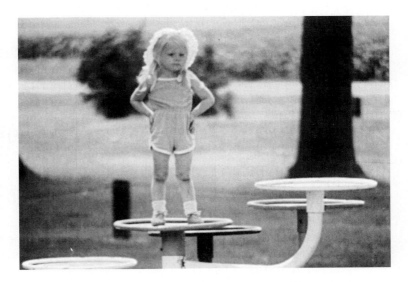

It is essential that professionals remember that just about all families care for their children and want the best for them, but barriers to collaboration may exist that will have to be overcome before success is possible (Dettmer et al., 1999). Many parents fear and mistrust school and agency personnel because of their own negative experiences as children or because of unpleasant experiences with other professionals. Overburdened by economic and personal hardships that create work schedule, transportation, and child care concerns, parents may find early childhood services to be one more challenge in their overtaxed lives. Some parents may fear being blamed for their child's condition or stereotyped because of their culture or lifestyle. Such cultural differences can make them uncomfortable or misunderstood. Hence, collaboration requires respect, trust, and cooperation, and it is the professional's responsibility to cope with and value differences in positive ways. Dettmer and colleagues (1999) advise the following mindset in working in this sensitive field:

1. Remember that the professional's place is on the parent's side as a team member working for the common goal of the child's success.
2. Be aware of feelings of defensiveness, take a deep breath and put those feelings aside.

3. Remember the focus is on the needs and interests of families and their children, not their values. Attack the problem, not the person.
4. Accept people as they are and stop wishing they were different.
5. Remember that most families are doing the best they can.
6. Respect family rights to values and opinions—even when they differ from yours.
7. Demonstrate open-mindedness and flexibility.

Even though family collaboration is mandated and challenging, its rewards are many (Dettmer et al., 1999). Children benefit from family involvement through more success in school, higher achievement, and more positive attitudes (Christenson & Cleary, 1990). Family members report greater feelings of self-worth, self-satisfaction, and increased motivation for enhancing the educational environment of the home (Hoover-Dempsey & Sandler, 1997; Murphy, 1981). Finally, professionals learn more about the children in their care and improve communication and advocacy in their communities.

COMMUNICATION BETWEEN PARENTS AND PROFESSIONALS

Communication, in its most basic form, is the ability of two or more people to send and receive messages. Of all the skills expected of early childhood professionals, communication skills rank among the most necessary. When Linda Davern (1996) interviewed parents regarding their suggestions for improving the quality of home-school relationships, they recommended the following:

1. Convey a clear, consistent message regarding the value of a child. See aspects aside from achievement and focus on the children's progress, rather than comparing them to other children.
2. Put yourself in the shoes of parents. Try to understand what it is like to have a child with a disability. Understand their frustration.
3. Expand your awareness of cultural diversity. Be aware of the cultural lenses through which you make judgments about children and families.
4. See individuals, and challenge stereotypes. Don't make assumptions about parents and their skills just because their child has a disability. Don't lump all parents together.
5. Persevere in building partnerships. Consider this a long-term commitment that takes time and flexibility.
6. Demonstrate an authentic interest in the parent's goals for the child. Work to diminish distance between professionals and parents while establishing connections. Avoid sending the message that you are the expert and the parent knows nothing.
7. Talk with parents about how they want to share information. Ask parents which school person they want to communicate with, how often, and through what means.
8. Use everyday language. Avoid jargon that confuses understanding.
9. Create effective forums for planning and problem solving. Formal IEP meetings can be very intimidating, so schedule regular less formal meetings where parents can be more comfortable.

Communicating well does not mean that each professional should interact with parents according to a rigid set of guidelines. Prerequisite to effective communication is learning the strengths and weaknesses of one's own interaction style and understanding how one's words and actions are interpreted. In short, effective communication grasps, with clarity, the difference between the intent of what is said and the interpretation of the message by the receiver. Several basic communication concepts or skills can enhance relationships between parents and professionals. These involve active listening, **perception checks,** and ways to accurately state needs.

CLOSE-UP

PARAEDUCATOR EXPERIENCES IN INCLUSIVE SETTINGS: HELPING, HOVERING, OR HOLDING THEIR OWN

The role of paraeducators has grown in recent years as more special education students attend regular programs with one-on-one assistance. In an effort to meet both the needs of the students and the teachers in inclusive settings, paraeducators have been hired to assist with behavioral and physical challenges specific to individual children. These staff members often become a child's personal "specialist" but hold a position on the teaching team that is poorly defined, presenting difficult challenges for the paraeducator. Interviews with 20 paraeducators revealed the following responsibilities: (1) keeping the student from being a bother to the teacher, (2) meeting the student's immediate needs, (3) being the "hub" and the "expert" on the child, and (4) representing inclusion to other team members. The following excerpts from these interviews illustrate each of these challenges.

Paraeducators felt their most pressing responsibility was making sure the regular teacher was not "burdened" by the inclusion student; that is, to make sure the inclusion experience was a positive one for all involved. One paraeducator stated, "It felt like a lot of pressure [being in the inclusive setting] because I . . . didn't want her [the inclusion student] to disturb the others and I didn't want her to disturb the teacher. So I felt responsible for every single little sound she made." Another pointed out, "I would address a behavior as it arose, before it got to a point where she'd [the teacher] notice it, and so there wasn't an opportunity for her to set a lot of limits with him, because . . . I never let it get to that point."

More than half the paraeducators felt their role was to address immediate daily needs of the student, which most often meant adapting an activity for the student's participation. One paraeducator noted, "The teachers I've been able to work with have been really open—receptive to everything about the program. I think I can walk up to a teacher and ask them what they're doing in class and then sometimes if I'm just at a loss, they'll give me some ideas on some alterations I can make." Another said, "It would take a lot of modifications so the child can participate more in the class. . . . And it was left for me to initiate, and they would say, 'Oh that sounds like a great idea'. . . . And I would end up doing it, and trying it."

Paraeducators felt they were the "hub" for a child, the liaison between all the various individuals who were involved with the inclusion child. This often meant they had to be the one to see that everyone's suggestions were implemented and were, in fact, the "expert" on the child. "I felt like . . . I was very much the hub, with the spokes coming in. . . . Sometimes I felt like it was hard to be the liaison, or the hub, the person who was the closest, but with the least to say. . . . It was just a frustrating situation to be in, as an assistant without the degree that gives me the right to say, 'Well, my expertise tells me that this is the case.' "

Sometimes the paraeducators felt they were responsible for representing the whole idea of inclusion to the rest of the school and community. They felt that how their students actually did would be a reflection on the inclusion movement. "What I get from a lot of people is that they don't really see that Cory is intelligent. They see the disability. . . . And it's a lot of education, talking to people about the student, 'Well you know she is very capable, she learns at a slower rate because of her disability, but she is quite capable of functioning . . . With adaptations, of course.'"

Paraeducators want to be a part of the child's team, from planning through implementation. They need teaming as a way to share their expertise, to clarify their roles, and to plan for a student's increased independence. They also need more training on accommodations and the support of other team members.

Source: Marks, S. U., Schrader, C., & Levine, M. (1999). *Exceptional Children, 65*(3), 315–328.

ACTIVE LISTENING

Active listening means that listeners (receivers of information) are attentive to a speaker on multiple levels: hearing, interpreting, sorting, and analyzing (see Table 10–3). It is the opposite of passive listening in which the recipient hears without understanding the intended message and without responding appropriately to the speaker. To illustrate the difference between active and passive listening, and ultimately, the effect they both have on communication and learning, consider this example:

> **Actively listening parent:** "I would very much like to have my child use his communication board on a more regular basis. Currently, he becomes very frustrated because he can't tell us what he needs." The parent frowns and looks sad.
>
> **Passively listening preschool teacher:** "All the students in my class are able to speak. We will have the speech language pathologist work with Andy so that he can speak as well." The teacher is fiddling with papers she needs for her next parent conference.
>
> **Actively listening parent:** "Perhaps you didn't read Andy's file carefully. His cerebral palsy is so involved that he is not able to make any understandable speech sounds. We have already had him evaluated by a speech therapist at St. Luke's and they created the communication board for him so he could develop his language skills." The parent shakes her

Table 10–3 Active listening

Skills	Description
Hearing	Understands and comprehends the words (spoken or written)
Interpreting	Is attentive to nuances, the larger context of the statement, and the political, cultural, and emotional dimensions of comments
Sorting	Categorizes information with other like information to increase the meaning or clarify intent
Analyzing	Compares information with other knowledge about the topic and draws conclusions

head and pushes a catalogue of language devices toward the child care provider.

Passively listening preschool teacher: (Still looking at her other papers.) "We have an excellent speech language pathologist. She will have Andy talking in no time. Andy can work with her during circle time since that is oral and Andy wouldn't be able to participate."

Actively listening parent: "We don't want Andy to miss out on circle time. He loves to be a part of the group. We can choose appropriate pictures to put on his communication board so he can respond with the rest of the children. He gets very frustrated when he is not allowed to be with the rest of the students." The parent's shoulders tighten and she leans forward, thumping the catalogue of language devices to emphasize the use of the communication board.

Passively listening preschool teacher: "Oh, we don't let the children bring toys to the circle. He has to be able to speak up like everyone else. Also, I've been meaning to talk to you about his behavior. He has been refusing to cooperate with our group activities. I'd like to send him to time out when this happens."

Actively listening parent: (She gives a big sigh.) "As I said, he gets very frustrated when he isn't able to communicate and when he isn't a part of the group. I don't think time out would be the right answer for this problem."

Passively listening preschool teacher: "Well, if you don't allow us to control his behavior, I don't know how Andy is ever going to be able to be a part of our class." She looks at the watch, ready to end the meeting.

Actively listening parent: "We seem to have a different understanding of Andy's problems. Perhaps we need to meet as a team again, so the speech language pathologist can also be involved. I'm concerned that you are not addressing Andy's communication needs." The parent's face is red, her hands are shaking as she pulls the catalogue back to her bag.

Passively listening preschool teacher: "That would be fine, because I have another parent coming now and can't talk any longer. It has been a pleasure meeting with you today." The child care provider smiles and shakes the parent's hand as she shuffles her papers together and heads toward the door to greet the next parent. The parent takes a deep breath, pulls her bag over her shoulder, and leaves, shaking her head as she goes.

When active listening is done well, relationships develop between the sender and the listener: partners hear and can respond to what their counterpart is saying; parents and children learn that what they have to say is important and respected; and professionals increase the probability that the right supports will be given parents. Unlike passive listening, which involves only one sender, active listening is an inclusive engagement between and among people. Here is an example where both parties are actively listening:

Actively listening preschool teacher: "We didn't address this in our last IEP meeting, but I think Cherise has matured in her language and self-help skills enough that she is ready to start toilet training. What do you think about this?" The teacher leans forward, looking the parent directly in the eye.

Actively listening parent: "Do you really think she could learn to go by herself? It would be such a relief to not have her in diapers, now that we are expecting another child." The parent smiles.

Actively listening preschool teacher: The teacher nods enthusiastically. "I just want to explain what this would involve and make sure we can work on this at both home and school. I'd like to check her every 15 minutes to see if there is a pattern to when she is wet and then start putting her on the potty at those most likely times each day. Can you do the same thing when she is at home with you in the afternoon and evening?" The teacher watches the parent's face and notices that her mouth falls a little.

Actively listening parent: "I don't think I could check every 15 minutes. We have the two older ones you know, so I'm always driving them to soccer or dance lessons; and Cherise's therapy sessions usually run at least 45 minutes and I don't like to disturb her once she is started in those." The parent sits back in her chair, pushing away from the table.

Actively listening preschool teacher: "Of course, you are probably on the go so much there isn't a lot of down-time where you could stop and do this every 15 minutes. Is there any period of time, like maybe the hour just before bed that you could work on this? I find kids learn toileting so much faster when we work on it at school and at home." The teacher raises her eyebrows in a hopeful gesture.

Actively listening parent: "Maybe I could ask my husband to watch Cherise when I take her older sister off to dance. That way she'd be home for the two hours before bed. Would that be enough to make a difference?" The parent leans on the table.

Actively listening preschool teacher: "I appreciate you rearranging your hectic schedule. I think that could make a big difference, and once Cherise is out of diapers, you'll have a little more free time with the new baby."

Actively listening parent: "I'm so glad you think we can do this. It would make a huge difference not to have two in diapers. Cherise will be happier too if she can be like the big girls." She hesitates. "But what if I can't carry through at home? What if she doesn't learn?"

Actively listening teacher: "I know it's harder to do these things at home when your hands are full. We'll keep working on it at school, and we might brainstorm another way to accomplish it at home. Cherise might not learn right away, but I've got some ways to motivate her. Perhaps we could use a buzzer that will let us know when she starts to wet, so we don't have to watch the clock. You just let me know if you don't think it's going well at home and we'll go back to the drawing board."

Actively listening parent: "Thank you for being so understanding. I'll give it my best shot." She rises and extends her hand. "I'm so glad you thought to work on this. It's like you read my mind."

Several specific communication strategies can be employed that will help you be a more effective communicator. The following suggestions may improve your relationships with other professionals and with the families with whom you work.

Avoid Binding Statements

Binding communications are habits of interaction that generally close or diminish the probability of continued conversation. By contrast, freeing communications are those habits of interaction that actually encourage expanded dialogue. The following examples illustrate a few habits that often lead to **binding communications:**

◆ Giving an overly enthusiastic response—responses that are generally based on what would be best for you
◆ Changing the subject without explanation
◆ Explaining others' behavior by interpreting their history (You act this way because your mother acted this way.)
◆ Providing direct advice and even persuasion (If I were you, this is what I would do.)
◆ Setting up expectations that bind the speaker to the past; this disallows change and innovation (You've never acted this way before; what's wrong?)
◆ Communicating expectations that bind the speaker to the future (I'm sure you'll figure this out and do such and such.)
◆ Denying feelings (You really don't mean that! Or, You really don't feel that way, do you?)
◆ Overgeneralizing (Everyone feels that way.); this diminishes the other; makes one feel like one's feelings or experiences really do not matter much
◆ Approving on personal grounds: praising the other for thinking, feeling, or acting in ways that you agree with, for conforming to your standards
◆ Disapproving on personal grounds: blaming or censuring the other for thinking, feeling, or acting in ways you do not like
◆ Commanding and ordering: telling the other what to do (including, Tell me what to do)
◆ Obligating emotionally: controlling through arousing feelings of shame and inferiority (How can you do this to me when I have done so much for you?)

In summary, binding statements are those comments that diminish the listener's desire to continue the conversation.

Use Freeing Statements

Freeing statements, such as "go on," "tell me more," "how do you feel about that?" actually increase the speaker's desire to continue and increase both personal autonomy and power. As a note of caution, professionals must use these statements sincerely and avoid assuming a therapeutic tone.

Avoid Killer Phrases

Killer phrases range from those comments that discourage further comment to those that break a person's spirit. Appropriately named for the effect they have on communication, killer phrases are generally (though not always) uttered in moments of frustration, anger, or depression. Early childhood professionals should recognize killer phrases and attribute no more to them than indications of weariness. As for the language of professionals, to the greatest extent possible, it should be void of killer phrases. The following are examples of killer phrases:

- It won't work.
- That's a swell idea, but. . .
- Good idea, but your family is different.
- It's all right in theory, but can you put it into practice?
- It's too academic (or it's too medical).
- We're rural (or we're too large).
- It's too simplistic.
- It needs more study.
- We've never done it that way.
- I haven't the time.
- I'm not ready for it. (You're not ready for it.)
- There are better ways than that!
- You haven't considered. . .
- Let's not step on anyone's toes.
- Why start anything now?
- The agency won't understand.

It is much easier for a professional to impose hurt on a parent than vice versa since professionals are generally supported in several ways by the power visited on them through training, social norms, and organizational structure. Therefore, the playing field is never level. In consideration of this relationship, professionals should prepare to weather killer phrases aimed at them without bowing to the temptation to respond in kind.

Allow and Respect "No"

Most novice professionals find themselves eager to pass on what they know and to support parents' decisions. Professionals simply do not set out to be offensive or to get in a family's way; yet it happens. It happens, against all intentions, because service providers fail to recognize the more basic needs of families, one of which is to not need a professional support person! In the course of each family or family system, there comes a time when parents and other members of the family wish to be left alone. Families may weary of professional conversations and interactions; they may well have priorities not shared by professional support persons.

Not wanting to discourage or seem ungrateful, parents will find various and subtle ways to say "Stay away for now." For a shy parent, avoidance may begin by simply canceling meetings or calling in ill. Others will tell the professional that the timing is bad and reschedule for some distant date. In such situations, it is the responsibility of a professional to analyze the communication as carefully as possible and to draw and confirm a conclusion. When it becomes apparent that a parent is asking for some free space from professionals, support for that request needs to be forthcoming. If professionals are unclear about a parent's actual intent, they need only ask parents directly: "Would you like my assistance? Please feel free to say no." If the parent answers "no," that answer must be accepted with the same dignity afforded the opposite response. In short, parents and caregivers need to be allowed to say "no" to support or services, (after all, it is their legal right to do so), and then be respected for saying it.

Use Perception Checks

Sometimes, despite best efforts, it is difficult to draw an accurate conclusion regarding the intent of a speaker. When this happens, it is possible to draw on a communication skill called a **perception check**. A perception check means that listeners check their perception or understanding of what was said (e.g., the parent doesn't want to waste the specialist's Saturday morning) against what the speaker intended to say (e.g., "My oldest child was sick all night, and I'm exhausted. Please leave me alone!"). A perception check is executed not by asking the speaker to repeat what was just said, but by saying, "This is what I understand you to mean . . ." This pattern allows the initial speaker to confirm or deny the perception.

Perception checks are especially important to use when more than two people are engaged in an interaction. During assessment sessions, in planning meetings, or in family consultations, early childhood professionals may find there is often a good deal of confusion about the intent or content of transactions or interactions. By using any of the following phrases, professionals can help keep the communication lines clear and open.

◆ I was listening to what you just said. Is (give explanation) what you mean?
◆ So many people have been offering comments. I'm a bit unsure of your position on (name the issue). Is (give explanation) what you meant?
◆ You just said, "no." Are you trying to accommodate my schedule, or is there really a better time for us to get together?

These three statements ask for clarification without judging the effectiveness or ability of the speaker.

Use Paraphrasing

Paraphrasing is another technique by which confirmation is obtained by restating the essence of the comment or conversation. In paraphrasing, listeners put into words what they think they have just heard. While a perception check seeks clarification (Is this what you meant?), paraphrasing seeks right direction. In the latter, the listener accepts responsibility for interpretation (e.g., "Another way to say what you just said is. . ." or "So what you just said is. . ."). Paraphrasing conclusions or using paraphrasing to confirm what is to be done next are the two most commonly used and highly productive forms of paraphrasing.

Use Descriptions of Behavior Rather than Descriptions of Feelings

There are a number of ways that parents, siblings, and professionals avoid participating in difficult or sensitive conversations. On one end of a continuum, people avoid engagement in difficult topics by withdrawing. On the other end of the continuum, people avoid a topic by engaging in unrelated conversations or behaviors. While these postures are perhaps admirable during a poker game, they generally complicate family discussions, interdisciplinary work, and most social interactions. When behaviors occur that range from withdrawal to unrelated engagement, there are two issues that must be confronted by listeners. First, what is the person indicating through her or his actions and words, or lack of action or words? Second, what is the parent, sibling, or professional really feeling?

Early childhood professionals working with parents and family members need to be especially aware of words, communication styles, and the feelings that ought to correspond to those words or gestures. For example, it is not uncommon to find a parent or professional colleague nodding the "yes" response, only to find out later they don't agree at all with what was being said. Because human beings sometimes experience a dissonance between what they intellectually believe and how they feel, professionals must be aware of discrepancies between descriptions of behaviors and descriptions of feelings.

Someone wishing to make clear the intent of a participant who suddenly pushes her chair back and withdraws from a discussion can interject, "I've noticed that you pulled out of the conversation [description of behavior]. Would you like to talk about what's going on for you at this time? [asking for description of feelings]." The person may well choose to say nothing because her feelings are still too close to the surface. In this case, the professional may return to the individual after a short while and ask again. The important thing to remember is to rest comfortably with a description of behavior (which is something you can see, feel, and observe) and refrain from making assumptions about feelings based on behavior (only your interpretation). A description of behavior can come from an observer; a description of feelings can come only from the person holding the feelings.

SPECIAL SKILLS FOR COMMUNICATING WITH PARENTS AT THE TIME OF DIAGNOSIS

In 1972, Korsch and Negrete investigated typical problems in communication between parents and physicians when difficult news needed to be delivered. Studying the pediatrician-parent interactions in a large urban hospital, Korsch and Negrete found that 76% of the parents felt satisfied with the communication at the time the information was delivered (usually diagnostic information). Yet, follow-up 10 and 30 days later revealed unsettling repercussions:

◆ 20% of the parents had no idea what was wrong with their child.
◆ 50% of the parents had no idea of the cause of the illness or disability.
◆ 26% of the parents had not mentioned their greatest concern about the child because they felt they were not encouraged to do so.
◆ 38% of the parents complied only in part with the physician's recommendations.
• 11% of the parents did not comply at all with any of the physician's recommendations.

ADVICE FOR TEACHERS: INTERVIEW WITH JAMES HOLDEN

The most important thing is to try to treat the child with a disability with as much similarity to other children as possible. Hold them, in so far as possible, to similar expectations: behavioral, cognitive, and emotional. Your instinct is to compensate for their disability, and you think the way to show concern is by doing special things for them to show that you really care. On the other hand, one of the greatest gifts to a child, particularly a child with a disability who may be separated from other children by the physical limitations of their disability, is to really give them a sense of inclusion, that they are really part of a group of children. You have to find the commonalty and the points of similarity which may involve getting past some superficial difference in order to tap into the point at which they're a child no different from any other child. That is an important gift.

As far as treating parents, my advice would be, to be brave in addressing issues. Sometimes, people are afraid to step on toes and so they tend to leave things unsaid or unspoken. That leads to confusion or may inadvertently communicate a lack of concern or caring or thought. I know I do this myself; if someone has had a death in the family, I talk about other things, thinking I'm being a good person by keeping their mind off this painful subject, when sometimes what they want to do is talk about that very thing. It requires a bit of courage to address issues in a very straightforward fashion. There is certainly the risk that the parent may be offended or you may inadvertently touch a sensitive nerve, and you're going to make some mistakes and say the wrong thing. But I think you're better off in the long run taking some risks, making some mistakes and getting better at it, than being too cautious about being direct. Even when it's painful, I think that the truth is more healing in the long run than euphemisms.

At the same time, I think that it is important to treat the child's disability in context. This is a child with a disability rather than a disability attached to a carrier. Sometimes you can get like a doctor; you get so tied up with the disease, and forget that a real live person is connected to it. You may think you're being good by devoting all your professional energy to the disability, but sometimes, you need to pull back and see the disability as a small part of a much larger person. Parents need to be reassured that you love their child. One of the most important things is for them to feel their child is in the hands of someone who really does care about the child.

This may be tough to do. It's hard to like your own children all of the time. But if you can do that and communicate it, that is what parents really appreciate. The bonds between you and the parents are much closer when you make a friend of a child with a disability. Parents can appreciate a teacher or a coach, but they really appreciate those people who can see in their child that special quality that lots of other people look away from. There are a lot of parents with a child whose disability causes other people to look away. Think of how much that must hurt and how desperately they want somebody to really like their child and see their child's good qualities.

It's hard to do it all the time, but if you can find the strength to engage at that level, that's the most important thing for a parent. I think that it's far more important than any of the technical skills, though there are many wonderful technical skills that you can learn. As a parent, I would rather have a person who knew nothing about the technical skills, but liked my kid and liked to play with him or work with her. I would pick that person any day over someone who had all of the technical skills in the world, but didn't care.

The Holden children.

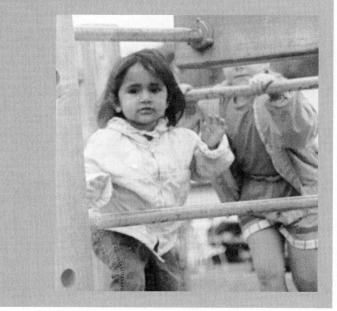

Nearly 25 years have passed since the Korsch and Negrete study. During that time, researchers have taken seriously the importance of determining how best to deliver difficult information to family members. Items of importance to this unique situation include (Turnbull & Turnbull, 1990):

◆ Provide full and honest information about the condition of a child.
◆ Repeat the information in many different ways and at many different times.
◆ Try to tell both parents at the same time.
◆ Avoid a patronizing or condescending attitude.
◆ Realize parents will need time to filter the information. Always schedule a follow-up meeting.
◆ Understand that parents may respond with anger. The anger is about the diagnosis—not about you.
◆ Discuss and practice strategies for informing brothers, sisters, and other family members.

CONFERENCING WITH PARENTS

Formal conferences between families and professionals are often structured around the child's individualized education program or arise from a particular concern on the part of the parent or the school or agency. They can be a source of considerable apprehension, especially for parents, if they are viewed as a problem rather than an opportunity to strengthen the cooperative ties between home and school (Perl, 1995). It is important to remember that the job of a professional is to bring out the best in people—to empower them, not to be overly directive or to "do for" them (Perl, 1995). This means monitoring reactions to parents and learning to communicate a genuine caring for them and their child. It means being an "enabler" by displaying a sincere sense of warmth and caring.

Building rapport is an important part of conferencing (Perl, 1995). Try to put parents at ease by beginning with pleasant informal conversation—"small talk." Offer coffee, a soft drink, or other refreshment. Hold the meeting around a table rather than on opposite sides of a desk. Use "door-opening statements" to encourage the parents to talk and to promote your own listening. Encourage parents to express concerns and make suggestions, even to "blow off steam" if they are upset or angry (Perl, 1995).

Try to be empathetic to the parent's situation and reflect the affect that is behind another person's words (Perl, 1995). That is, you may restate a parent's feelings in words or with your own facial expression. Sometimes you will need to clarify a parent's statement to make sure you are understanding. Notice nonverbal cues as well. Respond to and act on the concerns that are expressed.

RESPONDING TO FAMILY PRIORITIES

While a professional's role in the past may have been one of contributing expertise, it is now one that should be responsive to the priorities of the family. Above all, families and professionals join in a partnership that is truly collaborative in nature. In its best form, members are mutually engaged in the work to be accomplished and recognize the constraints placed on each other.

CONSTRAINTS AND CONFLICTS

An area of considerable constraint and a possible area for conflict between families and professionals that deserves special attention is time and the level of stress that time demands place on a family. Within the last decade, a number of researchers focused attention on the use of time as a critical resource of families with young children with disabilities. McLinden (1990) described time as the critical resource. Indeed, the amount of time demanded by caregiving responsibilities was the stressor most often mentioned by parents of children with disabilities. Brotherson and Goldstein (1992) described the availability of time within families in the following manner:

> Time is an example of a fundamental resource to family well-being that families can only partially generate and control themselves. To a large extent, a family's time is controlled externally by people, institutions, and events that impose expectations and requirements on the family. Time is a resource when it is available and when it can be negotiated and used; as with other resources, its absence often redefines time as a constraint. (p. 509)

While issues of time literally cross thousands of activities, the research of Brotherson and Goldstein (1992) and Brotherson and Martin (1992) found that most critical time issues fell into five categories:

1. Meeting the needs of the whole family
2. Decision making in partnerships
3. Working with the health care system
4. Professional demonstration of respect and sensitivity to families
5. Issues of working within service delivery systems across a variety of programs and agencies

Parents noted four supports that would help them in their use of time. The first of these is a need to fit therapy and education activities into the family's daily routine and environment. Brotherson and Goldstein (1992) wrote that parents' time was used more effectively when therapists integrated activities into the family's daily routines and home environment. Several parents stated that for professionals to know how to truly integrate activities into home life, the professionals had to spend time in their homes. Some parents also used time to frame the issue of transfer of knowledge from clinic to home. In part, this is a time issue, but it is also the issue of effective transferability of skills to the home environment and the material conditions of families' lives. Brotherson and Goldstein (1992) quoted a parent on this issue:

> In the past, the therapist would show me how to do this exercise on a nice round ball and wedges and then she turns around and says, "But you can do this with a dish towel and a beach ball." How am I going to get this together when I go home and try to do the exercises she's just told me about? This year we have been getting home PT and that has been very helpful, because they've got what you've got to work with and can show me how to work on the living room floor between the TV and stereo. (pp. 515–516)

Yet another dimension of the service in the home is the responsibility of professionals to develop interventions that fit families' schedules and environments. This may mean a radical shift in the working hours of professionals.

It is also critical that professionals listen to what parents know about their child and family. Perhaps the most common frustration of parents is when professionals discover what families have already told them. Having to repeat information or wait for the results of clinical assessments only to confirm what families already know frustrates and humiliates. Parents feel (whether it is true or not) they were not taken seriously and the information they offered was less than credible. This frustration frames the broader questions: (1) what information, provided by parents, needs to be reaffirmed by a professional, and what can be assumed? and (2) how can both parents and professionals learn to share information that results in the best use of time by both parties?

Today, professionals must learn to use technology for therapy and education activities as a way to work more efficiently. The advent of computer networks, conference call capabilities, faxes, e-mail, and 800-number phone lines provides communication with families that was not possible until recently. It is certainly consistent with professional obligation for early childhood educators to teach parents how to access and use those technologies that will free their time and lead to more consistent and less stressful communication.

CONFLICT WITH THE SCHOOL: INTERVIEW WITH MARSHA MOORE

It was important to us to live in a school district large enough to provide special education services to Michael, so just before his second birthday, we made the decision to look for employment in a larger town. After a year's search, we moved to Washington state. We focused our search for a home in an area where Michael could be served at a neighborhood school. We contacted the Association for Retarded Citizens to get recommendations for special education preschools. We visited the schools, talked with teachers and administrators, and finally made what we thought to be an informed decision. Two or three days after moving into our new home, and in the middle of unpacking, I called the school district to get information on how I would go about enrolling Michael in preschool. It was mid-August and I felt I didn't have much time to waste.

I was told that no decision would be made until Michael's developmental level could be evaluated by the school psychologist. Several days later, Mike and I drove out to the special education administration building for his assessment. I had dressed Michael in a little "preppy" outfit: short pants, knee socks, saddle shoes. I really had him "spiffed" up. The school psychologist took one look at him and commented that probably the only thing Michael needed was some interaction with some other children. I felt as if I'd just been told that the only problem Michael had was the lack of a stimulating environment, as if I had kept him in a closet all his life. The psychologist never told me outright that I was not providing Michael with the proper early childhood setting, but he clearly insinuated that school would "cure" everything. He also purposefully ignored the medical evaluations from Denver Children's Hospital and stated in a very patronizing manner that Michael was definitely not "autistic," as reported in his medical records. The psychologist "played" with Michael for almost two hours, and never managed to get him to respond. Michael was found eligible for special education preschool because he was two standard deviations below the mean in every domain.

From his office, I was sent over to meet Michael's preschool teacher who, at that point, was already setting up her classroom. We had left home at nine in the morning and it was now almost noon. Mike was getting cross. He was tired, he was hungry, and he was hot. The teacher sat Mike in the middle of the floor. He immediately stiffened and he threw himself back, banging his head on the carpet, howling loudly. He would not be comforted. She looked at him as if to say, "This is definitely not the kind of child we have in this classroom." She didn't say that, but that was the feeling I got. I was trying so hard to carry on a conversation, trying to be so polite, trying to get a rapport going with this teacher.

As I got up to leave, Michael was still crying. "We'll see you on the first day of school and you will bring him, right?" she instructed. I told her that he probably wouldn't ride the bus for the first few days, and that I had planned to bring him to school until he could get adjusted. The teacher continued, "And you will stay with him?" Well, I stayed every day for at least two weeks and then every other day for another month or two, because he just hated that new and strange environment. He had never been around other small children and he cried and cried, and wanted me to hold him.

Several months into school, right after Halloween, the director of special educa-tion phoned me and suggested that another program might be more suitable for Mike. This program was "specifically designed for children like Michael." She arranged to meet me at another school. I went, having no idea what the classroom would be like. When we opened the door, I found a large classroom with 8 or 10 children ranging in ages from about three to twelve or thirteen. Only one child could walk, a big boy who was taller than I was. Several children were lying on the floor on mats. One little girl was rocking back and forth on the floor; another was sitting in a rocker and shaking her head. I wondered what program was available for each of these children. Later I found that the room was called the "Severe and Profound Room," whatever that must mean!

It didn't take me long to realize that all of these other children should be in their own classes and not grouped together; it didn't seem appropriate to me that three-year-olds would be with twelve- or thirteen-year-olds. Whether they were develop-mentally on the same plateau or not, I just didn't think that was right. I remember feeling my cheeks and my ears getting very flushed. I had never had to fight a school system. I had never even thought about challenging anything that went on in school with my other children. My job as parent had been to support the school. I was a room mother, PTA officer, school carnival chairman. If our children had any prob-lems academically, I had always been able to collaborate with the teacher and often helped my child put in extra time at home. Discipline worked the same way. "So she's talking too much in class, we will see what we can do to take care of that right away." These simple problems were not even considered problems. Now how could I even think of taking a different path than the school suggested?

We visited the room for no more than 20 minutes when I stated that I would not allow Michael to be placed in this environment. The director wanted me to give it a trial run, but I held my ground and flatly refused. I told her I expected her to make the current placement work. I knew nothing of LRE then, but I soon would.

We completed an IEP for the original placement. Mike received a lot of help from an experienced physical therapist who worked for the school district. We were so pleased because by November of that same school year, Mike was up on his hands and knees, ready to crawl. Within a month he was actually pulling himself to stand, and by January he was crawling around. Soon, Mike was able to sit quietly and join circle time, and he was learning to eat finger-food at snack time. His teacher, al-though hesitant towards Michael in the beginning, structured her class in ways that allowed each child to work and learn at their own pace and towards their own goals. Well as you know, all good things must come to an end, and in February, she left school to have a baby. It's sad to say, but a program is only as good as the teacher.

When Mike started school the next year, the classroom situation was not good. After several conferences with the teacher, I started looking for help from specialists in the community. They recommended many things to facilitate Mike's progress, but the school did not provide what I was convinced he needed. For example, the school refused to work on toilet training although Michael had all the prerequisite skills. Be-cause he did not interact with the other children, he was often left to sit in the cor-ner and watch the other children play, as if he would learn how to play from watch-ing them. The most frustrating thing for me was that the school district disregarded

Mike's diagnosis of infantile autism. In fact, they not only disregarded it, but during an IEP meeting, they brought in another school psychologist to tell me that she was an expert on autism and Mike didn't have autism. I realize now that she didn't know what she was talking about, but at the time I didn't know as much and felt very intimidated by her professional expertise. I only felt angry and frustrated that they continually reminded me that I did not know my child as well as they knew him. In reality, they did not have a program for children with autism, so therefore, Michael was not autistic.

As the year progressed, I went to school once a week, sometimes twice a week. I was very quiet. If I participated in the circle time, it was only to help Mike do what the other children were doing. I held my tongue and never interrupted any classroom activity, no matter how inappropriate I felt it was. I called the teacher on a monthly basis to check on Mike's progress and ask questions that I felt were pertinent to his program. I often expressed my exasperation that Michael's program was not individualized to meet his needs. I was reminded that the "other" program was the individualized program!

When Michael started preschool the third year in the same classroom, I conferenced with the principal about what I had learned from the community specialist. I felt Mike needed more individual instruction. Mike seemed not to pay any attention to the other children in the classroom, and they were too socially delayed to interact effectively with him. I asked about bringing some kindergarten children into the classroom to act as appropriate role models for all of the children. The principal would not agree to any arrangement I suggested. There was absolutely no room for negotiation. I became more and more assertive, maybe even aggressive. I just got down right ornery.

I invited one of Michael's community autism specialists to visit his classroom in hopes that his recommendations would not fall on deaf ears. He met with the teacher, principal, and special education director and recommended one-on-one assistance, direct instruction, behavioral intervention, and other specifics. All recommendations were totally disregarded. No explanation was given. It was obvious to me that the district had a program and my child needed to fit that program. It didn't matter that the program was inappropriate for my child. What made me most angry was the reality that there were no data taken during the entire three years that Michael was in the preschool. There was no method to track Michael's progress or lack of progress. To me, that very fact indicated that Michael did not matter much.

Several weeks after the specialist had come in, the principal informed me that I made the teacher uncomfortable and that I was no longer allowed free access to the classroom. I obeyed the rules, but often would watch through the classroom door window until one day, the window blind was pulled. The principal met me in the hallway and asked me please to stay outside the school building unless I was there for a purpose other than to "harass" the teacher.

I was furious! I wrote various certified letters to the teacher, principal, and special education director to document Michael's inappropriate program as well as the unfair and illegal way I had been treated as a parent. I made a request to schedule an IEP meeting, and listed the goals and objectives that I believed were appropriate for Michael to work towards. I repeated the recommendations of the specialists I had used as consultants. In the meantime, I shared with the school staff an excellent book on IEP development, underlining everything I was requesting. I took a video to the principal about inclusion in the classroom. My information was politely refused. The school never responded to any of my half dozen certified letters.

Michael's IEP meetings were very tense and very stressful. Communication was terse and every one of my requests for Michael was met with blank stares, simply no response. I think the school staff thought that if they ignored me, I would go away or perhaps just give up. We must have had at least a dozen meetings, dozens of revised IEPs, and finally, Jim and I went to the Superintendent of our school district. We spent less than an hour with him and gave him copies of all the information and documentation we had concerning Michael's program.

Apparently he must have thought that we had some valid concerns. The district hired an aide to work with Michael and after continued advocacy for an integrated setting, we were finally given a six-week trial placement in a regular classroom. We got lucky. Mike had a wonderful first-grade teacher who made the placement a successful one, not only for Mike, but for everyone in the classroom. That year marked the beginning of a very different educational path which Michael and our family would follow over the next several years.

Professionals must provide time and consistency to develop trusting relationships with parents. Professionals who believe they can quickly meet with a family, assess their needs, and immediately participate in the development of an appropriate IFSP or IEP are badly mistaken. Time must be invested to develop and to maintain a relationship, even though an IFSP or IEP cannot be delayed beyond legal time limits. Services may begin while the process of association continues and a partnership is built.

Parents have also reported at least four common impositions on their time: (1) lack of coordination among professionals, (2) being overwhelmed with therapy and educational activities, (3) trying to access services not available in the community, and (4) lack of flexible and family-centered scheduling. In order to respond to these complaints professionals need to address the lack of flexibility within the structures of their organizations and the inherent difficulty in meeting all the needs of a whole family.

Cultural Constraints

Anne and Rutherford Turnbull (1996) offer a definition of culture that is especially relevant to professional relationships with families:

> Culture refers to many different factors that shape one's sense of group identity, including race, ethnicity, religion, geographical location, income status, gender, sexual orientation, disability status, and occupation. It is the framework within which individuals, families, or groups interpret their experiences and develop their visions of how they want to live their lives. (p. 56)

It is important that professionals are aware of their own cultural perceptions so that these do not unduly affect the way they interact with diverse families. They should also be knowledgeable of others' cultural values so that they understand the basis on which family decisions are made. Professionals must deal with stereotyping by recognizing that their cultural preferences are not superior; that making assumptions based on ethnicity can be quite misleading. Early educators must be sensitive to cultural differences that may be of concern to specific culturally diverse groups (Heward, 1996). Consider these examples:

◆ Caucasian educators generally place a high value on eye contact when talking with a student, but many African Americans engage in conversation without making eye contact at all times; they may even participate in unrelated activities while still paying attention to a conversation.

◆ Hispanic children may be reluctant to ask for help because they are accustomed to their families responding to nonverbal cues when help is needed. Hispanic children may work well in group projects but may not be motivated to strive for individual gain.

◆ Asian American parents may be reluctant to seek help for a child with disabilities, preferring instead to handle a child's abnormal behaviors within the family.

◆ American Indian children with disabilities may be so absorbed within the family and community that it is difficult to identify and provide services to these children and their families.

These and many other differences may interfere with a professional's understanding of the family and communication between school or agency and home unless early educators work hard to learn about a child's culture and customs.

For many Hispanics (a broad ethnic group which can include people whose families originally came from South and Central America, Mexico, Spain, and the Caribbean), children are the most important and valued assets, even when the family is in poor economic straits (Gonzales Alvarez, 1998). Having many children is considered a blessing, but having a child with a disability (as in most cultures) is very difficult. That child will always be viewed as sick, and if the disability is severe, will always be considered a child. Parents tend to feel sad about these children. Religion, often a strong influence within this culture, affects their perspective on a disability. Sometimes a child with a disability is seen as a punishment or curse from God, in which case the family may feel it is pointless to seek out services because that would go against God's will. A growing number of Hispanic families view the disability as fate, something that happened for a purpose. Mothers are more likely to seek services, since mothers are the main caretakers. But fathers are the decision makers and must be consulted on setting appointments and agreeing to intervention (Gonzales Alvarez, 1998).

To be effective for Hispanic families, service providers must become close to the family. Hospitality is important and home visits begin with food and conversation. Providers must be open to family invitations and become someone the family trusts. Speaking Spanish helps, but the language differs depending on the country of origin so one should recognize there will be differences. Hispanics tend to respect authority and may say they agree with recommendations when in fact they are not comfortable with the suggestions (Gonzales Alvarez, 1998).

Asian (another broad and varied ethnic group encompassing Chinese, Japanese, Korean, Vietnamese, Thai, Indonesian, and often other Pacific Islanders) families may consider matters involving a child with a disability to be private concerns, not to be openly discussed with others (Hyun & Fowler, 1995). For this reason, choosing an interpreter, when appropriate, can be an important and difficult decision. A community leader or clergyman may be respected and trusted to act in the capacity. The service provider must always treat the family formally; use Mr., Mrs., or Miss with the family name, learn simple greeting words, and use written materials prepared in the family's language. Many Asian families convey information through nonverbal communication such as silence or eye contact. Silence may mean respect or disagreement, direct eye contact is viewed as disrespectful. Encourage Asian families to bring people who are important to them to conferences and to choose a setting that is comfortable for them. If you make a home visit, it is usually common courtesy to remove one's shoes when entering. Greet older persons with a slight bow, and avoid crossing your legs when sitting. It is likely that food will be offered. If you meet in a public place, try to choose a private, quiet area.

As you plan interventions, remember that Asian childrearing may differ. For example, often young children do not self-feed but are assisted during mealtime. Infants rarely sleep alone and children under school age often sleep with their parents. Because teachers are often revered, the parents may feel it is appropriate for them to be dependent rather than active partners. Still, Asian origins are very diverse; each family is different and one must never assume something about a family based on cultural stereotype. Educators will be most effective if they are willing to learn about different people each time they meet a new family (Hyun & Fowler, 1995).

African American families have great diversity in their family living arrangements (Hunter, Pearson, Ialongo, & Kellam, 1998). There may be multigenerational family relationships, the sharing of child rearing and economic relationships across household boundaries, and a much greater role for fictive kin and parent surrogates. Grandparents, particularly grandmothers, are more likely to be actively involved in parenting children. Extended kin and nonrelatives play a significant role in child care, child management, rule setting, and discipline. This means important questions when providing support services: How do parents and other caregivers organize child care and parenting tasks? Who participates in the provision of care? and What is the role of parenting agents inside and outside of the household? (Hunter et al., 1998).

Cultural differences also abound even within "mainstream" America. One must be aware that a rural family may have different traditions and resources than an inner-city or suburban family. Regions of the United States may also vary in the way they relate family matters to professionals. Northeasterners may have different expectations than families from the deep South, for example. It is always important to get to know each individual family for its own heritage.

Other Constraints

When working with families, one must also consider the ecological context for the family. This may create different needs, varying with the child's type of disability and the family's resources (Duis, Summers, & Summers, 1997). For example, families with more cohesion tend to have less stress, as do families with higher incomes, while single-parent families are the most stressed regardless of income. Higher embarrassment ratings are linked with higher stress as is poor relationships between siblings (Duis et al., 1997). Sometimes, the needs of other family members take precedence

The family centered approach ensures that each family receives the unique set of services it requires.

over the specific needs of the child with disability, for example, when a parent becomes sick or loses a job. Often, educational needs may be a lower priority for families when compared to needs for such basics as food, shelter, child care, and health care (Bosch, 1996).

Financial needs can be a significant concern. Beyond hospitalization, families may also accumulate expenses for specialized equipment, therapy services, medications, and dietary supplements (Bosch, 1996). Sometimes private and public insurance coverage helps, but there are many gaps.

Young children with disabilities often have unusual or special caregiving needs that demand significant time and energy from their parents and contribute to fatigue (Bosch, 1996). Feeding difficulties or behavioral disturbances can add significant stress. A lack of communication skills, difficult temperaments, or the need for constant supervision adds to the strain. This creates stress on the usual routines of family life and makes finding respite difficult (Guralnick, 1998).

Emotional needs including grieving and reactions to stress are also important to consider (Bosch, 1996). Not all parents react in the same way and their reactions may change as the family life cycle changes. Often recurrent sadness appears when developmental milestones are missed, and may be more difficult than the impact of the original diagnosis (Bosch, 1996). Cultural values may inhibit a family from discussing personal issues with "outsiders" or prohibit their reliance on help outside the family (Bosch, 1996).

The greatest need perceived by parents is the requirement of information (Bosch, 1996). Families face an immediate "crisis of information" in regard to their child's current and anticipated health and development when a diagnosis is made (Guralnick, 1998). Parents of very young children with disabilities seek medical and diagnostic information. Those with older children want to know how to teach them, what services are currently available, and what their child might need in the future.

Parents need to establish their own priorities and choose the appropriate level and type of intervention that suits their family's needs (Bosch, 1996). But the following must always be considered. Adequate economic and institutional supports should be available to help families provide for their children with disabilities. Access to appropriate services should be facilitated through coordination among agencies. Informal supports may be as important as formal support. Extended family, friends, neighbors, and community should be assessed as resources. Professionals must behave competently, and this implies having a team of persons with different expertise available to provide information, resources, and support.

FORMING COLLABORATIVE TEAMS

Clearly, parental involvement in the education of children with disabilities produces academic, developmental, and social benefits, but professionals haven't been very successful in facilitating such involvement or in promoting collaboration as much as possible (Pruitt, Wandry, & Hollums, 1998). Parents are a key source for information about their children because of their firsthand knowledge of their children's physical, social, emotional, and cognitive traits (Hedrick, 1997). By working together, everyone benefits: parents, professionals, and children; and programs comply with the spirit of the federal law, not just the letter of the law (Duckworth & Kostell, 1999).

There are specific steps that can be taken to strengthen partnerships with families, such as increasing communication, using parent networks, and learning to understand family views and strengths in shared decision making (Turnbull & Turnbull, 1996). Collaborative strategies including one-on-one conferences, home visits, and parent panels are useful (Duckworth & Kostell, 1999), but the most important strategy may be the use of an effective collaborative team for planning, carrying out, and monitoring programs for young children.

Collaborative teams should be made up of all those who are essential in serving the young child with disabilities. This includes the parents (and extended family as appropriate), the teachers (both regular and special educators), the specialists and therapists who work directly with a child, such as an occupational or physical therapist, a family advocate, if desired, an administrator or designee who can commit program services, and someone who can interpret evaluation results as needed. Others who might be invited would include an interpreter, if needed, paraprofessionals who provide one-on-one aid to a child, and perhaps related medical personnel such as the visiting nurse or pediatrician.

Collaborative teaming has been initiated and researched in both regular and special education since the early 1970s (Johnson & Johnson, 1987; Kagan, 1991). While researchers lack agreement as to the essential components of collaborative teaming, at least five elements, or attributes, are common to most models of collaborative, or cooperative, teaming:

1. There is a common goal or set of goals to which all parties agree. The first order of business in team conduct is to determine the primary goal of the team. All other decisions, personal and team, should be measured against this fundamental intent.
2. There is an agreed-upon strategy for achieving each goal or set of goals (responsibilities). Members of a team collectively determine the most efficacious method(s). Even when the goal is quite clear, however, finding common ground on a method for achieving the goal can be a challenge.
3. There is a commitment to dignified and meaningful interactions, individual skill development, and task completion. In short, professional conduct is fundamental to team success.
4. There is a commitment to dependence on each other. In other words, teamwork cannot be completed if any one member fails in his or her responsibility. On the other hand, the entire team celebrates together when success is achieved because it was achieved collectively.
5. Individuals commit to a shared system of decision making and accountability. Components such as leadership, role assignments, agendas, and evaluation are determined together.

In addition, several other factors have been discussed in the literature and are believed necessary if a team is to function successfully and assert that they are indeed co-laboring:

◆ Trust building is essential. Smith and Auger (1986) contended that teams must have a way of building and maintaining trust. This trust is generated only over a period of time and, once developed, is the basis for mutual respect and security (Friend & Cook, 1990).

◆ Face-to-face interactions must occur. It is relatively simple today to communicate ideas without actually seeing our colleagues. We can usually e-mail, fax, phone, and voice mail ideas more quickly than scheduling and attending a meeting. However, these types of "interactions" are often not effective as a primary means of communicating. The sacrifice of time and effort made in order to hold meetings will eliminate many misunderstandings and conflicts that can set the team back unnecessarily (Thousand, Villa, & Nevin, 1994).

◆ Team members must acquire, refine, and practice small-group interpersonal skills. Most professional educators would agree that committee work can be torturous if decision makers lack basic skills to conduct small-group work.

◆ Collaboration should be voluntary. While individuals can be mandated through policy to work together, collaboration cannot be coerced from individuals (Friend & Cook, 1990).

◆ Collaboration requires equity among participants. Each member of a team must be equally valued, even though certain members may become more pivotal at different points in the process (Friend & Cook, 1990; Morgan, 1985). In collaboration, all members of a team are considered "experts" and may serve as consultant and/or consultee at different points in time.

The following discussion elaborates on these important attributes of collaborative teaming.

A Common Goal or Set of Goals to Which All Parties Agree

Persons new to participating in collaborative teaming on behalf of infants and young children with special needs often think they will be fairly comfortable with this first attribute. After all, it is relatively easy for physician, physical therapist, parents, or other caregivers, and educational interventionist, to agree upon an overriding desire to do what is best for the child. The problem is to define what constitutes "best." In determining and prioritizing goals, the conversation must be as clear and comprehensive as possible. As early interventionists seek to become vital and reliable members of teams, the following strategies should prove helpful:

1. Be clear about what you know and do not know. You are not expected to know other professional orientations, philosophies, and content as well as you know your own; do not pretend otherwise.
2. Listen. And listen some more. Think carefully about what you have heard and your actual ability to analyze it correctly. Do not screen out information at an early stage based on past experiences or personal biases.
3. Consider both the short- and long-term consequences of your position and the short- and long-term consequences of the other possibilities placed before the group.
4. Insist upon clarification. If a goal statement is ambiguous or unclear to one person, it may be unclear to others.
5. Check all assumptions underlying a goal before agreeing to support or reject it.
6. In setting goals on behalf of an infant or young child, be creative. Develop habits of conscience and imagination in order to move beyond personal experiences or the limits of one's education.

Agreement on the Strategy or Strategies for Achieving Each Goal

A common failure of teams operating in a collaborative fashion is to cooperatively arrive at goals, assign responsibilities, and then, not agree on strategies for reaching goals. One does not need to explore much of our service intervention history to discover the error of this oversight. When IEPs were initially established in the late 1970s, a student might have as many as three reading goals shared by two or more teachers (e.g., a regular classroom teacher, the resource room special educator, and the Title I specialist). By reviewing case studies of this period, it is possible to discover situations in which a classroom teacher used a linguistic approach, a Title I teacher used an eclectic approach, and the special educator used a phonetic/task analysis approach. The results of such a lack of coordination of strategies were disastrous.

It is easy to assume that the person or persons primarily responsible for a goal will know best how to achieve it, especially if the trust level is high on a team. While this may be true in the majority of cases, it is not always true. Working collaboratively means the team agrees they will take time to specify strategies that accomplish two things. First, collective decision making renders everyone accountable. If a strategy does not work, everyone needs to be part of analyzing the reasons why the strategy failed and defining a new one. Second, defining strategies helps clarify role responsibilities and expectations among members of the group.

A Commitment to Cooperative Interactions

What does commitment to cooperative interactions really mean? Thousand and Villa (1990) suggested that cooperation means opening ourselves to the will of the group as well as abandoning an individualistic orientation to work. But this simple answer is deceptive. Working in collaboration means entering into the potential uncertainty created when many minds must listen and decide together.

Commitment to collaborative interactions means accepting the responsibility to actively engage in conversation. More specifically, team members follow the rules of conversation and converse in such a way as to generate new ideas about issues under consideration. For example, some early childhood professionals are very capable, but very quiet. Silence means nonparticipation and will not do in the world of collaboration. It is essential that those who are quiet learn to speak out, and those who speak too much must learn to balance their input with silence.

Haroutunian-Gordon (1991) identified four rules of conversation that need to be understood and practiced in group problem solving.

1. Offer ideas that are supported by data (research or experience).
2. Ensure that individuals are listening carefully to one another.
3. Uncover and discuss contradictory evidence.
4. Allow members to build on one another's knowledge and comments and to validate new associations of information.

These skills require individual members to find value in collaboration itself. According to Kagan (1991), "Valuing collaboration means valuing empowerment, growth, and diversity. It means moving from programmatic to systematic thinking, from short- to long-term visions" (p. 93).

A Commitment to Positive Interdependence

Positive interdependence involves the recognition among team members that no one person can effectively address the diverse educational, social, medical, and psychological needs of any other person (Thousand & Villa, 1990; Thousand et al., 1994). Rather, team members know and feel that they are all responsible for the well-being of the organization and its mission.

Perhaps one of the most difficult tasks is for members of a team to articulate what they feel and know. This is worsened in every organization by fear. Fear is instilled when contributions are ignored, ridiculed, or discredited by those whose views are different from their own. The result of this unfortunate treatment is that bright women and men who are experienced listeners, polite, and reflective find the notion of initiating a new line of thinking, especially if it runs contrary to the mainline thinking of the group, to be too dangerous to consider. This passivity limits creativity and imagination—the very talents needed in team problem solving.

If collaborative teams are truly going to serve well, a practice of personal responsibility within a culture of shared and mutual responsibility must be developed. For example,

◆ Members of teams must learn not to let minor issues, which they find contrary to their own thinking or judgment, go unresolved. Differences must be addressed at the time the differences are first identified.

◆ Members must not be allowed to accept the long ramblings and dominating behaviors of certain members.

◆ Members must acknowledge the source of their input—whether they are speaking from opinion, fact, experience, intuition, or research.

◆ Members must confront, with compassion, those individuals or group behaviors that are obstructing the work and direction of the group. Likewise, feedback about tasks or responsibilities done well is equally necessary.

A special caution is offered to women in this regard: research on female/male interactions during classroom and business meetings reveals that, despite some awareness that they are welcomed to speak freely, women contribute only one third as much as their male counterparts (Cantor, 1992). Additionally, women report that, in general, they feel their comments are less valued and valuable than those of male colleagues. While it is not within the scope or intent of this chapter to address this issue, both male and female readers are encouraged to further explore their assumptions about formal and informal authority, which may have shades of gender bias—however subtle they may be.

CULTURE OF RESPECT

Early childhood professionals will be most effective if they not only cooperate with one another but truly collaborate. When done well, members come together to offer perspective, opinion, and recommendations from many different points of view. Again, in our society, members joining collaborative teams bring with them little experience in a group perspective paradigm. Villa, Thousand, Paolucci-Whitcomb, and Nevin (1990) discovered that the learning experiences of most professionals are the consequence of systems built on competition, not collaboration. Indeed, the educational experiences of most professionals and other specialists are highly competitive. Members of collaborative teams find that one of the first lessons is recognition that participating in noncompetitive modes of interaction is difficult after having participated in competitive school cultures for 12 or 16 or 20 years. It takes practice, reflection, analysis, and still more practice to develop a set of habits not previously taught or reinforced.

TEAMING AND IDEA

Federal law requires that early intervention services provided to children with disabilities or who are at risk be coordinated by a team of professionals and parents. Team members are expected to assist a child eligible for early intervention or school services and the child's family in receiving the rights, procedural safeguards, and services that are authorized to be provided (Roberts-DeGennaro, 1996). The team must draw together relevant professionals from various disciplines to share their expertise, decision making, and intervention skills with parents. To do so successfully requires trust in each other's competencies, trust in each other's opinions, and reliance on each other's skills (Roberts-DeGennaro, 1996). An attitude like this does not develop magically, it requires a great deal of time and energy devoted to working collaboratively. As professionals work together, they should be going through a series of steps that bring them closer and closer to a transdisciplinary, or role-sharing approach. Roberts-DeGennaro (1996) outlines these progressive stages well:

> **Step 1—Unidisciplinary:** Believing that (even alone) one's own discipline can make an important contribution to the habilitation of infants and toddlers with disabilities or at risk of disabling conditions.
> **Step 2—Intradisciplinary:** Recognizing also that other disciplines have important contributions to make to the habilitation of infants or toddlers with disabilities or at high risk of disabling conditions.
> **Step 3—Multidisciplinary:** Enunciating an activating philosophy that coordinated and comprehensive services based on the habilitation and developmental needs of infants and toddlers must be made available to all who are disabled or at high risk of disabling conditions.
> **Step 4—Interdisciplinary:** Being willing and able to work with other disciplines in the development of jointly planned programs for infants and toddlers with disabilities or at high risk of disabling conditions and being willing to assume responsibility for providing needed disciplinary services and treatment as part of the total program.
> **Step 5—Transdisciplinary:** Committing yourself to teaching, learning, and working together with other providers of services across traditional disciplinary boundaries.

In practice, this progression toward increased collaboration requires a number of regular activities. Here are a few guidelines for working on collaborative teams (Stump & Wilson, 1996).

1. Set a clear team purpose and identify what each individual brings to the team. Identify talents and abilities and how they can best be used collaboratively. Set expectations for each team member.
2. Establish schedules. Be consistent in when you meet, and set a specific amount of time for meetings. Plan to spend a lot of time when first working collaboratively.
3. Conduct meetings. Set a specific purpose for each meeting and stick to it until a plan is developed. List who is going to do what and set dates for task completion.
4. Share workload and responsibilities. Vary assignments so that members are not always doing the same thing. Be flexible about each member's time demands.
5. Share expertise. Identify shared and unique expertise. Share knowledge and skills.
6. Follow through. Check in to be sure that things agreed on have been completed.
7. Celebrate successes and shoulder failures together.
8. Keep the lines of communication open.

Early intervention teams coordinate several important components necessary for serving very young children with disabilities and their families; these include resource supports, social supports, and information and services (Guralnick, 1998). Resource supports include providing awareness of, access to, and coordination of services. It may also mean providing supplemental supports such as financial assistance or respite care. Social supports involve parent-to-parent groups, family counseling, and mobilization of family, friend, and community networks. Information and services include the formal intervention program (in home or center), parent-professional relationships (problem solving, decision making), and individual therapies.

If early intervention systems are working well, then services will be individually matched to the needs of the child and family (Guralnick, 1998). Some children and their families will require only surveillance or minimal supports, while others will require highly intensive, long-term programs. This implies that professionals must have a great deal of knowledge and the will to use it flexibly, according to the needs of individual families.

CLOSE-UP

ADDRESSING THE CHALLENGES OF FAMILIES WITH MULTIPLE RISKS

The shifts and realities that American families face today reflect growing social concerns that have profound implications for professionals who provide educational, health, and social services. Families have changed dramatically in composition and size, with growing numbers of single-parent households and blended families. Both parents are more likely to be in the workforce though it has become more difficult for families to stay out of poverty. Parental age is shifting, with more later childbearing at one end of the spectrum and more teen pregnancies at the other. Substance abuse leads to family problems and poses serious threats to caregiving for children. Children across the country are exposed to more violence in their communities and within their own homes. Many of today's families face not just one of these factors but live under the stress of multiple risks.

The stress associated with these many risks can sap parents' physical energy, undermine their sense of competence, and reduce their sense of control over their lives. Parents may find they are so overwhelmed in meeting basic needs that they cannot respond to specific developmental needs of their children. They may find it difficult to follow through, or may lack knowledge, resources, or motivation to even access services. When these families must turn to schools or agencies for assistance, they bring the impact of this stress with them. Children from these families may suffer the multiple stresses of poverty, risks from inadequate prenatal care, and deficits from the lack of nurturance, structure, and stimulation that would prepare them for life. Finally, these children may see little hope or success for the future.

Social support within the larger community may be a key factor to reducing parents' emotional strain and coercive parenting behavior. However, professionals must understand how to provide this support in effective ways. First, they must recognize that family problems do not come from single causes and thus, single interventions will probably not be effective. It is helpful in reaching out to multiple-risk families to: (1) provide a wide range of educational, health, and social services; (2) use family associates and paraprofessionals to assist families in gaining access to services; and (3) to employ home visitors to enhance contact with children's parents and caregivers. Such comprehensive services require a coordinated interagency response.

Service providers and educators need to engage effective interaction approaches to provide the most appropriate family support. They must give support at the earliest point for children and parents to establish positive and mutually satisfying relationships with one another. They must shift their focus from deficits to an emphasis on child and family strengths such as cognitive skills, goal-setting behaviors, family stability, and belief systems. Professionals must help build and encourage natural support systems from neighbors, friends, coworkers, and others within the family's community. Service providers must be respectful of cultural differences and able to listen to families as they express their needs, even though they may differ widely from that of the professional.

Service delivery must be comprehensive and coordinated and should provide a continuum of options that are community based and valued by the community members who are being served. Service providers must be advocates for all children, not just those labeled with specific needs. Educators and service providers must be willing to regularly cross traditional professional boundaries in order to offer options and individualize interventions to meet families' and children's needs. They cannot provide an inflexible, uniform, or routine kind of service to all families. Finally, professionals must also go beyond bureaucratic limitations to work with representatives from other agencies and outside the jurisdiction of their own areas.

Only an interactive, multilevel, coordinated approach can address the many challenges of families who experience multiple risks. A broad range of resources and services must be mobilized to counteract these risk factors. One must remember the African proverb, "It takes a whole village to raise a child."

Source: Hanson, M. J., & Carta, J. J.(1995). *Exceptional Children, 62*(3), 201–212.

Summary on Building Teams

Because of the unique mandate given to early childhood professionals to collaborate with and for families, it has been said that we have "the potential to be a guiding light to collaborators as they grapple with the complex issues inherent in today's unique social, political, and ideological context" (Kagan, 1991, p. 60). Still, Kagan labeled the collectivism effort as "naive idealism." She claimed that, as a whole, the movement is unlikely to be a panacea for our country's social ills. On a more modest level, however, she hoped that early childhood special education would be a beacon in the collaboration effort and that collaboration itself will be one necessary tool in efforts to improve care and education for young children with special needs.

Collaboration is the future (Dettmer et al., 1999). It is essential for achieving school reform, for responding to changing students' needs, and for insuring the development of global, economic, and technological productivity. The work each professional does as a part of a collaborative team adds to the framework for continued collaboration throughout the global village (Dettmer et al., 1999). A personal plan for today's small collaborative efforts may impact the future. Consider the following suggestions for encouraging collaboration on a wider scale (Dettmer et al., 1999):

1. Be a guest speaker about collaboration at community clubs and service organizations.
2. Develop a networking system that delivers positive "strokes" to school staff and families.
3. Inform colleagues of legislative and judicial activity.
4. Host sessions at conferences for school policy-makers and administrators.
5. Have an open house and invite school board members.
6. Send summer postcards to school personnel saying, "I am looking forward to working with you this year."
7. Serve as an officer and committee member to organizations that support your goals.

Bringing together all the team members of a special education student's program takes considerable effort and time, but it is an extremely important component (Marks, Schrader, & Levine, 1999). However, collaboration is more than just meeting together; its power lies in a team's capacity to merge its members' unique skills, to foster feelings of positive interdependence, to develop creative problem-solving skills, and to hold one another personally responsible for a student's success (Wood, 1998). It is only when individual members open themselves to each other's influence that the behaviors and attitudes necessary for collaboration can emerge. Those who effectively serve young children with disabilities and their families must be informed, caring, skilled, and flexible. They must believe in diversity, meeting individual needs, and supporting shared decision making. They must seek to strengthen alliances with parents and peers rather than achieving professional status by insulating themselves from those they serve (O'Shea, Williams, & Sattler, 1999). In short, effective teaming requires a commitment to children and families first, using multiple resources and skills to support our best efforts to their success.

STUDY GUIDE QUESTIONS

1. How would you describe family-centered practice to someone who is not in early intervention?
2. What would be the final measure of whether a family was empowered? What might you see that family doing?
3. What common negative assumptions about families of children with disabilities have grown from past research on these families? How has that changed in more recent years?
4. In your own words, how would you define "family"?
5. Describe the typical stages of the grief process and how they might be misused by professionals.
6. What is meant by family hardiness, and what are the three dimensions of family hardiness?
7. Give your own examples of specific communication skills that should be used and pitfalls that must be avoided when working with families.
8. How should one deliver difficult diagnostic information to families?
9. What have researchers learned about time as a family resource? What are the implications for early childhood professionals?
10. Give an example of how one's ethnic culture might affect the way a family treated a child with a disability.
11. What are some of the special needs faced by families of children with disabilities?
12. What are five elements that are desirable, if not key elements, in collaborative teaming? State these in your own words.
13. What guidelines should direct the regular activities of a collaborative team?

REFERENCES

Abbott, D. A., & Meredith, W. H. (1986). Strengths of parents with retarded children. *Family Relations, 35,* 371–375.

Able-Boone, H., Sandall, S. R., Stevens, E., & Frederick, L. (1992). Family support resources and needs: How early intervention can make a difference. *Infant-Toddler Intervention, 2*(2), 93–102.

Allen, D. A., & Affleck, G. (1985). Are we stereotyping parents? A postscript to Blacker. *Mental Retardation, 23*(4), 200–202.

Anderegg, M. L., Vergason, G. A., & Smith, M. C. (1992). A visual representation of the grief cycle for use by teachers with families of children with disabilities. *Remedial and Special Education, 13,* 17–23.

Beach Center on Families and Disability. (1995). Dads feel left out. *The Beach Center Newsletter, 6*(3). (*http://www.lsi.ukans.edu/beach/html/dis2.htm*).

Beach Center on Families and Disability. (Summer 1997). Family-centered service delivery. *The Beach Center Newsletter, 8*(2), (*http://www.lsi.ukans.edu/beach/html/fc1.htm*).

Beach Center on Families and Disability. (1998). Quality Indicators of Exemplary Family-Centered Programs. (*http://www.lsi.ukans.edu/beach/html/f19.htm*).

Beach Center on Families and Disability. (Summer 1998). Family stories. *The Beach Center Newsletter, 9*(1). (*http://www.lsi.ukans.edu/beach/html/sfam2.htm*).

Beach Center on Families and Disability. (1999). Quality Indicators of Exemplary Family-Centered Legislation. (*http://www.lsi.ukans.edu/beach/html/17.htm*).

Benson, B. A., & Gross, A. M. (1989). The effect of a congenitally handicapped child upon the marital dyad: A review of the literature. *Clinical Psychology Review, 9*(6), 747–758.

Bosch, L. A. (1996). Needs of parents of young children with developmental delay: Implications for social work practice. *Families in Society, 77*(8), 477–487.

Bradley, V. J., Knoll, J., & Agosta, J. M. (Eds.). (1992). *Emerging Issues in Family Support.* Washington, DC: American Association on Mental Retardation.

Breslau, N. (1983). Care of disabled children and women's time issue. *Medical Care, 21,* 620–629.

Brotherson, M. J., & Goldstein, B. (1992). Time as a resource and constraint for parents of young children with disabilities: Implications for early intervention services. *Topics in Early Childhood Special Education, 12,* 508–527.

Brotherson, M. J., & Martin, L. H. (1992). Building successful partnerships with families with young children with disabilities: Family, early interventionist, and physician perspectives. Paper presented at the Annual Conference of the Association for the Care of Children's Health, Atlanta.

Cantor, D. W. (1992). *Women in power: The secrets of leadership.* Boston: Houghton Mifflin.

Carr, J. (1988). Six-weeks to twenty-one years old: A longitudinal study of children with Down syndrome and their families. *Journal of Child Psychology and Psychiatry, 29*(4), 407–431.

Christenson, S. L., & Cleary, M. (1990). Consultation and the parent-educator partnership: A perspective. *Journal of Educational and Psychological Consultation, 1,* 219–241.

Cook, R. E., Tessier, A., & Klein, M. D. (1992). *Adapting early childhood curricula for children with special needs.* Upper Saddle River, NJ: Merrill/Prentice Hall.

Cox, A., Rutter, M., Newman, S., & Bartak, L. (1975). A comparative study of infantile autism and specific developmental receptive language disorders: Parental characteristics. *British Journal of Psychiatry, 126,* 146–159.

Darling, R. (1979). *Families against society: A study of reactions to children with birth defects.* London: SAGE.

Davern, L. (April, 1996). Listening to parents of children with disabilities. *Educational Leadership,* 61–63.

Dettmer, P., Dyck, N., & Thurston, L. P. (1999). *Consultation, collaboration, and teamwork.* (3rd ed.). Boston: Allyn & Bacon.

Duckworth, S. V., & Kostell, P. H. (1999). The parent panel: Supporting children with special needs. *Childhood education, 75*(4), 199–203.

Duis, S. S., Summers, M., & Summers, C. R. (1997). Parent versus child stress in diverse family types: An ecological approach. *Topics in Early Childhood Special Education, 17*(1), 53–73.

Dunlap, K. M. (1997). Family empowerment: One outcome of cooperative preschool education. *Child Welfare, 76*(4), 501–519.

Failla, S., & Jones, L. (1991). Families of children with developmental disabilities: An examination of family hardiness. *Research in Nursing and Health, 14,* 41–50.

Featherstone, H. (1980). *A difference in the family: Living with a disabled child.* New York: Penguin.

Fennel, M. (1999). The boy who could not speak. *Exceptional Parent, 29*(9), 132.

Francis, P. L., & Jones, F. A. (1984). Interactions of mothers and their developmentally-delayed infants: Age, parity, and gender effects. *Journal of Clinical Child Psychology, 13*(3), 268–273.

Friend, M., & Cook, L. (1990). Collaboration as a predictor for success in school reform. *Journal of Educational and Psychological Consultation, 1*(1), 69–86.

Gath, A. (1977). The impact of an abnormal child upon the parents. *British Journal of Psychiatry, 130,* 405–410.

Gath A., & Gumley, D. (1987). Retarded children and their siblings. *Journal of Child Psychology and Psychiatry, 28,* 715–730.

Gonzales Alvarez, L. I. (1998). A short course in sensitivity training. *Teaching Exceptional Children, 1,* 73–77.

Guralnick, M. J. (1998). Effectiveness of early intervention for vulnerable children: A developmental perspective. *American Journal on Mental Retardation, 102*(4), 319–345.

Hanson, M.J., & Carta, J. J. (1995). Addressing the challenges of families with multiple risks. *Exceptional Children, 62*(3), 201–212.

Haroutunian-Gordon, S. (1991). *Turning the soul: Teaching through conversation in the high school.* Chicago: University of Chicago Press.

Hedrick, L. (1997). Parents and professionals working together. In L. L. Dunlap (Ed.), *An introduction to early childhood special education* (pp. 118–136). Boston: Allyn and Bacon.

Heflinger, C. A., & Bickman, L. (1997). A theory-driven intervention and evaluation to explore family caregiver empowerment. *Journal of Emotional & Behavioral Disorders, 5*(3), 184–192.

Herman, S. E., Marcenko, M., & O'Hazel, K. L. (1996). Parents' perspectives on quality in family support programs. *Journal of Mental Health Administration 23*(2), 156–164.

Heward, W. L. (1996). *Exceptional children.* (5th ed.). Upper Saddle River, NJ: Merrill/Prentice Hall.

Hoover-Dempsey, K., & Sandler, H. (1997). Why do parents become involved in their children's education? *Review of Educational Research, 67*(1), 3–42.

Hunter, A. G., Pearson, J. L., Ialongo, N. S., & Kellam, S. G. (1998). Parenting alone to multiple caregivers: Childcare and parenting arrangements in black and white urban families. *Family Relations, 47*(4), 343–353.

Hyun, J. K., & Fowler, S. A. (1995). Respect, cultural sensitivity, and communication. *Teaching Exceptional Children,* 25–28.

Johnson, D. W., & Johnson, F. P. (1987). *Joining together.* (3rd ed.). Upper Saddle River, NJ: Prentice Hall.

Kagan, S. L. (1991). *United we stand: Collaboration for childcare and early childhood services.* New York: Teacher's College Press.

Kazak, A. E. (1986). Families with physically handicapped children: Social ecology and family systems. *Family Process, 25,* 265–281.

Kazak, A. E., & Marvin, R. S. (1984). Differences, difficulties and adaptation: Stress and social networks in families with a handicapped child. *Family Relations, 33,* 67–77.

Klemm, D., & Schimanski, C. (1999). Parent to parent: The crucial connection. *Exceptional Parent, 29*(9), 109–112.

Kobasa, S., Maddi, S., & Puccetti, M. (1982). Personality and exercise as buffers in the stress illness relationship. *Journal of Behavior Medicine, 5,* 391–403.

Korsch, B. M., & Negrete, V. F. (1972). Doctor-patient communication. *Scientific American, 227,* 66–74.

Kubler-Ross, E. (1969). *Locus of control: Current trends in theory and research.* Hillsdale, NJ: Earlbaum.

Marks, S. U., Schrader, C., & Levine, M. (1999). Paraeducator experiences in inclusive settings: Helping, hovering, or holding their own. *Exceptional Children, 65*(3), 315–328.

McCubbin, H. L., Nevin, R. S., Cauble, A. E., Larsen, A., Comeau, J. K., & Patterson, J. M. (1982). Family coping with chronic illness: The case of cerebral palsy. In H. I. McCubbin, A. E. Cauble, & J. M. Patterson (Eds.), *Family stress, coping, and social support* (pp. 169–188). Springfield, IL: Thomas.

McHale, S. M., & Gamble, W. C. (1989). Sibling relationships of children with disabled and nondisabled brothers and sisters. *Developmental Psychology, 25*(3), 421–429.

McLinden, S. E. (1990). Mothers' and fathers' reports of the effects of a young child with special needs on the family. *Journal of Early Intervention, 14,* 249–259.

Meyer, D. J., & Vadasy, P. F. (1994). *Sibshops: Workshops for siblings of children with special needs.* Baltimore: Brookes.

Morgan, S. R. (1985). *Children in crisis: A team approach in the schools.* Austin, TX: PRO-ED.

Moore, M. L., Howard, V. F., & McLaughlin, T. F. (In press). Siblings of children with disabilities: A review and analysis. *International Journal of Special Education.*

Murphy, A. T. (1981). *Special children, special parents: Personal issues with handicapped children.* Englewood Cliffs, NJ: Prentice Hall.

Murphy, A. T. (1982). The family with a handicapped child: A review of the literature. *Developmental and Behavioral Pediatrics, 3*(2), 73–82.

O'Shea, D. J., Williams, A. L., & Sattler, R. O. (1999). Collaboration across special education and general education: Preservice teachers' views. *Journal of Teacher Education, 50*(2), 147–157.

Orsillo, S. M., McCaffrey, R. J., & Fisher, J. M. (1993). Siblings of head-injured individuals: A population at risk. *Journal of Head Trauma Rehabilitation, 8*(1), 102–115.

Perl, J. (1995). Improving relationship skills for parent conferences. *Exceptional Children, 27*(1), 29–31.

Pollack, S. (1986). Human responses to diabetes mellitus. *Western Journal of Nursing Research, 11,* 265–280.

Pruitt, P., Wandry, D., & Hollums, D. (1998). Listen to us! Parents speak out about their interactions with special educators. *Preventing School Failure, 42*(4), 161–167.

Reed, E. W., & Reed, S. C. (1965). *Mental Retardation: A family study.* Philadelphia: Saunders.

Roberts-DeGennaro, M. (1996). An interdisciplinary training model in the field of early intervention. *Social Work in Education, 18*(1), 20–30.

Roos, P. (1985). Parents of mentally retarded children— misunderstood and mistreated. In A. P. Turnbull & H. R. Turnbull (Eds.), *Parents speak out: Views from the other side of the two-way mirror.* (2nd ed.), (pp. 245–257). Upper Saddle River, NJ: Merrill/Prentice Hall.

Roth, W. (1982). Poverty and the handicapped child. *Children and Youth Services Review, 4,* 67–75.

Schell, G. C. (1981). The young handicapped child: A family perspective. *Topics in Early Childhood Special Education, 1,* 21–27.

Seligman, M., & Darling, R. B. (1989). *Ordinary families special children: A systems approach to childhood disability.* New York: The Guilford Press.

Singer, G. H. S., & Nixon, C. (1996). A report on the concerns of parents of children with acquired brain injury. In G. H. S. Singer, A. Glang, & J. Williams (Eds.), *Children with acquired brain injury: Educating and supporting families* (pp. 23–52). Baltimore: Brookes.

Smith, S. D., & Auger, K. (1986). Conflict or cooperation? Keys to success in partnerships in education. *Action in Teacher Education, 7*(4), 1–9.

Stump, C. S., & Wilson, C. (1996). Collaboration: Making it happen. *Intervention in School & Clinic, 31*(5), 310–313.

Swick, K. J. (1996). Building healthy families: Early childhood educators can make a difference. *Journal of Instructional Psychology, 23*(1), 75–82.

Thousand, J. S., & Villa, R. (1990). Sharing expertise and responsibilities through teaching teams. In W. Stainback & S. Stainback (Eds.), *Support networks for inclusion schooling: Interdependent integrated education* (pp. 151–166). Baltimore: Paul H. Brookes.

Thousand, J. S., Villa, R., & Nevin, A. (1994). *Creativity and collaborative learning.* Baltimore: Paul H. Brookes.

Traustadottir, R. (1991). Mothers who care: Gender, disability, and family life. *Journal of Family Issues, 12*(2), 211–228.

Turbiville, V. P. (1995). Fathers, their children, and disability. *Infants and Young Children, 7*(4).

Turnbull, A. P. & Turnbull, H. R. (Eds.). (1985). *Parents speak out: Views from the other side of the two-way mirror* (2nd ed.), (pp. 245–257). Upper Saddle River, NJ: Merrill/Prentice Hall.

Turnbull, A. P., & Turnbull, H. R. (1990). *Families, professionals, and exceptionality: A special partnership.* (2nd ed.). Upper Saddle River, NJ: Merrill/Prentice Hall.

Turnbull, A. P., & Turnbull, H. R. (1996). *Families, professionals, and exceptionality: A special partnership.* (3rd ed.) Upper Saddle River, NJ: Merrill/Prentice Hall.

Vanderslice, V. (1984). Empowerment: A definition in progress. *Human Ecology Forum, 14*(1), 2–3.

Villa, R. A., Thousand, J. S., Paolucci-Whitcomb, P., & Nevin, A. (1990). In search of new paradigms for collaborative consultation. *Journal of Educational and Psychological Consultations, 1,* 279–292.

Werner, E., & Smith, R. (1982). *Vulnerable but invincible: A study of resilient children.* New York: McGraw-Hill.

Willoughby, J. C., & Glidden, L. M. (1995). Fathers helping out: Shared childcare and marital satisfaction of parents of children with disabilities. *American Journal on Mental Retardation, 99*(4), 399–406.

Wood, M. (1998). Whose job is it anyway? Educational roles in inclusion. *Exceptional Children, 64*(2), 181–195.

Young, D. M., & Roopnarine, J. L. (1994). Fathers' childcare involvement with children with and without disabilities. *Topics in Early Childhood Special Education, 14*(4), 488–502.

GLOSSARY

abduction: limbs move outward, away from the body

abruptio placenta: separation of placenta from the walls of the uterus prior to delivery

absence seizure: momentary interruption of on-going activity with a brief, blank stare

accommodation (mental): changing an existing mental schema (pattern) to fit new information

accommodation (visual): the process by which the eye adjusts to focus on near objects

acidotic: high levels of blood acid

active listening: attentiveness to a speaker on multiple levels: hearing, interpreting, sorting, and analyzing

acute stressors: events that place strain on a family and occur as periodic incidents related to a child's disability

adaptive reflexes: mature reflexes such as sucking and swallowing

adaptive skills: self-help, problem solving, responding appropriately to environmental demands

adduction: limbs move in toward the body

adolescent stage: time starting at about 10 to 16 years of age, depending on physical maturity, and extending to adulthood

adventitious: aquired after birth

advocacy: favoring and supporting the needs or cause of another

albinism: a congenital condition characterized by a lack of the pigment that gives color to skin, hair, and eyes

alleles: one of two alternative versions of a gene with complementary alleles residing on each of the two chromosomes in a pair

alpha-fetoprotein (AFT) screening: a blood test on a pregnant woman to detect neural tube deficits in her fetus

alveoli: tiny air sacs in the lungs which permit normal exchange of oxygen and carbon dioxide

amblyopia: dimness of vision not due to organic defect or refractive errors

amniocentesis: a procedure in which fluid is removed from the sac surrounding the fetus to determine if the fetus carries a genetic anomaly

amniotic sac: the membrane that surrounds the fetus and contains fluid that protects the fetus from physical shocks and maintains a constant temperature

anemia: a condition in which the amount of oxygen-carrying hemoglobin is below normal in the blood

anencephaly: a congenital malformation in which the brain does not develop and the skull, which would normally cover the brain, is absent

annual goals: targets for improvement that should be reached within one year's time

anomaly: a deviation in physical development

antibodies: a protein produced by the body in response to the presence of an antigen (chemical substance that causes the body to produce specific antibodies) and is capable of combining specifically with the antigen

antiviral: a group of drugs used to treat infection by a virus

apnea: breathing pauses due to immature central nervous system

asphyxia: loss of consciousness from interruption of breathing as in suffocation or drowning

associative play: individual children play with other children engaging in similar or even identical activities

astigmatism: a visual defect caused by unequal curvatures of the refractile surfaces (cornea, lens) of the eye, resulting in light rays not coming to focus at a point on the retina

asymmetrical tonic neck reflex (ATNR): a primitive reflex in which the limbs are extended on the side of the body toward which the head is turned but flexed on the opposite side; also called "fencer's reflex"

asymptomatic: showing no symptoms

at risk: used to refer to that class of infants who have been exposed to any one of a number of medical or environmental factors that may contribute to later developmental delay

ataxic cerebral palsy: cerebral damage that causes difficulty with coordination and balance

athetosis: variable muscle tone caused by noncortical cerebral damage, producing slow, writhing, and excessive movement

atonic seizure: sudden reduction in muscle tone, slumping

attachment: emotional bonding to another person

attention deficit hyperactivity disorder (ADHD): a combination of characteristics including inattention, impulsivity, and hyperactivity

attitude of science: the use of parsimony and empirical research to determine what is true

auditory nerve: vehicle of transmission of electrical energy from the ear to the temporal area of the brain

augmentative or alternative communication: using appliances or nonspeech systems to enhance a child's natural communication skills

autosome: any of the chromosomes other than the sex (X and Y) chromosomes in humans of which there are 22 pairs

axon: the nerve-cell process that carries impulses away from the nerve-cell body; any long nerve-cell process

babble: a combination of consonant and vowel sounds uttered by infants at about four months of age as they gain oral-motor control

Babinski reflex: a reflex in which stimulation applied to the sole of an infant's foot results in the infant spreading his or her toes

bacteria: a large group of typically one-celled, microscopic organisms widely distributed in air, water, soil, and the bodies of living plants and animals

behavioral assessment: examination of factors that govern children's behavior under given conditions

best practice: instructional and collaborative procedures based on current research and knowledge

binding communications: habits of interaction that generally close or diminish the probability of continued conversation

biological agents: microorganisms that cause damage to human cells by either living on cells or by causing inflammation of the cells and that travel throughout the body via the bloodstream or lymphatic system

biological risks: medical conditions that threaten to compromise a child's health, particularly perinatally, and are predictive of later delays

blended families: families including stepchildren and stepparents

bonding: attachment between infant and caregiver

bound morphemes: morphemes that cannot stand alone in meaning (-ed, -ing)

breath-holding spells: involuntary holding of breath

bronchopulmonary dysplasia (BPD): chronic lung disease resulting from respiratory distress syndrome

cardiovascular system: organ system including heart, veins, and arteries

carrier: individual who possesses a gene for a trait but does not express the characteristics

cataract: clouding or opacity of the lens of the eye

center-based programs: programs in which children are served in a central location

central nervous system (CNS): the brain and spinal cord

cephalo-caudal: the sequence of growth and development of motor skills that is progressively downward from head, to neck, to trunk, to hips, to legs, to feet, to toes

cerebral palsy: a nonprogressive neuromuscular condition affecting muscle tone, movement, reflexes, and posture

cerebrospinal fluid: a clear, colorless, odorless fluid that resembles water, is produced from blood through secretion and diffusion between the vascular system and the choroid plexuses in the brain, and protects the nervous system from injury by acting as a shock absorber

chancre: a lesion at the site of contact with an infected person

child abuse: the willful behavior by parents or guardians that harms a child in their care

child-directed instruction: flexible instruction that follows a child's lead in terms of interests and motivation

chorionic villus sampling (CVS): testing a small tissue sample from the chorion, or outer sac that surrounds the fetus, to determine if the fetus carries a genetic anomaly

chorioretinitis: inflammation of the retina and choroid

chromosome disorders: disorders caused by whole chromosomes or chromosome segments rather than a single gene or combination of genes

chromosomes: the basic genetic units that stay constant within a species and across generations (For example, normal human cells contain a complement of 46 chromosomes or 23 pairs.)

chronic stressors: constant pressure or strain on a family caused by concerns related to a child's disability

cirrhosis: interstitial inflammation of an organ, particularly the liver

cleft lip: a split in facial tissue that affects the lip and gum and may extend upward into the nose and may occur with a cleft palate

cleft palate: a split in facial tissue that affects the hard or soft palate (roof of mouth) and may occur with a cleft lip

clonic seizure: alternate contraction and relaxation of muscles

cochlea: the portion of the inner ear associated with the reception of sound waves, which lies in a cavity in the temporal bone and is shaped like a snail shell

cognition: thinking, mental processes

cognitive-developmental approach: a theory about how children learn that recognizes a natural, fixed sequence in which thinking processes emerge

collaboration: an interactive process that enables teams of people with diverse expertise to generate creative solutions to mutually defined problems

collaborative teaming: members agree to work together collectively to achieve common goals

communication: the ability of two or more people to send and receive messages; the most necessary skill of both parents and childhood educators

complex sentence: a sentence that contains at least one independent clause and at least one subordinate or dependent clause

compound sentence: a sentence that contains more than one independent clause and combines two or more ideas in a single sentence by using conjunctions, relative pronouns, or other linguistic linkages

Computerized Axial Tomography (CAT or CT): a procedure that uses X rays to view several planes of the body at one time to produce a three-dimensional image of body tissue

conceptual system: a set of principles that articulates a body of knowledge

concrete operations: the stage of cognitive development (at age 7–11 years) when children can use real objects to logically solve problems

conduction: heat loss to unwarmed surfaces (such as a mattress), and evaporation (heat loss through fluid loss through the skin)

conductive hearing loss: disruption of mechanical conduction of sound as it is transferred from the outer ear through the middle ear

congenital: present at birth

congenital heart defect: an abnormality of the heart present at birth

consensus building: guiding groups in decision making based on group agreement

consequate: to follow, contingent upon a specific behavior

consolidation: when disorganized behavior is replaced by more advanced developmental skills

continuum of services: options for educational placement that vary from least to most extensive or restrictive

contractures: a condition in which muscles and tendons shorten, causing rigidity and joint immobility

conversational postulates: subtle conversational rules that allow humans to converse in a reciprocal manner (i.e., initiating, turn taking, questioning, repairing a breakdown in conversation, maintaining interactions, and closing a conversation)

convection: heat loss with the delivery of unwarmed gases such as oxygen

cooing: vowel sound production that requires little motor control or use of the articulators (tongue, lips, palate, and teeth), which usually occurs in infants during the perlocutionary stage

cooperative play: children engage in organized play activities

coprolalia: involuntary use of vulgar or obscene gestures or language

cornea: the transparent epithelium (tissue covering internal and external surfaces) and connective tissue membrane that covers the anterior portion of the eye, which refracts light rays and channels that light through the fluid-filled anterior chamber

corrected gestational age: age adjusted to reflect premature delivery

cortical blindness: blindness that results when brain function interferes with processing of visual images

cortical visual impairments: a condition in which eye physiology is not impaired, yet there is a loss of visual ability caused by damage to the optic nerve or the cerebral tissue within the occipital portion of the brain

crawl: coordination of arms and legs to move across a surface on the abdomen

cruising: a child's movement by stepping sideways while holding on to furniture or some structure for support

cultural competence: knowledge of and respect for diverse beliefs, interpersonal styles, attitudes, and behaviors

culturally sensitive: awareness of different values and practices of divergent ethnic and cultural groups

cyanosis: a blue-tinged color to the skin, which can occur when blood bypasses the lungs, resulting in decreased oxygen being available to cells

cytomegalic inclusion viral infection (CMV): one of the family of herpes viruses that is common and produces no symptoms in adults but can cause malformations and brain damage to an unborn child

demographics: statistical characteristics of human populations

dentition: the development of teeth

deoxyribonucleic acid (DNA): a nucleic acid compound that carries the chemical coding needed to transmit genetic information from generation to generation

development: occurs when the complexity of a child's behavior increases

developmental delay: delayed progress experienced by infants and toddlers in one or more developmental areas: communication, physical development, adaptive behavior (feeding, dressing, toileting, etc.), cognition, and social/emotional development

developmentally appropriate: instruction that matches a child's abilities and interests according to age, skills, and cognitive level

developmental milestones: major indexes of development identified across developmental areas and across years and used to measure developmental progress

diabetes: any disorder characterized by excessive urine excretion, usually caused when the pancreas produces insufficient insulin

diplegia: cerebral palsy affecting all four extremities of the body, with greater involvement of the legs than of the trunk and arms

discretionary programs: allowed but not required by law

dominant gene: a gene that possesses sufficient genetic information for a characteristic to be expressed when only one allele carries the gene

duodenal atresia: a narrowing of the intestine

dyskinesia: a condition caused by noncortical cerebral damage (see athetosis)

eardrum: see tympanic membrane

early childhood stage: time from 3 years to 6 years of age

early intervention: period from birth to age 3 when services are delivered to infants and toddlers with developmental delays or at-risk conditions

ecological approach (to assessment): evaluations focus on children, their environment, and the interaction between the two

edema: swelling or filling with fluid

electroencephalography: a procedure that measures electrical potentials on the scalp to produce an analysis of brain activity

embedding: a process in which children add clauses internally to sentences (develops at 4 to 13 years of age)

embryonic stage: begins in the third week of pregnancy when cell differentiation permits the emergence of the central nervous system and circulatory system and is completed by the eighth week of gestation

empirical: relying on observation and experimentation

empowerment: encouraging individual reliance on self and providing understandable and practical information that can be used by families

encephalitis: inflammation of the brain

environmental risks: environmental conditions, such as poverty or abuse, that place infants and toddlers at risk for developmental delays

epilepsy: a condition of recurrent seizures

equilibrium reflex: the reflex that involuntarily causes the body to realign its trunk to a vertical posture after the body moves or is moved out of midline

established risks: diagnosed conditions that give infants and toddlers high probability of later delays in development

ethical standards: accepted professional guidelines for appropriate behavior toward others

eustachian tube: a continuous passage from the middle ear to the throat that acts as a safety tube, equalizing internal and external air pressure on the tympanic membrane

excited: activated to perform a function

exocrine glands: glands that secrete substances onto an inner surface of an organ or outside the body, such as salivary or sweat glands

exosystem: societal structures, such as local and state agencies or advocacy groups, that affect a child's life

expressive language: coded output message emitted by a child or adult

extension: the straightening of a joint that changes the angle between bones that meet in the joint; the opposite of flexion

external ear: the part of the ear responsible for collecting sound waves, consisting of the auricle, auditory canal, and tympanic membrane

extrapyramidal: outside the pyramidal nerve group; used to refer to noncortical cerebral damage

extremely low birth weight: less than 750 g (1 lb 10 oz)

failure to thrive: delay in physical and neurological growth in infancy and early childhood due to organic or environmental causes

family hardiness: a constellation of three dimensions: (1) control: the ability to influence events, (2) commitment: active involvement in events, and (3) challenge: viewing changes as opportunities for growth and development

family systems model: approaches families as complex organizations in which internal and external variables affect all members

Fetal Alcohol Effects (FAE): moderate birth defects caused by prenatal exposure to alcohol

Fetal Alcohol Syndrome (FAS): serious birth defects caused by prenatal exposure to alcohol

fetal blood sampling: a blood sample withdrawn from the umbilical cord to determine if the fetus carries a genetic anomaly

fetal stage: the stage of pregnancy from the ninth week through the ninth month

fine pincer grasp: grasp using the tips of the thumb and index finger in opposition

flexion: the bending of a joint; the opposite of extension

formal operations: the stage of cognitive development (at age 11 years and older) when humans develop abstract thinking; can classify and sort

freeing statements: habits of interaction that actually encourage expanded dialogue

full inclusion: to accept an individual with a disability as a full-time member of a regular social group and as a contributing participant

functional assessment: making changes in the circumstances and consequences for severe misbehavior in order to determine what is maintaining the behavior

functional skills: of immediate or future usefulness in the environment, such as self-feeding or mobility

functionality: degree to which skills are needed to operate as independently as possible in daily activities

gametes: the cells involved in reproduction (A sperm is a male gamete, and an ovum is a female gamete.) These germ cells have one half the number of chromosomes, one from each chromosome pair. When a sperm and ovum join during conception, the resultant cell has a full set of chromosomes, one of each chromosome pair from each parent.

gastrointestinal system: the part of the digestive system that consists of the mouth, esophagus, stomach, and intestine

gastrostomy tube: a tube or a gastric button through which feedings can be given directly into the stomach, bypassing the esophagus

generalization: transfer of skills to other settings, other caregivers, and other appropriate situations

generalized seizure: caused by activation of the entire brain; involves the whole body

genes: regions of a chromosome made up of molecules that collectively define a particular trait

genetic mapping: a process of learning the genetic code of humans by charting the relationships between specific genes and individual chromosomes

genotype: the combination of alleles inherited for a particular trait within an individual (The genotype can only be determined through cellular testing since the trait determined by the genotype may or may not be expressed.)

gestation: the period of intrauterine fetal development

gestational diabetes: acquisition of diabetes during pregnancy

glaucoma: a condition characterized by a buildup of pressure in the anterior chamber of the eye

grasp reflex: flexion of the hand in response to stimulation of the palm

gravida: the medical term for a pregnant woman; often used with a number to indicate the number of pregnancies a woman has had (a 3-gravida)

growth retardation: very small for age, weight less than the tenth percentile

group B streptococcus: a group of bacteria from the streptococcus family

group process: reflection by a group to determine what actions should be continued and what group behaviors should be changed in order to make collaborative efforts more effective

handling: therapeutic preparation for movement and positioning

hematoma: bruise or swelling filled with blood

hemiplegia: cerebral palsy affecting one side of the body

herpes: infection with the herpes simplex virus, causing small, painful blisters on the skin

heterozygote: when an individual has two different alleles for a particular trait (For example, a child who receives a normal gene from one parent and a gene for cystic fibrosis from the other parent will not express the disease from this heterozygote pair since the gene for cystic fibrosis is not dominant.)

home-based programs: programs in which children are served in their homes with instruction given primarily to the parents or caregivers

homozygote pair: when an individual has identical alleles for a certain trait (For example, when the gene for cystic fibrosis is inherited from both mother and father , the alleles form a homozygote pair and the child will express the disease.)

hydrocephalus: a condition in which there is an excessive accumulation of cerebrospinal fluid in the ventricles of the brain, causing the head to increase in size beyond two standard deviations above the mean on the standard growth chart

hyperopia: farsightedness; a condition in which parallel light rays come to focus beyond the retina because the refractile system is too weak or the eyeball is flattened

hypertonia: high muscle tone that limits joint movement

hypoglycemia: a condition in which there is a decreased amount of glucose available for use by cells

hypothermia: low body core temperature

hypotonia: low muscle tone that allows excessive joint movement

hypoxia: decreased oxygen flow

imitation: copy another's behavior or language

inclusion: to participate in the same activities as nondisabled peers

incontinence: inability to retain urine or feces

Individualized Education Program (IEP): an intervention plan developed by a team for a child (age 3–21 years) with a disability; includes a report of current performance, annual goals, instructional objectives, special education and related services, and an evaluation proposal

Individualized Family Service Plan (IFSP): an intervention plan developed by a team for an infant or toddler (birth to age 3) with a disability and for the child's family; includes identification of strengths and needs, a statement of expected outcomes, intervention and support services, and evaluation proposals for the child and the family

Individuals with Disabilities Education Act (IDEA): current federal legislation regarding the education of children with disabilities; provides for a free, appropriate education for all children with disabilities ages 3 to 21 and encourages services to infants and toddlers with disabilities or at risk for developmental delay

infancy: time from 30 days to 12 months of age

inflammation: redness, swelling, heat, and pain in tissue caused by injury or infection

inhibited: prevented from activating when not needed

inner ear: a fluid-filled chamber located in the temporal bone medial to the middle ear, containing the cochlea, the vestibule, and the semicircular canals

instructional objectives: expected outcomes of educational intervention within a short-term time frame; should state the observable behavior, the conditions or situation under which the behavior is expected, and the criterion, or how well the child must perform the behavior

integumentary system: organ system including skin, nails, hair, glands, muscles, ligaments, tendons, and fat tissue

Interagency Coordinating Council (ICC): agencies at the federal, state, and local levels that provide administration and service delivery for infants and toddlers with special needs

interdisciplinary model: the combination of expertise from several disciplines for evaluating, planning, and implementing intervention; a group whose members perform related tasks independently but interact collaboratively to meet goals

intracranial bleeding: bleeding in the brain; stroke

intraventricular hemorrhage (IHV): bleeding in the brain

invasive: a procedure that penetrates the body (such as surgery)

involvement: degree to which a child is affected motorically; ranges from mild to severe

ischemia: death of cells/tissue due to decreased blood flow and oxygen supply

jaundice: buildup of bilirubin (hyperbilirubinemia) in the basal ganglia

karyotype: the number and configuration of chromosomes

kin: immediate and extended family

kinship care: child care, housing, and so on, provided by members of the immediate or extended family other than the parents

late visual bloomers: those children who, like children with motor, language, and social developmental delays, experience maturational delays in visual ability, appearing to be blind at birth and during their first months of life, but usually developing normal visual ability by 18 months to 3 years of age

least restrictive environment: the most appropriate setting in which a child with a disability can be with typical peers to the greatest extent possible and still meet individual needs

lens: transparent convex structure of the eye just behind the pupil, whose curvature can be altered to focus on near or far objects

localization: identification of the orientation of a sound source

low birth weight: less than 2800 g (6 lb 3 oz) at birth

low vision: visual acuity at or less than 20/70 in the better eye with correction

macrosystem: the cultural and legislative/judicial contexts that affect a child, for example, IDEA legislation

magnetic resonance imaging (MRI): a procedure that uses magnetic force to draw ions to the edges of an internal organ to produce an image of normal and abnormal tissues

mandated: required by law

maturation: the universally observed sequence of biological changes as one ages; permits the development of psychological functions to evolve

Mean Length Utterance (MLU): an index of the sophistication of a child's language, acquired by measuring the frequency of morphemes in children's utterances

meconium: the thick, sticky, greenish-black feces passed by infants during the first day or two after birth

meconium aspiration syndrome: when the dark sticky mucous in the intestine of a fetus is expelled before birth and inhaled as the infant takes its first breaths

meiosis: cell division that produces sex cells, in which chromosomes divide and produce half the complement of 46 chromosomes in each of the resulting gametes

meninges: the covering that consists of three layers (arachnoid, dura mater, and pia mater) and surrounds the brain and spinal cord

meningitis: a condition in which infection occurs as the result of the entry of bacteria, producing inflammation of the meninges, which is the covering that surrounds the brain and spinal cord

meningocele: a neural tube defect that involves a soft tissue mass that is covered by skin, and does not contain nerves or nerve roots

mesosystem: relationships among microsystems in which a child sometimes spends time, for example, the relationship between teacher and parent

microbes: germs that are so small that they can only be seen through a microscope

microcephaly: very small head and brain; head circumference that falls at least two standard deviations below the mean on a standard growth chart for age

micropremature infant: an infant born at less than 600 g (1 lb 5 oz) or less than 25 weeks gestation

microsystem: the immediate environment in which a child spends the majority of time, for example, the childcare center

middle childhood stage: time from about 6 to 10 years of age

middle ear: a small air-filled chamber medial to the tympanic membrane containing three tiny bones: the malleus (hammer), incus (anvil), and stapes (stirrup)

milestones: behavioral markers or accomplishments of development

mitosis: cell division that produces two identical daughter cells, each containing the full set of 46 chromosomes; occurs in all body cell reproduction in which chromosomes replicate and the cell divides once to create two identical cells, as in the regeneration of skin cells

mitral valve: valve between the left atrium and the left ventricle; permits the left ventricle to contract and pump blood out of the aorta without regurgitation of blood back into left atrium

mobility: degree to which individual is able to move around her or his environment independently, with or without adaptive equipment

monoplegia: cerebral palsy affecting one extremity of the body

morbidity: diseased; pertaining to disease

moro reflex: a symmetrical abduction and extension of the arms followed by an adduction when a child's head is suddenly dropped backwards (as if the child were embracing something)

morpheme: the smallest part of a word that possesses meaning

morphological development: evolution of word structure and word parts

mortality: the death rate; the ratio of total number of deaths to the total number in the population

mosaicism: a portion of cells have 46 chromosomes and another percentage of the cells have a deletion or an extra chromosome

multidisciplinary: a group of professionals from several different disciplines who work independently but meet to exchange information and to present goals and progress reports

multifactored diagnostic evaluation: administration of more than one test to determine the presence of a disability; tests should be administered in all areas relevant to a child's perceived needs

myelin sheath: lipid material with protein arranged in layers around many axons to increase efficiency of electrical transmission during neural activity; gives white matter in the brain its color

myelinization: production of myelin around an axon

myelomeningocele: a condition in which both the spinal cord and its covering, the meninges, push through a spinal defect to the surface

myoclonic seizure: brief, shock-like muscle contractions

myopathies: diseases of muscle, usually degenerative

myopia: nearsightedness; a condition in which parallel light rays come to focus in front of the retina because the refractile system is too strong or the eyeball is elongated

natal: pertaining to birth—before, during, and immediately after

natural routines: activities that normally take place in the daily routine of infants and toddlers and their families

negative sentences: statements using "no," "not," "can't," and so on

neonate: an infant during the first four weeks after birth

neural tube defects: disorders in the development, closure, and formation of the neural groove, the vertebral column (which houses the spinal cord), or other soft tissue structures surrounding the nerves

neurological system: organ system including the brain, spinal cord, and nerves

neurons: cells responsible for receiving and sending messages

noncontingent helping: providing assistance without effort or request from the recipient

nondisjunction during meiosis: an incomplete detachment of the pairs of cells occurring during cell division to create either an ovum or sperm

noninvasive: a procedure that does not involve penetrating the body (such as ultrasonography)

nonorganic: without specific physical cause

normal development: a sequence of changes across time that is very similar for all children

norms: statistically determined age levels for developmental milestones

nystagmus: rapid involuntary oscillations or tremors of the eyeball; may be horizontal, vertical, or rotary

object permanence: the understanding that objects continue to exist even when they are out of sight

occipital: the back section of the head

optic nerve: transmits visual image from the eye to the brain

organic: specific physical causation

organism: a total living form; one individual

orientation: conceptual, perceptual, sensory, and body awareness of space and environment

ostomy: an opening made from an internal tube to an external source, allowing for passage of urine or stool from the body (usually to a collection pouch)

otitis media (middle ear disease): an inflammatory disease of the middle ear; may be acute otitis media or serous otitis media

overextension: children's language usage that commonly occurs due to a limited repertoire of words or when categories are defined too broadly, for example, referring to all men as "daddy"

ovum: an unfertilized female sex cell; egg

parachute reflex: extension of arms and legs toward the surface that results when an infant is held in a horizontal position and prone, and then lowered toward the floor

parallel play: children play independently even though they are near other children and engaged in similar activities

paraphrasing: the practice of the listener restating the heart of the conversation in order to confirm and clarify what was meant

paraplegia: cerebral palsy affecting the lower extremities of the body

paraprofessionals: staff who assist licensed or certified intervention specialists

parity: number of live births delivered by a woman

parsimony: the adoption of the simplest assumption in the formulation of a theory or the interpretation of data

partial complex seizure: seizures that commence from one cerebral hemisphere of the brain

patent ductus arteriosis (PDA): when the opening between the aorta and the pulmonary artery, which permits blood to bypass the lungs prenatally and normally closes shortly after birth, stays open after birth and diminishes flow from the aorta

pathogenic: capable of causing disease

perception checks: when a listener checks his or her perception or understanding of what was said in the course of a conversation in order to open up and clarify the communication

perinatal: relating to the period just before or just after birth

periventricular leukomalacia: development of cysts or fluid-filled holes in the brain

phenotype: refers to the observable expression, or appearance, of a genetically inherited characteristic in an individual

phenylketonuria (PKU): an error of metabolism that results in the buildup of an amino acid that causes brain degeneration

phonology: the study of speech sounds

placebo: a chemically inert substance given in place of a drug—sometimes has a positive effect if the person believes it will

placenta: a fleshy mass made up of villi or projectiles that insert themselves into the lining of the uterus to nurture a developing fetus

placenta previa: a condition in which the placenta implants itself near the cervix rather than the top of the uterus

plasticity: the quality of being plastic, or capable of being molded; in regard to neural function

positioning: treatment of postural and reflex abnormalities by careful, symmetrical placement and support of the body

positive interdependence: the dependency of each group member on each other member—successes and failures are collective deeds

positron emission tomography (PET): used to view tumors, seizures, etc.

postnatal: occurring after birth, with reference to the newborn

postural reflexes (adaptive reflexes): involuntary responses that supplement movement while preventing injury

predictive utility: providing accurate forecasts about what will happen

preexisting diabetes: diabetes that developed prior to pregnancy

premature labor: prior to 37 weeks of gestation

premature rupture of membranes: membranes of the water sac surrounding the fetus break prior to 37th week of pregnancy

prematurity: when a developing fetus is born prior to the 37th week of gestation

prenatal: preceding birth

preoperational stage: stage during which children reason through linguistic input and personal knowledge

present levels of performance: use of current evaluation information to summarize skills and abilities

presuppositions: judgments made about the listener in a conversation that allow us to modify the content and style of the communication (These judgments include assessment of social status, educational or developmental level, closeness of relationships, etc.)

primary social supports: informal support network comprised of close family, friends, and neighbors

primitive reflexes: involuntary motor responses to specific stimuli that interfere with movement if persistent

proactive stance: working to influence others positively toward a particular position

procedural safeguards: rights guaranteed to families of children eligible for services under IDEA

prolapse of umbilical cord: baby presses on the umbilical cord during delivery and decreases or stops blood flow (and oxygen supply)

prone: lying on the tummy

protective extension: reaching an arm out to prevent falling when pushed out of midline, either from sitting or standing position

protozoan: a member of the phylum comprising the simplest forms of the animal kingdom; a unicellular organism

proximal-distal: sequence of development that progresses from the center of the body outward toward the extremities

psychometric approach: assessment comparing a child to normal standards of development, intelligence, or achievement in order to determine performance discrepancies

pyramidal tract: the motor cortex and spinal cord

quadriplegia: cerebral palsy affecting all four extremities of the body

qualitative-developmental assessment: assessment in which a child's skills, as well as the child's approach to people and tasks, are evaluated according to a developmental sequence

radiation: heat loss through dissipation from the body into the air

range of motion: the degrees of movement for a limb or body part

range of normalcy: lower and upper limits of age at which developmental milestones are attained

range of reaction: the extent to which environment is likely to influence the sequence of development within individual children

receptive language: understanding of a message sent by another individual

recessive gene: a gene that does not possess sufficient genetic information for the characteristic to be expressed unless the gene is carried on both alleles

refinement: sequence of development that progresses from large muscle control to small muscle control

reflex integration: the disappearance of involuntary reflexes to allow for normal motor development

reinforcement: a change in stimulus, contingent upon a response, that results in an increase in the probability of that response

related services: additional support services that allow children to benefit from their educational experiences

relative clauses: a part of a sentence that describes a subject, for example, "I want a doll that wets."

renal system: organ system including the kidneys and bladder

replicate: to demonstrate again with the same results

residual vision: visual ability remaining to an individual with a visual loss

respiratory distress syndrome: collapse of alveoli in the lungs due to lack of surfactant production in premature infants

respiratory system: organ system including the lungs and airways

retina: the innermost layer of the eye; the neural layer containing the receptors for light

retinopathy of prematurity (ROP): overgrowth of connective tissue in the eyes due to excess oxygen given to premature infants; oxygenation that causes damage to the blood vessels supplying the retina and, in severe cases, detachment of the retina

Rh sensitization: blood type incompatibility of mother and fetus that causes a buildup of antigens in mother's blood

rooting reflex: occurs when an infant's cheek is lightly stroked and, in response, infant's head turns toward the stimulus

rubella: commonly called German measles; caused by a virus that usually produces only mild upper respiratory symptoms and a rash in the infected individual; can cause severe damage to a fetus and can result in spontaneous abortion

savant: an individual shows extreme aptitude in one area (e.g., music or mathematics)

scoliosis: spinal curvature of the lower back

screening: a relatively quick preliminary evaluation used to determine if a child should be referred for more in-depth assessment

secondary social supports: formal sources of support, such as health care providers, educators, and therapists, that are usually more temporary than primary social supports

seizure: abnormal electrical discharges in the brain that cause the body to tremor, lose consciousness, or move in uncontrollable ways

self-help skills: independent care including eating, dressing, toileting, and other personal responsibilities

self-stimulation: sensory input from personal tactile, visual, auditory, or other physical activity that ignores other people or objects in the environment (such as hand-flapping, lip smacking, biting, etc.)

semantic relationship: combinations of two or more words that possess more meaning than any one of the words uttered in isolation

semicircular canals: three canals in the temporal bone that lie approximately at right angles to one another, containing receptors for equilibrium, specifically for rotation

sensorimotor stage: takes place from birth to age two; represents children's primitive exploration of their environment, wherein children attempt to integrate sensory information with their own movement

sensorineural hearing loss: results from damage to the cochlea or auditory nerve

service coordinator: person assigned to family of a child with special needs who is responsible for seeing that family and child receive all the services for which they are eligible under Part H of IDEA

sex-linked disorders: transmitted through the parents on a sex chromsome (X or Y) so that it is common for individuals of only one gender to express the disorder

shunting: procedure that requires the surgical placement of a soft pliable plastic tube between the ventricle and either the heart or the peritoneal cavity in the abdomen to drain off excess cerebral spinal fluid

sickle cell crisis: in persons with sickle cell disease, frequent and severe painful episodes

social-affective play: interaction between adult and child that elicits pleasure responses from the child

socioeconomic: relating to income and social factors

solitary play: a child is involved with his or her own play and does not interact with others

spastic cerebral palsy: cerebral damage in which the muscles tighten and resist efforts to move

special education: specially designed instruction that includes adaptations that are significantly different from modifications normally made for typical students and are necessary to offset or reduce the adverse effects of the child's disability

spectator play: a young child observes the play of others but does not attempt to join them

speech acts: the speaker's intentions or purposes for communicating

spina bifida: refers to an incomplete spinal column and the relationship of the spinal cord and contents to the defect

spina bifida occulta: a defect in the vertebrae covering the spinal cord, with no exposure of the neural membranes or any evidence of nerve tissue in the defect

spinal tap: a procedure in which a hollow needle is used to draw cerebrospinal fluid from the spinal canal

stage theory response: the naming and sequential ordering of complex emotions that are normal under a given set of circumstances

startle reflex: occurs when a sudden noise or movement causes a child to throw its arms away from the body and then back toward the midline

status epilepticus: a prolonged seizure of 15 minutes or more that is a life-threatening condition

stepping reflex: step-like response that occurs when a child is held in a vertical position so that its feet touch a surface

strabismus: a condition in which the optical axes of the two eyes are not parallel; cross-eyed

supine: lying on the back

surfactant: a chemical agent needed for independent breathing that is not produced in sufficient quantity until the 32nd to 33rd week of pregnancy

syntax: rules that govern structural patterns of language utterances and sentences

systemic: pertaining to or affecting the body as a whole

teacher-directed instruction: highly structured instruction planned in advance and guided by the teacher

temperament: characteristic emotional response

teratogen: any agent or factor that causes physical defects in a developing embryo

term pregnancy: gestational period of at least 38 weeks

tertiary: third in order, as in tertiary service delivery in which a professional serves a parent who, in turn, serves a child

tertiary services: indirect services that benefit children or their families (For example, when service providers enable parents to implement activities to assist in the development of their children, the child is receiving tertiary services from the professional.)

toddler stage: time from 1 year to 3 years of age

tonic-clonic seizure: rigid muscular contraction and rapid alternation of contraction and relaxation of muscles

total communication: a combination of manual signing with oral methods of communication

toxemia of pregnancy: elevated maternal blood pressure during pregnancy

toxin: a poison

toxoplasmosis: a protozoan that is acquired by humans from contact with the feces of infected cats or birds and from the ingestion of raw or partially cooked meat; may result in premature delivery or spontaneous abortion

tracking: ability to follow moving objects with the eyes in several directions (vertically and horizontally)

transdisciplinary model: a group whose members share roles and combine assessment and treatment tasks so that they may be carried out by one professional

transition: change in growth and development that may result in unpredictable behavior or regression

transition plan: formal written plan that indicates activities and responsibility for those activities that will make the move from one program to the next as smoothly as possible

transition stressors: pressure on a family related to a child's disability and occurring at significant milestones in life

translocation: the existence of extra chromosomal material, which has become attached to another chromosome, varying in size from a piece of one arm to an entire chromosome

transplacental: substance crosses from maternal to fetal bloodstream, or vice versa, via the placenta

trimester: a period of three months, usually pertaining to gestational periods, for example, second trimester

triplegia: cerebral palsy affecting three extremities of the body

trisomy 21: the presence of an extra number 21 chromosome, which causes Down syndrome

tympanic membrane: (eardrum) a thin sheet of skin between the middle and inner ear that transmits sound vibrations

ultrasonography or ultrasound: a procedure that uses high-frequency sound waves to produce an image of an internal organ

umbilical cord: the cord that joins the bloodstream of the fetus at the abdomen to the bloodstream of the mother via the uterine lining

underextension: children's language usage that occurs when categories are defined too narrowly (For example, a young child may use the word "chair" when referring to a high chair or table chair, but not include the rocking chair or kitchen stool in the category.)

vaccines: consist of either active viral replications with decreased virulence or an inactive virus introduced into the human being to activate the immune system to produce antibodies, preventing an acute infection

varicella-zoster: a virus related to herpes responsible for chickenpox and shingles

ventricles: fluid-filled sacs that occupy space within and around the brain mass

very low birth weight: less than 1500 g (3 lb 5 oz)

vestibule: a small cavity or space at the entrance to a canal, such as that in the inner ear

viable: the age at which the fetus has the potential to live outside of the womb, about 26 to 28 weeks

viruses: the smallest known types of infectious agent that invade cells, take over, and make copies of themselves

visual acuity: acuteness of vision; the power of the visual apparatus to distinguish visual detail, such as recognizing a letter of the alphabet

vitreous humor: the colorless, transparent gel filling the cavity of the eye behind the lens

X rays: a form of invisible electromagnetic energy that allows a view of the size, shape, and movement of organs

INDEX